The Elementary School Teacher

THE UNIVERSITY OF CHICAGO PRESS
CHICAGO, ILLINOIS

Agents
THE BAKER & TAYLOR COMPANY
NEW YORK

THE CAMBRIDGE UNIVERSITY PRESS
LONDON AND EDINBURGH

THE

ELEMENTARY SCHOOL TEACHER

VOLUME XIII

SEPTEMBER, 1912—JUNE, 1913

THE UNIVERSITY OF CHICAGO PRESS
CHICAGO, ILLINOIS

Published
September, October, November, December, 1912
January, February, March, April, May, June, 1913

Composed and Printed By
The University of Chicago Press
Chicago, Illinois, U.S.A.

INDEX TO VOLUME XIII

INDEX TO ARTICLES

[The asterisk indicates authors of books reviewed]

INDEX TO AUTHORS

[The asterisk indicates authors of books reviewed]

VOLUME XIII NUMBER 1

THE ELEMENTARY SCHOOL TEACHER

SEPTEMBER, 1912

EDUCATIONAL NEWS AND EDITORIAL COMMENT

Editorial Announcement

The *Elementary School Teacher* will, beginning with the present number, conduct a department of educational news and editorial comment. This department takes the place of the editorial department as it has heretofore been carried on. The news notes will not aim to report personal matters, however interesting these may be, but will attempt to reflect in a large and general way the development of educational policies in different parts of the country. The editors invite the co-operation of friends of the Journal in securing information with regard to important educational movements. The present number will serve to illustrate the type of information which can be utilized in this department. Responsibility for the opinions which are expressed in the editorial comments should perhaps be placed very definitely so that there may be no commitment of all of the members of the faculty of the School of Education. Unless otherwise indicated, these editorial comments may be charged to the responsibility of the writer who signs this announcement.

CHARLES H. JUDD

Educational Politics Do Not Constitute Educational Leadership

The National Education Association held its summer meeting of 1912 in the city of Chicago. The attendance at the meeting was very large and many important papers were presented. The interest of members and of the people who read the newspapers was largely absorbed, however, in the political doings of this meeting. A candidate from New York City in presenting her claims made it perfectly obvious that negotiations had been carried on prior to the meeting by a very compact organization of teachers in the city of Chicago, which organization finally refused its support to this candidate because of her unwillingness to favor certain constitutional amendments which were to be presented on the floor of the association. It is doubtful whether the ordinary member of the National Education Association cares enough about the constitutional amendments under discussion to view with complacency the tendencies which have grown up within the organization when a systematic trade in offices is privately projected and publicly discussed as an accepted means of directing the policy of the association. The Board of Directors spent much of its time during the meeting in listening to charges and countercharges. Secretary Shepard, who since the meeting has resigned from his office, presented recommendations in regard to voting members which very reasonably aimed to prevent the domination of any given meeting by merely temporary members. In support of this he read an elaborate report in which he charged mispractices at the Boston meeting which had been continued since that meeting to the present. These charges were met by countercharges. The whole impression made on the innocent mind of a non-combatant is that the association is suffering from a temporary lapse of equilibrium. One notes with some satisfaction the election to the office of president of a man who by his past record is certainly clear from any implications of mixing with these politics in the National Education Association. Superintendent E. T. Fairchild, of the state of Kansas, is a vigorous school man who in his own state has stood for the improvement of the common schools and has not been deflected from the straight path of his own best judgment by any political influence.

It is hoped that when the next meeting of the National Education Association gathers no candidate will be able to stand before the association and assert with any show of veracity that he has been in negotiation with any group of teachers who can either promote or defeat his candidacy for office on such grounds as were discussed this year. What the members of the association want is an aggressive educational organization, free from petty politics and factional disputes. What the association needs is leaders in educational policy who will see to it that information is brought together which will benefit teachers, that co-operative influences are developed which will dignify and strengthen the teaching profession, that reports are prepared and acted upon which will improve American education. Let those who are interested chiefly in politics get out of the light.

Vacation Schools and All-Year Schools

At the end of the summer vacation one reads with much interest of the vacation schools which have been conducted by boards of education or organized through the co-operation of parents' associations and women's clubs. One reads of the special trade schools which have been in successful operation during the summer. For example, in Joliet, Ill., 200 boys were engaged in working daily at the Roosevelt School and held a very successful exhibition showing the chairs, benches, tables, and other pieces of furniture which they had made. In the same way at Lamoni, Iowa, a manual-training school was held during the summer and an exhibition was made at the Carlisle Building at the end of the summer's work. Like reports come from Columbus, Ohio, and many other cities and towns.

In New York, a novel feature of instruction was added in the summer schools when the children were given instruction in various safety devices, such as methods of getting on and off street cars, crossing the streets, etc.

In the Chicago vacation schools emphasis was laid upon sewing, cooking, physical education, housekeeping, and nature-study. Other examples could be found without end of this sort of activity all over the country during the summer vacation. Undoubtedly the ultimate result of this organization of vacation schools will be the extension of the school so that it will be in session throughout the year.

One characteristic item showing some of the difficulties in the way of such schools, which appeared in the *Indianapolis Star*, is a dispatch from Richmond, Ind. The dispatch in question says interviews obtained from the leading business men of Richmond show that the great majority of them are opposed to the plan of State Superintendent Greathouse to organize a twelve months' term in the public schools of the state. "The principal objection that Richmond business men have to the new idea is the additional expense and the consequent raising of the tax rate." This type of objection is likely to interfere with vacation schools for some time, but if the advantages can be clearly set forth by those who have had experience in such schools, the financial difficulties will ultimately disappear.

Textbook Adoptions

A subject of very general discussion during the summer vacation in various sections of the country is the adoption of textbooks by states. In the state of Oklahoma, the governor was induced by his investigations of the State Board of Education to call for the resignation of a number of members of the board. When these resignations were not forthcoming, the governor removed a number of members from the board. Just at the time that the governor was taking this action, the board met and passed the contracts for books for the coming year. The question of the legal validity of their action will have to be settled in the courts. In the meantime the acute character of the situation concentrates attention once more upon the importance of the book-purchasing issue as a matter of school organization.

In Kansas the possibility of increasing the amount of money which may be expended on books is one of the leading issues in the school campaign. Kansas operates under the old-fashioned law which makes it impossible to adopt books of suitable grade for the conduct of the schools of that state.

In California an amendment is proposed to the constitution which provides that the state shall print and distribute the textbooks for the children of the state. Opposition to this method of issuing the books has grown up in various quarters, and the so-called "teacher's amendment" is proposed in opposition to the movement above described. The so-called "teacher's amendment" is in favor of the local adoption of textbooks as distinguished from the general state adoption.

In Texas a committee nominates to the governor 30 school

officers. From among these the governor selects nine who with himself and the state superintendent of public instruction constitute the board for selecting textbooks to be used throughout the state.

These different methods of dealing with the question of state adoption of textbooks all make it clear that there are dangers besetting the large business transactions which are involved. Evidently there are advantages in favor of a widespread use of uniform textbooks. Pupils who have to transfer from school to school within the same state system are seriously disadvantaged by a lack of uniformity in the text employed in the different schools. On the other hand, the moment the selections are made on a large scale, dangers arise which are very real and which show themselves in a political way.

Rural Schools

From a number of different quarters the rural school problem is suggested as one of the most significant of modern educational problems. A report prepared at Teachers College of Columbia University by Mr. Burnham, director of the Department of Rural Schools in the West Michigan Normal School at Kalamazoo, contains a detailed description of the financial and domestic character of two counties, one in the state of Michigan, and one in the state of Ohio. On the basis of this study of sociological conditions, Mr. Burnham has investigated the schools in the various districts of these counties, and has given a very vivid picture of the general problem of rural school organization.

Mr. E. T. Fairchild, superintendent of public instruction in the state of Kansas, has published a monograph through the Bureau of Education in which he draws attention to the fact that a majority of the whole school population of the United States is obliged to spend its time in poorly organized rural schools. The teaching body is immature; the buildings are unsanitary; the schools are without equipment in either books or scientific apparatus of any kind; there is little or no supervision. These deplorable conditions affect the city schools which are in very much better condition than the rural schools. The city schools very frequently receive students from the country schools, and any lack of educational equipment in the latter will always be felt in the former. Mr. Fairchild, as the president of the National Education Association, will undoubtedly be able to bring his campaign for the betterment of rural schools to the attention of the country at large. Mr. Fairchild's criticism of the rural schools is supported by many other observers. For example, a similar report is made by Mr. Lindholm of the state of Wisconsin. Mr. Lindholm inspected 126 schools in twelve different counties. He found great differences between the different rural schools but in the main he points out that conditions are sadly in need of a remedy.

Unjustifiable Economy in Ohio

The schools of Ohio are suffering from a lack of funds. The last legislature passed a law which made the limits for all taxation ten mills. This law was passed with the avowed purpose of inducing the people of the state to come forward with their personal property and subject it to legitimate taxation. The device did not succeed, however, and the funds available in the state for public activities have been very materially reduced. The schools were the first public institution to suffer, in view of the fact that they depend upon immediate support and consume a very large part of the income of the community. All sorts of devices have been employed in the schools in an effort to meet the emergencies that have thus arisen. In some quarters the schools were closed early in the year. In other quarters school activities were curtailed. It is interesting to note that in some quarters this curtailment consisted in the dropping of the so-called "new subjects," while in others there was a uniform reduction in all of the activities of the school. In some quarters salaries were reduced. The outcome of this experiment in taxation is a matter of general interest to teachers and school officers. The lesson which Ohio furnishes to all educators is that there should be a very keen interest on the part of these officers in the problem of public finance. School officers could do no greater service for their communities than to bring to their attention such works as that of Professor Cubberley in which the whole matter of school taxation is made the subject of a careful scientific study. School officers themselves should be prepared to show as Professor Cubberley has clearly shown in his book that the efficiency of schools depends upon a sound policy of collection and distribution of school moneys. In the meantime Ohio is suffering from a noticeable exodus of good teachers and superintendents who are going to states which do not try to conduct their schools and other public activities on ten mills.

Teachers' Health

The *Kansas City Times* reports an innovation in the requirements for admission to the teaching staff in that city. "All persons teaching in Kansas City public schools beginning this fall must undergo a medical examination and produce a health certificate signed by the Health Commissioner." The requirement of good health has long been among the requirements in the statutes and in the rules of many city boards. If Kansas City is going to put the requirement into vigorous and effective operation, it will furnish an example of great interest to the country at large.

New York Investigation

Professor Hanus and his associates on the educational aspects of the school inquiry, carried on under the general direction of a committee of the Board of Estimate and Apportionment of New York City, submitted their report about July 1. The report is now in press, and it is expected that it will be ready for distribution some time in the autumn. No attempt was made to make an exhaustive inquiry into all the activities of the huge school system of New York City. It was found necessary, owing to the limitations of time and staff, to restrict the inquiry to important aspects of certain fields only. Nevertheless, the report is comprehensive and far reaching.

It is the present plan to publish the report in two parts—Part I to consist of the principal findings and recommendations; and Part II to consist of the series of monographs on which Part I is based. This arrangement makes it possible for the person who has a general interest in this inquiry to get from Part I the information he may wish, without reading technical details; the specialist will desire those details, and he will find them in Part II.

As the city of New York, under the charter, is printing only two thousand copies, it would be well for all who desire a copy of this report to write without delay to Hon. John Purroy Mitchel (president of the Board of Aldermen), 51 Chambers Street, New York City, who is chairman of the Committee on School Inquiry.

Private Organizations Aiding in Support of Public Education

The Public Education Association of New York City is an organization of citizens who are interested in the development of the school system of New York. This association is able to collect enough funds to support a well-equipped office which can be used for the investigation of school problems and for the measurement of the efficiency of the school system. The organization publishes a bulletin which can be secured by addressing the secretary of the association, Arthur W. Dunn. Bulletin No. 4 sets forth the desirability of continuing through some organization the investigation which has recently been carried on in New York City by a committee of the Board of Estimates and Appropriation. Some outside scrutiny of the work of schools, this bulletin argues, is better than the examination of the system merely through its executive officers. The bulletin also announces that the association will carry on the work of the Board of Estimates. Since the publication of this bulletin the press announces that one of the members of the committee which helped Professor Hanus carry on the investigation in New York, is to be continued by the Board of Estimates and Appropriation as special agent for the examination of the budget items submitted by the superintendent of public instruction. Whether this will lead to a modification of the plans of the Public Education Association or not is not announced. In any case it is evident that New York has learned through the investigations of the special committee the lesson of the very great importance of a continual supervision of the school system through the study of the results attained by the schools. In the second place, the existence of the Public Education Association illustrates very clearly an example of support of the schools which may very profitably be followed in other cities.

Milwaukee Trade School

In 1906, a trade school was organized by the Merchants and Manufacturers Association in Milwaukee. In 1907 this school was turned over to the public-school system of the city. Announcement was made on August 2 that the school opened with forty pupils, seven instructors, and one principal. The total capacity of the school is 120 pupils. As soon as the summer months are over, it is expected that the number will increase so as to reach the capacity of the school. A new wing to the building has been completed at a cost of $115,000, making the total cost of the buildings $250,000. This school illustrates the way in which a new type of educational work may be added to the public-school system after it has been initiated by private enterprise.

New Italian Methods

The Montessori method continues to be a subject of vigorous discussion. The Bureau of Education has issued a pamphlet prepared by Miss Anna Tolman Smith. This pamphlet sets forth the essential practices of the Montessori schools and gives a brief review of the method itself. A committee consisting of members of the faculty and student body of Teachers College visited Rome for the purpose of inspecting the schools. Committees from England have also inspected the schools. American travelers in Rome are said to congest the Montessori schools to such an extent that admission to the schools is being restricted. The apparatus which is supposed to make easy the introduction of the Montessori method is now on sale in this country at a price which seems to the casual observer to be considerably above the actual material value of the apparatus supplied. The public press is interested in reporting the monograph from the Bureau of Education and the various discussions which are held at mothers' meetings and educational gatherings. In the meantime, there is a very distinct note of conservatism in the reports of trained observers who have seen the system in operation. Evidently the difference between an Italian school and an American school has not been properly evaluated by those who were at first most enthusiastic for this Montessori method.

Sensory training which has been loudly praised as a part of the new method, and has been referred to as the natural and legitimate application of Wundtian psychology, is certainly very far from the teachings of Wundt and his followers. The virtues of the Montessori system, or at least most of them, can be matched by equally efficient devices in American schools without the introduction of the elaborate paraphernalia which is now regarded by some as necessary to the system as it comes from Italy.

THE MOTIVATION OF SEVENTH- AND EIGHTH-GRADE HISTORY WORK

SUPERINTENDENT G. M. WILSON
Connersville, Indiana

The work with the 8B pupils on the United States Constitution, as handled during the past two or three years, furnishes a good illustration of motivation in history work. It had been the custom to spend six weeks upon the study of the United States Constitution, at the beginning of the National Period. The pupils considered this work exceedingly difficult and uninteresting, and the teacher had real difficulty in getting good work done. Because of the difficulty of the situation, the teacher had spoken to me about the advisability of omitting this work on the Constitution. However, it appealed to me as a piece of work that should be done, since many of the pupils do not reach the American history work in the fourth year of high school, and many who do reach the fourth year of high school do not elect the American history work. With this thought in mind I suggested that we devise some means of making the work more interesting and profitable to the pupils. The suggestion was finally made that the teacher organize the grade into a Constitutional Convention, indicating to each pupil the character that he was to represent in such convention. The teacher was skeptical, both as to the feasibility of the plan, and as to her ability to carry out the plan. Accordingly, another term passed in which the work was done in the old way with the usual difficulty. When the time came for this work the next term, the suggestion of a Constitutional Convention was repeated to the teacher. She still hesitated to undertake it, but finally asked that some assistance be given her in organizing and starting the work. This was a normal situation, with the teacher in proper frame of mind, although a little skeptical as to results. We planned the work together very carefully. A sufficient number of Madison's

Journal of the Constitutional Convention was secured (six copies) to enable the class of thirty-five pupils to get along fairly well. Madison's *Journal* had been referred to on previous occasions, but it is a very difficult work to handle and no use had been made of it.

The Constitutional Convention was organized by electing George Washington (the teacher), president, and by electing some member (not necessarily Madison), secretary. A committee was appointed to draw up rules to govern the deliberations and discussions. This committee was required to report at the second session. After the adoption of the rules, Mr. Randolph was permitted to open the main discussion by presenting the Virginia plan. The work from this point was necessarily very greatly simplified. The teacher experienced no difficulty in getting a hearty response from the pupils. In fact, the next meeting of the Convention became the chief topic for conversation. A particular topic was assigned for the next meeting, say for illustration, *the length of the term for which the President shall be elected.* A pupil's work in preparation for the next session was to find out his view upon this subject. It was the duty of the pupil representing Mr. Pinckney to be prepared to present Mr. Pinckney's views to the Convention. The pupil representing Mr. Sherman was to be prepared to present Mr. Sherman's views, and so on throughout the list. It was the further duty of each pupil to know whether the man he represented introduced any resolutions having reference to the length of the term of the President. When the next session of the Convention was called (a week later), each pupil was prepared to present his views with reference to the topic assigned, to enter into the discussions, to make motions, and to vote. In fact, he was prepared to be a real member of the Constitutional Convention and have a part in the making of the United States Constitution.

After the first topic had been worked over in this way there was no longer any doubt as to the success of the plan. The teacher was as enthusiastic as the pupils. She is a thoroughly competent teacher, and this has contributed much to the success of the plan. Since the plan was adopted two and half years ago, there have been five 8B Constitutional Conventions. The six copies of Madison's

Journal which were in the Public Library have been almost completely worn out. The school has since bought additional copies.

While this special work is being carried on and the session of the Convention is being held about once a week, the other days of the week are given to a systematic study of the Constitution—the reasons for calling the Constitutional Convention, the defects of the Articles of Confederation, the great compromises of the Constitution, the organization of the different phases of the government, the opposition to the Constitution and its final adoption by the necessary number of states, and finally the election of the first President and the organization of the new government under the Constitution. But, it must be said that this work is conducted in quite a different spirit than formerly. The pupils seem to assume more or less of a proprietary interest in the United States Constitution. They understand just how difficult a matter it was to make the Constitution, the differences of view which prevailed, the compromises, the divisions, etc., which took place during the process of making the Constitution and bringing it into final form.

Topics which are treated in sessions of the Constitutional Convention vary, of course, from time to time. A session is usually held upon the *powers of Congress* in order to call special attention to the elastic clause of the Constitution (last paragraph, Art. I, sec. 8) and prepare for the use of this clause by Hamilton in his conflict with Jefferson during the organization of the government. A session is devoted to the regulation of commerce in order to emphasize the compromises based upon the regulation of commerce. Another topic which has been found very helpful and lends itself readily for treatment in the Convention, is the basis for representation in the lower house. Other topics in connection with the executive which have been treated from time to time are: (1) a single, dual, or triple executive; (2) powers of the executive; (3) manner of electing the executive; (4) eligibility for re-election.

The edition of Madison's *Journal* which we have been using is indexed by subjects and by persons. After the pupil becomes accustomed to the general plan of the *Journal* and learns how to use the index, he finds no difficulty in ascertaining his view upon any subject, by looking under his name in the index, and following through the points there indicated. He easily sees whether or not he has said anything upon the topic for discussion. The understanding is that in case he has said nothing he shall turn to the topic and read the views of one or two persons who do speak. This gives him the general line of argument. By keeping in mind his attitude in general it is possible for him to shape his views and say a word, even though he does not actually discuss the topic as indicated by the *Journal.* For instance, Alexander Hamilton when present was always conservative and doubted the advisability of conferring much power upon the poeple; while Wilson of Pennsylvania was thoroughly democratic, trusted the people, and sought at all times to give the people an opportunity to participate fully in the government. Wilson even favored the election of the President by direct vote. With his knowledge of the general attitude of Hamilton and Wilson, the pupils representing them would have little difficulty in properly representing them on almost any subject. And so it is with others although few are so easily represented as Hamilton and Wilson, since few are so consistent throughout.

In handling the Convention the teacher places all of the responsibility upon the pupils and so apparently has little to do in organizing or furthering the work. As a matter of fact, however, the teacher's work, especially when the work is being done for the first time, should be very carefully planned, and may require considerable extra time. The following gives the teacher's outline in preparation for the discussion of *the length of the term of the executive.* It will be noticed that with this outline before her, the teacher is prepared to say to Mr. Pinckney, in case Mr. Pinckney asks a question, "you will find your views explained on page 88." To Mr. Bedford she can say, "Your views as to the length of term, as also for re-eligibility, will be found on page 89." She can refer Mr. Hamilton to pages 183 and 185. Those not having a part in the discussion may be referred to the first plan on page 91, the plan as given in the first report of the Committee of the Whole on page 161, the further consideration of the report of the Committee of the Whole on the Executive on page 365, the agreement on the modification of the report of the Committee of the Whole on page

390, the unsettled opinion as to the length of the term as shown on page 422, the first mention of the present term on page 654.

The teacher's outline on the length of the term of the executive to which we have just been referring, follows:

LENGTH OF TERM OF THE EXECUTIVE

Terms of years left blank on Virginia plan (pp. 62 and 69).
Seven years agreed to in Committee of the Whole, discussion suggesting from two to eight years (p. 91).
Wilson moved for three years (pp. 88).
Pinckney moved for seven years (p. 88).
Sherman for three years, and against rotation (p. 88).
Mason for seven years and for prohibiting re-eligibility (p. 88).
Bedford against long term. Favored three years and eligibility for three terms (p. 89).
Ineligible after seven years agreed to by vote seven to two, Pennsylvania divided.
Final form of report of Committee of Whole on Virginia plan, seven year (p. 161).
New Jersey plan left years blank (p. 165).
Hamilton's plan favored life term of executive (p. 183), or "during good behavior" (p. 185).
Ninth resolution of Committee of Whole on Executive reported favoring seven years (p. 365).
Dr. McClurg moved "during good behavior" (p. 369). Seconded by Gov. Morris (p. 370). Opposed by Sherman, Mason (pp. 370–72).
Six years agreed upon (p. 390).
Mr. Williamson, ten or twelve years (p. 420).
Eleven, fifteen, twenty, and eight years suggested (p. 422).
Seven years agreed upon (p. 437).
Seven years in first draft of Constitution (p. 457).
Four years first mentioned in report of Committee of Eleven, Mr. Brearly, chairman Electors also proposed here (p. 654).
Mr. Rutledge moved to change to seven years. Failed (p. 664).
Four years in first complete draft (p. 707) and in final form (p. 756).

This illustration of motivized work on the Constitutional Convention has been worked out fully enough to enable any reader to take the idea and put it into practice. It is the belief of the author that our formal textbook work persists, because teachers are not helped to substitute something better and more life-giving. One of the aims of the present article is to aid such substitution.

This work on the Constitutional Convention uses the dramatic instinct, makes the pupil an actor of history, and gives interesting work which appeals to his best efforts.

History frequently fails of its purpose because it fails to live for the pupil. It is too often nothing more than verbal memory work. A sixteen-year-old girl once committed and recited to me the discovery of America by Cabot, without the least conception of the objective significance of what she was talking about. She had been permitted to recite in that way for so long, that I was forced to resort to drastic measures to awaken her.

History must live or it fails of its purpose. Dramatic treatment gives life. Last year a 7B class was plodding along with the situation in England and Holland that finally sent the Pilgrims to this country. It was a slow class and the teacher was thoroughly disheartened. "Don't blame the class," said I, "do something." The teacher was ready to do anything that promised relief. The next day English officers entered at recitation time with warrants for the arrest of twelve members of the class for not attending the Established Church services on the previous Sabbath. They were shackled and imprisoned. While in prison, they decided to leave for Holland in order to have religious liberty.

This was a new experience. The class was thoroughly aroused. The next day the class was in Holland, but they were suddenly interrupted by some of the children running into the room in their play, and to their amazement all of the conversation was in the Dutch language (6B pupils who were studying German played this part). A meeting was called and a decision reached to go to America in order that their children might grow up with English rather than Dutch, language, habits, and ideals.

By this time the class had entered fully into the spirit of the work. They "liked" history, and so did the teacher. From that time on the pupils were looking for opportunities to dramatize sections of the work. The teacher held back enough to make the pupils consider it a special favor, but continued to use this plan of motivizing and enriching the work.

A CHAPTER IN THE DEVELOPMENT OF ARITHMETIC TEACHING IN THE UNITED STATES

WALTER S. MONROE
The University of Chicago

III[1]

In considering methods of teaching a subject it is often profitable to investigate the methods which have been used in the teaching of this subject in the past. This is especially true of a subject, such as arithmetic, which has been taught since the time of the earliest schools without material change in content. In the case of arithmetic, a retrospective study of methodology is particularly illuminating, because the earliest method of instruction seems to have been considered efficient for a long period, there being practically no change until about 1825. The object of this paper is to give a notion of the arithmetic teaching in the schools of the latter part of the eighteenth and the beginning of the nineteenth century and to attempt an analysis of the method of instruction.

We have practically no record of the method of teaching arithmetic before the close of the Revolution, but several things lead us to believe that few changes were made in the method of teaching during the eighteenth century. We may then think of the schools of about 1800 as being typical, in respect to the teaching of arithmetic, of the schools of the eighteenth century. Concerning these schools we have the testimony of men who attended them.

It appears that in these schools arithmetic texts were seldom found in the hands of the pupils and it was unusual for the teacher to possess one. It is stated that many pupils never even saw an arithmetic. The master dictated or set "sums," as the problems were called, and the pupils worked them on scraps of paper. The teacher told the pupil the rule, and when the pupil had finished his "sum" he took it up to the teacher for approval, or disapproval. Often the teacher was surrounded by pupils waiting their turn.

[1] This article concludes the series begun in May and continued in June in the *Elementary School Teacher*.

As a rule each pupil had a blankbook made of a quire of paper folded and sewed together. This was his "Cyphering Book." After his work was approved by the master, the pupil carefully copied in his "Cyphering Book" the problem and its solution, together with the rule which the master had given him. The master usually possessed such a "Cyphering Book" which he had made as a pupil under his master and which now served as his source of "sums" and rules. It was also his criterion of correct answers and methods.

In Barnard's *Journal of American Education* we find a number of articles written by men who attended school about 1800. Some of their experiences seem to be so typical of the method of teaching arithmetic that we quote from them at some length.

". . . . At length, in 1790 or 1791, it was thought I was old enough to learn to *cypher*, and accordingly was permitted to go to school more constantly. I told the Master I wanted to learn to cypher. He set me a *sum* in simple addition—*five columns* of figures, and *six figures* in each column. All the instruction he gave me was—add the figures of the first column, carry one for every ten, and set the over-plus down under the column. I supposed he meant by the *first* column the left-hand column; but what he meant by carrying one for every ten was as much a mystery as Samson's riddle was to the Philistines. I worried my brains an hour or two, and showed the master the figures I made. You may judge what the amount was, when the columns were added from left to right. The master frowned and repeated his former instruction—add up the column *on the right*, carry one for every ten, and set down the remainder. Two or three afternoons (I did not go to school in the morning) were spent in this way, when I begged to be excused from learning to cypher, and the old gentleman with whom I lived thought it was time wasted; . . . . The next winter there was a teacher more communicative and better fitted for his place, and under him some progress was made in arithmetic, and I made a tolerable acquisition in the first four rules, according to Dilworth's *Schoolmaster's Assistant*, of which the teacher and one of the eldest boys had each a copy. The two following winters, 1794 and 1795, I mastered all the rules and examples in the first part of Dilworth; that is, through the various chapters of Rule of Three, Practice, Fellowship, Interest, etc., etc., to Geometrical Progression and Permutation."[1]

". . . . Printed arithmetics were not used in the Boston schools till after the writer left them, and the custom was for the master to write a problem or two in the manuscript of the pupil every other day. No boy was allowed to cypher till he was eleven years old, and writing and ciphering were never performed

[1] Joseph T. Buckingham, *Barnard's Journal*, XIII, 130.

on the same day. Master Tileston had been taught by Master Proctor, and all the sums he set for his pupils were copied exactly from his old manuscript. Any boy could copy the work from the manuscript of any further advanced than himself, and the writer never heard any explanation of any principle of arithmetic while he was at school. Indeed, the pupils believed that the master could not do the sums he set for them, and a story is told of the good old gentleman, which may not be true, but which is so characteristic as to afford a very just idea of the course of instruction, as well as of the simplicity of the superannuated pedagogue. It is said that a boy, who had done the sum set for him by Master Tileston, carried it up, as usual, for examination. The old gentleman, as usual, took out his manuscript, compared the slate with it, and pronounced it wrong. The boy went to his seat and reviewed his work, but finding no error in it returned to the desk and asked Mr. Tileston to be good enough to examine the work, for he could find no error in it. This was too much to require of him. He growled, as his habit when displeased, but he compared the sum again, and at last, with a triumphant smile, exclaimed, "See here, you *nurly* (gnarly) wretch, you have got it, 'If four tons of hay cost so much, what will seven tons cost?' when it should be, 'If four tons of *English* hay cost so and so.' Now go and do it all over again."[1]

As has been pointed out, arithmetic texts were scarcely used in the schools. To us this is probably the most conspicuous factor of this early teaching. This practice was probably due in the beginning to the fact that sufficient texts were not available to do otherwise.[2] But the continuance of a method of instruction which did not make use of a text cannot be due to texts not being available during the eighteenth century. Several texts by English authors were known in the colonies in the early part of the eighteenth century and by 1800 there had been at least fifteen arithmetic texts published by American authors.

Edmond Wingate published an *Artificial Arithmetic* in 1629. The fifteenth edition was published in 1726[3] and another edition in 1753.[4] Littlefield states: "A copy of the first edition is now in existence which was used in the Winslow family of Massachusetts for over one hundred years."[5]

[1] Wm. B. Fowle, *Barnard's Journal*, V, 336.

[2] There is evidence that arithmetic was taught in the colonies as early as 1665 and possibly as early as 1658. Suitable arithmetics were not known to any extent in the colonies until after 1700.

[3] A copy of this edition is in the Library of the University of Chicago.

[4] G. E. Littlefield, *Early New England Schools*, 163.

[5] *Ibid.*, 163.

Hodder's Arithmetic: or that Necessary Art made most easy, by James Hodder, writing master, was published in 1661. The twenty-fifth edition was printed in Boston in 1719.[1]

Cocker's *Vulgar Arithmetic, by Edward Cocker*, "Late Practitioner in the arts of Writing, Arithmetic and Engraving" was published in 1677. An edition of Cocker's *Arithmetic* was published in Philadelphia in 1779. It has been said that Cocker's *Arithmetic* "may be considered the father of modern arithmetics, as it furnished the plan which all of them have copied."

The Schoolmaster's Assistant, by Thomas Dilworth, was first published in 1743. It was republished in Philadelphia in 1769. I have a copy published in Philadelphia in 1790. The twenty-third edition was printed in Hartford in 1786; also an edition was printed in Wilmington in 1796, and one in New York in 1797. At the time of the Revolution and after until about 1800 it was more extensively used in this country than any other text.

That these texts did not become generally used in the schools and the method of instruction correspondingly changed seems to have been mainly due to a belief in the efficiency of the method of teaching arithmetic without a text.

To be sure, books were more expensive then than now, if we take into account the purchasing value of money. But this condition does not seem to have prevented the printing and distribution of religious writings and the almost universal use of the Psalter and Catechism in the schools. And certainly in the study of Latin, texts must have been used. "A printing press was set up at Cambridge (Massachusetts) as early as 1639, but it was wholly engaged in turning out controversial pamphlets of a religious nature."[2]

Another reason for believing that the efficiency of the "Cyphering Book" seems to have been accepted is that the first arithmetic published by an American author was a specific attempt to further the "Cyphering Book" method. Isaac Greenwood wrote *Arithmetic, Vulgar and Decimal: with the application thereof, to a variety*

[1] *Ibid.*, 167.

[2] Dexter, *History of Education in the United States*, 207.

of Cases in Trade, and Commerce,[1] which was published in 1729. He states what appears his chief purpose as follows:

"The Reader will observe, that the author has inserted under all those rules, where it was proper, Examples with Blanks for his practice. This was a principal End to the Undertaking; that such persons as were desirous thereof might have a comprehensive Collection of all the best Rules in the Art of Numbring, with examples wrought by themselves. And that nothing might be wanting to favour this design, the Impression is made upon several of the best Sorts of Paper. This Method is entirely new, ..."

The paper used in the book is thick, the type large. Words and phrases to which the author desires to call special attention are printed in italic characters, and, as more than half the book is, in the author's eyes, important, more than half is printed in italics. The method followed by the author seems to be in most cases to give the rule in each subject, then examples illustrating the rule, then examples for the student, and finally the proof. There is very little explanation aside from the rule. Each example has a "blank" beneath it for the student's "practice." There are no collections of examples, as in modern books. At times, though not always, terms, such as annuity, interest, etc., are explained.[2]

Greenwood's text seems to have not been well received and was used very little in the schools.[3] However, this same feature was utilized by Daniel Adams, who wrote *The Scholar's Arithmetic,* first published in 1801. In the preface of a revised edition, dated December 26, 1815, Mr. Adams writes as follows:

We have now the testimony of many respectable Teachers to believe, that this work, where it has been introduced into Schools, has proved a very kind assistant towards a more speedy and thorough improvement of Scholars

[1] J. M. Greenwood, "Notes on the History of American Textbooks on Arithmetic," *Report of Commissioner of Education for 1897-98,* 802. "There are two copies of this book in Harvard College library and one in the Library of Congress."

[2] *Ibid.,* 805.

[3] The second text by an American author was *A New and Complete System of Arithmetic, composed for the use of the citizens of the United States,* by Nicholas Pike in 1788. This is nearly sixty years after the appearance of Greenwood's text and apparently by this time the work of Greenwood was forgotten.

Pike says in the dedication of his text, "As this work is the first of the kind composed in America. . . . ." George Washington in his recommendation of Pike's book mentions that it is the first of its kind. That Pike did not know of Greenwood's book would seem to indicate that it made little impression and was soon forgotten, because Greenwood was professor of mathematics in Harvard College at the time he published his text and Pike graduated from Harvard.

in Numbers, and at the same time, has relieved masters of a heavy burden of writing out Rules and Questions, under which they have no long labored, to the manifest neglect of other parts of their schools.

To answer the several intentions of this work, it will be necessary that it should be put into the hands of every Arithmetician: the blank after each example is designed for the operation by the scholar, which being first wrought upon a slate, or waste paper, he may afterwards transcribe into his book.

This text apparently attained some popularity, for by 1815 it had gone through nine editions. I have seen a copy printed as late as 1824. I have a copy printed in 1820 which bears the imprint of the hand of some pupil who doubtless labored long over the involved and obscure problems.

Although we do not find other texts of this period making this specific provision for the "Cyphering Book" method, yet they were such that they contributed to this method of instruction. For the most part the texts were simply collections of rules and problems. Only occasionally do we find any attempt to explain or develop the rules and often the rules are not even illustrated by solving an example. Rules are given for every case. A set of rules are given for the Rule of Three with integers, another set is given for vulgar fractions, and still a third set for decimal fractions. Speaking of Dilworth's *Schoolmaster's Assistant*, Cajori says: "The whole book is nothing but a Pandora's box of disconnected rules. It appeals to memory exclusively and completely ignores the existence of reasoning powers in the mind of the learner."[1] (Dilworth's text was the most widely used book at the time of the Revolution and after to 1800.)

Such texts could serve for little more than a source of rules and problems. The extreme to which pupils and teacher alike depended upon the "rule" is shown by the following:

I quote the following from an article "Early School Days" in Indiana, contributed by Barnabas C. Hobbs. A law had just been passed requiring that teacher's examinations should be conducted by three county commissioners instead of the township trustees, as had been the practice before. "I shall not forget," says Hobbs, "my first experience under the new system. The only question asked me at my first examination was, 'What is the product

[1] F. Cajori, "The Teaching and History of Mathematics in the United States," *Circular of Information No. 3*, 1890.

of 25 cents by 25 cents?' We were not as exact then as people are now. We had only Pike's *Arithmetic*, which gave the sums and the rules. These were considered enough at that day. How could I tell the product of 25 cents by 25 cents, when such a problem could not be found in the book? The examiner thought it was $6\frac{1}{4}$ cents, but was not sure. I thought just as he did, but this looked too small to both of us. We discussed its merits for an hour or more, when he decided that he was sure I was qualified to teach school, and a first-class certificate was given me."[1]

We may appropriately characterize the arithmetic instruction up until about the close of the first quarter of the nineteenth century as the "Cyphering Book" method. Even though texts were used toward the close of this period, it seems that many of the essential features of the method were retained. The method persisted in some localities until well into the nineteenth century. Even today one occasionally finds a teacher who instructs his class without a text in the hands of the pupils. We retain certain features of the method when we require pupils to keep a notebook in which they record their work.

However, this is not the only phase of the method which seems worth considering. The instruction was largely individual. Each pupil worked on a problem of his own. When he had completed his work he took it to the teacher, and if he had not solved his problem, or had met with a difficulty, received individual attention.

The instructions given by the teacher were for his own benefit. Since there was no class instruction, there was no reason why the pupils should be kept together. If some pupils progressed less rapidly than the others, they did not hinder the work of those who were able to work more rapidly, and they in turn were not handicapped by being behind the class.

The writer does not wish to be understood as advocating the method of a hundred years ago as an efficient one for teaching arithmetic. An attempt to follow it under present conditions would most probably result in failure. And it must be admitted that for many of the practices of the teachers of this period we can present no justification. But it seems that what we have called the "Cyphering Book" method contains some features which are worthy of consideration.

[1] *Ibid.*, 16.

Toward the end of the first quarter of the nineteenth century the teachings of Pestalozzi began to receive attention in this country. We find his method of oral instruction incorporated in a text by Warren Colburn which was published in 1821. This text was adopted almost immediately by the schools and with its introduction we find the first marked change in the method of teaching. The decline of the "Cyphering Book" method accompanied the introduction of a new method.

CURRENT METHODS OF TEACHING HANDWRITING

FRANK N. FREEMAN
The University of Chicago

III[1]

Type of movement.—We turn now to the question of the type of movement and forms of drill which are used. It was stated in the early part of the discussion that the emphasis is very commonly laid upon the arm movement. As the arm movement component in the writing movement this component is variously described as "the fore-arm movement," "the muscular movement," or merely "the arm movement." None of these designations correctly describe the movement in question. The term "muscular movement" which is most commonly used is obviously a misnomer. The writer suggests that the most accurate designation is one which has been employed by McAllister, namely, "Arm movement with rest." This indicates that the movement is made by the whole arm moving from the shoulder, which is the case, and that the arm is not suspended, but rests upon the desk.

The majority of systems which are in use emphasize this arm movement with rest to a greater or less extent. The distinctions in current practice are two. The first distinction consists in the alternative between an exclusive arm movement and a movement which combines the arm and the fingers. Several writers insist upon entire exclusion of the finger component of the writing movement. The Palmer method perhaps represents most completely this attitude. Other systems defend the writing movement as most advantageous, which is a combination of the movements of the arm, hand, and fingers. This type of writing is recommended, for example, in the Bennett system, the California series, Spencer's Practical writing and the Whitehouse system. The movement of the hand about the wrist joint is ordinarily not mentioned, but when it is, it is for the purpose of condemning it.

[1] This article concludes the series begun in May and continued in June in the *Elementary School Teacher.*

The issue which is here raised has been discussed in a previous article in the present journal. It is not, therefore, necessary to consider it at length, but it will be sufficient to cite some authorities who favor the combined movement and to indicate briefly the function which the various component movements take in the combined movement. The only attempt at a scientific analysis of the writing movement, with reference to the part played by the fingers and the arm, has been made by Charles H. Judd. The report of this investigation may be found in *Genetic Psychology for Teachers*, chap. vi. The summary of the results which were found in this investigation may be stated in the words of the author:

> The general conclusion from a comparison of the large number of records of which the three reproduced represent the chief types, may be summed up briefly in the statement: In ordinary writing the fine formative movements are executed by the fingers; the movements which carry the fingers forward are executed by the hand or arm; and the pauses between groups of letters are utilized for long forward arm movements which bring the hand back into an easy working position (pp. 176, 177).

In the same place the author describes the type of writing which is characteristic of those who use predominantly the arm movement in the formation of letters:

> This writing is typical of a whole group of cases in which the movement is coarse, and more generally in which much less attention is given by the writer to questions of form.

We have here indicated a relation between movement and the form of writing which is somewhat different from that described in the quotation above given in the discussion of this question.

Another quotation from a prominent handwriting expert upholds the same position:

> It is possible to write entirely with the fore-arm movement without any separate action of the hand and fingers, and many superior penmen write in this manner. But the easiest, most rapid, and most perfect writing is that produced with the fore-arm movement used in connection with a slight action of the hand and fingers by which the small portions of the writing are produced.[1]

If one may venture a prediction it is that the more moderate procedure which recognizes the value and place of the movements of the fingers and the hand in the production of the letters will finally prevail against the extreme position taken by the advocates of the exclusive arm movement.

[1] A. S. Osborn, *Questioned Documents*, p. 108.

A second distinction in relation to this question is that between the practice which involves the use of the same type of movement through the grades, and the practice which allows a somewhat different form of movement in the earlier grades from that which is to be ultimately developed. All of the more moderate writers upon penmanship allow the child in the primary grades to use a movement which is described by one as "the relaxed finger movement," or by another as "the easy finger movement." There is a general agreement upon the evil of the cramped type of movement which was so characteristic of the writing in the earlier grades in the old days when the copy-book was not supplemented by any other means of teaching. This cramped movement is generally avoided by allowing the child at the beginning to write upon the blackboard and to make the transition to the ordinary sized writing upon paper by gradual steps. These steps include the use of crayon or large lead pencil and large sheets of rather rough paper throughout perhaps the first grade. In the second grade the paper may be reduced gradually to the ordinary size and the writing may likewise be reduced to the same extent. In this form of procedure the child is encouraged to write at first with much the same movement which he uses at the blackboard. This involves the arm movement without rest chiefly. As the child comes to write smaller and to use the finger movement more he tends to retain the same freedom which he has previously possessed. When he then comes in the third, fourth, or fifth grade to learn the arm movement with rest, in which the arm oscillates upon the muscle pad of the fore-arm, he is not required to make a complete transformation of his movement, but only to add to it a type of movement which he had not before acquired, and to co-ordinate it with the movements which he previously made.

This description represents the practice which is found in some systems which have studied most closely the psychology and pedagogy of writing, and in the opinion of the writer is the best method of developing the process. The introduction of the fore-arm movement with rest marks an advance to a much more accurate and finely adjusted writing movement, and should, therefore, be deferred until the child has already acquired some facility

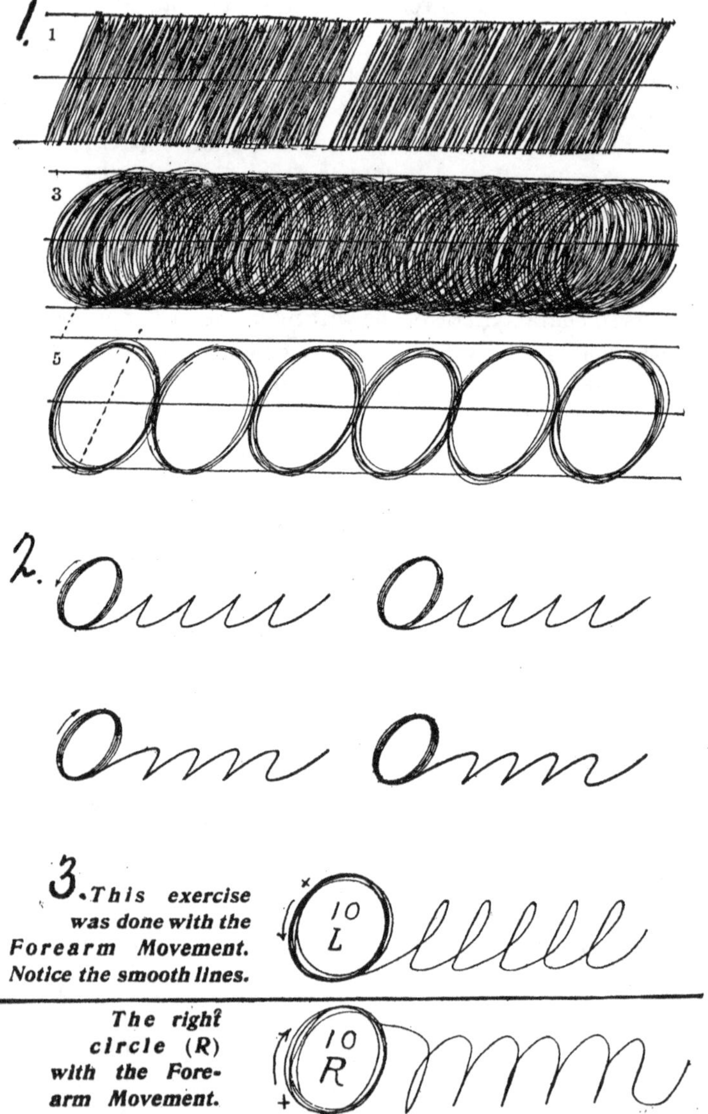

FIG. 5.—Illustrations of formal movement drills. 1. From the Palmer Primary cards for Grade II. These are also used with single spacing. 2. From the Economy system for Grade V. 3. From the *Whitehouse Copybooks* for Grade I. (Reproduced with the permission of the publishers.)

in the less exact use of the pencil, and until he has reached the stage in his development when he is capable of acquiring with facility a high degree of skill.

Movement drills.—We may now briefly review the types of drill which are used to secure the best form of writing movement. Certain drills are used pretty universally and the differences which exist are chiefly in matters of detail. We may distinguish in general two types of drill, one which is purely formal, and the other which is used in connection with the actual production of letters. Of the purely formal drills the most frequently used are the retraced oval

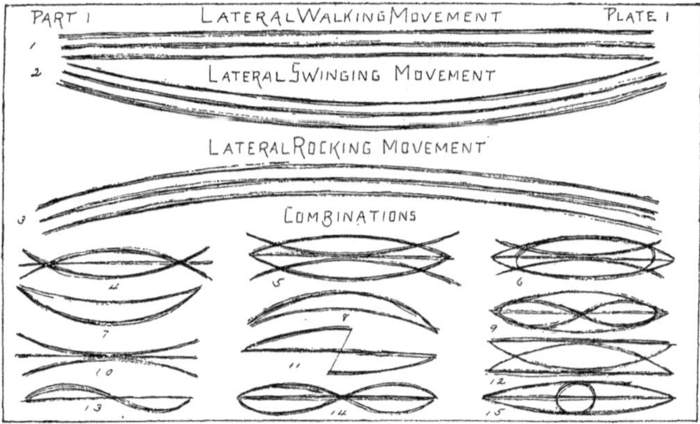

FIG. 6.—Illustrations of the lateral movement drills as used in the Bennett system. Reduced to one-half size. (Reproduced with the permission of the publisher.)

in both directions, the straight up-and-down stroke, and the retraced horizontal stroke. The continuous, progressive oval may be looked upon as a modification of the retraced oval. Somewhat less frequently used forms of drill are the continuous "*m*" stroke, "*u*" stroke, and "*l*" stroke (see Fig. 5). The aim of these drills is evidently to give the pupil practice in the use of the arm movement in the production of the letters.

Another type of drill is particularly directed toward the development of the arm component in carrying the hand along the line while the letters may be produced by the finger and the hand. This type of drill has been particularly developed in the Bennett method (see Fig. 6). This method in fact excludes entirely the oval and the up-and-down drills. The drills which are included in this method are the back-and-forth horizontal stroke, the so-called swinging and rocking stroke, and the development of the "*i*" and the "*n*" out of a combination of these strokes with an intervening downward stroke. This forward-and-backward movement is used even in the development of the letters themselves, as well as in the movement between the letters. Thus "*a*" is

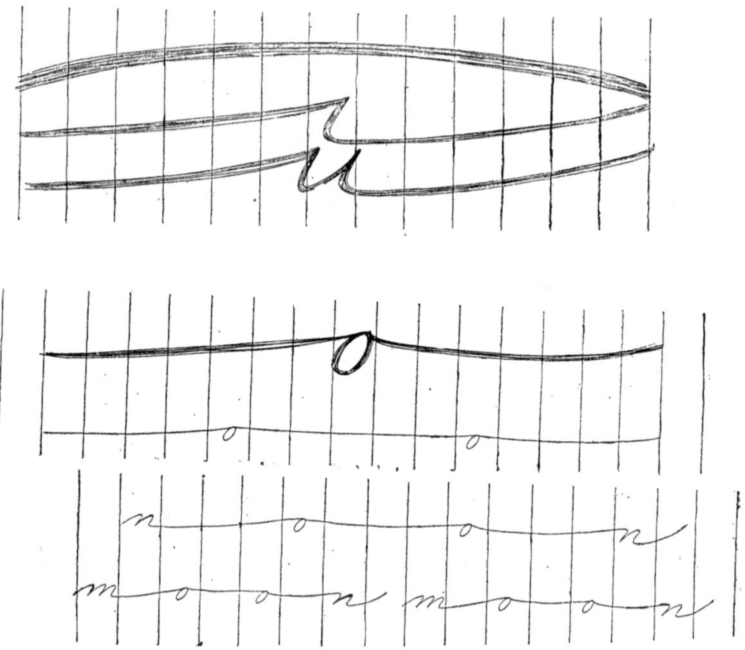

FIG. 7.—Illustrations of exercises with laterally spaced letters. From Houston's *Copy Slips* for Grade III. (Reproduced with the permission of the publisher.)

produced by a combination of the rocking and swinging movement with the downward movement following. This same lateral movement is emphasized in certain drills used by Houston, Berry, and others (see Fig. 7). These drills consist in a succession of letters which are connected by strokes an inch or more long. In such a drill it is necessary to combine smoothly the movement which produces the letters and the movement which carries the hand across the page. Since this touches upon the essential problem in the development of the writing co-ordination the writer believes that such drills are of the highest importance. The oval and the straight up-and-down stroke are useful to develop an easy, flowing movement, but lose some of their importance if one is not seeking to develop the exclusive arm movement with rest.

Only the commonly used formal drills have been here referred to since more labored forms are a matter for individual choice. A great many drills which consist in retracing letter forms or incorporating into the formation of the letter one of the formal drills, have been devised. These may be useful in compelling the pupil to use a free movement in the production of the letter, but are of less importance than the more formal drills.

Application of drills to letter-formation.—The application of the various formal drills to the different letters was touched upon in the description of the order of development of the letters. If this application is made a corresponding order of development will take place in the case of the formal drill. That is, the direct oval may be practiced in preparation for the drill upon the *i*, *u*, and *w*, and the capital letters *O*, *C*, *A*, *G*, *D*, and *E;* the reversed oval may be made the basis for the development of the *n*, *m*, and *v*, and the capital letters *I*, *J*, *P*, etc. Finally the straight up-and-down drill may be used to introduce the *t*, *d*, etc., and the loop drill in connection with the loop letters.

Rhythm and counting.—A very important aspect of the teaching of writing hitherto not mentioned is that of rhythm and the means of attaining rhythm. Experimental investigations have shown that one of the main differences between the writing of the child and of the adult is that the latter is very much more characterized by rhythm than the former. That is, the adult tends to write in time as though to music. The successive strokes, though very different in length, tend to approximate each other in time. It has also been shown that the use of an imposed rhythm, that is, the requirement that the child write according to a certain rhythm, tends to unify his writing and render it more mature in character.

This principle has been widely utilized in the teaching of writing. The main question in this connection concerns the rate of rhythm which is to be used and the manner of counting or of inducing the child to write in a rhythmical fashion.

The advocates of the free-arm movement have performed a good service to the pedagogy of writing by their insistence on the device of counting. They have not been so fortunate, however, in the choice of the rate of rhythm, particularly for the lower grades. As has been already mentioned, the rate of movement which is ordinarily chosen is 200 per minute, and no distinction is made between the different grades. The question of the rate of movement which is adapted to the different grades is easily susceptible of investigation. The writer has undertaken to determine the ability of children of different ages to make up-and-down strokes, with the result shown in the accompanying table. From this table it appears that three children of grade IB made between 70 and 79 double strokes per minute, and so on. (The column in which the median falls in each grade is indicated by printing the number in that column in black face.)

TABLE III

GROWTH IN RAPIDITY OF GRAPHIC MOVEMENT THROUGHOUT THE GRADES

Grade	60–69	70–79	80–89	90–99	100–109	110–119	120–129	130–139	140–149	150–159	160–169	170–179	180–189	190–199	200–209	210–219	220–229	230–239	240–249	250–259	260–269	270–279
IB . .	...	3	2	**2**	1	1	2	...	...	...	...	...	...	...	...	...	...	...	...	...	...	...
IIB . .	1	1	...	...	1	1	1	**3**	1	1	...	...	1	...	...	...	1	1	...	...	...	...
IIA . .	1	...	...	1	1	3	1	2	**2**	2	...	...	1	3	1	...	...	...	...	1	...	...
IIIB . .	...	...	1	1	2	3	**3**	...	...	...	1	1	2	1	1	...	...	...	...	...	...	...
IIIA . .	...	...	...	...	...	...	1	...	...	2	...	1	5	2	**5**	1	4	...	1	...	1	1
IVB . .	1	...	1	...	1	2	...	...	**2**	...	...	1	...	2	...	...	2	...	...	1	...	...
IV. . . .	...	...	...	...	1	2	1	...	2	...	3	3	**6**	2	3	1	2	...	4	...	...	...
V. . . .	...	...	...	...	...	1	2	1	...	2	3	1	7	**5**	2	7	...	1	1	...	1	...
VI. . . .	...	...	1	...	2	1	4	4	1	**4**	4	3	2	2	2	...	...	...	...	1	...	...
VII. . . .	...	...	...	...	...	...	1	1	1	...	3	3	1	**5**	2	4	3	2	2	1	...	...
VIII. . . .	...	...	...	...	...	1	1	1	3	4	5	**2**	1	2	5	3	2	3	...	...	...	...

Several facts appear from this table. In the first place, it is evident that there is wide variation in the ability of children in the same grade to write rapidly. In grades IIA and IVB the fastest child writes more than four times as fast as the slowest. It is clear that some provision must be made for these differences. When the pupils are writing in concert to a rhythm which is indicated by the teacher they must write at the same rate. When they are writing individually, however, some should write faster and some more slowly than this standard.

In the second place, it is evident that the rate of writing of a grade is influenced by the method of teaching as well as by the maturity of the pupils. Thus Grade IIIA is faster than the preceding and following grades, and Grade VI is slower. The full significance of this fact cannot be known unless the quality of the writing is also measured, but the fact remains.

Finally, in spite of variations among the individual grades, it is clear that there is a gradual increase in speed from the lower to the higher; and, if a uniform method were pursued throughout, this progression would, in all probability, be fairly regular. The particular standards which are suitable for the different grades must be established by more extended trial. A tentative set of standards may be proposed for trial and modification. The units refer to double strokes consisting of an upward and downward straight line with sharp angles at top and bottom. Grade I, 80–90; II–III, 125–50; IV, 175; V, 200; VI–VIII, 225–50. The speed of writing letters is about half as great as the speed of making double strokes.

There is some difference in procedure in the use of counting. The count is ordinarily made upon the down stroke. Sometimes, however, both the down stroke and the up stroke are counted, and in one case, that of the Bennett method, the count is upon the up stroke or the connecting stroke only. We have here a difference in procedure which is likely to have considerable influence upon the type of writing and which deserves attention. It is evident that emphasis will be placed upon the stroke which is made at the time the count is given. The ordinary procedure, then, places the emphasis on the downward stroke, whereas the Bennett method places the emphasis upon the connecting stroke and holds that the downward stroke will pretty largely take care of itself. The writer looks upon this as a very interesting idea but has no basis for judgment as to its merits, except the fact that it emphasizes the forward push of the hand. Since this is the element which is likely to be weak in the writing movement, it seems possible that a device which will emphasize it may prove worthy of adoption.

The time is ordinarily indicated by counting or by making a series of raps with a ruler, or hand claps, etc. Little, if any, use, so far as the writer knows, is made of music to indicate the time in writing, but the success with which music is used to mark time for marching, dancing, gymnastic exercises, etc., suggests that it would be well worth trying in this case also.

Style of alphabet.—The form of letter which is used as a model for the child is of a good deal of interest. There is a very strong tendency for the child to imitate the style of writing which is set before him. This can easily be verified by examining any set of samples of children's writing. They invariably resemble the copy in general style. The importance of this fact does not lie so much in the relative virtue of one form or another in itself so much as in the fact that certain styles of letter are more readily produced than others, and, therefore, involve a better type of movement. That this is so is an indication that the reverse of the opinion which is sometimes held, is, at least to a certain extent, true. The movement is the reflex of the form as much as the form is a reflex of the movement. It is important, then, as suggested in an earlier part of this article, that the letter be such as suggest fluency of movement. The writer believes that this can be best attained by the use of the reproduction of actual writing rather than of copies of engraved letters. See illustrations from the Bennett and the Palmer systems (Fig. 8).

These remarks will indicate the point of distinction of the various forms of alphabet which are used. We may perhaps classify the various styles of alphabet according to their probable ancestry. There are, in general, two strains which may be traced in the various styles. One originated in the Spencerian hand and was modified in the business colleges, and may be called the business or arm-movement style of writing. This writing usually has considerable slant, ranging about 60 degrees, though not so much slant as the Spencerian style. In form, the turns of the letters are relatively sharp and tend to become angular. Some of the systems, as the Bennett method, the Houston Copy Slips, the

Palmer method, etc., which use this style of writing, employ the reproduction of actual writing in their copies. Others, such as Spencer's Practical Writing, the California series, and the Standard Free-hand Writing, use an engraved style of script which suggests the written forms (see Fig. 9).

The other line of development originated in the vertical writing, which marked the introduction of a relatively new style of script.

FIG. 8.—Illustrations of copy reproduced from actual writing. 1. From the Bennett method, Grammar Series. 2. From the Palmer method. (Reproduced with the permission of the publishers.)

This writing was chiefly characterized by the extreme roundness and width of the turns, and hence by the breadth and squat appearance of the letters. These letters were also characterized by extreme simplicity, every possible superfluous stroke being omitted. When the vertical writing was, in general, given up, many systems used the same style of writing but modified it slightly by introducing some slant. Such a style is represented in the Whitehouse system, and Barnes's Natural Slant.

A third group of systems occupy an intermediate position between these two extremes, and almost every degree of difference may be found.

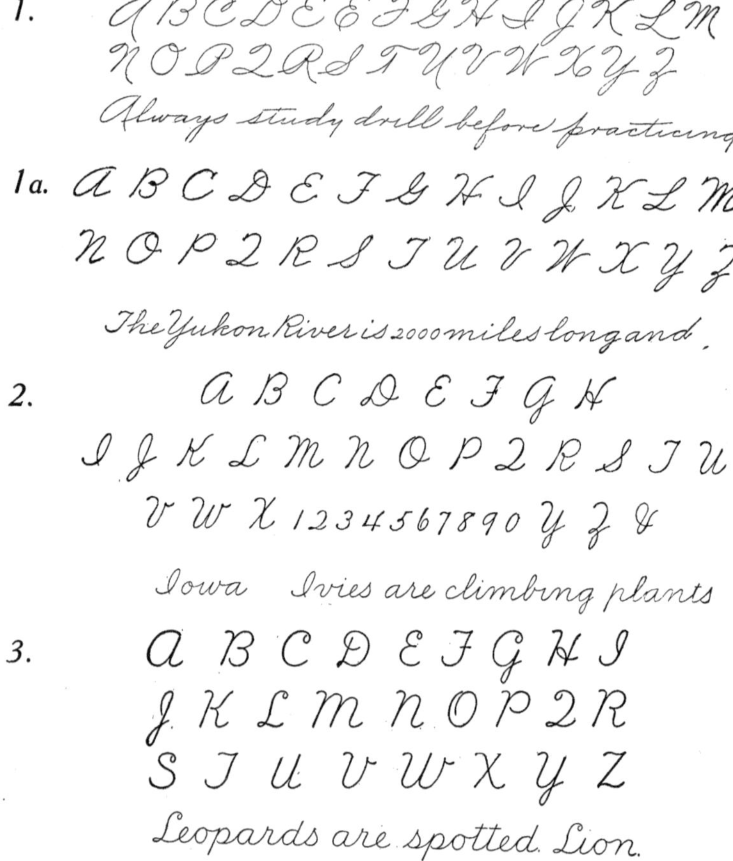

FIG. 9.—Illustrations of the three kinds of script. 1. The business, free-hand style; from the Palmer method. 1*a*. The same style engraved. From the Standard Free-Hand system. 2. Intermediate style from the Medial method. 3. The extremely round and simple style. From Barnes's *Natural Slant Penmanship*. (Reduced to ½.) (Reproduced with the permission of the publishers.)

The advantages claimed for the vertical style of letter and its successors are based upon the two points of legibility and economy. The legibility rests mainly on the relatively upright position of the strokes, and the economy upon the paucity of the strokes which are necessary to write the letters. The advantages upon the side of the opposing style of script are based upon considerations of ease and fluency of movement. The issue between legibility and fluency is clear cut. The writer believes, however, that the style of letter should be chosen on the basis of its adaptability to a fluent movement, rather than primarily on the basis of its legibility, since the legibility of writing depends, not so much upon the ideal which it is supposed to copy, as upon the degree which it approximates the ideal; and it is much more likely to approximate the ideal if it can be made with an easy, fluent movement. In regard to the economy supposed to be effected by lopping off certain of the strokes, such as the beginning up stroke of the *i* and *j*, it is to be said that simplicity of objective form does not necessarily mean simplicity of movement. The pen at the end of a word is usually at the bottom of a stroke. It therefore has to pass from the base line to the top of the letter through the air or upon the paper. Certain experimental results have shown that in similar cases, such as the crossing of the *t* or the *x*, it takes as long for the pen to pass through the air as it would take to make the stroke upon the paper. Furthermore, it is probable that there is more likely to be a considerable pause at the beginning of the stroke when it is started in such fashion as in the case of the letters referred to. It is easier to begin a letter by an introductory stroke so as to get one's bearings, so to speak. This, as well as other similar issues, may well be subjected to experimental investigation for final settlement.

The above principles will indicate without a more specific illustration the general type of letter which is most desirable. Considerable latitude as to details of form and style of letter may exist within the range of letters which meet the general principles laid down. A somewhat rounder and more nearly vertical style of script might well be used in the earlier, than in the later, grades.

Organization of work for the different grades.—The principles underlying the organization of the work for the different grades have been referred to in the discussion of the particular methods of teaching. They may here briefly be brought together. The question of the time of beginning writing in general was touched upon in discussing the replies from the questionnaire. It is held by a number of writers upon the pedagogy of handwriting that the ideal course to pursue, from the point of view of the writing itself, would be to defer the teaching of writing until the second or third year. This, however, appears to be impracticable, and the question remains as to the type of writing which shall be pursued in the different grades. Several of the systems which are under discussion make little or no distinction between the work to be given to the different grades. The courses are organized on the basis of a year's work and the pupil is put through the same work whatever his grade. The most thoroughgoing example of this type of procedure may be seen in the Palmer method. Certain of the other systems vary the work slightly in point of complexity in the different years, but in general repeat the same course. An example of this may be seen in the Steadman method.

On the other hand, the methods which lay little stress upon the movement drills, and which rely on the copy-book, may make little distinction between the work of the successive years, except in the subject-matter of what is written. In such case the first book may begin with one space letters and then introduce the multiple space letters in the course of the book, and defer the capital letters to the end of the first book or the beginning of the second. The size of the letters is usually decreased in the first two or three books. From this point on, longer words and sentences are used, and in the later books various business and social forms are introduced. But the formal side of the writing is very little changed. The chief respect in which a rational system of grading is introduced then, is in the distinction between the type of writing required in the lower and the higher grades, and the extent to which the specific writing instruction is given. Without stopping to detail the variations in method, we may outline a typical curriculum in writing, which aims to meet the different stages of development of the child.

In such a course the aim of writing in the different divisions of the school is radically different. In the primary grades the aim is to develop a fairly accurate perception of the form of the letters, and the ability to write with some facility, using free and not very precise movements. The writing for the child of these years is mainly a means of expression and not a matter of technical skill. The analogy may be drawn with the development of the child in drawing. The primary child does not draw to reproduce with accuracy the form of objects, but to express in a more or less symbolic way the ideas which he has in mind. In the same way, writing may be made a means of expression without undertaking to develop extreme accuracy.

In the intermediate grades the child should begin the formal drill which will enable him to acquire greater skill and fluency in writing. He is now interested in developing greater accuracy in his manual activities. He realizes the discrepancy between his earlier, rough attempts and the standard which is set before him. He becomes interested in the accurate use of tools and weapons, for the sake of development of skill for its own sake. This is the time, then, when he will be most interested in the formal drill in writing.

This development of skill and facility in the use of the pen should be accomplished, in the main, in two or three years. No particular difference in the type of training to be given in this group of years has been worked out. The best procedure, so far as we have basis for judging, is to determine upon an order of development of the letters and drills which is consistent and progressive, and go through this system in the two or three succeeding years of this period, placing special emphasis upon features which particular classes or individuals find most difficult. At the beginning of this period the form of the writing is likely to deteriorate for the time being. This is not at all a serious matter, and the form will soon improve if the drill is wisely chosen and the speed which is used is not too great.

If the two or three intermediate grades have been well trained, the aim in the upper grades may be merely to review that which has been already attained, and to develop somewhat greater speed and fluency. It is incorrect to assume, however, that the subsequent writing will take care of itself if the earlier training has been correct. It is probably not necessary to spend so much time upon drill at this time; but two or three short periods a week may profitably be spent in reviewing the drills which have been previously learned. In addition to this it is probably necessary to introduce some motive for the maintenance of careful writing in all the work. This might be done by holding occasional tests and giving grades on the basis of these tests, or by grading the writing which is done in other school exercises. This would emphasize the need of care, not merely in the writing lesson, but also in all written work. Experience shows that not even at the end of the elementary-school period can attention to writing be entirely withdrawn. Occasional drills might profitably be given even in the high-school period, and some attention be given to the excellence of the pupil's general writing.

This course in each part assumes the other parts and is an organic whole. What is said concerning each grade applies only in case the system is carried out throughout the grades. For example, if the training which is described for the intermediate grades is not given, it will be necessary to devote more time and energy to the writing in the upper grades, in order to secure good results. This principle of the organic unity of the whole course has often been flagrantly violated. Pupils have begun under one system and in the middle of their course a new system has been introduced, and it has often been the case in this way that the same person's handwriting has been torn up by the roots and reorganized two or three times. It is to be emphatically said that a relatively poor system carried through consistently is better than a continual shifting from one to the other, and it is to be hoped that the modern attempt to base the discussion of handwriting upon a scientific foundation will prevent the sudden and complete transitions from one extreme to another, which have characterized the past practice.

A THREE-FOOT SHELF FOR A TEACHER'S PROFESSIONAL LIBRARY[1]

Compiled by IRENE WARREN
Librarian, School of Education

Any collection as limited as this is certain to omit valuable books. These books are offered to the teachers of the elementary and secondary schools, as representative of the educational literature of today, and are indicative of the rapidly increasing and widening range of educational contributions.

Monroe, Paul, ed. Cyclopedia of education, vol. 1, 1911. Macmillan.
———. Textbook in the history of education, 1905. Macmillan.

Brown, E. E. The making of our middle schools, 1903. Longmans.
Dutton, S. T., and Snedden, David. The administration of public education in the United States, 1908. Macmillan.
Foght, H. W. The American rural schools, 1910. Macmillan.

Spencer, Herbert. Education: intellectual, moral and physical, 1900. Appleton.
Fröbel, F. W. A. The education of man, 1903. Appleton.

Locke, John. Some thoughts concerning education, 1902. Cambridge University.
Milton, John. Tractate on education, 1883. Cambridge University.
Pestalozzi, J. H. Leonard and Gertrude, 1885. Heath.
Rousseau, J. J. Émile, 1885. Ginn.

Dewey, John. School and society, 1900. University of Chicago Press.
Forbush, E. H. The coming generation, 1912. Appleton.
Perry, C. A. The wider use of the school plant, 1910. Charities Publication Committee.
Scott, C. A. Social education, 1908. Ginn.
Rugh, C. E., and others. Moral training in the public schools, 1907. Ginn.

Bolton, F. E. Principles of education, 1910. Scribner.
Bagley, W. C. The educative process, 1906. Macmillan.
James, William. Talks to teachers on psychology, 1902. Holt.

[1] Prepared for the Library Exhibit of the Library Section of the National Education Association.

Judd, C. H. Genetic psychology for teachers, 1903. Appleton.
Hall, G. S. Youth, 1906. Appleton.
Kirkpatrick, E. A. Fundamentals of child study, 1903. Macmillan.
Thorndike, E. L. Principles of teaching, 1906. Seiler.
Strayer, G. D. A brief course on the teaching process, 1911. Macmillan.

Bourne, H. E. Teaching of history and civics in the elementary and secondary schools, 1903. Longmans.
Carlton, F. T. Education and industrial evolution, 1908. Macmillan.
Carpenter, G. R., Baker, F. F., and Scott, F. N. The teaching of English in the elementary and the secondary schools, 1903. Longmans.
Comstock, A. B. Handbook of nature-study, 1911. Comstock.
Huey, E. B. The psychology and pedagogy of reading, 1908. Macmillan.

Cornell, W. S. Health and medical inspection of school children, 1912. F. A. Davis Co.
Palmer, G. H., and Palmer, A.F. The teacher. 1908. Houghton.

BOOK REVIEWS

Examples of Industrial Education. By FRANK M. LEAVITT. Ginn & Co. Pp. viii+330.

Professor Leavitt defines industrial education as the training which should be given to that large group of children who are not going to higher schools. The higher schools are vocational in a very proper sense of the term, but they are limited in scope, not preparing for the simpler and more common industries. The opportunities offered by the higher schools are therefore inadequate from the point of view of the great majority of the people.

The second part of Professor Leavitt's discussion sets forth the sources of the present vigorous demand for a modification of our American schools in the direction of more industrial training. Organized labor when it is clear as to the meaning of such training, the manufacturer who wants better labor, the professional educator, and finally the social worker who sees the conditions under which most boys and girls live, all unite in demanding a reorganization of our school system. No mere addition to the course of study will satisfy this demand, there must be a genuine remodeling of the school.

The third part of the book describes what has been done at different centers in the United States in the organizing of industrial courses. Many summaries of this type have appeared in recent years in reports of commissions and in reports of committees. This summary is, however, more complete and consequently more valuable to the student than any of the other reports. It classifies the schools also in such a way as to define clearly the underlying principle exemplified in the different experiments.

The book is well adapted for use as a textbook with teachers' classes. The individual teacher, whatever his part in the elementary school, will also find it profitable to acquaint himself or herself with the movement which is exercising so powerful an influence in present-day elementary education.

Professor Leavitt's recommendation for a solution of the problem presented in his summary of existing conditions is tempered by a recognition of the necessity of dealing with the present schools and reorganizing them rather than merely adding to them. He is prepared accordingly to favor several plans as particular circumstances may dictate in various cases. Some differentiation from the sixth grade on is the general solution of the problem, and much preparatory work can be carried on below the fifth grade in anticipation of the reorganization which is to be entered upon at the sixth grade. The exact character of this differentiation and of the preparatory work remains to be worked out in subsequent studies.

CHARLES H. JUDD

A Scale for Measuring the Quality of Handwriting of School Children. By LEONARD P. AYRES, Department of School Hygiene, Russell Sage Foundation. New York, 1912.

This report sets forth the results of an investigation of the legibility of handwriting and of an attempt to construct a scale for the measurement of legibility on the basis of this investigation. As a basis for the study a large number of samples of the handwriting in the upper school grades were collected from forty cities in widely different parts of the United States. Of the samples which were returned 1,578 were found to be satisfactory and were used for the investigation. The method by which the samples were graded was to measure the average time which was required by ten investigators to read the individual samples. For this method it was necessary that the content of the different samples be not the same; on the other hand it was necessary that they be of approximately equal difficulty. These requirements were met by using the same subject-matter but throwing the words out of their natural order. Thirty different arrangements of the words were made.

After the time of reading the samples had been measured they were arranged in order on the basis of this measurement. The distribution of the papers was then investigated in order to determine whether it followed any law, particularly whether it accorded with the normal distribution. It was found in a preliminary examination that the samples did apparently fall into such a distribution. Assuming a normal distribution, then, the samples were divided into steps of equal interval by separating them into such groups as would be produced in the normal distribution by dividing it into equal steps. It was found that the successive steps which were thus marked off and which have been described as equal in legibility were not exactly equal in the time which was required to read them. They rather formed a series which progressed with approximately the ratio of 117 per cent. This was due to the fact that there was greater difference in the time required to read the samples which represented the successive steps in the lower part of the scale than in the upper part. In other words, a progression by (assumed) equal steps in the objective quality of the writing corresponded to a progression by regularly diminishing steps in the speed at which the writing could be read, or the subjective legibility. The actual series of steps nearly approximated a regular progression so that a theoretical series, in which there was a regular progression of 117.2 per cent between the successive steps, was substituted for the actual one.

This gives us a series of samples, then, which are assumed to progress by equal steps in legibility from the lowest to the highest. The whole range of distribution was divided into ten steps and designated by the numbers 1 to 100, but only those from 20 to 90 are actually represented upon the scale. This form of division is used because it corresponds to the grading in common use.

In order to meet one of the criticisms to which the Thorndike scale is subject, the author selected and furnishes for each step in the scale a sample of three styles of writing. These styles are distinguished according to their slant into vertical, medium slant, and extreme slant writing. There are then in the scale three parallel series of samples, and in measuring any particular sample, the style of writing on the scale which it most nearly resembles is to be chosen for comparison. This device is undoubtedly calculated to make the grading of writing by means of the scale very much easier.

It may be pointed out, however, that there are difficulties in using the scale as it stands as a means of grading the writing of the children in the different school grades. This is due to the fact that a different standard should be required of the children in the different years. For example, the writing which is equal to quality 60 may be perfectly satisfactory for a sixth-grade child but not for an eighth-grade child. Therefore, in order to make the grade conform to the grading in the other school subjects the measurements in the lower grades must be transmuted into other terms. This difficulty might be overcome by fixing a standard for attainment by the different grades and designating this standard by the mark 90 for that grade. The development of such a standard makes a suitable problem for investigation.

Another difficulty which will be met in applying the scale for grading writing is that the greater part of the writing of the school children will fall within the middle divisions of the scale. That is, according to the law of normal distribution which was found to apply to the writing of school children, approximately one-half of the cases fall between the grades 40 and 60 upon the scale and one-quarter fall below grade 40. This means that if 70 per cent were taken as the passing mark, as it ordinarily is in school work, three-quarters of the children would fail to pass. Obviously, then, the results of measurement by the scale cannot be used directly to express the grade of the child's writing.

The other purpose for which the scale is intended is for the survey of writing of children in different school systems and under different methods of instruction. It is intended, in other words, to be used as a tool for investigation. From this point of view, as also from the point of view of practical use in the schoolroom, the scale by itself is very deficient for the reason that it measures only one of the essential characteristics of good writing. The acquirement of speed is as essential in learning to write as the acquirement of legibility. It is, therefore, not sufficient in judging a child's writing to measure merely the legibility. The scale as it stands can be used, however, as a basis for a part of the test, and is probably adequate, provided it is supplemented by a measurement of speed.

As a measurement merely of the scale of legibility, the scale appears to be very well constructed. The fact that it conforms so closely to the normal distribution gives a presumption in its favor. The fact that it was constructed on the basis of objective measurement rather than of mere subjective judgment is also a strong point in its favor. It cannot be applied, of course, by the same method of objective measurement by which it was constructed, but the fact that it is based upon a perfectly clear and unambiguous quality of writing will doubtless make the results of its application fairly uniform and reliable. Whether or not this expectation will be confirmed by trial remains to be seen, but at any rate the scale merits careful trial under various conditions. If it proves to be an accurate means of measurement it will furnish an exceptional means of comparing writing in widely different places because of the prominence of the agency which stands sponsor for it.

FRANK N. FREEMAN

THE UNIVERSITY OF CHICAGO

BOOKS RECEIVED

AMERICAN BOOK CO., CHICAGO

A Study of the Paragraph. By HELEN THOMAS. Cloth. Pp. 125. $0.50.
Elementary Physiology. By JOHN CALVIN WILLIS. Cloth. Illustrated. Pp. 400. $0.80.
Trading and Exploring. By AGNES VINTON LUTHER. Cloth. Illustrated.

APPLETON & CO., NEW YORK

A Fifth Reader. By CLARENCE F. CARROLL and SARAH C. BROOKS. Cloth. Illustrated. Pp. 479. $0.45.

CAMBRIDGE UNIVERSITY PRESS

Cambridge Geographical Text Books. By A. J. DICKS. Cloth. Illustrated. Pp. 362. $1.00.
A First German Book on the Direct Method. By G. T. Ungoed. Cloth. Pp. 177. $0.80.
The Revised English Grammar. By ALFRED S. WEST. Cloth. Pp. 329. $0.60.
Heroes, Hero-Worship and the Heroic in History. Edited by GEORGE WHERRY. Cloth. Pp. 277. $0.45.
A First Year Latin Book. By JOHN THOMPSON. Cloth. Pp. 227. $0.50.
Prehistoric Man. By W. L. H. DUCKWORTH. Cloth. Pp. 156. $0.40.
Caesar in Britain and Belgium. By J. H. SLEEMAN. Cloth. Pp. 123. $0.45.

THE CENTURY CO., NEW YORK

The Westward Movement.
The Colonists and the Revolution.
Explorers and Settlers.
A New Nation.
The Progress of a United People.
The Civil War. Edited by CHARLES L. BARSTOW. Cloth. Illustrated.

FORBES & CO., CHICAGO

False Modesty. By E. B. LOWRY, M.D. Cloth. Pp. 110. $0.50.

GINN & CO., CHICAGO

The Normal Child and Primary Education. By ARNOLD L. GESELL. Cloth. Illustrated. Pp. 340. $1.25.
The Pierce Spellers. Books One and Two. By WALTER MERTON PIERCE. Cloth. Pp. 110. Book One, $0.18. Book Two, $0.20.
The Expression Primer. By LILIAN E. TALBERT. Cloth. Illustrated. $0.30.
The Friendship of Nations. A Story of the Peace Movement for Young People. By LUCILE GULLIVER. Cloth. Illustrated. Pp. 293. $0.60.

Fine and Industrial Arts in Elementary Schools. By WALTER SARGENT. Cloth. Illustrated. Pp. 132.

Pageants and Pageantry. By ESTHER WILLARD BATES with an Introduction by WILLIAM ORR. Cloth. Illustrated. Pp. 294.

HARPER & BROTHERS, NEW YORK

Festivals and Plays. By PERCIVAL CHUBB and His Associates. Cloth. Pp. 403.

D. C. HEATH & CO., BOSTON

The Industrial Primer. By MARY B. GRUBB and FRANCES LILIAN TAYLOR. Cloth. Illustrated. Pp. 127. $0.30.

Introductory American History. By HENRY ELDRIDGE BOURNE and ELBERT J. BENTON. Cloth. Illustrated. Pp. 264.

HOUGHTON MIFFLIN CO., BOSTON

Two Years before the Mast. By RICHARD HENRY DANA, JR. Cloth. Illustrated. Pp. 524. $0.60.

The Life of Christopher Columbus. By CHARLES W. MOORES. Cloth. Illustrated. Pp. 117. $0.25.

Letters from Colonial Children. By EVA MARCH TAPPAN. Cloth. Illustrated. Pp. 319. $0.65.

Winter. By DALLAS LORE SHARP. Cloth. Illustrated. Pp. 148. $0.60.

A History of the United States. By REUBEN GOLD THWAITES and CALVIN NOYES KENDALL. Cloth. Illustrated. Pp. 471. $1.00.

First Year in Number. By FRANKLIN S. HOYT and HARRIET E. PEET. Cloth. Illustrated. Pp. 129. $0.35.

The Spring of the Year. By DALLAS LORE SHARP. Cloth. Illustrated. Pp. 148. $0.60.

Children's Classics in Dramatic Form. Book Five. Cloth. Illustrated. Pp. 326. $0.60.

Fourth Reader. By JAMES H. VAN SICKLE and WILHELMINA SEEGMILLER. Cloth. Illustrated. Pp. 275. $0.55.

THE MACMILLAN CO., NEW YORK

The Utopia of Sir Thomas More. Edited by WILLIAM DALLAM ARMES. Cloth. Pp. 346. $0.60.

English Composition in Theory and Practice. By HENRY SEIDEL CANBY and Others. Cloth. Pp. 465. $1.25.

The Literary Reader. By KATE F. OSWELL and C. B. GILBERT. Cloth. Pp. 591. $0.65.

Education. By EDWARD L. THORNDIKE. Cloth. Pp. 292. $1.25.

Nature Stories. By MARY GARDNER. Cloth. Illustrated. Pp. 255. $0.40.

The American Secondary School and Some of Its Problems. By JULIUS SACHS. Cloth. Pp. 295. $1.10.

Everyday English. Book One. By FRANKLIN T. BAKER and ASHLEY H. THORNDIKE. Cloth. Illustrated. Pp. 240. $0.35.

RAND McNALLY & CO., CHICAGO

The Water-Babies. A Fairy Tale for a Land-Baby. By CHARLES KINGSLEY. Edited by SARAH WILLARD HIESTAND. Cloth. Illustrated. Pp. 382.

SCOTT, FORESMAN & CO., CHICAGO

Selected Letters of Pliny. Edited by HUGH MACMASTER KINGERY. Cloth. Pp. 242.

WARWICK & YORK, BALTIMORE

The Outlines of Educational Psychology. An Introduction to the Science of Education. By WILLIAM HENRY PYLE. Cloth. Pp. 247. $1.25.

WASHINGTON GOVERNMENT PRINTING OFFICE

Country Schools for City Boys. By WILLIAM STARR MYERS. Paper. Pp. 22.

Report of the Commissioner of Education for the Year Ended June 30, 1911.

CURRENT EDUCATIONAL LITERATURE IN THE PERIODICALS[1]

IRENE WARREN
Librarian, School of Education, The University of Chicago

ANDREWS, CHARLTON. The stage and education. Educa. 32:608–13. (Je. '12.)

ANTIN, MARY. First aid to the alien. Outl. 101:481–85. (29 Je. '12.)

BARNES, EARL. The feminizing of culture. Atlan. 109:770–76. (Je. '12.)

BARTON, JAMES W. The combination of the social with the physical work at the University of Toronto. Am. Phys. Educa. R. 17:343–49. (My. '12.)

BASHFORD, HARRY M. Teaching printing in Denver public schools. Print. Art 19:383–84. (Jl. '12.)

BECK, CARL. A university show. Harp. W. 56:22. (27 Jl. '12.)

BLAICH, LYDIA R. The Gregg scholarships of the Indianapolis public schools. El. School T. 12:460–62. (Je. '12.)

BLAN, LOUIS B. Are we taking proper care of the health of our school children? Pedagog. Sem. 19:220–27. (Je. '12.)

Bolting school-teachers. Lit. D. 45:148–49. (27 Jl. '12.)

BOLTON, FREDERICK E. Public education of exceptional children. Educa. R. 44:62–69. (Je. '12.)

BONNELL, CLARENCE. The first week at the beginning of the school year in the high-school woodworking shop. Man. Train. M. 13:401–15. (Je. '12.)

[1] Abbreviations.—Amer. Phys. Educa. Rev., American Physical Educational Review; Atlan., Atlantic Monthly; Cent., Century; Colum. Univ. Q., Columbia University Quarterly; Educa., Education; Educa. Bi-mo., Educational Bi-monthly; Educa. R., Educational Review; Educa. Rec. (Lond.), Educational Record (London); El. School T., Elementary School Teacher; English J., English Journal; Harp. W., Harper's Weekly; J. of Educa. (Bost.), Journal of Education (Boston); J. of Educa. Psychol., Journal of Educational Psychology; J. of Psycho-Asthenics, Journal of Psycho-Asthenics; Kan. School M., Kansas School Magazine; Kind. R., Kindergarten Review; Lib. J., Library Journal; Lit. D., Literary Digest; Man. Train. M., Manual Training Magazine; Outl., Outlook; Pedagog. Sem., Pedagogical Seminary; Pop. Sci. Mo., Popular Science Monthly; Print. Art, Printing Art; Psychol. Clinic, Psychological Clinic; Pub. Lib., Public Libraries; R. of Rs., Review of Reviews; School and Home Educa., School and Home Education; School R., School Review; Sci. Am., Scientific American; Sci. Am. Sup., Scientific American Supplement; Teach. Coll. Rec., Teachers College Record; Train. School M. (N.J.), Training School Magazine (New Jersey); Univ. of Chic. M., University of Chicago Magazine.

BRINTON, CHRISTIAN. A master of make-believe. Cent. 84:340–52. (Jl. '12.)

BRUÈRE, MARTHA B. How shall we learn to keep house? Outl. 101:536–41. (6 Jl. '12.)

———. Launching the child. Outl. 101:75–80. (11 My. '12.)

BRUÈRE, ROBERT W. Dilemma of the public school. Harper 125:213–19. (Jl. '12.)

BRYAN, WILLIAM LOWE. Economy in university administration. Science 36:41–45. (12 Jl. '12.)

BUMANN, A. M. Manual training, yesterday and today. Kan. School M. 1:205–12. (My. '12.)

BURNHAM, WM. H. Suggestion in school hygiene. Pedagog. Sem. 19:228–49. (Je. '12.)

BUTLER, NATHANIEL. Report of the twenty-fourth educational conference of the academies and high schools in relations with the University of Chicago. School R. 20:383–400. (Je. '12.)

CALL, ARTHUR DEERIN. Dr. Dawson's inductive study of school children. Psychol. Clinic 6:61–68. (My. '12.)

———. The growth of the moral ideal. Educa. 32:546–59. (My. '12.)

CARSON, JESSIE M. The children's share in a public library. Lib. J. 37:251–56. (My. '12.)

CATTELL, J. MCKEEN. University control. Science 35:797–808. (24 My. '12.)

CHASE, ARTHUR MINTURN. Children of the street. Outl. 101:686–94. (27 Jl. '12.)

CHURCHMAN, PHILIP H. The sliding scale and academic standards. Educa. R. 44:25–34. (Je. '12.)

CLARK, S. H. A new plan for a contest in public speaking. School R. 20:379–82. (Je. '12.)

(The) college not the sheriff. Outl. 101:381–82. (22 Je. '12.)

COLVIN, STEPHEN S. Marks and the marking system as an incentive. Educa. 32:560–72. (My. '12.)

COOK, JOHN W. History of education, XIX. School and Home Educa. 31:373–79. (My. '12.)

COOK, W. A. Shall we teach spelling by rule? J. of Educa. Psychol. 3:316–25. (Je. '12.)

COULTER, JOHN G. The student's appreciation and response as elicited by biology. School and Home Educa. 31:379–85. (My. '12.)

DEARBORN, GEORGE V. N. The sthenic index in education. Pedagog. Sem. 19:166–85. (Je. '12.)

DIMAN, JOHN B. The ideal as an incentive. Educa. 32:573–77. (My. '12.)

EDGERTON, FREDERICK WILLIAM. A recent experiment with magazine literature. English J. 1:278–83. (My. '12.)

Education by mail. Harp. W. 56:27. (18 My. 12.)

Educational reactionaries. Lit. D. 44:1256. (15 Je. '12.)

Effinger, John R. La ligue pour la culture française. School R. 20:401–6. (Je. '12.)

Eliot, Charles W. School instruction in sex hygiene. J. of Educa. (Bost.) 75:595–97. (30 My. '12.)

Ellis, Havelock. Rousseau today. Atlan. 109:784–94. (Je. '12.)

Fernald, Guy G. An achievement capacity test: a preliminary report. J. of Educa. Psychol. 3:331–36. (Je. '12.)

Foster, William T. Scientific distribution of grades at Reed College. Science 35:887–89. (7 Je. '12.)

Freeman, Frank N. Current methods of teaching handwriting. II. El. School T. 12:481–93. (Je. '12.)

(A) friend of East-side children. Lit. D. 45:65. (13 Jl. '12.)

Gates, Frederick T. The country school of to-morrow. World's Work 24:460–66. (Ag. '12.)

Gayler, G. W. Elimination and vocational training. Psychol. Clinic 6:69–73. (My. '12.)

George, Anna E. Dr. Maria Montessori. Good Housekeeping 55:24–29. (Jl. '12.)

———. The first Montessori school in America. McClure 39:177–87. (Je. '12.)

Gilliams, E. Leslie. Investigating the child. Harp. W. 56:13–14. (8 Je. '12.)

(The) girl graduate. Harp. W. 56:6. (8 Je. '12.)

Greenwood, James M. New York City School Report for the year 1911. Educa. R. 43:508–18. (My. '12.)

Gruenberg, Sidonie Matzner. What is the Montessori method? Sci. Amer. 106:564–65. (22 Je. '12.)

Hall, G. Stanley. Children's rights. Kan. School M. 1:183–87. (My. '12.)

Herts, Alice Minnie. The power of dramatic instinct. Outl. 101:492–95. (29 Je. '12.)

Hitchcock, Alfred M. A composition on red ink. English J. 1:273–77. (My. '12.)

Hollingworth, H. L. The psychology of efficiency in work. Sci. Am. Sup. 74:59. (27 Jl. '12.)

Howerth, Ira Woods. Patriotism, instinctive and intelligent. Educa. R. 44:13–24. (Je. '12.)

Hutchinson, Woods. Children as cabbages. Good Housekeeping 54:676–82. (My. '12.)

———. We and our children. Psychol. Clinic 6:122–23. (Je. '12.)

Hyde, Henry M. Science's challenge to business. Harp. W. 56:21–22. (27 Jl. '12.)

Jesse, Richard Henry. President and faculties in state universities. Educa. R. 44:1–12. (Je. '12.)

JOHNSON, ROSWELL H., and GREGG, JESSIE M. Three new psychometric tests. Pedagog. Sem. 19:201–3. (Je. '12.)

KAYSER, C. F. May the modern languages be regarded as a satisfactory substitute for the classics? Educa. R. 43:449–60. (My. '12.)

KENNARD, BEULAH. Restoring a birthright. Child (Chicago) 1:7–10. (Mr. '12.)

KENNEDY, JOHN. The Batavia plan after fourteen years of trial. El. School T. 12:449–59. (Je. '12.)

KING, IRVING. The place of certain kindergarten principles in modern educational theory. Kind. R. 22:643–54. (Je. '12.)

KINGSLEY, SHERMAN C. Community recognition of children's rights and needs. Child (Chicago) 1:7–10. (Jl. '12.)

KUHLMANN, F. The present status of the Binet and Simon tests of intelligence of children. J. of Psycho-Asthenics 16:113–39. (Mr. '12.)

LARKIN, JOHN. Princeton's new president. Harp. W. 56:10. (18 My. '12.)

LEONARD, WILLIAM J. The place of art in the American college. Educa. 32:597–607. (Je. '12.)

LEVINE, MICHAEL. Treatment of stuttering, stammering, and lisping in a New York City school. Psychol. Clinic 6:93–106. (Je. '12.)

LURTON, FREEMAN E. Retardation in fifty-five western towns. J. of Educa. Psychol. 3:326–30. (Je. '12.)

LUTHER, FLAVEL S. Moral standards in college. Educa. 32:539–45. (My. '12.)

MCANDRESS, J. MACE. The history of education in the normal school. Educa. 32:614–19. (Je. '12.)

MCCONN, CHARLES MAXWELL. Students' ranking of English classics. English J. 1:257–72. (My. '12.)

MCCOURT, WALTER EDWARD. A philosophy of geography. Pop. Sci. Mo. 80:587–96. (Je. '12.)

MCCRACKEN, ELIZABETH. American children. Outl. 101:427–35. (22 Je. '12.)

MCKEEVER, WILLIAM A. The Kansas teacher and the cigarette law. Kan. School M. 1:198–200. (My. '12.)

———. The public schools and the subnormal child. Normal Instructor 21:11–12. (Je. '12.)

MCMANIS, JOHN T. The history of arithmetic in the elementary schools of America, 1825–1850. Educa. Bi-mo. 6:397–412. (Je. '12.)

MCMURTRIE, DOUGLAS C. Educating the crippled child. Educa. 32:636–42. (Je. '12.)

MACVEAGH, FRANKLIN. Education and the voter. Univ. of Chic. M. 4:300–308. (Jl. '12.)

MACY, MARY SUTTON. The vegetative child: a biological study of early child life. Child 2:625–47. (My. '12.)

MAIN, JOSIAH. Sequence of science and agriculture in the high school. III. Kan. School M. 1:188–97. (My. '12.)

MARKUS, HENRY F. A scheme for grading in manual training. Man. Train. M. 13:450–51. (Je. '12.)

MARTIN, GEORGE H. The peculiar obligation of the public high school. Educa. R. 43:461–71. (My. '12.)

MEARNS, WILLIAM HUGHES. The high school: its manners and customs. Outl. 101:581–85. (13 Jl. '12.)

MILES, DUDLEY H. The dramatic museum at Columbia University. R. of Rs. 46:67–70. (Jl. '12.)

MILLIS, JAMES F. Appeal to the play instinct in teaching arithmetic. Educa. Bi-mo. 6:386–96. (Je. '12.)

MONROE, WALTER S. Warren Colburn on the teaching of arithmetic, together with an analysis of his arithmetic texts. II. El. School T. 12:463–80. (Je. '12.)

MOOGRIDGE, GEORGE, and HEALY, WILLIAM. A feeble-minded genius. J. of Psycho-Asthenics 16:93–102. (Mr. '12.)

MORROW, LOUISE, and BRIDGMAN, OLGA. Delinquent girls tested by the Binet scale. Train. School M. (N.J.) 9:33–36. (My. '12.)

MOSS, EDWARD BAYARD. America's athletic missionaries. Harp. W. 56:8–9. (27 Jl. '12.)

———. When grandfather "made" the 'varsity nine. Harp. W. 56:12–13. (13 Jl. '12.)

MURPHY, J. PRENTICE. A community program for child care. Child (Chicago) 1:21–23. (Jl. '12.)

NEWHALL, CHARLES W. The real problem in secondary mathematics. Educa. R. 43:472–82. (My. '12.)

NEYSTROM, PAUL H. A commercial course for high schools. Educa. R. 43:483–98. (My. '12.)

———. Advertising the public library. Pub. Lib. 17:199–202. (Je. '12.)

NICOLSON, FRANK W. Family records of graduates of Wesleyan University. Science 36:74–76. (19 Jl. '12.)

NICHOLSON, KATHLEEN. The Michigan schools. Educa. R. 44:55–61. (Je. '12.)

OSBORNE, LUCY A. The school luncheon. Pedagog. Sem. 19:204–19. (Je. '12.)

O'SHEA, M. V. Enduring verities in education. Kind. R. 22:655–59. (Je. '12.)

———. The Montessori method of teaching. Dial 52:392–94. (16 My. '12.)

PEARCE, R. M. Chance and the prepared mind. Science 35:941–56. (21 Je. '12.)

PEARCE, RICHARD M. Research in medicine. Pop. Sci. Mo. 81:5–18. (Jl. '12.)

PEIRCE, GEORGE J. The opportunity of the endowed university. Science 35:973–77. (28 Je. '12.)

(A) penniless philanthropist. Lit. D. 44:1352–54. (29 Je. '12.)

PHILLIPS, BYRON A. Retardation in the elementary schools of Philadelphia. Psychol. Clinic 6:107–21. (Je. '12.)

PHILLIPS, PAUL C. The extension of athletic sports to the whole student body at Amherst. Am. Phys. Educa. R. 17:339–42. (My. '12.)

PHILLIPS, WILBUR C. Community planning for infant welfare work. Child (Chicago) 1:16–20. (Jl. '12.)

PRICE, ANNA MAY. Libraries and the commission form of government in Illinois. Pub. Lib. 17:216–18. (Je. '12.)

Public pensions to widows. Child (Chicago) 1:31–54. (Jl. '12.)

ALMY, FREDERIC. Experiences and observations which lead me to oppose such a law.

KINGSLEY, SHERMAN C. Introduction.

PINCKNEY, MERRITT W. Experiences and observations which lead me to favor such a law.

PUTMAN, HERBERT. The quick in the "dead." Lib. J. 37:325–45. (My. '12.)

RADOSAVLJEVICH, PAUL R. What are the principles of modern reforms in school subjects? Educa. Bi-mo. 6:413–24. (Je. '12.)

RAPEER, LOUIS W. Tentative standard plan for the medical supervision of schools. School and Home Educa. 31:367–72. (My. '12.)

RAYCROFT, JOSEPH E. Hygiene and physical education at Princeton University. Am. Phys. Educa. R. 17:333–38. (My. '12.)

(A) retrospect. Educa. Rec. (Lond.) 18:417–37. (Je. '12.)

I. Monitorial schools and their successes: A contribution towards a history of school practice in the nineteenth century. By W.

II. Lancaster's writings—(*continued*). By Principal SALMON.

RICHARDS, JOSEPH W. Helps to studying. Pop. Sci. Mo. 81:193–96. (Ag. '12.)

ST. JOHN, EUGENE. A technical trade school for pressmen. Print. Art 19: 301–4. (Je. '12.)

SANFORD, EDMUND C. Methods of research in education. J. of Educa. Psychol. 3:303–15. (Je. '12.)

SAUNDERS, LEONARD DOUGLAS. Cruelty in childhood and some of its results. Child 2:657–62. (My. '12.)

SCHMITT, CLARA. The Binet-Simon tests of mental ability. Pedagog. Sem. 19:186–200. (Je. '12.)

(A) science library for children. Science 36:46. (12 Jl. '12.)

SCOTT, FRED NEWTON. Verbal taboos. School R. 20:361–78. (Je. '12.)

SCUDDAY, LOUISE. Fifteen minutes a day. Good Housekeeping 54:708–11. (My. '12.)

SIMPKINS, RUPERT R. Legislation for the last three years on vocational education. School R. 20:407–16. (Je. '12.)

SMALLWOOD, JULIAN C. The teaching of experimental engineering. Educa. R. 44:35–44. (Je. '12.)

SMITH, DAVID EUGENE. Chinese mathematics. Pop. Sci. Mo. 80:597–601. (Je. '12.)

———. The present teaching of mathematics in Germany. Teach. Coll. Rec. 13:5–124. (Mr. '12.)

SMITH, FRANKLIN O. A rational basis for determining fitness for college entrance. Pedagog. Sem. 19:137–53. (Je. '12.)

STEARNS, ALFRED E. Moral standards in the schools. Educa. 32:529–38. (My. '12.)

STEEVES, HARRISON ROSS. The cultivation of ideas in the college writing course. Educa. R. 44:45–54. (Je. '12.)

STEVENS, THOMAS WOOD. The pageant as a school exercise. School Arts Book 11:1003–11. (Je. '12.)

STODDARD, FRANCIS HOVEY. The college preparatory school: which shall the boy choose? Lit. D. 45:155–56, 158. (27 Jl. '12.)

STONE, JOHN C. The nature and purpose of a problem. Educa. Bi-mo. 6:379–85. (Je. '12.)

STOREY, THOMAS A. Statistical record, College of the City of New York. Am. Phys. Educa. R. 17:350–60. (My. '12.)

STOWE, A. MONROE. Our textbook problem. Kan. School M. 1:201–4. (My. '12.)

SULLIVAN, J. W. N. Henri Poincaré. Sci. Am. 107:78. (27 Jl. '12.)

TAYLOR, CHARLES KEEN. Athletics and the boy. Psychol. Clinic 6:74–78. (My. '12.)

TAYLOR, JAMES P. The doomed pupil. Educa. R. 43:499–507. (My. '12.)

Teaching the world by mail. Harp. W. 56:26. (18 My. '12.)

TERMAN, LEWIS M. The Binet-Simon scale for measuring intelligence. J. of Psycho-Asthenics 16:103–12. (Mr. '12.)

———. Some evils of school life. Harp. W. 56:24. (20 Jl. '12.)

THOMSON, GODFREY H. College camps for boys. Child 2:648–56. (My. '12.)

TUCKER, WILLIAM JEWETT. Administrative problems of the historic college. Educa. R. 43:433–48. (My. '12.)

TUCKERMAN, FREDERICK. Henry James Clark—teacher and investigator. Science 35:725–30. (10 My. '12.)

(A) university exposition. World's Work 24:381–82. (Ag. '12.)

WALLIS, WILSON D. The Oxford system versus our own. Pedagog. Sem. 19:154–65. (Je. '12.)

WARD, R. DEC. Abbott Lawrence Rotch. Science 35:808–11. (24 My. '12.)

Wetter, A. A. Great educators, VI. Horace Mann. Educa. 32:643–47. (Je. '12.)

Wild, Laura H. Training for social efficiency. Educa. 32:624–35. (Je. '12.)

Williams, Talcott. The School of Journalism. Colum. Univ. Q. 14:235–48. (Je. '12.)

Winship, A. E. Looking about. J. of Educa. (Bost.) 75:625–26. (6 Je. '12.)

Wirt, William. The place of the public school in a community program for child welfare. Child (Chicago) 1:11–15. (Jl. '12.)

Woman's work for better cities. Lit. D. 45:49–50. (13 Jl. '12.)

Wood, Thomas Denison, and Reesor, Mary. Health instruction in the elementary school. Teach. Coll. Rec. 13:1–140. (My. '12.)

Woods, Elizabeth L. Recent experiments in committing to memory. Pedagog. Sem. 19:250–79. (Je. '12.)

Zimmern, Elsie M. A new training school for children's nurses. Child. 2:671–76. (My. '12.)

The Constructive Bible Studies and Other Textbooks for Religious Education (A fully graded series)

Published by THE UNIVERSITY OF CHICAGO PRESS, CHICAGO, ILLINOIS

A study of the titles illustrated above will show that play, music, stories with handwork, the fresh interest in books, hero-worship, the historical and literary instincts, are successively employed to present social, ethical, and religious truths at just the stage of development when these instrumentalities make their strongest appeals.

Features not shown in the photograph are: the attractive color in the bindings, appealing strongly to the eye and taste of the pupil; the numerous artistic and instructive illustrations; the illuminating maps; the clear, large type; the careful editing; the interesting form of presentation of each lesson, both to teacher and pupil.

The six volumes on the left are all guides for the teacher, the work of the pupil in those grades being in notebook or other expressional form.

VOLUME XIII NUMBER 2

THE ELEMENTARY SCHOOL TEACHER

OCTOBER, 1912

EDUCATIONAL NEWS AND EDITORIAL COMMENT

School Buildings

In Los Angeles a school building one story high is being built around three sides of a quadrangle 240×250 ft. A playground 190 ft. square will be inclosed by this building. There will be sixteen rooms, all lighted and ventilated from both sides. A double roof is to cover the whole so as to protect the rooms from excessive heat. This plan is, of course, best adapted to a warm climate, but it suggests the problem of school architecture as a living and important problem.

In Cincinnati the Health Department has taken a lively interest in the remodeling of several buildings. It recommends that two neighboring schools should be merged and the site of one used for a playground. The new building should have open-air rooms and more window space for ventilation.

In Tulsa, Oklahoma, an elementary school is to be built on the cottage plan with more air and light for each unit than can be obtained in the common school building.

In Gary, Indiana, the buildings have been planned with a view to using the corridors for entertainments and play; there are also swimming pools, shops, and large playgrounds connected with each building. By a lengthening of the school day, and a distribution of the children throughout the different parts of the building and grounds, the expense of this more elaborate equipment is so distributed that the cost per capita is less than in the ordinary school.

In Chicago a report of the Elizabeth McCormick Memorial Fund states that of 367 children who attended four schools on roofs and seven in open window rooms, 90 per cent improved decidedly in general physical condition, 15 per cent sufficiently to be discharged as cured, 75 per cent gained in weight from two to eight and one-half pounds. The children in these schools are kept in the fresh air the year round, are given from two to three meals a day, and are required to rest at least one hour during the school period.

All these examples call attention to the fact that a change in the methods and scope of education calls for a change in school buildings. If play is useful in education, there must be a place for play. If the health of a child is a matter of legitimate concern on the part of the teacher, there must be more fresh air and more space for exercise. The school building is an embodiment of educational ideals and a modern school cannot flourish in an old-fashioned building, modeled after a private dwelling or a barn.

An All-Year-Round School

The Belmont Avenue and Seventh Avenue schools in Newark, N.J., were kept open during the past summer, and regular work was carried on in order to test the feasibility of a continuous school session. These schools were chosen because the population is such that most of the children in these districts are obliged to stay at home during vacation.

The average attendance of fourteen hundred children enrolled was 93 per cent. The enrolment represented 70 per cent of the total school population in these districts. The health of both pupils and teachers was good, because the windows were kept open all the time. There was more fresh air than usual in the rooms. The work was satisfactory in grade, more children being promoted at the end of the course than in the regular classes at other times in the year. The cost of conducting the schools was $6,500. By a very slight change in the organization of classes, the pupils are enabled to get the full advantage of their work during the summer, and will complete their elementary-school courses sooner by one-fourth than they could under the old vacation plan.

It will require only a few more experiments of this kind actually carried to successful completion to persuade school boards and teachers that a continuous school session is the only economical, efficient, and justifiable type of school organization.

Public Interest in Schools

Evidence of public interest in schools is nowhere more strikingly furnished than in reports of non-educational organizations which investigate from time to time the efficiency of public schools. The city of Cleveland has in the past two years had a trying experience in school matters. Politics have to an unjustifiable extent controlled the action of the School Board. It is interesting to note that an organization of Cleveland citizens, namely the Cleveland Engineering Society, has raised in definite form the question which the Board of Education ought to have faced some time ago: the question of efficiency of the school system. The engineers find that the efficiency of the system according to their standards is less than 50 per cent. The committee points out that frequent changes in policy affecting the course of study and promotion are demoralizing and incompatible with highest efficiency. Any form of dissension in the school organization is harmful.

These are wholesome words and should sink deep into the minds of all teachers and all boards of education. The slight respect with which business men and engineers frequently look upon school organization is due in very large measure to the instability of school plans and the short and uncertain tenure of school officers.

A different type of example of public interest in school matters is to be found in two reports recently issued by public associations in the city of Chicago. The City Club through its School Committee, and the Commercial Club through its special agent, Mr. Cooley, have both investigated the needs of the Chicago schools in respect to industrial education. Mr. Cooley's report is reviewed on a later page. The report of the City Club will be reviewed fully in a later issue of this Journal. The two reports are diametrically opposed in that one advocates separate vocational schools of secondary grade, the other advocates a genuine reform within the elementary schools, making much of the work of these schools vocational in type. The two programs will come up for legislative recognition in the state of Illinois during the coming winter. It is highly important that school officers be prepared to discuss the two plans fully and intelligently. One plan is being advocated and tried in Massachusetts, the other in New York. It is possible to get reports from both of these states.

Michigan Course of Study

The law of 1911 gives the State Superintendent of Schools in Michigan the authority to outline the course of study which must be followed in every district in the state. Heretofore this authority was vested in the district boards. One of the most important changes made in the new course is that requiring agriculture to be taught in every district school in the state. There is a practical difficulty in the way of this change in the fact that teachers are not prepared to give the course. A beginning is therefore all that is required at this time, namely, one-half year of agriculture in the eighth grade. However, a course of nature-study dealing with home gardening, crop planting, and other related subjects is introduced earlier. Later the course in agriculture is to be enlarged. The rural school is to be ruralized rather than allowed to go on reflecting in a weak and inefficient way the city schools.

Summer School for Teachers

The statistics from the summer schools of universities and normal schools show that the movement is progressing at a rapid rate. Fifteen years ago teachers felt that they must have a long vacation. This vacation was supposed to be of necessity a period of complete relaxation. Today a very respectable minority of the teachers of the country spend a major part of their time in study. The University of Chicago with its regular summer quarter and Columbia University with its shorter term of six weeks lead in point of numbers and in richness of curriculum. Each of these institutions had during the past summer the largest enrolment in its history, both passing the 3,500 mark. The Summer School of the South, one of the most influential factors in the educational reawakening of the South, enrolled nearly 2,500 teachers. Normal schools all over the country report more students than ever before. Commissioner Claxton at the end of a trip including a number of these institutions declared the movement one of the most significant in the educational history of the country. Such it certainly is. No longer can the teacher rest content with a normal-school training completed years ago. He must get himself into contact with the current enlargements in science, with the recent advances in methods of study and instruction. He must learn of new types of educational organization and must study the efficiency of the new courses of study which are being tried out in parts of the country remote from his own home. It means much for the development of the schools of this country that teachers come together in this way to renew their student activities and prepare themselves to carry home the most progressive educational ideas.

Teachers' Organization

Several speakers and writers have recently called attention to the importance of developing a new type of Teachers' Association in this country. The utter failure of our present National Association to deal with professional problems is too conspicuous to need further comment. The Department of Superintendence is in a better position than the general Association to do something really worthy of the teaching profession. The English Guild furnishes a model to which we in America might well turn attention.

The promising line of organization is that which is suggested by the success of summer schools. Teachers can set up standards of professional efficiency and can develop the machinery for requiring conformity to these standards. They can judge schools better than any other agents of the public. They can supervise appointments better than irresponsible teachers' agencies which take an unwarranted percentage from teachers. The discussion of these problems is fortunately becoming more common where teachers come together. The idea that a teachers' meeting is a picnic or an excursion is gradually becoming less and less common. In short, the time is ripe for some strong and efficient organization like the Department of Superintendence to crystallize the movement toward a real teachers' association in America.

Grading Pupils on Home Work

The State Superintendent of Instruction in Missouri and the Rural School Inspector have devised a plan whereby a closer co-operation shall be established between the home and the school in the training of the children. A report card has been prepared on which the parent is to send to the school a statement of the home work of each pupil. Superintendent Evans comments on the plan as follows:

"This home work may be domestic, helping the mother, or it may be agricultural, helping the father, or of whatever character provided it be not aimless. Parents, especially in rural communities, have not been asked or invited to co-operate with the teacher in any definite, systematic way to correlate the work of the home with that of the school and as a result many pupils have been educated away from the farm and have formed a distaste for home life on the farm.

"Because the school has paid little attention to industrial education and the parent has failed to co-operate with the school in a way that would tend to attract the attention of the pupil to good sweeping, dusting, sewing, cooking, washing, tending stock, milking, caring for poultry, plowing, and industrial work generally, thousands of pupils have left the farms, rushed to the cities, and become consumers instead of producers.

"To the end that the attention of every pupil in the rural schools of the state may be directed toward the things that make better homes, more efficient citizens, this department has issued a definite and systematic method of reporting quarterly from teacher to parent on the progress made by the pupil in the school studies and a report from the parent to the teacher on the progress made by the pupil in such simple, but important, subjects as sweeping, dusting, cake-baking, bread-making, sewing, washing dishes, for the girls, and for the boys, currying horses, feeding stock, milking, caring for poultry.

"This report is to be signed by the teacher as the parent signs the report from the teacher.

"If this method is used efficiently by county superintendents and teachers throughout the state, a long step will be taken in the direction of better co-operation between the school and community."

Devices other than the grading of home work have been adopted in other states with a view to encouraging out-of-school work.

Encouraging Home Work

In the state of Oregon the Bankers' Association in co-operation with the school authorities supports a director of home agricultural work. Of the 125,000 school children of that state 75,000 are reported to be engaged in systematic agricultural work. In Idaho the State Department of Education is succeeding with the aid of the officers of the State Fair in bringing to the capital the children from the different counties in the state who have shown the highest degree of efficiency in potato raising and domestic work. This visit to the State Fair will be made the occasion for instruction to these children in agriculture and domestic science. In Iowa good roads clubs are formed among the boys and prizes are given to individuals and to clubs. In Wisconsin the following announcement is published:

"With the co-operation of the Wisconsin Experiment Association a corn-growing contest has been arranged for the school children of the county. The object is to stimulate an interest in, and disseminate information relative to, the proper selection of seed corn and modern methods of corn culture.

"A number of rules and regulations have been made to cover the contest. Exhibitors must be boys or girls between ten and eighteen years of age, attending school in the county. Golden Glow Wisconsin No. 12 seed will be used and no exhibitor will be allowed to enter more than one sample in any one class, but may enter in each of the three classes, namely sweepstakes, single ear, and corn on stalks. All samples in township classes will consist of ten ears, and all samples in 'corn on stalk' shall consist of not less than three stalks.

"Twenty-one premiums of $2.00 each will be offered. There will be twenty-one second premiums of $1.00 each, and twenty-one premiums of 50 cents each.

"The boy scoring highest in the sweepstakes class, and the boy scoring highest in the corn-on-stalk class will each receive a scholarship to the boys' one-week course in grain-judging at Madison.

"A special premium of $5.00 is offered to the teacher whose pupil receives first premium. This prize is offered by J. P. Bonzelet, of Eden.

"The contest will be conducted in conjunction with the county fair."

One brief item comes to hand showing that this type of interest is not confined to rural communities. The Poultry Association of the city of Buffalo, N.Y., offers through the Board of Education to give free instruction in the breeding and care of fowl to the school children of that city.

These examples could be supplemented by descriptions of experiments in other states and cities. Each undertaking of this type shows how large a margin of unused energy there is among the boys and girls of the country and how urgently the demand for organized employment of this energy is felt by educators.

Out-of-School Reading

A typical example of library development is reported by the librarian of the city of Chicago. The figures which he presents for books circulated through the public schools during the last five years are as follows:

1907–8	666
1908–9	621
1909–10	1,362
1910–11	60,586
1911–12	77,996

These figures represent the growth of a new policy on the part of the library and a new interest in the schools. In some quarters it will doubtless be necessary for teachers to take the initiative in cultivating an interest in good outside reading and in creating the opportunity for such reading. Such out-of-school reading proves, as does out-of-school agricultural work, the possibility of extending widely the influence of the school.

A Course in Morals

The State Normal School at Greeley, Colorado, announces a course in moral education to be offered to Junior and Senior students in that institution. The course as announced emphasizes the rights and value of morals and the importance of personal hygiene.

The Montessori Method

The *New York Globe and Commercial Advertiser* of August 16 contains long interviews with Dr. Kilpatrick, Dr. Hillegas, and Miss Moore, members of the Committee of Teachers College who visited Rome to inspect the Montessori schools. The general tone of these interviews is in agreement with the following statement quoted directly from one:

"Mme. Montessori has really not contributed any thoughts essentially new to education. She has rediscovered or revived some educational doctrines which were known over a hundred years ago, and some of which were rejected by advanced American educators about thirty years ago. Mme. Montessori no doubt was sincere in her work, and she still is convinced that she has invented a new system of education. It is probably true that she worked out her method quite independently and that she did not know that her doctrines had already been proclaimed by educators years ago."

There is always danger of misjudging systems of education either because of overenthusiasm or overconservatism. It is to be hoped that the observations which lie back of these interviews may be put into form which will help American teachers who have not been in the schools of Rome to form just opinions on these new methods which have been so widely discussed.

MONTESSORI AND FROEBELIAN MATERIALS AND METHODS

LUELLA A. PALMER

This article is written merely to start a discussion with regard to the possible combination of Montessori and Froebelian materials and methods as suggested by Dr. Holmes in his introduction to Dr. Montessori's book. No definite conclusions can be reached yet, for several reasons: (1) Mme. Montessori herself feels that her system is not thoroughly worked out; (2) there are few schools even among those called by her name which have accepted the most fundamental principle of the Dottoressa's teaching, the right of the child to liberty; (3) it takes the sifting of time and the judgment of many minds to discover the truly permanent in any system.

It is not necessary to describe in detail the Montessori materials. Those interested in the new method have read either Dr. Montessori's book or the articles which give accurate descriptions and which have appeared in various magazines. They fall naturally into three groups as indicated by Dr. Holmes: those for sense training, physical training, and social training. The sense materials are such as the frames for buttoning or hooking, and the insets, plane and solid; the materials for physical training are such as the stairway, swing, rope ladder; the social materials are those used in the home activities such as preparing and serving food, cleaning, and dressing.

We can easily believe that Froebel would be in hearty sympathy with the physical and social training as advocated by Mme. Montessori, but where in her system the physical education would merely make provision for the exercise of the muscles and through these influence the human side of the child, Froebel would see a more direct spiritual effect in the experience itself. Froebel would hold that the child feels an exhilaration in the act of swinging such as Stevenson has expressed in

How would you like to go up in a swing,
  Up in the air so blue?
Oh, I do think it the pleasantest thing
  Ever a child can do!

Up in the air and over the wall,
  Till I can see so wide
Rivers and trees and cattle and all
  Over the country side.

In the social education there would probably be the same difference. The Montessori training, by having the children do necessary things together, is fundamental but would lack the exercise of the imagination which would be given by the social game of Froebel. In the game the child would see in epitome the forms and results of social co-operation and so have these ideas brought to consciousness with much more distinctness. Muscle exercise is developing and lessons in serving our neighbors are ethical, but these can be given the highest significance by cultivating the imagination at the same time.

Let us confine the discussion to the question, Do the Montessori and Froebelian materials and method for sense and hand training have any relation to each other, are they equivalent, do they supplement each other or do they overlap?

The first Montessori materials, those for fastening cloth together, are not duplicated in any way by the Froebelian materials. They give a child an opportunity to repeat some of the operations which he sees carried on around him and which often relate to him very personally. For this reason he is much interested in them. By isolating these operations and giving them under conditions which make it possible for him to practice them and test whether he can do them properly, the first step is taken in the scientific study of the environment, which is by isolating and concentrating on particular problems. Attention is paid to material and its limitations, there is only one correct solution, there can be no intermediates between right and wrong in working out the problem. The very simplicity of having only two alternatives, but one of which is right, gives a little child a sense of security in solving the problem and of mastery when the definite, easily seen end is accomplished.

In all probability when a child uses this material it will not be the first time that he has studied his environment in this way, isolating certain actions and testing control; but Montessori has devised the simplest educational material which can be supplied for such study. (Little children will often for ten minutes at a time open and shut a drawer or drop and pick up a stone.)

The insets of different kinds isolate certain facts of the environment as to form and size. These materials, also, are so planned that there is but one correct solution to the problem presented. The child feels that there is some definite relation between the removable objects and the openings. Unless he finds out the right relation and puts each object in its proper place, he will be left with something that does not "fit." After several attempts a child about three years of age finds this state of affairs unsatisfactory.

When the flat insets are used with the cards the child corrects his own error. If he has not succeeded in finding a form which will completely cover the filled form or the outline or line, he has no one to blame but himself, his observation has been at fault, the material always offers a perfect solution.

With the long and broad stairs and the tower there is but one right way to show a satisfactory relation between the objects presented. The material again isolates a definite thing to be learned in proportion. Although by combining the different parts of the long stair, number values in addition, subtraction, and multiplication can be seen, this is a use which is secondary to its original purpose and is far too difficult for the child who is only ready to distinguish the differences in proportion.

With the foregoing materials the child would probably stumble on a correct solution even if he had no teacher near him to offer suggestions. With the color tablets the different textures of cloth, and the rough and smooth tracing, the teacher must take the initiative by supplying words to accompany the discrimination. She must also be at hand to show the next step when the child is ready to proceed. The eye and fingers soon become sensitive to differences in shade and texture but there is always a possibility of mistake which can be determined only by social approval or the reverse.

All of the above Montessori materials have tested sense discrimination, they have been sense gymnastics, they have called for observation and eye and muscle identification. They have given the child skill in controlling certain activities of his body, and the pleasure obtained has been from the accuracy with which he has been able to learn from matter and conform to its laws.

If we turn to the Froebelian materials we find that they can be used somewhat as those of Mme. Montessori but that a new element enters in which brings a different educational advantage.

The six prismatic balls can be used for sense discrimination, but while the Montessori color tablets have suggested by their form that they be laid upon the table, the balls suggest motion. As soon as motion is involved there comes a possibility of choice. The roundness says to the child, "grasp," "roll," "toss," "bounce," the string says, "swing," "drag," "twirl." So, although the material limits the child, there is so much latitude within these limitations that the child feels free. Instead of learning but one thing from his material, he learns several and experiments with his knowledge and exercises his human prerogative of choice in using material in several possible ways according to his own desire.

Just as soon as motion, choice, freedom, enter in, the material becomes food for the imagination. Stability points toward unchangeable law, choice in movement points toward infinite possible variations. The imagination is set free. Whereas with the flat object there has been only the desire to find a similar color, now, with the moving object, there is desire to find something similar in motion. So we have a "wheel," a "bird," a "pussy," and the many other ideas which flit through children's minds, and they are many, for moving objects attract a child's attention.

The three objects of Froebel's second gift, the wooden ball, cube, and cylinder, invite to a comparison in form and also to a comparison in motion. With these objects the errors in motion correct themselves, the cube will do but one thing, stand still; the ball will do but one thing, roll; the cylinder will do either. After learning the possibilities of the material a child must have in mind some definite thing which he wishes to do in order to confirm his knowledge or find his error. He must make a choice in thought and then test his knowledge of material by his ability to carry out his idea. In the Montessori tower and stair the material has always said, "Do one thing." With Froebel's second gift the material says, "What will you do?" and then the child tests whether his idea is in accord with the idea in the material. Mme. Montessori thinks that children "rarely recognize solid geometric form."[1] According to her the ball, cube, and cylinder would not be as useful for little children in promoting the observation of form in the external world as plane figures. If this is granted, it means that these objects cannot be used as Montessori uses her form material but that they can be used in the distinctive way in which Froebel's material has the advantage, as types of motion. It is interesting to note that in play children almost invariably prefer the ball or cylinder to the more stable cube.

With Froebel's building-materials there are many variations which can be worked out. If one cube of the third gift (a cube divided into eight small cubes) is taken, there are many possible ways of placing another cube in relation to it, back, front, right, left, or on top, corner to corner or corner to face. The test is whether the resulting form embodies the child's idea as nearly as he can express it with the material at his command. The observation demanded is not only of the material itself but of form in the outside world. As the building-gifts progress, more and more possible variations present themselves until a child is able to represent quite complex objects. After he has used blocks of varying shapes, a child will be able to test his knowledge of the material by having the choice presented to him of which material will best carry out the idea which he wishes to represent.

The tablets (wooden circles, squares, triangles) and rings are in shape much like the insets and outlines of the Montessori materials. They invite to discrimination in form, but besides this they leave the child free to make arrangement in many different ways. Montessori feels that the geometrical analysis suggested by Froebel is too hard for little children except as called for in application to everyday living.[2] She thinks that each form should be

[1] Maria Montessori, *The Montessori Method*, p. 238.

[2] *Ibid.*, p. 243.

observed as a whole rather than as made up of parts.[1] To consider it in the latter way would be to deal with abstractions when the child is able to understand only the concrete.

Sticks and seeds like the other Froebelian materials are capable of being used in two ways, to show the limits of straight lines and points and also to show that by combination and arrangement they can be adapted to expressing an idea which the child has in mind.

In the "occupations" of Froebel (the materials which cannot be returned to their original form after the child has used them) there are many ways of varying the results. Paper, crayon, clay give many possibilities both in the discoveries about the material itself to which they lead and in the expression of ideas to which they lend themselves. Weaving and card sewing are more like the Montessori materials in that the choice is very restricted; the expression is limited to ideas about the material itself; imagination, interpretation cannot enter in. Both of these occupations are considered by Mme. Montessori too severe a strain on the eyes of little children.[2] Folding is considered by her "hand gymnastics"; she does not feel the value of the imaginative use of the objects made. Clay and drawing, which Froebel felt gave great opportunity for the creative use of the imagination and consequently an educative use, Mme. Montessori considers uneducative.[3] Yet she feels that they are necessary in order that the teacher may study the "psychic individuality" of the child and find out how much of the knowledge implicit in the regular lessons has been assimilated.[4]

It would seem as though the Montessori and Froebelian materials were not equivalent, that they were intended to supplement each other. One lays emphasis on a single property of matter at a time, the other offers several for discrimination and consideration. One draws attention to the inert properties of matter which pertain to lower forms of nature, the other includes motion and possible position, the attributes of higher types of life. Montessori emphasizes the more primitive attitude of the child as a learner

[1] *Op. cit.*, p. 236.

[2] *Ibid.*, p. 162.

[3] *Ibid.*

[4] *Ibid.*, p. 241.

from material, Froebel suggests experimenting and learning from material but also using it to carry out human ideas. A child must advance from the study of simple isolated ideas to those of more complexity as found in daily experience. Matter and motion are both in the scheme of the universe, both have discoverable laws and need to be understood to give complete control of the outer world. A child presents various tendencies at the same time. Both the scientific attitude and the interpretative are necessary for well-rounded living.

In the function of the teacher, Froebel and Montessori do not completely agree. This is because of their fundamental difference in philosophy, which is also at the basis of their divergence in materials and methods. Montessori feels that the teacher should be at hand, to help a child in his effort to realize the relation between concrete material and himself. Froebel felt that the teacher's place was, not only to supply didactic material which the child could manipulate, but also to arouse ideas so that the child would seek to embody them in material. With Montessori, the teacher appeals only through the material which she presents; with Froebel, she appeals through the material and also by presenting some idea which it would be possible to express by conforming to the laws in the material.

Both Montessori and Froebel impress the fact that the teacher should study each child individually, and should present materials in a progressive way when the child shows that he is ready for the next step. Where Montessori would leave the child alone to learn as the race has, Froebel might suggest an idea to follow which would hasten the process of learning. Montessori seems to see no middle course between letting entirely alone and a form of dictation.[1] As for instance after a child is taught "blue," she would have the teacher make no application so that some day the child will be able to discover with great joy that the sky is blue. The only alternate she sees to this is pointing to the sky and saying, "What color is that?" and then teaching "blue."[2]

[1] On p. 115 Montessori suggests the value of a *generalized* observation, given by the adult: "We experience the joy of having crystallized an impression which we had before only imperfectly felt."

[2] Montessori, *op. cit.*, p. 110.

Would the Froebelian course be to make the child's senses alert by suggesting after the lesson, that he might find something else blue? The joy of later discovery would probably be as great and be made in a shorter time.

There seems to be but one right method with the Montessori materials, that of letting the child learn the one lesson which was intended by its isolation. This is satisfying and educative for young children. It is like drawing single strokes. These may please little ones for a while but soon they want a result which calls for more knowledge and control.

As Froebelian materials suggest different kinds of knowledge to be gained from the material itself and also the manipulation of the material for the purpose of interpretation as well as control, so there might be various methods by which these materials could be made educative. In an article entitled, "Principles Underlying the Organization of Kindergarten Materials,"[1] I have suggested the following:

> When a child reaches kindergarten age, he is ready to use material in several different ways. (1) There is still much that he may learn by actual contact, many actions may still be impulsive responses to the qualities of the matter presented. (2) Many of the child's actions may be dictated by an adult or be imitations of copies set for him. (3) A child may be led to improve upon some form which he made while experimenting with the material. (4) Some idea may be stimulated, which in order to be complete must, through the expending of the full amount of effort, arrive at a goal. This method may be called either the suggestive or purposive; if viewed from the teacher's side, it is suggestive, from the child's it is purposive. It is founded upon the principles which Froebel realized as most educative because they organize experience.
>
> A very simple illustration of the above methods may be given in the use of the divided cubes of the fifth gift. (1) A child might be left free to discover the possible uses of the half-cubes, for instance, for a slanting roof. (2) Some form with such a roof might be dictated or be imitated. (3) Some form that a child had accidentally made, might be repeated with suggested improvements. (4) A different kind of material might be used as a stimulus, such as a picture of a barn, in order to arouse the desire to make such a form, and the blocks then placed in the child's hands. A double stimulus would be applied through picture material and block material. The child would have a more or less

[1] Paper presented for discussion at the Training Teachers Session of the International Kindergarten Union, 1911.

definite idea to express, would put forth effort in trying to accomplish it satisfactorily, would control means to bring about the end which he feels of value, and would discover the possibilities of the material itself. The more developed children can be led to understand why man uses the sloping roofs, and for them the stimulus provided might have been in the form of a little problem, how to make a roof which would shed rain. Sometimes the older children may have an idea so clearly in mind that they can make a choice of the familiar material which they think would be best adapted to carry it out.

These different methods represent the different uses which man has made of his environment in gaining control over it. Each has some value in developing the right attitude toward the surroundings. None should be omitted in the kindergarten, none used exclusively. (1) If experiment is never allowed in the use of materials the children will not learn how to investigate, they will be helpless when confronted with any new problem, they will never advance beyond their companions but will lose the exquisite joy of discovery and contribute nothing to the knowledge of their own world. If no other method were used there would be only slow progress. A tendency would be formed to be governed by the moment's interest and not to sum up or connect. Respect might be lost for material, and effort would lie dormant if no product could be conceived better than the one chanced upon. (2) If a child never imitated a good copy or followed a dictation he would miss some of the uses of the material which he was capable of appreciating, but not discovering for himself. If this method were used exclusively, it would develop a habit of following blindly and the idea of taking the initiative would never be formed. (3) Where there is no repetition for the sake of improvement, there is a tendency to be satisfied with results that have not demanded a child's best effort, many things are attempted but nothing done well. A child can measure himself and gain fresh impetus for further effort when he sees two similar products placed side by side, one the result of today's work and the other of last week's. If this is the only method employed, the child uses each material for itself, never in relation to any other. It gives him a disconnected view of his environment, he will not feel the unity of thought underlying its various expressions in material. (4) If the purposive method is never used, the materials will never be organized upon the highest basis. A desirable end in view demands a child's best effort, right stimulation will not only call forth self activity to conceive that end, but also require that in its accomplishment control shall be gained over the particular material used and its relation shown to other materials through thought. If this method should be used exclusively, it would defeat its own object, the children would become discouraged and effort paralyzed because they would be tasked to arrive at a result before they could control the means through which to attain it.

The period between four and six years is the time when there is a decided change in the character of the purpose for which materials are used. At four, the gratification of the passing moment is all that is sought; at six, the result and simple means by which it is attained are much enjoyed. These facts should in a general way decide the kind of method predominant at the beginning of the kindergarten and that at its close. It should be mainly experimental at the beginning and purposive toward the end.

The Montessori method with materials is (1), the first of those suggested above, that of learning by actual contact. The methods for Froebelian materials may be many, as stated above, progressing in harmony with the material.

"Method" is larger than the mere using of sense materials; it includes all the means by which the ultimate goal is to be reached as well as the goal itself. The ultimate aims in education of Montessori and Froebel appear to be nearer alike than the roads by which they would reach them. Compare the two following quotations.

> The mother [in instructing Lena how to read] now resembles here in her action the sun, which in spring awakens the slumbering power in seeds and buds, which slowly rousing, further nourishes and strengthens itself. And so it is to be with all human education.[1]
>
> And such is our duty toward the child, to give a ray of light and to go on our way. . . . . To stimulate life—leaving it then free to develop, to unfold—herein lies the first task of the educator."[2]

We can imagine Montessori writing in simpler words:

> We are repeatedly impressed with the conviction that everything which is to be done for the true human development of the child, and all efforts which are to be made for such an education as will satisfy the needs of all sides of its being, must be connected with, and proceed from, the fostering of the impulse to employment, and the oversight of the first employment of the child.[3]

For Montessori the employment would signify "work," for Froebel it would involve a freer element "play." He felt that earnest play held the same values for a child as work does for the adult.

This employment for Mme. Montessori is to aim at the development of the will-power. "The method which is the subject of this book contains in every part an exercise for the will-power, when the child completes co-ordinated actions directed toward a given end, when he repeats patiently his exercises, he is training his positive

[1] Froebel, *Education by Development*, p. 15.

[2] Montessori, *op. cit.*, p. 115.

[3] Froebel, *Pedagogics of the Kindergarten*, p. 24.

will-power."[1] For Froebel the will-power is more a means than an end. "It is the conquering . . . . of the outward hindrance of life by one's own will-power and one's own enhanced power of action, which preserves to man peace, joy, and freedom in his own consciousness, and thus elevates him to that likeness to God for which he was destined."[2]

The desired result, the harmony between child and environment are expressed by Froebel thus: "One willingly makes oneself at home where one can act freely; and on the other hand, one can act freely where one has made oneself at home."[3] In the Montessori schools where Mme. Montessori's principles are thoroughly understood and carried out, a result is seen similar to the above description in actual practice; the children are free and self-controlled. Surely these schools are approximating Froebel's dream of "an institution for self-instruction, self-education, and self-cultivation of mankind."[4] The principal difference is shown in his next sentence: "Individual cultivation of the same through *play*, creative self-activity, and spontaneous self-instruction."[5] The idea of play, of cultivation of the imagination, which Froebel gives as the first means, is that activity of the human mind which has resulted in works of art, in painting, music, and literature. It is this cultural side which seems to be lacking in the Montessori schools and upon which Froebel lays so much stress.

Mme. Montessori is restricted in materials and methods with materials, but she is free in actual practice because she feels so intensely the individual's right to follow his own life. Froebel's materials and possible methods are freer, but when he described his practice he became more circumscribed. Froebel's discovery of the educational value of simple sense materials was so startling that he had to impress the fact upon his contemporaries. When he planned lessons for little children he was so anxious for adults as well as children to find the knowledge that he knew was implicit in the materials, that he sometimes forgot just how the little child ought to approach them and so he dictated uses which would have

[1] Montessori, *op. cit.*, p. 364.

[2] Froebel, *Pedagogics of the Kindergarten*, p. 26.

[3] *Ibid.*, p. 27. [4] *Ibid.*, p. 6. [5] *Ibid.*

been more educative if the child had discovered them for himself. Constant obedience to the word of an individual is slavish, but following the suggestion of a self-determined end sets free. Montessori with the calm patience born of waiting for the slow development of defective children is willing to let a child discover knowledge in order that he may gain something better, the *habit* of acquiring knowledge, the attitude of mind involved in "attention, comparison, and judgment."[1]

The foregoing discussion has tried to suggest the feasibility of combining the different materials and methods into one system for the education of little children. There must be an elimination of some of the materials in order that the child may gain sufficient control over others to make their use valuable. Choice might be based upon the degree to which the materials carry out the characteristic aims of the two educators, the discovery and control of the properties of matter, and the interpretation through material. This is a question which admits of much debate. Perhaps the following might be discarded for children between three and six years of age: (1) Intricate forms of plane insets, many of the "stuffs" and shades and tints; these might be used later and in place of them at this age the child might study the more variable and complex properties of matter as shown in Froebelian material. (2) The Froebelian tablets and rings; these are meager in interpretative possibilities, and the properties of plane surfaces as well as number and proportion can be studied better through the Montessori material. (3) Weaving and card sewing can be postponed until a later period, not only because the eye and hand will then be stronger, but because they are not good as material for interpretation. They might be employed as advance steps of the Montessori material and method.

With the use of Froebelian methods should be kept in mind the great principle which makes the Montessori children so free. The object to be accomplished is never just the will of the teacher, there is always a third something in control, where it does not mean conforming to the limits which the material itself sets, it should be an end realized by the individual child, a task which

[1] Montessori, *op. cit.*, p. 360.

he sets himself. "Once the habit of work is formed, we must supervise it with scrupulous accuracy, graduating the exercises as experience has taught us. In our effort to establish discipline, we must rigorously apply the principles of the method. It is not to be obtained by words; no man learns self-discipline through hearing another man speak. The phenomenon of discipline needs as preparation a series of *complete actions* such as are presupposed in the genuine application of a really educative method. The end is obtained by developing activity in spontaneous work."[1] The truly educative method is to have the child realize the immediate goal toward which he is working and which he has selected or helped to select, to let him make a choice of means by which he will arrive there, and then *to control himself* enough to accomplish this end. This gives training in self-discipline.

If this principle is accepted in the use of Froebelian material it will do away with much uniformity in results. As the material is variable and designedly so, each individual may carry out the same idea in a different way. The uniformity heretofore required has been on the supposition that the result obtained—the object seen—was the thing of value to the child; this is not true as Montessori shows in her illustration of the child filling his pail with gravel.[2] It was the act of filling, not the full pail which was of value to the child. It is the way in which a result is obtained which determines whether it is educative, it must be attained by self-impulsion toward some self-determined end.[3]

Although the result of accomplishing diverse things with the same material, is exactly contrary to that achieved by the use of Montessori materials, which by their very nature require uniformity, the use of the same method will produce this opposite effect because of the variable nature of the kindergarten material. It is this method founded upon the principle of "spontaneous activity" which Montessori insists makes for self-discipline.

Mme. Montessori sees self-development coming through the conquest of self-determined ends. In order that the child may

[1] Montessori, *op. cit.*, p. 350. [2] *Ibid.*, p. 355.

[3] Dr. Dewey says: "It is better to get an externally efficient *method* of getting a result than the mechanical result. It is better to fail intelligently than to succeed accidentally."

gain the habit of striving toward an end and accomplishing what he set out to do, she supplies material which will lead to gradually more difficult attainments. It is the very simplicity of her first materials which make them so educative for little children; they provide an easily attainable goal but one which represents a completed action. Of the separate actions leading to the game of silence Montessori says: "These actions being directed toward an end have no longer the appearance of disorder, but of work. This is discipline which represents an end to be attained by means of a number of conquests. The child disciplined in this way is no longer the child he was at first, who knows how to be good passively; but he is an individual who has made himself better—who has made a great step forward, who has conquered his future in his present."[1] "He is learning how to become his own master."[2]

It must be remembered that "master" for Montessori means almost wholly one who controls himself in order to conform to some established standard; the emphasis is on stability. This is excellent training for little children especially in this age of nervous frenzy in invention and quick change of custom, but there should also be education which prepares for the freer aspect of life. It is this emphasis on stability which gives the children in the Montessori schools their characteristic poise and freedom. With more emphasis on the changeable side of living, the children would not appear so self-controlled but might be better prepared for progress in life.

Whatever the limitations that are felt in the Montessori philosophy, material, and method, there can be but one judgment with regard to the purpose of method as expressed thus: "The greatest triumph of our educational method should always be this: to bring about the spontaneous progress of the child."[3]

As stated in the beginning, this article is only intended to provoke discussion. The Montessori idea of respecting the individual development and needs of each child appeals very strongly to kindergartners. As they long to give little children the best opportunities for self-cultivation which can be obtained, they try to be neither hasty in giving up the good in the old theory and practice, nor slow in accepting what is of value in the new.

[1] Montessori, *op. cit.*, p. 352. [2] *Ibid.*, p. 366. [3] *Ibid.*, p. 228.

THE NEED, PURPOSE, AND POSSIBILITIES OF INDUSTRIAL EDUCATION IN THE ELEMENTARY SCHOOL[1]

FRANK M. LEAVITT
The University of Chicago

The time at my disposal is brief and the subject of industrial education is a large one; therefore I desire to define the specific phases of it about which I am to speak. The discussion will be limited first of all, obviously, by the terms used in the title of the paper, "industrial education" and "the elementary school," and those must be examined briefly.

Industrial education still means different things to different people. As used in this discussion it will mean a complete and adequate scheme of education for the future industrial worker. This scheme includes not only the industrial work but all the related mathematics, science, and art appropriate to the grade of practical work undertaken, and the necessary English, civics, and hygiene.

Many industrial workers will receive training in continuation schools, in trade schools, in high schools, and even in higher technical institutions, but these, for the time being, are not under consideration. The title limits our discussion to the *elementary* schools.

What the elementary school is, and what it ought to be, cannot be disposed of in a single sentence. This unit in our school system has not always been called "elementary," but the names "grammar" and "common" were formerly used and are still heard occasionally. A generation ago the expression "a common school education" meant the training given to that large majority of school children who never had any intention of going to a "high" school. It was superimposed upon the "primary" school of

[1] Read at the annual meeting of the Western Drawing and Manual Training Association, Cincinnati, Ohio, May 3, 1912.

three grades and, together with the primary school, comprised a nine-year course. There still remain school systems with nine elementary grades.

These schools were, in a measure, finishing schools. They were supposed to give the fundamentals of a general education—to provide the pupils with the common tools of an English education. That these schools were efficient, for their time, is only too clearly shown by the countless number of men and women who have attained eminent success in later life with only this training as an educational foundation. No one thought of criticizing the common or grammar school because only a small percentage of its graduates went to the high school. Preparation for high school was not the primary purpose of such schools. What the purpose was may be stated in the words of John Stuart Mill found in his inaugural address at the University of St. Andrews in 1867: "Education makes a man a more intelligent shoemaker, if that be his occupation, but not by teaching him how to make shoes; it does so by the mental exercise it gives and the habits it impresses." At that time there was little doubt that somewhere the boy would be taught to be a shoemaker, a machinist, a salesman, a bookkeeper, or what not, but it was believed that he would be more intelligent, both in his business and outside of it, because of the sharpening and the habitual drill which he was to receive in the school.

It has remained practically for our own day to decree that the main function of the elementary school shall be to select those children who are qualified to continue their education in the high school and to *prepare* them to do so. Without further exposition of facts let me state my main contention in this matter and say that, if the primary purpose of the elementary school is to lay the foundation for a secondary education, and to select those who are competent to take that work with value to themselves, then the elementary school consumes too many of the precious years before the fourteenth birthday of the pupil in giving this preparation, and it imposes tests which make it impossible for many pupils to reach high school at all. Among the rejected is some of the best material in the schools.

When it becomes an established fact that the purpose of the elementary school is the laying of this foundation and the selecting of the pupils best suited for the diversified work in high schools; when there are but six elementary grades, and when the methods employed in these grades are encouraging, instead of repressive, to the concrete-minded children, then there will be no need whatsoever for industrial education in the elementary school. Until that time shall come, I maintain that the most important part of industrial education must be given in connection with the work of grades 7 and 8 of our present elementary school.

In passing it may be noted that, in 1910, the New York State Education Department recommended a six-year elementary school, and also that, for the past two years, two school systems, one on the Atlantic and the other on the Pacific coast, have been administering a six-year elementary school, with a lower and an upper high school. In this lower high school, work such as we are now advocating for the upper grades of the traditional elementary school is made possible.

It will thus be seen that the present organization of our school systems into elementary and high schools of eight and four years respectively, and the consequent domination of the higher over the lower constitutes one of the greatest "needs" for industrial education in the elementary school.

I will present now for your consideration, a few other reasons why industrial education is needed in these schools *as they now exist*. I shall endeavor to state these reasons without argument, merely desiring to bring the several questions forward for discussion as concisely as is consistent with an adequate understanding of their import. The statements follow.

Perhaps the least important reason which I have to suggest is that the wages of some children, even at the early age of fourteen years, are needed for the support of some dependent. I believe that there are relatively few such cases, but there must be some children so situated. The least that the school can do for them is to make them so efficient that their childish service may be worth more than untrained, irresponsible, child labor. Experience has demonstrated this to be possible.

The second reason is closely related to the first, but applies to a much larger percentage of our children. In common with the world in general, industry today demands specialists, or at least requires specialized training for its successful workers. This specialized training is being furnished more and more by secondary schools and the higher institutions of learning. More subjects have been added to the curricula of secondary and higher schools since the Civil War than had been offered in all school courses prior to that time, and these subjects have been introduced largely in the interests of vocational education. Since the elementary school fails to deliver 75 per cent of its children to the higher schools where these vocational subjects are taught, but allows them to go, entirely unprepared, into their life-work, there is a need for something of vocational content in the grades to help this 75 per cent in their competitive struggle with the more fortunate 25 per cent.

Again, the industrial development of the country requires in the industrial workers, the vast majority of whom receive their only school training in the elementary grades, a much higher degree of industrial intelligence, and a keener industrial interest or curiosity than can possibly be awakened or created in the low-grade industrial occupations themselves. The child who, as Dr. Felix Adler says, has been "pitchforked into industry" at an early age, is too near the great unintelligible organization to see it as it really is. The perspective is distorted, and even the good things about it, the necessary economies and the efficient management, seem altogether selfish, heartless, cruel, and inhuman to the young worker. He sees only the grinding wheels which seem to have caught him in their ceaseless whirling, and he feels as lacking in intelligence as they, and as hopeless of an opportunity to perform any other function in the complex process. Beyond a doubt something of this marvelous organization might be demonstrated to those children by the proper kind of work given in connection with their studies at, or preferably before, the time when they will undoubtedly leave school. This whole matter can be so explained and illustrated that children will be a little more discriminating in their selection of jobs, and also a little better able to see the necessity for rigid regulations and apparent severities. Such knowledge would enable them so to adjust themselves to the burden, that they can carry it more easily and more hopefully, and with a reasonable certainty that faithful and intelligent work will bring reward here as elsewhere. No one has time to teach them all this after they have entered a mill or factory. Certainly if they are to make their entry into industry through the mill door, it is of more vital importance that they learn something in school of the methods and meaning of modern industry than that they acquire proficiency in figuring bank discount and partial payments, or in computing interest on promissory notes or in distinguishing between a participle and an infinitive. Therefore there is need, in some communities, of a certain type of industrial education because it will *deter* children from entering low-grade industrial occupations, or will lead them to defer such entry as long as possible, and because it will enable some to rise through such work, instead of being crushed by it, provided they must enter it eventually.

There are four other reasons which may be urged—reasons relating to supposed defects in our traditional educational ideals and practices. The first of these is that this type of education is needed, for boys especially, because it brings more men teachers into the schools. Without overlooking the fact that women are generally better teachers than men, it is nevertheless to be regretted that the majority of boys leave school without having come into contact with a male teacher, except for matters of discipline. Furthermore, the men thus brought into the schools will be of a somewhat different mental attitude and fiber and should serve to hold the balance true and to give a more practical flavor to education.

It has been said, and it is probably true, that our traditional school system tends to create a disinclination to hard work of any kind but especially to manual work, even when such work requires a high order of thinking and promises ample financial and social reward. Referring to the work of Pestalozzi, in his *Educational Reformers*, Quick says, "To many people in the present day it might seem that education, when quite successful, would qualify *laborers* to become *clerks*. This was not the notion of Pestalozzi." It has been noted by all writers on child-study that the child loves activity of almost any sort. It is noticed that children like to *play* at work, but it is also to be observed that children enjoy real work when done in company with their elders. Perhaps they do not care to be set about some uninteresting and disagreeable job, which their elders are also anxious to avoid, but, given companionship in their task, children generally *like to work*. It is a fundamental need in our education that the schools shall address themselves to the problem of so guiding and stimulating this interest in work that it will not have disappeared entirely in the child of seventeen or eighteen years of age. To utilize this almost instinctive desire of children, at the time it appears, training in real work becomes necessary in the grades.

Another distinctly educational reason for urging industrial work in the grades is that it is here that most children reach the period of early adolescence. It seems to be true that our present system of education makes little provision for this mysterious and difficult period of the pupil's school life. If there is any one thing true about the period it is that, during it, the peculiar tastes and desires of the *individual* must be carefully studied, and must be utilized as a motive power if the best results are to be achieved. This period brings to thousands of our children the awakening of vocational interests, the more so when they are hungry and poorly clothed and are without spending money or the means of getting it. These vocational interests must, therefore, be brought into the school work and there utilized as an incentive for vigorous effort on the part of the child. Since with so many of our city children this vocational motive is derived directly from the low-grade industrial occupations above mentioned, the introduction of industrial education would seem to be a necessary educational measure.

And then this introduction of real industrial work into the elementary school is necessary because the first and most important function of the school should be to teach children to *succeed*. Our present schools too often allow children to remain in them for years (often until the children desert the school altogether and forever), without ever experiencing the *joy of success*. After all, is there anything better that the school can do in eight years than to see that children form the habit of successful effort? For my part I would rather a child would *succeed* in industrial work than to acquire the habit of *failing* in his arithmetic, geography, and language work, and of accepting the situation with entire equanimity and indifference. It is undoubtedly true that large numbers of our children will succeed mainly, at this time in their lives, with concrete, creative work of a thoroughly practical and utilitarian nature. Therefore industrial education is needed in the elementary school for the purpose of showing some children how to succeed, and thus inciting them, through the joy of achievement, to still further accomplishment in this and in other fields.

There remain on my list of needs three others, more or less closely related to those already discussed, but having in mind chiefly the benefit which will accrue to society at large, rather than to the individual child or to the school system.

First I would note the advance which is being made by the National Child Labor Committee and other child-saving agencies in securing and enforcing school attendance laws and other measures regulating or preventing child labor. We must all recognize the desirability of such progress, but it raises, nevertheless, a serious question. No generation of men has yet been raised without the advantages, whatever they may be, that inhere in the intimate, personal, and early acquaintance with the difficulties and the joys of real productive labor. Whether this early acquaintance with real work and responsibility provides an *indispensable* element in the education of the race cannot be proven in a generation, but there is a growing belief that such is indeed the case. If one holds to that theory there appears to be but one solution of the problem, namely, to introduce industrial education into the grades as a substitute for child labor.

Industrial education is needed in the elementary schools as a preventive of juvenile delinquency. Existing industrial conditions render it difficult, if not impossible, for children of fourteen or fifteen years of age to satisfy their natural desire to earn money. Even if they leave school and go to work, investigation shows that employment is extremely irregular and poorly paid. Such labor is often uninteresting, and so fails to hold the attention of the child, or to develop in him any enthusiasm for the work. The result is a great deal of idleness which is undoubtedly conducive to delinquency.

It is said that 95 per cent of boy delinquents have committed crimes against property. Most of these crimes would not be committed if money were plenty or even adequate to the barest needs of the family. It seems to be a fact that delinquency is on the increase, both in Europe and America. It would further appear that work of a distinctly vocational nature and promising the development of greater earning power would retain large numbers of the fourteen- and fifteen-year-old children in school, especially if the work were begun a year or two before the end of the compulsory school period.

However this may be, it is thoroughly well understood that the methods employed in the reformation of these delinquents, in reform schools and in penitentiaries, include a liberal amount of training in the practical arts and industries and in continual opportunity for the doing of work needed to maintain the daily life of the institution. A careful study of these schools, and of other schools for the unfortunate or less fortunate of our children, seems to prove beyond peradventure, the efficiency of these methods. They are employed, in many of these institutions, in training children of the same age and possessing the same general characteristics as the less progressive members of our elementary schools, and this fact leads to the belief that the same or similar methods applied in our public schools would be preventive and thus render less and less necessary our reformatory institutions. If this be true, industrial education is badly needed in our elementary schools.

And finally, I would urge as the last of the three social reasons and the last on my list this, that industrial education is needed to bring to our young people a finer appreciation of the joy and pleasure to be derived from productive work. This is needed as a corrective for the present tendency of our schools, in common with our civilization in general, to over-emphasize the pleasures to be gained by consumption and by passive entertainment.

The schools teach our young people, and rightly so, to desire and to enjoy poetry, music, art, travel, the drama, beautiful clothes, beautiful houses, both as to architecture and in interior furnishings, and many other things of like nature. The schools develop a strong desire to enjoy such things but give very little idea of how these wants can be satisfied, leaving the inevitable conclusion that money is the one and almost the only source of enjoyment. It should not be hard to convince a body composed of teachers of the manual arts that, while all the above-mentioned means of securing enjoyment are good, there has been omitted one which really brings a more lasting joy and one which may be, perhaps *must* be, combined with the love of the beautiful, and that is the joy which is found *in the making*. Children may be taught the joy *in making* for the better employment of their leisure, as well as the sterner joy *in productive labor* which will enable them to get a little more satisfaction out of their daily work. This interest, like so many other vital interests, is peculiarly susceptible of development in the child of twelve to sixteen years of age, and therefore should be the peculiar care of the elementary school.

If we turn from the consideration of the needs for industrial training in the grades to ask what the purpose of such training is we may feel that, obviously, the purpose is simply to meet the demonstrated needs and that nothing more need be said. I believe, however, that it is worth while making one general and inclusive statement regarding the purpose of elementary industrial education in addition to all which has been said in, or may be implied from, the foregoing. There are certain types of industrial schools which have a single, definite purpose, and rightly so; but any industrial work in the grades must be distinguished by a double purpose or it will be unworthy of our approval.

Industrial education in the grades must meet, in some measure, one or all of the needs which we have discussed. It must show the joy in productive labor, must serve to interest children in the industrial world, must enable the young worker to enter an occupation with some special training which will better prepare him to succeed in it, it must give him a respect for honest labor and teach him the satisfaction in work well done, it must give him some comprehension of the great industrial organizations of our country and some notion of the dangers, difficulties, and possibilities of success which are presented by them; but this is only half the purpose. The other half consists in so presenting this industrial material that the children will be led, consciously or unconsciously, to a better understanding of what education is, of what the schools can do to promote it, of what advantages may come from a better mastery of the tools of knowledge, in short, so as to interest him in what we have commonly called "education" but which perhaps is better described by the more homely term "schooling."

This second purpose, perhaps the more important of the two, is an attempt to harness that great motive power, *the vocational interest*, in the service of stimulating elementary education as it is now employed in secondary and higher education. It is not to be doubted that some students pursue their college courses with the admonition of Solomon in their hearts, "Get wisdom, and with all thy getting get understanding," but I firmly believe that, if these courses were known to be devoid of vocational significance there would be an exodus from our institutions of learning, both of students and instructors. The vocational motive is potent with most of those who are receiving a liberal education, and it is the *purpose* of industrial education in the elementary school to provide an equally vital inducement to study for those children who can have but a few years of contact with the schools and who do not come at their life-work by way of the professions.

And finally, we are to consider the possibility of such work in the grades of the public schools. I shall be pleased to leave the details of these question for the discussion of those who follow me. I will say, however, that the best answer to the question that I can give is that, within three years, a dozen or more such classes or schools have been organized experimentally and have met with unexpected success. Merely to mention the location of these schools would show the widespread and growing interest in this work. Beginning at the Atlantic Ocean and ignoring the industrial schools which maintain a separate organization, that is, which require the children to leave the established pathway which leads to the high school and to the university, we find a line of these *elementary industrial schools* under one name and another as far as to the Pacific. Within a few weeks, Boston, the city which first experimented with this type of school work, has fixed the status of the work by establishing seven "pre-vocational centers," so called. Fitchburg, Mass., Cleveland, Cincinnati, Indianapolis, Springfield, Ill., Evanston, St. Louis, St. Paul, Los Angeles, and Seattle have all *demonstrated* the possibility of industrial education in the elementary school.

Whatever may be the superiority of other types of industrial schools, it is certain that these will touch more pupils and at a time when to touch is strongly to impress. It is also true that whatever may be the relation of other industrial schools to the present school system and to the present corps of teachers, the elementary industrial work will be most effective when conducted under the direction of the manual-training authorities. This presents to the manual-training teachers of the country one of the most important and interesting educational problems now under consideration. It is my firm belief that manual-training teachers will rise to the occasion and will work out a solution of this problem which will be of great and lasting good to the entire school system.

THE RELIABILITY OF STANDARD SCORES IN ADDING ABILITY

ARTHUR S. OTIS AND PERCY E. DAVIDSON
Leland Stanford Junior University

In[1] the effort to set up standard scores in arithmetic, or standards in any school subject for that matter, it is necessary to keep in mind the different purposes to which such scores may be put. Stone[2] measured school systems. Courtis[3] invites us "to measure the efficiency of the entire school, not the individual ability of the few." Others would doubtless urge "finding the individual." Perhaps the practical uses of scales or standards in the branches of the curriculum may be reduced to three. There is, first, the great desirability from the administrative point of view of determining the efficiency of instruction in groups, large and small. The purpose here is to learn of the effect of school conditions as exhibited in the achievements of classes, schools, and systems in comparison one with another. The idiosyncrasies of individuals are of concern only when they tend to differentiate a group from what is usual among school groups. There is, also, quite as important a need of standards in properly locating an individual child either as an entrant to a class or as a candidate for promotion. And standards are required for the purpose of disclosing the peculiar weaknesses which act as causes of backwardness in the more general abilities. It is plain that a standard score might be derived in such fashion as to serve one of these purposes without adequately satisfying the others.

The usefulness of standards for the analysis of pedagogical backwardness may not be obvious. Suppose that by the applica-

[1] The writers of the paper are under obligations to the following persons for considerate co-operation in the gathering of data: Superintendent Alexander Sheriffs, of San Jose, Cal.; Principals L. Bruch, A. L. Dornberger, V. Dornberger, J. E. Hancock, J. Manzer, R. A. Lee, of the same place; Principal M. L. Trace, of Hester; Dr. Margaret Shallenberger and Miss Henrietta Riebson, of the Normal Training School, San Jose.

[2] *Arithmetical Abilities and Some Factors Determining Them.* Columbia University.

[3] "Standard Scores in Arithmetic," *Elementary School Teacher*, November, 1911.

tion of a standard test in addition it appears that a certain child is seriously retarded in this general ability. It becomes necessary to discover just wherein his weakness consists before subjecting him to a course of corrective training. Our knowledge of the complexity of mental processes makes it likely that the factors conditioning even so simple an ability as adding are very numerous. Even a casual analysis shows four subsidiary processes that may, and in fact do, vary independently, weakness in any one of which may serve to pull the child below the average in adding. These are: the ability to make all the possible combinations of single digits with average rapidity and accuracy; the ability to hold securely in mind numbers of two- and three-place value while adding in the next digit or combination of digits in "running up" a column; the ability to "carry" from one column what is "over" to the column next on the left; and the ability to write down figures with average speed. The further analysis of these four constituent processes would doubtless lead into intricate psychological issues, which may or may not be required practically for the economical use of time in corrective treatment. But, in any case, it appears that before anything positive can be said of the weakness of the backward child in question, norms for each of these processes must be found. Once they are known, the performance of the child may be compared with them, and specially devised exercises may be employed to bring him up to standard at just those points, and those only, with which his backwardness in adding is associated. Practice in making the addition of single digits is not appropriate in a case where the difficulty consists in holding number meanings in mind. The processes may be as unlike as association and attention span. If improvement does not come from the use of the exercise selected, the situation calls for further analysis, one possible outcome being the discovery of fundamental defect. Norms or standards of performance are of course required for each factor distinguished.

AIMS OF THE PRESENT STUDY AND SUMMARY

From what has been said it is apparent that there are at least three kinds of pedagogical tests, which may be characterized severally, after their unlike functions, as administrative, grading, and diagnostic tests. The first kind relates to groups, the last two relate to individuals. The third is comparable to the clinical test for mentality, except that it aims frankly at the analysis of specialized training rather than inherent capacity or "general intelligence." It may well happen, of course, that a given test may serve all three purposes, but it need not, and doubtless many tests will be devised for one of these purposes only.

This study took its departure from an attempt to use the Courtis "Standard Scores in Arithmetic" to measure arithmetical backwardness in a class of backward boys. These boys were at quite different points in their arithmetical training, and it was desired to grade them with reference to the average attainments of normal public-school children in order to estimate the time needed to bring them up with their classes. It was necessary, too, to locate their arrests and peculiarities as closely as might be so that their further training could be applied where it would do the most good. The Courtis tests, although used chiefly for the measurement of groups, are recommended for individuals, and several of them are of diagnostic value in the sense that they test abilities that are fairly elementary and at the same time highly important elements in the more inclusive abilities of which they are a part.

The Courtis scores were derived from a single performance from each individual. They are averages from the work of some nine thousand children in different parts of the country, and they may be taken as true measures of the average single performance in the processes they examine. Undoubtedly the average of single trials from large groups may be safely compared with them. But it seemed questionable, considering the possibility of accidental error from one performance, to measure individuals and small groups by means of them. It thus became necessary to consider the significance of one trial as an index to the standing of any individual in the abilities in question. The Courtis Test No. 1 on the addition combinations was chosen for examination.

This study, then, is an attempt to ascertain: first, the approximate reliability of a single score as a measure of an individual's status in the ability to make the addition combinations in writing; second, the number of scores required of an individual in order to obtain a desirable degree of reliability; and third, the size of a group that may be measured with reasonable accuracy by means of one score from each member of the group.

With reference to the first aim it should be explained that by "unreliability" is meant the probable deviation of an actual single score from a hypothetical single score which would accurately place the individual on a scale of status. This hypothetical score was derived as follows. Twenty-five tests were given each individual, and the median, or the thirteenth highest score, was regarded as the measure of the individual's ability to write the addition combinations. It will be seen at once that if an individual began with a score of 55 combinations and attained a median of 75, his first score could not be said to be in error to the amount of 20 combinations, due to the fact that the median is uniformly higher than the first as a result of practice. It was therefore assumed that the middle measure of all the first scores of 202 children (51 combinations) would represent the same relative position on the scale of status as the middle measure of all the medians (70 combinations). The hypothetical first score was consequently considered to be for each individual fifty-one seventieths of his median. The deviation of the actual first score from the hypothetical first was then found in each case.

This deviation in the 202 cases examined varied from no combinations up to 26, with a middle measure of four combinations and an average of slightly over five. That is to say, any individual's score from one performance has one chance in two of deviating less than four combinations, and one chance in four of deviating ten or more, from that measure which would properly place him on a scale of status in this ability. This would seem to make one performance altogether too uncertain as a test of an individual's standing for purposes either of grading or of diagnosis.

In regard to the second purpose of the study it was found that safely to measure the ability of an eighth-grade child to write the addition combinations probably twenty-five trials are required. This number will practically assure a result correct within three combinations. If a smaller reliability will suffice for any purpose the appropriate number of trials may be noted from the table given farther on.

As to the reliability of a single score from each member of a group for purposes of group measurement, on the average, measures of groups of 25 were in error approximately 1.7 combinations, groups of 50 were in error approximately 1.2 combinations, groups of 100 approximately 0.7 combination. This applies to eighth-grade groups.

PROCEDURE

Printed blanks for making the tests were prepared. The print and arrangement of the Courtis Test No. 1 were exactly duplicated for the first minute. This test consists of 120 combinations, including the hundred possible ones and twenty duplicates arranged in groups of five such that each five presented approximately the same difficulty as any other five. Four other slightly altered arrangements of the same test were made to occupy the remaining four of the five minutes devoted to adding on each of the five days.

Two hundred and seventy eighth-grade children in the eight larger grammar schools of San Jose, Cal., were given the tests. The desirability of having all the tests given by the same person—one of the writers—made it impossible to present them at the same time in all the schools. Each school was tested at about the same time on the succeeding days with insignificant exceptions. The one marked alteration of this order was with some fifty children in one school who were given the tests for the fifth day after a lapse of fourteen days. An examination of the returns from this group revealed a barely perceptible fall for which slight allowance was made. A formula was memorized and spoken to each class at the beginning, drawn in such a way as to insure a sympathetic and complete understanding of the test and a quick response to the signals. The children were encouraged to write as many combinations in the minute as they could without error, but emphasis was placed upon accuracy. Throughout incentive prevailed, as it seemed, from motives of individual and school rivalry and personal improvement. There was no evidence of fatigue. Time was taken by stop-watch. Close observation of the pupils showed that in a few cases figures were improperly added on after the final signal but it is felt that the amount of this that was unnoticed by the examiners and uncorrected was really negligible. A rest of about thirty seconds occurred between each two trials.

From a preliminary study it had been concluded that five minutes' adding with rests of about half a minute avoided fatigue and preserved incentive satisfactorily. For various reasons twenty-five was chosen as the number of the tests from which a measure of status might be derived. This point on the practice curve was considered to be sufficiently far advanced practically to eliminate accidental error and yet not so far advanced as to involve learning ability unduly. Any number must be, perforce, the result both of some practice and of some accidental error. As to the effect of practice, it is evident no sharp line can be drawn between status and learning ability, in view of the fact that practice effects are marked after the first performance. It is merely a question of arbitrarily deciding upon the amount of practice which shall fairly be admitted in determining status. Surely children are entitled to the amount of improvement they can make in an hour's time, before being classified for a course of training of any considerable duration.

THE DATA

The number of combinations written each minute and the number of errors made were ascertained for each individual. The papers of twenty children who missed the fifth day were included. The decision as to how to deal with errors was made with difficulty. Courtis regards them as negligible in his test. The present writers supposed that such haste as would result in errors would at the same time increase the number of combinations written per minute, and various attempts were made to evaluate errors in terms of time, that is, to find the smaller number of combinations which might be assumed to have been written in the event that errors had not been made. It was then a matter of surprise to discover that scores containing many errors did not average as many combinations as scores without them, which seems to point to some third factor as being responsible for errors and smaller scores alike. For lack of a better term this factor may be called the "predisposition of the moment." In any case, because of the smaller scores of the children making many errors and an observed erratic character of their performance, a somewhat complicated process of elimination was substituted.

The papers of any individual who made more than two errors in any one minute throughout the twenty-five were set aside, provided that in the event of not more than three errors appearing in one minute the results might be included when there were not more than five errors in one day and not more than ten in the five days. Some half-dozen children escaped on this provision. The papers of any individual who made more than five errors in any one day and more than fifteen in the five days were set aside without exception. No errors at all was thought to be too exacting, and inconsistent with our adult practice in which we work with moderate care and check for mistakes. The papers thus selected were considered to represent a reasonable degree of accuracy. The result of the selection was as follows:

	25 Tests (5 Days)	20 Tests (4 Days)	Total
Accepted	182	20	202
Rejected	65	3	68
Total	247	23	270

Figs. 1, 2, and 3 on the accompanying plate show the actual scores of three pupils selected to illustrate the possible variation among individuals. Of the twenty-five scores of each of the 202 individuals were found: the average of the first two scores, the average of the first three, four, five; the median of the first seven, of the first thirteen, nineteen, and the whole twenty-five, being respectively the fourth, seventh, tenth, and thirteenth highest. In the cases of the twenty pupils who took the test four days only, the twelfth highest was found to be the value which most nearly approximated the probable value of the median. These values for the three pupils represented in Figs. 1, 2, and 3 are shown as the longer lines in Figs. 1*a*, 2*a*, and 3*a*.

The median of the 202 first scores was found, also the median of

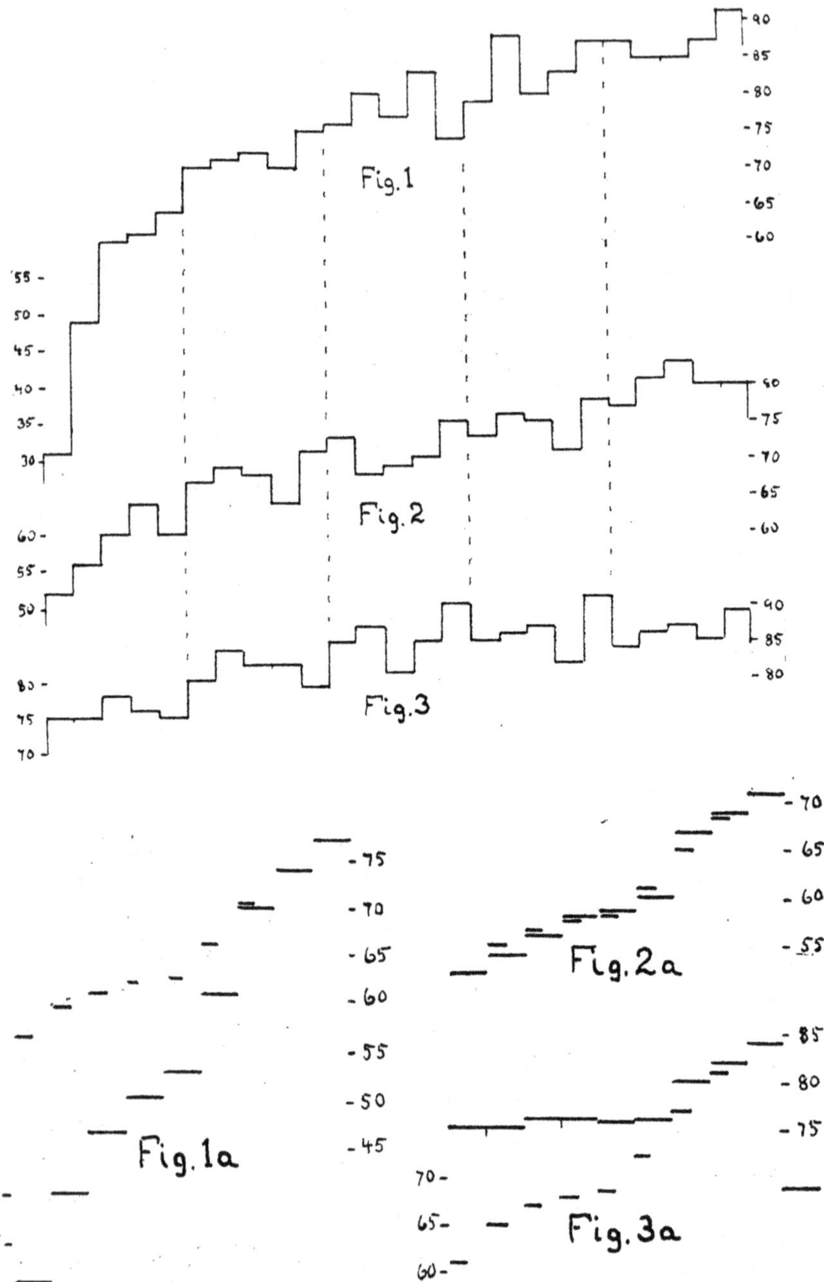
Fig. 1
55 -
50 -
45 -
40 -
35 -
30
- 90
- 85
- 80
- 75
- 70
- 65
- 60
Fig. 2
60 -
55 -
50
80
- 75
- 70
- 65
- 60
Fig. 3
80 -
75
70
- 90
- 85
- 80
Fig. 1a
- 75
- 70
- 65
- 60
- 55
- 50
- 45
40 -
35 -
Fig. 2a
- 70
- 65
- 60
- 55
Fig. 3a
- 85
- 80
- 75
70 -
65 -
60 -

the averages of the first two, of the first three, and so on, for each of the above quantities. These are shown in the following table:

	Combinations
The median of the 202 first scores	51
The median of the 202 averages of the 1st and 2d scores	54
The median of the 202 averages of the 1st, 2d, and 3d scores	55½
The median of the 202 averages of the 1st, 2d, 3d, and 4th scores	56½
The median of the 202 averages of the 1st, 2d, 3d, 4th, and 5th scores	57
The median of the 202 medians of the first 7 scores	60
The median of the 202 medians of the first 13 scores	64
The median of the 202 medians of the first 19 scores	67
The median of the 202 medians of all 25 scores	70
The median of the 202 medians of the actual highest scores	79

The first scores varied from 28 to 88 combinations, the middle half falling between 42 and 60. The medians of the twenty-five scores in the 202 cases varied from 42 to 107 combinations, the

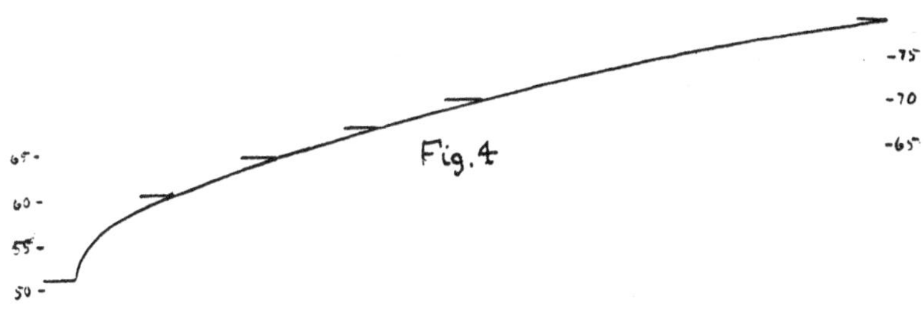

middle half falling between 62 and 80. The quantities of the table are plotted on the plate (Fig. 4*a*). From these was constructed an idealized practice curve (Fig. 4) upon which appear six selected values.

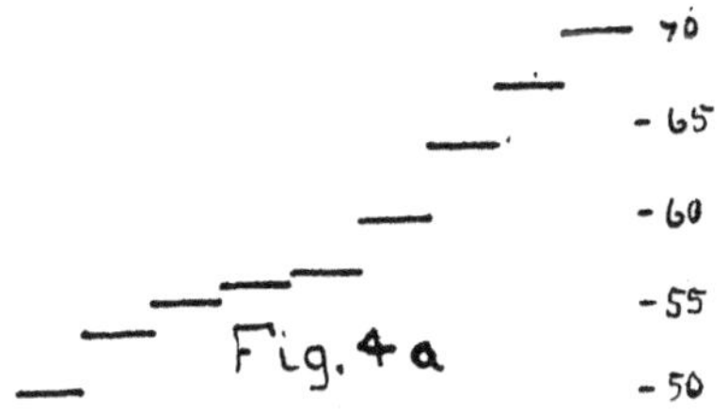

Hypothetical first scores, or first scores which would locate each individual upon the scale of status in correct relation to every other individual, were computed, as explained previously, by taking fifty-one seventieths of each individual's median. Hypothetical values of the averages of the first two scores were computed by taking fifty-four seventieths of the median in each case, and so on for the other values shown in the table above. These values for the three individuals represented in Figs. 1, 2, and 3 are shown as the shorter lines in Figs. 1*a*, 2*a*, and 3*a*.

Figs. 1*a*, 2*a*, and 3*a* may be interpreted thus: In the case of the first pupil, from some cause, the first score (the longer line) lacks 26 combinations of equaling that hypothetical first score (the shorter line) which would place him correctly on the scale of status. The average of the first two scores brings him within 19 combinations of the corresponding hypothetical value, the average of the first three scores within 14 combinations of its hypothetical value, and so on. The second pupil would vary but little in relative position by any number of measurements, so closely does his actual performance approximate the hypothetical. The case of the third pupil is quite the opposite of the first. Because of slight improvement the first score would rank this pupil far too high.

Out of 182 cases where all twenty-five tests were taken the first scores deviated from the hypothetical values by between zero and one combination in 26 cases, by between one and two combinations in 18 cases, in order as follows:

Combinations..	0	1	2	3	4	5	6	7	8	9	10	11	12	13	14	15	16
Cases....		26	18	25	23	17	11	9	8	12	8	7	4	4	3	0	3

Combinations..	17	18	19	20	21	22	23	24	25	26
Cases....	1	1	0	0	0	0	0	1	0	1

The percentage of deviation is not given. It would not augment the obtained degree of accuracy appreciably. The values of the

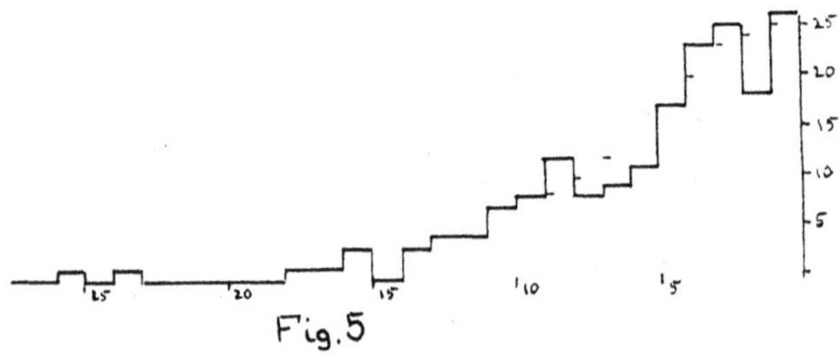

Fig. 5

table are plotted in Fig. 5 of the plate. Fifty per cent of the first scores were in error four or more combinations, 10 per cent were in error 11 combinations, one score was in error 26 combinations. These and the amounts of error for the average of the first two scores, the first three, and so on, are shown in the following table.

Cases	50 Per cent	10 Per cent	One Case
First score	4 combinations	11 combinations	26 combinations
Average of 1st and 2d scores	3.5	9	25
Average of 1st, 2d, 3d	3	8	21
Average of 1st, 2d, 3d, 4th	2.85	7	20
Average of 1st, 2d, 3d, 4th, 5th	2.76	7	19
Median of first 7 scores	2.55	6	18
Median of first 13 scores	2.15	5	10
Median of first 19 scores	1.5	3	5
Median of first 25 scores	1 (probably)	2 (probably)	3 (probably)

The values in the 50 per cent column of the table are plotted in Fig. 6 of the plate where each value shows the median deviation of the value represented directly above in Fig. 4*a*. It appears that any individual eighth-grade child tested in the addition combinations by one trial stands one chance in ten of being displaced from his true standing by 11 combinations. From two trials the displacement would be nine combinations, and so on, as indicated in the 10 per cent column of the table.

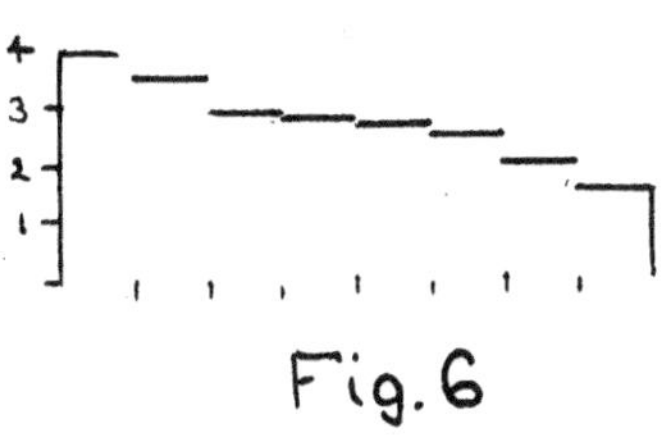

The procedure for finding the reliability of group averages based upon one score from each member of the group was as follows. The averages of all the firsts and of all the medians in the 202 cases were found. They were respectively 51.5 and 69 combinations and form a ratio of 0.748. Two hundred of the individuals, chosen by chance, were distributed into eight groups of twenty-five. These groups were treated in the way individuals had been treated in the first part of the study. The averages of the first scores and of the medians of twenty-five scores were found for each group of twenty-five. Hypothetical averages of first scores were found by taking 0.748 of the actual averages of first scores. The average deviation of the hypothetical averages of first scores from the actual averages of first scores for the eight groups was approximately 1.7 combinations. The two hundred individuals were then distributed into eight chance groups of fifty and eight chance groups of one hundred. The approximate average deviation in these cases was respectively 1.2 and 0.7 combinations.

CONCLUSIONS

The study was conducted primarily in the hope of learning something of the value of standard scores for the measurement and understanding of the work of individuals in arithmetic by means of comparatively few samples. Test No. 1 of the Courtis series was chosen for study because averages had been found for it from a large number of children and because it was considered comparatively elementary. There is, of course, no telling how representative the process of adding single digits is. It is probably as simple as any process in arithmetic, and the presumption would be that the reliability of a single or a few trials in this process would be far greater than that of the more complicated processes which make up the important practical abilities in the subject. The results of the study show that a single or a few trials must be used with caution in determining the status of individuals in these abilities.

The unreliability of a few trials may be shown again by reference to the standard scores of Courtis based upon the results of the best 30 per cent of his group of some nine thousand children. His averages for this test range from 26 for the third grade up to 65 for the ninth grade, a difference of 39 combinations. Many of the children of the group studied here made up this amount of difference during the twenty-five trials, the average difference between the first and last being 28 combinations. Often the difference between several grades would be covered in the first two or three trials. A child's place on the Courtis scale would thus depend largely upon the number of trials he made.

The question remains as to whether it is possible to use the valuable scores of Courtis for the measurement of individuals. Because of the unreliability of one score from an individual it is clear that such a single score cannot be compared directly with an average of Courtis. And of course it is impossible to measure the average of several scores of an individual against an average of first scores of many individuals. If, however, we may assume that the curve of improvement based upon 202 returns (Fig. 4) is representative of the rate of improvement of so large a group as the 1,370 eighth-grade children of Courtis, then we have a basis upon which to proceed. The average of first scores of the 202 children of this study is 51.5 combinations and the average of the median of twenty-five trials is 69. If about the same ratio should exist in the larger group of Courtis, which seems likely, the average of medians of twenty-five trials to correspond would be 69/51.5 of 57, his average of first scores, or 76.4 combinations. We may then say that the median of any eighth-grade pupil's twenty-five successive trials should approximate 76 combinations to compare favorably with what is normal in the country. Of the San Jose group about 33 per cent made this score. Or, if Courtis' standard score for the eighth grade of 63 combinations be used, then the pupil's median should approximate 84 combinations. Only 12.5 per cent of the San Jose group reached this score.

The conclusions of the study require qualification in that it has been assumed that a first trial is a definite thing, whereas it is of course largely relative to what has preceded it of a similar nature. Probably the 202 children of this group, as well as the eighth-grade children from whom the Courtis scores were derived, had not had practice in adding in the form of the test for several years, although the daily work in arithmetic must have given some continuous practice incidentally. Children practiced systematically on the precise form of the test would probably be more reliably measured by one trial if this should be made during or immediately after the training. Nothing can be said here of what this increased reliability would amount to. It would probably not justify the use of one or a few trials for a formal classification of individuals.

From a certain point of view the usefulness of the Courtis Test No. 1 may be questioned. It is plainly not a test of addition even when addition is limited to the handling of columns of figures and the rational side of the topic is disregarded. As has been noted, the ordinary process of addition is much more complicated than writing the sums of single digits. The value of the test as a measure of addition as usually met with can be determined only after its correlation with the more inclusive process has been ascertained. It is doubtful whether the correlation is sufficiently high to warrant the use of the test for grading. Undoubtedly the better way would be to make use of a test more typical of addition as such. Unfortunately Courtis does not have a test of addition except as a part of a larger one on the four fundamentals. This has the effect of concealing the standing in any one fundamental process and so makes it inconvenient to discover just what special training a pupil needs. As an aid in the analysis of backwardness in addition when this has been found with the use of a satisfactory grading test, Test No. 1 would seem to be important—just how important can be known only after its correlation with adding ability has been determined, along with the correlations of the other important components of the ability, whatever they are.

A final word should be said of the ability examined by the test on the addition combinations. It has been understood throughout the paper as the ability to write with reasonable accuracy and intelligibility the sums of the possible combinations of single digits with average or normal speed. Accuracy and intelligibility in writing have been defined practically by eliminating returns passing certain limits, limits which have been described in the matter of accuracy. The limit of intelligibility was a rough one. If the figures could be definitely made out the papers were accepted.

But this raises a question. How is the writing of figures related to readiness of response in supplying the sums of the combinations mentally? Some children are doubtless held back very much by the difficulty of manipulating the pen or pencil. Others write about as fast as they can add. Just how children range between these limits is unknown. Perhaps this need not be a matter of concern for purposes of grading, for the ability to write combinations is a practical one that may be treated as a unit. But in searching for causes of backwardness it would be wholly desirable to distinguish between standing in writing figures and standing in readiness and accuracy of association in the combination of numbers as such. It is therefore quite possible that an oral response will prove more satisfactory for this purpose. It hardly seems possible that the amount of improvement shown by the 202 children of this study is to be explained in terms of increased readiness of mental association alone. In fact, a noticeable depreciation in the quality of the writing and other signs of haste arouses the suspicion that a considerable part of it came from an increased facilitation of a neuromuscular sort in the manipulation of the writing instrument. But the determination of these issues must be left for future study.

BOOK REVIEWS

Mental Fatigue. By Max Offner; translated by G. M. Whipple. Warwick and York. Pp. vi+133.

This book is of the type of a number of works which have recently been written for the purpose of presenting in summary form for the convenience of teachers and educators the results of experimental investigations in a particular field which have a bearing upon educational practice. Of a similar nature are Watt's book on *Memory*, Heck's on *Formal Discipline*, Miss Thompson's on *Writing*, and Meumann's comprehensive work, which indeed includes all the fields which have been made the subject of investigation. Such books meet a very widespread demand and are evidence of the fruit which the new effort to apply the scientific method to the solution of educational problems is already bearing. The author of *Mental Fatigue* has presented a comprehensive and critical, and for the most part clear and concise, discussion of the literature of the subject. The interpretations and applications which follow the more technical presentation are given with due caution and reserve, and yet offer reasonably definite suggestions for practice.

After defining fatigue and drawing a distinction between mental and physical fatigue, the author discusses the various methods which have been tried for the measurement of fatigue. These are divided in general into physiological and psychological, according as the process which is tested is a physiological or a mental activity. The physiological methods assume that there is a close relationship between diminution in the capacity for physical and for mental work—sufficiently so that the degree of diminution in physical efficiency may be taken as a measure of mental fatigue. This relation has been found not to be so simple as was assumed, however, and resort has accordingly been had to the use of mental processes, such as the ability to discriminate between sensations or the speed and accuracy of computation, memory, etc., and it is upon the results of such tests that most of the conclusions are based.

In the next section the discussion deals mainly with the relation between fatigue and other factors in their effect upon the efficiency of work. The fluctuations in efficiency do not give a simple picture of the course of fatigue because of the effect of such factors as practice, "warming up," the initial and final spurt, etc. It is this complication which makes the testing of fatigue difficult. The author shows in this section the part which each of these factors may be expected to play.

Under the caption "Laws of Fatigue" are shown the course which fatigue itself may be expected to take, and the variations which occur in different persons and at different ages. This section also takes up in some detail the application of the principles of fatigue to the length of lesson periods, the length and distribution of pauses, longer and shorter, and to the fatigue effect of various studies and of various kinds and conditions of work. Finally in the last section certain general conclusions upon mental hygiene are drawn.

The book will be found of interest not only to teachers but to all as well who are concerned in the development of mental efficiency.

Frank N. Freeman

The University of Chicago

Fine and Industrial Arts in Elementary Schools. By WALTER SARGENT. Ginn & Co. Pp. 132.

Readers of the *Elementary School Teacher* will remember the articles by Professor Sargent which appeared in this journal two years ago. The present volume is a revision and enlargement of that series of articles.

The first two chapters deal with general principles and state the reasons why drawing, constructive work, and design should be included in the elementary course. The remaining five chapters contain detailed recommendations for the work of each of the grades.

The book commends itself to the student of elementary education because it seeks to find a place for art in elementary education which will put drawing and manual activity on the level with all the other subjects taught in the school. If drawing and constructive work are to take such a place in the schools, they must be organized so that from year to year the pupil shall progress and secure genuine mental development from his training. That it is very difficult to get a progressive series of exercises in drawing and constructive work everyone knows who has seen children struggling with school drawing-books and with repetitious manual-training exercises. In the second place, handwork of all types must be related to reading, writing, and number work. This can be done only when the value of practical activity for the training of powers of mind which are on a level with those trained in the intellectual subjects is understood and emphasized.

Professor Sargent has stated these principles in such a way as to stimulate the most wholesome thinking on the part of the elementary-school teachers and supervisors. Furthermore, he has illustrated the way in which the principles may be carried into practice from grade to grade.

C. H. JUDD

The Yearbook of the Francis W. Parker School. The Social Motive in School Work. Published by the Faculty of the School. Pp. 139. 35 cents.

The Francis W. Parker School was established as a memorial to Colonel Parker and it has continued to carry out the educational policy which he inaugurated. The present publication is the first of a series which is promised by the faculty of this school. It contains the reports of a number of different activities of the school. A general introductory statement of principles with which the volume opens is followed by an account of Investigation Lane. This account relates the way in which some land back of the school has been put to use as a means of educating the children through activity, and at the same time producing much experience that is valuable for the social life of the children and for their other school work. Later sections of the monograph give examples of the way in which the dramatic instinct of children may be employed. The organization of the music of the school is discussed. The print shop is reported in general and in some special details that are of importance in the work of the seventh grade. Altogether, the monograph is very suggestive of lines of activity which may be taken up in elementary education.

The authors of the book call attention in their announcement to the fact that the school is unhampered by traditions, and is therefore free to experiment in the course of study and in the methods of organizing teaching. The best characteristic of the volume is its treatment in a definite, concrete way of the work which is actually being carried on in the school. One can see in these reports the vigorous life of a real school. The stimulus that comes from such concrete reports will certainly not be lost in the application of the general principles here set forth to schools less fortunate in equipment and in freedom to carry on experimentation.

C. H. J.

The Child in the City. A series of papers presented at the conferences held during the Chicago Child Welfare Exhibit. Edited by SOPHONISBA P. BRECKINRIDGE. Published by the Chicago School of Civics and Philanthropy.

During May, 1911, there was held at the Coliseum in the city of Chicago an exhibit of all of the activities in the city which are directed toward the improvement of conditions surrounding children in the home, in the school, on the street, or in the playground. This exhibit included not only the private and public educational agencies but also the philanthropic and medical activities which aim at the improvement of the hygienic conditions and moral conditions in the city.

This Child Welfare Exhibit was an enlargement of the exhibit which had been held in New York City a few months earlier. The materials from New York were brought to the Coliseum, and were supplemented by exhibition material from the city of Chicago itself. One notable feature of the exhibit was the series of conferences at which educators, philanthropists, and social workers discussed the various problems of child welfare. The addresses given at these conferences have now been brought together in a bulky volume edited by Miss Breckinridge. The book supplies a very good general survey of the activities in the city which make for the benefit of children. The addresses are divided into nine sections. After a brief introductory section which gives the addresses made at the opening of the exhibit, there is a section dealing with personal service. This section reports three addresses by Richard C. Cabot. Following this are sections on the physical care of children, on the school and the child, on special groups of children, on the working child, on the law and the child, on libraries and museums, on social and civic problems of childhood, and finally two addresses, one by Mrs. McCormick, whose generosity made possible the exhibit, and one by Mrs. Blaine who contributed with Mrs. McCormick to the support of the enterprise, and was largely instrumental in its organization. In each of these sections there is reported a number of addresses by specialists engaged in practical work with children. It would be difficult to select for detailed discussion any special papers from among the large numbers here presented.

The book ought to stimulate others to a similar series of conferences. The wholesome influence of these conferences in Chicago is felt long after the close of the exhibit itself. As a means of arousing the consciousness of a city to the necessity of improvement in all of these different lines of activity, nothing can be stronger than the united presentation of the different types of social activity in behalf of children. The material side of this exhibit was expensive, and probably cannot be reproduced in very many centers, but the conferences which are set forth in this volume could be reproduced at relatively slight expense, and the benefit of a series of such conferences is attested by the contents of the book itself.

C. H. J.

Vocational Education in Europe. Report to the Commercial Club of Chicago by EDWARD G. COOLEY. Published by the Commercial Club. Pp. 347.

This volume contains a report of an investigation which was carried on by Mr. Cooley during a year of visitation of European schools. A very full statement is made of the schools of Germany which have to do with vocational training. In somewhat briefer compass the industrial education of Austria is summarized and the industrial education of Switzerland. The volume gives the course of study of the various institutions, and some statement of their organization and support.

The part of the book which will undoubtedly be of most interest to general readers is that which sets forth the conclusions which Mr. Cooley has drawn from his studies. Mr. Cooley believes that there should be a general elementary education extending through a period of eight years before there is any special effort to give trade instruction. These eight years should be followed in the case of people who are going into industry by special instruction in the trades. This special instruction is the function of a group of institutions not yet fully organized in our American educational system. "Special schools managed by specially trained teachers a part of whom at least must be practical men from the industries" must be added to the general education system of the country. These schools will be of secondary grade and will provide for pupils who would not naturally go on with the general schools that are now in existence at the level of the high school and beyond.

Mr. Cooley makes one significant statement in his first general conclusion based upon his studies. He believes that it is worth while for us to attempt in America to revive and reorganize in some fashion the apprenticeship system which has fallen into disuse in our present-day civilization.

Whatever may be the individual opinion of various investigators and experimenters with regard to the best methods of introducing vocational education into American schools, there can be little doubt that Mr. Cooley's book will be read with very great interest by all teachers and supervisors of elementary schools. Probably the largest divergence of opinion will center about his position that this work is of secondary grade only and is not suitable for the general elementary school even in its upper classes. The practice is becoming so widespread of undertaking some industrial work in the later years of the elementary school that there will be very little disposition to accept without qualification Mr. Cooley's general position. In the meantime, a careful perusal of his reports from Europe will be of interest to all students of the subject. So far as the present reviewer can make out from a study of the first part of the book, there is relatively little justification for the belief that our American system is shut up to the one possibility which Mr. Cooley advocates. The freedom of our American school organization is so great and the virtues of much of the industrial training which Mr. Cooley has observed are so obvious that it would seem much more direct to advocate the conclusion that our American elementary schools should take on as a part of their regular work some of the types of training that have been found to be of such importance in the older civilizations of Europe.

C. H. J.

Social Aspects of Education. By IRVING KING. New York: Macmillan, 1912. Pp. xvi+425.

Educational literature bearing upon the social aspects of education has been very voluminous of late. It is to be found scattered, however, through numberless books periodicals of every type, pamphlets, special bulletins, reports of local organizations, scattered speeches, etc. To cover the field it has been necessary to read a multitude of incoherent and repetitious matters. We have needed for economy in reading and for perspective and organization a book that would treat in systematic and related fashion the various social aspects of education; and at the same time present accounts of representative social movements that would adequately illustrate each particular aspect described.

Professor King's book does this for us in an admirable manner. Most of the important social movements relating to education are treated. They are grouped according to their relationships. Each is briefly but clearly interpreted in the beginning of the chapter devoted to it. The main body of the chapter is then given to source-materials illustrative of the movement in question written by one intimately in contact with it. Some of the writers drawn upon are: Dewey, Leipziger, Mero, Dean, Cooley, Royce, Burnham, Reeder, Kerschensteiner, Butterfield, E. J. Ward, Louise M. Greene, Colin A. Scott, Franklin W. Johnson, Professor G. H. Mead. Each writer naturally treats his specialty.

The book is divided into two parts. The first deals with the relations of the school as an institution to society in general and to all other social institutions that it is designed, or at least expected, to serve. The second part treats of the social life within the school in its bearing on the socialization of the pupils, the studies, methods, and school government.

Topics covered under Part I are: the social view of education; social origins of educational agencies; social opportunities of rural schools; home and school relationships; schools as social and civic centers; extension work among adults; the playground movement; social value of school gardens; vocational education; vocational guidance; education as a factor in social progress and social reform. Topics treated under Part II are: social life of the school; social organizations within the school; self-government in schools; social aspects of mental development; social atmosphere of the school as related to the learning process; corporate life of the school as related to moral education.

The book presents an excellent introduction to the field. It also points the way for intensive specialized work. Each chapter is followed by a list of problems and topics for further research, and by a full and carefully selected bibliography.

J. F. Bobbitt

The University of Chicago

CURRENT EDUCATIONAL LITERATURE IN THE PERIODICALS[1]

IRENE WARREN
Librarian, School of Education, The University of Chicago

AYRES, MAY. The rich town and the poor schools. Survey 28:603–9. (3 Ag. '12.)

COLTON, ELIZABETH AVERY. Standards of southern colleges for women. School R. 20:458–75. (S. '12.)

Doctorates conferred by American universities. Science 36:129–39. (2 Ag. '12.)

FREEMAN, FRANK N. Current methods of teaching handwriting. III. El. School T. 13:25–40. (S. '12.)

JAMES, EDMUND J. The national university. Science 36:202–10. (16 Ag. '12.)

JUDD, CHARLES H. Educational news and editorial comment. El. School T. 13:1–10. (S. '12.)

JUDSON, HARRY PRATT. Waste in educational curricula. School R. 20:433–41. (S. '12.)

KOCH, C. VON. Chautauqua: growth of popular education. Chaut. 67:183–93. (Ag. '12.)

KRAUSE, LOUISE B. Contribution of library science to efficiency in business. Pub. Lib. 17:247–51. (Jl. '12.)

LACY, ERNEST. Reconciliation between the ideal and the real in literature. Pub. Lib. 17:243–47. (Jl. '12.)

LEUPP, CONSTANCE D. Campaigning for babies' lives. McClure 39:361–73. (Ag. '12.)

Making the blind hear light: Fournier d'Albe's Optophone. Sci. Am. Sup. 74:71. (3 Ag. '12.)

MARTIN, HERBERT. Problems in philosophy which affect present educational ideals. Kind. R. 23:1–9. (S. '12.)

MONROE, WALTER S. A chapter in the development of arithmetic teaching in the United States. III. El. School T. 13:17–24. (S. '12.)

"Moonlight schools." Lit. D. 45:261. (17 Ag. '12.)

MORROW, PRINCE A. Eugenics and child welfare. Child (Chicago) 1:7–10. (Ag. '12.)

Our public school system a failure. Lit. D. 45:188. (3 Ag. '12.)

[1] *Abbreviations.*—Chaut., Chautauquan; Child Wel. M., Child Welfare Magazine; El. School T., Elementary School Teacher; J. of Educa. (Bost.), Journal of Education (Boston); Lit. D., Literary Digest; Outl., Outlook; Pub. Lib., Public Libraries; Sci. Am. Sup., Scientific American Supplement; School R., School Review.

ROBBINS, JANE E. The new schoolboy. Outl. 101:880–83. (17 Ag. '12.)

STARCH, DANIEL, and ELLIOTT, EDWARD C. Reliability of the grading of high-school work in English. School R. 20:442–57. (S. '12.)

STRAUS, ESTHER. Recent tendencies in children's literature. Pub. Lib. 17: 252–56. (Jl. '12.)

TAPLIN, HARRY BLAKE. Camp Hale, a social experiment. Survey 28:619–25. (3 Ag. '12.)

TERRY, H. L. Two lines of high-school reading. School R. 20:476–82. (S. '12.)

VAN HISE, CHARLES RICHARD. A national university, a national asset; an instrumentality for advanced research. Science 36:193–201. (16 Ag. '12.)

Vocational disabilities due to defective color sense, a handicap more common than generally supposed. Sci. Am. Sup. 74:75. (3 Ag. '12.)

WARD, GILBERT O. Elementary library instruction. Pub. Lib. 17:260–62. (Jl. '12.)

WARREN, IRENE. A three-foot shelf for a teacher's professional library. El. School T. 13:41–42. (S. '12.)

WILD, LAURA H. The Montessori system and our schools for the deaf. J. of Educa. (Boston) 76:176. (22 Ag. '12.)

WILSON, G. M. The motivation of seventh- and eighth-grade history work. El. School T. 13:11–16. (S. '12.)

(The) work of a council of parent-teacher associations. Child Wel. M. 6: 420–23. (Ag. '12.)

ZACHERT, ADELINE B. Creed of the children's librarian. Pub. Lib. 17:257–59. (Jl. '12.

VOLUME XIII NUMBER 3

THE ELEMENTARY SCHOOL TEACHER

NOVEMBER, 1912

EDUCATIONAL NEWS AND EDITORIAL COMMENT

A Paper Edited by Patrons of Schools

A publication entitled *The Child Welfare Bulletin* is issued by the Child Welfare League of Peoria, Illinois. The first number of this bulletin contains articles on child welfare, the mothers' pension law in Illinois, the Proctor endowment recreation center, home and school associations, and a number of local matters, such as official notes of the Peoria Betterment Association, Peoria Woman's Club, Mothers' Club, Association of Commerce, and Child Welfare League.

This bulletin is to be published every month, and is in the hands of a committee of editors appointed by the League. Copies can be secured by communicating with Mrs. M. L. Fowler, 101 South Institute Place, Peoria, Illinois.

The publication represents a type of movement which in one form or another is becoming very common in the cities in the Middle West. Attention has been called in an earlier number of this Journal to the volume published after the Chicago Child Welfare Exhibit. The periodical now at hand shows another method of distributing information about all the agencies that make for the betterment of the conditions surrounding children.

Philippine School Exhibit

During the past winter an exhibit of work done in the Philippine schools has been shown in various cities in this country. Mr. White, the Director of Education in the Philippine Islands, and Mr. Briggs, the agent of the school system in this country, have been present with this exhibit at various centers, and have given information with regard to the work which is being done for the native Filipinos. The schools have broken away from the traditional notions about education and have introduced a large amount of handwork. The result has been that the Filipinos have progressed rapidly in industrial lines, and have at the same time taken on in connection with their industrial training much of the best which can be offered in occidental art and general training.

A new magazine is being published under the direction of Mr. White. The first number of the first volume appeared in July, 1912, and has just come to hand. It shows the different types of work which are undertaken in the schools, and gives in addition general information about the organization of the schools in the Philippines.

Educational Meetings

With the opening of schools after the summer vacation come announcements of the educational meetings which are to be held during the autumn. Many state associations and smaller associations are announcing full programs. There are in the list two meetings which may with propriety be mentioned as having general importance for teachers in all parts of the country. The National Council of Teachers of English will meet in Chicago on November 28 and 29. This council has dealt up to this time very largely with the problems of secondary and college instruction in English. There is a department which will discuss elementary instruction in English. The National Council promises to stir up much interest in the vital problems of instruction in the vernacular.

English has been accepted in the school curriculum without serious objection by all educational parties, and yet it has been recognized on every hand that it is very difficult to administer a course in English which shall be genuinely productive of mental training. The content of many English courses becomes highly attenuated. The compositions which are written are very often of the most artificial kind. There is repetition almost without limit, and duplication in the different schools. If any department of American education needs to seriously discuss its problems, it is the department of English.

Another organization which is to have a meeting of general interest is the National Association for the Study and Education of Exceptional Children. This Association will meet in New York on October 30 and 31. The topics which will be discussed at this meeting are, first, the exceptionally bright child, second, the retarded child, and third, rational human eugenics.

Much has been said in recent discussion about the importance of developing special school methods for children who advance more rapidly than normal children. Such especially bright children are undoubtedly important to the life of the community in a much higher degree than children who are retarded. Bright children need to be treated in a fashion peculiar to their own needs. During the summer quarter Professor Witmer of the University of Pennsylvania conducted a class of exceptionally bright children for the purpose of showing that methods of instruction for such children ought to be developed and discussed by all teachers.

Less comment is needed to emphasize the necessity of dealing with retarded children. They represent a problem which the school has long recognized as an urgent problem, and one difficult to solve.

As for human eugenics, it may be doubted whether the school can do much along these lines, but the consideration of problems of human heredity by scientifically trained experts is certainly timely.

Colleges and the Teaching Profession

Interesting evidence of the development of the teaching profession appears in a monograph which has just been published by the Bureau of Education of the United States. This monograph, prepared by Mr. B. B. Burritt, shows that teaching is now the dominant profession of college graduates. Twenty-five per cent of the graduates of thirty-seven representative colleges enter this profession. Formerly the graduates of colleges went into the professions of law or the ministry. Since 1880 there has been a rapid movement toward a wider distribution of college graduates among the types of activity demanded by the community. Today 20 per cent of college graduates go into business. Law takes 15 per cent, medicine 6 or 7, engineering 3 or 4, while the ministry takes only 5 or 6 per cent. It is not uncommon for college graduates to take positions in the elementary school. With the growth of departments of education and normal departments in universities, the relation between the elementary school and the college is likely to become increasingly intimate.

Night Schools

No phase of school organization arouses more popular interest than the night schools which are conducted for the benefit of older and younger students in the community. From all parts of the country come announcements of the opening of all sorts of night schools. The following examples may give some notion of the range of subjects which are covered in these schools, and of the different types of classes which are organized in different cities. In Milwaukee, Wisconsin, there are to be evening recreation schools under the Recreation Board established by the legislature. There are to be industrial schools where trades and useful arts are taught. There will be social center work, and finally, the elementary subjects, such as arithmetic, reading, and writing, will be coupled with cooking, sewing, and domestic arts. In Los Angeles, California, the following list of classes is enumerated: English, Spanish, Latin, mathematics, science, bookkeeping, shorthand, typewriting, cooking, sewing, history, civics, and citizenship. Libraries and reading-rooms are open for any members of the community who wish to use them. In Buffalo the registration was announced as including 6,775 persons. Courses are announced in carpentry, cabinet-making, electrical construction, and in shoe repairing. Some of the largest classes are in sewing, dressmaking, and millinery. Instruction is given in hair-dressing and manicuring. The usual school subjects are also represented in regular classes in all the schools.

In New York City the classes are divided into senior classes junior classes, and classes for foreigners. Junior classes are composed of pupils between the ages of fourteen and eighteen, who are not attending school. Senior classes take pupils who are not attending day schools, and who have completed the sixth year of the elementary day course, or its equivalent. The subjects taught in the senior classes are reading, arithmetic, penmanship, bookkeeping, composition, drawing, stenography, sewing, millinery, dressmaking, cooking. Special trade instruction is also given as local conditions may require. In the junior classes the instruction is in English, reading, spelling, meaning and use of words, arithmetic, penmanship, geography, bookkeeping, hygiene, physical training, American history, and civics.

The miscellaneous character of the work which is done in many of these schools shows very definitely the broad view which is taken of the function of the school. It would have been quite impossible twenty years ago to have persuaded the ordinary superintendent of schools that the different subjects now enumerated at these different centers fall within the province of the public school. It would also have been difficult to have secured from boards of education the funds necessary to support these classes. At the present time there is the heartiest indorsement of this work, and the community is evidently satisfied to extend as widely and as rapidly as possible the range of subjects with which these night schools deal.

The effect of the night school upon the day school is very marked. One announcement from Montclair, New Jersey, states that the night school is to conduct classes which will help the day pupils in their studying. It has been the practice for some time in Hibbing, in the state of Minnesota, to open the schools in the evening so that pupils who do not have proper places for study at home may study in the school buildings and prepare their work for the sessions of the following day.

Tests of Arithmetic in Schools

Mr. Courtis, who for several years has been working on arithmetic tests, and has published in this Journal a number of reports of his investigations, has begun the issue of a bulletin dealing with the tests on which he has reported in his earlier articles. This first annual bulletin contains a statement of the expenditures which Mr. Courtis has incurred in the printing of his standard tests. It also gives an account of the extent to which these tests have been used by others, and shows how the results obtained from various centers which have used the tests up to this time can be employed in the standardizing and comparing of work done in individual schools.

The bulletin is accompanied by a general descriptive circular and a price list. Mr. Courtis seeks in this way to secure a wider field of co-operation in research, and a wider opportunity to apply his tests as an educational measuring-rod. He was employed by the investigation committee in New York to apply these tests to the New York city schools. His report will appear as a part of the New York report.

The *Elementary School Teacher* has always been very glad of the opportunity to promote the interests of this work. The efficiency with which the tests have been prepared and the practical character of the results justify a widespread interest on the part of students of education, and of practical teachers, in these methods of standardizing the work in arithmetic.

Montessori Lectures

The American committee organized to promote the Montessori methods of teaching in this country announces that Doctor Montessori will give a course for the training of teachers, beginning in January, 1913, and lasting for four months. This course is to be given in Rome, and applications will be received for enrolment at 443 Fourth Avenue, New York City.

The opportunity thus offered of visiting Rome may be attractive to some American teachers. They will undoubtedly get much benefit from contact with the civilization of that city, and from observation of all the remains of Roman art and architecture. They may be stimulated to a new interest in educational principles, although a careful perusal of the material that up to this time has been put out by Dr. Montessori would hardly arouse in one any expectation of anything very novel or clear along educational lines. There are good American kindergartens, and many good elementary schools in America, which deserve more recognition than has been accorded to this Italian system; but human nature seems to be organized in such a way that happenings in Rome excite more interest and arouse more confidence than the commonplace work which is going on in the school that is near at hand.

The *Elementary School Teacher* is very glad to recommend the trip to Rome to anyone who can make it. Further responsibility for this announcement must attach to the American committee which has urgently requested that the announcement be made.

Tardiness Interpreted as Absence

The city of Joliet, Illinois, is attempting to deal with the problem of tardiness at school. The legal department of the school system has obtained the ruling from the State Superintendent of Public Instruction that tardiness six days in any given month may be considered as equivalent to absence for six days in the month. Parents permitting this degree of tardiness will then be open to a prosecution under the compulsory attendance act.

It is reported that this somewhat drastic attitude on the part of the legal department has already resulted in the bringing back of several pupils through the truant officer.

Home Study to Be Replaced by School Study

The superintendent of the Pittsburgh schools proposes, according to the *Post* of that city, that children shall do their studying in the schoolroom, rather than be burdened with the necessity of study at home. It is argued that children ought to be able to study under the guidance of teachers more economically, and the distractions which interrupt study can be more readily removed in the school than under the ordinary conditions of family life. Attention is also called to the fact that the school is shirking its responsibility by unloading on the home the obligation of supervising home study.

This pronouncement with regard to method of study raises a number of interesting questions. In the first place, it must be recognized that there is great truth in the contention that children have been sent home to do work which it is quite impossible for them to do economically. Teachers have forgotten the difficulties of independent study in many cases, and have imposed upon children tasks which are in excess of their ability. In the second place, a miscellaneous assignment of home study by different teachers in the school is likely to result in conflicts which the child cannot solve. If he is called upon to study three or four different subjects, he will not know which one is most important on a given evening.

Furthermore, there is much truth in the contention that distractions at home make study difficult.

On the other hand, it is to be pointed out that children cultivate a certain independence when they are required to be their own guides. They might conceivably learn how to use books more efficiently because the teacher is not accessible. Moreover, parents are very frequently brought into contact with the school through the questions which the children raise at home in a way that would be quite impossible if all of the studying were done in the schools.

We shall probably come, in the long run, to some sort of a combination of the two methods of study. In the meantime it is very suggestive that a superintendent of schools should call attention to the necessity of more work of this type in the school itself.

Foreign Language as Elementary Subject

In the city of Grand Rapids, Michigan, Superintendent Greeson has been advocating the beginning of Latin, and perhaps German, in the grammar grades. He draws attention to the fact that pupils in the grammar grades are able to learn these subjects much more easily than high-school pupils. In order to test this recommendation an experiment is to be tried in the junior high school during the coming year. Pupils are to be allowed, if they so desire, to assume work in addition to the regular course of study. A large number express themselves as desirous of beginning Latin. It should be added that other optional courses, such as shop work, were also offered. For the moment, however, attention may be centered upon the problem of language instruction in the grammar grades.

It has long been the recognized practice in German and French schools to begin instruction in languages during the elementary period. It is true, as Superintendent Greeson points out, that the younger children learn to pronounce in these languages more easily than do older pupils in the higher schools. With some modification of the method of instruction it is possible to introduce in the upper grades of the grammar school the grammatical studies which will prepare for high-school work, and for a study of the literature of the language. There can be little doubt that in the future there will be a growing tendency to introduce languages into the elementary schools. Whether Latin will succeed in holding its place as an instrument of education when the elementary school begins to interest itself in language instruction is very doubtful. The culture represented by Latin is certainly remote from the interests of elementary school children, whereas the culture represented by French and German can be made very useful for elementary training. The modern languages have also shown themselves very much more flexible in the matter of methods of instruction.

On the other hand, Latin is being tried in the experiment above referred to, and may be used as a very helpful instrument for instruction in English grammar. It may therefore succeed in securing a place in elementary instruction which will justify it as an elective along with the modern languages.

Finally, the experiment in Grand Rapids suggests an important extension of school organization in the fact that work is being offered to elementary school children, and is being taken by these pupils, in addition to the regular school program. The time is certainly at hand when the school ought to offer out of the regular hours many educational opportunities which will be accepted by the pupils who find themselves without proper engagements to occupy their time after school.

The Wider Use of Schools

It is very seldom that school interests are seriously considered in a presidential campaign. The fact that two of the candidates for the presidency of the United States have declared themselves in favor of the use of school buildings for general community uses shows that the community at large has finally realized the advantages of a wider use of the school building. For some time educational leaders have been urging the organization of debating clubs and mothers' clubs in the school buildings. Now it is proposed that political rallies be permitted in school buildings, and that the polling-places on election days be in these public-school buildings. Judge Lindsey is moving in the state of Colorado in the direction of a constitutional amendment which shall not only make this possible, but sure. Boards of education are taking action which makes it possible for communities to use the school in the way suggested. This is true, for example, of the Board of Education in the city of Chicago. The movement, which began with a few limited lectures and general meetings, thus promises to become a widespread movement.

New York School Budget

The extent to which school expenditures increase in a great municipality is very seldom realized by the individual member of a school staff. The largest school budget in this country is that of New York City. The budget which was adopted by the School Board and is to be presented to the financial officers of the city of New York for the year 1913 amounts to $38,318,650.00.

Age Limits of Elementary Education

Indications appear in several quarters that the age limit for elementary school attendance is likely to be changed in the near future. An amendment to the constitution of Missouri is proposed, and will be submitted to the voters in that state at the general election in November of this year. This amendment provides that the school attendance shall begin at five instead of six years of age. It also provides that persons over twenty years of age may receive free instruction. The present maximum age is twenty years, and the minimum age is six.

This constitutional amendment recognizes the importance of kindergarten training on the one hand, and continuation work or regular school work for older pupils, on the other. It also paves the way for a general discussion of the importance of giving to every citizen the benefit of as much training as he can take.

Another type of recommendation comes from the Illinois Federation of Labor, which, according to its president, will advocate an extension of the compulsory education period to sixteen years of age. The incorrect assumption which underlies our present state laws has become very obvious through recent investigations. When it was assumed that the ordinary child would complete the elementary school course at the age of fourteen, no account was taken of the usual retardation, which holds children back and allows them to leave school before they have reached the eighth grade. If the limit of school is to be defined in terms of the pupil's age, that age should certainly be set at sixteen years. Better still would be the adoption of state laws which defines the period of elementary education in terms of the number of grades which the pupil must complete. At all events it is a wholesome indication of general interest in the matter when the labor unions see the importance of extending the school period beyond the fourteen-year age limit.

Shooting as Educational Exercise

The War Department has taken an interest in a form of training which certain public schools have adopted. Acting Secretary of War Oliver has written to the governor of every state asking that action be taken to put rifle practice in the public schools directly in charge of the National Guards, and urges that every boy over twelve years of age be put under instruction in the handling of firearms. Furthermore, Secretary Oliver announces that the Department will offer a trophy to be awarded to that school which shows the highest degree of efficiency in marksmanship. This trophy is to be competed for by clubs of ten boys from each school.

Shooting is recommended by the Secretary on a variety of grounds. In the first place, it is a form of exercise which gives training in accuracy. In the second place, it teaches the dangers of abuse of firearms as well as the value of their use. Finally, it is a form of training which can be taken up by each individual, rather than a form of training which can be participated in only by the few boys who are members of a limited team.

A SURVEY OF THE SOCIAL-CENTER MOVEMENT

CLARENCE ARTHUR PERRY
Russell Sage Foundation

RECREATIONAL

The most solid and conspicuous progress in the socialization of school property has occurred in that phase of it which is denoted by the evening recreation center. Two years ago there were only fifteen cities in which any of the schoolhouses were used as winter play centers under the direction of *paid workers*. During the past season that number reached forty-three, and the total number of school buildings in the cities where play leaders were employed for winter evening activities was one hundred and sixty-nine.

Reports from thirteen cities showed the expenditure of $117,-631 for the maintenance of recreation centers during the season of 1911-12. Of this amount $100,000 was reported by New York City, where forty-eight centers were operated. In that city five years ago the nightly attendance at the evening recreation centers averaged over 9,500. During the season just passed the average nightly attendance was over 17,500.

Chicago, which began two years ago with only two public-school recreation centers, supported sixteen during the winter of 1911–12. The recreational work which has been carried on for a number of years in the Philadelphia schools by the Home and School League and its affiliated organizations has so thoroughly demonstrated the wisdom of community provision for a larger play life that the superintendent of schools in his last annual report has recommended that the work be placed under the control of the Board of Public Education.

In Boston the Women's Municipal League has established a popular neighborhood center in the East Boston High School. The undertaking was directed by a couple of skilled social workers who settled in the district and spent three months in investigating and making acquaintances before opening the social center. Intensive club work has been the leading characteristic of this interesting experiment which attained such a pronounced success that next year it is to be conducted, along with four new centers, by the School Committee.

In St. Louis the first definite experiment in the social use of the public schoolhouse has been made by the Neighborhood Association. It rented Franklin School from the Board of Education and used it as a meeting-place for clubs and the carrying-on of various recreational and social activities.

Milwaukee has during the past year employed a field secretary of the Playground and Recreation Association of America to make a recreational survey. On the basis of its findings a comprehensive plan was drawn up. Through a referendum the city authorized its board of school directors to levy a two-tenths of a mill tax for social- and recreation-center work, which will yield next year about $88,000. A director and staff have been employed to start this work.

The Massachusetts State Legislature during the past year enacted a law authorizing the use of public-school property in Boston for social, civic, and other purposes. As the result of an agitation for social centers which had been waged in Washington, D.C., a bill was introduced in the United States Senate authorizing the Board of Education to use public-school buildings as centers of recreation and for other supplementary educational purposes.

In many cities organized agitations are being carried on to secure the use of school buildings for social- and recreation-center work. In Duluth this is being urged by the Board of Public Welfare. In Youngstown, Ohio, over $7,000 was raised in a campaign for playgrounds and recreation centers which was carried on by the local playground association. In Cincinnati, where the schoolhouses have been open for evening gymnasium classes for years, the proposition of a more thorough expansion of the social-center idea is being vigorously advocated. The Evanston Welfare Association of Cincinnati made a social survey of a certain district and thereby developed facts which make a strong argument for providing wholesome recreation in public-school buildings.

The same topic is very much to the front in Racine, Wis., where the school officials and local civic organizations are waging an active campaign.

The men's club of one of the large churches of Springfield, Mass., has secured the use of one of the public schools for neighborhood-center work. In Paterson, N.J., the Woman's College Club has agitated the subject of social-center work in that city. The Social Service Council of Portland, Ore., representing twenty-five local philanthropic organizations, is also seeking the opening of the public-school buildings as substitutes for the dance halls.

The above instances are simply representative of the organizations and their methods; they do not constitute, by any means, a complete record of all the bodies which are working to further this movement.

The superintendents of some fifty cities other than those included in the foregoing summaries reported schoolhouses which were locally known as "recreation or social centers"; and although on closer inspection of their reports it appears that many of these buildings were used only for monthly parent-teacher meetings or bimonthly entertainments, nevertheless the fact of their being thus reported is indicative of the new attitude of school officials respecting the recreational use of school property.

These fifty do not embrace, even approximately, all of the cities in which incipient social centers are developing. The increasingly frequent desire to extend the privileges of the school building for recreational purposes, even when the board's funds do not permit organized activities, is well illustrated by an extract from the report of a superintendent in the Far West:

> Our schoolhouses have been used as social centers by permitting the pupils in the respective grades, in charge of their teacher, to have little parties. Also, the teachers of the respective schools have held social gatherings at which the teachers of the city have been invited, together with other persons interested in educational work. Schoolhouses were allowed to be used, free of all cost, by outside organizations for consistent purposes. Parents' meetings were held in all the schools, closing with some exercises in which the pupils take part. We hope to do more of this the coming year.

Since many of the parent-teacher associations have recreational and entertaining features upon their programs, they cannot be overlooked in this survey. Some notion of the number of these associations can be gained from the fact that the National Congress of Mothers, with which the majority of them are affiliated, has branches in over thirty states, the number of local groups making up the state bodies ranging from twenty to one hundred and seventy.

SOCIAL

The terrible facts regarding the extent and causes of the social evil as revealed by the report of the Chicago Vice Commission have given a new impetus to the movement of providing substitutes for the vicious dance hall. In the effort to find a place where young men and women may come together in a social way under wholesome auspices, welfare workers are turning more and more to the public schools. In New York City the opportunity for social dancing was afforded during the past season in over a dozen of the recreation centers. In Jersey City the School Extension Committee has been instrumental in opening three of the public schools for social dancing one night a week. From the outset the school board furnished heat, light, and janitor service, and after the work won the approval of the community it employed a trained supervisor to direct it, retaining the Extension Committee in an advisory capacity. In a dozen or so other cities the question of social dancing in the public schools is being very actively discussed.

CIVIC

Voting is now carried on in public schoolhouses in over a half-dozen cities. In Los Angeles, where it was inaugurated recently, the city expects to save $50,000 a year rental. The proposal to do the same thing in New York and several other cities is now being seriously considered.

The advanced position taken by some of the boards of education in California is well illustrated by the latitude which is allowed in Long Beach. Here the various political parties are permitted to hold their caucuses and other meetings in the school buildings, and they have also been used as polling-places for the past five years without interfering with school work. A couple of the outlying schools are used for Sunday-school purposes.

One of the most significant developments during the past year occurred in several cities in Ohio, where, during the recent agitation which preceded the constitutional convention, many of the public schoolhouses were used as campaign grounds in the fight for new constitutional changes. In Cleveland, meetings in advocacy of the initiative and referendum were held in school buildings under the auspices of the local Federation of Labor. Conservative members of the school board attempted to restrict the use of buildings for these discussions, but the popular approval of such use was so manifest that the rule was finally passed that schools could be obtained for meetings upon the presentation of a petition signed by twelve voters of the school district and upon the payment of $3.00 to compensate the caretaker of the building for his extra service.

The increasing tendency to bring about local improvements through mass meetings in public-school buildings is very marked. In the public press every now and then one sees instances like that at Chelsea, Mass., where a hearing was held by the joint committees on highways and public property to get the consensus of opinion in regard to a new playground; in Newark, N.J., where a mass meeting was held in the Hamburg School with a view to obtaining a new public bath on the east side; and in Brooklyn, where the Evergreen Board of Trade called the citizens together in the public school to talk over the questions of sewage and water supply.

To meet this rising public sentiment school boards are beginning to pass freer regulations regarding the use of school buildings by outside organizations. In Milwaukee public schoolhouses may be obtained for meetings of civic associations for the discussion of non-partisan questions whenever three or more reputable citizens make a written request. In several eastern cities boards are now considering the passage of regulations equally liberal in character. In Wisconsin the state law says that school boards "may grant the request of any responsible inhabitant of the district to occupy the schoolhouse for such public meetings as will, in the judgment of the board, aid in disseminating intelligence and promoting good morals. . . . ." In Oregon the state legislature has enacted a law covering the extended use of school buildings which makes no restriction upon free discussion except that all religious and political bodies be given equal rights and privileges. Kentucky has passed a law in the last legislature permitting the use of schoolhouses as places of worship during vacation time.

MISCELLANEOUS ACTIVITIES

A western superintendent writes: "The high-school building was used about four evenings a week by the Y.W.C.A., local art association, equal franchise association, and for social purposes by the high-school students. Charge for the use of the building was made by the board of education only when the organization using it charged an admission fee." This is indicative of the growing practice of permitting the use of schoolhouses by all sorts of social or philanthropic organizations. In a large number of cities school boards are preparing for this general community use of the schoolhouse by providing suitable auditoriums in all of their new ward buildings. In many places the Boy Scouts and other young people's clubs are making their headquarters in the public schoolhouse. In Oklahoma a country school teacher in Cleveland County has been arranging lectures and entertainments in the rural schools. Many of them have had lyceum courses of from two to six numbers, and sometimes as many as twelve meetings are held simultaneously in one county.

In Brooklyn, N.Y., a small committee of citizens during the past season secured the Commercial High School for a series of free concerts and lectures on social and civic subjects on Sunday evenings. The course included ten concerts given by high-class quartettes and other groups of well-known musicians. These alternated with the lectures by persons prominently identified with various kinds of social work. The attendance at the first four concerts averaged 1,500 people and the attendance at the lectures ran from 400 to 800. At these meetings a new departure was made by allowing a collection to be taken toward defraying expenses. In this way the committee hoped to relieve the audience of the feeling of being pauperized, and at the same time the income assisted in the extension of the undertaking.

The superintendent of the schools in Alma, Kan., has promoted public meetings among the citizens of the school district. The meetings were held sometimes in the afternoon, but more often in the evening, and musical features enlivened the evening entertainment. The school children addressed and carried printed invitations to their parents, and others were sent through the mail. The discussions were focused upon matters of common community interest. Starting from the standpoint of sentiments that already existed, the attention of the auditors was gradually directed to new viewpoints and new ways of co-operating for community betterment. Among the topics discussed were school athletics, musical instruction in the grades, school libraries, and student government. As the result of one meeting the purchase of a tract of land for athletics and agriculture was authorized. Social hygiene was the subject of one of the discussions, and a public sentiment is now developing that will permit the giving of systematic instruction in eugenics and wholesome sex hygiene.

Significant of the serious effort which is being made to work out the methods through which the public schoolhouses are to be more completely socialized is the formation during the past winter of the New York Social Center Committee for the Wider Use of the School Plant. The committee was formed upon the initiative of the People's Institute. Its fourteen members were selected from such organizations as the Association of Neighborhood Workers, Public Education Association, Playground and Recreation Association of America, Ethical Culture Society, Russell Sage Foundation, and the People's Institute. It was formed for the purpose of co-operating with the local board of education in not only co-ordinating the evening recreation center and public lecture work already being maintained in public schoolhouses, but with the view also of demonstrating how a single schoolhouse could be made the focusing point for the largest possible number of the various activities of one neighborhood. The committee has employed an expert to give his whole time to the work.

AGENCIES ENGAGED IN PROMOTING SOCIAL CENTERS

Chief among these is the University of Wisconsin, which has added to its University Extension Division Edward J. Ward, the organizer and director of the Rochester social centers. As "adviser on civic and social center development," Mr. Ward has been able to stimulate this work not only throughout Wisconsin but in many other states. Working in co-operation with the Social Center Association of America, which was founded by Mrs. Frances G. Vandergrift and Mrs. David Kirk, the University Extension Division held during four days in October, 1911, a "National Conference upon Civic and Social Center Development." This gathering was addressed by two governors, the president of the University of Wisconsin, and many other men who are prominent in the nation's affairs. Following the conference a permanent organization having the same name as the provisional one above mentioned was effected, with the following officers: president, Dr. Josiah Strong; first vice-president, Frank P. Walsh; secretary, Edward J. Ward; treasurer, George W. Harris; second vice-president, Dr. George M. Forbes; third vice-president, Louis D. Brandeis; fourth vice-president, Dr. Frank Strong. Since its formation the addresses delivered at the Madison conference have been published and circulated through the Extension Division of the Wisconsin state university.

Following upon the leadership of Wisconsin, the state universities of Virginia, California, Kansas, Missouri, Texas, and Oklahoma have become the propagandists of the social center as a part of their extension work. In Texas this is taking the form of sending out bulletins describing model schoolhouses which are adapted to social-center work and of carrying on a campaign to stimulate the formation of parent-teacher associations. Another force in the same state which is effectively spreading the social-center idea is *Farm and Ranch*. Its proprietor, Colonel Frank P. Holland, financed in February, 1911, the Southwestern Conference on Social Centers. Edward J. Ward was the leading speaker and the conference was attended by 350 delegates. Its two sessions were devoted to the consideration of southwestern problems and the best ways of furthering a "get-together" movement. By promoting the purchase of school libraries and through frequent articles upon the social-center idea carrying practical suggestions for their establishment, this periodical is exerting a strong and far-reaching influence upon the movement.

The National Municipal League at its meeting in November, 1910, at Buffalo, devoted one of its principal sessions to the report of its School Extension Committee. This committee was made up of nineteen members, and a summary of the papers contributed by these members was presented at the meeting.

The National Education Association at its July, 1911, meeting in San Francisco passed a resolution of which the following is an excerpt:

> The school buildings of our land and the grounds surrounding them should be open to the pupils and to their parents and families as recreation centers outside of the regular school hours. They should become the radiating centers of social and cultural activity in the neighborhood, in a spirit of civic unity and co-operation, omitting however all activities and exercises tending to promote division or discord.

The United States Bureau of Education is now sending out bulletins describing the progress of social- and recreation-center work throughout the country. The social-service commissions of a number of the leading religious denominations are now promoting the wider use of the school plant. The Social Service Committee of the New York Federation of Churches and Christian Organizations passed the following resolutions:

> That the community should regard the school building as its property, to be turned to every possible community use. That the sense of the community should commend the work already done and demand the further extension of the use of the school buildings, outside of school hours, until the needs of the city be more fully met as regards summer vacation schools, supervised playgrounds, and evening recreation centers for physical, social, literary, and other activities of young people and adults. That the use of school buildings for polling-places and other civic activities be urged as far as practicable.

In connection with the Men and Religion Forward Movement during the past winter, the "wider use" idea was advocated in some seventy conferences in the leading cities of the country. Each of these meetings was attended by representatives of near-by cities and towns, so that the social use of school buildings was in that way brought to the attention of leaders in the religious life of a large number of communities throughout the country.

During the past three years the Russell Sage Foundation has been promoting the more extended use of school property in various ways. The results of a year and a half's study of methods of utilizing the school plant were published in December, 1910, in a 400-page book entitled *Wider Use of the School Plant.* The Foundation through its Division of Recreation has supplemented this work by publishing a number of pamphlets dealing with practical aspects of the subject, among those recently issued being a bulletin that describes the social-center features now appearing in the newer elementary-school architecture. It is also promoting the cause by furnishing a lecture service and a large number of lantern slides for loaning. In co-operation with one of the leading motion-picture film manufacturers, it recently produced and has given wide publicity to a photo-play entitled "Charlie's Reform," which demonstrates the efficiency of the schoolhouse social center as an antidote to the low dance hall and the saloon.

The 1911 *Yearbook* of the National Society for the Study of Education was devoted to a treatment of city and rural schools as community centers.

The above catalogue of facts does not purport to be an accurate statement of the extent of this movement. Its manifestations are so varied, are appearing so rapidly and in so many different localities, that any quantitative statement becomes untrue a month after its utterance. In general the summaries given above are probably under- rather than over-statements. If they give some notion of the speed and scope of the movement they will have served their purpose.

PREPARING PUPILS TO LIVE

FRANK R. PAGE
Staten Island Academy, New Brighton, New York

The Staten Island Academy is a private coeducational day school situated in New Brighton, Staten Island, within the limits of New York City. The school has been in existence twenty-eight years. During its first twenty-three years it was locally known as a preparatory school of good reputation. There was an elementary department, the object of which was the preparation of pupils for the academic department. The school was through and through a "preparatory" school.

Five years ago the aim of the school changed. It is still, incidentally, a college preparatory school, but it aims to be primarily a life preparatory school. This is the story of the change and its result in the elementary department.

The Staten Island Academy began by adopting an educational creed, a crude creed, but a good working one, with some pedagogy in it and a good deal of common sense. This is the creed condensed: Education is preparation for life, using the word in its big sense, life as opposed to existence. Preparation requires, first, acquaintance with the world in which the living is to be done, not a cobwebby schoolroom acquaintance, but a real vital acquaintance. School must teach not merely textbooks but *real things*. Second, school must wake pupils up so they *will* live. School subjects must have a "push"; they must be in touch with things outside school. Finally, school work must be interesting; it must appear to pupils as worth while. School should not merely make pupils work; it should make them *want* to work.

It works out like this. In a class in geography the children are studying New York City, studying it by trips, by talks, through pictures, maps, and guidebooks. They study its historic buildings, its skyscrapers, its shipping, its transportation facilities, Wall Street, Riverside Drive, Fifth Avenue, Central Park, the East

Side, the Pennsylvania Station, the Public Library, the Custom House, the Aquarium. They take imaginary trips to other cities in this country and abroad, getting information from Baedeckers, books of travel, railway and steamship folders and time tables. They study the railway lines and steamship routes. They visit

SEMAPHORE SIGNALING

the "Mauretania." They figure the expense of the trip. They listen to stereopticon talks on the city they are to visit and different pupils give stereopticon talks themselves for the benefit of the rest of the class. They correspond with pupils in other cities, exchanging postcards and pictures and accounts of the sights to be seen. In a word, they approach the subject in the common-sense way that you and I would approach it—if we want to go to San Francisco or Paris or London or Japan, what route shall we choose and what shall we see and when do we arrive? Because geography is alive the pupils are awake and alert and interested. They talk geography *outside* of school.

Arithmetic is more of a problem. The school is working to make it a means rather than an end of education. Primary classes have miniature stores in the schoolroom with scales and measures and toy money and make-believe merchandise which they can really weigh and measure. The children take turns in keeping store, at buying, at account keeping, and are not only being developed into a wide-awake lot of young arithmeticians, but are incidentally getting acquainted with real things, actual prices, and the reason for adding and multiplying and tables of weights and measures. Making a play of school, you say? Possibly, but common sense will tell us that it is wise to teach children the things for which the process stands, as well as merely the process, and that arithmetic is a *real thing*, not just an opportunity for manipulating figures.

In older classes pupils study insurance, banks, stocks and bonds, taxation; study them concretely, by visits, through the newspapers, by specimens, by talks. They study them because they are things one ought to know; they constitute a pupil's acquaintance—elementary, naturally—with the business world. *Incidentally*, insight is gained, and skill too, in the arithmetical operations that underlie these real things. Pupils of the eighth grade have based some of their arithmetic on a study of the budget of the city of New York and are not only developing skill in performing problems, but are learning to see the use of arithmetic as well as getting their eyes opened to facts that will make them more useful citizens.

The eighth grade, who have completed the study of American history, are making a study of the government of New York City—studying it by means of trips to the engine house, the police station, the borough hall, the city hall; by visits to the meetings of the local board, the Board of Aldermen, and the Board of Estimate; by talks given by city officials, and by reports on newspapers and magazine articles. New York holds annually a "budget exhibit," a sort of fair, the purpose of which is to show concretely how the city money is spent in the various departments. The class visit this and get much information for use during the year. The Borough President responded to the invitation of the pupils and gave them an informal talk on the government of the Borough of Richmond and its relation to the city government. Following his talk, he invited the class to the borough hall where the office of each department

TEACHING ARITHMETIC BY PLAYING STORE

was visited and the heads of the departments showed and told the pupils interesting things about methods of street cleaning and garbage disposal, the fire alarm system, the water supply, and the sewerage system. The class have become interested in newspaper reading and are getting a good acquaintance with current news relating to city government.

You and I do better work, are willing even to submit to drudgery and grind, if we have an object in view. The same rule works with school children. What a deadly bore letter writing used to be!

We wrote letters to imaginary people, letters which no one ever saw except the teacher, and she only to blue pencil mark; letters whose ultimate destination was the waste paper basket. In our school today pupils write real letters to real people about real things. And they get answers. And they write again and again. And the teacher couldn't keep them from writing letters, and from learning how to write letters, even if she tried.

Making compositions worth while is solving for us the problem of composition writing. Briefly our plan is this. Composition is not regarded as a formal exercise but as a real thing. Instead of "writing compositions" the pupils "make books." They use a special kind of paper without the red margin lines and with horizontal writing lines terminating an inch from each side of the sheet. A written page on this paper presents a neater appearance than on the ordinary composition paper. Each sheet is punched in the left margin, one hole near the top and the other an equal distance from the bottom. There are round-headed brass fasteners for binding. Each composition makes a chapter in the book and is inserted when finished. The chapters are illustrated with drawings, with pictures collected from magazines, with postcards and photographs. Pupils collect or design initial letters and head pieces and tail pieces. At the end of the year a real preface and table of contents are added, and real covers of real cover stock with an appropriate design planned and executed by the authors. And then the book is *taken home*. Composition subjects are drawn always from the pupil's own experience or from things with which he is familiar. Besides the personal experience stories, composition books are made in connection with the study of geography, history, literature, and nature, thus reinforcing the lessons in these subjects. The pupil looks on this kind of composition as worth while; it is interesting, too, and he likes to compose; so because it is interesting and worth while he does his best work; he takes pains. Note again that the interest is not an artificially created one; the children do not simply play at writing. The interest is innate and natural. Children have as much right to be interested in their work as I have in mine. The method is based on the soundest kind of common sense and results prove its truth.

The school is trying to instil more life into the class recitation. Instead of looking on a recitation in history, for example, as a "test" directed by the teacher to be ultimately rewarded by her with a "mark," it is looked on as a "lecture" delivered by the pupils *to* the pupils. The recitation becomes thus a sort of clearing house for ideas and opinions and facts. Occasionally a class, particularly in geography, give a "program" to which different pupils contribute; a program, say, based on the country just studied.

A History Lesson Conducted by the Class

One pupil reads a composition, another tells some of its legends, one reads an account of some of its famous men, others show pictures of its famous buildings and works of art, others sing its songs, the class unite in singing its national hymn. Guests are invited; another class, perhaps, comes in. The program is written out and distributed. It is an occasion to be looked forward to by the participants. They have an incentive and they work and study with a will to produce something worth while.

The object of the course in literature is, first, to acquaint the children with good books, second, to make them want to read them. Literature begins in the first grade. In the elementary school they read the Greek and Norse myths, stories from Homer and the great Greek writers and from Virgil; they hear the stories and legends of the mediaeval ages—Beowulf, Siegfried, Roland, King Arthur, Robin Hood; they learn about and read a little from Chaucer and Dante, Milton, Cervantes, and Shakespeare, Wordsworth, Scott, Dickens, Hawthorne, Tennyson, and other great landmarks of literature. The relation of the different authors to each other and to the age in which they lived is seen. The great events in history are talked about and their relation to the great ages of the world is shown. The pupil gets a bird's-eye view of history and literature. As an aid, the school makes use of a chart. The basis of the chart is a straight line representing all time. For each author or work talked about a pyramid is erected at the appropriate point in time. The height of the pyramid represents the relative rank of the author; the color denotes his nationality. As different epochs are talked of they are marked off and named in the line. To show historical events, flags are drawn below the line, different colors standing for different nations. So the children see how the age of Pericles followed the Persian wars and they understand why it followed; they see the relation between Demosthenes and Alexander; they see the relation of the fall of Rome to the Dark Ages, and they see the relation of those ages to literature; they see the relation of the fall of Constantinople to the Renaissance, and the relation of the Renaissance to literature; they see the relation of the Ages of Chivalry to the Crusades, and the relation of Cervantes to the tales of Chivalry, and so on. It is a sort of framework upon which the pupil may go on building.

We try to have the children look on a piece of literature just as you or I would, as a pleasant thing to be enjoyed, not as a thing to be studied and dug out. The teacher does not sacrifice the true significance of a piece of writing to "looking up definitions" and "allusions." Philological discussion is not the children's entrance to literature. There are frequent pleasant and familiar conversations between pupils and teacher on books read outside of school. The children keep lists of the books that they read. Incidentally they are guided to choose books by authors instead of pleasant-sounding titles.

In the last grade of the elementary school a beginning is made in teaching literary appreciation. Here is the work of that class in literature: First the class read selections from "King's Treasuries" in Ruskin's *Sesame and Lilies*. The pupils note the difference between a "book of the hour" and a "book of all time," and the teacher tries to arouse in them the desire to enter and explore and know these book "treasuries." Then the class read one or two of the "Adventures of Sherlock Holmes," and a study of the plot as exemplified in these stories. Next the question is asked, "What besides just the story makes a piece of writing good literature?" The children read selections from Hopkinson Smith, Mary Wilkins Freeman, from Margaret Deland's *Old Chester Tales* and Dickens' *Christmas Carol*, and find that answers are lifelike characters and effective descriptions. Then *The Merchant of Venice* is read and its characters discussed and compared with characters from these other readings. This is followed by a study of poetry in which an answer is sought to this question: "What is true poetry and how, apart from meter, does it differ from prose?" The class read Bryant's "To a Waterfowl," "The Yellow Violet," "Thanatopsis," Celia Thaxter's "The Sandpiper," Gray's "Elegy," the opening stanzas of Keat's "Endymion," Wordsworth's "Daffodils," and many others. They are led to see the beauty and effectiveness of figurative language. They see poetry as an inspirer and as an interpreter of nature. They see that a poet is born, not made; that he sees and hears things that we cannot see and hear, and that by revealing these things to us he makes our lives nobler and better. The year's work ends usually with a study of American magazines.

Our first grade has the spirit of the kindergarten. There is a morning talk which gives the little child his introduction to literature and history and nature and industry. The reading lesson consists of sentences relating to the talk. Writing and composition, too, consist of sentences and, later on, of little stories related to the talk. The drawing is illustrative of the child's own ideas. He is encouraged to draw freely what he, not the teacher, sees. There is much dramatizing, but it does not conform to a model; it is the children's own expression. Some of the best and most educative work done in the beginners' class comes under the head of "busy work." We find in the fact that the teacher is engaged with one division of the class a real opportunity for the other division to work spontaneously and happily by themselves. Some of the best of the "busy work" consists of blocks of light wood, big blocks the size of bricks. A large rug, nine by twelve feet, is laid on the floor in a corner of the room and here groups of children busy

The Kindergarten Spirit in the First Grade

themselves with making things with the blocks. There are toys too, brought from home—pasteboard houses, soldiers, trains of cars, horses, boats. The children plan and build a castle, a ferry slip, a railway station, a village, a whole city. They are free to originate and develop what they please. Besides, there is a big sand table with smaller blocks and toys. Sometimes groups work at illustrating with drawings or paper cuttings the little stories they have written. Always they are free to express themselves.

Naturally our school takes many trips to study "real things." Nearly always these are taken in school time, for we do not regard them as extras but as a most legitimate and vital part of school work. Here is a list of some not already mentioned: the Metropolitan Museum, the Natural History Museum, the Hispanic Museum, Ellis Island, Fraunces Tavern, St. Paul's Chapel, the Stock Exchange, the Gas Works, a Telephone Exchange, the Pennsylvania Terminal Station, Doubleday, Page & Co.'s, the *New York Herald* Building, Midland Beach to study marine life, the Quarantine Station, botanical trips, tree-study trips, physical-geography trips.

School work is further supplemented by an annual series of lectures delivered by men and women famous as orators, writers, travelers, and explorers, and as authorities in many and varied branches of knowledge. When the course was first given it came in the evening and we found it difficult to get the pupils together. So for four years the lectures have been given on a school-day morning, occupying usually two recitation periods. We conceived the idea of selling enough season tickets to parents to pay the cost of the course and thus admit pupils free. This was easy to do, for the lectures have been of high grade, and parents, especially mothers, have been as much interested as the children. Most of the lectures have been illustrated with the stereopticon and more recently with motion pictures. Here are some of the speakers and their subjects: Edward Howard Griggs, "Venice," "Florence," "The Use of the Margin"; Booker T. Washington, "Tuskegee"; Peter McQueen, "Central Africa"; Frederick Monsen, "The Land of the Navajo, Mexico"; William E. Griffis, "Holland"; John Barrett, "How Uncle Sam's Prestige Abroad Concerns American Boys"; Toyokichi Iyenaga, "Picturesque Japan"; Charles T. Hill, "Fighting a Fire"; Earl Barnes, "Different Kinds of Great Men"; Daniel Gregory Mason, "The Listener's Share in Music"; Frank L. Blanchard, "The Making of a Newspaper"; Henry Oldys, "Bird Notes"; Charles W. Furlong, "The Sahara and Its Caravans"; John G. Brady, "Alaska"; Dan Beard, "How to Do Things"; Arthur A. Stoughton, "The Ten Best Buildings in the World"; Charles A. Eastman, "An Indian Boyhood"; Henry T. Bailey, "The Enjoyment of Pictures"; Raymond C. Osburn, "The New York Aquarium"; Seumas MacManus, "A Merry Ramble about Ireland"; E. M. Newman, "Russia"; Henry van Dyke, Reading from his Stories; Maud Ballington Booth, "The Need of Our Country's Prisoners."

School walls tend to restrict and confine education. Some ways we found to surmount them have been mentioned, but still we sought a means to do more for the education of the *whole* boy and the *whole* girl. Two years ago we found it in the Boy Scout

Log Cabin Built by the Boy Scouts

movement, which we incorporated into school work. The teacher of physical training, who is also in charge of the manual training, is our Scout Master. On two afternoons of the week at the close of school and on Saturday mornings the boys go out to the woods, for although Staten Island is within the city limits, it has acres and miles of fields and woods. The Scouts have the use of a tract of several acres including a small pond, within a half hour's ride of the school. Here during the past year the boys have built a log cabin and have made several pieces of furniture for it. Here they build the camp fire and here they occasionally spend the night. They are learning about camping and building and woodcraft; they study the trees and flowers and birds; they learn to swim and manage a boat and canoe; they have instruction in telegraphing and semaphore signaling, in first aid to the injured; and above all these, they are acquiring manliness and self-reliance.

A few months ago a similar organization was formed among the girls, known as the Camp Fire Girls. They, too, have been

THE CAMP FIRE GIRLS BUILDING THE CAMP FIRE

given the use of a tract of land in the country and at least once a week they go out with the director of physical training for girls.

Does it all pay? Have the changes in the school justified themselves? Unqualifiedly, yes. Pupils love school. They are interested in school work. They are wide awake. Incidentally, they are better prepared for the examinations which once were the end and aim of the teaching. And we feel, in fact we know, that when the time comes to begin living, real living, for which school is preparation, our boys and girls will have fewer new adjustments to make, fewer things to unlearn, fewer new things to learn, because of this preparatory schooling.

STUDIES IN PRINCIPLES OF EDUCATION

CHARLES H. JUDD
The University of Chicago

VI. INITIATIVE OR THE DISCOVERY OF PROBLEMS

The principle of self-activity has been stated by a number of writers in such terms as the following: The pupil should be brought face to face with some problem which will challenge his maximum ability. This problem may arise out of his desire to construct something, or it may grow out of his desire to take part in some social activity. In either case he will come to realize the need of more training. He is then supposed to seek this training without any compulsion from others. If, for example, he wishes to make a flying machine, he will read about the construction of flying machines, and will give himself the necessary arithmetic to work out the dimensions which are described in the reading-matter that he takes in hand. The problem which is in his mind becomes thus an adequate motive for reading and for the study of arithmetic. Again, if a child wishes to take part in some game, he will submit to discomfort for the sake of the social enjoyment which he can derive from contact with his companions. The same kind of motives ought to be utilized in regular school work. Children should be confronted by problems in construction and by social opportunities. Reading should grow out of these adequate self-realized motives. Number-work should be mastered in the solution of real constructive designs. In all of these cases a realization of the problem is the important step in education. The educational process will, it is assumed, take care of itself through the student's self-activity, if only he can be brought to realize the desirability of the concentration which the teacher wishes him to exhibit.

One of the best sources for problems of this sort, it is said, is the manual-training workshop. All children have a natural desire to possess boats and cages and boxes, and if they are called upon to construct these things their studies can be made to grow out of their natural desires. Again, attention is called to the fact that there are certain fundamental needs of life which may be utilized. Every child needs food, and a good deal of emphasis has been laid in recent educational discussions upon the desire for food as a natural problem which can be used in organizing school work. In like fashion it is urged that interest in clothing may be used as the basis of a course of study.

The first criticism which is to be made of many of these assertions rises from the fact that a child may have a need without in any wise realizing that need, or regarding it as a genuine motive for his own personal concentration of attention. Thus while it is true that a child has need of food, there is very seldom in civilized society any recognition of this need on the part of the child. For the most part the food products of the community are brought to the child through an elaborate social machinery which removes him far from the natural sources of the food supply. No demand has ever been made upon him personally and he has no realization of the labor which society expends in the collection and preparation of food. To realize that there is here a personal problem involves something more than the mere natural existence of a necessity. One must have enough experience to form some idea of his own relation to the rest of the world before he can understand his need. Not only so, but he must realize also the connection between any effort which he may be able to put forth and the satisfaction of this need. Thus, continuing the illustration of a moment ago, it is perfectly clear that a child may have a natural need for food, and may be brought to a realization of the fact that he needs this food, but he may have very great difficulty in recognizing the fact that the cultivation of the ability to write a letter is in any way connected with the satisfaction of his natural need. Between the letter and the satisfaction of his need must stand a realization of the fact that a letter is a means of communication and that some means of communication is necessary in order to bring him into that social contact with the people about him which will serve to supply his natural need.

We see from this illustration that the recognition of a problem is itself a step in education. One must have enough of a view of the world to realize his relations to the world, and this he can attain only through some study of himself and the conditions which surround him.

A second criticism of the general position which holds that a child will exert himself if he can only realize that there is a problem before him, can be formulated in the statement that the motives for action do not arise from the mere affirmation of certain needs. Very frequently a person may give assent to his need in a certain direction, and yet not have the necessary energy to carry him through the activities which would satisfy this need. The motive for action must in some cases be made very strong. This very frequently means that there must be a realization of the evil consequences of a failure to meet the problem. For example, a child may be persuaded in a general way of the necessity of knowing something about numbers. He may even have clearly before him the advantages of being able to measure or otherwise deal with number problems. And yet this realization of the advantage may not be strong enough to lead him to exert himself. There is many an artisan and mechanic in the world who realizes in a general way the advantage of an advanced education. He is confronted every day with evidences that he could occupy a more comfortable position in the world if he would concentrate his mind upon certain information which is offered to him. The correspondence schools which have grown up in this country have very little difficulty in persuading men that it is desirable to begin home study. The very great majority of those who register in the courses offered by these schools do not have the enthusiasm which will carry them through the courses. They are intellectually persuaded at the beginning of their work that there is a problem to be solved, and that the way in which they should solve this problem is through the acquisition of more knowledge. But as soon as they begin the arduous task of pursuing the knowledge necessary to advancement they lose sight of the problem which they have once seen. Their motives are not strong enough to carry them forward and they stop the work. In the same way children in the elementary schools do not easily hold to lines of work which demand concentration over long periods of time. The fact is that enthusiasm and energy in such cases rest upon a broad training which prepares one to realize the fact that education has certain remote ends as well as immediate ends. Breadth of vision therefore is an important part of one's devotion to any task. This breadth of vision can be cultivated only by a kind of training which will give a view of remote consequences, and this view of remote consequences must in many cases be cultivated without depending upon any problem which can be presented at the moment. Furthermore, as indicated above, the view of the remoter consequences should include certain negative factors. The evil consequences of omission can be utilized as real and legitimate motives for present training. Thus Spencer calls attention to the important educational influence of starvation, both real and imagined. The savage who never looks into the future or stores food for future need suffers from time to time because of his lack of foresight. He ultimately comes to realize the importance of storing food, and cultivates foresight in order that he may avoid future suffering. His education in this case has grown out of the desire to avoid an unfavorable consequence. Once the race has mastered this lesson, children can be taught to store food without passing through the actual distress of starvation. What we do in anticipating direct needs we may do also in preparing for indirect activities. Thus we call the attention of a child in the school to the fact that he will not be able to take a high place in society if he does not learn to read. Consequently he begins to exert himself with a view to avoiding undesirable consequences which amount to a social punishment. Such negative considerations are often quite as educative and frequently more stimulating than any positive motives which can be presented.

If the foregoing discussion has served its purpose it has made it clear that the realization of problems is itself a matter of training. A child must learn how to see the problems of life. He must have some intellectual guidance in his discovery of the types of activity which it is necessary for him to take up. The business of the school therefore is not merely to help him solve those problems which he now realizes, but the still more important business of the school is to give him that mental training which will open up to him problems that he could not have realized from his own limited experience. Furthermore, it is the business of the intelligent guide of the child's training to look far enough into the child's future to anticipate those problems which are going to arise in later years and to lay the foundation in the school work of the solutions which will be advantageous when, in the future, these problems actually appear. The conventional training given in the schools has been of this anticipatory type. Any example borrowed from the regular work of the ordinary school can accordingly be utilized to illustrate what is meant. Thus, the child does not recognize at all the advantages of a systematic statement of the principles of mechanics. He is interested at the beginning of life in the consideration of certain toys. Each of these toys involves a mechanical principle. After he has dealt with the simple mechanical principle in the form in which it appears in his handwork his attention should be drawn to the fact that there is in this situation not merely an opportunity to do something in a constructive way, but there is also an opportunity to understand the situation with which he has had to deal. He may not understand the importance of formulating what he has done in a general principle. He must be led to realize the importance of understanding what he has done. He will treat the principle at first as a mere accessory to his real constructive interest; but gradually, through the consideration of those principles which he learns in this formal way, he will come to realize that there are other similar principles which he does not know at the present time. The study of principles will thus open his mind to the importance of a general training in the principles of mechanics. If this cycle of training can be given in its entirety the child can be taught to use abstract principles. He will then be in possession of a new instrument of progress no less important than that which he gains by solving the constructive problems which he understands at the beginning of his study. The pupil has thus established a type of thought which will carry him beyond anything that he can discover through his relations to concrete objects alone. The school has opened up his mind to the recognition of an entirely new kind of problem.

Take another illustration, this time from community life. All communities have from the beginning been in need of some sort of sanitary regulations. Primitive peoples met these demands in a very simple way, by leaving the sites which they had occupied for a time. In other words, instead of trying to devise sanitary principles of community organization, they evaded the problem. Most untrained people evade problems rather than develop through their contact with problems. Somewhat later the moving about of communities became more and more difficult, and evasion became increasingly difficult, and yet the problems of sanitation were not for a long time actually discovered and realized. Sooner or later some of the more intelligent members of the community saw that if a community was to live permanently on a single site steps must be taken to provide sanitary conditions. The educational struggle began at this point. Those members of the community who were sufficiently in advance of the others to realize the necessity of sanitation have had to exert themselves strenuously in order to persuade the other members of the community that there is such a problem as the sanitary problem. One cannot convince an ignorant man of the necessities of sanitation without taking steps to present to his mind in some vivid way needs which have existed all along but have never been comprehended. The vivid presentation includes training in the comprehension of facts which the untrained man has misinterpreted in his superstitions or overlooked altogether. The facts have indeed been before his eyes and are undoubtedly of great importance to him and to those with whom he is immediately connected. But he needed training in order to realize how these facts touched his conduct. We undertake exhibitions and we provide means of instruction for the community in order that the problem of sanitation may be recognized as a problem. The educational effort in such a case as this is directed, not toward the solution of a problem, but toward the cultivation of a realization of the problem.

Practically all of the systematic work of the sciences is of the type just described. Thus when we have put together that which is known in any field of science, we have at the same time stated certain requirements for the extension of knowledge which could not have been understood before. A science creates its problems. In the elementary school a study of plants, even though it be very elementary in character, may create a realization of the need of further study of the conditions under which plants grow. The science creates its own new problems, and each step that is taken in intellectual development is a step in the realization of new demands for knowledge as well as a satisfaction of the demands which went before. In this sense all education is a succession of problems. Indeed, we may go a step farther in emphasizing the importance of pointing out problems. No one ever realized the problems of life in a large way who depended solely upon his own experience and his own consciousness. An educated individual should be keen enough in accepting the suggestions of those who are about him and of all the sciences which he studies to realize that civilization has developed a world of problems that never could occur to the untrained individual. The appreciation of literature and art, the intelligent study of economic needs, are all problems of the trained mind; they are not natural problems.

This view of education, that it consists in training the individual to see and realize problems, is in strict comformity with the psychological analysis of children's minds. The young child in the primary grades is willing to take his problems without any immediate reference to his own personal needs, if only someone will suggest problems. Thus if the teacher is interested in training the child in the first grade how to read, the child will regard that as a problem merely because it is of importance to the teacher. He does not assert his own personal needs. Indeed, he has no very marked personal needs. He is willing to receive society's general directions as they come from the teacher, and he is willing to try to satisfy the demands which society makes upon him. The one great source of his problems is social suggestion. During this period we ought to prepare the child with all of the instruments for the realization of new problems in his future experience. He ought, in other words, to learn the elements of reading and the elements of number-work.

In the intermediate grades there is a wholly different attitude. This is a period of discovery of one's own personality and one's own needs. At this stage the child must have problems which grow out of his own immediate interests. This is the period for constructive activities and the period for a statement of social demands which surround the child in terms of the child's own contact with those demands. It is a mistake to believe that the problems in the intermediate grades are of the same type as the problems in the lower grades; or, to put the matter in the other form, it is a mistake to assume that children in the early years must have their problems formulated with as great deference to their individual needs as children in the intermediate grades. Finally, when we reach the upper grades of the elementary school, children ought to have been trained to look beyond their own personal needs. Children in the intermediate grades, while they are given problems in accordance with their needs, should come to realize that there are problems in society which do not relate to them personally. They should have their attention drawn to these problems constantly. Even though these problems are not pushed to a solution in the intermediate grades, there ought to be in the mind of the child who arrives in the seventh grade a great variety of problems which carry him toward the higher forms of knowledge. He will thus have gained new and productive interests which will carry him forward. Unless there is a new type of interest in the mind of the child at this stage of his training, a type of interest that is to be described as an insight into larger needs, elementary education is all that the child is likely to seek or be willing to take on. He is satisfied to enter one of the practical walks of life and to give up the effort at intellectual comprehension of his environment. On the other hand, if he has been led to take a broad interest in the problems which other people are taking up, this broader insight will be the beginning of a new and much more productive kind of educational endeavor.

Not merely the solution of problems suggested by one's own experiences, then, constitutes the end and aim of school training, but the discovery of new problems is an important part of education. Youth is a period of learning to see problems as well as a period of learning to solve problems. Indeed, the progressive phase of education is not found in skill, but rather in alertness to see new opportunities. Education, if it is to carry the student forward, must open up many new problems, thus substituting a scientific view of the world for the view suggested by the consideration of personal needs.

BOOK REVIEWS

Education: A First Book. By EDWARD L. THORNDIKE. New York: Macmillan, 1912. Pp. 292.

We have long needed—and still need—for students just beginning their studies in education an introductory book that would exhibit in bold outlines the broad fundamental aspects and problems of education. Many books under various titles have recently appeared which attempt to perform this service. But unfortunately for us, each partially fails for one reason or another—incompleteness in the survey, disproportion of elements, equality of emphasis on specific and general, oversight of the social milieu, failure to recognize individual differences, or some special bias, academic, psychological, or biological. Professor Thorndike's book is the latest contribution to the list.

After a preliminary eight pages on the meaning and value of education, he divides the problems of education into five groups: (1) the aims of education; (2) the raw material or subjects of education, by which he means the individuals to be trained; (3) the means and agents of education, by which he refers to teachers, books, appliances, buildings, grounds; (4) the methods of education; (5) the results of education.

Under the aims of education, he shows first how values depend upon the power to satisfy human wants, proximate or ultimate. With this as a basis he then discusses the various aims: happiness, utility, service, morality, perfectionism, natural development, knowledge, mental discipline, culture, skill. Reason is shown to be superior to custom in the choice of aims.

In the section on the material for education, there is first a discussion of certain general facts, laws, and relationships: the fact that the individual always finds himself within some specific situation, to some selected element or group of elements of which he must make response; intellect and character are due to intelligible causes; the physiological basis of human nature, especially the neurological; the varieties of human nature, due to sex, to remote ancestry, to near ancestry, to chance variations, and to degree of maturity. He then discusses the original nature of man: his unlearned tendencies, his individualistic and social instincts, his original interests and play, together with the possibility of using all these things in the process of education. And finally, he discusses the learning process as looked at psychologically: the laws of habit formation, the selective activities of attention, the improvement of practice, and the possible transfer of the results of practice.

In the discussion of the means of education, he considers the educative effect of everything with which the individual comes into contact; the knowledge that is of most worth; the relative values of the studies, and the basis on which they are to be measured; the problems relating to the election of studies; the arrangement of studies into sequences and correlations; the relative efficiency of men and women teachers; and the relation of personal to textbook teaching.

In the section on the methods of education, after making clear the possible variety in the methods that may be employed, he takes up for brief consideration the following topics and methods: methods of forming habits; methods of intellectual analysis; verbal versus realistic methods; inductive methods; expressive methods;

telling and showing; questioning and developing methods; the method of discovery; methods in moral education; and finally, teaching pupils how to study.

In the section on the results of education, he discusses the effects of both formal and informal education, showing that the effect is individual and transitory, not affecting the heredity-bearing germ-plasm. Thorndike's methods of measuring writing and composition, and the methods of Rice, Stone, and Courtis are presented to illustrate accurate methods of measuring educational results.

The final section of the book is devoted to a consideration of the general status of education in the United States at the present time: the student body, age and number at the various levels of progress, length of training, retardation, elimination, selective screening of the mass, and ratings; the teaching body, sex, quality and quantity of training, experience, salaries, and public esteem; the organization of the curriculum of the various grades and classes of schools; and finally, the fiscal aspects of American education.

All these matters are covered within the space of 281 pages. The well-informed specialist when he would write a general treatise is so overconscious of each of the multitudinous details which every teacher must know that he simply cannot persuade himself to leave any of them out, even though this is necessary for showing the broad fundamental aspects in heavy outline. The result reminds one of those ancient etchings of landscapes in which leaf is separated from leaf as clearly as tree is separated from tree. General proportion demands restraint in the use of details, and inequalities in emphasis.

The book appears to be meant for education within a social vacuum. The tremendous significance of modern social movements for education, their bearing upon educational purposes and aims, upon the raw material of education, upon differentiation in the work, upon the reorganization of the studies and the textbooks, upon the vital training of teachers before and during service, and upon standards of measuring results, appear to be so negligible as scarcely to require mention. A beginner's book that does not portray the fundamental social relationships of education in clear, strong outline is sure to work harm by giving a false initial impression of the place and purpose of education in the general human economy. The first general impression should, it would seem, furnish all the central nuclei about which all later ideas in the field might be associated. It should furnish the ground-plan that is never to be changed in the genesis of one's professional mental content. In this ground-plan, certainly the social relationships must not be slighted or omitted.

J. F. BOBBITT

An Elementary English Grammar. By ALMA BLOUNT and CLARK S. NORTHUP. New York: Henry Holt & Co., 1912. Pp. xi+264. 12 mo. 60 cents.

The authors of *An Elementary English Grammar*, Alma Blount, of the Michigan State Normal College, and Clark S. Northup, of Cornell University, have succeeded as well as anyone before them in accomplishing the important feat of writing an interesting and scholarly grammar. To single out matters for specific praise in this book is easy. In the maze of grammatical terminology the authors have threaded their way circumspectly. There are only a few terms to cavil at. In the exercises given, the material is extraordinarily simple, direct, and vital. Pupils working through the exercises under the guidance of even uninspired teachers having no love for grammar would surely understand the fundamentals on completing the book. The "additional sentences for practice" here and there in the book are uplifting in tone and free from difficult syntactical puzzles; many of the sentences are from writers like Emerson, Wordsworth, Hawthorne, Holmes, and Lowell, with the author's name appended to the quotation. The definitions are crisp, and on the whole clear and accurate; they are worked up to by easy sentences. In fact, the inductive method followed by the authors is worthy of particular praise.

Some details of the book must be criticized adversely. The authors would have done well to use the terms *regular* and *irregular* for verbs instead of *weak* and *strong*. *Gender* is preferable to *sex-reference*. The term *verb*, with modifiers and complements, would do away with the awkward though common phraseology of *predicate*, simple and complete. The term *direct object*, chosen by the authors as an equivalent, appears preferable to *object complement*, the term selected. The conjugation of the verb *See* is rather eccentric on pp. 248–50. The division is into the groups present stem, past stem, tense phrases, progressive phrases, modal phrases, modal progressive phrases, *do*-phrases, verbal phrases, passive tense-phrases, passive progressive phrases, passive modal phrases, and passive verbal phrases. This arrangement is unfortunate in a book the general spirit of which is conservative.

Regarding the main order of items in the book there is bound to be difference of opinion. Here is the order chosen by the authors: I, The Sentence and the Parts of Speech; II, Predicate Complements; III, The Inflection of Nouns; IV, Phrases and Various Uses of Nouns and Pronouns; V, Compound and Complex Sentences; VI, Classes and Inflections of Pronouns; VII, Classes and Inflections of Adjectives and Adverbs; VIII, The Inflection of Verbs; IX, Verbals; X, Verb-Phrases; XI, Some Questions of Usage. Have teachers in general found this order or some other order the satisfactory one in English Grammar classes?

CHARLES ROBERT GASTON

RICHMOND HILL
NEW YORK CITY

School Agriculture with Experiments and Exercises. By MILO N. WOOD, Principal, High School, Pittsville, Wisconsin. New York: Orange Judd Co., 1912. Pp. xv+339.

School Agriculture is intended for use as a textbook in rural and graded schools. The materials of the book are the same as those presented in several recent texts in agriculture, and perhaps three things may distinguish this book from others. There is a good balance in the use of the different fields of science that compose agriculture, there being a fair representation each of soil studies, plant studies, horticulture, animal husbandry, and rural economics. The extreme simplicity of presentation makes the book readable to an elementary student. This simplicity is sometimes secured at the expense of a brevity which may do injustice to facts, as, for example, when the idea is given that starch is practically the only product of the work of green plants. The illustrations are abundant, and some of them are designed to present to the student the very best type of plant or animal, to the end that good standards may be established. The book unifies about country life the various facts and experiments, and evinces less evidence of being made up of unorganized extracts from various sciences than is usual in texts in agriculture. It is not stated whether the particular plans for presentation as included in this book have been tried in the kind of situations to which the book is dedicated.

OTIS W. CALDWELL

CURRENT EDUCATIONAL LITERATURE IN THE PERIODICALS[1]

IRENE WARREN[2]
Librarian, School of Education, The University of Chicago

BRADFORD, MARY D. The kindergarten and its relation to retardation. Kind. R. 23:67–72. (O. '12.)

A study comparing the intelligence, advancement in school, etc., of children with and without kindergarten training.

BRESLICH, ERNST R. Teaching high-school pupils how to study. School R. 20:505–15. (O. '12.)

Describes an experiment as to the relative value of the usual form of home-study in mathematics as compared with "supervised study," having as its chief aim the teaching of how to study.

BURNHAM, WILLIAM H. The problems of child hygiene. Pedagog. Sem. 19:395–402. (S. '12.)

A survey of the topic.

CIPRIANI, CHARLOTTE J. The use of phonetics and the phonograph in the teaching of elementary French. School R. 20:516–25. (O. '12.)

Teaching French as a living language so as to secure right pronunciation and easy understanding of its spoken forms.

DAGGETT, STUART. Method and scope of high school economics. Hist. Teachers M. 3:172–76. (O. '12.)

DAVIS, C. O. The history, organization, and administration of the teachers' appointment office of the University of Michigan. School R. 20:532–58. (O. '12.)

A very satisfactory presentation of the methods employed in placing their graduating educational workers.

DELL, JOHN A. Some observations on the learning of sensible material. J. of Educa. Psychol. 3:401–6. (S. '12.)

An experiment upon the influence of sequence in learning unorganized and organized facts.

[1] *Abbreviations.*—Atlan., Atlantic; Atlan. Educa. J., Atlantic Educational Journal; Educa., Education; Educa. R., Educational Review; El. School T., Elementary School Teacher; Hist. Teachers M., History Teachers Magazine; J. of Educa. Psychol., Journal of Educational Psychology; Kind. R., Kindergarten Review; Lit. D., Literary Digest; Pedagog. Sem., Pedagogical Seminary; Pop. Sci. Mo., Popular Science Monthly; Q.J. of U. of N.D., Quarterly Journal of the University of North Dakota; Relig. Educa., Religious Education; School R., School Review; Sci. Am., Scientific American; Teach. Coll. Rec., Teachers College Record; Voca. Educa., Vocational Education.

[2] Annotations by John F. Bobbitt and Frank N. Freeman.

DUFFY, FRANK. Industrial education and what labor unions are doing to promote it. Voca. Educa. 2:28–35. (S. '12.)

Voices the claim of the industrial worker for a fair share in the training given in the public schools.

GEDDES, JAMES, JR., and TESSON, M. LOUIS. Oral instruction in modern languages. Educa. 33:27–35. (S. '12.)

Presents briefly a method of oral instruction, and discusses its advantages.

GRIFFIN, JOSEPH T. Practical illustrations of the law of apperception. Pedagog. Sem. 19:403–15. (S. '12.)

Illustrations and application to general method in the five formal steps and to various school subjects.

GRIGGS, A. O. The pedagogy of mathematics. Pedagog. Sem. 19:350–75. (S. '12.)

A critical study of the methods of teaching mathematics, specially in the early years. With a bibliography.

HENDERSON, CHARLES RICHMOND. To help the helpless child. World's Work 24:627–30. (O. '12.)

HICKS, FREDERICK C. Newspaper libraries. Educa. R. 44:174–90. (S. '12.)

Discusses the libraries found in the newspaper offices of New York City, under the topics: organization, care and use of clippings, bound files of newspapers, and indexing of newspapers.

HILLEGAS, MILO B. A scale for the measurement of quality in English composition by young people. Teach. Coll. Rec. 13:1–54. (S. '12.)

History in the secondary school. Hist. Teachers M. 3:179–83. (O. '12.)

EVANS, ELDON C. The use of the blackboard.

GOODWIN, FRANK P. Social science courses for commercial students.

VIOLETTE, E. M. Setting the problem.

HOLMES, W. H. The Montessori methods. Educa. 33:1–10. (S. '12.)

A brief statement of the Montessori methods, and a critically fair valuation of them.

How lightning calculators calculate. Lit. D. 45:514. (28 S. '12.)

Industrial education in the Philippines. Science 36:396–97. (27 S. '12.)

KEYSER, CASSIUS J. The humanization of the teaching of mathematics. Educa. R. 44:140–56. (S. '12.)

A literary and philosophical idealization of mathematics as it is related to human life.

KLINE, LINUS W. A study in the psychology of spelling. J. of Educa. Psychology. 3:381–400. (S. '12.)

An experiment to compare the relative efficiency of learning to spell by methods which conform or do not conform to the individual's imagery type.

KUNZ, GEORGE F. Professor Dr. Paul Walden. Sci. Am. 107:260. (28 S. '12.)

LADD, A. J. The work of the pioneers. Q.J. of U. of N.D. 3:3–30. (O. '12.)

LEAVITT, FRANK M. The need, purpose, and possibilities of industrial education in the elementary school. El. School T. 13:80–90. (O. '12.)

———. Vocational purpose in the manual training high school, Indianapolis, Indiana. Voca. Educa. 2:36–52. (S. 12.)

Discusses the vocational possibilities of a typical manual training high school.

MARTIN, E. S. A father to his freshman son. Atlan. 110:441–46. (O. '12.)

A sensible man of the world presents his valuation of the various opportunities of the modern college and its life.

NEWELL, BERTHA PAYNE. Aspects of the first three gifts and some Montessori materials. Kind. R. 23:73–79. (O. '12.)

A discussion of the appropriate age for the use of the first three gifts and of certain of the Montessori materials.

OTIS, ARTHUR S., AND DAVIDSON, PERCY E. The reliability of standard scores in adding ability. El. School T. 13:91–105. (O. '12.)

PALMER, LUELLA A. Montessori and Froebelian materials and methods. El. School T. 13:66–79. (O. '12.)

PEARL, RAYMOND. The first International Eugenics Congress. Science 36:395–96. (27 S. '12.)

PENROSE, STEPHEN B. L. The organization of a standard college. Educa. R. 44:119–27. (S. '12.)

Discusses very briefly faculty organization and administration, and the supervision and direction of student life.

PERRY, ELIZABETH H. A working library for the supervisor of the manual arts. School Arts M. 12:132–35. (O. '12.)

PILLSBURY, W. B. Rousseau's contribution to psychology, philosophy, and education. Pop. Sci. Mo. 81:331–35. (O. '12.)

A brief account of Rousseau's mental and moral character and of the influence of his writings.

RANLETT, ALICE. Shall Latin go? Educa. 33:11–18. (S. '12.)

Ridicule for modern progressive educational movements, and an idealization of older ideals.

RICHARDSON, R. F. The learning process in the acquisition of skill. Pedagog. Sem. 19:376–94. (S. '12.)

A general discussion of the factors and conditions of learning. With a bibliography.

RIORDON, RAYMOND. How a neighborhood built its own public school and is making it self-maintaining. Craftsman 23:69–74. (O. '12.)

SCOON, R. M. Oxford—a contrast. Educa. R. 44:157–73. (S. '12.)

Describes the work at Oxford, and points out its superiority over American education.

SHOWERMAN, GRANT. Clothes and the man. Educa. R. 14:109–18. (S. '12.)

A plea for placing clothes, furniture, and household decorations on a basis of art rather than fashion; literary not educational.

SHULER, ELLIS W. The passing of the recapitulation theory and its misapplication to teaching. Educa. R. 44:191–96. (S. '12.)

SMITH, C. ALPHONSO. State history in the public school. Hist. Teachers M. 3:176–78. (O. '12.)

SMITH, FRANK WEBSTER. The normal school ideal. Educa. 33:19–26. (S. '12.)

Pleads for a more functional co-ordination of the elements of the normal school curriculum.

SNEDDEN, DAVID. Debatable issues in vocational education. Voca. Educa. 2:1–12. (S. '12.)

Enumerates nine generally accepted principles. Discusses six debatable questions: 1. Vocational and liberal education in the same school; 2. Vocational courses possible under school conditions; 3. The period from 14 to 16 years of age; 4. The amount of productive work desirable; 5. Part time work; 6. The program of evening work.

SNEDDEN, DAVID. Differentiated programs of study for older children in elementary schools. Educa. R. 44:128–39. (S. '12.)

Discusses the training of pupils 12 to 16 years of age.

SQUIRE, CARRIE RANSOM. Graded mental tests. Pt. 1. J. of Educa. Psychol. 3:363–80. (S. '12.)

The report of an experiment to determine the normal performance of children of the ages (mental, physiological, and chronological) of six to thirteen in tests of a variety of mental processes.

STARBUCK, EDWIN D. Report of the commission appointed in 1911 to investigate the preparation of religious leaders in universities and colleges. Relig. Educa. 7:329–48. (O. '12.)

STEVENS, THOMAS WOOD. The making of a dramatic pageant. Atlan. Educa. J. 8:13–16. (S. '12.)

A description of the nature and method of construction of a dramatic pageant.

TAYLOR, JOHN ADAMS. The evolution of college debating. Q.J. of U. of N.D. 3:31–46. (O. '12.)

TROWBRIDGE, ADA WILSON. The home school of Providence. Voca. Educa. 2:13–27. (S. '12.)

Describes a public school in a city flat building, that is both a home and a school, training girls in living fashion for household occupations.

UEDA, TADAICHI. The psychology of justice. Pedagog. Sem. 19:297–349. (S. '12.)

An account of the various forms of the sentiment of justice with particular reference to the replies to a questionnaire. With a bibliography.

WIENER, WILLIAM. Home-study reform. School R. 20:526–31. (O. '12.)

Presents arguments for school study periods to fill up the working day, and leave the evening hours free for children as they are for adults.

VOLUME XIII NUMBER 4

THE ELEMENTARY SCHOOL TEACHER

DECEMBER, 1912

EDUCATIONAL NEWS AND EDITORIAL COMMENT

New York State Educational Building

On October 17 New York state dedicated in Albany a building which is to be devoted to the business of the State Department of Education. The first floor is given over to administrative offices. On the floor above is a vaulted corridor leading to a reference reading-room. There are libraries of medicine, law, and legislation, and there is a periodical room connected with these libraries.

The building has already cost five and a half millions of dollars. It is a monument to the most highly centralized and fully developed educational department in any state in the Union.

The ceremonies of dedication were preceded by an elaborate educational program. On Tuesday the first part of the program was devoted to the discussion of problems relating to libraries and museums. In the afternoon elementary and secondary education were the topics. On Wednesday educational extension and private schools were taken up in the forenoon, and universities and professional schools were discussed in the afternoon.

The program indicates the range of interest which is served by the Department of Education of New York state. More than any other state department, this deals with the whole range of public education. The material expression of New York's interest in education, in this building, will undoubtedly draw the attention of other states to the importance of organizing in a more complete way their educational work. A central office which is not relegated to some remote corner of the state house, but is a place to which all of the school and college officers of the state may go for conferences and for material which will help them in their work, is certainly an indication of the type of attitude which must be taken toward education.

The federal government might with propriety be called upon to take note of the wisdom of following the example of New York state in this matter.

Department of Superintendence

A preliminary announcement is made of the session of the Department of Superintendence. The Department will meet in Philadelphia on February 25. The meeting will continue during the remainder of the week. This date is set at a time which will make it possible for the members of the department to go on to Washington and attend the inauguration ceremonies.

A number of affiliated organizations will meet with the department. Among these are the National Society for the Scientific Study of Education, the College Teachers of Education, the National Association of School Accounting Officers, the Kindergarten Section of the National Association, and the Department of Higher Education. Announcement is also made that the National Council of Education will meet at this time.

The session on Tuesday, February 25, will be given to the National Council. On Wednesday there will be a forenoon meeting occupied by the preliminary exercises, including addresses of welcome. These will be followed by a discussion of "Team Play between Schoolmaster and Layman," by Mr. Prosser, and "Team Play between City Superintendent and City," by Mr. Cary. In the afternoon there will be a discussion of uniform standardization in school administration, curriculum, etc. The members of the program who have already consented to take part are Mr. Draper and Mr. McMurry. In the evening there will be a paper on the "Development of Professional Spirit and Initiative of Teachers," by Mr. Judd, and a paper on "Rhythm in Education," by Mr. Joseph Lee. In all probability the Commissioner of Education of the United States will also appear at this time.

The Thursday forenoon program will be devoted to a discussion of "The Outcome of a Few Experiments in Developing a School System." A number of practical men are to appear in this discussion: Superintendent Meek, Superintendent Condon, Superintendent Francis, and others.

The business meeting of the department will be held at 11 o'clock on Thursday. In the afternoon there will be round tables and departmental meetings. There will be a round table for superintendents of large cities, conducted by Superintendent Edson; a round table for state and county superintendents conducted under the presidency of Mr. Blair of Illinois. The round table for superintendents of small cities will be conducted by Mr. Gruff, of Omaha.

In the evening Mr. Schaeffer will deliver an address on "Limitations of Examinations," and David Starr Jordan will speak on "Ideals."

Friday forenoon will be used for the reports of committees. The committee which was appointed to investigate the cost of living and the salaries of teachers will make a report, and the committee which is to discuss Economy of Time in the Elementary School will also make a report.

In the afternoon the subject will be the "Testing of Efficiency of School Administration." Messrs. Hanus, Bailey, and Spaulding, and others will appear on this program.

Research Aids Offered by Bureau of Education

The Bureau of Education of the United States has never been more active than it is at the present time in distributing educational information to students and school officers throughout the United States. A recent note from the Bureau calls attention to the fact that the Bureau is now prepared to accommodate commissions and committees appointed by state boards of education and by local associations for the purpose of investigating particular phases of education. Committees and commissions will be provided with a place to work and will, so far as possible, be aided in pursuing investigations through the library of the Bureau. Further than this, the Bureau is prepared to co-operate with such committees and commissions in collecting information from all parts of the country. The department has the advantage of being able to frank its communications, and can in this way collect information which would be very expensive if it were brought together by a separate commission.

Furthermore, the Bureau is prepared to supply documents from its library to individuals who are at work at home. These individuals can borrow, through institutional or public libraries, the works which the Bureau has carefully collected, including a large number of textbooks. For example, anyone who is about to prepare a textbook on any subject can thus secure the benefit of the example of many other books which have gone before in that particular field.

A monthly bulletin is issued by the Bureau, giving a full record of current educational publications. This bulletin should be in the hands of every school official. The articles and books which come out during the month are referred to, and in many cases epitomized in such a way that the student can find through these references whether the book is one that he should secure for his own personal use.

Comments on Equal Pay in New York

Comment is made in two newspapers on the experience of New York City which results from the passing of the equal-pay law. The *Detroit Free Press* of October 24 writes as follows: "Application of the principle of equal pay for men and women has had the inevitable result in New York City. It has practically driven men out of the field. The school authorities find themselves unable to increase the pay of the women to the amount that had been received by the men, and the only thing they can do is to reduce the salaries of the men. The latter cannot support themselves and their families on the lessened stipend, which is quite adequate for the maintenance of a single woman. The result may bring a little selfish gratification to women teachers, for in the readjustment they have gained somewhat at the expense of their male associates, but it means grievous loss to the school system."

The editorial continues to comment on the impossibility of maintaining the teaching staff as it was constituted before this legislation was passed.

The *Boston Transcript* referring to the same matter, writes as follows: "New York City is now reaping the full fruits of the equal-pay policy that a yielding legislature and school board put into effect in the public schools. Feminization, the evils of which have so often been pointed out, is virtually a fact, and it will probably be many many years before any movement in the opposite direction is instituted. In the list of teachers now eligible for appointment there are the names of six hundred and eighty-eight women, and of not a single man, and this situation is not an accident. It is the result of the operation of inflexible economic laws. Everyone connected with the vicious equal-pay proposition, which raises women's salaries by reducing those of men, was warned long in advance of the certain results."

These two quotations are cited not for the purpose of advocating or answering the conclusions which are there set forth. They are quoted because they represent very definitely the reaction of two leading newspapers upon the situation which has arisen in New York City. It may and it may not be advantageous for the number of women to increase in the schools. Many superintendents would be perfectly clear that it is better to have a well qualified woman than a badly qualified man, and they may be prepared to support, as a legitimate matter of school policy, the maintenance of a faculty made up primarily of strong women who can receive an adequate salary, rather than of a mixture of men and women, both of whom receive inadequate pay. But the fact is that the people who support the schools are interested in the outcome of such legislation as that which was carried through in New York City, and the attitude of other communities will be based upon the experience of New York City, and upon the comments which are reported in the public press.

Normal Extension

An experiment in normal extension work is being tried by the State Normal School at Macomb, Ill. There go out from this normal school instructors who conduct in the neighboring cities and towns extension courses for teachers. The work of the normal school is in this way brought to the teachers who are in the field and who are not able to suspend their regular duties for the purpose of study at the institution itself. Bulletins are issued in which outline courses are presented; these outlines are used in connection with certain textbooks which are to be read by the students, and lectures which are given by members of the normal-school staff. The teachers in the neighboring towns are able through such courses to secure certificates and credentials from the normal school which they were not able to secure as students before entering upon their professional work.

The effort of public institutions to spread their influence through the organization of extension work is exhibited in many of the higher institutions, especially in the state universities in the Middle West. There is certainly no reason why the normal school should not serve its territory in the same way, and the discovery of this method of enlarging the range of influence of the normal school is an important addition to normal-school organization.

Material for Bird-Study

The National Association of Audubon Societies calls attention to the fact that it has a considerable sum of money to expend in distributing literature and pictures which shall promote the study of birds in the public schools. The association is prepared to send the magazine *Bird Lore*, the usual cost of which is one dollar, to any teacher who will make application and show that she is able to make use of this publication for work in the school. Other material, such as pictures to be used in connection with the work of the school, will also be supplied on application.

Anyone desiring further information about this offer is recommended to write to Mr. T. Gilbert Pearson, secretary of the association, at 1974 Broadway, New York City.

Public Health

The Bureau of Education sends the following news item: "The state of Minnesota has engaged Dr. Ernest B. Hoag, a health expert, to travel about the state and demonstrate to the citizens that rational conservation of the mental and physical health of children is possible and practicable with the means already at hand. Three plans are proposed: (1) organization with a medical officer and a nurse or nurses; (2) organization with a school nurse or nurses only; (3) organization by the employment of a simple non-medical health-survey on the part of the teacher only. To make it possible for every community, however small, to possess the necessary technical knowledge, the State Board of Health will maintain at the state capital a "clearing-house of information concerning child hygiene, medical supervision, the teaching of school hygiene, and the like."

This action on the part of the state of Minnesota is a clear indication that the public is coming to recognize that the prevention of disease is more economical than the cure of disease. The whole matter of public health is a matter of education and public organization.

Vocational Guidance

A conference was held in New York City on October 23 to 26, dealing with the general problem of vocational guidance. There was an exhibit of material on vocational guidance in the New York Public Library, and addresses were made by numerous workers who are interested in developing a better system of vocational guidance in the public schools.

The arguments in favor of vocational guidance are sufficiently familiar, so that we need not at this time report that phase of the discussion. A suggestion which ought to stimulate study was made by one of the speakers who pointed out that no teacher in New York City, or anywhere else, has the right to attempt to guide a child in the choice of his life-work, since there is no adequate knowledge of the relation between certain specialized forms of capacity, and the demands for certain trades. This fact that we do not know now how to direct children should be the strongest possible stimulus toward investigation of this problem. It ought to be possible to discover, in the first place, by an examination of the various trades, what qualities are needed, and in the second place it ought to be possible to discover which children in the school have those qualities that will best prepare them for special lines of work. This kind of an investigation offers an inviting field to the scientifically trained student of education who is also engaged in giving instruction in the schools. This is one of the problems which is not a problem of subject-matter at all, but must be recognized by teachers as a legitimate field for the exercise of the best possible scientific training.

Professor John R. Commons, a member of the Wisconsin Industrial Commission, proposes that the school-houses shall be used as vocational bureaus; that boys and girls on the one hand, and adults on the other, shall find here an opportunity to register for employment. Giving Mr. Commons' own statement of the case, it may be said: "There is need of an organized market for labor. If each public schoolhouse had a director of its social-center service, he would be supplied with blanks from the main employment office. A workman, by going to the school nearest his house of residence, could immediately be connected with the whole organized labor market of the state."

Employment Bureaus in Schools

This suggestion for the extension of social-center work and the development of the vocational-guidance work through the school, is justified by the experience of teachers who know that without formal organization of the movement schools now serve as centers where employers often find those who fill the places which they have vacant.

Two news items call attention to the probable importance in the future of moving pictures in the city schools. The Brooklyn Teachers' Association held an exhibit to test the success of moving pictures, and many of the members of the association came to the conclusion that these pictures could be used with very great advantage in the ordinary work of the school. Much science material and much geographical material certainly can be presented in this way better than in any other way. The Bureau of Education also calls attention to the fact that the use of moving pictures in education has had a real impetus in German official circles. The Prussian minister of education is considering the feasibility of employing moving pictures in certain courses in higher educational institutions, and a number of film manufacturers are being given an opportunity to show the authorities what films they have that can be adapted to educational purposes.

Moving Pictures

The use of the moving picture in schools has become common in the schools of Gary, and has frequently been commented upon as an important part of the work in those schools. One of the principals in a school in Paterson, N.J., gives an account of competition in kind which he felt called upon to carry on against the moving-picture show which established itself immediately across the street from the school building.

All these cases go to show the importance not only of acquiring new methods of presenting interesting material to children in the schools, but also the importance of preparing children to appreciate proper kinds of recreation material.

Free Textbooks

The issue of whether or not free textbooks shall be supplied to the children of the Indiana schools was one of the important matters discussed in the recent campaign. Senator Beveridge advocated the giving of free textbooks to all the children in the public schools of Indiana. It was replied that this would increase the tax levy upon the state to such an extent that it would jeopardize the school work. It was replied again in answer to this objection that the distribution of expense for the conduct of public schools is a legitimate charge upon all the people in the state, whether or not they send children to the schools, and that the cost of textbooks is a part of this necessary public expense.

In the state of California the matter was a subject of vigorous discussion in terms of a constitutional amendment which was proposed in that state. It was argued there that the chief objection to the use of public textbooks is to be found in the fact that disease is spread by passing books around from family to family. It was also argued that better textbooks can be made by independent book companies in competition with each other than can be manufactured by the state department.

In the city of Cleveland the same general question has come up in a somewhat different form. The discussion in Cleveland, however, was not carried on so much with regard to the merits of the case for and against free textbooks, as in terms of a very heated political discussion which has followed the reorganization of the school system. In that controversy one of the labor unions took a hand because of its interest in the methods of manufacturing textbooks.

These various indications show the keen interest of the public in the matter of textbooks, and raise several questions which sooner or later will have to be met in all of the different states. The disadvantages of public textbooks, and the advantages, on the other hand, of supplying everybody with textbooks free of cost to the individual family, certainly must be regarded as a part of the problem of public education.

Rural Schools of Wisconsin

The Training School for Public Service has prepared a report on the conditions and needs of the rural schools of Wisconsin. This report opens with a brief general statement of the factors which make for progress in rural schools. Following upon this statement is a careful analysis of a number of cases of school expenditures throughout the various districts of the state. These studies of the actual practices of the small rural school boards indicate that there is a large amount of petty graft and irregularity in the work of these school boards. Accounts are evidently kept very loosely in many districts, and charges are made which do not seem to be justified when one studies the actual needs of the schools.

Later in the report matters of instruction and supervision are taken up in detail. Facts are brought out which are of importance not only to Wisconsin, but to students of rural education in all parts of the country. For example, it is shown that out of 128 teachers visited and reported on, 56 had taught in their present schools less than one year, 39 had taught one year, 20 had taught two years, 9 had taught 3 years, and only 4 had taught for four years or more. This shows that the rural school certainly has in the districts canvassed no continuity of purpose or control.

The number of visits of supervision made at the different schools is also a matter of interest. Out of 131 schools 17 were not visited during the year by either state inspector or county superintendent; 66 were visited once by the county superintendent, 30 were visited twice by the county superintendent, 8 were visited by the state school inspector, and 18 were unable to supply information with regard to supervision.

PLANS FOR GRADE LESSONS

JOHN W. HALL
University of Cincinnati

The following plans are the outgrowth of students' work in methods in the University of Cincinnati. They are prepared for the students' own use in their teaching and seem to be of sufficient merit to warrant a somewhat wide circulation. Two ideas are emphasized—the richness of subject-matter and the organization of this material into good thought problems.

RECLAIMING THE SWAMP LAND IN MINNESOTA[1]

JEANNETTE C. STONE

(To be taken up after the study of irrigation and in contrast to it, in considering agriculture in the United States.)

Precede study with such arithmetic problems in percentage as the following:

In Tarr and McMurry's *New Geography* (second book), turn to the tables on population (p. 425).

1. Find the percentage of increase in the population of Minnesota during the last 10 years (16 per cent).

2. In the State of Wisconsin in the last 10 years ($12\frac{1}{2}$ per cent).

3. In the State of Ohio in the last 10 years ($13\frac{1}{2}$ per cent).

Let us compare the percentages of the increase in population in these states. What do the figures show us?

Ans. People are going to Minnesota.

Show Swamp Map of state.

Let us look at this map of the state of Minnesota.

What do you learn about the condition of the land there? (Swamp land.)

How much of the state is covered with the swamps?

Ans. Over two-thirds.

If you were going to farm, then, would you go to Minnesota? Why not?

But let us turn to the map on p. 183.

What do you learn from this map?

What do the statistics show?

Ans. Minnesota is the state leading in the production of wheat.

Turn to page 402.

[1] This plan is accompanied by an interesting collection of pictures and newspaper items which unfortunately cannot be adequately reproduced—ED.

What part of the supply of wheat raised in the United States comes from Minnesota?

Ans. Over 1/10.

Why do you suppose then that so many people have gone to Minnesota?

Ans. To take up wheat-raising.

Aim. *Let us find out, then, what conditions exist in Minnesota, which have made it the greatest wheat-producing state in our country.*

Name the requirements necessary for the raising of wheat.

Ans. Temperature; Rainfall; Soil.

Take up each topic in turn.

Temperature.—The average temperature in the state of Minnesota is 42°.

Explain what an "average temperature" is, telling that sometimes in the state of Minnesota the temperature goes 26° below zero in the winter and 98° above in summer.

Do the same for the state of Ohio (ave. 52°). How much difference?

Of course this difference in temperature will make some difference in the kind of products raised, but it certainly will not prevent the carrying on of agriculture. We know this fact to be true from the statistics in regard to the amount of wheat raised.

Rainfall.—Turn to p. 214. Find the average rainfall for the state of Minnesota. (20–30 in.) For the state of Ohio (30–40 in.). Compare. Do we have sufficient rainfall in this state for farming?

Ans. More than enough.

Do you think, then, that the rainfall in the State of Minnesota will be sufficient?

We have now determined that the temperature is mild enough for carrying on agriculture and that the rainfall is sufficient.

Soil.—Let us find out if Minnesota has any advantage over other parts of the country in respect to the conditions of the soil.

Turn to the map on p. 8. Read Secs. 3 and 4, "Extent of the Great Glacier and Changes That the Glacier Made." Also p. 10, (3) "Changes Made upon Our Farming." Read to find out:

What some of the effects of the work of the Great Glacier were on the state of Minnesota?

How would this benefit the composition of the mold?

After the formation of the lakes and swamps how could the fertility of the soil be increased?

Ans. By decaying animal and vegetable matter.

Knowing then, that the temperature in the state of Minnesota is not too severe for carrying on agriculture, that the rainfall is sufficient, that the soil is fertile, what would be the difficulty in farming?

Ans. Swamps.

Show picture of swamps.

What are some of the difficulties in trying to farm swamp land?

GETTING RID OF THE SWAMPS

The whole question, then, of carrying on agriculture in the state of Minnesota hinged on the project of getting rid of the swamps.

Do you know of any country in Europe that has had a similar problem to meet?

Ans. Holland.

Turn to the top of p. 278.

How did the Hollanders meet this problem?

Ans. Dikes and drainage ditches.

What advantage has the position of the state of Minnesota over that of Holland?

Ans. No surrounding ocean, therefore no need of dikes.

MEANS OF ACCOMPLISHMENT

If the state of Minnesota has been made more fit for carrying on agriculture how has this condition been accomplished?

Ans. By building drainage ditches.

Who would be interested in the building of these ditches?

Ans. Land-owners, counties and state.

Very often large sections of the land were wholly uninhabited, as much sometimes as a whole county. In such a case no one cared for the land, for it was unfit for use.

Would anyone be very interested in improving it?

As the population of the state increased, however, much of this swamp land was investigated and in 1886 one of the judges of the state by an open letter, published in the newspapers, called the attention of the public to the condition of the land and the opportunities which it offered for improvement.

So, for an example, let us take Marshall and Beltrami counties, shown here on the map, and find out how the building of ditches progressed there. In other counties much the same thing happened.

The richness of this land and the fact that it was capable of being easily well drained was first noticed by a civil engineer or a surveyor, W. R. Hoag, in company with an attorney, William J. Brown, on a trip through that territory in 1900.

What might a civil engineer and a lawyer do toward furthering the building of ditches in these counties?

Suppose the people became interested, could they and would they undertake this plan alone? Why not?

Ans. Cost.

But in the state of Minnesota, as soon as the importance of draining the land was realized, money was set aside for this purpose by the state.

Why would the legislators think it an important thing to improve the land?

Ans. Get people to come there.

How could the lawyer help the people in these counties under these conditions?

Ans. Advising them in securing the improvement, drawing up petitions, etc.

This was what happened in these counties. The people drew up a petition, with Mr. Brown's help. This petition was presented to the legislature and the money finally granted for the building of certain ditches, which Mr. Hoag, the civil engineer, had planned. The United States government has also recently made such appropriations.

BUILDING OF THE DITCHES

What are some of the things you would like to know about the building of these ditches?

Ans. Width, length, depth, shape. Process of building, etc., what becomes of the water drained off, cost.

PROCESS OF BUILDING

From what you already know about the condition of swamp lands, that is, the fact that they contain stagnant pools of water, rank with vegetation etc., what do you think would be some of the dangers of such an undertaking to the workmen?

Ans. Sinking in the mud. Mosquitoes.

It certainly would be difficult for surveyors to get around without sinking in the mud, for their work takes them everywhere. Can you think of a way by which they might avoid sinking in the mud?

Ans. Use of stilts.

Their instruments are even set on stilts.

Why wouldn't you expect to find mosquitoes in Minnesota?

Ans. Too cold.

But strange to say in spite of the cold, the mosquito pest is perhaps the most disagreeable thing about the whole state. The mosquitoes are hatched in the latter part of the summer in large numbers. So great that the people cannot even sit out on their porches unless they are screened. Fortunately the pest lasts only about a month.

What advantage could the workmen take of this?

Ans. Work where there are none.

From this standpoint, what will be one of the results derived from draining the land?

Ans. Fewer mosquitoes.

Before actually building the ditch, what would the workmen have to know?

Ans. Where to build it.

The civil engineers or the surveyors determine this part of the work.

Draw diagram on board (p. 175).

From this diagram, if you were the engineer, where would you plan to run the ditches? Why?

Ans. Outlet to carry away water drained.

But suppose the river isn't wide and deep enough to carry away all the water drained off. What would happen?

Ans. Water would spread over the land.

That is exactly what did happen.

How could this condition be remedied?

Ans. Deepen the river channel.

And that is exactly what they did do. They deepened Thief River by means of dredges.

How many have seen the dredge-boats along the Ohio River? You know then how they would go about this part of the work.

Now we are ready to find out how they were going actually to dig the ditches throughout the counties. You have all seen men digging ditches in the city in laying pipes, repairing sewers, etc.

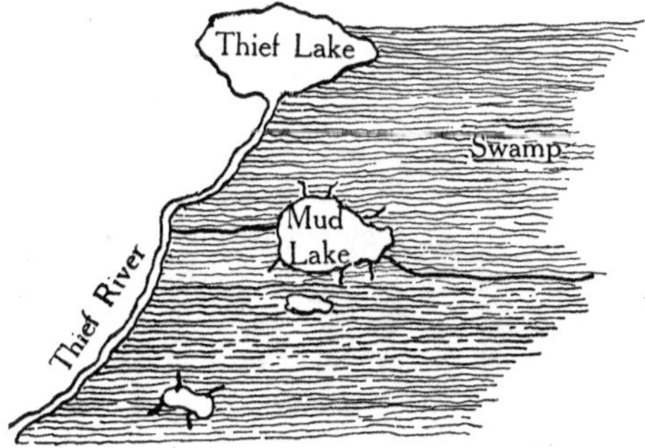

How do they do it? Why wouldn't this be a good way to dig ditches in Minnesota?

Ans. Too slow. Laborers hard to get. Cost.

Has anyone ever seen ditches dug in any other way?

Ans. By machines.

Show pictures. What advantages would this way of digging ditches have over the other?

Some of these machines are made so that horses or oxen can be used to draw them. Others are propelled by steam engines. These are called "traction engines."

Where do you suppose people would get these machines out in the swamp country?

Ans. Ship them in.

It is an interesting fact to know that some of the best machines shipped there are made in our own state, at Findlay, Ohio.

When this ditch-digger is in operation, as you see in the picture, it heaps up dirt along the side. Can you think of any use that might be made of this?

Ans. Since the side of the ditch is thus made higher than the land around it, it would serve as a splendid road in that country.

What would be the advantage of a road built in this manner?

Let's find out, now, just what building these ditches would mean.

ARITHMETIC PROBLEM

The contract that was let out to Mr. Hoag called for the building of 498 miles of ditches and the building of the same number of miles of highway within 2 years.

One of the first things we have to consider is the length of time the men can work in a year. Why?

1. Suppose the contractor found that the work could be carried on during six months of the year, working 8 hours per day. How much of the ditch and the road must be complete per day in order to finish the contract in the given time?

Ans. $1\frac{2}{5}$ mile.

2. The ditch is 20 ft. wide and 9 ft deep. How much dirt would have to be removed per day? per hour? per min.?

Ans. 1,330,560 cu. ft., 163,820 cu. ft., 274 cu. ft.

3. If one ditching machine will remove 18 cu. ft. per min., how many machines will this contractor be required to buy to complete the contract within 2 years?

4. If it takes 3 men to handle one machine and they receive on an average $2.00 per day, what will be the cost of labor to complete the work?

Ans. $27,648.

5. If it costs $2.50 per acre to drain land, and $20 per acre to irrigate land, find the difference in cost in improving 480 acres of land.

From what you already know about irrigation give reasons for its being so much more expensive.

Besides the fertility of the soil, the climate, the ease of draining the land, etc., there is another reason for so many people coming especially to this part of the country.

At one time much of this land was set aside as an Indian Reservation. Does anyone know what has become of the Indians?

Since there are very few Indians left, they no longer need this land.

What would be the best thing for the government to do with such lands?

The government has opened this land up as homestead land, and as we have already found out, is even assisting in building the ditches.

Can you see how this will in any way affect the settlement of Canada?

Ans. Turn the tide of immigration.

On the whole, how will the improvement of this land benefit the United States?

What effect has the building of the drainage system had on the state of Minnesota?

Ans. Made it the greatest wheat-producing state in the Union.

A LESSON PLAN FOR THE STUDY OF ALASKA

ELMORE C. WALTHER

Aim: In what ways is Alaska a profitable possession of the United States?

What interested the Russians in Alaska?

Why should the fur industry interest the Russians more than the Americans?

What must the Russians do in order to prevent the Canadians from taking furs on Russian territory?

Would this be worth while?

At what other disadvantages would Russia be in protecting this great strip of territory?

What other countries, besides Russia, would make inroads on the fur resources of Alaska?

What effect would this have on the present industry? in the future?

What must the United States do in order to protect this industry?

Suggest some plan to accomplish this. Read text, p. 150 (Sealing)[1]; read *R.C.G.*, §218.

Would this industry alone pay the United States to keep this vast territory?

What, then, must we do in order to make Alaska worth while? (Develop the resources.)

FISHING

Why would this industry be the easiest to develop?

What physical conditions would make the fish of Alaska desirable?

Why would they be easy to catch?

Where would they be more abundant, in the open sea, or near the shore? (Reasons.)

Make an outline map of Alaska. Show the extent of the 100-fathom and 200-fathom depths. Locate the places where the different fish abound. Use *R.C.G.*, p. 211; text, p. 188.

During what season are salmon most easily caught? How and where? (Teacher add information.)

What reasons can you give for locating the fish canneries in Alaska?

Where in Alaska, would you locate them so as to be easily operated in the spring? Draw conclusion after studying (*a*) Isothermal charts, text, pp. 225 and 226; (*b*) Ocean current charts, text, p. 220.

COAL AND LUMBER

What would we need in order to establish a fish cannery in Alaska? (1) Machinery; (2) Fishing Craft; (3) Fuel.

What material would be most easily accessible for fuel?

[1] Abbreviations: Text used: Tarr and McMurry, Second Book; *R.C.G.* = *Robinson's Commercial Geography*. Material for Reports can be obtained from recent articles on Alaska in: *The Review of Reviews*, *The Outlook*, *The Technical World*.

Would it be wise to continue to use timber for fuel?

To what extent could Alaska furnish her home industries with fuel? (Report: "The Coal Resources of Alaska").

AGRICULTURAL POSSIBILITIES

Where would most of the fish canned in Alaska be sold?

Look up the population of Alaska and compare with U.S.; Ohio; Hamilton Co.; Cincinnati; text, p. 424; p. 30, Appendix.

Would any be sold in Alaska? (Reasons.)

Do you think that Alaska will be a future for the fishing industry?

Upon what food do you think the Alaskans will live, besides fish? (text, p. 152).

Where could vegetables be raised in Alaska? Determine from rainfall map, p. 213 (text); isothermal charts, pp. 225 and 226 (text).

To whom would you sell this garden truck?

What other crops could you raise?

MINERAL RESOURCES

What industry would the remainder of the people be engaged in? (text, p. 151).

What has been responsible for the rapid development of that country? (Report: "Gold Mining in Alaska," the "Copper Resources of Alaska," the "Tin Resources of Alaska").

Would it be advisable to invest much money in farm lands in Alaska as yet? (Read last ¶ of text, p. 152.)

What kinds of people would you expect to find in Alaska? (Races of Mankind chart; text, Fig. 329).

Which of the races is most responsible for the development of that country?

Of what advantage would it be to Uncle Sam to educate these people? (Report: The Awakening of Alaska).

Summary: In what way has Secretary W. H. Seward shown himself to be a far-sighted statesman when he said: "The Pacific Ocean, its shores, its islands, and the vast region beyond will become the chief theater of events in the world's great hereafter"?

Test: Write an account suitable for a railroad folder, making Alaska as attractive as possible for: (*a*) The tourist, (*b*) The farmer, (*c*) The stock-raiser, (*d*) The prospector, (*e*) The miner and promoter, (*f*) The hunter.

Indicate (or cut out and paste in your account) the pictures that you would use to illustrate this folder.

For what railroad line would you make this folder?

A TEST IN GEOGRAPHY AT CLOSE OF STUDY OF AFRICA

FREDERICK D. COTTER

This set of examination questions is prepared with the idea that an examination should test primarily a child's ability to use the facts which he has acquired; that in the examination itself there should be growth along this line; and that knowledge should also be increased.

Children are to be allowed to use geographies and any other books from which they may gather information. They are not to communicate with each other or receive any help from the teacher.

A certain wealthy Englishman named Cecil Rhodes had become interested in Africa. He had done much to develop the country and now was in the Southern Park in the Transvaal. It occurred to him that a railroad from Cairo in the north to Cape Town in the south would do more to help out his idea of developing Africa, than anything else. What arguments would he use to induce people to invest their money in this scheme (use books). Suggest a good namc for this railroad. Use your maps and decide the best route for this railroad. Give four or five good reasons for the route you selected. Trace on the blank map of Africa the route you selected.

What difficulties would be met with in this undertaking with regard to labor? (*a*) Where would they get unskilled laborers? Why? (*b*) Where would they get the skilled workers (engineers, superintendent)? What are the dangers to health of the workers? How would they be overcome?

Where would the material for the construction of the road probably be obtained? Why? What would be the cost per mile of building this railroad compared with the cost per mile in the United States? Give one or two reasons for this. Where would they obtain their rolling stock? What fuel would they use? Why? Where would they get it? Would there be more passenger or freight trains? Why? What would be the occupations of the people who traveled on this road? What would the principal articles of freight be (*a*) from the coast to the interior of the land; (*b*) from the interior to the coast?

Effect of this railroad.

Name four or five results on the continent.

Give four or five ways in which this railroad would benefit England. In what countries would there be magazine and newspaper articles about this railroad?

Think about whether this project would have any effect on the United States.

APPRENTICESHIP UNDER THE ENGLISH GILD SYSTEM

J. F. SCOTT
Madison, Wisconsin

If history is to be used effectively to shed light upon present problems it must be used guardedly; for the exact conditions of the past are never reproduced in the present. Many a problem of bygone ages has reappeared in modern times, but with so different a setting that the solution attained in the past may be ineffective today. So in the case of the problem of industrial education, which has become so prominent since the disappearance of the American frontier, it must not be forgotten by those who propose a revival of the apprenticeship system that times have changed and that apprenticeship, as it existed in England from the thirteenth to the nineteenth century, would be utterly out of place in the majority of occupations today. On the other hand the system was, in its time, a success; for no institution could have lasted as long as this did unless it had met certain vital social needs. It accomplished certain results for the individual and for society which we expect the industrial training of today to accomplish. A study of certain of its phases may, then, be of some use.

The success of the apprenticeship system during the Middle Ages and the period of the Renaissance was largely due to two factors: First, the close personal relationship and identity of interest existing between master and apprentice; and second, the supervision of master and apprentice by the craft gilds. These factors were fostered by the social and economic conditions of the Middle Ages, but passed away under the changed economy of modern times. To the loss of the proper personal relationship and identity of interest existing between master and apprentice and to the lack of adequate supervision over this relationship is partially due the decay of the apprenticeship system.

As Sombart points out, one can only understand the relation

of the master to his "Hilfspersonen" by remembering that all handicrafts had their origin in family life. Journeymen and apprentices entered completely into the family circle and in the common activity found a bond of union.[1] The reciprocal duties of master and apprentice are set forth in a general way in the indentures—articles of agreement at the time of binding—many of which are preserved in ancient records.[2] These indentures show that the chief duty of the apprentice was to serve his master faithfully, not only in his master's business, but in the performance of household tasks or other services; the master was obliged to teach the lad his trade, to house, feed, and clothe him. More than this, he was supposed to give the youth such moral and religious training as a boy of immature years would naturally require.[3] In a word it was the master's duty to prepare the boy to be not merely a good craftsman but a good citizen as well.[4] Finally the closeness of the personal relationship between the two is clearly brought out by the fact that not rarely the apprentice led his master's daughter a blushing bride to the altar.[5]

The apprenticeship system, as it existed in mediaeval times, offered opportunity to the apprentice of learning all branches of his trade. The shop was small; master and apprentice often worked side by side at the same bench. The master himself worked at all processes of his handicraft, and therefore it was comparatively easy for him to teach all processes to the lad at his side. It was comparatively easy, too, for the lad to follow all the

[1] Sombart, *Der moderne Kapitalismus*, I, 118; *vide* also Strype's ed. of Stow's *Survey of London*, II, 331.

[2] Bateson, *Leicester*, III, 50; Cunningham, *Growth of English Industry and Commerce, Early and Middle Ages*, pp. 349–50; Noble, *Ironmongers*, pp. 44–45; Clode, *Early History of the Merchant Taylors*, I, 344; Hibbert, *English Gilds*, pp. 52–53; Madox, *Formulare Anglicanum*, No. clxxviii; Bird, *Law Selections*, pp. 76 ff; Ashley, *Economic History and Theory*, II, 86, refers to a number of others.

[3] An ordinance of the Shoemaker's Gild of Carlisle provides that no master shall allow his apprentice to play cards in the master's house (Ferguson and Nanson, *Gilds of Carlisle*, p. 179). Some gilds required masters to see that apprentices went to church (Welch, *Pewterers*, I, 223; *Clothworkers' Ordinances*, pp. 133, 134; *vide* also Cunningham, "Growth of English Industry," etc., *Modern Times*, Part II, 629–30).

[4] "London 'Prentices," *Colburn Magazine*, V, 174, quoted from the *Cities' Advocate*, printed 1629; Strype's ed. of Stow's *Survey of London*, II, 331.

[5] *Ibid.*

workings of his master and to imitate them. The number of apprentices being small the master could give each one a large part of his attention. Furthermore, as there were but few apprentices[1] and journeymen, there was but little division of labor and therefore but little of the modern tendency to keep a boy employed on one or two processes to the exclusion of all others. It was to the interest of the master that the apprentice be able to assist him at every process of the craft. To the master, too, accrued the profits of the apprentice's toil during the latter's term of service,[2] and the more skilful the boy, the greater the profits of his employer.

In the same way the apprenticeship system favored the development of artistic ability. The long term of service, usually seven years in England, somewhat less on the Continent,[3] gave opportunity for the acquirement of that refinement of skill so necessary to the true artist. The careful, individual attention given by the right sort of master to the apprentice enabled the latter to avoid superficiality, while the master's own work furnished a worthy example for the lad's imitative powers. Then, too, since whatever the apprentice earned went to his master, the young man was forced to find his rewards, not in immediate pecuniary gain, which might tempt him to quick, superficial work, but in his master's praise and in the joy of artistic creation. Finally the fact that he was one day to be a master himself would naturally lead the apprentice to a desire to acquire a knowledge of all processes of his craft and to a dexterity of hand and artistic skill in construction. In general, then, the interests of master and apprentice in the

[1] From the fifteenth century onward, however, the English gilds had frequently to forbid masters to take more than two, three, or four apprentices. This prohibition the wealthier masters resented and came more and more to disregard. Harris, *Coventry Leet Book*, I, 92; Smith, T., *English Gilds*, pp. 315, 316; Wadmore, *Skinners*, p. 26; Young, *Barber-Surgeons*, p. 64; Lambert, J. M., *Two Thousand Years of Gild Life*, p. 206; Welch, *Pewterers*, I, iii; *ibid.*, pp. 185, 237–38; Smith, Adam, *Wealth of Nations* (Cannan ed.) I, 121, etc.

[2] "Whatever the Apprentice gets of his own labour, or of his Master's Occupation or Stock, he getteth to him whose apprentice he is."—Strype's ed. of Stow's *Survey of London*, II, 434.

[3] Brentano, *History of Gilds*, p. cxxix. While the period of apprenticeship was shorter on the Continent than in England, the period of journeyman service was longer. This period of journeymanship fostered the development of artistic skill.

days of handicraft were identical. Apart from the matter of personal attachment between the two, it was to the economic interest of each that the apprentice should become a skilled, artistic master-craftsman.

The results of the apprenticeship system are to be found in the artistic handicraft work of the later Middle Ages and the Renaissance. While it may be true, as Sombart says, that the finest productions are the work of artists who chose to express themselves through the crafts, rather than the work of skilled artisans,[1] yet there are proofs that there were many artisans of high artistic ability. Sombart shows that it is unsafe to judge the craftsmanship of the Renaissance by the treasures of our "Arts and Crafts" museums, treasures which possess unusual artistic merit and which he holds to be the work of artists. On the other hand there are certain relics in these museums which are preserved, not for their artistic value, but for their historic or antiquarian worth, as interesting witnesses to a bygone age. A suit of armor, for example, would find a niche in the museum whether it possessed artistic merit or not. Yet if one takes into consideration the lack of machinery in mediaeval times it must be admitted that even the average suit of armor is a work of art. And it is the work of an armorer—an artisan—not an artist who chose to express himself through the medium of armor-manufacture.

As further proof of the artistic instinct and power of the mediaeval craftsman take some of the exquisite details in the cathedrals. The carvings on the pews or the walls, the wonderful ironwork and other details indicate the skilled hand and aesthetic feeling of the craftsman. So numerous are these details that it is impossible to think of them as the work of artists rather than of artisans. It is hardly possible that the obscene carvings so often tucked away in odd corners or cornices—carvings so incongruous with the majestic spiritual ideal dominating the great structure—were planned by

[1] "Die Renaissancezeit hat ein so herrliches Kunstgewerbe nicht deshalb besessen, weil die Handwerker Künstler, sondern weil die Künstler Handwerker waren, richtiger." *Der moderne Kapitalismus*, I, 85. Sombart's estimate of the artistic ability of the average craftsman is, I think, too low. *Vide* his discussion of this in I, 85, and compare with the evidence presented above.

the architect; they are far more likely to be the expression of the coarse but artistic sense of humor of some long-forgotten artisan.

Jacquemart tells us that the artisans known as joiners developed the handicraft of making and decorating furniture in a wonderful manner. They approached the sculptors in artistic power.[1] It is not necessary to multiply examples. Enough has been said to show that dexterity of hand and power of artistic expression were widespread in the days when the apprenticeship system flourished.

The efficiency of the apprenticeship system was guarded by gild supervision. It may be objected that I have praised the mediaeval apprenticeship system too highly, that I have represented an ideal condition of affairs. It may be pointed out that masters sometimes ill treated their apprentices, neglected them, and failed to instruct them properly, and that apprentices were sometimes idle, thievish, and faithless. All this is true, even of the mediaeval system, though most of the examples of such bad conduct come from the seventeenth and eighteenth centuries. In mediaeval times the danger of such bad consequences was lessened by the fact that both master and apprentice were responsible to the gild. The gilds passed many ordinances to regulate the conduct of master and apprentice,[2] and these ordinances were enforced in the gild courts.[3] Such supervision over conduct was far more

[1] *History of Furniture*, p. 22.

[2] *Vide* in this connection Welch, *Pewterers*, I, 4; Riley, *Memorials of London Life*, pp. 243, 247; Herbert, *London Livery Companies*, I, 13; Harris, *Coventry Leet Book*, Part III, 671; Young, *Barber-Surgeons*, p. 181, etc.

[3] "The authority of the craft, even after it had altogether fallen into the hands of its wealthier members, continued to be used for the protection alike of apprentices and of journeymen against the violence of their employers."—Ashley, *Economic History and Theory*, II, 106.

The following case arose in the court of the Pewterers' Company of London in 1559. "At the same Courte John Smythe Sometime apprentice with Geffery Mathewe was commytted to warde by the Mr [master of the company] wardens and assystance for that he had promysed to serve a certayne tyme with John Cutler as maye apeare the last yeare and after his promys within ii days after went to maydstone and wrought with a Tynkerd and made hym mowlds."—Welch, *Pewterers*, I, 207.

Clode, C. M., *Early History of Merchant Taylors*, I, 209: "'Apprentices were under the care of the Company, and masters were fined for ill treatment. . . . . In the case of misusing an apprentice an entry of April 2d, 1563, shows that very sum-

effective when the towns were small and the actions of the gild members open to close scrutiny than when the towns had grown to cities and less was known of the private life of master and apprentice.

The supervision of the gild was not confined to observation and control of conduct but was extended to the actual work of instruction as well. Sometimes the gilds specified what the master should teach. Thus the Clockmakers of London in 1632 provided that every person of their trade should "teach and instruct his said Apprentice and Apprentices in such manner and form as their Predecessors have done, which is to keep daily him and them in his House, and there by himself or his sufficient Journeyman, teach or instruct them in the making of Cases or Boxes of Silver or Brass, and likewise the several Springs belonging to a Watch, Clock or Larum, and likewise all other particular and peculiar things belonging to such Watches, Clocks, Larums, Mathematical Instruments, and Sun-Dials his or their Master shall teach and instruct them in."[1] The Apothecaries and the Barber-Surgeons of London made rather elaborate provision for the matters to be taught their apprentices;[2] but as a rule it was not necessary for the gilds to specify the subject-matter, as the masters knew perfectly well what was expected of them.

While the gilds did not usually specify what was to be taught they did take measures to see that the teaching was properly done. They did not intend to allow apprenticeship to become a farce nor

mary measures were taken against his master, thus, 'The Wardens have comyted Thomas Palmer to pryson for that he hath broken Henry Bourefelde his apprentice's hedd without any just cause. Henry Bourfelde by composition had comytted his two apprentices to serve with Thomas Palmer during and for so long time and such consideration as they were agreed. And for that the said Thomas Palmer hath not only evill used himself towards the said apprentices, but also for that they have not had of hym sufficient meate and drynke as they ought to have had' " (p. 209).

"Jan. 12, 1571, in case where cassock had been made too small, Master and Wardens ordered that defendant pay the plaintiff forty shillings 'and shall take to hym self the said garment to make his best pffit accordingly' " (*ibid.*, p. 210; from records of the company).

[1] Atkins, *Clockmakers*, p. 44.

[2] Barrett, *History of the Apothecaries of London*, p. xxxiii; *ibid.*, pp. 197–98; Young, *Barber-Surgeons*, pp. 309–10.

to permit the apprentice to become a master at the end of seven years whether or not he was a skilled craftsman. One of the objects of the gilds was the maintenance of a high standard of production and for this they were responsible to the community.[1] In at least one case, that of the Cappers of Coventry, it was a duty of the principal master of the craft to go round the city annually, examining every apprentice to see that he was receiving proper instruction from his master.

Practically all the gilds insisted on some sort of an examination of the apprentice at the end of his term.[2] At first the examination merely took the form of a requirement that the master or other "able men" testify to the fitness of the apprentice to "occupy" his craft.[3] Later on, however, the gilds insisted that the apprentice be examined by the masters or chief officers of the company and proved "sufficient and able to occupie."[4] Thus the Clothworkers of London insisted that the candidate for mastership "shear and worke" in the Common Hall of the gild before the Master, Wardens, and certain of the assistants.[5] The Shoemakers' Gild of Carlisle required that the apprentice, after completing his term "have foure paire of shoes given him to worke"; if the shoes were well wrought he was to be admitted a journeyman, but if not he

[1] Webb, *History of Trade Unionism*, p. 17.

[2] Bickley, *Little Red Book of Bristol*, II, 96; "Ordinances of the Skinners," 1408; *ibid.*, p. 104, "Ordinances of the Cordwainers"; *Hist. Mss. Comm.*, *Twelfth Report*, IX, 521, "Ordinances of the Butchers of Gloucester," 1454; *ibid.*, *Fourteenth Report*, VIII, 135, "Ordinances of the Weavers of Bury St. Edmunds," 1477; Black, W. H., *Leathersellers*, p. 123, "Ordinances of the Pouchmakers," 1501; "Clothworkers' Ordinances," p. 26; Welch, *Pewterers*, II, 243; Fox, F. F., *Merchant Taylors of Bristol*, p. 61. Many other examples might be adduced.

[3] *Munimenta, Gildhallae Lond.*, III, 442. *Liber Memorandorum*, "Ordinance of the Cordwainers," 1272; Coote, *Transactions of the London and Middlesex Historical Society*, IV (1871), 30; Sharpe, *Calendar of Letter-Books*, Letter Book E, p. 13; Hudson, and Tingey, *Records of Norwich*, I, 178; Kerry, in the *Antiquary*, XXIII, 28; Bickley, *Little Red Book of Bristol*, I, 38; *ibid.*, II, 87.

[4] The first requirement of this sort which I have seen was one made by the Fullers of Northampton about the middle of the fifteenth century. Markham and Cox, *Records of Norhampton*, I, 292; see also "Ordinances of the Weavers of Bury St. Edmunds," *Hist. Mss. Comm.*, *Fourteenth Report*, VIII, 135.

[5] "Clothworkers' Ordinances," p. 26, *Ordinances of 1531–32*.

must be a "hireman."[1] Rather more complicated examinations were laid down in the ordinances of the Barber-Surgeons and the Apothecaries,[2] examinations which must have done much toward changing the craft of "barbery" into the science of surgery, the art of the apothecaries into the science of medicine.

The difficulty of the examination must have varied greatly in different gilds, being probably rather a hard test in such crafts as the Apothecaries and Barber-Surgeons, the practice of whose arts required some skill, and rather a simple matter with the Fullers and other mechanical crafts. There can be no doubt that it must have done much toward holding the apprentice to a high standard of workmanship. Its efficacy, of course, varied with the standards of the individual gilds. It seems to me that in the case of the industrial arts the examination system would be more effective than examinations upon book-knowledge. The candidate required to make a pair of shoes before the craft masters must be possessed of real skill in his art in order to do well. Dexterity of hand cannot be "crammed." Thus the strength of the apprenticeship system was greatly increased by the gilds through their surveillance of the relations between master and apprentice and through their examination system.

Whatever may have been its weak points the mediaeval apprenticeship system is by no means to be despised; it was well adapted to the social and economic conditions of the time. The household, the small shop, and the gild were the great factors in industrial life. There was little capital, little machinery, no factory system, no great gulf between employer and employee. The apprentice became a part of his master's household and was given a home and instruction in a trade at but little expense save that of time. If the master did his duty, skill and artistic ability were developed in the lad. At the end of his term of service he passed into the

[1] Ferguson and Nanson, *Gilds of Carlisle*, pp. 179–80, "Shoemakers' Ordinances," 1595. The Bakers of York required that the apprentice, after completing his term, "shall at his first settinge up bake a batche of bread, and entreat the Searchers to come and se the same, whether it be well, lawfulllye and workmanlie wrought and done or no."—Smith, L.T., *Archaeological Review*, I, 222.

[2] Young, *Barber-Surgeons*, p. 310; Barrett, *History of the Apothecaries*, p. xxxiii.

ranks of the master craftsmen and looked forward to a life of comparative economic security and perhaps of some honor as a skilled artisan, merchant, or citizen. He might even hope to become Lord Mayor of London. If there was little opportunity for him to rise out of his class there was great opportunity for him to rise in it.

On the other hand the apprentice was an important asset to the master, giving him increasingly valuable aid in his craft work, attending to his customers, and performing irksome menial duties for the master, the master's wife, and other members of the household. Broadly speaking, the interests of master and man did not conflict, but were in large measure identical. Such a relationship grew from the fact that the household and the small shop were the foundations of industry.

Master and apprentice were held to their duty by the craft gild. By means of its general supervision, and especially by means of the examination system, the gild was able to see that a certain standard of workmanship was maintained. Towns were small, gild members few, concealment of bad conduct difficult, so that gild supervision could be made very effective.

We need not hesitate to affirm that the result of this system of apprenticeship was the development of well-wrought and even artistic productions. It can scarcely be denied that the superiority of the later Middle Ages and of the Renaissance over the early Middle Ages, in the field of the industrial arts, was due in some degree to the apprenticeship system. The system offered opportunity for the development of skill and artistic ability, and while it is true that not every apprentice took advantage of this opportunity, some apprentices did, and produced good work. On the whole, the institution met the needs of mediaeval and early modern times as a system of industrial education.

In a subsequent article it will be shown that the system of apprenticeship declined in the seventeenth and eighteenth centuries as the result of changed social and economic conditions; and that the existence of some of these conditions today will operate to render a revival of the institution, an inadequate solution of the present problem of industrial education.

OBSERVATIONS CONCERNING THE ORGANIZATION OF SCHOOLS AND CERTAIN PHASES OF EDUCATIONAL WORK IN GERMANY

GEORGE KOEPPEL
Principal Twenty-first Street School, Milwaukee, Wis.

The organization and administration of schools and school systems is of such vast importance, and naturally of such great interest to a principal, that I gave a great deal of attention to the study of the organization and management of schools. As to special fields, I studied the following phases of educational activity:

a) Schools for those children whose progress has been retarded; akin to our ungraded classes.

b) Schools for backward or exceptional children.

c) Parental schools.

d) Continuation and trade schools.

e) Open-air schools (*Waldschulen*) and recreation resorts in the woods (*Walderholungsstätten*).

f) Physical education: Gymnastics, playgrounds, outings, *Schülerwanderungen*, vacation colonies.

It was at all times my effort to find the best of what is *thoroughly typical* of the educational policy of the places visited, and I shall not report on anything that is exceptional, unusual, or simply experimental. I shall restrict myself to pointing out what seems to me particularly worthy of our attention.

Our system of public education is so different from that of the countries which I visited that it seems necessary to point out briefly the essential differences in order to avoid referring to them repeatedly in the remarks that are to follow.

At least two parallel systems of schools exist in Germany, and each is represented by several types of schools. With us, all pupils have to pass the eight grades of the elementary school before they are admitted to the high schools, and there is practically no other way of reaching these schools. High schools are the direct continuation of the district schools and depend entirely upon the preparation that is given all pupils alike in the elementary schools. Not so in Europe. Generally speaking, all pupils who will probably receive but an elementary education and who will leave school at the age of fourteen or fifteen, attend the lower grade of schools (*Gemeindeschule, Volksschule, Districtschule, Mittelschule, Bürgerschule*), while most pupils who probably will receive what corresponds to our high-school and college education enter after three to four years of preparation, *at the age of nine to ten years*, the higher schools (*Realschule, Oberrealschule, Realgymnasium, Reformgymnasium, Gymnasium*). These higher schools often have an elementary department that prepares the young pupils in three years for the lowest class of the institution. A good pupil of the common schools may, at the end of the fourth year, enter the lowest class of the higher schools by examination. The courses of the higher schools are carefully planned to meet from the very beginning the conditions required by the higher aim. As an example of the broadness of the foundation may be mentioned that the youngest pupils study, besides the common branches, French five hours, natural science two hours, history two hours per week in *Realschulen*, and eight or nine hours of Latin in *Gymnasia*.

This very early parallelism of the elementary schools and of the higher institutions is one of the most interesting and prominent distinctions from our system, and while apparently less democratic, it is in reality of advantage to the vast majority of both classes of pupils.

The sole function of the elementary school is the preparation of pupils for the ordinary walks of life, and matter and method are planned with this aim definitely in view.

In the higher schools, the long courses of training in definite subjects, harmoniously arranged from grade to grade and *continued through a number of years*, produce a degree of thoroughness and power that cannot be attained in another way. These schools provide a high degree of general culture and also prepare for the universities and highest technical schools.

A student of schools and systems will, of course, make comparison with the educational conditions at home and use the system that he knows best as a standard of measurement. It is, however, necessary, when comparing the efficiency of our system with that of Germany, to keep distinctly in mind that in Germany these two great classes of schools operate side by side, and that it would evidently be incorrect and unfair to compare our common school below the high school with the *Volksschule* alone. The only reasonable procedure is to consider the average age of pupils attending our grades, and compare broadness and depth of subject-matter taught, the methods of instruction, and the proficiency attained by pupils of corresponding age without reference to the kind of school they attend.

To give an idea of the comprehensive nature of even the elementary courses, and of the time devoted to the several branches in the various grades, I insert the weekly program for the lowest type of elementary schools.

ELEMENTARY SCHOOLS

WEEKLY TIME TABLE OF THE GEMEINDESCHULEN OF BERLIN
NUMBER OF HOURS PER WEEK FOR EACH STUDY AND GRADE

	First Grade	Second Grade	Third Grade	Fourth Grade	Fifth Grade	Sixth Grade	Seventh Grade	Eighth Grade
Religion	3	3	3	4	4	4	4	4
Reading, language, spelling	8	7	7	6	6	6	6	6
Object Lessons	2	2	2	..	..	..	..	..
Geography	..	..	..	2	2	2	2	2
History	..	..	..	2	2	2	2	3
Arithmetic	4	4	4	4	4	4	4	4
Geometry	..	..	..	..	..	3	3	3
Nature-study, including physiology, elementary physics, and chemistry	..	..	..	2	2	4	4	3
Drawing	..	1	2	2	2	2	2	2
Writing	..	2	2	2	2	1	1	1
Singing	1	1	2	2	2	2	2	2
Gymnastics	2	2	2	2	2	2	2	2
Total hours	20	22	24	28	28	32	32	32

Manual training, bathing (shower baths), swimming, attendance on playground games and sports are optional.

In examining this table we find that ample time is given to the fundamental branches, but we note especially that the range of subjects taught in this lowest class of elementary schools provides for its pupils a broader and more comprehensive training than we give in our district schools. Indeed, our course absolutely lacks instruction in branches that are both useful in their training value and practical for life.

In the lowest grades stories from history are taught in connection with reading and object lessons, but from the fourth grade upward regular lessons in history are given two hours, and in the eighth grade three hours a week.

Geometry is taught in the *sixth*, *seventh*, and *eighth* grades, three hours a week, besides four hours of arithmetic a week throughout the course.

Regular lessons in nature-study are given in all grades, but in addition *elementary physics and chemistry* are taught in the *sixth, seventh*, and *eighth grades* two or three hours a week. Excellent illustrative material, apparatus, and supplies are furnished to make this instruction effective, and the pupils of these schools acquire a good knowledge of common things and of natural laws and phenomena of which our boys and girls are sadly ignorant. The teaching of elementary physics is especially valuable for the training it supplies in logical thinking and in definiteness of oral and written expression. My observations lead me to recommend an early reintroduction of elementary physics into our district-school course.

The following weekly time table is representative of one type of the higher schools, the *Oberrealschule*. The lower five or six classes are attended by children of the average age of nine to fourteen or fifteen years and may therefore be approximately compared to our classes from the fourth to the eighth grade inclusive. The heavy line in the table marks off these grades from the higher grades.

In addition to these subjects the following are optional: Latin, manual training, shorthand, orchestral music. From this course it appears that in the grades corresponding to our fourth to eighth a broad and solid foundation is laid not only in the common branches but also in history, mathematics, the natural sciences, physics, chemistry, French, and English, and that *all* these sub-

WEEKLY TIME TABLE OF AN OBERREALSCHULE AT CHARLOTTENBURG

NUMBER OF HOURS PER WEEK FOR EACH STUDY AND GRADE

	Grade VI	Grade V	Grade IV	Grade IIIB	Grade IIIA	Grade IIB	Grade IIA	Grade IB	Grade IA
Age on entering	9.55	10.7	11.91	13.3	14.33	15.5	16.6	17.17	18.17
Religion	3	2	2	2	2	2	2	2	2
German	6	5	4	4	4	3	4	4	4
Geography	2	2	2	2	2	1	1	1	1
History	..	..	3	2	2	2	3	3	3
Arithmetic	4	4	..	..	..	..	..	..	..
Mathematics	..	..	6	5	5	5	5	5	5
Natural science	2	2	2	2	2	2	..	..	..
Physics	..	..	..	..	2	2	3	3	3
Chemistry	..	..	..	..	..	2	3	3	{3 (2)*
French	6	6	6	6	5	5	4	4	4
English	..	..	..	5	4	4	4	4	4
Drawing, freehand	..	2	2	2	2	2	2	2	2
Drawing, linear	..	..	..	..	(2)	(2)	(2)	(2)	(2)*
Writing	2	2	2	1	1	..	..	..	..
Singing	2	2	2	2	2	2	2	2	2
Gymnastics	3	3	3	3	3	3	3	3	3
	30	30	34	36	36	35	36	36	36
Optional	..	..	..	..	2	2	2	2	4
Total hours per week	30	30	34	36	38	37	38	38	40

*Optional.

jects are *continued throughout the course*, every pupil being required to take all these lessons. The graduates of this school have received instruction in

Natural sciences . . . . . 6 years
Physics . . . . . 5 years
Chemistry . . . . . 4 years
Mathematics . . . . . 7 years
History . . . . . 7 years
Geography . . . . . 9 years
German . . . . . 9 years
French . . . . . 9 years
English . . . . . 6 years

This long-continued application to a somewhat limited number of subjects provides an excellent scientific and modern classical training, and results in a surprising accuracy of knowledge and remarkable thoroughness in the students.

Other conditions that contribute to this result need special mention.

The pupils of these schools are taught from thirty to forty hours a week (including recesses) which is largely in excess of the time that our pupils spend in school.

As the lessons are distributed over six forenoons and one to three afternoons, and as recesses are frequent, the pupils are not overburdened.

Homework is required of the pupils of all grades.

It is clear that greater progress is possible and that more time can be taken for reviews and for deepening and broadening the instruction than where the actual school time per week is so exceedingly limited as with us. Eighty per cent of our pupils attend school but twenty-five hours a week including recesses. *The time spent in school by German pupils therefore exceeds* our time in the fourth and fifth grades by 20 per cent, in the sixth grade by 36 per cent, and in the seventh and eighth grades by about 48 per cent!

The cheerfulness and vigor displayed by the boys during their gymnastic exercises and games as well as in their sports on the playground are proof that the time given to their studies is not excessive.

A distinctive feature in all types of higher schools is the *class organization* of students throughout the course. The members of the upper grades, corresponding in age, approximately to those in our high-school grades, are formed into classes, each being assigned to a certain classroom where all instruction is given excepting laboratory work. Each class is in charge of a class teacher (*ordinarius*) who is especially responsible for the welfare of his class. This teacher instructs his class usually in one or two branches, and other teachers, specialists in their fields, enter the room successively to take charge of the class so that each group or class as a unit is *during the whole school day* under the direct supervision, instruction, and guidance of a teacher. In the school quoted, for instance, one Senior class numbering but 15 students, and another Senior class numbering 25 students, remained each intact as an organization for one year, and were every minute of the school time under the influence of a number of very fine men who are excellent teachers; and so are all the classes of this school and of the schools of its type.

Considering the fact that *our pupils of the high schools* usually take four studies of 45 minutes each per day, they are *under this direct influence of their teachers only 15 hours each week*, while German pupils of equal rank *enjoy this advantage more than thirty hours* each week.

This continuous influence of teachers, the class organization, and the definiteness of subjects studied for many years, easily account for the frequent reports of the excellency of the German higher schools.

It needs to be added that teaching is a profession in Germany and that all teachers of these higher schools are men of excellent preparation for their work.

Concerning the work required of teachers, the principle prevails in all classes of schools that the quantity of work is reduced as the teacher's years of service increase. The *Oberrealschule* No. 1 of Charlottenburg, mentioned above, contains *18 classes*, but the *number of teachers employed is 28;* 13 of these teach from 21–24 hours a week, including recesses; 13 teach 20 hours a week, including recesses; 2 teach 17 hours a week, including recesses. Their lessons are irregularly distributed during the week according to the requirements of classes.

A FUNDAMENTAL PRINCIPLE OF SUCCESS

One of the most prominent merits of German schools is the conscious and succcessful effort of teachers to make all instruction as far as possible objective. On the outer walls of a Dresden school building, one of the great principles of education, as announced by Pestalozzi, is inscribed in gilt letters: "Der Ursprung und das Fundament aller Erkenntniss ist die Anschauung. Von dieser Form hat der Unterricht auszugehen."

This principle seems to be the soul of the teachers' work in all schools of Germany, and in elementary schools in particular; it pervades all educational activity, and produces very good, often excellent teaching. The teachers do not merely conduct recitations or hear lessons, but teach the subject in hand till the pupils have comprehended it, till they have gained a clear, definite, vivid, and lasting knowledge of the lesson. To enable the teachers to apply this great fundamental principle, an astonishing wealth of material (*Lehrmittel*) is at his command. The liberality with which the common schools in Germany are fitted out with all sorts of material devised to make good teaching more effective by appealing directly to the senses is one of the features that cannot be too strongly emphasized. Every school building has one or more rooms, large and conveniently located, where this *Anschauungsmaterial* is systematically arranged and easily accessible. Good cupboards, stands, supports, drawers, and other fixtures are provided to hold and protect these things. A definite sum of money for each class is appropriated each year for the enlargement of this collection. Besides maps and globes we may find here a large variety of excellent pictures of large size illustrating nearly all subjects taught in geography, nature-study, physiology, hygiene, first aid to the injured, history, the progress of civilization, and all fields of human activity. All these pictorial illustrations are large enough to be distinctly seen by all members of the class, and many are designed by artists.

The same subjects are also illustrated by collections of natural or artificial specimens of natural and industrial products, and also by models. A detailed description of these *Lehrmittel* cannot here be attempted as the field is almost boundless, and reference must be made to one of the large catalogues[1] to gain a faint idea of the richness of these accessories to effective teaching. The manufacture of this instructional material has become an important industry in Germany.

All *elementary* schools have a collection of apparatus and supplies for the teaching of elementary physics and chemistry, and in many of these schools a special "physics room" is provided to which classes of the sixth, seventh, and eighth grades go to receive instruction in these branches.

A very large room or hall is fitted up in most schools for the work in drawing. The tables are provided with stands for the models, and good collections of models such as needed in modern courses

[1] *Schulwart Katalog: Lehrmittel.* Leipzig und Berlin: F. Volkmar.

in drawing are furnished. In some cities a small sum of money is allowed each drawing teacher to buy flowers and other natural objects that cannot be procured from the school garden. Fine and very large glass cases placed in these drawing-rooms hold and protect the drawing-models and the material. The instruction in drawing is in nearly all cases given by teachers who are specially trained for the work. Ample opportunity is, however, given the regular teachers to attend courses that introduce them to the requirements of modern drawing in weekly lessons that often extend throughout the year. These courses are here mentioned because the ability of teachers to sketch and illustrate rapidly stands in close relation to objective teaching.

The most important exponents of the fundamental idea of instruction through *Anschauung* are the numerous museums. While all of these have a strongly educational influence, there is one type of museum whose only purpose is instructional, and of this class probably the grandest example is the Deutsche Museum at Munich. Here the triumphs of human genius over nature and its forces are demonstrated by very extensive collections of originals and models covering nearly all departments of human endeavor; and here the inspection and observation of realities and processes that are difficult to understand from description or from books impresses one with the truth and the importance of the great principle "The origin and foundation of all knowledge is *Anschauung*. From this form all teaching has to proceed."

[*To be continued*]

BOOK REVIEWS

Peter Ramus and the Educational Reformation of the Sixteenth Century. By FRANK PIERREPONT GRAVES, PH.D. New York: Macmillan, 1912. Pp. xi+226. $1.25.

This monograph by Professor Graves is an interesting example of the recent tendency in writing the history of education to emphasize the development of educational practice. Peter Ramus (1515–1572) is treated as the great progressive leader at the University of Paris in the contest "between the conservative forces of scholasticism, ecclesiasticism, and the masters of the university colleges, on the one hand, and the progressive alliance of humanism, Protestantism, and the royal lecturers, on the other." The educational reforms of Ramus in France were similar to those of Melanchthon and Sturm in Germany, but before the appearance of the present treatise there has existed no extensive account of his work in English. The author's experience as a student and professor of the classical languages before specializing in education has made possible this account which is based almost entirely upon Latin sources.

The first half of the book is primarily biographical in character, but the events in the life of Ramus are so related to the general social development and the life of the university as to present a concrete picture and narrative of the whole movement in which he played a part. The story is well told and would be of interest to all students of the history of education.

The second half of the book is a more technical discussion of the educational reforms inaugurated by Ramus. It is of interest to the special student who is concerned with the detailed history of higher education, especially with changes in the curriculum and methods of instruction.

S. CHESTER PARKER

Great Educators of Three Centuries, Their Work and Its Influence on Modern Education. By FRANK PIERREPONT GRAVES, PH.D. New York: Macmillan, 1912. Pp. ix+289. $1.10.

In this book Professor Graves has reverted to the type of historical treatment of education represented by Quick's *Educational Reformers*, Munroe's *The Educational Ideal*, and Laurie's *Educational Opinion since the Renaissance*. The author recognizes in his preface that such books do not present the history of education, but justifies his work on the basis of its service to the more general reader.

In order to secure the interest that attaches to such a personal treatment of the history of education and justifies it, the account of each individual must be made sufficiently full to bring out his personality. In the cases where the author has done this the chapters are very interesting and hold the reader's attention in the same way as does the biographical part of the Peter Ramus reviewed above. The chapters on Rousseau, Pestalozzi, and part of the one on Froebel are especially good from this point of view. On the other hand, the interest of the general reader is likely to flag when abstract classifications and philosophical discussion are presented. This tends to be the case in some of the earlier briefer chapters where there is much reference to "humanism," "humanistic-realism," "sense-realism," and "social-realism," and in some parts of the chapter on Herbart. These portions however are not frequent, and in general the book possesses the same charm that gave Quick's *Educational Reformers* such a long life.

There is a strong emphasis throughout on the influence exerted by each reformer on educational practice, and wherever possible the practical developments in America have been traced.

The educators treated are Milton, Bacon, Ratich, Comenius, Locke, Franke, Rousseau, Basedow, Pestalozzi, Herbart, Froebel, Lancaster and Bell, Mann and Spencer. A little over half of the book is devoted to the five chapters on Rousseau, Basedow, Pestalozzi, Herbart, and Froebel.

S. CHESTER PARKER

Berry's Writing Book and Primer. B. D. Berry & Co., 1912.

This writing-book is constructed on the same principles as the other Berry writing-books, with colored pictures illustrating rhymes or quotations having literary value. The content of this primer is the Edward Lear A B C rhymes. The writing is nearly one-half inch high and so is better adapted to beginners than the ordinary first book. If one uses copy-books this is the best one for beginners with which the reviewer is acquainted.

F. N. F.

UNIVERSITY OF CHICAGO

The Outlines of Educational Psychology. By WILLIAM H. PYLE. Boston: Warwick & York, 1911. Pp. x+254.

The book opens with a brief introductory chapter in which it is pointed out that sociology teaches the aim of education, biology and psychology teach the nature of the child, and psychology explains the essential nature of the educational processes. The kind of psychology in which the author is interested is functional, biological, and evolutionary psychology. He takes up accordingly as his first problem heredity and the inherited modes of adjustment which the child brings into the school. The individualistic instincts such as fear, anger, etc., are described and their pedagogical importance is briefly discussed. In like fashion the social instincts, environmental instincts (migration, collecting), the adaptive instincts (play and imitation) are treated at length. After instinct comes habit. The nature of habit, the training of habit, the problems of drill, and the moral value of habit are each treated in turn. Finally, there are three chapters on memory, attention, and fatigue. The book has in its appendices some charts for use in school inspection.

The book illustrates very strikingly the author's view of the intimate dependence of education on inheritance. One-half of the book is gone before the discussion of instincts is completed. The higher processes of thought and reasoning get no attention. That most vital and significant mode of social adjustment, language, is left out. The combative tendencies are dwelt upon, but the constructive adjustments which appear in the industrial arts are not explained. The sphere of intellectual activities which are commonly treated under the terms abstraction, generalization, and conception, in short the whole world of scientific reasoning, is as if it were not.

There can be no doubt that instinct is important in education; and in common with such books as those of Kirkpatrick, the present outlines give some insight into the productive studies of human behavior which have lately bridged over the gap between human and animal psychology. The teacher who is offered these studies as the major part of educational psychology, however, is likely to regard the author as one-sided and as out of touch with the school. Whatever else the school does, it teaches language, and this topic is not mentioned in Dr. Pyle's index. Nor are reading or number.

C. H. J.

A Manual of Shoemaking and Leather and Rubber Products. By WILLIAM H. DOOLEY. Boston: Little, Brown & Co., 1912. Pp. 279.

This book contains, first, a general account of the preparation of leather, second, an account of the parts of the shoe with which the manufacturer has to deal in constructing a shoe, also accounts of the anatomy of the human foot to which the shoe has to be fitted, of the organization of the large manufacturing concerns that turn out shoes, and finally of the history of footwear.

The volume was prepared for use in the Linn Industrial School, and represents the effort of that school to give to children who are being trained in one of the trades some general insight into the industry with which they are to be connected. Through this book they are to be trained in the methods of reading, and in the methods of securing information about their work. The skill that they cultivate in the trade class is thus to be supplemented by the intellectual power which they cultivate through the study of a manual relating to their trade.

The type of material which appears in this book is very suggestive for teachers in schools other than industrial schools. There can be no doubt at all that children of the fourth and fifth grades, and children of the upper grades of the elementary school are very much interested in the manufacturing processes by which common articles are produced. Children will read this practical description of manufacturing processes, when they find the ordinary literature which is supplied to them in reading-books very irksome. It is surprising that teachers do not see the importance of getting together material of this type, and putting it in form for children's reading.

It is doubtful whether a good deal of this manual in its present form would be useful in the lower grades. Some of the information is rather technical, and some of the chapters deal with the names of parts of objects in such detail that the chapter would not be useful as ordinary reading-matter. At the same time there are chapters, such as "The General History of Footwear," and the account of the way in which a shoe is made, which without much change would be of interest to all children.

The time will certainly come when teachers will prepare manuals similar to this with regard to the making of lead pencils, the making of various fabrics and ordinary pieces of furniture. The volume is therefore one which can be commended to the attention of teachers as an excellent illustration of writing in a field as yet unoccupied, but very important for the development of children's interests in the schools.

C. H. J.

BOOKS RECEIVED

AMERICAN BOOK CO., CHICAGO

Rabenort's Geography. North and South America. (Exclusive of the United States.) By William Rabenort. Cloth. Illustrated. Pp. 230. $0.50.

Rabenort's Geography. Europe. By William Rabenort. Cloth. Illustrated. Pp. 231. $0.50.

William's Choice Literature. Compiled and arranged by Sherman Williams. Cloth. Illustrated.

Book One. Pp. 144. $0.20.
Book Two. Pp. 160. $0.25.
Book Three. Pp. 192. $0.28.
Book Four. Pp. 256. 0.35.
Book Five. Pp. 320. $0.40.
Book Six. Pp. 400. $0.45.
Book Seven. Pp. 512. $0.50.

General Science. By Bertha M. Clark. Cloth. Illustrated. Pp. 363. $0.80.

Laboratory Manual in General Science. By Bertha M. Clark. Cloth. Illustrated. Pp. 96. $0.40.

Fifty Famous People. By James Baldwin. Cloth. Illustrated. Pp. 190. $0.35.

A First Latin Reader. By H. C. Nutting. Cloth. Pp. 250. $0.60.

Pupil's Notebook and Study Outline in English History. By Francis A. Smith. Pp. 142. $0.25.

GINN & CO., CHICAGO

Old Time Hawaiians and Their Work. By Mary S. Lawrence. Cloth. Illustrated. Pp. 172. $0.60.

Heimatlos. By Johanna Spyri. Translated by Emma Stelter Hopkins. Cloth.

Work and Play with Numbers. By George Wentworth and David E. Smith. Cloth. Illustrated. Pp. 144. $0.35.

HASTINGS, BATTLE CREEK, MICH.

Education. The Old and the New. Published by the Author, William P. Hastings. Cloth. Illustrated. Pp. 299. $1.00.

D. C. HEATH & CO., CHICAGO

Health in Home and Town. By Bertha Millard Brown. Cloth. Illustrated. Pp. 312.

Grammar Grade Speller. By Edwin S. Richards. Cloth. Pp. 188.

HINDS, NOBLE & ELDRIDGE, NEW YORK

The Most Practical Theme Tablet. Devised by George Morey Miller. Per pad, $0.20.

HOUGHTON, MIFFLIN CO., BOSTON

Fifth Reader. By James H. Van Sickle and Wilhelmina Seegmiller. Cloth. Illustrated. Pp. 278. $0.55.

THE MACMILLAN CO., NEW YORK

When We Were Wee. By Martha Young. Cloth. Illustrated. Pp. 153. $0.40.

Stories Grandmother Told. By Kate Forrest Oswell. Cloth. Illustrated. Pp. 246. $0.40.

The Teaching of Mathematics in Secondary Schools. By Arthur Schultze. Cloth. Illustrated. Pp. 367. $1.25.

Teaching in School and College. By William Lyon Phelps. Cloth. Pp. 186. $1.00.

Thought-Building in Composition. By Robert Wilson Neal. Cloth. Pp. 170. $0.80.

THE MANUAL ARTS PRESS

Manual Arts for Vocational Ends. By Fred D. Cranshaw. Cloth. Pp. 99. $0.85.

NEWARK, N.J., BOARD OF EDUCATION

Newark. In the Public Schools of Newark. Prepared by J. Wilmer Kennedy. Cloth. Illustrated. Pp. 213.

ORANGE JUDD CO., NEW YORK

School Agriculture. By Milo N. Wood. Cloth. Illustrated. Pp. 340. $0.90.

SILVER, BURDETT & CO., BOSTON

A Practice Book in Arithmetic. By Harriet E. Sharp. Paper.

STEWART & KIDD CO., CINCINNATI

Mind Cure and Other Essays. By Philip Zenner. Cloth. Illustrated. $1.25.

CURRENT EDUCATIONAL LITERATURE IN THE PERIODICALS[1]

IRENE WARREN[2]
Librarian, School of Education, The University of Chicago

ABELSON, A. R. Tests for mental deficiency in childhood. Child (London) 3:1–17. (O. '02.)

A description of a number of tests given by the author and the conclusions drawn from them.

ADAMS, JOHN. An objective standard in education. School W. 14:367–71. (O. '12).

Presidential address before the section on education in the British Association for the Advancement of Science. Gives illustrations of the application of the scientific method to education.

Address of President Taft at the Fifteenth International Congress on Hygiene and Demography. Science 36:504–8. (18 O. '12.)

ANDREWS, E. BENJAMIN. The crusade for the country school. Educa. R. 44:385–96. (N. '12).

Announcement of a Montessori training course. McClure 50:82. (N. '12.)

ASHLEY, M. L. Aims, difficulties, and possibilities in teaching psychology to normal school students. Educa. Bi-mo. 7:1–8. (O. '12.)

BAGLEY, WILLIAM C. The professional training of high school teachers. West. J. of Educa. 5:347–45. (O. '12.)

BERRY, CHARLES SCOTT. A comparison of the Binet tests of 1908 and 1911. J. of Educa. Psychol. 3:444–51. (O. '12.)

A description of the two-test series and a report of the application of both series to forty-five children.

BOVERI, THEODOR. Anton Dohrn. Science 36:453–68. (11 O. '12.)

British schools spoiling the boy. Lit. D. 45:556. (5 O. '12.)

BROOKMAN, THIRMUTHIS. An appeal to school women. Educa. Bi-mo. 7:41–45. (O. '12.)

BURNHAM, WILLIAM H. Suggestions in elementary education. Am. Phys. Educa. R. 17:540–46. (O. '12.)

[1] Abbreviations.—Am. Phys. Educa. R., American Physical Educational Review; Atlan., Atlantic; Cent., Century; Educa., Education; Educa. Bi-mo., Educational Bi-monthly; Educa. R., Educational Review; Educa. Rec. (Lond.), Educational Record (London); El. School T., Elementary School Teacher; English J., English Journal; Geographical T., Geographical Teacher; Harp. W., Harper's Weekly; J. of Educa. Psychol., Journal of Educational Psychology; Lit. D., Literary Digest; Liv. Age, Living Age; Man. Train. M., Manual Training Magazine; Outl., Outlook; Pop. Sci. Mo., Popular Science Monthly; Psychol. Clinic, Psychological Clinic; School B., School Bulletin; School R., School Review; School W., School World; Sci. Am., Scientific American; Scrib. M., Scribner's Magazine; Voca. Educa., Vocational Education; West. J. of Educa., Western Journal of Education.

[2] Annotations by John F. Bobbitt and Frank N. Freeman.

CABOT, ARTHUR TRACY. Tuberculosis and the schools. Atlan. 110:704–8. (N. '12.)

CALL, ARTHUR DEERIN. The specialized or vocational versus the composite high school. Voca. Educa. 2:110–18. (N. '12.)

COLWELL, LEWIS W. Some observations concerning the teaching of primary arithmetic. Educa. Bi-mo. 7:19–25. (O. '12.)

COSSAR, J. The teaching of geography in Scottish primary schools. Geographical T. 6:261–66. (Je. '12.)

A general survey of subject-matter and method in accordance with the memorandum issued by the Scotch Education Department.

DAKIN, W. S. Vocational service for men in service. Voca. Educa. 2:89–109. (N. '12.)

DANIEL, Roland B. The secondary industrial school, Columbus, Georgia. Voca. Educa. 2:119–38. (N. '12.)

DAVIS, JESSE B. Vocational and moral guidance through English composition. English J. 1:457–65. (O. '12.)

The report of a successful trial of a plan to find material for high-school composition in the pupils' study of his vocational qualifications and responsibilities and the vocational opportunities of the world about him.

DYKE, PAUL VAN. College life. Scrib. M. 52:619–23. (N. '12.)

"A word to fathers who have not been to college but whose sons want to go." Minimizes the evils of college life and magnifies the virtues.

FISHER, WILLARD J. The drift in secondary education. Science 36:587–90. (1 N. '12.)

FISHPAW, CLARA BROOKS. The training of rural teachers. Educa. 33:79–83. (O. '12.)

FITZGERALD, ELLEN. Reading to write. Educa. Bi-mo. 7:36–40. (O. '12.)

FORDYCE, CHARLES. College ethics. Educa. 33:71–78. (O. '12.)

FRANK, MAUDE M. Dramatization of school classics. English J. 1:476–81. (O. '12.)

The author describes a satisfactory trial plan of securing interest in *Ivanhoe* and the *Odyssey* in the first year of high school by means of informal, rough-and-ready dramatization.

From red schoolhouse to Greek Parthenon. Lit. D. 45:786–87. (2 N. '12.)

GAYLER, G. W. Enrolment by grades in fourteen school systems of central Illinois. Psychol. Clinic 6:140–43. (O. '12.)

A brief statistical study.

GODDARD, HENRY H. The hygiene of the backward child. Am. Phys. Educa. R. 17:537–39. (O. '12.)

On the treatment of the child who is inherently feeble-minded.

GREGG, F. M. Social hygiene. Educa. 33:100–104. (O. '12.)

GULICK, LUTHER H. American School Hygiene Association. Am. Phys. Educa. R. 17:547–54. (O. '12.)

GULICK, LUTHER H. Report of the Committee on Heating and Ventilating. Discussion of the report.

HALE, H. O. The kinematograph in school. School W. 14:361–64. (O. '12.)

An account of the uses to which the kinematograph may be put in various subjects, such as geography, history, biology, etc.

HAYES, D. W. The training of teachers for rural schools. West. J. of Educa. 5:355-62. (O. '12.)

HINES, L. N. A study in retardation. Am. Phys. Educa. R. 17:534-36. (O. '12.)

A study to determine the share which physical defects have in causing retardation.

HOBBS, W. W., AND OTHERS. An inquiry into the causes of student delinquency. School R. 20:593-612. (N. '12.)

A questionnaire study on why high-school pupils fail to pass.

HODGMAN, T. MOREY. Functional changes in the college. Educa. R. 44:240-48. (O. '12.)

A discussion of the changes in the small college necessary to make it fit present demands.

HUGHES, HELEN SARD. English literature and the college freshman. School R. 20:583-92. (N. '12.)

Reports the results of a minor statistical test of the knowledge of English literature acquired in the high school.

HURLBATT, ETHEL. The teaching of hygiene in the public schools. Am. Phys. Educa. R. 17:525-33. (O. '12.)

Advocates regular specific training in hygiene, by properly qualified teachers, and discusses other requirements.

HUTCHISON, JEAN. Textile industries and their practical application to education. Educa. Bi-mo. 7:64-68. (O. '12.)

Its only fault. Lit. D. 45:558. (5 O. '12.)

JASTROW, JOSEPH. The administrative peril in education. Pop. Sci. Mo. 81:495-515. (N. '12.)

A vigorous protest against "externalism" in university administration, and a plea for democracy in management.

JUDD, CHARLES H. Studies in principles of education. El. School T. 13:146-53. (N. '12.)

A discussion of the need not only of providing an opportunity for the child to solve the problems which he apprehends, but also of training him to discover problems he would not otherwise see.

KATSCHER, LEOPOLD. Educational gardening. Child (London) 3:18-24. (O. '12.)

An account of the important experiments in educational gardening with particular emphasis upon the last ten years.

KING, CHARLES A. Pre-vocational training. Educa. 33:105-8. (O. '12.)

LANSING, MARION FLORENCE. Seventy-five years of higher education for women. Outl. 102:360-65. (19 O. '12.)

LASELLE, MARY A. The special transfer class at the Newton Technical High School. Educa. 33:109-11. (O. '12.)

LYON, E. P. The migration of students. Science 36:533-43. (25 O. '12.)

A discussion of the principles which should govern the transfer of students from one institution to another.

MCANDREW, WILLIAM. One remedy for education. World's Work 25:72-79. (N. '12.)

MCCRACKEN, ELIZABETH. Going to school. 1. American children. Outl. 102:425-33. (26 O. '12.)

A gossipy discussion of the greater variety, pleasureableness, and normality of the schools of today as compared with those of a generation ago.

MACDOUGALL, ROBERT. The child's speech. 1. The impulse to speech. J. of Educa. Psychol. 3:423–29. (O. '12.)

A discussion of the hereditary and environmental factors which underlie the impulse to speech.

MCMANIS, JOHN T. The study of children in the normal school. Educa. Bi-mo. 7:69–73. (O. '12.)

MARTINDALE, W. C. How Detroit cares for her backward children. Psychol. Clinic 6:125–30. (O. '12.)

An account of the examinations made of children who are suspected of being defective and of the method of their assignment and treatment.

MASON, WILLIAM A. Art education, retrospective and prospective. Man. Train. M. 14:1–9. (O. '12.)

The author advocates a combination of the "mechanical and artistic elements" in art teaching.

MAXWELL, WILLIAM H. School achievement in New York. Educa. R. 44: 275–309. (O. '12.)

A record of the development of the New York City school system since the consolidation of the city in 1898.

MILLER, E. A. The organization of a college department of education. School R. 20:613–22. (N. '12.)

Discusses the desirability of practice teaching and observation in college for training high-school teachers, for which courses credit toward a degree should be given.

MORGAN, ALEXANDER. Education and social progress. Educa. R. 44:368–84. (N. '12.)

MÜHLHOFF, KÄTHE. The Schullehrerin in Prussia. Educa. R. 44:234–39. (O. '12.)

Account of the status, preparation, salary, and work of the woman teacher in Prussia.

MUIR, JOHN. My boyhood. Atlan. 110:577–87. (N. '12.)

MURRAY, JOHN P. New Jersey school conditions. Educa. R. 44:397–412. (N. '12.)

Of education. Harp. W. 56:8. (5 O. '12.)

OSBORN, HENRY FAIRFIELD. The state museum and state progress. Science 36:493–504. (18 O. '12.)

PAGE, FRANK R. Preparing pupils to live. El. School T. 13:134–45. (N. '12.)

An outline of the methods used in the Staten Island Academy, where school activities are made as much as possible like life outside of school.

PALMER, GLENN E. Culture and efficiency through composition. English J. 1:488–92. (O. '12.)

An attempt to reconcile the two aims expressed in the title in teaching Freshman English in college.

PAUL, HARRY G. The teaching of lyric poetry. English J. 1:466–75. (O. '12.)

Discusses details of method for the high school.

(The) peril of externalism. Dial 53:321–23. (1 N. '12.)

PERRY, CLARENCE ARTHUR. A survey of the social-center movement. El. School T. 13:124–33. (N. '12.)

A catalogue of the advances which have been made in the last two years, since the publication of the author's book, *The Wider Use of the School Plant.*

PETERS, W. Pedagogy at the Berlin Psychological Congress. J. of Educa. Psychol. 3:452–57. (O. '12.)

An abstract of the discussions presented at the congress.

PRICE, WILLIAM RALEIGH. Aims and methods in modern language instruction. Educa. R. 44:257–74. (O. '12.)

The author advocates facility in reading as an aim, as distinguished from the "reform method" and discusses the report of the State Examination Board of New York in this connection.

PRINCE, JOHN T. Moral training in public schools. Educa. 33:65–70. (O. '12.)

PROSSER, C. A. Vocational education in Europe, by E. G. Cooley. A review. Voca. Educa. 2:139–47. (N. '12.)

Religion of the college girl. Lit. D. 45:792. (2 N. '12.)

RICKERT, EDITH. The fraternity idea among college women. What docs it stand for? Cent. 85:97–106. (N. '12.)

Presents fairly the arguments for and against the existence of women's fraternities in our colleges.

ROGERS, MARY. A case from the Indiana University clinic. Psychol. Clinic 6:144–51. (O. '12.)

A clinical study.

RUSK, ROBERT R. Movements in handwriting. School W. 14:379–81. (O. '12.)

A review of experimental investigations of the writing movement and their practical applications to methods of teaching.

SALMON, PRINCIPAL. Lancaster's writings. Educa. Rec. (Lond.) 18:468–84. (O. '12.)

(The) School of Journalism of Columbia University. Science 36:470–72. (11 O. '12.)

SMITH, H. BOMPAS. Education at the British Association. School W. 14: 364–66. (O. '12.)

A brief résumé of the papers and discussions at this year's meeting of the educational section.

SQUIRE, CARRIE RANSOM. Graded mental tests. II. Association, construction and invention. J. of Educa. Psychol. 3:430–43. (O. '12.)

Continuation of the report begun in the September number.

STEVENS, ELLEN YALE. The Montessori method and the American kindergarten. McClure 50:77–82. (N. '12.)

A popular description of the method.

STEVENS, NEIL E. Educational advertising. School R. 20:577–82. (N. '12.)

Argues that the way to interest parents in schools is not by the production of irrelevant programs and displays.

STEWART, CHARLES A. Appointment and promotion of college instructors. Educa. R. 44:249–56. (O. '12.)

An argument for the fuller recognition of teaching efficiency as a basis for appointment promotion.

STEWART, J. A. New York State education building. Sci. Am. 107:366. (2 N. '12.)

STONE, JOHN C. Some sources of failure to solve a problem. Educa. Bi-mo. 7:26–35. (O. '12.)

STRATTON, CLARENCE. How can the university be of more help to the secondary school? English J. 1:482–87. (O. '12.)

A plea for higher entrance standards in English in order to stimulate the high school to higher standard.

SUMMERS, L. L. Woodwork in the lower grades. Man. Train. M. 14:10–23. (O. '12.)

A detailed account of manual work given in the first five grades of the elementary school and of its correlations with other studies.

TANNER, GEORGE W. The library situation in Chicago high schools. Educa. Bi-mo. 7:9–15. (O. '12.)

TAYLOR, JAMES M. College education for girls in America. I. Educa. R. 44:217–33. (O. '12.)

A history of the opportunities for college education open to women prior to the founding of Vassar.

TAYLOR, JAMES M. College education for girls in America. II. Educa. R. 44:325–47. (N. '12.)

TAYLOR, JOSEPH S. Measurement of educational efficiency. Educa. R. 44: 348–67. (N. '12.)

TERMAN, LEWIS M. A survey of mentally defective children in the schools of San Luis Obispo, California. Psychol. Clinic 6:131–39. (O. '12.)

An illustration of the method of testing and treating backward children in school.

TOMBO, RUDOLF, JR. The geographical distribution of the student body at a number of universities and colleges. Science 36:543–50. (25 O. '12.)

A study of the statistics for the year 1910–11.

Two years in a Canadian university. Liv. Age 275:203–13. (26 O. '12.)

WARD, EDWARD J. The school-house or the saloon. Outl. 102:487–88. (2 N. '12.)

WASHINGTON, BOOKER T. Is the Negro having a fair chance? Cent. 85: 46–55. (N. '12.)

He compares the situation of the Negroes of the United States with that of the Negroes in other countries, and shows the superiority of the opportunities and treatment in the United States.

WHITNEY, FRANK P. Equality and the schools. Educa. 33:84–90. (O. '12.)

WILD, LAURA H. Training for social efficiency. Educa. 33:91–99. (O. '12.)

William Henry Maxwell, 1887–1912. School B. 39:25–26. (O. '12.)

VOLUME XIII NUMBER 5

THE ELEMENTARY SCHOOL TEACHER

JANUARY 1913

EDUCATIONAL NEWS AND EDITORIAL COMMENT

The Indiana Commission on Vocational Education

The last legislature of the state of Indiana appointed a commission to investigate the general problem of industrial and agricultural courses throughout the state. This commission was also empowered to develop a plan for future promotion of this sort of work in the schools of the state. The commission is prepared now to make its report and has given a preliminary statement of its work before educational meetings. It finds, as every other commission of this type has found, that there is grave need in all of the communities of the state for industrial and vocational training. It finds also that very little of this work has been done in the state, and that the courses which have been undertaken have been carried forward very unsystematically. The commission deplores the lack of attention to this work. One point in particular may be brought out, since the report is offered to the people of the state as a whole. Attention is drawn to the fact that the communities are not at all alive to the importance of such training. Most of these communities believe in the traditional school, and, since they do not recognize the urgency of the problem, are unprepared for the recommendations to be made by the commission.

After reviewing the whole situation and referring to the practices in other states and countries, the commission recommends first that school authorities in cities, towns, and townships be given power to establish and maintain vocational schools in departments including trade classes and agricultural classes as their local situation may warrant, and to levy a tax in support of the same. The commission further recommends that state aid in amounts equal to two-thirds of the sum expended by the local authorities in instruction in vocational and technical subjects be supplied, in order that the work of the schools may be carried on more efficiently.

The further recommendations of the commission work out in detail this general plan. A number of co-operative agencies are provided through state universities and through state departments for the supervision and promotion of this type of training.

It is to be noted that the report of this commission, which undoubtedly will have much influence in formulating the policy not only in the state of Indiana but in neighboring states as well, is distinctly in favor of a reorganization of the elementary school rather than the development of a parallel school system. In this particular the report of the commission departs radically from the plan which is being developed in the state of Massachusetts and imitates the New York state plan.

From the point of view of the present writer, this report of the Indiana commission is in keeping with the best policies that can be advocated for all of the middle western states.

National Society for the Scientific Study of Education

"Supervision of City and Rural Schools" is the topic to be discussed in 1913 Yearbooks of the National Society for the Study of Education. This continues the policy which has prevailed in recent years of discussing, in a concrete practical way, certain fundamental aspects of the administration of city and rural schools. The Yearbook on *City School Supervision* is being prepared primarily by Dr. J. F. Bobbitt of the Department of Education of the University of Chicago. A supplementary discussion is to be provided by Professor John Hall of the University of Cincinnati. A unified, scholarly, practical outline discussion of the problems and attempted solutions in this line is greatly needed.

The Yearbook which deals with *Rural School Supervision* was planned by Mr. A. C. Monahan, specialist in agricultural education of the National Bureau of Education. It will contain a general introduction by Mr. Monahan and special articles dealing with typical schemes of rural supervision such as the "District Plans of West Virginia and Oregon"; "New England Townships and Union Districts"; "State Supervisors of Rural Elementary Schools in the South"; "County Supervision in Illinois, in Baltimore County, Md., and in Berks County, Pa."; "Supervision of Rural Schools for Negroes." The contributors include L. J. Hanifan, state supervisor of West Virginia, J. E. Warren, state inspector in Massachusetts, Wallace Lund and Wicliffe Rose, of the Southern Education Board, State Superintendent Blair of Illinois, A. S. Cook of Baltimore County, Md., E. M. Rapp of Berks County, Pa., and Jackson Davis, state supervisor for Virginia. A bibliography is provided through the courtesy of Mr. J. D. Wolcott of the Library of the Bureau of Education.

The Yearbooks go to press soon and will be distributed about February 1. They will be discussed at the annual meeting in Philadelphia on Monday evening, February 24.

Books and Art, Collected and Distributed by the Bureau of Education

The Bureau of Education asks that attention be called to the fact that two types of donations are needed to complete the library collection of the bureau. First, the bureau is anxious to secure all sorts of current educational material. Reports from educational associations, boards, and societies of state, county, and city departments of education are urgently needed if the record of school systems and educational activities is to be complete. Second, the bureau requests that all sorts of textbooks be sent to the library. If anyone has a textbook fifty years old, or one hundred years old, this material will be very valuable in helping to fill out the history of American education. Indeed, we are coming to recognize in general that the history of education needs to be rewritten in terms of such concrete material as the bureau is now attempting to collect. The typical history of education contains reviews of the statements of those who had written their ideas about what ought to be done in the schools. Future histories of education are going to contain more and more information about what was in the actual textbooks employed, what the classroom exercises consisted in, how the children were graded in the different schools. These concrete matters about actual school practice are by no means as easy to get together as the remarks of educational writers, and yet it is perfectly clear that within the next generation, students of the history of education will learn to recognize the importance of this type of material which the bureau is now bringing together, as contrasted with the somewhat vague and nebulous opinions for the most part offered to students of educational institutions.

The bureau also makes an announcement which is of very large interest, because it calls attention to the possibility of developing the loan collection plan. The art museum of the city of Boston made it possible some years ago for towns throughout Massachusetts to receive material of this sort. The development of a national method of loaning art material is a very welcome addition to school equipment.

It will soon be possible for any city school to have a drawing exhibit of national significance practically without cost. Dr. Henry Turner Bailey and Mr. Royal B. Farnum are preparing for the United States Bureau of Education an exhibit of the best examples of drawing and art work in the elementary, high, and normal schools of the United States, as well as one or two of the art schools. The exhibit is to be sent to any city desiring it upon payment of the cost of transportation from the city last using it. The transportation charges will be small.

The exhibit is not to be a large one, but it is being selected with unusual care, so as to show the work that will be most suggestive to teachers, children, and school officers. It will be ready for shipment about January 1, but cities desiring it should make application at once to the Commissioner of Education, Washington, D.C., in order that it may be dispatched to as many localities as possible with the least expense to each of them.

Shall the School Day Be Shortened?

In recent addresses before state associations, the Commissioner of Education of the United States has advocated the reduction of the school day. The formula which he has employed is somewhat as follows: It would be very well for us to have three, or perhaps even two hours of schooling in the morning, this to be continued during a long period, indeed during the whole life of any citizen. The remainder of the day should be spent in useful occupation of some sort or other.

Such a statement as this sounds very reactionary in contrast with the plea which is frequently being heard in all parts of the country for a larger school opportunity. It is not unusual to hear a fuller school day advocated because this fuller school day corresponds more exactly to the hours which have been found essential in business. Thus the Boston School of Commerce found it desirable to increase the length of its school day for exactly this reason.

The Commissioner's remarks will undoubtedly be more truly interpreted by referring to some of the details of the plan which he advocates. His plan is advocated primarily with a view to giving children in the lower school some opportunity to find suitable engagements for their powers and interests in farm work, in house work, and in constructive activities. Indeed, the plan was not discussed in detail in its application to city schools but was made most emphatic with reference to rural schools. Furthermore, the Commissioner states explicitly that it is his desire that the school shall supplement and enlarge this opportunity for real labor, that the opportunity for real labor shall furnish the material out of which the school work shall grow. Thus, the advocacy of a shorter school day turns out to be after all the advocacy of a somewhat different program for the child's supervised work. For two hours in the morning, or three, he shall devote himself to the studies which give him the scientific principles on which his work is based during the rest of the day when he is not in school. During the remainder of the day he shall go, for purposes of employment and for purposes of enrichment of experience, into the practical world. Presumably if the practical world which surrounds the child does not offer the opportunities for suitable occupation, it will be the business of society to see that the remaining hours of the day are equipped with opportunities for recreation and for work. In other words, if the city child is to be brought into this program advocated by the Commissioner, it will be necessary for some sort of an institutional supervision to be provided for these extra hours. The school probably can do this as well as any other institution, and we shall be led, in keeping with the spirit of the Commissioner's comments, to provide after all for a longer rather than a shorter school day. It is certainly desirable that the educational world, in the discussion of matters of this type, should be very fully informed as to the actual machinery which is to be set in motion in order to make valid a contention that the school day should be reduced in length. The clamor for an increase in school opportunity is much too loud to be suppressed by the general theoretical statement that we can leave children to collect experiences for themselves, if only these experiences can somehow be coordinated with the work of the school. The serious problem of the school at the present time is to keep the child's time and energy systematically organized and utilized. In order to perfect this extremely difficult program, it will be necessary for us to keep our eyes clearly upon the necessity of some social contribution to the whole organization of the child's energy and time.

Shall Teachers Be Promoted with Their Grades?

Another interesting doctrine which the Commissioner of Education has been advocating in his recent addresses is the doctrine that a teacher should be promoted with her class. It would be very much better, the Commissioner holds, for the fourth-grade teacher to go forward into the fifth grade with the class, carrying along the knowledge of personal peculiarities and achievements of the children, than that the children should be transferred, or, as he picturesquely puts it, "pitched," from one teacher to another.

The experiment which the Commissioner here advocates has been tried from time to time with very great advantages to the children. On the other hand, it is to be pointed out that the teacher who is successful in the primary grades may miss very seriously the problems of the intermediate or upper grades. If our educational psychology has shown us anything with regard to the development of children, it is that that development is periodic in character, involving from time to time very radical changes in interest and in methods of study on the part of the children. The teacher would probably have to readjust quite as radically as the children, and the changes would not be so certain if the teacher went forward with her class. Indeed, it is very frequently true that the change in social environment which comes with the transition from grade to grade is the very best opportunity for arousing in children characteristics which they have not up to this time exhibited. Parents do not recognize the radical changes in interest and in mental qualifications of children because they deal with them too intimately and continuously. The problem which is suggested by the Commissioner's discussion is an interesting one, and should call for the report of experiences from all quarters where experience has been collected, but that a radical change should be made in our public-school system so as to carry the teachers forward is not immediately obvious without more evidence than is now at hand.

Various Types of Teachers' Agencies

Two significant announcements have recently been made with regard to the methods of securing appointments for qualified teachers. Mr. C. A. Prosser, secretary of the National Society for the Promotion of Industrial Education, announces that his office will conduct a registration bureau for those teachers who are prepared to give instruction in industrial subjects. This registration will not include recommendation, and it will not be the business of Mr. Prosser's office to select teachers for given places, although naturally enough the office will sooner or later come to exercise some advisory functions. For the present, however, the bureau is to be conducted in such a way that anyone wishing a teacher of this sort will consult it merely for information rather than for selective advice.

An announcement made by the department of education of Massachusetts states that, by act of the legislature in 1911, the state board of education is required to establish a teachers' bureau. The object of the bureau is to assist superintendents in finding the right teachers, and teachers in finding the right places. Plans for developing this work are now under way, and a comprehensive system of registering and classifying is being worked out. By law a registration fee of two dollars is charged to the applicant. There is no other fee. In addition to the information obtained by the customary registration blank, it is intended to accumulate first-hand information concerning teachers and their work by members of the staff. All the information obtainable will be placed at the disposal of the inquiring superintendent. Teachers will not be notified of vacancies for which they are expected to apply, unless the bureau is requested to notify them.

In this connection it is interesting to note that practically every college and university in the country is now conducting a free registration bureau through which superintendents become acquainted with the graduates who are qualified to fill high-school positions and even positions in the elementary schools. Every normal school is also a center for distribution of information about available candidates. In addition to these public institutions there are a large group of teachers' agencies engaged in the business of finding places for teachers and finding teachers for superintendents who wish to fill vacancies. The fact that certain of the educational institutions of the country and certain organized societies are beginning to deal with this matter is undoubtedly significant for the future. There is no reason why state teachers' associations, and sectional associations should not become very helpful agencies in the distribution of information. Indeed, there are many teachers who have experienced through teachers' agencies the unfortunate results of overkeen competition and of a purely business attitude toward the question of placing teachers. Very frequently the teachers' agency renders very slight service and collects an unduly large proportion of the subsequent salary. In other cases the teachers' agency undoubtedly does render a service which justifies its commission. The co-operative method of dealing with the problem would be more economical for teachers than the present business methods employed by teachers' agencies. Mr. Prosser's bureau and the registration system which is required in Massachusetts are suggestive examples which ought to be followed by other institutions of like type.

School Banks in Canada

The Consular and Trade Report gives an interesting account of the growth of the Canadian penny bank system in the public schools. The organization of school penny banks in the Dominion of Canada is regulated by an act of Parliament. A large number of these banks have been established throughout the various provinces. During the fiscal year ending June 30, 1911, deposits increased from $142,000 to $175,000. The depositors received 3 per cent interest, and it is understood that the government pays to the banks $3\frac{1}{2}$ per cent on these special deposits. Certain banks in each town offer their services in handling these accounts, in which there is no profit, in the hope that the children, depositing in these school banks, may eventually become depositors in a larger way. Deposits are made each morning by the students with the teacher, and an employee of the bank goes to the school to receive the money so collected. Each depositor has a passbook in which deposits are entered by the teacher. The withdrawals are entered by the bank. The books are supplied by the school board, and paid for out of school funds.

The Panama-Pacific Exposition

The preliminary announcements of the Panama-Pacific International Exposition to be held in San Francisco in 1915 make emphatic reference to the educational features of this exposition. It is planned that there shall be a series of educational conferences. Teachers' associations and conventions are invited to become a part of the general organization of this exposition, and there will undoubtedly be an elaborate collection of material from American and foreign schools. The interest of teachers in the general exposition is of course urgently solicited, and the probability that educational meetings will be an important part of the organization is set forth in the preliminary circulars.

Marking Systems

The methods of marking pupils in school are constantly subjected to adverse criticism both by students and by the instructors who have to employ marking systems. How nearly a student has approached to some theoretical maximum is very difficult to determine, and certainly more difficult to express. Again and again it has been pointed out that it would probably be better to subdivide the problem in some way, to call attention to the fact that a certain pupil has initiative, that he prepares his lessons carefully, that he exhibits good powers of memory and concentration, that he knows how to reason. In short, it would be better if the general problem could be so subdivided that the mark finally given to the student would signify something with regard to each of these different traits which his school work is supposed to cultivate and perfect.

The various schemes which have been suggested for this sort of grading are re-examined at most teachers' meetings, and it is with a view to exciting discussions along this line that the note is here inserted. It would be very desirable to hear from those who have tried any of these methods of special rating of school children.

This item is suggested by the fact that Dr. L. C. Wooster, head of the Biological Science Department at the Kansas Normal School, recently proposed the following subdivision of one hundred points.

	Perfect Grade
Power of initiative	24
Power of inductive reasoning	24
Memory of general principles	24
Power of deductive reasoning	20
Memory of words	8
	100

PRINCIPLES OF REVISION OF A COURSE OF STUDY APPLIED TO GEOGRAPHY

J. L. STOCKTON
Winona, Minn.

In an attempt to correct an overcrowded curriculum, there are at least three ways in which the problem may be attacked.

I. Elimination of unnecessary subject-matter (A) through careful attention to the aims of the course, and (B) by the presentation of subject-matter in the form of problems, thereby providing for something more than a *mere listing of facts*, and automatically limiting the exploration of relatively unimportant bypaths.

II. Such taking account of relations between various elements of the subject-matter as will provide for right *cumulative effect*. That is to say, wherever possible, the first thing taught should (through grade after grade) lead up to, and reinforce later material. The whole should also be knit together by *review problems* which present new aspects of old material, and serve as drills and reviews of important points.

III. Integration of subjects, in other words cutting down the number of subjects because of recognition of the fact that phases of the same subject have crept into the curriculum under various names, and can be put together so that the same results may be obtained with less skipping from subject to subject.

The following course in "Environment" has been prepared as an attempt to apply these principles. This course is meant to take the place of elementary science, nature-study, school gardening, and geography of the first three grades, and to merge into the geography of the fourth grade (see fourth-grade outline). Geography is regarded as "relation of the earth to life," and the early grades are devoted to the gathering of facts (earth facts and life facts), which are to be related causally in later grades (beginning with real home geography in fourth grade) where the child is more mature. Some spatial relations are dealt with in each grade.

TENTATIVE COURSE OF STUDY IN ENVIRONMENT

TO TAKE THE PLACE OF REGULAR COURSE IN NATURE-STUDY, ELEMENTARY SCIENCE, SCHOOL GARDENING, AND GEOGRAPHY, IN THE STATE NORMAL SCHOOL AT WINONA, MINN.

GRADE I

I. *Natural environment.*

Study trees, because (1) there are plenty within easy reach on our campus, (2) they are large and present easily comprehended gross features, (3) they are stationary and easily observed again and again, and for relatively long periods (N.B.—These considerations overbalance the fact that children's interests are more primarily in moving animal life.)

The problem in regard to trees is one of *recognition and appreciation* only.

In animal life, work for recognition of such common animals as will be likely to be met with in the reading or in the child's own restricted experience. Most of the children will be familiar with many of these, but some will be ignorant of a part of the last, and there should be a general checking up, covering such creatures as cats, dogs, chickens, rabbits, squirrels, foxes, cows and calves, horses and colts, sheep, turtles, ants, grasshoppers, butterflies, crickets, bees, etc.

Children in this grade should begin to learn how to care for a canary and for plants, but should not be given full care and responsibility. Assistance should be permitted and encouraged, attention being drawn to the details of what must be done.

Do gardening in order that the children may see *many things grow*, in order that they may get the concept that things do grow—that they come from seeds planted in the ground and develop through the various stages to maturity. Note all kinds of plant life—vegetables, cereals, flowers, weeds—but for the above-mentioned purpose specifically.

Cultivate a general appreciative observation of the whole environment as opportunity presents itself, but do *specific* work as outlined above.

In none of the work suggested for this grade should scientific analysis be expected. Let the child recognize by picking out the characteristics which appeal to him.

II. *Artificial environment.*

Study three stores: (1) dry goods, (2) meat market, (3) grocery. Find out definitely what is kept in each store. Notice particular things. Learn generalization "store."

Study local *home*. Make this study from the *fact* side.

To aid in future geography work give some attention to the spatial relation of direction and distance. Let the children learn the directions by actual field work (view from top of building or similar device). Do not deal with maps or symbols of other kinds at this point.

GRADE II

I. *Natural environment.*

Recognition and appreciation of local flowers and shrubs.

Review problem: To find and recognize away from the campus the trees we learned to know on the campus last year. Tell how we know them. (Still let the child be largely independent as to the distinguishing features he selects.)

Gardening (spring): Review and clinch main features of fall visit to farm (see below).

Problem: To recognize what the farmer plants, and actually to plant it, and to recognize it when it grows.

Distinction between weeds and valuable garden plants. What animals and insects do we discover are helpful to our gardens, and what are harmful? Recognition of what common animals of the environment are domestic and what are wild.

Appreciation as in Grade I.

II. *Artificial environment.*

Other local stores than those studied in first grade. Recognize and tell what these stores have for the home, and what they get from the farm.

Visit the farm, familiarizing the children with farm conditions, becoming at home on the farm, wearing off strangeness, recognizing fields, animals, housing, fruits, grains, etc.

(Manual-training course should make application of all of this in construction work, etc.)

Transportation: Recognition of modes of getting from farm to town and about town.

Distinction between domestic and wild birds: Care for a bird in the schoolroom.

Continue first-grade work in direction and distance, but in field work only, without relation to maps or diagrams.

GRADE III

I. *Natural environment.*

Recognition and appreciation of birds.

Review problem: What kinds of trees, flowers, and shrubs did we see while looking for birds?

What makes an animal a good domestic animal?

How can our domestic animals take care of themselves, and how can we help to take care of them?

What kinds of flowers and weeds have seeds that are good food for birds? Do the birds all eat the same kind of seeds? Of insects?

What birds are helpful to our gardens? For what other reasons do we like birds? How can we help them? Kodak-hunting vs. gun-hunting.

Gardening (fall): Harvesting of normal department spring garden. Compare what was seen on the farm with what was seen in the school garden.

Care of house plants (winter) and planting of bulbs: One motive—to have Easter lilies.

II. *Artificial environment.*

Factories of Winona—Problems: What do they make? What raw materials do they use? Where do the raw materials come from? What are the uses of the products? How many of them come into our homes direct from the factory, and how many through the stores?

N.B.—Work with spatial relations of distance and direction should be continued in this grade, but still through actual experience, instead of through the medium of maps or diagrams. The direction of the farm from the school, etc., suggest the character of the available material. Pointing in various directions; walking in various directions; using names north, south, east, and west until they are very familiar in actual practice—all of this should be woven in until it is too familiar to allow the child to become confused.

GRADE IV

Beginning with this grade the course should be definitely called *geography,* but should include the necessary elements of the other subjects, no subject called elementary science, nature-study, or school gardening being put upon the program separately. The first three grades have been collecting *facts*—facts about the *earth,* and facts about *life.* They are in the fourth grade to begin to relate those facts into the science of geography, geography being regarded as the "relation of earth to life." These relations are of course mainly *causal.* The basis for geography is another relation—the spatial. These spatial relations are (as already provided in this course) to be emphasized in each one of the first three grades, and to be summed up and applied to maps and charts in the latter part of the fourth grade now under discussion (see below).

Home geography: 6 months. Use Dodge's *Home Geography* outline as found in his first book, but treat the subjects as treated in McMurry's discussion. (Tarr and McMurry's *Geography.*)

4 B Grade. Do topics 1 to 10 inclusive, omitting topic 4.

4 A Grade. Do remaining topics in Dodge, *Home Geography* outline, and spend three months on *Homes in other Lands,* as an introduction to a first *extensive* view of the "world as a whole," going from *consequence* to *cause.* Make this study of homes by means of a series of type studies, gathering the facts which will tend to build up in the child's mind an idea of the heat belts, so that he has roughly blocked out in his mind the "world as a whole" divided into zones. Use *Seven Little Sisters* and *Each and All,* in so far as they are applicable to this work.

Map study: Map study should come *after* the child has something to map. Hence, as has been intimated in previous grades, it would be left until the study of home geography in the fourth grade has gone far enough to give the child at least an elementary need for symbols of geographic areas. But the fact that his necessity does appear should be recognized, and along with it the other fact that it takes very careful initiation into the use of the symbol in order to be sure that it does not supplant the real thing, but *only comes to stand for the real thing.*

Spatial relations having been well cared for in the preceding grades, this knowledge can be relied upon as an aid in the understanding of the map idea. Directions on the map should be developed first by plots of ground used to represent larger areas, then by sketches on paper made by laying the paper upon which a sketch is to be made flat on the floor, where the real directions may be observed and marked. Hang on north wall. Afterward, the simple details may be filled in as becomes necessary or desirable. Do not give to the child, at first, maps completed by someone else and ask him to interpret them, but stimulate and encourage him to make maps for himself, summing up his knowledge of home geography relations. Some of the gross theory of drawing to a scale will need to be taught. Teach the child to see the map as a symbol of a reality (which reality at this point is largely within his own experience).

Credit for valuable constructive criticism of this course is due to the critic teachers of the Winona Normal School.

BIBLIOGRAPHIES, BRIEFS, AND ORAL EXPOSITION IN NORMAL SCHOOLS[1]

S. CHESTER PARKER
University of Chicago

I desire to comment on three phases of co-operative training in English which are possible in normal schools, namely, (1) training in the use of books and libraries, that is, systematic bibliographical work, (2) training in the organization of material in the form of expository briefs, and (3) training in oral exposition.

The possibilities of this type of co-operative English work are probably greater in a normal school which emphasizes two-year courses for high-school graduates than in any other educational institution above the elementary school. These large possibilities are due to the fact that such a normal school theoretically should be, and often is, more unified in its organization than other institutions. This greater unification results from several factors which include (1) the very definite professional aim, namely, training teachers for elementary schools, (2) the relatively brief period for doing this. The combination of these factors results in a very rigid selection of those courses of instruction which are essential and the definite elimination of those courses which do not have a large applied value. Hence in a given department, few courses will be offered, and these will soon become definitely standardized. When this standardization is once effected, the attention of the department is no longer concentrated on the selection of its subject-matter, but upon the most effective teaching of the subject to the normal-school students. This effective teaching may very well include the three forms of co-operative English work mentioned above, namely, training in systematic bibliographical work, in writing expository briefs, and in oral exposition, and this work may be required uniformly throughout the institution in all departments.

[1] A paper presented before the National Council of English Teachers, Chicago, November 29, 1912.

These forms of activity are of vital importance in the effective teaching of every subject; they are as important in history, geography, and nature-study as they are in English. In this respect they differ from some of the more formal aspects of English work, such as correct spelling, correct forms of speech, sentence structure, etc., in which the instructor who is not a specialist in English is often not interested and of which he is commonly not competent to judge. I shall take up briefly each of the forms of co-operative work for special consideration.

The necessity of training in systematic bibliographical work is easily demonstrated. Many school buildings are being provided with selected libraries; special library collections for children are provided in many cities; supplementary reading by children is growing in all subjects; and the teacher is expected to be constantly developing a body of supplementary subject-matter and informing herself concerning the larger aspects of the topics she is teaching. The difficulties encountered by teachers in connection with some of these new demands are illustrated in connection with the making of lesson plans in practice teaching, especially in the content subjects. Student teachers are commonly not considered competent to teach any topics except those of which they have had an intensive treatment in departmental courses. Yet very few of the topics they will have to teach in actual school work are covered in these courses. One practice teacher was referred to a departmental head for assistance on a topic which had not been covered in the course. He referred her to a dozen or more large volumes. She worked on them twenty-five hours and came back with the report that there was nothing in them on the topic. This waste of time was partly the fault of the instructor, partly of the system for not providing bibliographical training, and partly the fault of the student.

I was in a Junior class in history in college in which the instructor assigned us individual topics to work up for reports. He said, "Your first step will be to prepare a bibliography." Half of the class had never heard of a bibliography and had never done any systematic reference work.

Training along this line should provide for the following:

(*a*) a short course (from five to ten lessons) by an expert, on the use of standard reference systems and bibliographical aids; (*b*) frequent assignments in all departments of topics to be worked up; (*c*) the requirement of a representative or fairly complete bibliography as the first step in working a topic; (*d*) this bibliography should include not merely exact references, but also a brief description of each reference based on a cursory examination of it.

The second phase of co-operative English work, namely, the preparation of expository briefs, might well take the place of much of the writing of long term papers and other papers which is often required. There is entirely too much of the writing (or often copying) of long papers made up of undigested, unorganized ideas. There is entirely too little of the careful, thoughtful organization of ideas derived from a variety of sources, and of the concise expression of these ideas freed from the lumber of unnecessary words. One remedy is to be found in the requirement that many reports should be put in the form of expository briefs.

By an expository brief I mean the presentation of material in the form of clear, concise, complete statements or sentences, so subdivided, paragraphed, and numbered as to indicate clearly the relative value and subordination of the various points. Hence it differs from the ordinary outline or ordinary summary. This difference must be elaborated to students but need not be here.

The advantages of this type of writing for the student are obvious. It is a mechanical device which practically forces him to attend to the number, relation, and organization of his ideas. In the ordinary long paper these factors do not stand out clearly. The training in concise, exact expression that results is also important.

From the standpoint of the instructor for whom the paper is written the use of the brief is a great time-saver. He can read it in much shorter time and can more easily estimate just what the student has accomplished.

Not only term papers, but also notes on readings can be put in this form to advantage. In one of my undergraduate classes I require students to read periodical articles on the teaching of special subjects and to report on them in the form of briefs. I can read thirty of these, representing three hundred pages of periodical reading, in two hours. I usually make note of such references and items as interest me. The advantage to the instructor is obvious in this case. Lesson plans put up in the form of briefs make the student much more conscious of the problems of subject-matter and method which confront him in his teaching. Moreover, the plans may be much more quickly read by the critic teacher.

The preliminary training in the making of briefs should be provided in the department of English, and a uniform style established which should prevail in all departments.

The third phase of co-operative work in English, namely, training in oral exposition, is intimately related to the other two, for the oral reports on topics which might be required in all subjects should be preceded by systematic bibliographical work and careful organization of the reports in the form of written briefs.

The great value for teachers of training in systematic, artistic oral exposition is shown in the high grade of this type of work in the schools of Germany. We are not likely to carry exposition by the teacher to the extreme to which it is carried in Germany, but it deserves to play a considerable part in our instruction as supplementary to textbooks and to development lessons. Many of our teachers are especially deficient in oral exposition. They have no standards of excellence and no skill. They may be somewhat skilled in oral narration, but the rambling, hodge-podge, unorganized character of their expository oral discourses is often appalling. Even the experienced teachers whom we find as graduate students in our departments of education are often lamentably weak along this line. Their class reports have been characterized by one instructor as "unmitigated bores."

Again, the remedy is preliminary training in the English department, supplemented by regular oral reports in all other departments. These reports may vary from three minutes to a half-hour in length, and a definite technique of giving them should be developed. This should include very definite and clear assignments by the teacher followed by the bibliographies and briefs prepared by the students as described above. In making a short oral report the student should not have any notes in his hand, but his brief or some of its more important points should be written on the board. An immature student in the normal school, before presenting his first long oral report to the class, might be required to rehearse it before a committee of two or three students from the class, and the instructor. This provides the necessary audience, breaks the performer in gradually, and saves the time of the class if the report is found to be unsatisfactory for presentation.

From the standpoint of the special department, this method of reporting is, in my estimation, a useful device for freeing individual reports from some of the objections that have been urged against them. From the standpoint of training in expression it provides the first essential, namely, an audience-situation, that is, the pupil with something to say and the group for whom it will be significant.

I first became acquainted with this type of co-operative English work in a high school which I attended. The principal was a teacher of English and provided for this much co-operative work throughout the departments. For purely departmental purposes I have used it in the department of education with all grades of students from those of the normal school to candidates for the Doctor's degree, and I am convinced that it has contributed to the efficiency and interest of everyone concerned, including the instructor.

OBSERVATIONS CONCERNING THE ORGANIZATION OF SCHOOLS AND CERTAIN PHASES OF EDUCATIONAL WORK IN GERMANY. II

GEORGE KOEPPEL
Principal Twenty-first Street School, Milwaukee, Wis.

SPECIAL HELP SCHOOLS

Hilfsschulen.—The establishment of special help classes for children whose progress in school is retarded and the *organization of such classes into schools* has made great progress in all parts of Germany, and large and small cities, even villages, conduct such schools.

I am at present not referring to institutions for the feebleminded where children of lower types of mental weakness are educated to a certain degree of usefulness, but to schools that are established for pupils who are unable to do the regular work required in the courses of the elementary schools in the usual time, and who occupy a place intermediate between the so-called normal pupils and those who are properly placed in institutions for the feebleminded or idiotic.

Most of the pupils of the *Hilfsschulen* are congenitally weak in intelligence, while in many others faulty development, sickness, or unfavorable surroundings are either the cause of their backwardness or reinforce their innate weakness. Feeble-mindedness is a relative term. We know well enough that in classes of so-called normal children there is no approach to evenness of mentality and that in such classes we have to deal with children who, from the most intelligent member down to the dullest, represent many degrees of congenital endowment, and that not a few of them are *comparatively* feeble-minded. That the latter class is unable to follow the instruction devised for pupils of higher powers is evident; they will not profit by it themselves and moreover become a burden to the class.

Similar considerations led in Milwaukee to a great deal of agitation in favor of ungraded classes and to their establishment. In other American cities, various other arrangements are used experimentally in consideration of the inequality of the natural ability of pupils, in order that at least the two great classes of normal pupils and backward pupils may each have a better chance of progress.

In Germany, Switzerland, and Austria, the movement of caring for these weaker pupils has taken large proportions, and many of the foremost educators, school physicians, and medical specialists are intensely interested in furthering it. Every other year a convention is held where prominent delegates from all parts of the empire and from neighboring countries discuss conditions and means of progress in this particular field. I attended a similar congress, held July 5 and 6 in Altdorf, Switzerland, where an exhaustive report on the *Hilfsschulen* of Switzerland was made and various problems pertaining to mentally and morally backward pupils were discussed by able educators and alienists. The earnestness and ability of these men and their devotion to a difficult and somewhat uninviting phase of work were highly inspiring.

Wherever I investigated these schools for backward children, in Berlin, Charlottenburg, Wittenau, Lübeck, Hamburg, Leipzig, Chemnitz, Dresden, Zürich, I found my opinion confirmed that ungraded classes are not more than makeshifts. Unless the backward pupils of a larger district are brought together to form classes, each representing a grade, and these organized into a school, very much valuable time and effort must be wasted without really benefiting the pupils, not to speak of the excessive burden that is put on the teacher.

Years of experience and observation in special help classes in Germany have demonstrated the fact that the great majority of these children *need a reduced course of study* and special training in schools organized for their need. The late superintendent, Dr. Bertram of Berlin, who had been very reluctant in introducing this innovation, was forced to admit that very few pupils, properly assigned to a special help class, develop sufficiently to carry the work in the regular classes, and that their interests are best served by promotion through the grades of the *Hilfsschule*. Nothing, of course, prevents a retransfer to the regular grade in favorable cases.

About 1 per cent of the pupils of German elementary schools are found in *Hilfsschulen*. Before being assigned to one of these, a pupil has been tested usually a year and a half in the regular first grade and is then transferred to the *Hilfsschule* upon the judgment of his teachers and the school physician. The records kept for each child by teachers and physicians are highly interesting and instructive. I am prepared to report specially on these records if required.

As many of the pupils have attended school nearly two years before entering the *Hilfsschule*, the organization of the latter comprises six grades. The classes, each containing but one section, are *very small*. In Charlottenburg the number of pupils assigned to a teacher and class is 12 in the lower grades, 14 in the middle grades, and 16 in the upper grades. In Berlin and other cities the numbers are very slightly higher, 14, 16, and 18 pupils per class respectively. It is this organization of primary classes of 12 to 14 pupils, *all being of one group or section*, that permits of a degree of individual attention and care by the teacher that is next to ideal.

One school of this kind that I visited was composed of nine classes. This small school had three shops, one for clay-modeling, one for pasteboard work, and one for woodwork. There was also a large exhibition room, a kind of museum, showing in genetic progression the work to be done along all the lines of activity in that school. A large *Lehrmittel* room was also provided which contained a rich supply of material for object lessons, so much needed with backward children. While manual training is optional for children of the elementary schools it is considered absolutely essential in the training of backward pupils. Singing, gymnastics, walks in the city, to parks, and to the woods form part of the program.

Stutterers and stammerers are instructed 2–4 hours a week by specialists.

To show the reduced and simplified course of these schools,

I insert the weekly time table of the *Hilfsschulen* at Berlin for comparison with that of the regular classes on p. 191.

HILFSSCHULE—BERLIN

HOURS PER WEEK

	Grade 6 (lowest)	Grade 5	Grade 4	Grade 3	Grade 2	Grade 1 (highest)
Religion	3	3	3	3	3	3
Reading, writing, language, spelling	5	5	5	5	6	6
Arithmetic	4	4	4	4	4	4
Object lessons	4	4	4	4	6	6
Manual training	4	4	4	4	4	4
Drawing	..	..	1	1	1	1
Singing	1	1	1	1	2	2
Gymnastics—games	1	1	2	2	2	2
	22	22	24	24	28	28

The large amount of time given to object lessons and manual training is worthy of attention. The elements of geography, history, and nature-study are taught as object lessons. The teachers present only what is most essential and practical and an especial effort is made in these schools to make the instruction vivid, real, and objective. Slow progress, repetitions, frequent reviews, presentation of the subject-matter from various viewpoints are of great value and of necessity with backward pupils. These processes cause even the duller pupils to comprehend things that would remain Greek to them during the more rapid and comprehensive instruction in the regular classes. The feeling of satisfaction and joy that comes to the backward pupils when they discover that they learn to know and to do things which were formerly dead to them acts as a stimulus to their interest in new matters and to their hopefulness of making further progress. But it is clear that the separation of these backward pupils is not only a very decided advantage to them but also to the regular classes. A considerable portion of the school time and a much greater portion of the teacher's nervous energy is saved by their removal, and time and energy may now be applied to a more evenly graded class, one that is more nearly capable of receiving instruction as a body; and therefore better mastery of the subject-matter and more rapid progress is insured.

Hilfsschule pupils who leave school at the age of fourteen or fifteen years have an opportunity, in fact they are obliged, to continue their school studies and their manual work a number of hours each week, in a continuation school especially organized for their needs.

SCHOOLS FOR THE FEEBLE-MINDED

A study of the institutions for the training of children of low mentality is instructive from many points of view but particularly for the lessons in patience and skill exhibited by the teachers who make a specialty of this work. Some of these institutions are models of that type of schools that have full control of the child's education, regulating and guiding every step of his life for a number of years. One of the grandest examples of this class is the Landes-Erziehungs-Anstalt in Altendorf near Chemnitz.

Its location is very healthful and ideal, on gently sloping ground near the Crimmitschau forest, overlooking city and surrounding country. The city of Chemnitz agreed to preserve the forest in its present extent "forever" and grant admission to the woods to the members of the school at all times. The grounds belonging to the school cover an area of about 170 acres, about two-thirds of which is used for gardening and farming. A rectangle about 1,300 feet wide and 1,650 feet long contains the beautiful buildings which are surrounded by tastefully arranged gardens, ample playgrounds and fine gravel walks. Among the thirty-eight buildings which are constructed in the villa style, may be mentioned three schoolhouses, a chapel, a gymnasium, a central bathhouse, kitchen and dining-hall, several buildings containing shops, an administration building, dwelling-houses for the pupils and for the officers and teachers, a dairy, a central heating and lighting plant, and a hospital. No two of these buildings are alike, each presenting an architectural individuality of its own, and yet the whole complex impressing the observer with its harmony of conception. This school can accommodate only eight hundred pupils, but the cost of the buildings and their outfit amounted to about four and a half million marks, more than a million dollars.

Careful attention to modern hygienic requirements, the most scrupulous order, neatness, and cleanliness are apparent throughout. Classrooms and living-rooms are made comfortable by a liberal supply of good furniture, and the cheerfulness of the occupants is promoted by pictures, decorations, songbirds, aquariums, and plants.

Each of the three school buildings has only nine classrooms, but in addition, each has two *Lehrmittel* rooms well supplied with material for object lessons. One of the classrooms in each school building is very large and is furnished with a grand piano for instruction in music.

The accompanying pictures show the exterior and interior of the hall for gymnastic exercises, which also serves as assembly hall on special occasions, and is provided with a stage.

The teachers of Milwaukee and their friends have long been hoping for the establishment of a parental school. If ever this dream should be realized, a careful study of the plans, in all their details, of the Landes-Erziehungs-Anstalt near Chemnitz should not be neglected.

The methods of education and of instruction in these schools are based on the results of psychological research confirmed by long experience with mentally weak children. The fundamental principle is the stimulation to conscious and voluntary activity. Not the mechanical acquisition of a quantity of knowledge but the training to useful work is the main object of all educational processes in these institutions. The classes in school and the "families" out of school are *very small*, numbering *about twelve pupils*, and each is composed of pupils that are physically and mentally as nearly equal in grade as possible. This careful grading of classes is considered as absolutely fundamental for success. The development of the work through ten steps or grades and the numerous classes within this range, enable the teachers to place each child where he can do his best.

The four lowest grades comprise the *Vorschule*, the preparatory department, whose function is the training of the pupils' senses to observe properly the objects that surround them and to form concepts of these and of their qualities by numerous activities. A considerable portion of time is devoted to practical exercises in attending to themselves; learning to know the articles of dress,

Gymnastic Hall

Interior of Gymnastic Hall

their use, their material; utensils used in washing and bathing and the application of these. Regular use of the toothbrush is insisted upon. The pupils learn by frequent exercises to dress and undress and to aid each other in doing so, to clean their clothing and shoes, and to habituate themselves to orderliness in hanging or placing articles of dress and other objects, and in keeping their rooms in an orderly and neat condition. They have exercises in finding their way in the room and in the house, in the yard, on playgrounds, and in gardens, also to the places that have been visited on walks in the neighborhood. Polite behavior is also established by daily exercise.

A glance at the program for these lower four grades shows that only a small part of the time is devoted to regular school work, and during that time there is hardly a minute when the children are not "acting out" what is being taught. The lessons last 45 minutes and each is followed by 15 minutes' recess on the playground.

The distribution of work, in hours per week, is as follows for the *preparatory four grades or steps:*

	Grade I	Grade II	Grade III	Grade IV
Object lessons	6	6	6	5
Reading	..	..	..	4
Counting exercises	..	..	..	2
Singing	1	1	2	2
Gymnastics and play	4	3	3	3
Attending to themselves	6	6	4	4
Sorting of substances	..	2	2	1
Work with colored beads	3	3	..	..
Building	2	2	..	..
Folding and weaving	..	2	3	2
Placing colored sticks	..	..	2	2
Braiding	..	..	2	2
Claywork	..	..	1	1
Work with mosaic blocks	..	..	..	1
Total hours per week	22	25	25	29

The principal aim of this plan is to acquaint the pupils with objects, their qualities and properties; to train their perceptive faculty. Nothing is memorized but everything is learned by experience. In the *six grades of the school proper* the work, in hours per week, is distributed as follows:

	Grade VI (Lowest)	Grade V	Grade IV	Grade III	Grade II	Grade I (Highest)
Religion	..	4	4	4	4	4
Story telling	3	..	..	..	..	..
Reading, writing, language, spelling	6	6	6	6	6	6
Arithmetic	3	3	3	3	3	3
Object lessons	4	3	3	3	1	1
Home geography	..	..	..	1	2	2
Singing	2	2	2	2	2	2
Drawing	1	1	1	1	2	2
Gymnastics and play	3	3	3	3	3	3
Manual Training	**9**	**9**	**10**	**10**	**11**	**13**
	31	31	32	33	34	36

In the higher grades, too, the development of manual skill is a prominent feature.

The processes by which it is attempted to reach the aim of this school, the training to conscious voluntary activity, are very interesting and instructive, and particularly so in the preparatory department where children of very low mentality are found, but these methods cannot be discussed in this report, as only a detailed and extended description would be of value, and that would form a special report.

Not a few of the weak-minded children who are found capable of training when first examined and observed, reach a point in their development where they come to an intellectual standstill and where they can no longer progress with their class in school or in the shops. To prevent retrogression, these children are instructed in school a short time every day and during the greater part of the day are trained to do some useful work within their capacity in so-called "work classes." One of these classes was composed of girls who had reached but the third grade of the preparatory department, two of boys who had reached but the second and fourth grades respectively of that department, while with others arrest of development occurred in one of the grades of the regular school.

Nowhere is demonstrated more clearly that with the best of teaching the progress of pupils must vary greatly in consequence of the natural endowment and of intercurring developmental conditions over which the educator has absolutely no control.

The institutions for feeble-minded children in Wittenau near Berlin and in Alsterdorf near Hamburg are organized and conducted, in theory and practice, essentially on the same principles; everywhere we find systematic efforts of promoting the physical conditions of the child and of arousing and stimulating his feeble mental powers by constant activity. The pupils are employed in a variety of occupations and are finally trained in one, so that they may become competent and possibly independent workers in some trade.

The literature concerning the education of weak and backward children is quite rich in Germany and the institutions mentioned above, as well as the *Hilfsschulen*, are liberally supplied with these books. A small school in Dresden of ten classes and 140 pupils is provided with a library of several hundred of such special works for the use of the teachers.

[*To be continued*]

ANALYSIS OF COLBURN'S ARITHMETICS. IV

WALTER S. MONROE
Kansas State Normal School

The appearance of Warren Colburn's arithmetics (*First Lessons* and *Sequel*), marked the beginning of a new epoch in the development of arithmetic and arithmetic teaching in the United States. The principal features of these texts may be classed under three heads: (1) the introduction of oral instruction, (2) his ideas about the subject-matter of arithmetic and its organization, and (3) his recognition of sound educational principles. It is the purpose of the writer to present evidence of these features from Colburn's writings.

ORAL INSTRUCTION

To appreciate the significance of Warren Colburn's introduction of oral instruction into arithmetic teaching, it is necessary to recount briefly the method of instruction prevailing before his time. This method may be characterized as the "Cyphering Book" method. In the earlier times rarely did either the teacher or pupil possess a text. Each pupil was provided with a blankbook made of a quire of paper folded and sewed together. The teacher either dictated or set "sums" which the pupil worked on scraps of paper. After the work had been approved by the teacher it was carefully copied in the "Cyphering Book." Such rules as the pupil needed were given by the teacher. Thus the arithmetic work was written as well as being deductive.

Later, when arithmetic texts began to be used in the schools, the method of instruction was not materially changed. For example, in beginning addition the pupil was first given the rule and then as the first problem asked to find the sum of several numbers, some of which were often composed of five or six digits. And similarly in other topics, the first problems were such as to require the use of pencil and paper. Since the numbers were so large that they were beyond the comprehension of the pupil, the work must have appeared to him as a mere juggling with written symbols.

In contrast to this, Colburn does not provide for written computations in the *First Lessons*. In fact he does not introduce the number symbols at all in the first third of the book. Thus the pupil is compelled to perform the operation mentally and to give the result orally. Furthermore, the quantities of the problems throughout the book are small enough to bring the number within the comprehension of the pupil and also so small that he may do the problems mentally. It is therefore probable that pupils solved the problems of the *First Lessons* without recourse to written calculation. When there were no "sums" to be done on paper or slate and submitted to the teacher for inspection, it became necessary for the teacher to hear the pupils give an oral solution of the problem. Thus at least in the case of the younger pupils arithmetic teaching came to be largely oral after the appearance of the *First Lessons.*

Oral instruction required the operations to be performed mentally, i.e., without recourse to written symbols, and the method of oral instruction is probably most widely known as "mental arithmetic."

This feature is not made prominent in the *Sequel* but close connection is made between "operations performed in the mind" and the "application of figures to these operations."

THE SUBJECT-MATTER OF ARITHMETIC AND ITS ORGANIZATION

In his analysis of the subject-matter of arithmetic, Colburn distinguishes between the processes of arithmetic, which he calls "principles," and the applications of arithmetic, which he designates as "subjects." To him the "principles" mean arithmetic and the applications merely a field for the exercise of these principles. Denominate numbers, mensuration, percentage, interest, etc., are not taken as the basis for separate chapters, or even distinct topics. "To give the learner a knowledge of the principles" is his purpose, and to this end the problems are grouped about the principles.

Colburn takes the position that "when the principles are well understood, very few subjects will require a particular rule, and if the pupil is properly introduced to them, he will understand them better without a rule than with one." This is to say, for example, that if a pupil understands well the relation between a product and its factors in all its phases, percentage and its applications require no particular rule and will present no difficulty to the learner. At most, the learner will need to be told the meaning of the new terms used in expressing the problem.

As we would naturally expect from such a point of view, the applications of arithmetic do not influence nor determine the structure of Colburn's texts. To give an idea of the content of the texts and the organization of the subject-matter, the section headings of the *Sequel* are given below.

I. Numeration and notation.
II. Addition.
III. Multiplication, when the multiplier is a single figure.
IV. Compound numbers, factors, and multiplication, when the multiplier is a compound number.
V. Multiplication, when the multiplier is 10, 100, 1000, etc.
VI. Multiplication, when the multiplier is 20, 300, etc.
VII. Multiplication, when the multiplier consists of any number of figures.
VIII. Subtraction.
IX. Division, to find how many times one number is contained in another.
X. Division. Explanation of fractions. Their notation. What is to be done with the remainder after division.
XI. Division, when the divisor is 10, 100, etc.
XII. To find what part of one number another is, or to find the ratio of one number to another.
XIII. To change an improper fraction to a whole or mixed number.
XIV. To change a whole or mixed number to an improper fraction.
XV. To multiply a fraction by a whole number, by multiplying the numerator.
XVI. Division, to divide a number into parts. To multiply a whole number by a fraction.
XVII. To divide a fraction by a whole number. To multiply a fraction by a fraction.
XVIII. To multiply a fraction by dividing the denominator. Two ways to multiply, and two ways to divide a fraction.
XIX. Addition and subtraction of fractions. To reduce them to a common denominator. To reduce them to lower terms.
XX. Contractions in division.
XXI. How to find the divisors of numbers. To find the greatest common divisor of two or more numbers. To reduce fractions to their lowest terms.
XXII. To find the least common multiple of two or more numbers. To reduce fractions to the least common denominator.
XXIII. To divide a whole number by a fraction, or a fraction by a fraction, when the purpose is to find how many times the divisor is con-

tained in the dividend. To find the ratio of a fraction and a whole number, or of two fractions.

XXIV. To divide a whole number by a fraction, or a fraction by a fraction; a part of a number being given to find the whole. This is on the same principle as that of dividing a number into parts.

XXV. Decimal fractions. Numeration and notation of them.

XXVI. Addition and subtraction of decimals. To change a common fraction to a decimal.

XXVII. Multiplication of decimals.

XXVIII. Division of decimals.

XXIX. Circulating decimals. Proof of multiplication and division by casting out 9's.

Even the subdivisions and order of the "principles" are unusual. Multiplication of integers follows addition instead of subtraction. In fractions, multiplication is placed first and is followed by addition and subtraction. Both multiplication and division of fractions are divided into several cases.

The *Sequel* is divided into two parts. The first consists of graded lists of problems with an occasional suggestive note to define some new term or to interpret the meaning of the problem. "The second part contains a development of the principles" based upon problems.

The two parts are to be studied together, when the pupil is old enough to comprehend the second part by reading it himself. When he has performed all the examples in an article in the first part, he should be required to recite the corresponding article in the second part, not verbatim, but to give a good account of the reasoning. When the principle is well understood, the rules[1] which are printed in italics should be committed to memory.

The Table of Contents of the *Sequel* makes no mention of any of the applications of arithmetic, several of which usually have a chapter devoted to them. However, one must remember that it is Colburn's plan to teach the principles through their use in solving problems. He says:

As the purpose is to give the learner a knowledge of the principles, it is necessary to have the variety of examples under each principle as great as possible. The usual method of arrangement, according to subjects, has been on this account entirely rejected, and the arrangement has been made according to principles. Many different subjects come under the same principle; and different parts of the same subject frequently come under different principles.

[1] Few rules are given and such as are given are placed at the end of a section. The rule is the result of a process of development. Colburn gives rules only for the principles.

Colburn mentions the following "subjects" as being specifically included in the text: Compound Multiplication, Addition, Subtraction, and Division; Simple Interest, Commission, Insurance, Duties, and Premiums, Common Discount, Compound Interest, Discount, Barter, Loss and Gain, Simple Fellowship, Compound Fellowship, Equation of Payments, Alligation Medial, Alligation Alternate, Square and Cubic Measure, Duodecimals, Taxes, Mensuration, Geographical and Astronomical Questions, Exchange, Tables of Denominate Numbers.

Colburn omits some topics entirely. He specifically mentions the Rule of Three, Position, and Powers and Roots. The reasons he gives for their omission are:

> Those who understand the principles sufficiently to comprehend the nature of the rule of three, can do much better without it than with it, for when used, it obscures, rather than illustrates the subject to which it is applied.
>
> . . . . This (the rule of Position) is an artificial rule, the principle of which cannot be well understood without the aid of Algebra; and when Algebra is understood, Position is useless. Besides, all the examples which can be performed by Position, may be performed much more easily, and in a manner perfectly intelligible, without it.
>
> Powers and Roots, though arithmetical operations, come more properly within the province of Algebra.

It is interesting to note that some of the omissions which Colburn made nearly a century ago are still considered by some individuals to be debatable.

Not only in his arrangement of topics but also in the very subject-matter itself does Colburn differ radically from the writers of arithmetic who preceded him. In Daboll's *Schoolmaster's Assistant*, which was probably more extensively used in the United States after 1800 than any other arithmetic before Colburn's, the pupil was introduced to the subject as follows:

> Arithmetic is the art of computing by numbers, and has five principal rules for its operations, viz., Numeration, Addition, Subtraction, Multiplication, and Division.
>
> NUMERATION
>
> Numeration is the art of numbering. It teaches to express the value of any proposed number by the following characters, or figures:
>
> 1, 2, 3, 4, 5, 6, 7, 8, 9, 0—or cypher.
>
> Besides the simple value of figures, each has a local value, which depends upon the place it stands in, viz., any figure in the place of units, represents

only its simplest value, or so many ones, but in the second place, or place of tens, it becomes so many tens, or ten times its simple value. . . . .

In the *Scholar's Arithmetic* by Daniel Adams, which was another widely used book in Colburn's time, the subject is begun as follows:

Arithmetic is the art or science which treats of numbers.

It is of two kinds, theoretical and practical.

The theory of arithmetic explains the nature and quality of numbers, and demonstrates the reason of practical operations. Considered in this sense, arithmetic is a science.

Practical arithmetic shows the method of working by numbers, so as to be most useful and expeditious for business. In this sense arithmetic is an art.

There are six pages of definitions of this sort and an explanation of the system of notation before any problems are given.

Contrast these with the way Colburn introduces the pupil to arithmetic:

FROM "FIRST LESSONS"[1]

1. How many thumbs have you on your right hand? how many on your left? how many on both together?

2. How many hands have you?

3. If you have two nuts in one hand, and one in the other, how many have you in both?

4. How many fingers have you on one hand?

5. If you count the thumb with the fingers, how many will it make?

6. If you shut your thumb and one finger, and leave the rest open, how many will be open?

7. If you have two cents in one hand, and two in the other, how many have you in both?

8. James has two apples, and William has three; if James gives his apples to William, how many will William have?

FROM "SEQUEL"[2]

1. James has 3 cents and Charles has 5; how many have both?

2. Charles bought 3 buns for 16 cents, a quart of cherries for 8 cents, and 2 oranges for 12 cents; how many cents did he lay out?

3. A man bought a hat for 8 dollars, a coat for 27 dollars, a pair of boots for 5 dollars, and a vest for 7 dollars; how many dollars did the whole come to?

In Adams' *Scholar's Arithmetic* division is begun as follows:

Simple division teaches, having two numbers given of the same denomination, to find how many times one of the given numbers contains the other.

[1] This and all other citations in this article from the *First Lessons* refer to an edition of 1847.

[2] This and all other citations from the *Sequel* refer to the edition of 1826.

Thus, it may be required to know how many times 21 contains 7; the answer is 3 times. The larger number (21) or number to be divided, is called the *Dividend;* the lesser number (7) or number to divide by, is called the *Divisor;* and the answer obtained (3) the *Quotient.*

After the operation, should there be anything left of the dividend, it is called the *Remainder.* This part, however, is uncertain; sometimes there is no remainder. When it does happen it will always be less than the divisor, if the work be right, and of the same name with the dividend.

RULE

1. "Assume as many figures on the left hand of the dividend as contain the divisor once or oftener; find how many times they contain it, and place the answer as the highest figure of the quotient.

2. "Multiply the divisor by the figure you have found, and place the product under the part of the dividend from which it was obtained.

3. "Subtract the product from the figures above it.

4. "Bring down the next figure of the dividend to the remainder and divide the number it makes up as before."

When you have brought down a figure to the remainder, if the number it makes up be still less than the divisor, a cypher must be placed in the quotient, and another figure brought down.

One example, "Divide 127 by 5," is worked out and explained. Two other problems with divisors of two digits are worked out but not explained. In all there are 11 problems in the list, all abstract.

Colburn begins division in the *First Lessons* by asking, "How many apples, at one cent apiece, can you buy for four cents?"

Twenty-three problems of this sort are given before any attempt is made to consider division as a process. Then it is first considered in a practical problem, and immediately following, the same combination is called for in an abstract problem.

These quotations are typical of the texts of Daboll and Adams. They are also illustrative of the prevailing attitude toward the subject-matter of arithmetic before Colburn's texts appeared. It is very evident that he had a different notion of the subject-matter of arithmetic.

Colburn invariably introduces a topic or a new combination by a "practical question." If the topic or combination is new, the "practical question" is followed by the same problem in abstract form. For example, the following is taken from p. 94 of the *First Lessons:*

1. If a yard of cloth cost 3 dollars, what will 1 half of a yard cost?
2. What is 1 half of 3?

3. If a barrel of beer cost 5 dollars, what will 1 half of a barrel cost?
4. What is 1 half of 5?
5. If 2 barrels of cider cost 7 dollars, what is that a barrel?
6. What is 1 half of 7?
7. What is 1 half of 9?
8. What is 1 half of 11?

One phase of the organization of the subject-matter is Colburn's treatment of the symbols of notation which seems to exemplify one of his fundamental notions of arithmetic. For example, he wishes the pupil to learn that two objects and one object make a total of three objects; that five plums and four plums are nine plums, and *not* that the symbols 2+1 equal the symbol 3, or the symbols 5+4 equal the symbol 9. As a means to this end, in the *First Lessons*, the characters 1, 2, 3, ... are not given until p. 50 and the system of notation and numeration is not given beyond 10 until p. 69. Before these symbols and the system of notation and numeration are given, the pupil has learned the four fundamental operations for integers. The symbols are introduced by saying, "Instead of writing the names of numbers, it is usual to express them by particular characters called figures." Thus before the pupil is asked to learn the number symbols, he doubtless has felt the need for them. For this reason he is more likely to appreciate their meaning and usefulness.

Another feature of Colburn's texts is that, so far as I am aware, they represent the first explicit attempt to write a series of arithmetic texts. The *Sequel* is a continuation of the *First Lessons* and yet begins with the first of arithmetic. The *Sequel* is the equivalent in scope and type of problems to the other arithmetics of that time, but the *First Lessons* is a pioneer in a new field. The author intended it to be especially adapted to young children. It is stated in the edition of 1847 that "almost any child of five or six years is capable of understanding more than half the book, and those of seven or eight years old can understand the whole of it."

[*To be continued*]

BOOK REVIEWS

The Learning Process. By S. S. COLVIN. New York: Macmillan, 1911. Pp. xxv+336.

The scope of this book is broader than might be inferred from the title. It is, in fact, a textbook upon educational psychology. The general standpoint of the author is indicated by the title. The book is not, however, a discussion of the learning process in so far as the learning process means specifically the acquirement of knowledge or skill. It includes these forms of development, but also includes a general analysis of the psychological processes which are usually treated in introductory psychology. The appropriateness of the title lies in the fact that the point of view from which the various topics are treated is the functional point of view. The mental life, that is, is treated as a means to the adaptation of the individual to the conditions of his life, and this adaptation may be spoken of as learning in its broadest sense.

The book may, then, be regarded as educational, first, because it deals with mental processes from the functional standpoint. In the second place, there are in the course of the discussion frequent references to the application of the principles evolved to the teaching and the learning processes. There is also considerable reference to the development of the various functions in the child, which further adapts the treatment to the needs of education.

We may say that the book is a general psychology rewritten in such a way as to make it applicable to education. The order and selection of topics are the same as those which would be found in a general textbook of psychology. For example, in the early chapters occur the topics reflex action, instinct and habit, sensation and perception. These are followed by chapters upon imagination, memory, association, attention and interest, and the higher thought-processes. Interspersed among these chapters are chapters in which the special application of the matter which is treated in a more theoretical way in the previous chapters is made to education. The fact that the book is in the main the conventional type above described is further shown by the absence of material which has been developed recently, based upon the experimental analysis of school subjects—such material, for example, as is found in the works on experimental education by Meumann and Rusk. Such material unquestionably must be incorporated into a textbook upon educational psychology if it is not in fact made the basis of such a treatment.

Although the *Learning Process* does not, then, make a very radical departure from the traditional text of educational psychology, nevertheless it gives much material which is of value to the teacher. The author has evidently had contact with educational problems and uses frequent illustrations from the schoolroom to make clear the principles which he is describing. In the more general processes, such as habit, memory, learning in the narrow sense of the acquisition of skill, and the transfer of training and of fatigue, the discussion is of the sort which is needed in an educational psychology. The treatment of some of the other psychological processes, such as perception, imagination, association, etc., is rather too general and far removed from the actual problems of education best to fulfil the needs of an educational psychology.

The book, however, will be tried with a good deal of interest since it goes farther than previous texts in the field, and is in some respects the most satisfactory attempt to cover the new field of educational psychology which has yet been made. The book is adapted for use with classes in normal schools or colleges who have had no psychology and who are taking a beginning course in educational psychology.

FRANK N. FREEMAN

UNIVERSITY OF CHICAGO

A Report on Vocational Training in Chicago and in Other Cities. By GEORGE H. MEAD, ERNEST A. WREIDT, WILLIAM J. BOGAN, Subcommittee of the Committee on Public Education, 1910–11, of the City Club of Chicago. Published by the City Club of Chicago, 1912. Pp. xiii+315.

This report consists of four sections. In the first section the recommendations which the committee has to make as a result of its investigations are set forth in detail. In the second section a large body of information about schools is presented. The first chapters of this section show the extent of retardation and elimination and the waste suffered by the individual and by society through a failure of the ordinary school to provide for children from fourteen to sixteen years of age. The next chapters present a study of the attitude of organized labor toward the whole matter of industrial education. Then follow a number of chapters describing the efforts which are being made in Chicago and in other cities to develop school agencies which can meet the demand for improved industrial training of children. The reports on schools are based on visitations made by one of the members of the committee and are very comprehensive, including all the typical industrial schools and classes in this country.

Part three reports the facts regarding business colleges and commercial schools. Curiously enough the business colleges have grown up and flourished in this country altogether out of relation to the trade schools. In Germany the trade school came first and the commercial course grew up as a departmental course within the trade school. In America the wages commanded by those who are trained to do clerical work furnished a practical motive for the private organization of commercial courses long before any system of industrial education was seriously considered. The fact that this report deals with the commercial schools distinguishes it from the ordinary reports of commissions on industrial education. Most of the reports on industrial education have reviewed the industrial schools as does the second section of this report, but few refer to the problem presented by the business colleges and commercial schools.

The fourth section of the report gives the results of a series of tests in which boys who left school to go to work as soon as the law permitted, regardless of their advancement in the grades, are investigated with reference to their ability to solve simple problems in arithmetic, with reference to their ability to understand and write simple English, and with reference to their knowledge on simple matters of civil government and history. These tests show that such boys are very deficient in all lines in which they were tested. The significance of these results is very great. The work done in the schools evidently does not carry over into life, and life of the ordinary type does not stimulate mental activity of the kind cultivated in the school.

The large body of convincing information which the report contains will do much to promote interest in the development of industrial education. The first section of the report will do much to help direct this interest into the right channel. There are many sentences in this part of the report which are worth quoting. The following extracts give an idea of the position of the subcommittee:

"Our elementary school curriculum undertakes more than can be accomplished by a large percentage of the children during the period of eight school years. The over-age of one-third of the children is convincing evidence that they cannot complete this curriculum inside of the time during which the law keeps them in school; and neither the interest of the child nor that of his parents keeps him there when the law has withdrawn its hand" (p. 4).

"In the opinion of your committee, a discussion of the question of reducing the content of the curriculum of the American school or of increasing the school time while the content of the curriculum remains the same would have only academic interest. The influences which have forced continually new material into that curriculum are fundamental influences in our schools and in the community at large. They are as American as are our public schools. There is no reason to believe that the elementary school curriculum will be cut down and school time increased to such an extent that over-age will disappear and thus automatically eliminate elimination. Nor would it be reasonable to simply adopt the other half of the German program and to try to meet the ineffective education which follows upon elimination by continuation classes (pp. 5 and 6).

"Again, it is the generally accepted judgment of educators that the boy and girl in the neighborhood of fourteen are so much interested in the society into which they expect to enter and the occupations of men and women in that society, that a school which does not appeal to the vocational motive is bound to lose the interest of a great number of these children" (p. 6).

"The first part of our recommendation is, therefore, a plan worked out in some detail, of a type of school in which half of the time in the seventh and eighth grades may be given to vocational work, while during the other half of the school time we are confident that as much can be accomplished in the academic studies as is accomplished today. We recommend for these vocational grades a school day of six hours instead of the present five hours and a rearrangement of the time given to different subjects" (p. 7).

"Our great contention is that vocational training be introduced into our school system as an essential part of its education—in no illiberal sense and with no intention of separating out a class of workingmen's children who are to receive trade training at the expense of academic training. We are convinced by what we have found elsewhere in America, as well as in other countries, that such a division is unnecessary. We are convinced that just as liberal a training can be given in the vocational school as that given in the present academic schools. Indeed, we feel that the vocational training will be more liberal if its full educational possibilities are worked out" (p. 9).

The conclusions to which this committee comes are diametrically opposed to those which underlie the Massachusetts plan and to those which Mr. Cooley presents in his report to the Commercial Club of Chicago. The position defended in the present report is however so typically American, so clearly feasible as a school program, and so simple to put into operation as contrasted with the plan of special and separate schools, that it is certainly worthy of careful consideration before any other course is adopted. It is the belief of the present reviewer that it is the position which will ultimately be universally adopted in American schools.

C. H. J.

BOOKS RECEIVED

AMERICAN BOOK CO., NEW YORK

High School Geography, Physical, Economic, and Regional. By CHARLES REDWAY DRYER, Professor of Geography and Geology, Indiana State Normal School. Half Leather. Illustrated. Pp. 536. $1.30.

Essentials of French. By VICTOR E. FRANCOIS, PH.D., Associate Professor of French in the College of the City of New York. Cloth. Pp. 426. $0.90.

Physical Laboratory Guide. By FREDERICK C. REEVE. Cloth. 12mo, pp. 192. Illustrated. $0.60.

Plane and Solid Geometry. By C. A. HART and DAVID D. FELDMAN. Edited by J. H. and VIRGIL SNYDER. Cloth. Illustrated. Pp. 496. $1.25.

Seth of Colorado. A Story of the Settlement of Denver. By JAMES OTIS. Cloth, 12mo, pp. 147. Illustrated. $0.35.

Bookkeeping and Accounting Exercises. By R. J. BENNETT. Cloth. Illustrated. Part I. Pp. 96. $0.40. Part II. Pp. 112. $0.45.

Manual of Experimental Botany. By FRANK OWEN PAYNE, M.Sc. Cloth. 12mo, pp. 272. Illustrated. $0.75.

Forge Work. By WILLIAM L. ILGEN. Edited by CHARLES F. MOORE. Cloth. Illustrated. 12mo, pp. 210. $0.80.

"Masterpieces of the English Drama Series." *Webster and Tourneur.* Pp. 464. *Christopher Marlowe.* Pp. 426. *Beaumont and Fletcher.* Pp. 414. Edited by FELIX E. SCHELLING, Professor of English Literature, University of Pennsylvania. Cloth. 12mo, $0.70, each.

Hygiene for the Worker (Crampton's "Hygiene Series"). By WILLIAM H. TOLMAN, PH.D., and ADELAIDE WOOD GUTHRIE. Edited by C. WARD CRAMPTON, M.D. Cloth. Illustrated. Pp. 231. $0.50.

English Grammar. By LILLIAN G. KIMBALL. Cloth. Illustrated. 12mo, pp. 271. $0.60.

D. APPLETON & CO., NEW YORK

Principles of Educational Practice. By PAUL KLAPPER, PH.D., Instructor of Education, College of the City of New York. Cloth. Pp. 476.

A Reader for the Eighth Grade. By CLARENCE F. CARROLL and SARAH C. BROOKS. Cloth. Pp. 286.

A. S. BARNES CO., NEW YORK

After Long Years and Other Stories. Translations from the German by SOPHIE A. MILLER and AGNES M. DUNNE. ("Sunshine and Shadow Series.") Cloth. Illustrated. Pp. 241.

THE CENTURY CO., NEW YORK

Famous Pictures. Famous Pictures Described with Anecdotes of the Painters. By CHARLES L. BARSTOW. Cloth. 78 Illustrations. Pp. 239. $0.60.

DOUBLEDAY, PAGE & CO., NEW YORK

New Demands in Education. By JAMES PHINNEY MUNROE. Cloth. Pp. 312. $1.25.

GINN & CO., NEW YORK

The Dramatic Method of Teaching. By HARRIET FINLEY-JOHNSON. Edited by ELLEN M. CYR. Cloth. Illustrated. Pp. 199. $1.00.

Education as Growth or the Culture of Character. By L. H. JONES, A.M., President Michigan State Normal College. Cloth. Pp. 275.

A Dramatic Version of Greek Myths and Hero Tales. By FANNY COMSTOCK. Cloth. Illustrated. Pp. 191. $0.45.

HARPER & BROTHERS, NEW YORK

The Montessori System, in Theory and Practice. By DR. THEODATE L. SMITH of Clark University. Cloth. Illustrated. Pp. 78. $0.60.

D. C. HEATH & CO., NEW YORK

Lessons in the Speaking and Writing of English. Book One, *Language Lessons.* By JOHN M. MANLY, Head of the Department of English, University of Chicago, and ELIZA R. BAILEY. Cloth. Illustrated. Pp. 299. $0.45.

Civics in Simple Lessons for Foreigners. By ANNA A. PLASS. Cloth. Illustrated. Pp. 187.

HENRY HOLT & CO., NEW YORK

A Montessori Mother. By DOROTHY CANFIELD FISHER. Cloth. Illustrated. Pp. 240. $1.25.

HOUGHTON MIFFLIN CO., NEW YORK

English for Foreigners. By SARA R. O'BRIEN. Book Two. Cloth. Illustrated Pp. 248. $0.70.

Sixth Reader. "The Riverside Readers." By JAMES H. VAN SICKLE and WILHELMINA SEEGMILLER, assisted by FRANCES JENKINS. Cloth. Illustrated. Pp. 276. $0.55.

LITTLE BROWN & CO., BOSTON

The English History Story-Book. By ALBERT F. BLAISDELL and FRANCIS K. BALL. Cloth. Illustrated. Pp. 198. $0.50.

LONGMANS, GREEN & CO., NEW YORK

Atalanta's Race and The Proud King. (From *The Earthly Paradise.*) By WILLIAM MORRIS. With introduction and Notes. Cloth. Pp. 60. $0.35.

MACMILLAN CO., NEW YORK

The Administration of Public Education in the United States. By SAMUEL TRAIN DUTTON, LL.D., Professor of School Administration in Teachers College, Columbia University, and DAVID SNEDDEN, PH.D., Commissioner of Education, State of Massachusetts. Cloth. Pp. 607.

The Art of Education. By IRA WOODS HOWERTH, A.M., PH.D., Professor of Education in the University of California. Cloth. Pp. 237.

Great Opera Stories ("Everychild's Series"). Translated from Old German Original Sources by MILLICENT S. BENDER. Cloth. Illustrated. Pp. 186.

Historical Plays for Children ("Everychild's Series"). By GRACE E. BIRD and MAUDE STARLING. Cloth. Illustrated. Pp. 292. $0.40.

Nonsense Dialogues for the Youngest Readers ("Everychild's Series"). By ELLEN E. KENYON-WARNER. Cloth. Illustrated. Pp. 168. $0.40.

CHARLES E. MERRILL CO., NEW YORK

The Merrill Speller. By J. ORMOND WILSON. Cloth. Book One. Pp. 132. Book Two. Pp. 251.

Durell's Elementary Arithmetic. Pp. 410. $0.48.

Durell's Advanced Arithemtic. Pp. 484. $0.64. By FLETCHER DURELL, PH.D., and ELIZABETH HALL. Cloth. Illustrated.

THE MANUAL ARTS PRESS, PEORIA, ILL.

Manual Training Toys for the Boy's Workshop. By HARRIS W. MOORE. Cloth. Illustrated. Pp. 111. $1.00.

STEWART & KIDD CO., CINCINNATI

The Soul and Sex in Education. By JIRAH D. BUCK, M.D. Cloth. Pp. 175. $1.25.

ROW, PETERSON & CO., CHICAGO

"Reading-Literature Series." *First Reader*. Pp. 134. *Second Reader*. Pp. 191. *Third Reader*. Pp. 256. Adapted and Graded by HARRIETTE TAYLOR TREADWELL AND MARGARET FREE. Cloth. Illustrated.

WARWICK & YORK, BALTIMORE

The Outlines of Educational Psychology. An Introduction to the Science of Education. By WILLIAM HENRY PYLE, PH.D., University of Missouri. Cloth. Enlarged Edition. With Charts. Pp. 268.

JOHN WILEY & SONS, NEW YORK

Elements of Plane Trigonometry, High-School Edition. By ROBERT E. MORITZ. Cloth. Illustrated. Pp. 323. $1.00.

CURRENT EDUCATIONAL LITERATURE IN THE PERIODICALS[1]

IRENE WARREN[2]
Librarian, School of Education, University of Chicago

Abbott, P. The fifth International Congress of Mathematics. School W. 14:416–19. (N. '12.)

Affleck, G. B. Bibliography of physical training and hygiene, May–August, 1912. Am. Phys. Educa. R. 17:624–36. (N. '12.)

Arnold, Frank R. Bicentenary viewpoints of Rousseau. Educa. 33:135–37. (N. '12.)

Brereton, Cloudesley. The character-forming influence of vocational education. J. of Educa. (Lond.) 44:779–80. (N. '12.)

Bronk, Isabelle. Experiences of a non-native teacher of modern languages. Educa. 33:150–58. (N. '12.)

Brown, J. C. An investigation on the value of drill work in the fundamental operations of arithmetic. J. of Educa. Psychol. 3:485–92. (N. '12.)

In the investigation reported in this paper, the pupils who had been drilled did uniformly and considerably better than the others.

Carringer, M. A. The ten year old boy and his books. Educa. 33:166–69. (N. '12.)

Charles, Fred. The second Moral Education Congress. School W. 14:419–21. (N. '12.)

Clark, Herbert F. An experiment in concentration. Psychol. Clinic 6:178–79. (N. '12.)

The effect of permission to leave school when tasks were finished upon a group of boys in a special school.

(The) Cleveland meeting of the American Association for the Advancement of Science. Science 36:707–10. (22 N. '12.)

Preliminary program, directory of meetings, etc.

[1] *Abbreviations.*—Am. Phys. Educa. R., American Physical Educational Review; Cent., Century; Child Wel. M., Child Welfare Magazine; Educa., Education; El. School T., Elementary School Teacher; English J., English Journal; J. of Educa. (Bost.), Journal of Education (Boston); J. of Educa. (Lond.), Journal of Education (London); J. of Educa. Psychol., Journal of Educational Psychology; Lit. D., Literary Digest; Man. Train. M., Manual Training Magazine; Outl., Outlook; Pop. El. M., Popular Electricity Magazine; Pop. Sci. Mo., Popular Science Monthly; Psychol. Clinic., Psychological Clinic; School R., School Review; School W., School World; Sci. Am. Sup., Scientific American Supplement; Tech. World M., Technical World Magazine.

[2] Annotations by Dr. Frank N. Freeman.

Colby, Lester B. Great new school for Texas. Tech. World M. 18:388–91. (D. '12.)

Crichton-Browne, James. Child study and school hygiene. Child (London) 3:105–16. (N. '12.)

Crossley, M. L. The function of a college education. Educa. 33:129–34. (N. '12.)

Drinker, Cecil K. Undergraduate research work in medical schools. Science 36:729–38. (29 N. '12.)

An investigation of the opportunities for undergraduate research in selected American medical schools.

Du Breuil, Alice Jouveau. Written composition in the high school. English J. 1:537–46. (N. '12.)

Dumville, Benjamin. The methods of teaching reading in the early stages. School W. 14:408–13. (N. '13.)

A comparison of the method of phonetic analysis with the "Look and Say" method to the advantage of the latter.

England's athletic schoolboy. Lit. D. 45:905. (16 N. '12.)

Foxley, Barbara. How children learn to read. School W. 14:413–16. (N. '12.)

A comparison of the phonetic and "common-sense" methods to the advantage of the latter.

Gallienne, Richard le. Children in fiction. Harper 126:73–78. (D. '12.)

Gayler, G. W. Are the elementary schools getting a square deal? Psychol. Clinic 6:174–77. (N. '12.)

A comparison of the salaries and per capita expenses in the elementary and high school.

Hall, John W. Plans for grade lessons in geography. El. School T. 13:171–79. (D. '12).

Hays, Willet M. A national university. Science 36:723–29. (29 N. '12.)

A criticism of certain features of the scheme presented by Presidents Van Hise and James, together with certain positive suggestions.

Hein, Leon F. A. The cost of materials for manual training in the elementary grades. Man. Train. M. 14:129–37. (D. '12.)

Hill, David Spence. The need of practical co-operation of educational and of medical departments in modern universities. Science 36:647–59. (15 N. '12.)

Howe, Charles B. The future of the manual training high school in vocational education. Man. Train. M. 14:105–14. (D. '12.)

(An) industrial university. Pop. El. M. 5:859–60. (D. '12.)

Johnson, Alvin S. The child and social reform. Dial 53:380–83. (16 N. '12.)

King, Irving, and Johnson, Harry. The writing abilities of the elementary and grammar school pupils of a city school system measured by the Ayres scale. J. of Educa. Psychol. 3:514–20. (N. '12.)

The results of the application of the Ayres test to the eight grades and a table showing the variability among eight judges.

Kirkpatrick, E. A. Financial training of children. Child Wel. M. 7:73–78. (N. '12.)

Koeppel, George. Observations concerning the organization of schools and certain phases of educational work in Germany. El. School T. 13:189–97. (D. '12.)

Leslie, R. Murray. Child welfare and industrial insurance. Child (London) 3:117–24. (N. '12.)

McCracken, Elizabeth. Children in bookland. Outl. 102:686–92. (23 N. '12.)

MacDougall, Robert. The child's speech. II. J. of Educa. Psychol. 3:507–13. (N. '12.)

The influence of the mother's speech as a model for the child.

Moorhead. F. G. College for egg buyers. Tech. World M. 18:396–98. (D. '12.)

Noyes, Ernest C. Progress in standardizing the measurement of composition. English J. 1:532–36. (N. '12.)

A popular description of the Thorndike-Hillegas method, with approval.

O'Leary, Raphael D. Pity the poor teacher. English J. 1:552–56. (N. '12.)

Paul, Harry G. The teaching of lyric poetry. II. English J. 1:521–31. (N. '12.)

Porter, Elizabeth Crane. A pageant of progress. Outl. 102:653–59. (23 N. '12.)

Prince, John T. Moral training in public schools. Educa. 33:138–43. (N. '12.)

Raycroft, J. E. The athletic research society. Am. Phys. Educa. R. 17:585–98. (N. '12.)

Rickert, Edith. Exclusiveness among college women. Cent. 85:227–35. (D. '12.)

Riis, Jacob A. The New York newsboy. Cent. 85:247–55. (D. '12.)

Robinson, Edward Van Dyke. The reorganization of the grades and the high school. School R. 20:665–88. (D. '12.)

Rogers, A. K. The function of the American college. Pop. Sci. Mo. 81:574–81. (D. '12.)

Ryle, E. A three years' Latin course. School W. 14:401–4. (N. '12.)

Sargent, D. A. Defects in the school curriculum in physical training as shown by the disabilities of college students. Am. Phys. Educa. R. 17:602–7. (N. '12.)

Schools for tractioneers. Sci. Am. Sup. 74:348. (30 N. '12.)

Schurman, J. G. Faculty participation in university government. Science 36:703–7. (22 N. '12.)

A formal proposal to extend to professors representation upon the governing bodies of the university.

Scott, J. F. Apprenticeship under the English gild system. El. School T. 13:180–87. (D. '12.)

Scovel, Mary C. The theater: a second grade problem. Man. Train. M. 14:115–28. (D. '12.)

Sisson, Edward O. College students' comments on their own high-school training. School R. 20:649–64. (D. '12.)

Smith, F. The psychology of adult reading. School W. 14:404–8. (N. '12.)

A brief account of the results of the experiments on reading—no new material.

Smith, Harlan I. The educational work of a great museum. Science 36: 659–64. (15 N. '12.)

A description of the ways in which a museum may extend the scope of its influences.

Smith, Simeon Conant. Poetic triteness. English J. 1:547–51. (N. '12.)

Snow, Mary S. Essentials in education. J. of Educa. (Bost.) 76:507–8. (14 N. '12.)

Squire, Carrie Ransom. Graded mental tests. III. J. of Educa. Psychol. 3:493–506. (N. '12.)

A continuation of the report on graded tests to include the higher mental processes. Also a classification of abilities in all the tests according to age.

Stowe, Lyman Beecher. Training city boys for country life. Outl. 102: 537–41. (9 N. '12.)

Stowe, Lyman Beecher. Training city boys for country life. II. Outl. 102:584–91. (16 N. '12.)

Thorn-Wright, Doris. Oral reading in its relation to the study of literature. English J. 1:557–61. (N. '12.)

Utsurikawa, Nenozo. The status of Japanese students in America: past and present. Educa. 33:144–49. (N. '12.)

Wallin, J. E. Aspects of infant and child orthogenesis. Psychol. Clinic 6:153–73. (N. '12.)

A critical consideration of the methods of eugenics and of euthenics in promoting the mental and physical welfare of the child.

Wild, Laura H. Training for social efficiency—the relation of art, industry and education. Educa. 33:159–65. (N. '12.)

Woodrow Wilson at college. Lit. D. 45:970–72. (23 N. '12.)

VOLUME XIII NUMBER 6

THE ELEMENTARY SCHOOL TEACHER

FEBRUARY 1913

EDUCATIONAL NEWS AND EDITORIAL COMMENT

The Chicago University Dinner at the Meeting of the Department of Superintendence

In connection with the meeting of the Department of Superintendence in Philadelphia during the last week in February there will be a dinner of the former students and graduates of the University of Chicago. Placards will be posted announcing the exact time and place of this dinner. The dinner will occur on Wednesday evening. It will be the third annual event of this type. The dinner originated in imitation of the example of Teachers College which has for a number of years had a reunion of its former students and graduates at this time. The dinner of Teachers College is held on Tuesdays so that no conflict is possible between the two gatherings. All who read this notice are requested to spread the information so that the attendance at these dinners may be as large as possible.

Investigation of the School System

The Portland, Ore., public-school system is to be investigated under the direction of a special committee of five taxpayers appointed at a recent meeting. This committee is to employ educational and financial experts and is to make a report of its findings to the Board of Education. The committee was created at the annual meeting of taxpayers of school district No. 1. An appropriation of $7,500 was made to meet the necessary expenses of the investigation. In providing for the investigation, attention was called to the fact that the disbursement of funds had increased six times in the course of the last ten years. This large increase in expenditures seemed to the citizens of the district to justify a careful inquiry into the efficiency of the school system. The author of the resolution providing for the inquiry stated, however, that he wished to repudiate the statement made at the meeting that the resolution was intended to reflect upon the school management. The resolution merely expresses, he asserts, the conviction of its supporters that evidence of the efficiency of the school system should be presented to those who provide the funds for the maintenance of schools.

This new example of the eagerness of taxpayers to know something about the efficiency of their school system draws the attention of teachers and school officers once more to the importance of preparing to show the efficiency of their schools before the question is raised by outside agencies.

In contrast with the initiation of an inquiry by taxpayers is the example of Boise, Idaho. In that city an investigation was recently made at the invitation of the Board of Education and Superintendent by three educational experts, with the result that the school system was shown to be in sound condition in both its financial and educational organization. A number of suggestions were offered in the report of the experts, which, if accepted, will make for enlargement of the work of the school. It will probably be easier for the Board to secure these enlargements from the community because of the co-operation of those who were drawn in from the outside to consider the educational problems of the city. The taxpayers in Boise have cheerfully contributed large amounts to the maintenance of their schools. The Board of Education is undoubtedly wise in anticipating the demand of these taxpayers for evidence that the school system is doing its work efficiently.

These and other examples teach one further lesson. There ought to be some organized agencies for the examination of school systems. Committees of taxpayers and even boards of education find it difficult to secure proper co-operation from educational experts in the conduct of such examinations. If an authoritative group of experts could be organized it would make investigations of this type very much simpler to conduct and in the long run very much more productive of benefit to the school systems.

The Public Education Association of the City of New York

This association is made up of the citizens of New York and its immediate environs. The association employs a permanent secretary, and collects funds with which it undertakes different kinds of activity. *Bulletin No. 7*, recently issued, sets forth the different types of activity which this association will carry on during the coming year.

First, it seeks to give a full and fair hearing to the report of the School Inquiry Committee. Second, it carries on continuously investigations which throw light upon the school budget. Third, it co-operates, whenever the opportunity offers, with the public authorities. For example, two years ago, when a proposition was made for a radical revision of the New York City charter, especially that chapter dealing with the school system, this association collected and distributed a great body of information which led to the abandonment of the revision which had been projected by the mayor and others. Fourth, the association keeps a man who is technically trained in the field to study the problem of compulsory education. Fifth, it makes a study of the problem of vocational training. Last year a survey was made of the school children of two districts to find out what occupations those children entered who left school to go to work. Other related problems are also studied under this general head. Sixth, the association employed last year a trained investigator who worked with the department of ungraded classes investigating cases of mental defectives in the school. This work is directly associated with the seventh line of work, in which the association co-operates with the departments of health and charities to secure proper hygienic and moral conditions for the children in the public schools. Eighth, the association employs nine visiting teachers who carry on their work in thirteen schools. These visiting teachers deal with the cases of children who do not measure up to the school standards, but who are not truant or defective. The work of these visiting teachers is of such importance that a large number of principals in the public schools have requested that teachers be sent to their districts. Ninth, the association conducts a school for boys in the Tombs Prison. Finally, the association has established a bureau which will furnish information with regard to educational matters to anyone in the country who asks for such information. Students of education in all parts of the country, and school officers are at liberty to take advantage of this co-operation if they wish to learn anything about the school system of New York City.

This example of public voluntary co-operation with the school system indicates the large interest which the public feels in educational matters. While the activities of this association are more varied than could be the activities of a smaller association, there is no reason why this New York example should not be followed in smaller centers throughout the United States. A careful investigation of school conditions would make it clear that in every quarter some additional activities can advantageously be taken up by co-operating organizations.

Home Study

So long as the critics of the schools deal with general matters such as the course of study and the efficiency of school discipline, they are not likely to excite either the parents who are fairly well satisfied or the teachers who know that the schools are doing good work. To be sure, there break out from time to time local storms of protest either against the new subjects, which are then designated fads, or against the old subjects, which are regarded by some as so antiquated that they ought not to be permitted. But these local storms attract little attention.

When some critic of the school system leaves these more general problems and begins to deal with the problem of home study, principals and teachers are sure to hear from interested fathers and mothers, especially from those who agree with the critics that there ought to be no home study. During the last month the newspapers have quoted freely from the recent discussions of home study in the *Ladies Home Journal*, and have expressed various opinions on the matter. It will be interesting to see how this matter is dealt with in some of the different discussions.

Thus one ex-superintendent of schools in a large eastern city is quoted by the press of Cleveland, Ohio, as saying that "little children ought never to be permitted to have home study interfere with their play." The superintendent of schools in this same city is quoted as making the following statement: "There should be no home study in any of the lower grades. However, in the upper grades it is better that a little home work be begun to prepare the child for the high school and independent work. It is out of the question to have no home work in the high school."

The *Times* of Oklahoma City, Okla., has the following editorial:

> The schools are now closed for the Christmas holidays. There would be a tremendous jolt felt by the whole futile system if, before the schools open again after the holidays, each father would convince himself of the wisdom of having his child's lessons end with school hours, just as his own business ends with office hours; in other words, that there should be no books brought home; no lessons studied in the evening. Of the physical and mental folly of evening study by a child every parent can easily satisfy himself.

In the *Daily Herald* of Quincy, Ill., there is a somewhat different expression of opinion quoted from the superintendent with approval:

> It is clearly the teacher's duty to train children how to use books, how to acquire facts therefrom, and how to do school work efficiently and successfully. It is not the duty of fathers and mothers to teach their children at night for the purpose of getting them ready to recite their lessons the next day. I am opposed to any practice of so-called home work that will interfere with the child's recreation and full quota of sleep. However, I am not ready to assent that a certain amount of voluntary, judicious home work "flattens everything out into a dead level of listlessness". . . . I am not ready to concede that all home work is a waste of time and energy, and that its complete abolition is a requisite to the improvement in the education of children. I believe there is a tendency on the part of many to exaggerate the amount of home work, etc.

From other centers one might quote the opinions of physicians who have been brought into the discussion by parents or school authorities. These physicians are variously of the opinion that school work is damaging, and that school work is necessary in order to train children. Some physicians believe that home work is sure to produce all of the ills of life, while others believe that evenings can very profitably be filled by some regular work assigned by the school.

The whole matter is certainly one of great importance to school officers and parents. The time will never come when legitimate exercise of one's mental powers is not desirable after school has closed. What the exact form of this mental exercise shall be remains to be determined by wisely directed experiment. There can be no doubt at all that the mistake has sometimes been made of requiring too much work. Sometimes the school has committed the more reprehensible mistake of requiring pupils to work out tasks for which they were not prepared. Anyone who attempts, on the basis of either one of these general charges, to make a universal statement that there shall or shall not be home study fails to recognize the real educational problem. The real educational problem is so to organize the home work of the child that it shall be productive and wholesome. Moreover, this home work should be so organized that there shall be co-operation between the home and the school. There can be no doubt at all that some children work more rapidly than others. The school cannot equalize the rate at which children move by throwing the responsibility upon the home for leveling up the work of the slow child with that of the fast child. The school must co-operate with the home in differentiating the children. In short, this problem involves all the problems of school administration and classification. The school which is called upon to do its work without any outside preparation will undoubtedly be demanding very shortly that its time be extended so that it may adequately fulfil the serious obligations which it is assuming. If individual administrators and teachers need support in the face of the public criticisms which have been scattered about very freely during the last few months, this is perhaps the strongest statement that can be made of their side of the case. The complicated problem of transmitting modern civilization cannot be solved in the short hours which are now devoted to actual school exercises. If parents object to home study, a complete reorganization of the school day and the school year is required and would be welcomed by educational officers. This would mean more and better equipment of schools and an increase in the teaching staff.

Credit for Home Work

Attention was called some months ago to the fact that the state superintendent in Missouri had arranged to recognize in the schools work done at home. A blank was to be filled out by the parents indicating the different kinds of activities of the child at home, together with some statement as to the quality of this work. This blank was to be received and signed by the teacher in the same way that the teacher's report is received and signed by the parent. There now comes from the Bureau of Education at Washington a statement to the effect that the same practice is being adopted on an extensive scale in Oregon. A number of home activities, such as building fires, milking the cow, splitting and carrying wood, dusting furniture, making beds, sewing, etc., are enumerated as the types for which credit will be given. "The work is definitely measured and allowed for. The child desiring credit for home tasks brings to school a slip signed by the parent testifying to what he has done. Ten per cent is added to the general examination result of all pupils who enter and continue in the voluntary contest to see which can obtain the most of such credits. This experiment has been tried with satisfactory results at one point in the state and is now attracting the attention of all the county superintendents."

Adjustment of the Elementary Course to Individual Pupils

At a meeting of the New York State Council of Elementary School Principals and Teachers, held during the recent holiday week, Principal L. V. Arnold of Amsterdam, N.Y., outlined a plan of organization which is followed in that city. There are two parallel courses, one a seven-year and the other an eight-year course. The distribution of students between these two courses is made at the end of the first year. By making this division between the students, one group can be carried forward much more rapidly than the other. The result is that at the end of two and one-half years the pupils in the seven-year course are doing the same work that those in the eight-year course do at the end of the third year. Transfers are made between the two divisions as occasion may demand. The arrangement keeps all of the pupils working at the maximum of their ability, and in many cases saves a year or more of the child's time as he progresses through the school. This plan is of special interest because it concentrates attention upon the possibility of saving time in the elementary school in the early part of the course. Teacher and parent alike are likely to overlook this possibility. The child is supposed to be progressing satisfactorily if he keeps up with his grade and the rate at which the grade is progressing is less thought of than it is later. In the later years of the school course when the child is ready to leave school or be advanced into a higher school the question of economy comes acutely to the consciousness of school officers and parents. If the general principles of efficiency and economy can be put into operation in such a way that the lower grades will contribute their full share to the education of the children, economies in the later years of the elementary school would be much more easily effected and would probably be less urgently demanded.

Educating Miners

Notice has been sent out by the Bureau of Education at Washington calling attention to the experiment which is being made at Ellsworth and Cokeburg, Pa., in the development of special courses of education in the schools for children who are sure to spend their lives in the mining industry. Mr. E. E. Bach has been employed by the mining companies as "sociological superintendent." He is preparing courses in elementary mining, first aid to the injured, and business forms. These courses are introduced as early as the sixth grade so that boys may be encouraged to remain in school. The girls are given courses in domestic science and other lines of work appropriate to home-making. The traditional school subjects are being modified so as to correlate with this vocational demand.

In Germany educators have long seen the importance of training the children in each community to be efficient in the industries of that community. This special experiment, therefore, has the justification of successful experience in Germany behind it. The special modification in the traditional courses undoubtedly will require much ingenuity and experimentation to perfect it. The statements which are made in the notice from the Bureau of Education would seem to indicate that the adjustments in these courses have not as yet gone very far. Thus it is reported that spelling lessons contain words taken from the state mining law, and English exercises deal with mining life. In all probability these relatively direct adaptations of the course to the interests of the community will later be supplemented by more radical adjustments of the course.

Corporal Punishment

A recent court decision in Texas justifies a school teacher in administering corporal punishment. The teacher in this case was charged with assault and battery. The matter was investigated by the Board of Trustees and the trustees sustained the teacher in her action. The court now holds that the evidence is in favor of the teacher. This adds another to the long list of court decisions which constitute interesting reading for the school administrator and for the teacher.

Several speakers at educational gatherings have recently called attention to the importance of a careful consideration of the whole matter of corporal punishment. Professor Elliott, speaking before a number of associations, has reviewed the history of corporal punishment in the schools, reminding his hearers of the universal practice of the earlier schools in using the rod as an instrument of education. Professor Meeker, of Princeton, has expressed himself as distinctly in favor of the use of corporal punishment on occasion as an instrument of school discipline. In New York City, where the regulations of the Board of Education prohibit the use of corporal punishment, there have arisen grave doubts in the minds of many principals and observers of the schools whether it will not be necessary in the near future to restore corporal punishment as a means of discipline. Indeed, it is understood that among the recommendations of the committee of inquiry there will probably be reference made to the lack of control which is exhibited in some of the New York schools and the absolute necessity of re-establishing this control through vigorous means of punishment.

Suggestions for an Improved School Seating

The medical inspector of the schools in Kansas City, Mo., calls attention to the familiar fact that the conventional school desk is in need of modification in order to produce a proper posture during sitting and studying. He suggests a chair which shall have in front of it a desk that slopes in such a way as to hold a book in front of the pupil who is reading or studying in the position in which it is usually held and at the level of the eyes. The present flat desk which lies before the pupil as he works evidently needs to be modified for a good many school activities. The problem of storing books and other material which is solved in the ordinary school desk by a drawer in front of the pupil is being solved in the newer experiments in school seating by placing a drawer under the seat of the chair. This makes difficult the adjustment of the seat in height, but removes the desk from in front of the child where it is not needed for most of the activities of the school.

Public Interest in Vocational Education

No better evidence can be given of the public interest in educational problems than the large amount of newspaper space which is being devoted to the discussion of industrial education and its effects upon the general work of the school. The *Chicago Tribune* has been conducting during the past month a series of articles on industrial schools and their relation to the general school system. The Illinois legislature will be called upon during its present session to provide for industrial education throughout the state. In order that the opinion of all classes in regard to the best type of education may be secured, the *Tribune* has secured statements from professional educators, business men, philanthropic workers, and labor leaders.

There have been presented in these articles strong arguments in behalf of better child-labor legislation. There have been various suggestions for reforms in the elementary school. There have been pleas for prevocational courses and citations of the facts which make it clear that vocational education is necessary. It is hardly necessary to review all of these matters which are well understood by educational readers. One statement which is characteristic of a type of thinker not always heard in educational discussions may be singled out for special reference. It is the statement which was made by Mr. Edwin R. Wright on December 29. Mr. Wright is the president of the Illinois Federation of Labor and his statement presents in a very vivid way the attitude of a labor leader on the whole problem of education. He says:

> The worker demands industrial education. . . . . The present agitation is not the work of enthusiastic schoolmasters or of long-haired altruists. It is not even new. The great correspondence schools are not philanthropic but business institutions. For years the worker has striven to help himself to a

better understanding of his craft and to a higher wage. He desires to master the calling he expects to follow as his life-work. He knows he never will as an individual own the factory or shop or mine in which he works, but he may become foreman or even superintendent, and he is willing to work for the position.

There is much in the article which is of no immediate significance to the school officer; but a clear expression of skepticism with regard to the efficiency of present school organization appears in such passages as the following:

> If I stopped here I would be classed as a common scold or a wooden-headed labor skate, but I don't propose to stop before I present the larger view generally held by the workers and try to carry their ideas to a more fitting conclusion.
>
> Education is out of joint. We know it, and judging from the columns of space given the subject just now nearly everyone has a remedy of some kind. After 600 words of assorted gibberish, a writer in New York informs the readers of a downstate paper that the schools of Illinois are ideal. He is a schoolbook man. For him the schools are ideal.
>
> Everything of any value must be paid for. We workers expect to pay for vocational schools, but from now on we want better value for our money. We are losing faith in politician, business man, and schoolmaster. Here in Illinois we pay a dollar a week for every child in school. Other states have just as good schools for much less money. Why so, Mr. Politician?

Without continuing to quote from this article of Mr. Wright's we may conclude that these paragraphs furnish evidence of the general interest of everyone in the problem of school efficiency.

School of Industrial Arts, of Trenton, N.J.

The school of industrial arts of Trenton, N.J., is supported jointly by the state of New Jersey and the city of Trenton. Its purpose is to provide instruction for students of all ages and interests and its aim is to develop and improve the industries of the state through the training of skilled laborers in all branches of industrial art. The school offers 46 separate courses of study. These courses are conducted during the day and in the evening so as to be accessible to workers in the factories and shops in the city as well as to students who devote their whole time to study.

The institution began in the evening mechanical drawing school conducted by Joseph Crampton for ten years previous to 1898.

This evening mechanical drawing school was supported by the Board of Education. In 1897 the mayor of Trenton appointed a committee to consider plans for the enlargement of this class into an art school. On April 4, 1898, the school was opened on its present general plan. It has at the present time a large independent equipment and the variety of its courses can be seen from the following selected titles taken from its catalogue. Courses are given in: free-hand drawing, figure composition, costume designing, bookbinding, mechanical drawing, pottery painting, architectural drawing, general chemistry, applied electricity, English, millinery, applied physics, domestic art, etc.

By a combination with the State Normal School situated at Trenton, normal courses are offered to those who wish to become teachers in schools. Through this combination the school is able to issue a certificate which will be recognized by the state department of education.

CONTROL OF THE INDUSTRIAL SCHOOLS OF GERMANY

F. W. ROMAN
University of South Dakota[1]

The direction and government of industrial education in Germany does not come under the jurisdiction of the empire, but is left to the several states. Nevertheless, indirectly, imperial legislation has had a great influence in forwarding industrial education (Lexis, *Das technische Unterrichtswesen*, pp. 17–25).

The main point of this imperial legislation lies in Section 120 of the *Reichsgewerbeordnung*, which provides that the school districts or communes *may* compel boys under the age of eighteen years to attend an industrial or commercial school. The same provision may be made to apply to girls of the same age, if they are engaged in commerical or clerical work. Parents who refuse to send the children are subject to a fine. Attendance upon a guild school or other continuation school will not free the pupil from attending the school established under this law, unless the instruction given has been sanctioned as at least equal in grade and quantity to that in the regular school. Employers are obliged to give workers under eighteen years of age the necessary time to attend such schools.

Most states have additional legislation which is much more comprehensive and mandatory than the above-mentioned *Reichsgewerbeordnung.*

The question, What authority shall control these schools? has been variously answered. The table on the following page shows the departments that now control in the states named.

We see that the three states, Prussia, Saxony, and Hessen, have a dual school organization, that is, the public schools are under a different state department from the ones indicated in the table.

[1] In view of the discussions which are going on in the United States of the methods of organizing industrial education Mr. Roman's discussion is very timely. Professor Roman is an economist and sociologist and recently completed at the University of Berlin an exhaustive study of German industrial schools.—EDITOR.

The other three, Bavaria, Würtemberg, and Baden, have put the trade schools in charge of the state department of education, which also controls the public schools.

State	Department of the State	Division of This Department	Local Control
Prussia.............	Ministry of Commerce and Industry	Permanent Commission of Industrial Education	Trade-school director
Bavaria............	Ministry of Schools and Churches	....	Directors of the higher schools and district-school inspectors
Saxony.............	Ministry of Interior	....	Trade-school inspector
Würtemberg........	Ministry of Education	Commission of Industrial Education	....
Baden.............	Ministry of Education	Trade-school supervisor	Trade-school inspector
Hessen.............	Ministry of Interior	Trade Bureau	Trade-school inspector

In Würtemberg, the commission which has local control of the industrial schools must always have the director of the public schools as one of its members, and that means that he practically controls both trade and public schools. As director of the public schools, he has a life-position, and consequently a permanent place on the trade-school commission.

In Baden, the arrangement is very much the same.

In Bavaria, the director of the high schools and the district-school inspector have direct charge of the industrial schools. This accounts for the fact that Dr. Kerschensteiner has been able to bring Munich to the front in trade-school development. Being in charge of both the public schools and the trade schools, he has been able to do a great deal in the public school which prepares the pupils for their future trade-school work. There has been no time wasted in having two types of schools fighting each other.

So far as any one city comes into consideration, Munich leads all Germany in its trade-school development, both in efficiency and in the number of boys and girls reached by the system. Munich is a great argument for a united school system!

So far as whole states come into consideration, Würtemberg and Baden lead. They were the first to develop such schools, and are still leading in efficiency of organization, number of boys and girls in attendance per capita population, and also in amount of money spent. It seemed to me the Germans were quite unanimous in this conclusion. This again is due in no small degree to the united action for which the school organization provides.

In Prussia, we find a unique situation which must be changed before decided advancement can be made in further trade-school development. The Ministry for Schools and Churches which controls the public schools is always headed by a theologian, that is, a man who has gone through a theological seminary, and has had long experience as pastor and officer in church circles. For this reason the public-school system is very conservative in all that it teaches. Religion as a study in the curriculum is strictly insisted upon for one hour per day throughout the school course.

In 1884 the industrial schools of Prussia were transferred from the Ministry of Schools and Churches to the Ministry of Commerce and Industry. This move represented one of Bismarck's successful efforts to get something completely out of the hands of the clergy, with whom he usually quarreled. Industrial education has made some great strides since the establishment of the dual organization, but only in so far as it has been possible to develop under the legislation which was in force at the time of separation. The dropping of religion from the curriculum, and the emphasizing of the practical rather than the "bookish" studies offended the clerical party. This, in turn, has resulted in a constant warfare between the two factions ever since. Up to the present time Prussia has not been able to get legislation making industrial education compulsory except for the provinces of West Prussia and Posen. The two parties cannot agree on the question of religion. Both parties want to make attendance compulsory from the ages of fourteen to seventeen. The clerical party wants a guaranty that one hour per week shall be given over to their hands for religious instruction. The other party claims that religious teaching has no place in a trade school. As it is now, only the districts or communes can make attendance compulsory. The result is that for the most part Prussia has only voluntary trade-school attendance.

Is it desirable to have the dual organization which now exists in Prussia? Does specialization of work and aims justify a separate trade school board? Herr Director Haese of the Charlottenburg-Berlin trade schools, and Herr Director Haumann of the Berlin trade schools gave answers to these questions, which may be considered typical of the opinion of numbers of teachers whom I interviewed.

Under normal conditions a dual organization would not be the best. However, for Prussia, both men favored the separation, but both made it quite clear that they favored separation only because it keeps them out of the control of the clergy and makes it possible to use the hour formerly devoted to religion to some trade or literary study. By continuing the fight long enough, they hope to get compulsory trade education for Prussia without being dominated by the influence of the clergy.

Both stated emphatically that as far as trade-school efficiency itself is concerned, it would be better to have but one board of control. Two public-school systems in the same city create jealousy. This divides the interests of the people, since much energy which ought to be used constructively is constantly being wasted in dealing with controversial matters. A dual organization tends to create a feeling of class division in society, thus undermining democracy. There is a lack of co-operation between the schools while a united system could do much in the grades toward paving the way for trade schools. Teachers in the public schools which are under the control of the clergy, and teachers in the trade schools which are under domination hostile to the clergy, find themselves in a relation which makes co-operation difficult or impossible. If there were only one organization, the same plant could be utilized to much better advantage. A certain amount of the trade-school work must necessarily be done in the evening, the day-school teachers must be employed to some extent, because it is not always possible to get two full corps of teachers. This renders it necessary for the trade-school board to make terms with the day-school board. There is always more or less trouble growing out of these arrangements. The day-school teachers who teach in the evening trade schools are under two boards and this proves to be a constant source of trouble. The present type of organization is unnecessarily expensive, because there are duplications in the work as well as in equipment. Even the officers have to be duplicated. Thus there are two directors' salaries to be paid. One such officer could often do the work more efficiently for the community than it is being done by two directors.

A SEVEN-YEAR ELEMENTARY SCHOOL

OFFICERS OF THE SCHOOL OF EDUCATION
University of Chicago

The Elementary School of the University of Chicago has been working for some years on the problem of saving the time of the pupils so that they may enter the High School at an earlier period than has been the custom in the regular eight-year course which has up to this time been administered in this school. It is evident to all students of education that in one way or another time is wasted, or at least not as well spent as it might be. Teachers realizing that they have more time than is required to cover a given amount of work relax somewhat in their instruction and the class is less well instructed than it might be. Lack of activity on the part of the pupils is then interpreted as due to the difficulty of the course and further reduction of the requirements follows until the rate of intellectual movement in the upper grades is distinctly slow. This manifests itself in many schools in an error which everyone tries to avoid but is likely to fall into either in the elementary school or in the first year of high school, namely the error of excessive reviewing. In the case of the University schools there was undoubtedly repetition in several of the high-school courses of matter and methods which had been adequately taken up in the elementary schools. In some other schools excessive reviewing appears in the seventh grade. This reviewing is repeated in the early part of the eighth grade, and the latter half of the eighth grade is very commonly given over to a general review of the work that has been done in the elementary school, in preparation for the high school. All this reviewing, even where it has been consciously carried out, seems to be regarded as ineffective, for as soon as the student enters the high school, he finds himself dealing, as indicated above, in many of the subjects, with materials and methods which he has canvassed before in the elementary school. The natural result of such repetition is that the student manifests no interest in the work that is offered to him in the first year of the high school because he has already become acquainted with it in the upper grades of the grammar school.

If it is urged that this reviewing is necessary on the principle that the elementary work must be done with great care so as to avoid any possibility of failure in the high school, there is double reason for the contention that the high school must recognize exactly what has been accomplished in the elementary grades, and the teachers in the high school ought to be called upon to take advantage immediately of all of the preparation which the children have for advanced work. The fact is, however, that high schools and elementary schools very often have little or no articulation. For example, a committee of the National Council of English Teachers declared the problem of relating elementary English to high-school English to be a new and unsolved problem. It is evident to the student of education that in most schools students bear the burden of maladjustment in these matters. The elementary school is overanxious and overburdened with strict supervision, while the high school is neglectful of its duties. The student is made to repeat unnecessarily and is left in a bewildered state of mind because the teachers have not worked out an adjustment.

It was the belief that the school could work out the relation more efficiently that prompted the University schools to attack the problem of economy. Teachers in the High School were called into conference with the teachers in the later years of the Elementary School, and the matter of each of the different subjects was canvassed in detail in order to find out exactly what was being done in the seventh grade and in the eighth grade and in the first year of the High School, and how far all the different lines of work were interrelated.

It should be noted perhaps at the outset that the program of the Elementary School is somewhat fuller than the ordinary program in public schools of elementary grade. For example, all of the children of the University Elementary School take one foreign language beginning with the fourth or fifth grade. The result is that each pupil arrives at the eighth grade with some speaking knowledge of either French or German, according as he may have elected to take the one language or the other during his elementary course. Furthermore, it may be pointed out that the Elementary School gives a good deal of attention to nature-study. Work in the garden alternates with studies in physics, hygiene, general zoölogy, and botany. This type of work is cultivated to a degree unusual in elementary schools. In like fashion, a good deal of emphasis is laid on the cultivation of skill through manual arts and the development of knowledge of the industries. Sewing, weaving, and constructive work are taught in the lower grades; the girls are given more complete courses in sewing in the upper grades, while the boys take shopwork; both boys and girls take printing in the upper grades. In short, the effort to economize time is not to be confused with any effort to reduce the elementary course to its lowest possible terms in point of content. The undertaking is to be described rather by saying that the school is organized to include all that can legitimately be included in an elementary education. Its full content is then to be administered in such a way as to save as much time as can be saved by the best possible organization. It should be explicitly noted, therefore, that the reduction of time involves no curtailment of the various extra lines of work. The work in foreign language, in science, and in handwork is recognized as altogether as important as other lines of work in the school; and it was understood from the outset that if the reduction of time was to be legitimately made, it must be made in such a way as not to jeopardize the interests of these special subjects. The whole attention of the school was concentrated upon the problem of a more effective correlation of the two schools without depriving the students of anything.

The type of economy which it was the aim of the school to secure can best be illustrated by referring to the various subjects of instruction. Thus, the High-School teachers did not find it easily possible to take advantage of the training which had been given in the Elementary School in modern languages. The German teachers and the French teachers of the High School held that the kind of work which had been done in the Elementary School did not correspond exactly to the work that had been done in the High

School in the first-year course. They found therefore that students who came from the Elementary School could not be admitted to the second year of the High-School classes without interfering in some degree with the ordinary organization of the courses. The organization was therefore inhospitable to the child. The pupil had done such work as was required of him, but little or no recognition could be given to the elementary work by the High-School departments because their organization did not connect directly with the elementary work. A second example of failure to articulate appears in the science work. For a long time the students from the Elementary School were put into the same kind of science work as children who came to the High School from elementary schools where less attention had been given to science. Again, elementary manual training was given in the High School and was required of all, including those who had done similar work in the University Elementary School.

It would have been altogether disastrous to the organization of the two schools to have made any sudden move. In the first place, the teachers who would have been involved in any such sudden arrangement would not have had time to adjust their work, and the children would have experienced the ill effects of an experiment for which the teaching corps had relatively little sympathy. The first step therefore was to bring together the various members of different departments, and to establish relations which would make it easily possible for the High-School teachers and the Elementary-School teachers to look at the problem from the same point of view. For example, the modern-language teachers were called upon to examine each other's work and to suggest any modifications that were necessary in order to allow the children to pass directly from the elementary work into the advanced stages of the work in the High School. Indeed, certain forms of organization were undertaken to make this transition easy. It was said, for example, that children who come from the Elementary School are somewhat less mature than the children who have passed through the first year of high school. For two years, therefore, the children who came from the Elementary School, and had taken a good deal of German, have been allowed to do a small amount of German during the first year of the High School until they should obtain the maturity supposed to be necessary in order to make it possible for them to stand on an exact equality with the students in the second year of the High School. This compromise organization is on the whole not very satisfactory, but it furnishes a method of passing without shock from the general inco-ordination with which the organization started to the final arrangement in which it hoped the adjustment will be complete. In the meantime the teacher of the Elementary School has been called upon to give some of the work in the first year of the High School, and modifications have gradually been made in the work of both the Elementary School and the first year of the High School until there seems to be reasonable promise of a complete co-ordination.

The English departments of the two schools were asked to meet together and to canvass in detail all of the work given in the eighth grade and the work given in the first year of the High School. This careful study of the problem very soon brought out the result that both schools were dealing with the same type of material, and in much the same fashion. Only very slight modifications were necessary in order to justify the promotion of the children who had done the work of the eighth grade in the Elementary School directly into the second year of the High School. This promotion into the second year of the High School avoided all of the repetitions that had formerly been committed in the first year of the High School.

So far as science was concerned, it was very simple to allow the children from the Elementary School to omit the first-year science course. In the University High School this first-year science course is a general course dealing with phenomena that are at once physical and biological. The problem of giving credit for this science course is perhaps not as simple as the problem of giving credit in the other departments, but the permission, indeed the requirement, to omit the first year of science in the High School has been put into full operation.

The discussion of manual training led to a modification of the course as administered in the High School, so that now elementary handwork is not required of first-year children who have had such work in the Elementary School. This readjustment is generally advantageous, because not only the University Elementary School, but many other schools also, are introducing enough handwork to justify a somewhat more advanced type of work when the pupils enter the first year of the High School.

The problem of mathematics was somewhat more complicated. The traditional division between arithmetic and algebra, which marks the boundary line between the elementary and the high school, is not so easy to transcend. There can be very little doubt to the mind of the careful observer that this traditional division is not justified by the needs of pupils. A great deal of the work that is done in arithmetic in the Elementary School in the later years is valuable merely because it presents complicated opportunities for developing reasoning processes in the children. As a training in mathematics these problems are of very doubtful value. They involve only the relatively simpler mathematical processes, and these mathematical processes are imbedded in a situation which must be visualized and disentangled before the student can properly apply what he knows about arithmetical operations. It would be very much more educative, in many cases, to solve these complicated problems that are given in arithmetic by algebraical formulas. For example, if a symbol of the unknown quantity could be employed in the calculations, the method of solving the problem would be better from the point of view of the child's development. If the principles of solving the equation were understood, the solution of many an arithmetical problem would be rendered very easy. Yet there is a strong tradition against the introduction of the unknown quantity and the simpler methods of solving equations into the elementary-school course. From time to time algebra has been taught in the upper grades of some elementary school only to be timidly dropped because of the anxiety of someone about the traditions of elementary education. In spite of reason the high school has accordingly kept its hold on algebra and its methods. In the same way, geometry has traditionally been the property of the high school. Little by little the elementary school has been introducing certain constructive problems which deal with the simpler properties of space, but even here it has not been regarded as heretical to call such work by the name of geometry because geometry has always been given as a high-school course.

The experiment in the University Elementary School proceeded therefore very cautiously in this matter of mathematics. The mathematical work usually required of the eighth grade was completed in due form. Last year, with an eighth grade that had advanced well in matters mathematical, a certain amount of high-school work was tentatively undertaken, and it was found that the eighth grade could take, in addition to its regular arithmetic, approximately half a year of high-school work in algebra and geometry. It should be said that the mathematical course given in the University High School consists of certain algebraical and geometrical problems which are worked out together. Exactly the same course was followed with the eighth grade. In order to corroborate the judgment of the instructors that the eighth grade had done the work satisfactorily, a test prepared by the High-School department was given at the end of the half-year course. This test was just the same as the test which was administered at the same stage to the classes in the High School; furthermore the papers were graded by the instructors in the High School, and the eighth-grade children succeeded in the tests fully as well as the High-School children had succeeded. There was a good deal of enthusiasm in the class for the work, and the general result upon the children of the whole experiment has been very gratifying. They have been willing to work, and they have shown enthusiasm about the progress which has interested their instructors as well as themselves. They have gone on in the High School this year with unabated success.

This year's eighth-grade class is doing from the first practically high-school mathematics, with the result that at the end of this year the present eighth grade will have, instead of half a year's mathematics to its credit, practically all of the first-year high-school work.

Such an adjustment as has been described in mathematics is not altogether satisfactory. The changes ought to be made farther down in the elementary course, and it is hoped that the work may proceed from this point in such fashion that in the sixth and seventh grades certain mathematical formulas that have always been given in algebra shall be gradually introduced. The use of co-ordinate paper and co-ordinate sections on the blackboard has long been common in the elementary course in mathematics. There is no reason why this should not be enlarged to the point of including a good deal of material that is ordinarily presented in geometry. In other words, the work in mathematics will gradually but certainly be worked over so as to articulate very much more intimately the work of the elementary school with that of the high school. There will ultimately be no break which has to be bridged over by the study of high-school mathematics in the eighth grade.

There are two eighth-grade subjects which are not fully dealt with in the preceding paragraphs. These are history and geography. A certain amount of history is commonly taught in the eighth grade. There is also a completion of the work in geography. If these two subjects are entirely omitted, the elementary course is likely to be incomplete, and if, on the other hand, they are carried up into the high school, they raise a number of questions which are not commonly understood by first-year teachers of the high school. Thus we find very few high-school classes which have any general geography. This practice, however, of completing geography in the elementary school is peculiar to the United States. If one visits European institutions one finds that geography is a respectable science which has its place in university classes and in the upper years of the secondary schools. There is no reason at all why we should not consider as part of our American readjustment the problem of putting into the high school a certain amount of geography. Indeed, such a change in the high-school course is advocated in many meetings of teachers of science. If the history taught in higher institutions is to be made intelligent, it is very clear that there ought to be some review of the geography which has been studied in the elementary school. At the present time the geography which finds its place in some high-school courses is a form of physical geography, strictly related to the science of geology. That there should be some general earth science in the high school is recognized widely enough to command serious attention, and the suggestion which ought to be carried out in some form or other is that there is such a readjustment of the elementary-school geography that there shall be no loss to the individual pupil from the ultimate omission of the present eighth-grade course.

Again, with regard to history, the problem is one of general readjustment. At the present time the eighth grade in the University Elementary School is carrying on the history and geography which have been for some years usual in this grade. The result is a program which is somewhat heavier than the program of students who are doing similar work in the first year of the High School. The heavy program is an incident of readjustment, however, and will probably be avoided in the future.

As a matter of administrative convenience, all of the readjustments which have been described above have been made without changing in any way the designations of the classes of pupils concerned. That is, up to this time the eighth grade has been continued as an elementary-school class. Children who have succeeded in doing the work in modern language, English, etc., have been passed into the second year of the High School, and there have been allowed to go forward with high-school work, taking advanced credits for the work which they did in the Elementary School.

There is no final reason why the first year of the High School should be circumvented in this way rather than that the eighth grade be abolished. Indeed, there are many reasons why it would be advantageous to omit the eighth grade and allow the children to begin their work with the regular course of the High School. It is planned for next year that the eighth grade shall be entirely omitted. The seventh-grade children will be promoted directly into the first year of the High School, and will carry on the work which is this year being done in the eighth grade, in the first-year class of the High School. This decision needs perhaps to be defended in detail. The purely local considerations are of no great importance. It is essential that the question be faced in some general form. In the effort to deal in a general way with the whole matter, considerations of the following type are of importance. Is the eighth grade in its organization and in its method of conduct of work more like the high-school class or more like the general elementary course? Do the students gain any social and personal advantages by being classified as high-school students, which they would miss if they continued to be members of the elementary school?

The considerations which led the officers of the University schools to decide on the abolition of the eighth grade are as follows: First of all, the general departmental type of work which has been carried on for years in the eighth grade is of the high-school type. Students have been brought into contact with special teachers for each of the subjects in the upper grades, and this type of instruction seems to give the highest degree of efficiency. The student is mature enough so that he is not crippled by his lack of continuous contact with his instructor. Furthermore, this departmental type of organization makes it possible to defer in some degree to the special needs of the individual child. It is possible, in other words, to introduce some elective opportunity which will differentiate the course and adjust it somewhat more readily to the interests of the individual. Sometimes a child falls behind in a single subject. If the elementary type of organization continues, it is extremely difficult to carry him forward in his other subjects because of this single deficiency, whereas in the high school a deficiency in a single subject is not very serious for the general organization of the student's program. Apart therefore from the general advantages of election there is the possibility of adjusting the student's work in detail, and this adjustment is more readily carried on under the formula of high-school instruction than it is under the general formula of elementary organization. Indeed, the upper grades are even now, although they remain in the elementary schools, taking on the freer form of organization which makes election possible.

Again there are many considerations which tend to attach the children of the upper years of the elementary school to the adolescent group as distinguished from the elementary group. A general social consciousness and a desire for the simpler forms of social life which are known in the high school and are cultivated by adolescent children, begin to appear in students of the eighth grade. There is no reason at all why such students should not, under careful supervision, be allowed to share in some of the larger liberties which are accorded to high-school students as distinguished from students in the elementary school. The interest that is aroused in the minds of these students who are just beginning to realize their social opportunities and obligations is also a distinct advantage in stimulating them to do better and more elaborate work. They can be thrown on their own responsibility with more definite consciousness on their own part and on the part of the teacher, that they are to be held responsible for their own conduct and for their social organization. They can be relied upon to organize more fully their home work. They can be appealed to in a variety of ways because of the classification which is accorded to them, whereas if they were continued in the elementary school they would feel on the whole more dependent than they do as members of the high-school community.

From the point of view of the instructorial organization also, it is doubtless advantageous for the students to be classified in the high school. They come in contact more frequently with men, and this is a distinct advantage, especially for the boys.

The question immediately arises whether this process of economy and condensation can legitimately be carried a step farther than it has been carried in the University Elementary School.

In reply to the question thus raised, it may be said that the effort of the Elementary School has not been in this case to work out to its final stages the whole experiment of readjustment. The effort which has attracted the attention and interest of the officers of the University schools up to this point is the effort to co-ordinate the work of the two schools. It is a mere accident that a single grade, rather than a grade and a half, has been eliminated as a result of this experiment. Perhaps the condensation of the course can go farther. It is the judgment of those who are in closest contact with this experiment that it is probably not desirable to attempt to reduce any further the time spent on the subjects discussed up to this point. If there is lack of economy in the High-School organization from this point on, that lack of economy can probably be corrected most advantageously by a fusion between the High School and the Junior College similar to that which has been worked out between the Elementary School and the High School. Whether or not the seventh grade should be classified with the High School or the Elementary School is another question not to be confused with the question of economy. That detail of organization may or may not be worked out by reducing the Elementary School to a six-year school. The work which is now done in the seventh grade will undoubtedly have to be done somewhere, and in much the same form in which it is now done. If that can be carried on better by High-School officers and under the classification of the students in the High School, there is certainly no objection to this new type of organization. If this change in the classification of the seventh grade were made, no such opportunity for further economy of time and energy on the part of pupils as that which has been recognized in the present readjustment of the University Elementary School is likely to be discovered. From the point of view therefore of economy, the present experiment may be regarded as fairly closed. From the point of view of the possible reorganization of the Elementary School, the present experiment does not aim to be at all definitive. It may be desirable to work over this organization much more completely than it is worked over at the present time, but any such administrative readjustment of the Elementary School and the High School will in no wise affect the conclusion of the present experiment. One year has been saved. Whatever the classification, or whatever the type of organization ultimately adopted, this saving of a single year is a definite and final economy which will operate to the advantage of the student, whatever the form of organization through which he passes.

The suggestion has been offered above that a similar economy can be effected in the High School. This is not the proper place in which to discuss this economy, but it cannot be repeated with too great emphasis that the failure to recognize the possibilities of economy usually grows out of the fact that two different institutions are organized under different managements and with different faculties. The one great virtue of this particular experiment is that it calls attention to the fact that a conference between teachers who have to deal with the same children will very frequently bring out opportunities of economy that would be entirely lost sight of if these conferences were not held. It is also to be noted that the children feel, somewhat vaguely perhaps, this lack of economy. Indeed, it is frequently true that the lack of enthusiasm on the part of the children is the best possible indication that the school organization is defective. That teachers should be slow to discover the significance of these symptoms that appear in the listless children who refuse to be enthusiastic about reviews is simply another indication of the necessity of a careful and complete survey of the work of every instructor, giving him an opportunity to place his own individual task in the general light of all the educational activities which surround his own individual work. The eighth-grade teacher may have done his work conscientiously, but until he recognizes that it is his duty to carry the children forward as far as it is possible for them legitimately to go, he has not done his whole duty. This full duty may carry him into the domain of the high school. This should not deter him from the utmost efforts to economize the time of the pupils. The gravest menace to our school organization is that which grows out of the fact that all work of one type is terminated at the end of the eighth grade, and begins anew in an entirely different environment and with an entirely different set of officers in the first year of the high school. To transcend these limitations of institutional organization is one of the opportunities of the teacher who recognizes the fact that economy of the children's energy and time is more significant than any of the traditions of present-day school organization.

OBSERVATIONS CONCERNING THE ORGANIZATION OF SCHOOLS AND CERTAIN PHASES OF EDUCATIONAL WORK IN GERMANY. III

GEORGE KOEPPEL
Principal Twenty-first Street School, Milwaukee, Wis.

REFORM OF SCHOOL SYSTEMS

In all discussions concerning school reforms two leading ideas constantly recur and are emphasized by educators of the foremost rank.

First, the *growing necessity of raising the efficiency of the individual*, because the development of modern life, especially of the industrial conditions, makes excessive demands upon the nations who are leaders in culture and human progress, and because no people can hope to retain its place in the march of civilization or to attain supremacy in culture, unless all educational factors are so modified and intensified as to give each individual that training which will lead to the fullest development of which his innate powers are capable.

The second idea depends upon the first. If every individual is to be educated to greatest efficiency, *elementary school systems*, schools, and classes *must be organized and graded according to the mental and physical ability of pupils.* This ability varies greatly in children of the same age on account of the inherited mental and physical endowment; and these innate variations are increased, especially in large cities, by the numerous and divers economic and social conditions surrounding the children, and by the constant shifting of the population.

The failure that resulted from attempting to teach pupils of such widely different powers together in one class caused the *reconstruction of school systems on the basis of differentiation of pupils according to their ability.* These systems are so organized that they comprise: (1) schools for pupils of average ability; (2) schools for pupils who have failed to do the regular grade work; (3) schools for backward children (*Hilfsschulen*); (4) schools for pupils who have shown unusual ability, diligence, and moral conduct; (5) a school for feeble-minded pupils.

The separation of feeble-minded children in institutions and of backward children in *Hilfsschulen* had been so long established and the resulting benefits were so apparent, that the abovementioned further steps in the classification of the so-called normal children easily suggested themselves.

Some of the most progressive cities in Germany have succeeded in carrying this educational reform to a high degree of perfection and educators throughout Germany are discussing the system and its possible improvements and modifications most seriously. Men of the highest rank and of international reputation, as Professor Rein of Jena, regard this organization as fundamental for all future uplift of popular education.

While there are variations in details of execution in various cities, the organization of the Mannheim public schools may be considered a model of its type and will therefore be briefly discussed.

The elementary schools (*Volksschulen*) of Mannheim were attended last year by 22,677 pupils, which number does not include the pupils who attended the higher elementary schools (*Bürgerschulen*, tuition fee charged) nor the pupils of the higher types of schools.

It should be distinctly understood that the organization here to be outlined is that of the lowest class of schools, the free elementary *Volksschule*.

The city is divided into six school districts, each containing six schools. One or two of these schools in each district are central schools where all pupils of that district who are members of the special system of classes to be mentioned are brought together.

The pupils who are able to pursue the prescribed course of study with success are promoted through eight grades and form the *main system*. The membership of these classes is *45 pupils*.

Those who are unusually backward are transferred to the school for the feeble-minded or to the *Hilfsschulen*, the latter being organized in some of the central district schools. These special help schools have before been described; the *membership of each class is from 14 to 18 pupils*.

The weaker pupils of the main system who have not reached the aim of the class and fail of promotion because of lack of ability, sickness, laziness, or other cause, are transferred to special classes called *Förderklassen*. These are also centralized and organized in one of the buildings of each school district. The *membership of these classes is 30 pupils*, and the system consists naturally of seven grades, the lowest containing the pupils of the first grade of the main system who could not do the grade work satisfactorily in a year.

This system of *Förderschulen* was composed last year of 93 classes with 2,764 pupils, an average of nearly 30 pupils to the class. On account of the small number of children in each class the opportunity of giving them individual attention is considerably increased, and it was originally expected by the advocates of this system that pupils could be so trained in these special classes that they might be promoted to the higher *main* class at the end of the year. The superintendent of the Mannheim schools, Dr. Sickinger, the chief promoter of this reform, was an ardent believer in the doctrine that these slower pupils could be advanced to a degree that would enable them to keep step with the pupils of the regular classes. Experience has, however, definitely demonstrated that conditions which are beyond the reach of the teachers render such success impossible. Only 131 of the 2,764 could be promoted to the higher grades of the *main* system, 125 failed completely, while the great body of about 2,500 were promoted to the next higher class within the same system. Dr. Sickinger reports in regard to this experience that—

> It *again* shows that the majority of the pupils [of the *Förder* system] is merely able to progress *within this system*, and that a small number (125), in spite of the improved conditions, could not even succeed in this. Certainly it is evident that the attainment of the requirements of the regular course of study is *a matter of impossibility* for the pupils of the *Förderschulen*. As the result of this conviction, the preparation of a *special course of study* adapted to the needs of these schools has become a necessity.

The considerations that led to the establishment of a special system of *Förderklassen* parallel to the regular schools have more recently resulted in a separation of the best pupils of the four upper grades of the main system, and to the organization of these classes of select pupils into schools. This reform logically followed from the application of the fundamental idea of the Mannheim system that "all educational agencies must be adapted to the individual capacity of the pupil." Since special schools, special courses, and special teaching had been found just and beneficial for various types of children *below* average ability, it was only fair to make special provision for the more extensive and intensive training of those children who surpass the average pupils of the regular classes in mental endowment, vigor, diligence, and moral conduct.

Those children who have given evidence of these qualifications during the first four years of their school life are admitted to these special schools and receive in the four upper grades the same instruction that is given in the higher elementary schools (the *Bürgerschulen*). It is evident that rapid progress and thoroughness of work is possible in these classes composed of the best pupils selected from a number of the surrounding district schools. The course of study for these select schools is enriched by increasing the subject-matter in arithmetic and geometry, in elementary physics, chemistry, and nature-study, and by the addition of four hours of French each week.

The *select pupils* of the fifth grades are taught in their respective schools, but those of the sixth, seventh, and eighth grades are brought together from a larger territory and are formed into classes that are *organized into schools in centrally located buildings*.

It is only fair to mention here that while the other features of the Mannheim system have found general recognition, the practice of removing the best from the less gifted pupils of a class is a matter of question much debated in educational circles of Germany.

The horizontal differentiation of pupils of the same grade in the Mannheim elementary schools and the resulting interrelations of the four parallel systems described above are synoptically expressed in the scheme shown on p. 291. This system can easily be varied to suit local conditions, and other cities have introduced it with such modifications. The results obtained have been declared very satisfactory by government inspectors and educators of rank.

Wonders cannot be worked by any system, but proper organization can supply such conditions that permit placing children where the instruction, the subject-matter, and all other educational factors are adapted to their ability. While these arrangements are in themselves of great benefit to the pupils, they prepare the way for another great advantage that cannot be overrated. The teacher is relieved of much strain and anxiety and saves much

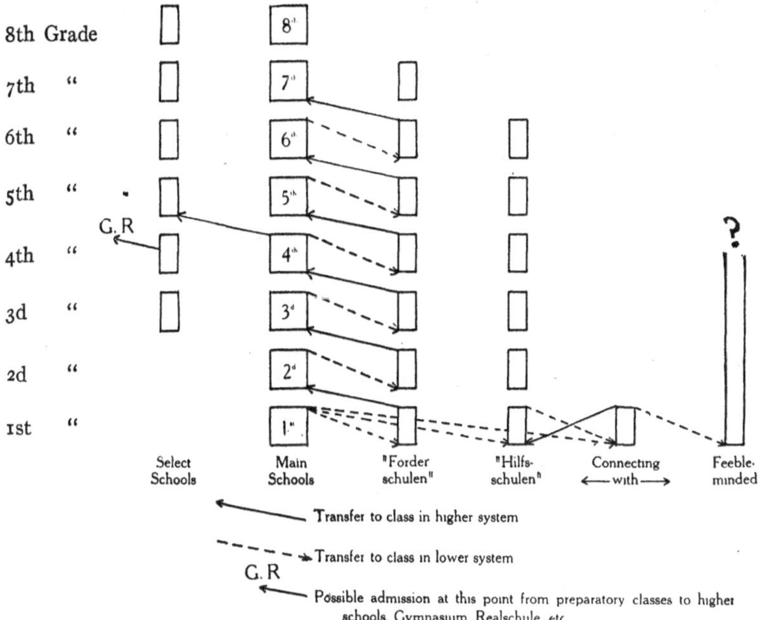

nervous energy by the exclusion of those pupils who are not properly members of his group and who are a burden to him and to his class. The improved conditions reduce the chances of irritation and consequently conserve the energy and enhance the cheerfulness of the teacher; and cheerfulness is fundamental to an educator's success.

Differentiation of pupils according to ability and centralization of differentiated classes to form schools of their kind are the keynotes of the success of this system.

CONTINUATION SCHOOLS

One of the greatest achievements in popular education in Germany is the extensive, systematic, and thorough provision for the continued training of boys and young men while they are employed in various trades and occupations. This training tends to raise the general efficiency of the young generation and is one of the factors of the surprising cultural and industrial progress of Germany. These schools are of various types and cover the whole field of industrial activity; they are in operation from early morning till night and even on Sunday. The simplest type is the obligatory continuation school that must be attended by all boys till they are at least seventeen years of age. From a somewhat extended district the boys are gathered and formed into classes according to their trade and at the same time according to their previous preparation. In the Berlin schools about one thousand classes with thirty thousand students were in operation last year in this type of school alone. Each class contains members of a certain trade only and the variety of occupations represented is very great. There are classes for bricklayers, masons, painters, carpenters, machinists, blacksmiths, tinsmiths, coppersmiths, precision mechanics, electro-mechanics, goldsmiths, tailors, bakers, confectioners, cooks, waiters, chimney-sweepers, and others. Among them were 149 classes of commercial apprentices with an attendance of 4,416.

The particular trade of the members of the class forms the basis and center of all instruction. While the work must of necessity have a cultural effect, it is planned to be of practical utility. All classes are taught the rights and duties of citizenship. The course comprises three years, in some places even four years. Each class attends school from six to nine hours a week, *not* in the evening but *during regular business hours*. At the beginning of a semester, the time for each class is fixed and the employers are notified. The apprentices are excused by their employers regularly and without fail. Sufficient time must be allowed them to go home and get ready for school, as they are expected to appear in class clean in person and dress. Attendance and deportment at these schools are very satisfactory. The discipline presents little difficulty as the teachers are efficient disciplinarians and are effectively supported and protected by law.

There was at first opposition to these *day* continuation schools on the part of employers, as these were unwilling to lose the services of their apprentices so many hours a week, but the increased efficiency and skill of the boys resulting from the training received at school gradually silenced the opposition, and now the great value of these schools is so generally recognized that the combined efforts of the government, the employers, and the educators are turned to the problems of highest practical efficiency.

The continuation schools for girls reinforce and broaden the training which the girls have received in the elementary schools, and are intended specially "to give intellectual stimulation toward gaining a serious view of life and to foster the desire and skill for woman's work." Besides the fundamental branches, the following subjects are taught: bookkeeping, commercial correspondence, commercial geography, typewriting, shorthand, drawing, designing, French, English; ironing, repairing of clothing, sewing, machine sewing, machine embroidering, cutting of undergarments, dressmaking, artistic fancy work, cooking, hygiene, dietetics, gymnastics, and singing. Special continuation schools are established for mentally backward youths and girls, for the deaf, and for the blind.

For ambitious young people schools of a higher type are in operation. In these the students may elect to study branches, or do practical work, not taught at the obligatory schools. Most of these secondary schools are evening and Sunday schools, and *all are crowded with students, although attendance at these schools does not exempt the student from the regular work in the obligatory schools.* The commercial schools of this type teach all the advanced commercial branches including commercial law, political economy, English, French, Italian, Spanish, and Russian.

[*To be continued*]

ANALYSIS OF COLBURN'S ARITHMETICS. V

WALTER S. MONROE
Kansas State Normal School

Colburn's treatment of percentage, interest, etc., is perhaps typical of his attitude toward the applications of arithmetic. On p. 28 of the *Sequel*, in sec. VII, on multiplication, this paragraph is given immediately preceding the first problem on interest:

Interest is a reward allowed by a debtor to a creditor for the use of money. It is reckoned by the hundred, hence the rate is called so much per cent or per centum. *Per centum* is Latin, signifying by the hundred. 6 per cent signifies 6 dollars on a hundred dollars, 6 cents on a hundred cents, £6 on £100, etc., so 5 per cent signifies 5 dollars on 100 dollars, etc. Insurance, commission, and premiums of every kind are reckoned in this way. Discount is so much per cent to be taken out of the principal.

Colburn evidently considers this sufficient explanation for such problems as the following, for he gives nothing additional either here or in Part II.

44. What is the interest of $43.00 for 1 year at 6 per cent?

47. What is the interest of $247.00 for 3 years at 7 per cent?

49. I imported some books from England, for which I paid $150.00 there. The duties in Boston were 15 per cent, the freight $5.00. What did the books cost me?

53. A merchant bought a quantity of goods for 243 dollars, and sold them so as to gain 15 per cent; how much did he gain, and how much did he sell them for?

The next mention of percentage is on p. 77, sec. XXIV. This problem is given:

119. A merchant sold a quantity of goods for $273.00, by which he gained 10 per cent on the first cost. How much did they cost?

Following the problem, is this note:

Note.—10 per cent is 10 dollars on a 100 dollars, that is, $\frac{10}{100}$. 10 per cent of the first cost therefore is $\frac{10}{100}$ of the first cost. Consequently $273.00 must be $\frac{110}{100}$ of the first cost.

A little farther on in the list we find the following problems and notes:

122. A merchant sold a quantity of goods for $983.00, by which he lost 12 per cent. How much did the goods cost and how much did he lose?

Note.—If he lost 12 per cent, that is $\frac{12}{100}$, he must have sold for $\frac{88}{100}$ of what it cost him.

124. A merchant sold a quantity of goods for $87.00 more than he gave for them, by which he gained 13 per cent of the first cost. How much did the goods cost him, and how much did he sell them for?

Note.—Since 13 per cent is $\frac{13}{100}$, $87.00 must be $\frac{13}{100}$ of the first cost.

130. A man having put a sum of money at interest at 6 per cent, at the end of 1 year received 13 dollars for interest. What was the principal?

Note.—Since 6 per cent is $\frac{6}{100}$ of the whole, 13 dollars must be $\frac{6}{100}$ of the principal.

132. A man put a sum of money at interest for 1 year, at 6 per cent, and at the end of the year he received for the principal and interest 237 dollars. What was the principal?

Note.—Since 6 per cent is $\frac{6}{100}$, if this be added to the principal it will make $\frac{106}{100}$, therefore $237 must be $\frac{106}{100}$ of the principal. When interest is added to the principal the whole is called the *amount.*

133. What sum of money put at interest at 6 per cent will gain $53 in 2 years?

Note.—6 per cent for 1 year will be 12 per cent for 2 years, 3 per cent for 6 months, 1 per cent for 2 months, etc.

138. Suppose I owe a man, $287 to be paid in one year without interest, and I wish to pay it now; how much ought I to pay him, when the usual rate is 6 per cent?

Note.—It is evident that I ought to pay him such a sum, as put at interest for 1 year will amount to $287. The question therefore is like those above. This is sometimes called *discount.*

Later in the sections on decimal fractions, special methods for interest are given in the same way, i.e., by means of a note following a problem which calls for a special method.

EDUCATIONAL PRINCIPLES RECOGNIZED. THE INDUCTIVE METHOD

In the titles of both his arithmetics,[1] Colburn explicitly states that the method of presentation is inductive rather than deductive. We have already alluded to the instruction of Colburn's time as being a drill in the manipulation of written symbols as opposed to oral instruction which he introduced. This "old system" was also deductive. The rule was given to the pupil in the beginning and he was expected to interpret it and apply it to problems. In

[1] The full titles of the texts in the later editions are: *First Lessons, Intellectual Arithmetic upon the Inductive Method of Instruction,* and *Arithmetic upon the Inductive Method of Instruction: Being a Sequel to Intellectual Arithmetic.* These titles are taken from editions of 1847 and 1828 respectively. Even his algebra has the title, *An Introduction to Algebra upon the Inductive Method of Instruction.*

some of the better texts the rule was followed by two or three problems worked by the rule and explained. The presentation of division quoted from the *Scholar's Arithmetic* on p. 31 is a typical illustration of the deductive method.

The inductive method which Colburn presented is the reverse of this. The way in which he develops the topics of arithmetic may be illustrated by his development of division in the *Sequel*.

In Part I, p. 32, he begins division with these problems:

1. How many oranges, at 6 cents apiece, can you buy for 36 cents?
2. How many barrels of cider, at 3 dollars a barrel, can be bought for 27 dollars?
3. How many bushels of apples, at 4 shillings a bushel, can you buy for 56 shillings?
4. How many barrels of flour, at 7 dollars a barrel, can you buy for 98 dollars?
5. How many dollars are there in 96 shillings?

The table of English money is given following problem 5, and the list is continued with problems of this type. These problems are such that the pupil probably was able to solve the first ones intuitively. The list consists of 128 problems of gradually increasing difficulty. The last 22 only are abstract and they are intended simply for drill.

In Part II, p. 142, which is to be studied with Part I, we find:

A boy having 32 apples wished to divide them equally among 8 of his companions; How many must he give them apiece?

If the boy were not accustomed to calculating, he would probably divide them, by giving one to each of the boys, and then another, and so on. But to give them one apiece would take 8 apples, and one apiece again would take 8 more, and so on. The question then is, to see how many times 8 may be taken from 32; or, which is the same thing, to see how many times 8 is contained in 32. It is contained four times. *Ans.* 4 each.

A boy having 32 apples was able to give 8 to each of his companions. How many companions had he?

This question, though different from the other, we perceive, is to be performed exactly like it. That is, it is the question to see how many times 8 is contained in 32. We take away 8 for one boy, and then 8 for another, and so on.

A man having 54 cents, laid them all out for oranges, at 6 cents apiece. How many did he buy?

It is evident that as many times as 6 cents can be taken from 54 cents, so many oranges can he buy. *Ans.* 9 oranges.

A man bought 9 oranges for 54 cents; how much did he give apiece?

In this example we wish to divide the number 54 into 9 equal parts, in the same manner as in the first question we wish to divide 32 into 8 equal parts. Let us observe, that if the oranges had been only one cent apiece, nine of them would come to 9 cents; if they had been 2 cents apiece, they would come to twice nine cents; if they had been 3 cents apiece, they would come to 3 times 9 cents, and so on. Hence the question is to see how many times 9 is contained in 54. *Ans.* 6 cents apiece.

In all the above questions the purpose was to see how many times a small number is contained in a larger one, and they may be performed by subtraction. If we examine them again we shall find also, that the question was, in the two first, to see what number 8 must be multiplied by, in order to produce 32; and in the third, to see what the number 6 must be multiplied by, to produce 54; in the fourth, to see what number 9 must be multiplied by, or rather what number must be multiplied by 9, in order to produce 54.

The operation by which questions of this kind are performed is called *division*. In the last example, 54, which is the number to be divided, is called the *dividend;* 9, which is the number divided by, is called the *divisor;* and 6, which is the number of times 9 is contained in 54, is called the *quotient.*

Mr. Colburn then goes on to tell how to prove division and following this takes up the case when the combination is not one that has occurred in the multiplication table.

At 3 cents apiece, how many pears may be bought for 57 cents?

It is evident that as many pears may be bought, as there are 3 cents in 57 cents. But the solution of this question does not appear so easy as the last, on account of the greater number of times which the divisor is contained in the dividend. If we separate 57 into two parts it will appear more easy.

$$57=30+27$$

We know by the table of Pythagoras[1] that 3 is contained in 30 ten times, and in 27 nine times, consequently it is contained in 57 nineteen times, and the answer is 19 pears.

This same method is explained for four more problems in which he points out how the breaking up of the dividend may be determined. He then continues:

It is not always convenient to resolve the number into parts in this manner at first, but we may do it as we perform the operation.

In 126 days how many weeks?

[1] Multiplication table.

Operation

126=70+56 Instead of resolving it in this manner, we will write it down as follows:

```
Dividend 126 (7 Divisor
          70
          __  __
          56  10
          56   8
          __  __
              18 quotient
```

I observe that 7 cannot be contained 100 times in 126, I therefore call the two first figures on the left 12 tens or 120, rejecting the 6 for the present. 7 is contained more than once and not so much as twice in 12, consequently in 12 tens it is contained more than 10 times and less than 20 times. I take 10 times 7 or 70 out of 126, and there remains 56. Then 7 is contained 8 times in 56, and 18 times in 126. *Ans.* 18 weeks.

From this the development is continued through four more problems, the last only being abstract and having a divisor of five digits. The rule is then stated, the last thing in the section.

MOTIVATION

The development of a motive by means of problems which especially appeal to children and by causing the child to feel a need for the process or definition before it is given to him is an important feature of both texts. The types of problems are well illustrated by those already given.

A feeling of need for the process is created by introducing each topic by problems. The very plan of dividing the texts into two parts and thus separating the problems from the development of the principles operates to create motive for the study of the principles. Even in the development of the principles, the rules are not stated until after the explanation of the operation which is itself based upon a problem. Whatever drill seems necessary is not given until after a considerable number of problems have been solved by the pupil. Colburn clearly states his attitude toward rules. He says:

> To succeed in this (i.e., teaching arithmetic to children), however, it is more necessary to furnish occasions for them to exercise their own skill in performing examples, rather than to give them rules.

But even these devices do not represent all that Colburn has done to motivate the arithmetic work. His style of writing and his ability to see things from the child's point of view assist materially in this respect. But the way he guides the learner in the development of the principles adds a touch of genius to the whole work. The following is from the *Sequel*, p. 168:

A boy wishes to divide $\frac{3}{4}$ of an orange equally between two other boys; how much must he give them apiece?

If he had 3 oranges to divide, he might give them 1 apiece, and then divide the other into two equal parts, and give one part to each, and each would have $1\frac{1}{2}$ orange. Or he might cut them all into two equal parts each, which would make six parts, and give 3 parts to each, that is, $\frac{3}{2} = 1\frac{1}{2}$, as before. But according to the question, he has $\frac{3}{4}$ or 3 pieces, consequently he may give 1 piece to each, and then cut the other into two equal parts, and give 1 part to each, then each will have $\frac{1}{4}$ and $\frac{1}{2}$ of $\frac{1}{4}$. But if a thing be cut into four equal parts and then each part into two equal parts, the whole will be cut into 8 equal parts or eighths; consequently $\frac{1}{2}$ of $\frac{1}{4}$ is $\frac{1}{8}$. Each will have $\frac{1}{4}$ and $\frac{1}{8}$ of an orange. Or he may cut each of the three parts into two equal parts, and give $\frac{1}{2}$ of each part to each boy, and then each will have 3 parts, that is $\frac{3}{8}$. Therefore $\frac{1}{2}$ of $\frac{3}{4}$ is $\frac{3}{8}$. *Ans.* $\frac{3}{8}$.

Two more problems are similarly explained, though somewhat more briefly. He then draws a conclusion as follows:

In the last three problems the division is performed by multiplying the denominator. In general, if the denominator of a fraction be multiplied by 2, the unit will be divided into twice as many parts, consequently the parts will be only one half as large as before, and if the same number of the small parts be taken, as was taken of the large, the value of the fraction will be one half as much. If the denominator be multiplied by three, each part will be divided into three parts, and the same number of parts be taken, the fraction will be one third of the value of the first. Finally if the denominator be multiplied by any number, the parts will be so many times smaller. Therefore, *to divide a fraction, if the numerator cannot be divided exactly by the divisor, multiply the denominator by the divisor.*

In the above illustration and also the development of division which we have already quoted, Colburn takes as his point of departure a crude, intuitional way of handling the problem. This way is one which the pupil would probably discover for himself. It is only after he has presumably found this way rather cumbersome that a shorter way and rule are given to him. On just this point Colburn makes clear his attitude in the preface of the *Sequel:*

When the pupil is to learn the use of figures for the first time, it is best to explain to him the nature of them as in Art. I, to about three or four places; and then require him to write some numbers. Then give him some of the first examples as in Art. II, without telling him what to do. He will discover what is to be done, and invent a way to do it. Let him perform several in his own way, and then suggest some method a little different from his, and nearer the common method. If he readily comprehends it, he will be pleased with it, and adopt it. If he does not, his mind is not yet prepared for it, and should be allowed to continue his own way longer, and then it should be suggested again. After he is familiar with that, suggest another method, somewhat nearer the common method, and so on, until he learns the best method. Never urge him to adopt any method until he understands it, and is pleased with it. In some of the articles, it may perhaps be necessary for young pupils to perform more examples than are given in the book.

When the pupil is to commence multiplication, give him one of the first examples in Art. III, as if it were an example in Addition. He will write it down as such. But if he is familiar with the "First Lessons," he will probably perform it as multiplication without knowing it. When he does this, suggest to him, that he need not write the number but once. Afterwards recommend to him to write a number to show how many times he repeated it, lest he should forget it. Then tell him it is Multiplication. Proceed in a similar manner with the other rules.

One general maxim to be observed with pupils of every age is never to tell them directly how to perform any example. If a pupil is unable to perform an example, it is generally because he does not fully comprehend the object of it. The object should be explained, and some questions asked, which will have a tendency to recall the principles necessary. If this does not succeed, his mind is not prepared for it, and he must be required to examine it more by himself, and to review some of the principles which it involves. It is useless for him to perform it before his mind is prepared for it. After he has been told, he is satisfied, and will not be willing to examine the principle, and he will be no better prepared for another case of the same kind, than he was before. When the pupil knows that he is not to be told, he learns to depend upon himself; and when he once contracts the habit of understanding what he does, he will not easily be prevailed on to do anything which he does not understand.

Several considerations induce the author to think, that when a principle is to be taught, practical questions should first be proposed, care being taken to select such as will show the combination in the simplest manner, and that the numbers be so small that the operation shall not be difficult. When a proper idea is formed of the nature and use of the combination, the method of solving these questions with large numbers should be attended to. This method, on trial, has succeeded beyond his expectations. Practical examples not only show at once the object to be accomplished, but they greatly assist the imagination in unfolding the principle and discovering the operations requisite for the solution.

Oral instruction and the *inductive method* are the features of Colburn's books which have received general recognition, and which were most effective in changing school practices. These two features were the essential components of the "new system" of teaching arithmetic to which Colburn makes reference in his address on the "Teaching of Arithmetic." Other features of his books have not been appreciated except by few. This is true of his concept of the subject-matter of arithmetic and its structure, the omission of certain topics, creating a motive for a process before it is presented, minimizing abstract drill and putting it after the concrete problems. Some of these things have been recognized within the past few years and others are now only beginning to be appreciated.

But, notwithstanding this failure to appreciate certain features, sufficient recognition was accorded oral instruction and the inductive method to change within a very few years both the actual teaching of arithmetic and the contemporary texts. The *Scholar's Arithmetic* by Daniel Adams has been cited as an example of the old type of text. In 1827 Mr. Adams published *Adams' New Arithmetic*. In the preface he says:

> The *Scholar's Arithmetic*, published in 1801, is synthetic. If that is a *fault* of the work, it is a fault of the *times* in which it appeared. The analytic or inductive method of teaching, as now applied to elementary instruction, is among the improvements of later years. Its introduction is ascribed to PESTALOZZI, a distinguished teacher in Switzerland. It has been applied to arithmetic, with great ingenuity, by MR. COLBURN, in our own country.
>
> The analytic is unquestionably the best method of *acquiring* knowledge; the synthetic is the best method of *recapitulating*, or *reviewing* it. In a treatise designed for school education, *both* methods are useful. Such is the plan of the present undertaking, which the author, occupied as he is with other objects and pursuits, would willingly have foreborne, but that, the demand for the *Scholar's Arithmetic* still continuing, an obligation, incurred by long-continued and extended patronage, did not allow him to decline the labour of a revisal, which should adapt it to the present more enlightened views of teaching this science in our schools. In doing this, however, it has been necessary to make a new work.

Speaking of the *First Lessons*, Mr. Page said in 1843 in addressing the American Institute of Instruction:

The reason, the understanding, is addressed, and led on step by step, till the whole is taken into the mind and becomes a part of it. The memory is little thought of, yet the memory cannot let it slip; for what has been drunk in, as it were, by the understanding, and made a part of the mind, the mind never forgets! To how many a way-worn and weary pupil under the old system; to how many a proficient, who could number his half dozen authors, and twice that number of manuscript cyphering books; to how many a *teacher* even, who had taught the old system, winter after winter, and yet saw but as "through a glass darkly"; to how many such, was this book on its appearance *Their First Lessons in Arithmetic?* WARREN COLBURN's name should be written in a conspicuous place, in letters of gold, for this service.

BOOK REVIEWS

A Cyclopedia of Education. Vol. III. Edited by PAUL MONROE. New York: Macmillan, 1912. Pp. 682. $5.00.

The third volume of this important work has appeared in one year after the second volume, and a year and nine months after the first volume. The general comments which were made upon the appearance of the first volume are appropriate to this one and need not be repeated. The main criticism to be made is that a disproportionate amount of space is devoted to subjects which possess only an antiquarian interest, or which are not particularly related to education. As illustrations of the first sort of article may be cited the one and a half pages which are given to the discussion of the history of the term "high school," and the one-page treatment of the use of the term "glomery," which is merely a corruption of the word "grammar." Examples to illustrate the second type of article are found in the numerous biographies of men who had little or no special relation to education except that they were great scientists, philosophers, or literary men. Such are the articles on Galen, Galileo, and Francis Galton. With this prefatory criticism we may turn to a consideration of the more important topics which are treated in this volume.

Two groups of articles which are among the most important of any in the cyclopedia concern state and national systems of education. The most important representative of this type of article in the present volume is the article on Germany. In the compass of forty pages is given a comprehensive survey of the historical development and of the aims and spirit of German education written by the late Professor Wilhelm Münch, and surveys of the present organization of the elementary schools, the secondary schools, and the universities by men equipped to treat of those topics. The training and status of teachers, the curricula of the various schools, and statistics of attendance and of expenditures are given in detail. There are similar articles, though not so extended, upon the systems of Greece, Hungary, India, Ireland, Italy, and Japan. The article upon Japan was written by Baron Kikuchi, and is interesting as the expression of the point of view of the Japanese themselves. A similar interest attaches to the article upon the education of the American Indian.

This volume also contains a goodly number of articles which treat of the various subjects of study in the school or college. Among the longer articles appear titles on geography, geology, history, household arts, Latin, language and literature, and law. These articles commonly treat of the history of the subject in the schools, various conceptions of its value and methods of teaching it. Sometimes, as in the case of household arts, the teaching of the subject in various countries is treated separately.

Among the educational institutions which receive extended treatment are the high school and the kindergarten. An article which is particularly timely is one on industrial education, which gives in detail the forms of industrial education in vogue in the United States, England, Germany, and France. An authoritative article on growth is written by Professor Boas. This important article, however, is given only twice as much space as the article on the history of the term "high school" referred to above.

Some very interesting articles in the field of psychology deserve mention. Professor Judd has treated the genesis and development of imagination and of language in a way which throws light upon mental development in general. Professor Dewey's article on interest gives a very clear and satisfactory analysis of this much-disputed question, and the article on imitation gives clearly the point of view of his school on that subject. Professor Watson presents clearly the topics of habit and instinct.

These citations will be sufficient to indicate the value of the cyclopedia, both to the general student of education who desires brief and compendious treatment, and also in many cases to the specialist who desires the latest information or an authoritative presentation of views.

FRANK N. FREEMAN

UNIVERSITY OF CHICAGO

A Revision of the Binet-Simon System for Measuring the Intelligence of Children. BY F. KUHLMANN. *Journal of Psycho-Asthenics.* Monograph Supplements. Vol. I, No. 1, September, 1912. Pp. 41+11 plates.

This is a somewhat more radical and complete revision of the Binet scale than the others which have been made by Goddard, and Terman and Childs, but is of the same general nature. The monograph contains a full description and directions for the use of the Binet scale, modified and enlarged, and an introduction which gives an account of the changes which have been made and general directions for the conduct of the test. The revision consists in the standardization of procedure, in shifting of tests from one age to another, in the elimination of certain tests and the addition of others, and in the extension of the scale so as to be applicable to younger children. All of the figures which are necessary in the use of the scale are given in plates, and a list of other materials which are necessary is appended. The author does not give results of the application of the scale, but states that his standard for the determination of ages in which a test belongs is the ability of 75 per cent of the children of that age to pass the test. The monograph is useful as an attempt to make the Binet tests more accurate, but does not proceed in the direction in which a test series for maturity must ultimately be worked out, namely, in the standardization of a group of the same tests which shall be applied throughout the period from early childhood to maturity, instead of a selection of miscellaneous groups of tests many of which are different for successive ages.

FRANK N. FREEMAN

School Organization and the Individual Child. By W. H. HOLMES, PH.D. Worcester, Mass.: The Davis Press, 1912.

A modern book without a table of contents gives one a shock as he attempts to make his way into its pages; such a book we have in the present volume. The chapters one after another confirm somewhat the impression which is made by this first lack of a systematic introduction. These chapters contain interesting descriptive accounts of many of the different methods that are employed in different parts of the United States to give individual instruction and individual promotion to children in elementary schools. The several plans of individual treatment of pupils are reviewed, each under the name of the city where the plan is to be found in operation. Diagrams illustrate the way in which grades can be made to overlap and in which given devices can be employed for bringing the children into more intimate contact with individual teachers. One fails to find in these descriptive accounts any critical evaluation of the success of various experiments. It is not made clear at all that the Batavia method, for example, is better or worse than the St. Louis method. It does not appear that the Mannheim plan of grading has demonstrated advantages over the ordinary plan; and yet the author seems to have arrived, so far as his own opinion is concerned, at some very definite conclusions with regard to the way in which these various suggestions can be carried out most advantageously. He has accordingly offered suggestions for individual classification and instruction, thus summing up his own estimate of the success of the different methods, and lauding the virtues of organization which seem to him to be of the greatest advantage in the school. Such a series of suggestions will hardly influence practical school people and certainly do not appeal to the careful student of education who is demanding these days, more and more, a definite scientific study of the efficiency of different systems. Indeed, the book gives one the impression of superficiality just in the degree in which it fails to insist upon a careful evaluation of the different experiments which are discussed.

After the 197 pages of descriptive matter and suggestions of the type to which reference has been made, we reach the second division of the book, which deals with subnormal children. Nowhere in the literature of education is a better descriptive account to be found of the different efforts which are being made in this country to deal with defective children. The student of this particular problem will be encouraged to find the amount of work which can be reported for the United States along these lines. Here again, however, there is a lack of scientific evaluation of the different types of work. There is for example an account of the Binet tests and another of the after-care of cases which have been treated, which make it appear that the author has been industrious in bringing together a large amount of material, but has not been especially competent in distinguishing between the sources of his materials.

The appendices contain a number of blanks and reports which will be of interest to the student of these problems. There is also a bibliography, and finally an index, which makes it possible to use the book after one has gone through it systematically. On the whole, the book will be found very useful as a descriptive account of the various experiments which it reports. It is unfortunate that it does so little to stimulate any careful scientific investigation of the problems to which it refers.

C. H. J.

CURRENT EDUCATIONAL LITERATURE IN THE PERIODICALS[1]

IRENE WARREN[2]
Librarian, School of Education, University of Chicago

Andress, J. Mace. The Sunday-school and educational progress. Educa. R. 44:502–6. (D. '12.)

Angell, James Rowland. The duplication of school work by the college. School R. 21:1–10. (Ja. '13.)

Baker, Elizabeth W. The problem of two vocabularies. Educa. 33:238–42. (D. '12.)

A plan to overcome the disparity between the pupil's classroom and ordinary speech by creating greater stimulus to expression in the classroom.

Bawden, William T. Second National Conference on Vocational Guidance. Voca. Educa. 2:209–17. (Ja. '13.)

Boas, Franz. The growth of children. Science 36:815–18. (13 D. '12.)

A critical discussion of recently determined facts regarding variability in growth.

Butler, Nicholas Murray. The service of the university. Educa. R. 44:511–20. (D. '12.)

Chapman, John Jay. A nation's responsibility. Educa. R. 44:460–65. (D. '12.)

Children in the canneries. Lit. D. 45:1110–12. (14 D. '12.)

Cooley, Edwin G. The need for vocational schools. Educa. R. 44:433–50. (D. '12.)

Cunliffe, John W. College English composition. English J. 1:591–600. (D. '12.)

A discussion of aims and methods.

Davenport, Eugene. Unity in vocational education. Voca. Educa. 2:186–88. (Ja. '13.)

Dean, Arthur D. The mission of the technical high school. Voca. Educa. 2:177–85. (Ja. '13.)

[1] *Abbreviations.*—Child Wel. M., Child Welfare Magazine; Educa., Education; Educa. R., Educational Review; El. School T., Elementary School Teacher; English J., English Journal; Lit. D., Literary Digest; Psychol. Clinic, Psychological Clinic; School R., School Review; Voca. Educa., Vocational Education; West. J. of Educa., Western Journal of Education.

[2] Annotations by Dr. Frank N. Freeman.

Fleagle, B. E. Oral English in the high school. English J. 1:611–18. (D. '12.)

A description of methods and devices used by the author.

Foerster, Norman. Literature and the undergraduate. Dial 54:3–5. (1 Ja. '13.)

Ford, R. Clyde. Circulating libraries in France. West. J. of Educa. 5:448–53. (D. '13.)

Good and bad in college fraternities. Lit. D. 45:1179–80. (21 D. '12.)

Gutzmer, A. The work done by the German Subcommittee of the Teaching of Mathematics. Science 36:818–20. (13 D. '12.)

A brief description of the subject-matter of the report.

Hahn, Walter L. A plea for out-of-door zoölogy. School R. 21:50–54. (Ja. '13.)

Hunsaker, A. F. Civics in the secondary schools. Educa. 33:228–37. (D. '12.)

Value, aims, and methods.

Johnson, Franklin W. The Hillegas-Thorndike scale for the measurement of quality in English composition by young people. School R. 21:39–49. (Ja. '13.)

Judd, Charles H. The meaning of secondary education. School R. 21:11–25. (Ja. '13.)

Kahn, Joseph. Why teachers fail: fundamental causes and remedies. Educa. 33:193–199. (D. '12.)

A reduction of main causes of failure to inability to understand and apply the principles of the science of pedagogy.

Kent, William. Academic efficiency. Science 36:841–50. (20 D. '12.)

A proposal program for the investigation of educational efficiency according to the methods which are being introduced into industry.

Koeppel, George. Observations concerning the organization of schools and certain phases of educational work in Germany. II. El. School T. (Ja. '13.)

Lathrop, Julia C. The federal children's bureau. Child Wel. M. 7:117–20 (D. '12.)

The need of registration of births.

Leavitt, Frank M. The continuation school: Cincinnati's examples. Voca. Educa. 2:218–34. (Ja. '13.)

Martin, E. S. Old-fashioned children. Harper 126:237–46. (Ja. '13.)

Maxwell, William H. My ideals as superintendent. Educa. R. 44:451–59. (D. '12.)

Monroe, Walter S. Analysis of Colburn's arithmetics. IV. El. School T. (Ja. '13.)

Morton, William Henry Stephenson. Retardation in Nebraska. Psychol. Clinic 6:181–97. (D. '12.)

A statistical investigation of the amount of retardation in smaller cities of Nebraska with discussion of results.

Parker, S. Chester. Bibliographies, briefs, and oral exposition in normal schools. El. School T. (Ja. '13.)

Practical education in Canada. Lit. D. 45:1118–19. (14 D. '12.)

Price, William R. The second year of a modern language. School R. 21:26–38. (Ja. '13.)

Prosser, Charles A. Facilities for industrial education. Voca. Educa. 2:189–203. (Ja. '13.)

Ragland, Fannie. Development of agricultural education in the rural schools of Ohio. Voca. Educa. 2:204–8. (Ja. '13.)

Rapeer, Louis W. Outlines of educational hygiene, emphasizing medical supervision. Educa. 33:200–207. (D. '12.)

Raymer, J. W. Advisory systems in high schools. Educa. R. 44:466–91. (D. '12.)

Riordan, Raymond. Does vocational training fail to build character or create a conscious citizenship? Craftsman 23:449–53. (Ja. '13.)

Smith, Frank Webster. The normal school ideal. Educa. 33:223–27. (D. '12.)

The value of certain of the courses in the normal school.

Stockton, J. L. Principles of a revision of a course of study applied to geography. El. School T. (Ja. '13.)

(A) strike to end school night-work. Lit. D. 45:1125–26. (14 D. '12.)

Tombo, Rudolf, Jr. University registration statistics. Science 36:887–94. (27 D. '12.)

Town, Clara Harrison. The borderland between feeblemindedness and insanity. Psychol. Clinic 6:198–202. (D. '12.)

A detailed description of a case which is not satisfactorily included in the usual classifications but which manifests symptoms of insanity and feeblemindedness.

Wild, Laura H. Training for social efficiency: the relation of health to efficiency. Educa. 33:208–22. (D. '12.)

Wilhelm Münch. Educa. R. 44:507–10. (D. '12.)

Woolley, Edwin C. Student's use of the dictionary Educa. R. 44:492–501. (D. '12.)

VOLUME XIII NUMBER 7

THE ELEMENTARY SCHOOL TEACHER

MARCH 1913

EDUCATIONAL NEWS AND EDITORIAL COMMENT

New York School Inquiry

The New York school inquiry has continued to attract attention during the month. Preliminary reports have been put into the hands of the New York newspapers, and widespread comment has been heard on the various recommendations of the Committee of Inquiry. Professor Hanus was good enough to supply the *Elementary School Teacher* with the following summary which constitutes the closing paragraphs of his general summary of the report:

It is clear that in spite of the progress the public-school system of New York City has made since the consolidation, it is seriously defective. It needs thorough reorganization in respect to its administration by the Board of Education and the supervisory staff; and in respect to its general system of supervision. The Board of Education needs a clear conception of its functions, and should come to close quarters with its work. The Board of Superintendents fulfils no useful function and should be abolished. In the general system of supervision, helpful co-operation under leadership should replace bureaucratic control. The Board of Examiners is decidedly efficient, but needs reorganization to improve and maintain its efficiency. The courses of study for elementary schools and for high schools need thoroughgoing revision, and flexibility should replace rigidity in their administration. The quality of the teaching in the elementary schools, at least, is in general not good, though sometimes good to excellent. The provisions for the discovery, segregation, and appropriate treatment of mentally defective children are quite inadequate, and need immediate attention. The compulsory attendance service is inefficient; it emphasizes police functions rather than preventive measures, and the staff greatly needs reorganization on a functional basis. The recognized advantages of intermediate schools in relieving congestion have not led to the further establishment of such schools, and no attempt has been made to realize the exceptional educational opportunities these schools afford; promotions and non-promotions are not studied so as to yield a real basis for a maximum rate of promotion; part-time classes should be abolished; the estimated need of teachers for elementary schools and for high schools is not based on indisputable and well-organized data. The provision for industrial education is so meager as to be almost negligible; neither industrial nor commercial education is so maintained as to secure the necessary effective co-operation of industry and commerce, and co-operative and continuation schools are wholly absent. Habitual self-scrutiny and an appeal to well-conducted investigations and experiments to secure the necessary data to confirm or refute educational opinion and furnish the regulative for all the activities of the school system and for its adequate financial support are lacking.

National Education Association and the Million Dollar Fund

The executive officers of the National Education Association have authorized a campaign for the collection of a million dollars. This fund is to be used, according to the official announcement, for the purpose of promoting the activities of the Association. A statement is given of the resources and expenses of the organization, and it is evident from this statement that the society is in need of funds if it is to carry on anything beyond the most routine activities. The official announcement also suggests, although in a very nebulous way, that the fund is to promote scientific studies.

Comment on this announcement may be ungracious if it is not enthusiastic at the present very immature stage of the campaign. Everyone is so familiar with large endowments for educational undertakings that the effort to secure a million dollars seems less pretentious at the present time than ever before in the history of the country. Yet it is to be pointed out that people who are to be intrusted with this amount of money shall have a definite program of expenditure to present to the philanthropists who are called upon to contribute funds. One is led to inquire, therefore, what are the probable channels through which the National Association would be likely to direct the income from such funds. If the Committee on Rural Education is to be supported in its endeavor to bring the rural schools to the level of efficiency of city schools, there can be little doubt that enthusiastic support for that undertaking would be forthcoming. If the Committee on Economy of Time in the Public Schools could be assured that its work would be supported and carried on in such a way as to lead to definite economies in school practice, there would be justification in asking for public support. In short, one might enumerate a long list of investigations that need to be made.

On the other hand one must admit that there is a danger that the income from a million dollars will be used in investigations which are not easily recognized as of great public importance. The National Education Association has unfortunately not kept its reputation perfectly clear during the last few years in the matter of a scramble for office. There have been certain domestic infelicities within the organization that lead one to fear that an increased income would create a temptation for new trouble rather than a cure for ancient wrongs. Would it not be well, now that the campaign has been announced, for some of the leading members of this organization to get together and plan definite lines of scientific research, contributing their time and energy to the cause until they have raised that cause to the level of obvious necessity? If educational workers are to convince people of this country that they are to be trusted with large endowments, they must continue for a time to make the sacrifices which are so familiar to every school worker. Committees must meet and time and energy must be spent in the voluntary effort to better schools. This voluntary energy must prove its capacity to bring about useful reforms in education. Useful reforms will then get proper support.

An Apprentice School

The *Handbook for the School for Apprentices* of the Lakeside Press of Chicago describes an experiment in industrial education which is worthy of general attention. The school was organized in July, 1908. It grew out of the need of a large printing establishment for properly qualified workmen. The school is in the printing plant itself, and is supplied with all of the appliances of an ordinary school. Boys are taken into this school at the level which is known as that of "pre-apprentices." At this stage they spend one and three-fourths hours daily doing academic work. This time is devoted to lessons in design, mathematics, English, elementary science, and history. The rest of the time is spent in shop work. The boys thus become acquainted with all the foundations of the art to which they are to devote themselves when they become qualified workmen. The pre-apprentice course is completed at the end of two years. The boys are sixteen years of age at this time. They now enter the factory as regular apprentices and learn some one of the trades in the different branches of the printing business.

The contact which the boys have had with practical work in the pre-apprenticeship period helps them to find the phases of the work which are most congenial to them. At the same time, the foremen of the different departments have an opportunity to learn the characteristics of the different boys, so that a selection of work is made which is advantageous to the establishment as well as to the boys themselves. During the period of apprenticeship the boys have an opportunity to continue their studies. Indeed, they have learned one important lesson in the school in which they were prepared for their apprenticeship, namely, the lesson of combining practical industry with academic work. Such schools as this undoubtedly furnish encouragement to those who are disposed to regard the problem of industrial education as a problem of a type somewhat different from that which is faced in the ordinary school. On the other hand, it requires very little modification of the usual school program to take advantage of this example. Printing is so closely related to the regular school work that there is every justification for the introduction of printing into the regular school course. The design which can be taught in the printing class is more practical in character and quite as perfect in form as that which is taught in the regular drawing class. The students can be made to appreciate books through their contact with the methods of making books perhaps even better than through the study of books which are put into their hands in finished form. The advantages of academic training are emphasized by the use made of these subjects in the Lakeside School quite as much as are the advantages of practical courses.

The Conference for Education in Texas

The Conference for Education in Texas was organized in 1907 and is composed of citizens of the state who are sufficiently interested in its educational progress to give to the cause their service, their money, and their moral support. It has an executive board composed of prominent laymen as well as some of the leading educators of the state. A salaried secretary is employed and an office is maintained in the capital of the state from which most of the work of the organization is done.

The Conference has led state-wide campaigns which have resulted in four constitutional amendments which are of immense value to the schools from both a financial and an administrative point of view. It also furnishes model plans for school buildings and has sent out more than 400,000 bulletins in behalf of rural high schools, school buildings, and educational progress.

The work of the Conference can best be summed up by saying that it serves as a great publicity bureau for the educational forces of the state, and is in line with the policies adopted by other great activities of the state.

So far it has been maintained by the voluntary contributions of the teachers of the state. In this way more than $30,000 has been raised. A movement is now under way to raise a permanent endowment fund from subscriptions of all those who are interested in the educational progress in the state.

Conservative men are free to say that the efforts of the Conference will advance education in Texas more in the next ten years than would otherwise be possible in twenty-five years.

C. T. GRAY

The following news item is quoted in full from the announcement of the Bureau of Education:

Facts about Teachers

Not more than one in every five public-school teachers in the United States is professionally trained to the extent of being a graduate of a teachers' training course, according to a bulletin on rural-school teachers just issued by the United States Bureau of Education. In fact, A. C. Monahan and R. H. Wright, the authors of the bulletin, point out that this ratio represents only the highest possible estimate; that the actual conditions are even less favorable.

It is in the rural schools that the problem of securing competent teachers has been most acute. The attention of educational leaders has in the past been occupied by the rapid growth of the urban systems and the rural schools have been neglected. The trained teachers, themselves often the product of the country, have been attracted to the cities and towns by higher salaries and better prospects. There was formerly little inclination to appraise rural teaching at its full value, either in pay or position, and the better teachers left the country schools as soon as they gained experience.

Raising the standard of rural teachers by dignifying rural-school work as a special field of high importance is already attracting better trained teachers to the country. It is now generally demanded that the teacher for the country school have a special training for the work. "The rural teacher," says the bulletin, "needs the same courses in education and the same general methods of teaching as the town or city teacher. He needs, however, in place of some of the academic subjects of secondary or collegiate grade, additional courses in natural and physical sciences, particularly in their applications, and in nature-study, elementary agriculture, domestic economy, sanitation, rural economics, and rural sociology."

Three main agencies are attempting to meet the demand for trained rural teachers: the normal school, the county training school, and the high school. The bulletin describes the work of each of these agencies and selects typical examples from different sections of the country for more detailed description. State normal schools at Bellingham, Wash., Harrisonburg, Va., and Athens, Ga., are discussed as examples of normal schools that offer regular courses for rural-school teachers, based on the special needs of their respective localities.

In other state normals there are departments of rural education, as in those of Michigan; the Illinois State Normal School at Normal; the Kirksville Normal School at Kirksville, Mo.; and five Wisconsin normal schools. The rural education department of the Western State Normal School at Kalamazoo, Mich., is considered typical of this group. One-year courses for rural teachers are offered at Valley City, N.Dak., Lewiston, Idaho, and Greenville, N.C. Certain county normal schools are designed solely for the preparation of rural teachers, as in Wisconsin. So great has been the lack of trained teachers in rural education that the high schools have been pressed into service. Thirteen states have organized teacher-training courses in the public high schools or in close connection with them.

Clark Educational Museum

A publication has just come to hand from Clark University which contains the catalogue of the Department of School Hygiene of the Educational Museum of that University. New York and Chicago have enjoyed, within the past two years, an opportunity to see in a very complete form exhibits of all of the municipal activities undertaken for child-welfare. These exhibits are of such large educational value that they will undoubtedly be repeated in some form in the future. In the meantime, Clark University and several other institutions for the training of teachers have recognized the advantages of such exhibitions of material to the extent of beginning permanent collections of the type represented in this catalogue. The Clark Hygiene Museum contains exhibits of appliances for the prevention of diseases, for the proper nutrition of young children and school children; it contains drawings and suggestions for school buildings and for school sanitation; and it deals with the problems of the playground and testing apparatus. It also gives material dealing with normal and abnormal physiological development. The catalogue now issued contains a list of firms from whom material can be obtained, in this way making it possible for other institutions to take advantage of the experience of this museum.

Compulsory Education

In the state of Tennessee the legislature is considering a bill which, if enacted into a law, will give that state compulsory education. The northern states have had compulsory education long enough so that the objections to such laws are no longer heard in these states. The discussion going on in Tennessee gives an opportunity to look back into the history of compulsory education in a very concrete and vivid way. The *Nashville Banner* discusses the matter in the following editorial:

A correspondent who is opposed to compulsory education in a communication published elsewhere on this page, says: "The education of my children is more my private business than it is the public business."

What is written here is not intended to be controversial or to make any argument pro or con on the subject of compulsory education. It is intended only to remark that the sentiment expressed by this correspondent—and it is a very common sentiment—shows in quite an interesting way the difference between the old idea and the new—the simple plan of a pioneer democracy and the progressive thought of a populous state.

The education of a man's children, according to the latter view, does not mean more to him than it does to the public. A man may be stupid, illiterate, or selfish, but advanced thought does not concede that he has the right, moral or otherwise, to afflict the state with future citizens of his own kind simply because he prefers that sort or is careless of his public duty.

A man's children are his charge, but not his slaves. They are also the children of the state, and it is the state's duty to see that they have every advantage it is able to give them.

A man can be compelled to bear arms and fight battles in defense of the country. He must also defend it against the backwardness and brutality that come of an ignorant citizenship.

If the state for the state's good proposes to educate the children of the state, people too ignorant and prejudiced to appreciate the value of education should not be allowed to thwart that design and impose ignorance upon the children.

The parent has no right to maim or imprison a child. He has no more right to cripple its intellect or to deprive it of the advantage of education.

This is the modern view and the view that prevails in most advanced communities. It is not tyranny to the parent but justice to the child and to the state itself.

A parent would be punished under the law for starving a child's body, why should he be allowed to starve its mind?

This same correspondent says: "We, the common people of the rural districts, know better what we need than the people of wealth and leisure in the towns and cities do." We can give the correspondent perfect assurance that "the people of wealth and leisure" in the cities, or elsewhere, are not worrying about school problems. They are in the main a selfish lot who devote little attention to anything but their own pleasure and advantage and some of them object to being taxed for school purposes. Plans for educational advancement come from men and women who think and who are mostly toilers, as much so as those who delve in the fields. They are people who believe in the elevation of the masses, in equal advantage, and would as far as possible abolish the causes that lead to poverty and human degradation. The "people of wealth and leisure" don't worry with such things.

And, furthermore, what is done in this respect must be done by the people themselves through their representatives in the Legislature, and the rural population in Tennessee is still much greater than that of the towns and cities.

Public Teachers' Agency

The following news item reports a type of co-operation which teachers should interest themselves in promoting. Either State Departments or Teachers' Associations should do this work. The item is copied from the *Minneapolis Journal*.

The teachers of Minnesota, through the State Educational Association, are asking for the establishment of a state teachers' agency in connection with the office of the State Superintendent of Public Instruction. There is merit in the suggestion. The teachers' agencies are the present intermediaries between school boards needing teachers and teachers needing employment. It is an important work well discharged, but the whole burden of its expense falls on the teachers, who are already underpaid. The fee of 5 per cent of salary is collected from the teacher for whom a position is found. The revenues to the agencies are estimated at fifty thousand dollars a year or more. A state teachers' agency could, it is believed, be maintained in effective operation for thirty-five hundred dollars a year. It would be a fine and helpful thing and would save the poor teacher money he or she can ill afford to lose.

Another educational reform that commends itself to the judgment is that designed to make county superintendents appointive, non-political officials. This change is asked for by the State Association of County Superintendents, who realize better than anyone else what a handicap politics and partisanship are to their work. The measure suggested provides that the county superintendents, instead of being elected as now, be appointed by a county school board made up of representatives from each of the school districts. The bill would put this important position somewhat on a par with that of superintendent of city schools. The effort to require candidates to have certain attainments along professional lines failed for constitutional reasons. The right to run for office could not be thus abridged! The measure now offered evades this difficulty and seeks to put this important office on a securely non-partisan and professional basis.

The following paragraph is clipped from the *Tribune* of Duluth, Minn.:

An Experiment in Pupil Government

Municipal government will hereafter play a prominent part in the day's work at the Longfellow School, Sixtieth Avenue West and Elinor Street. The administration of the conduct of the pupils will be in charge of the Young Citizens' Association. This association is modeled on the plan of the political parties, with the exception that there is no "opposition" to stir up trouble. At an election held the first of the week, a complete set of city officers was elected. They will take their oaths of office this morning and will assume their duties Monday. The plan of government is on the same order as under the old ward system. The association was formed for two purposes—to instil in the minds of the pupils a knowledge of and interest in the administration of municipal affairs and to bring more closely to home the responsibilities of self-government. The pupils will participate in the making of all laws governing their conduct and the officers will see that these laws are observed. The workings of the various departments will be explained and it is probable that, later on, various city officials will be requested to speak on some of the mooted questions.

A ruling given by the Indiana attorney-general is reported in the *Indianapolis News* as follows:

What Is the Limit of the Legal School Age?

Attorney-General Honan today gave an opinion to Charles A. Greathouse, state superintendent of public instruction, in which he held that the usual decision of school officials and parents with regard to the legality of taking children out of school as soon as they are fourteen years old, is not correct. Mr. Honan's opinion, which was requested by the state superintendent to clear up numerous questions on the subject, is that under the truancy laws the child must attend school "between the ages of seven and fourteen years inclusive." The statute means that the child must attend school until the close of his fourteenth year, the attorney-general held. The usual interpretation of the law throughout Indiana has been that of allowing the child to leave school—if such action was desired—at the beginning of the fourteenth year, thus evading the law by an entire year, according to the state official.

John J. Walsh, state factory inspector, under whose jurisdiction the enforcement of the child-labor laws in Indiana falls, said today that he had been enforcing the child-labor laws only up to the time the child entered his fourteenth year. He said, however, that he would examine the truancy law at once and confer with the attorney-general as to whether the latter's opinion would affect the administration of the child-labor law. The child-labor law uses the phrase "no child under fourteen years" in handling the age limit proposition.

The ruling seems to be of very doubtful validity. The question which it raises is, however, one of large general importance.

Longer Terms for School Officers

School officers everywhere will recognize the wisdom of the state superintendent of Colorado as exhibited in the recommendation reported in the following news item copied from the *Denver Post:*

In the biennial report just issued by Mrs. Helen M. Wixson, state superintendent of public instruction, a number of recommendations have been made to the legislature.

The most important is the recommendation that the terms of the superintendent of public instruction and county superintendents be increased from two to four years and that the offices be taken out of politics by holding a special election, the names of candidates to go on by petition and there being no indication of the politics of the candidate.

It is urged by Mrs. Wixson that it is impossible to get plans well under way and obtain results in less than four years.

"Our schools are among the best, but there is always room for improvement and nothing would give greater impetus to growth than a change in the constitution providing for a four-year term in the office of state and also of county superintendent and the removal of these offices from the turmoil of politics," says the report.

Other legislation recommended is provision for a state school visitor who shall relieve the state school superintendent of public instruction of the necessity of traveling over the state constantly, to keep watch over the schools; the formulation of a law for medical examination of school children by specialists and trained nurses; publication and use of the state course of study.

The Bureau of Education has issued a statement with regard to the place of women in the public schools. The facts reported in this news item are as follows:

Women in Administration of Public Schools

How women have advanced from the educational ranks to the highest administrative positions in the public schools is interestingly revealed in figures just compiled by the United States Bureau of Education. Four states—Colorado, Idaho, Washington, and Wyoming—have women at the head of their state school systems, and there are now 495 women county superintendents in the United States, nearly double the number of ten years ago.

In some states women appear to have almost a monopoly of the higher positions in the public-school system. Wyoming has a woman state superintendent; the deputy state superintendent is a woman; and of the fourteen counties in the state, all but one are directed educationally by women. In Montana, where there are thirty counties, only one man is reported as holding the position of county superintendent.

The increase in the number of women county superintendents is most conspicuous in the West, but is not confined to that section. New York reports 42 women "district superintendents," as against 12 "school commissioners" in 1900. Other states showing marked increases are—Iowa, from 13 in 1900 to 44 in 1912; Kansas, from 26 in 1900 to 49 in 1912; Nebraska, from 10 to 42 in the same period; North Dakota from 10 to 24; Oklahoma, 7 to 14. In only two states is a decrease reported—Tennessee had 9 in 1900 and only 5 in 1912, and Utah has one less than a decade ago.

Together with the advancement of women in the administrative branch of education has come a demand for women on local school boards, and this demand has been recognized in many communities. The following cities of 100,000 population or over report one or more women on the school board: New York, Chicago, Cleveland, San Francisco, Milwaukee, Washington, Indianapolis, Rochester, St. Paul, Denver, Columbus, Worcester, Grand Rapids, Cambridge, and Fall River. Numerous smaller municipalities have adopted the idea.

The important place assigned to women in American education has become so usual as to excite little comment in this country; yet American conditions in this respect are the reverse of those of most nations. It is probably safe to say that in no other country in the world are there as many women teachers proportionally as in the United States; in fact men teachers greatly outnumber the women in most European countries.

In many of the cases described above the explanation of the fact that women have been advanced to high administrative positions is to be found in the fact that in the states where the women have been enfranchised the one political office which it is easy to turn over to them is the office of school superintendent in either state or county. The fact that the women have filled the ranks of teachers in the school is so familiar that it is not a subject for frequent comment, but this new fact that school administration is coming into the hands of women in many states is a unique development worthy of comment.

THE REPORT OF THE NEW YORK SCHOOL INQUIRY

THE SYSTEM OF GENERAL SUPERVISION AND THE BOARD OF EXAMINERS

EDWARD C. ELLIOTT

On January 27, 1912, the Committee on School Inquiry of the Board of Estimate and Apportionment of New York City made public the special report dealing with the system of general supervision and the work of the Board of Examiners. This report dealt with the school system as to its organization and operation "higher up," and contained recommendations of far-reaching importance. In view of the widespread interest in the work of the Inquiry, the presentation of the following general survey of the contents of the report, together with the specific recommendations resulting therefrom, may be considered timely.

This special report is a document of 144 printed pages, and is prefaced by an analytical summary prepared by Professor Hanus, who was in general charge of the educational aspects of the School Inquiry. The nine separate sections of the report will be treated in order.

The first section deals with the general scope of the report, the methods pursued in the Inquiry, and a discussion of the fundamental nature of school control, in which the distinctive characteristics and differences of the legislative, administrative, supervisory, and inspectorial forms of control are indicated. The conclusion of this section is significant:

> All of the evidence considered during the conduct of this portion of the Inquiry has revealed and emphasized this important fact, namely, that there seems to be nowhere, at least within the school system, a clear and conscious discrimination between those activities of control that are administrative in character, and those that are supervisory or inspectorial. The absence of this distinction in the minds of those charged with the main responsibility has been, it is believed, an important factor in retarding the progress and complicating the development of the public-school system (p. 9).

The second section gives a brief historical statement of the development of the existing plan of school organization and control since the passage of the Greater New York charter in 1897. On the basis of the study made of the relationship and interdependence of the several boards, officers, and other instrumentalities that constitute the existing scheme of school control, and after a study of the general principles under which this control is operative, the conclusion was reached that—

The schools have been maintained under a form of control that is distinctly administrative and mechanical; a form of control that has not kept a single eye on the real substance and worth of teaching and education. The schools have not been kept, however, under the influence of that effective supervision and inspection which gives unity, purpose, and high standard of attainment to the work of teachers. *There is a striking lack of consciousness within the school system of the radical difference between merely keeping the schools in operation, and keeping the schools in operation so as to produce tangible results of high quality. The organization of the school has been from the top down, rather than from the bottom up; a procedure as obstructive to progress and real growth in education as it is in other human institutions* (p. 17).

The third section deals with the school as the unit for supervision, with special reference to the situation existing in the elementary schools. A general summary of the principal findings of this portion of the report is as follows:

a) The number of supervisors (principals, etc.) provided for elementary schools is entirely adequate for effective supervision.

b) The salary schedules are such as to attract men and women of competence.

c) The tendency is to appoint men and women whose education, training, and experience have been too exclusively within the city.

d) The position of the principal is primarily administrative, rather than supervisory.

e) The system of rating the efficiency of principals is not such as to distinguish the competent from the incompetent (pp. 32–33).

The fourth section considers the organization, status, and functions of the staff of district superintendents.

The major results of this consideration are:

a) While the general theory of the plan of the district superintendent in the supervisory organization is a sound one, this theory is not, as to its essential elements, carried out in practice.

b) The supervisory districts are too large to permit the district superintendents properly to fulfil their responsibilities as supervisors. Many of these should be transferred to the principals of schools.

c) The existing method of selecting district superintendents too narrowly confines choice to those whose education, training, and experience have been entirely within the city.

d) The absence of a definite and high standard of qualification for selection and retention of district superintendents has limited the supervisory usefulness of these officers.

e) The relation between the Board of Superintendents and the district superintendents is such as to restrict unnecessarily the freedom, initiative, and responsibility of the latter with respect to matters of fundamental educational importance. Provision should be made for the larger participation of the district superintendents in the making of educational policies (pp. 41–42).

As to the supervision of the special branches, including kindergartens, as presented in the fifth section the report concludes:

a) Under existing conditions the number of directors and assistant directors, excepting for the kindergarten, is sufficient to secure proper supervision of the special subjects. The relation of the director to the principal and the district superintendent is in need of clearer definition, and his responsibility for the scope and method of his subject should be recognized.

b) Special teachers in certain of the special subjects should be made unnecessary by requiring competency on the part of regular teachers.

c) More adequate provisions should be made for the supervision of the kindergarten by the appointment of additional assistant directors, and by making elementary school principals responsible for the supervision of the kindergartens to the same degree as they are for the other classes (p. 48).

Obviously, the most important section of the report deals with the office of the city superintendent, the organization and functions of the Board of Superintendents, and the activities of the associate superintendents. The following paragraphs are significant of the results of the inquiry upon these points:

The limitations of this inquiry make it impossible to do more than to express a series of general judgments and recommendations regarding the office of the city superintendent as at present constituted. Concerning one important feature of the particular issue, the members of the staff engaged on the educational aspects of the School Inquiry are unanimously agreed—that the centralization of large administrative and supervisory authority in the city superintendent, as provided for by the revised charter, was absolutely necessary for the creation of a scheme of responsible school direction free from those prejudices and partisanships that have so often disorganized the institutions and public service of the city. That the schools of Greater New York have, during the past decade, been consolidated into a coherent whole is due, without question, to the perseverance, foresight, and wisdom of the present city superintendent. His unyielding loyalty to certain of the fundamental principles of school control has brought the policy of centralization to a successful end. No serious study of the facts and circumstances of the development of the school system could lead to any other conclusion.

The city superintendent has achieved distinguished success in protecting the school system and the teaching staff from the selfish influences that are always found in the public service of a great city—and this is conspicuous success. Through his long term of office, he has naturally aroused strong personal and organized opposition to his policies; but no competent and principled man could do otherwise.

No other educational leader of this generation has had a task of such magnitude and complexity. It is very improbable that any other man could have succeeded as he has in unifying the school system and harmonizing the educational forces of the city. Through his service and performances, the office of city superintendent of schools in this country has been greatly magnified. He has made the New York public-school system one of nation-wide significance.

Mechanical consolidation, with the resulting standardization of aims and values, has been effected. The next epoch of educational control will need to be dominated by the idea of establishing a scheme of *decentralized*, *co-operative*, *expert* supervision. Military standards of authority and organization cannot be permanently adapted to the enterprise of education. Education, particularly public education, is a great *co-operative* undertaking, and, therefore, must make provision for the initiative, independence, and creative activity of every individual charged with responsibility. The administrative efficiency of a great, complex school system demands a high degree of centralization of administrative power. On the other hand, the supervisory efficiency of the school system is conditioned by a degree of co-operation which has not yet been fully comprehended by the city superintendent. Machinery *stifles individuality; co-operative effort expands individuality.* The teaching of children and the direction of their education are dependent, ultimately, upon freedom, not repression.

The pre-eminent difficulty of the existing situation arises, as has already been pointed out, from the failure clearly to distinguish between effective administrative control and effective supervisory control. In so far as the city superintendent is an administrative officer, his powers should be broad and direct. As a supervisory officer, he should be the executive agent of the supervisory and teaching staff. In several respects his administrative authority should be enlarged. This is especially true with regard to many of the activities now under the control of the Board of Superintendents. The scope and method of his supervisory functions need to be submitted to thorough study and investigation, far more thorough than is possible during the present inquiry. Consequently, it has been recommended that the Bureau of Investigation and Appraisal, as proposed in this report, undertake to define the legitimate functions of the city superintendent as a supervisory officer, with the end of securing to the schools the benefits of the great amount of productive power which, under the present organization, must be latent. The proposed plan of reorganization of the supervisory staff and the creation of the Supervisory Council is merely suggestive of the idea of efficient, co-operative organization (p. 52).

The variety of evidence considered justifies the positions taken in the report that the attitude of the city superintendent and the associate superintendents, acting either in an individual official capacity, or collectively, as the Board of Superintendents, toward the members of the teaching and supervisory staff has discouraged competent criticism of the methods and effectiveness of the school system, and has prevented the development of a necessary spirit of co-operation within the school organization; that the present machinery of control represented by the city superintendent, the Board of Superintendents, and the associate superintendents is too complicated for effective administration, and too bureaucratic for effective supervision; that a larger concentration of authority over matters of routine and administrative character in the city superintendent, and a reorganization of the supervisory control so as to provide for a wider, responsible participation of the members of the teaching and supervisory staff in the making and oversight of educational policies, are necessary.

From one point of view the body controlling the qualifications of those appointed to the teaching and supervisory staff in a metropolitan city is the key to the effectiveness of the educational work accomplished. During the seven years, 1905–12, the Board of Examiners for the city examined over 90,000 persons for certificates. This Board licensed over 60,000 candidates. The most important conclusions concerning the Board of Examiners are:

a) The Board of Examiners, by its methods and standards, determines the character of the demands made upon the supervisory staff.

b) The Board of Examiners has a tremendous annual task in conducting the wide variation of examinations of many thousands of candidates for teachers' licenses.

c) The method and standards of the Board of Examiners have been such as to select the more fit of those presenting themselves for examination.

d) The Board of Examiners has sought constantly to adapt itself in a progressive way to the changing needs of the school system.

e) The constitution of the Board of Examiners so as to include the city superintendent is to be desired.

f) The enlargement of the Board of Examiners would contribute to its effectiveness (p. 75).

The eighth section of the report considers critically the methods and standards employed for determining teaching efficiency. The general conclusions are as follows:

a) The determination of the fitness or unfitness of teachers for continuance and promotion in the school system represents the chief task of the supervisory staff and the best test of its service to the schools.

b) The certainty with which the initial probationary license is renewed to permanency may be largely accounted for by formality that characterizes the inspections and reports upon service.

c) The approval of service as "fit and meritorious" does not depend upon thorough and impersonal inspections necessary for obtaining any true measure of a teacher's efficiency.

d) The means and methods for the regular annual and semiannual ratings of teachers and principals are not such as to produce results commensurate with the labor involved or calculated to raise the level of teaching performance within the schools.

e) The principle of "superior merit," for teachers in high schools, introduced by the salary legislation of 1911 is a valid one, capable of serviceable extension to the teachers in elementary schools (p. 84).

The ninth and last section of the report contains the four important recommendations for the reorganization of the supervisory staff:

(1) That appropriate steps be taken to secure the necessary legislation for the abolishment of the Board of Superintendents and the position of associate city superintendent; and that a careful, detailed study be made of the powers and duties now belonging to the city superintendent, to the Board of Superintendents, and to the associate city superintendents, to the end of securing a more efficient and economical distribution of the necessary administrative and supervisory powers and duties among the city superintendent, the proposed Supervisory Council, the district superintendents, and the principals of schools.

(2) That appropriate steps be taken to secure the creation of a Supervisory Council to be composed of the city superintendent, all of the district superintendents, and a selected number of directors, principals of training schools, principals of high schools, principals of elementary schools, and representatives from the teaching staff in the various types and grades of schools.

(3) That there be established, as an integral part of the system of school control, a Bureau of Division of Investigation and Appraisal.

(4) That the Board of Examiners be reorganized so as to provide for nine members, including the city superintendent of schools, *ex officio;* the service of the eight appointed members to be arranged so as to permit each member to devote every fourth year to supervisory, or other special duty in the school system (pp. 85–90).

THE RELIABILITY OF SINGLE MEASUREMENTS WITH STANDARD TESTS

S. A. COURTIS
Liggett School, Detroit, Mich.

A recent article in this Journal gave the results and conclusions of a study of the reliability of single measurements in the derivation of standard scores in adding. The tests used (Test No. 1 of the Courtis series, see Fig. 1, below) measured the ability to write the answers to the fundamental combinations in addition.

For the purpose and the results of the study the writer has only the highest praise; the article as a whole is a valuable, a suggestive, and a much-needed contribution to the work of standardization. With certain features of the method of the study, however, and with the conclusions drawn from the data, the writer wishes to take issue. In the present article he will attempt to make clear his reasons for believing the method faulty, and, with the aid of additional data from certain investigations of his own, will try to so interpret the results obtained by the authors as to reverse their conclusions.

A brief summary of the method, results, and conclusions of the article are presented herewith as a basis for the present discussion. For a really adequate explanation of essential details reference must, of course, be made to the original paper.

Two hundred and seventy eighth-grade children in the eight larger grammar schools of San Jose, Cal., were given a practice series of twenty-five tests, five on each of five days. The tests used each day consisted of one like that shown in Fig. 1 and four slightly altered arrangements of it. These were given under carefully controlled conditions to all. The paper of any individual who made more than two errors in any one minute was rejected (68 cases, or 25 per cent of total number), leaving a selected group of 202 papers, chosen as representing a reasonable degree of accuracy as the basis for the discussion of the article.

In the first test the scores varied from 28 to 88 combinations, a range of 60 combinations, the middle half falling between 42 and 60. The median of the first scores was 51 combinations. The medians of the twenty-five scores in the 202 cases varied from 42 to 107 combinations, a range of 65 combinations, the middle half falling between 62 and 80. The median of the group was 70 combinations. From this data it is evident that the first score of the

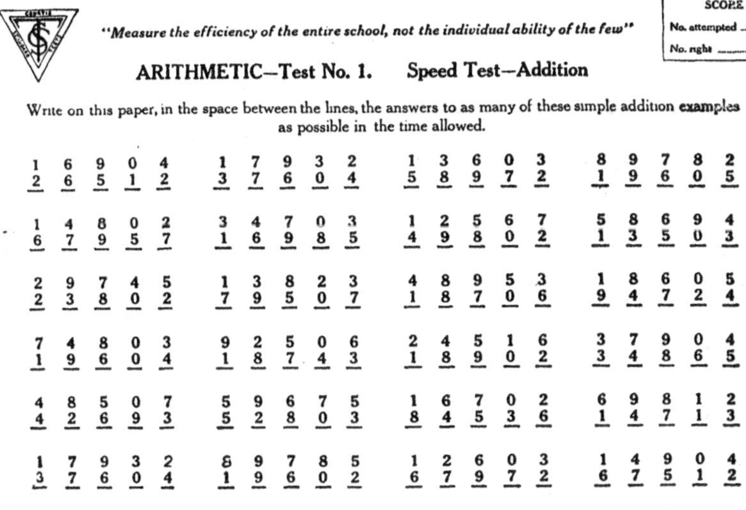

SCORE
No. attempted ....
No. right ....

"*Measure the efficiency of the entire school, not the individual ability of the few*"

ARITHMETIC—Test No. 1. Speed Test—Addition

Write on this paper, in the space between the lines, the answers to as many of these simple addition examples as possible in the time allowed.

1 6 9 0 4 1 7 9 3 2 1 3 6 0 3 8 9 7 8 2
2 6 5 1 2 3 7 6 0 4 5 8 9 7 2 1 9 6 0 5

1 4 8 0 2 3 4 7 0 3 1 2 5 6 7 5 8 6 9 4
6 7 9 5 7 1 6 9 8 5 4 9 8 0 2 1 3 5 0 3

2 9 7 4 5 1 3 8 2 3 4 8 9 5 3 1 8 6 0 5
2 3 8 0 2 7 9 5 0 7 1 8 7 0 6 9 4 7 2 4

7 4 8 0 3 9 2 5 0 6 2 4 5 1 6 3 7 9 0 4
1 9 6 0 4 1 8 7 4 3 1 8 9 0 2 3 4 8 6 5

4 8 5 0 7 5 9 6 7 5 1 6 7 0 2 6 9 8 1 2
4 2 6 9 3 5 2 8 0 3 8 4 5 3 6 1 4 7 1 3

1 7 9 3 2 8 9 7 8 5 1 2 6 0 3 1 4 9 0 4
3 7 6 0 4 1 9 6 0 2 6 7 9 7 2 6 7 5 1 2

Name .... *School* .... *Grade* ....

FIG. 1

group as a whole is fifty-one seventieths of the median score. On the basis of this relation it became possible to compute for each individual a hypothetical first score from his median score and this was done. That is, on the assumption that the middle measure of all the first scores of 202 children represents the same relative position on the scale of status as the middle measure of all medians, the hypothetical first score for each individual represents the real measure of his initial ability. For it is a measure derived from twenty-five scores with the practice effect eliminated. The difference between the actual and hypothetical first scores was then found for each individual with the following results:

Out of 182 cases where all twenty-five tests were taken the first scores deviated from the hypothetical values by between zero and one combination in twenty-six cases, by between one and two combinations in eighteen cases, in order as follows:

Combinations	0	1	2	3	4	5	6	7	8	9	10	11	12	13	14	15	16
Cases	26	18	25	23	17	11	9	8	12	8	7	4	4	3	0	3	

Combinations	17	18	19	20	21	22	23	24	25	26
Cases	1	1	0	0	0	0	0	1	0	1

The individual scores showed a large practice effect, the average difference between the first and last scores being 28 combinations. There were marked individual differences both in the total amount of the practice effect, in the variation in successive scores, and in the form of the practice curves.

The conclusions drawn from this study were:

1. That one performance is altogether too uncertain as a test of an individual for purposes of grading or of diagnosis.

2. That twenty-five trials would be necessary to safely measure the ability of an eighth-grade child to write the addition combinations.

3. That from a certain point of view the usefulness of the test may be questioned owing to the uncertainty as to what it measures.

4. That the practice effect was probably to be explained not in terms of increased readiness of mental association but from an increased facilitation of neuro-muscular sort in the manipulation of the writing instrument.

Taking up the discussion of these conclusions in the reverse order, the writer can express at once his basic criticism of the whole study by saying that the addition test shown was put to a use for which it was not intended. It is not surprising, therefore, that undesirable results were obtained and the suspicions of the authors aroused as to the usefulness of the test itself. The writer will accordingly attempt to make clear the real purpose of the test, and will try to prove that, while rightly used the test does measure a valuable ability, the ability generated by its repeated use is specific and may be largely valueless.

The evolution of the series of tests, of which the one under discussion is a member, has been described in previous articles in this

Journal and the description need not be repeated here.[1] It is sufficient to say that they are the end-products of a long series of experiments, in the course of which most of the questions and criticisms that are likely to occur to a person considering the use of standard tests for the first time, were raised and answered.

The purpose of the series as a whole was to enable the writer to study and bring under control the fundamental abilities in abstract work with whole numbers—the abilities represented by Test 7 of the series, of which column addition is a part. In the analysis of the mistakes of Test 7, however, the necessity for diagnostic tests of the simpler component abilities was soon perceived and tests Nos. 1 to 5 were constructed.

For as the authors of the study show clearly, since the ability to add a column of figures involves the control of four or five elemental abilities, tests that disclose weakness in one or more of the components enable a teacher to concentrate his efforts on the exact cause of failure, and so to increase the efficiency of his teaching. What it was proposed to do then was to cross-section the minds of the children and to try to control the complex ability through control of the component elements.

All measurements of mental facts, however, appear to differ from measurements of physical facts in this particular, that the conditions under which the measurements are made can never be reproduced again exactly. In the physical world the length of a brass rod is unchanged by the mere measurement of its length, although in the last analysis this is pure assumption, as the time element changes from one measurement to another and the time conditions cannot be reproduced at will. At least it is possible to say that the length is apparently unaffected by measurement. In dealing with the mental facts, however, we do not even assume that we can reproduce the conditions, as the mind itself is so very

[1] The subject-matter of each test is as follows:

Test No. 1. Addition (Combinations, 0–9)
2. Subtraction (Combinations, 0–9)
3. Multiplication (Combinations, 0–9)
4. Division (Combinations, 0–9)
5. Copying figures (rate of motor activity)
6. Speed Reasoning (judgment of operation to be used in simple one-step problems)
7. Fundamentals (abstract examples in the four operations)
8. Reasoning (two-step problems)

evidently affected by the measurement. To write the answers to the addition combinations in Test 1 is to increase by one the number of times we have responded to these visual stimuli, and the law of habit formation leads us to suppose that the character of our response to that stimulation in the future will in some degree be affected by the increase.

A careful examination of the situation, however, shows that measurement of mental facts is more complex than measurement of physical facts for another reason, measurement must be made indirectly. We compare length with length, but we cannot so measure readiness of response. Instead we resort to indirect measurement. In column addition readiness of response to a stimulation partly visual, partly mental is a factor determining ability.

But in the attempt to measure that factor by Test 1 we supply a stimulus that is wholly visual and we really measure the resulting motor achievement. At least four types of factors play a part in determining that achievement; the purely physical, as contrast between printing and paper, lighting conditions, hardness of pencil, etc.; the purely physiological, as state of health, fatigue, bodily structure, etc.; the purely psychological, as emotional state, degree of conscious control, etc.; and the factors directly involved in the control of the sensori-motor machinery. In repeated testing there is great danger, therefore, that any change observed may be due to the influence of factors *other than those it is desired to measure*, and the term "reliability" as applied to mental measurements needs definition.

In physical measurements, where the quality of thing measured is apparently not affected by the measurement, and all causes of variation in the result are external, the median of twenty-five measurements is more reliable than a single measurement, as the chance errors produced by the external causes are now positive, now negative, and tend more and more to destroy each other as the number of measurements is increased. In mental measurements, however, the fact that the thing to be measured may be changed by the measurement and the fact that, even if it is not changed, the actual achievements by which it is measured may vary because of changes in other factors, alters the situation completely. A reliable measure of a quality is one that accurately reflects the degree of that quality in the person at the time the measurement is made. If a practice series produces changes in the factors determining achievement, then twenty-five measurements or any derived value based upon them may be more unreliable than a single measurement. The real question of reliability as applied to a measurement of readiness of association in the case of the addition combinations resolves itself into two questions: Is readiness of association a sufficiently definite and stable quality to permit of its being measured at all? If so, is it the determining factor in the achievement by which it is measured?

It must be evident that as readiness of association cannot be isolated and measured directly, no final answer to either of these questions can be made. Yet where the same inference can be drawn from several different types of data, its truth becomes reasonably certain.

The experiences of the writer that many children and adults show great constancy of performance in various situations led him to assume at the outset of the testing work that knowledge of the tables was a definite and stable quantity capable of exact measurement and only recently has he had occasion to question that opinion. The authors of the study under discussion evidently were of the same opinion and their reluctance to credit the practice effect to increased readiness of association would seem to show that they did not entirely abandon it. A priori, it would seem that an ability slowly built up through six or seven years of constant repetition—thousands of repetitions for each combination—and permanent enough to endure through life in spite of periods of disuse years long, must be both definite enough to permit of exact measurement and stable enough to be practically unaffected by the measurement.

However, a-priori reasoning is unsatisfactory when more direct evidence can be obtained and in this case such evidence is not wanting.

In the results from measurements of groups, the individual variations caused by minor factors tend to destroy each other, leaving in high relief only those effects common to all members of the group. It is possible, therefore, to correlate ability to work abstract examples of Test 7 (the four operations) with the total of the scores in the first four speed tests (the addition, subtraction, multiplication, and division combinations) on the basis of returns from many large groups of children.

TABLE I

Relation between ability to work in the four operations, simple examples with whole numbers (Test 7), and knowledge of the tables (total of scores in Tests 1 to 4). Average scores of various grades of children from third through twelfth, in Boston, New York, Detroit, and of the tabulations to determine standard scores, 55,200 children in all. Scores for Test 7 are the number of examples attempted and the number right in twelve minutes. For totals, the sum of the number of answers per minute in each of the four speed tests (the addition, subtraction, multiplication, and division combinations).

No. of Children in Group	Average Scores of Group in			No. of Children in Group	Average Scores of Group in		
	Attempts Test 7	Rights Test 7	Totals 1 to 4		Attempts Test 7	Rights Test 7	Totals 1 to 4
472....	5.4	1.7	87	244....	12.0	8.3	178
525....	5.4	1.7	72	410....	12.0	8.8	185
2,278....	5.6	1.4	86	5,670....	12.5	7.0	176
345....	6.2	2.4	95	2,129....	12.5	7.4	182
481....	6.4	2.7	102	264....	12.5	7.8	179
1,222....	6.6	3.6	102	405....	12.8	9.0	177
2,655....	6.9	2.8	109	209....	12.8	8.9	185
356....	7.5	3.9	117	1,370....	13.1	8.9	189
5,520....	7.8	4.0	137	328....	13.5	9.2	197
276....	7.8	4.8	137	412....	13.7	9.5	198
530....	8.0	5.9	136	4,771....	14.0	8.5	194
5,396....	8.8	4.2	128	216....	14.0	9.5	191
1,177....	9.0	5.3	130	151....	14.4	9.4	198
2,710....	9.2	4.7	135	368....	14.5	9.8	209
476....	9.5	6.1	153	169....	14.9	10.8	202
484....	9.9	7.6	165	179....	15.4	10.5	232
335....	10.0	6.3	149	4,502....	15.7	10.1	219
1,282....	10.3	6.9	152	440....	15.7	10.9	224
260....	10.8	7.3	151	120....	16.0	11.0	230
425....	10.8	6.5	161	257....	16.1	11.5	227
2,518....	10.9	6.5	163	464....	16.8	12.6	233
5,836....	10.9	5.8	157	131....	17.2	11.8	242
1,432....	11.5	7.6	167				
				55,200			

The writer has recently had opportunity to carry through, with a trained force of examiners and with mechanical timing, tests of school children in Detroit (2), New York, and Boston. The Boston test was made at the beginning of the year (October), the first Detroit test in January, the second in June, the New York test in April. He has also the returns from the investigation to determine standard scores, representing between three hundred and four hundred classes in sixty to seventy schools in ten states. The average scores made by each group of children examined (eighth grade, seventh grade, sixth grade, etc.) in each of the two traits are given in Table I, arranged without respect to either city or grade, but solely on a basis of size of scores in Test 7. The number of children in each group is also given. All grades from third to twelfth are represented and a few scores are from normal-school students. Returns from rather more than 55,000 children in 45 divisions are represented in the table.

It is evident both from the table and from the graphic representation of the data (Fig. 2) that the correlation between speed work (ability to attempt examples) and knowledge of the tables is positive and high. (Pearson coefficient of correlation $=+0.98$.) That is, in general the ability to complete any number of examples in Test 7 in a given time (say eleven examples in the twelve minutes allowed for this test) occurs with a corresponding score in knowledge of the tables (in this case 160 combinations in four minutes) without respect to either grade, city, or time of year. For accuracy (number of examples right) the correlation is also positive but slightly lower. Given the score made in one of these tests by any large group of children, the score made in the other tests can be computed by the formula: $C=13.3A+13.3$ and $C=15.4R+55$ in which C is the total score in the combinations, A the score in number of examples attempted, and R the number of examples right. Weighing the various results in proportion to the number of children in the groups, the average deviation of the actual from the computed values are $C_A=3.2$, $C_R=9.1$. That is, in general, knowledge of the tables, or readiness of response, determines speed of work and to a lesser degree accuracy also.

In considering these results the reader should be careful not to infer too much. It is quite certain that each of the two traits is a definite measurable quantity, that they have a functional relation to each other in that for every value of one there is a corresponding value of the other, but the causal relation of the two is by no means proven. Or if this relation be granted, these results alone do not show which of the two is the cause and which the effect. It may be that a child in whom has been built up a very great control over the fundamental number associations may *for that reason* be able

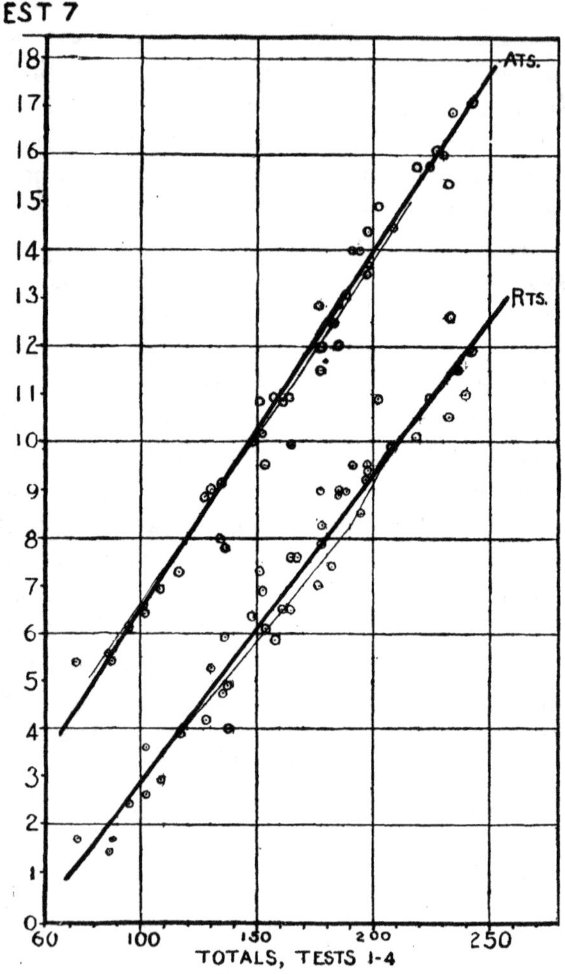

FIG. 2.—Relation between ability to work abstract examples in Test 7 and Knowledge of the Tables on basis of scores of 55,000 children in Detroit, Boston, New York, and in 60 to 70 schools in ten states. Ability to attempt examples is almost exactly proportional to degree of knowledge of tables. The relation is less exact in case of examples right. Light lines represent the scores previously selected as standard.

to attempt a large number of examples. But it may also be that it is the ability to work a large number of examples which enables him to make a high score in the tables. It might even be that the two have no direct relation, both being but expression in different ways of the same basic facts—a retentive memory, a short reaction time, and a perfect muscular control. Whatever the explanation, of the facts themselves there is no question. One of the most striking results of the testing work has been the marvelous agreement, both in average score and in range of distribution, of results from schools in widely separated localities. Whether returns are received from a small public school in Virginia, a country school in Kansas, a private school in a northern state, or a large public school in New York City, a seventh-grade class will make about the same average scores in the various tests. Slightly higher scores in some tests, it is true, do occur but at a cost of lower scores in other tests. The product of teaching in arithmetic seems to be determined mainly by factors that must be common to all schools rather than by the artificial differences created by teachers, methods of work, and courses of study.

In this connection it is interesting to compare the scores selected as standards from the measurement of a few thousand children in many schools—mainly schools in smaller cities and towns—with the relations shown in the graph which were derived from six times as many children from a few school systems. The standard scores are represented by the light lines in the figure. It is evident that the standard scores are not far wrong even in "Rights," where the greatest differences occur.

TABLE II

Distribution of scores in the tables (Tests 1–4) made by a group of 928 children, each of whom had a score of 12 examples right in Test 7

Scores in tables	90	120	150	180	210	240	270	300	330	360
Number making score	2	25	169	293	236	139	68	18	6	2

The reader should be careful, also, to remember that a relation may be true in general but not at all true of certain individuals, and that an average score hides the range of individual variation. In Table II, for instance, is given the distribution in one of these traits (total score of four speed tests) of a group of children having the same score in the other trait (Test 7, rights). FIG. 3 shows the same facts graphically. Although these 958 children all had exactly twelve examples right in Test 7 and should by the relation in Fig. 2 have a score of 240 in the tables, their actual scores range from 90 to 360.

That is, the children at one end of the distribution have four times the equipment in knowledge of the tables of the children at the other end, yet were able to get no more examples right.

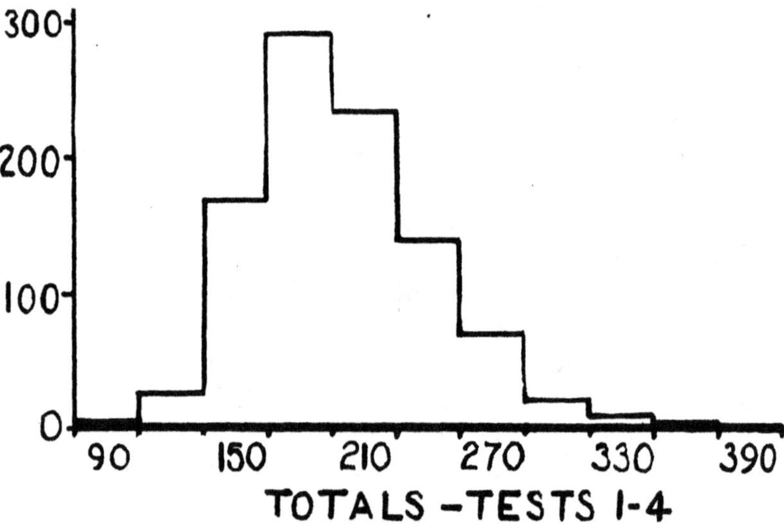

FIG. 3.—Distribution of scores in the tables (Tests 1–4) made by a group of 958 children, each of whom had a score of 12 examples right in Test 7. Average score =201.

The mode is at 180 to 210, and in Table III is given the distribution in Test 7 of about 5,564 children, all of whom have a score of 180 to 210 in the tables. The range here is greater than before, some children failing in every example attempted, others having a perfect score of 19 examples right. Moreover the average falls, not at 12 as it should by the previous figure, but at 8.1, more nearly the point in accord with the computed value.

A similar range of variation has been found in all schools so far examined, and the necessity for, and the value of, a study of the reliability of the first scores must be apparent at once. The interpretation to be placed upon such results depends almost wholly upon one's opinion as to the reliability of "first" scores. The writer feels, however, that on the basis of the evidence presented

TABLE III

Distribution of scores in Test 7, rights made by a group of 5,564 children, each of whom had a score of 180 to 210 in the tables

Scores in Test 7, rights...	0	1	2	3	4	5	6	7	8	9	10	11	12	13	14	15	16	17	18	19
Number making score....	189	137	222	252	366	422	495	534	598	559	499	418	293	264	141	90	49	29	6	1

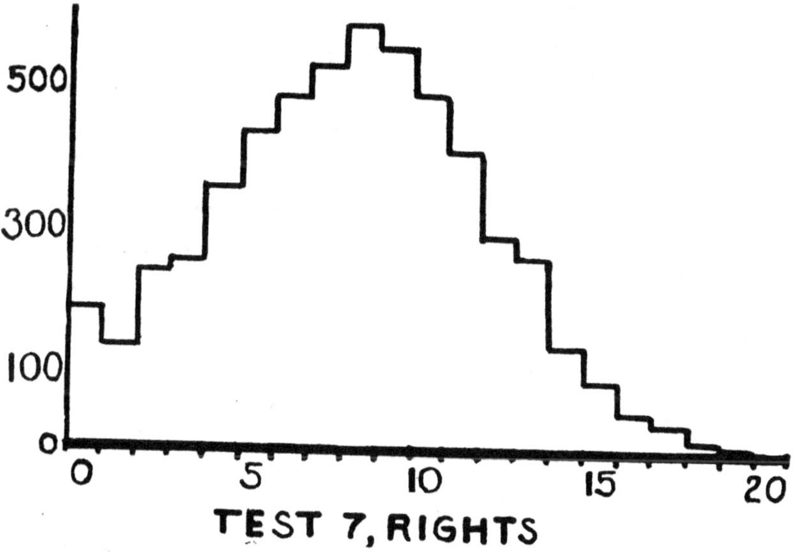

FIG. 4.—Distribution of scores in Test 7, rights made by a group of 5,564 children, each of whom had a score of 180 to 210 combinations. Average score, 8.1 examples.

above it is possible to answer in the affirmative the first of the two questions proposed. Readiness of association in the case of the fundamental combinations *is* a sufficiently definite and stable trait to admit of measurement. The second question may then be discussed.

If readiness of association is in itself a stable quantity, and further, if it is the determining factor in the achievement by which it is measured, then repeated tests of an individual ought to show only slight fluctuations above and below a certain constant value. If, on the other hand, it is not a determining factor, all sorts of variations are possible. Further, since measurement of the abilities of many school children show in general a constant relation between

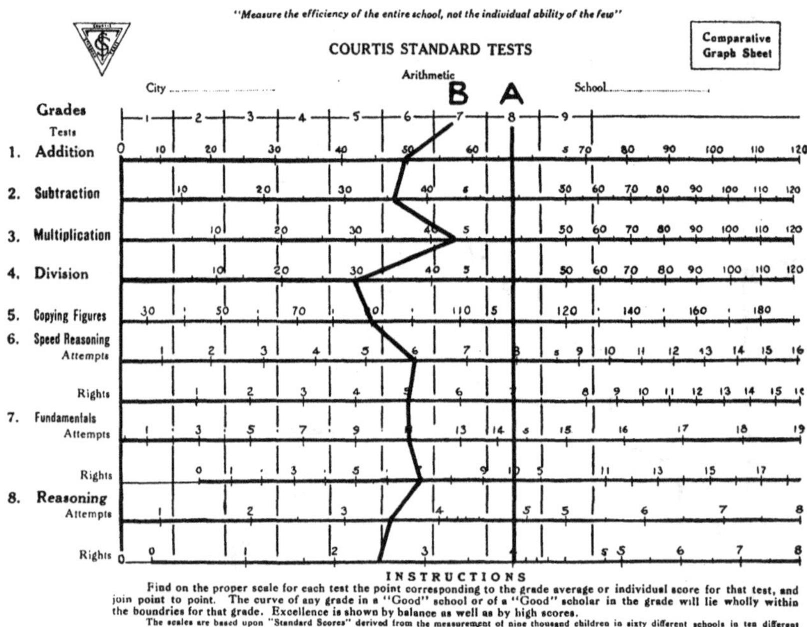

FIG. 5.—Comparative Graph Sheet, a device for comparing individual scores, or class averages, with standard scores. *A* represents an ideal curve of a standard individual, *B* the actual curve of the most nearly standard individual found among 1,500 twelve-year-old children.

scores in Test 7 and knowledge of the tables, this and the foregoing can be used as criteria in judging particular cases. The results of the study being discussed show clearly that great changes in scores are produced by repeated measurement and the writer is disposed to agree with the authors in assigning the practice effect to changes in factors *other* than the one to be measured. The ability generated by practice is the specific ability to write answers to the particular test and not increased readiness of association. For the latter would presumably function in Test 7, while the former does not.

To show this, a device adopted by the writer for making graphic use of the scores of either individuals or classes for diagnostic purposes must be explained. It is called a comparative graph sheet and is illustrated in Fig. 5. Along the horizontal lines representing the various tests scales are so drawn that the standard score for each grade falls directly below the grade. As a result the curve of a standard grade or individual is a straight line as shown at *A*.

Such balance of development is seldom found and *B* represents the most nearly perfect curve found, in the examination of the scores of about 1,500 twelve-year-old boys and girls.

In Fig. 6 is shown the specific character of the ability generated by repeated uses of the tests as drill exercises. Curves *A* and *B* are from two eighth-grade sections in a large city school. Section *A* worked directly upon Tests 1–4 throughout the year and large practice effect and high average scores in the tests of the elemental combinations resulted. It is to be noted, however, that in Test 7, in which these elemental abilities are put to use, the curves of the two sections agree.

That is, the higher scores in the elemental tests in the four operations that were made by Section *A* do not mean greater ability to work more abstract examples in a given time. Precisely similar results can be shown for other classes and for individuals where the tests have been *misused* in this same way.

It should be apparent, therefore, that the large practice effects obtained in the study under discussion probably have the significance that the authors attach to them; that is, the larger gains were caused by greater speed in "getting started," more rapid writing due, as the authors suggest, to degeneration of the form of the figures written, and to other changes of a similar nature, not to greater knowledge or control of the proper associations. In a "first" test there is a certain cautious watchfulness, a guarding against surprises. The child works as rapidly as he can but his attention is on the *arithmetical* phase of the work. At any subsequent test, however, he knows what to expect. He can take his attention from the arithmetical work and bend all his energies to securing speed. In the writer's experience a second test shows quite uniformly a rise in scores of from 10 to 15 per cent. Repeating the test twenty-five times in five days would afford ample opportunity for such improvement, particularly if the children were by the proper phrasing of the instruction given a strong incentive.

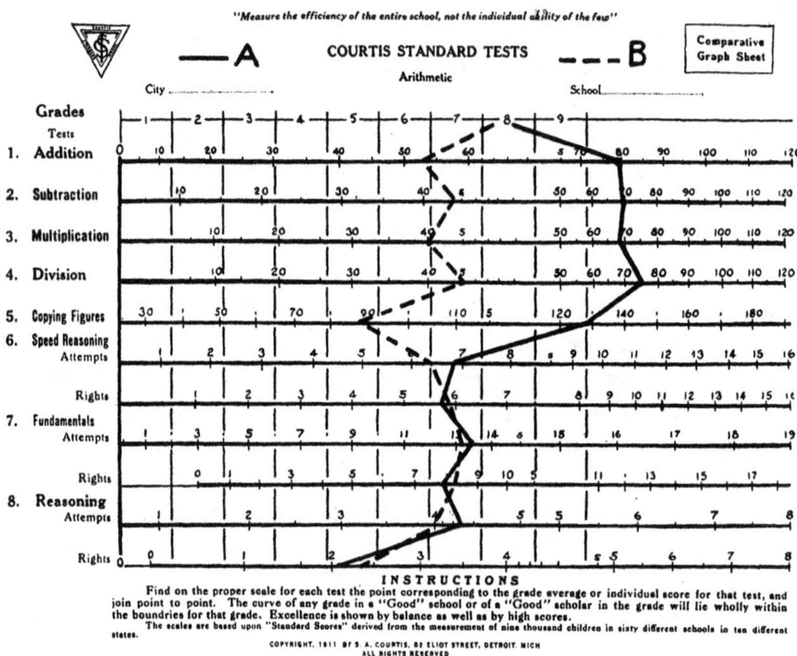

FIG. 6.—Comparison of grade averages of two sections of an eighth-grade class in a large city school. Section *A* was drilled on Tests 1–4 through the year. Section *B* was not practiced. The fact that the scores agree in Test 7 shows that the ability generated by the repeated use of the tests was specific, and did not transfer.

To the writer, therefore, the study seems to yield more of a measure of the amount of change in the achievement that can be produced by practice than any data bearing upon the reliability of the first scores as measures of the readiness of association, and as such evidence as that presented above proves that the increase in skill does not transfer to practical work, he is still of the opinion that the first scores are more reliable as a base for detecting individual defect than the twenty-fifth score or the median of the twenty-five scores.

It is particularly to be noted that in a general way the variation within the class was little changed by the practice. By the first scores the extreme range of the class was 60 combinations (88−28), the range of the middle half of the group being 18 combinations. The extreme range of the medians of the twenty-five scores was 65 combinations (107−42), roughly a 10 per cent increase, while the range of the middle half was still 18 combinations (80−62). It is to be noted also that the extreme range of the class was 60 combinations, and was more than twice the average practice effects of the twenty-five trials. To the writer, these facts all have the same explanation.

In the first scores and in all subsequent scores the determining factor in the differences between the achievements of different individuals is the readiness of associations. Under practice, however, the absolute scores change for causes and by amounts which vary from individual to individual. The greater the practice, the greater the differences produced by the practice effects. The first scores, therefore, in which the effects of other factors are at a minimum, measure more reliably than any other actual difference in the readiness of association.

In this connection it may be well to state for the benefit of all the writer's idea of the proper use of the tests. They are not a method of instruction. The first six of the eight tests cover abilities which should be developed through oral work and never through written practice as such. Neither are the tests examinations for promotion. The abilities covered are too simple and the conditions of the testing too artificial to be of value from this point of view. The tests are, however, comparative rulers for arithmetic, and if given not more than four times a year, reflect accurately the great complex changes produced by school work. The results are of value, therefore, to all who are making a critical study of school conditions, whether from the point of view of administration—the determination of efficient methods, the comparison of efficiency of teaching from school to school, or system to system, characteristics of the course of study, etc.—or from the point of view of the teacher of the individual child. The fundamental idea of the system, however, is that of comparison on basis of a *sample* obtained under set conditions. First scores, as have been pointed out, are proved by this very study to represent more nearly the existing conditions than any other scores, and if the tests are given only at long intervals, all the complications due to the introduction of other factors are avoided.

Before leaving the discussion of the nature of the practice effect, it will be necessary to consider the effect of the rejection of the papers of the inaccurate workers. The authors express much surprise at their discovery that papers having high scores were in general free from mistakes. The writer made the same discovery some years ago and it is written in the folder of instructions to scorers (Folder C), in the manual, and in other discussions of the same sort. The statements, however, probably need revision, as in saying that "Courtis regards them [the errors] as negligible in these tests" (p. 96), the authors show they have failed to get the idea the writer intended to express. From the scoring of many hundreds of papers it has been determined that in general the errors in the addition test will average from 1 per cent to 3 per cent of the answers written, and in *general* that it would be better to expend in other ways the time and effort needed to detect this small number of errors

The purpose of the search for errors is to discover those who do not know their tables, but, since "scores containing many errors did not average as many combinations as scores without them, which seems to point to some third factor as being responsible for errors and smaller scores alike," it is possible to detect such children by their small scores and there is no need to search for mistakes. The authors call the factor determining both errors and small scores the "predisposition of *the moment*" [the italics are mine], but elsewhere the writer has arrayed the data that prove this factor is the basic factor in the learning process—the specialization of the mental abilities of the individual by the forces of heredity. Measurement of whole families, of twins, of the behavior of twins under practice, etc., proves that each individual responds selectively to school training on the basis of his natural aptitudes. One child can learn addition readily but is unable to master subtraction, the next does well in subtraction but cannot learn addition. The authors speak of an "observed erratic character of their performance" in discussing the elimination of those making small scores. The writer, curious to see for himself the character of such performance, gave the next day after reading the article five successive tests to a girl with a very marked and stubborn weakness in division, a girl who after two years of special work still averages four errors per minute. Her scores in order were 46 (first), 42, 30, 34, 28 (fifth). The decline in the scores is due almost wholly to the fatigue caused by the great effort that *for her* is necessary to do such work. In the study, therefore, the elimination had the effect of selecting those who by nature were able to respond to the kind of practice they were to undergo and even this selected group responded in very different ways to the practice series, as is shown by the increase in the extreme range, previously noted, and by the differences in the sample practice curves shown. Had the results in the entire unselected group been used, these differences would have been more marked and the hopelessness of attempting to eliminate the individual practice effect on the basis of a general idealized practice curve more apparent. For any discussion of the individual, the results from that individual alone must be used—his behavior is an individual matter. For general laws of mental behavior, results from large groups eliminate all the idiosyncrasies of individuals. The writer, therefore, does not regard the "hypothetical first scores" as being in any way the true measures of the initial ability of individuals.

The data of the study, however, may be made to yield information as to the size of the chance errors in such mental measurements. In Fig. 7, the figure on p. 98 of the article is reproduced, but through each curve a line has been drawn to represent the growth in ability, the practice curve of the individual. The actual scores in the successive tests fall now above and now below the practice curves in the usual manner of measurements containing chance errors. That is, the writer interprets the curves to mean that any one score is determined by two major factors (assumed for the present to be "readiness of association" and "practice effect") and by a number of minor factors. The "predisposition of the moment," in the sense of the combination or opposition of the minor factors, determines the variation of the score. By scaling the scores from the curves and finding the differences between the ideal and the actual

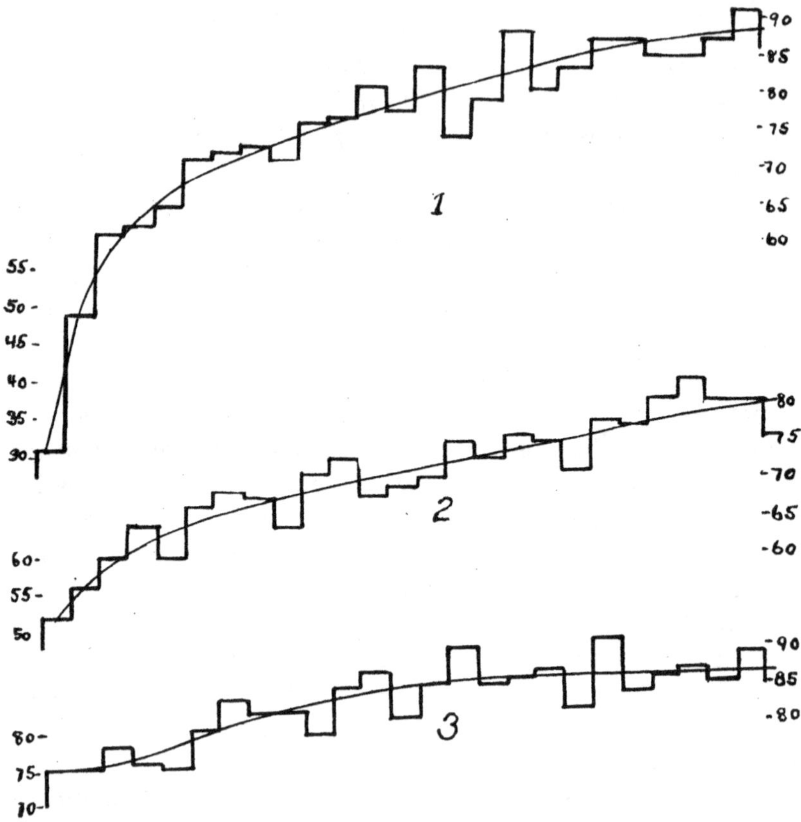

FIG. 7.—Three individual practice curves and graphs of the actual scores, showing variation caused by chance errors.

values, the writer secured an average deviation of 2.1 from the seventy-two differences. Even if the difference between each score and the next is used as a measure of the effect of the chance errors, the average variation would be increased to but 3.7. The distribution of these differences is as follows:

DISTRIBUTION OF DIFFERENCES SHOWING THE NUMBER OF CASES OF EACH SIZE

Size of deviations	0	1	2	3	4	5	6	7	8	9	10	11	18	Average Difference
Variation from curve......	11	18	19	10	7	6	0	1	...	...	....	....	.....	2.1
Variation from preceding score......	6	14	12	5	14	8	2	6	1	1	2	1	... 1	3.7

The writer is sorry not to have the full data from all the curves, including those of the children who made many errors. It is to be hoped the authors will supply the deficiency.

The significance of deviations of this order will be discussed below.

Turning now from the discussion of the results of the study, the writer will present data of his own bearing on the nature of the relation between scores in Test 1 and scores in column addition (conclusion three, above), other data showing the effect of chance errors, and will comment on the diagnostic interpretation of individual curves on the comparative graph sheet. Until such a complete discussion of the facts in the case has been presented, he will be unable to take up the first two conclusions drawn from the study.

OBSERVATIONS CONCERNING THE ORGANIZATION OF SCHOOLS AND CERTAIN PHASES OF EDUCATIONAL WORK IN GERMANY. IV

(*Concluded*)

GEORGE KOEPPEL
Principal Twenty-first Street School, Milwaukee, Wis.

TRADE SCHOOLS

The obligatory continuation schools have developed in some places into trade schools. It is freely admitted in Germany that the most perfect system of obligatory trade schools is found in the city of Munich. English admirers considered it so excellent that a bill has been presented in Parliament intended to establish such schools in England. The details of the Munich organization are stated in the bill giving full credit to its excellencies.

In Munich six large and a number of smaller trade school buildings are exclusively used for the theoretical and practical instruction of the apprentices of the various trades. These buildings contain shops that are fitted out with the most modern equipment in tools, apparatus, and machinery. The instructors are teachers, engineers, architects, artists, and master-mechanics.

The aim of the schools is *the formation of the habit of careful and exact work* and the systematic introduction to all the essential details of the work required in the respective trades. The school is to counteract the tendency of modern shops to turn the boys' work to profit by limiting them to a few manipulations in a small field of their trade, leaving them helpless and ignorant in regard to all the rest.

A nation that is in the race for industrial supremacy cannot hope to win unless its workers are trained to be exact, thorough, and intelligent. The trade schools are doing a grand work toward the accomplishment of this aim, while their influence as ethical and cultural centers on the army of adolescent youths is hardly less pronounced. The feature to be specially emphasized is the *compulsory attendance of all boys till they are at least seventeen years* old, which places them under educative and protective influence during that period of life when they are in special need of guidance and advice.

The co-operation of employers with these schools is wonderful; individuals and corporations make voluntary contributions to funds, donate material, tools, models, and the most expensive machinery. All factors seem to combine to make the trade schools a growing success.

The courses extend over three, in some trades over four years, and are carefully graded. Attendance beyond the legal requirements is encouraged.

All trade schools have special classes for journeymen in which skilled workmen receive advanced theoretic and practical instruction. Many are fitted to take responsible positions and some develop into successful teachers of the schools which they have so long attended.

It is remarkable to what extent the study of science and art supplements the practical work done in the shop. Drawing and painting in all their branches, especially with reference to the artistic trades, is fundamental, as well as the study of style and of beautiful productions of former centuries. While famous historic models are carefully studied and imitated, originality of conception and design is also encouraged.

The workers are warned from the beginning, and learn to appreciate during the course, that modern mechanics and artisans require, besides practical and artistic skill, a scientific training, and that considerable knowledge of mathematics, physics, chemistry, mechanics, and statics is indispensable to the highest success. Especially in the schools for the building trades these subjects find extensive room in the programs.

At a fine exhibition of the furniture industry and of interior decoration, held last summer at Berlin, a very notable feature was the exhibit of the Berlin trade school for cabinet-makers, turners, and wood-carvers. It represented in a most striking and beautiful manner the great ability of the members of that school and the splendid work done under the influence of competent instruction, and of the devoted study of some of the most famous furniture of former times. Several of the most artistic pieces had each a value of $450. The exhibit was not for sale, but remains with the school for instructional purposes. This school is exceptionally well supplied with historical models.

Course for masters of various trades are also conducted. I visited such a class in Zürich that was attended by more than twenty masters who had come from all parts of Switzerland to spend ten days perfecting themselves in the latest developments of lithography. The progress of the art was discussed in lectures and illustrated by practical demonstrations in the shops.

It is evident that such extensive, systematic, and successful provisions for training the workers, from the masters down to the youngest apprentices, must result in elevating considerably the efficiency and productive power of the nation.

The large and fine collections of the museums of the large and many of the smaller cities supplement very effectively the efforts of the schools. A most beautiful building, housing a school for the artistic trades in Dresden, is directly connected with a museum. The trade school in Zürich, Switzerland, an excellent institution, is adjacent to the National Museum containing most precious collections, among them many interiors taken from famous homes, convents, castles, and public buildings. The refining influence of these beautiful objects of the past cannot be overestimated.

Excellent classified collections of materials, photographs, engravings, books, and periodicals are at the service of the learners in the trade schools.

The school at Zürich has arranged regular exhibits of various trades that have proved very instructive, not only to the members of the school and to tradesmen, but also to the public, who are admitted free of charge. These exhibits are changing every three or four weeks. When I visited the school, the exhibition rooms had been transformed into a suite of many apartments furnished and decorated completely to illustrate beauty and comfort in homes of the middle class. This was to be followed by an exhibit of homes for laborers, and later by one of the most exquisite furnishings of houses for the wealthy. Artists, manufacturers, and merchants furnish all that is needed and co-operate with the director of the school to make these exhibits models of taste and workmanship.

In connection with the trade schools may be mentioned the powerful influence that comes from the grand collections of the Deutsche Museum at Munich containing the masterpieces of natural science and technology in original models and demonstrations. Each branch of human industry is represented in its development by numerous models, and the collections constitute one of the grandest examples of objective teaching that can be imagined. The mining of ores, the preparation and working of metals, for instance, is so plainly and amply illustrated that no other form of instruction can equal it. Stones used as building-material are represented by portions of buildings, some of them hundreds of years old, to show the effects of weathering on various materials under the same climatic conditions. The development of house-building, of bridge-building, of ship-building, of electro-technics, is illustrated in the same manner. These few examples may suffice to indicate the valuable aid which the trade and technical schools derive from these precious collections.

The great fundamental principle, so prominent in German schools, of teaching objectively by appealing directly to the senses, finds its most perfect exemplification in such masterly and comprehensive exhibits of models as those of the Deutsche Museum.

PHYSICAL CARE

Physical training receives much attention in Germany and Switzerland. Large and well-equipped halls for *gymnastic exercises* are connected with nearly all schools and many of the playgrounds are fitted out with apparatus. Two to three hours a week of the regular class time are set aside for systematic gymnastic drill. The pupils of all classes of schools are obliged to take part in these exercises. Besides the regular school grounds, many *playgrounds* have been established, and the movement for increasing their number is advancing very rapidly. Some of the playgrounds are truly ideal and are located in beautiful surroundings. In some cities attendance at play is compulsory and all classes receive the benefits of healthful sports under the leadership of teachers who have taken special courses to fit them for this work.

The modern school buildings are provided with *shower baths.* These are very roomy, light, airy, and invitingly bright, being constructed of white tiles. They are constantly in operation, classes using them in rotation; attendance of pupils, however, is optional with the parents.

Where rivers or lakes present the opportunities, open-air bathing is encouraged and *swimming* is taught.

Medical inspection is general and the records kept are very interesting. Some of these are extensive, giving a minute account of the family and personal history, others are simple and brief. The records of the backward and exceptional children are the most instructive and include the observations of teachers during the years of the child's school attendance.

At the annual congress of the association for school hygiene which was held from May 31 to June 2 at Dessau, the question of the extent of medical supervision and the extent of the records to be kept was one of the subjects of reports and animated discussions. These conventions are attended by prominent school physicians and specialists, educators, representatives of educational departments of states, and by military officers; they are of great importance, as they tend to unify the efforts for the physical welfare of the children in all parts of the empire.

Several cities have established *open-air schools in the woods* (*Waldschulen*) for sickly children, and my visits to these schools at Charlottenburg near Berlin and at Wesloe near Lübeck convinced me that a great deal can be done for the relief and cure of children in poor health by simple and rather inexpensive means, while at the same time instruction in the essentials of school work is continued.

These schools are located in fine old forests on carefully selected grounds. The buildings are few and of simple construction, just offering protection against unfavorable weather. The children spend all day in the open air. Nearly all instruction is given in the forenoon and every lesson is followed by a period of play or active exercise. After the noonday meal a long period of enforced rest is considered very essential, and this is followed by play, work in the school garden, observations in connection with nature-study, construction of geographical reliefs in sand, and similar occupations; there are also occasional excursions to places in the neighborhood.

The meals are simple but nourishing; milk is given several times a day. In the evening the children walk a short distance to reach the car that takes them home.

Besides these *Waldschulen* there are numerous *recreation resorts in the woods* (*Walderholungsstätten*) that are conducted in the same manner without furnishing regular and systematic instruction. Improvement of health by constant life in the fresh air, by play, gardening, and other pleasant occupations, by rest and proper feeding, is the aim of these resorts.

The members of the forest schools and resorts are selected by teachers and school physicians; medical supervision is, of course, more frequent, more exact and minute than that of the regular pupils. The number of applicants is always greater than the capacity of schools and resorts. The parents who are able to do so, pay for the transportation and feeding of their children. The results of the open-air life are very satisfactory, as nearly all children gain in weight, strength, cheerfulness, and ability to work.

The degenerating influences of city life on the population of large cities are felt in Germany as elsewhere, and it is recognized that a return to nature is one of the most potent remedies. As the poorer children living in crowded quarters are especially in need of recreation and removal from the city, many thousands of them are sent every year to the sea coast, to lake resorts in the woods, and to the mountains, where they remain in groups of 25 or 30 for three or four weeks. This branch of physical care is splendidly organized under the name of *vacation colonies* and cannot be too highly recommended.

Frequent *outings of classes* to the woods or other scenes of beauty, also to places of historic interest in the neighborhood of cities, are a prominent feature of school life in Germany and Switzerland. Not only do these outings furnish recreation and enrich the knowledge of children, but the contact with nature has a most salutary influence in elevating and purifying the emotions. The joys of a day of roaming in the fields and woods in cheerful company bring strength and hope to the hearts of all children, but especially of those who live under discouraging conditions.

The most perfect form of outings are the *Schülerwanderungen*. These are carefully planned wanderings on foot, usually lasting five or six days, in the most beautiful regions of the country. Thousands of pupils of the three upper grades are formed into groups of about twenty-five boys or girls and each group is placed under the leadership of a sympathetic teacher who has made himself thoroughly familiar with the region to be visited. The preparations for the trip, the discussions between the leader and his group, the study of guidebooks and maps are very interesting and profitable preliminaries. When the time for departure arrives, the children are taken by train, at small expense, to the starting-point of their tramp, and then begins for them an experience that no teaching at school can equal and whose impressions will last a lifetime. During the days of their wanderings, the beauty of nature brings constantly to the children new and pure delights as they proceed. Mind and body are refreshed, hundreds of new and wonderful impressions are gained, and the souls of all are filled with love for the beauty of their fatherland. The friendly relationship that this delightful experience creates between pupils and teachers is valuable to both; they learn to know each other better than at school, and the gratitude of the children for all that teachers do for them during these excursions is an ample reward.

Among all the great and good impressions received in my travels, the remembrance of the numerous classes of happy boys and girls that I met in the beautiful mountains of Saxony and Bohemia, and in Switzerland, the cheerfulness of these children, their pure delight in the wonders of nature, and their joyful and beautiful songs will never be forgotten.

BOOK REVIEWS

"EDUCATION FOR LIFE IN AMERICAN HIGH SCHOOLS." By DR. WILHELM STEITZ, PH.D. *Neue Jahrbücher*, August, 1912.

In the August number of the *Neue Jahrbücher*, Dr. Wilhelm Steitz, Prussian exchange teacher in the University High School for the year 1910–11, writes on "Education for Life in the American High Schools" ("*Die Erziehung für das Leben an den amerikanischen High Schools*"). He begins by saying that, like most German visitors to American schools, he has received the impression that they do not rank as high as the German schools in scholarship, exact knowledge, and especially historical interpretation. But, he continues, the American schools do not aim at scholarship in the same degree as the German schools, but rather at "education for life." The German schools of course also claim to prepare their students for life, but they try to accomplish this end by means of the scholarly and thorough training given their students in a course in general education. They pursue an indirect method, whereas the American takes the direct way, as he says. Dr. Steitz then proceeds to show what he means by "education for life," basing his observations in the main on his experience at the University High School.

He describes in detail and in an interesting and sympathetic manner those features of the American system which are designed to give social training to the pupils. He discusses the high-school publications, the monthlies, dailies, weeklies, and the annuals, the weekly assembly, athletics, debating, the organization of the classes with their officers and committees, the various clubs, and the school dances. He sees in the large number of short stories in the publications the influence of our monthly magazines, which abound in the form of literary entertainment most agreeable to the nature of the American. Viewed from a pedagogical standpoint, he thinks this form of composition deserves only encouragement, and he finds the stories well written. In the large-typed and sensational headlines and in the optimistic tone and fondness for exaggeration he sees the influence of the daily press.

He discusses the weekly assembly at length and notes especially the training in public speaking which the pupils receive. He finds that the boys and girls speak with assurance and in a simple manner appropriate to the occasion. He observes in the assemblies also that fostering of the spirit of loyalty to the school which is lacking in German schools. The writer remembers, for instance, that in his school days the football enthusiasts remained in ignorance of the victories of the boat crew of their own school.

In the discussion of athletics, the writer is struck by the highly developed system of contests that prevails. After noting that we aim to develop the quality of leadership in the captains, the ability to work for a common cause on the part of the teams, and loyalty on the part of the onlookers, he points out how the athletic contests further the sympathetic relations between teachers and pupils because of the common interest and enthusiasm that they arouse. The contests are, however, so numerous, so exciting, and so time-absorbing that they must of necessity interfere with the ability of the pupils to do scholarly work.

After a sympathetic discussion of the above and many similar features of our educational system, the writer concludes that these things demand so much of the pupil's time and energy that his scholarly attainments cannot be very marked. It seems to him that these features could be introduced into the German system only by sacrificing something of the thorough training that is now given.

The writer then proceeds to compare the results of the two systems of education. The American method is undoubtedly successful in America. For one thing, the pupils have more *Schulfreudigkeit.* They take more pleasure and interest in their school life than German pupils. This, however, is confined only to the features outlined above. When it comes to the studies the *Schulverdrossenheit* is greater with us than among the German pupils. He also considers an important element the greater assurance of bearing and greater self-possession of American students, qualities which so often determine one's success in life. The German graduate of a gymnasium, the *Abiturient,* is an awkward figure in comparison with the high-school Senior. The outward assurance of the Senior is, however, in marked contrast to his intellectual immaturity, his lack of interests in higher intellectual questions, and his ignorance. Early independence in practical matters characterizes the American pupil, but this is probably primarily due to the environment afforded by a new country still rich in possibilities for advancement and to the fact that children are treated as grown-ups much earlier than is customary in Germany. But though the young American shows a greater independence in practical matters, this cannot be said of his independence in intellectual matters. The independent thinkers in America are fewer and the intellectual uniformity is greater than in Germany. The *Abiturient* has a larger capital in the way of possibilities for further intellectual development and the ability to work. The German can acquire at the university and in military service those things in which the young American excels; but the desire for serious thought and study must be implanted early or it will never really exist.

The article is well written and proves the author a careful observer and sympathetic interpreter of conditions widely different from those to be found in the schools of his own country. Such inaccuracies as appear are few and generally unimportant. While we readily agree when he speaks of our admiration for the German educational system, we are surprised at his statement that whenever in America there is a demand for a *höhere Arbeitskraft* we look for a German trained in Germany.

LYDIA M. SCHMIDT

UNIVERSITY HIGH SCHOOL
CHICAGO, ILL.

BOOKS RECEIVED

AMERICAN BOOK CO.

Antoine of Oregon. By JAMES OTIS. Cloth. Pp. 149. Illustrated. Price $0.35.

Hygiene for the Worker. By WILLIAM H. TOLMAN and ADELAIDE WOOD GUTHRIE. Edited by C. WARD CRAMPTON. Cloth. Pp. 231.

Language Lessons for Little People. By JOHN MORROW. Cloth. Pp. 80. Illustrated. Price $0.25.

Kreuz und quer durch Deutsche Lande. By ROBERT MEZGER and WILHELM MUELLER. Cloth. Pp. 260. Price $0.60.

Forge Work. By WILLIAM L. ILGEN. With editorial revision by CHARLES F. MOORE. Cloth. Illustrated. Pp. 210.

The Swallow Book. Gathered by DR. GIUSEPPE PITRÈ. Arranged by ADA WALKER CAMEHL. Cloth. Illustrated. Pp. 158. Price $0.35.

HOUGHTON MIFFLIN CO.

The Teaching of English Classics in the Grammar Grades. Riverside Literature Series. By EUGENE CLARENCE WARRINER. Paper. Pp. 126. Price $0.15.

Word Mastery. By FLORENCE AKIN. Cloth. Illustrated. Pp. 124. Price $0.25.

Selected Stories from the Arabian Nights. Edited by SAMUEL ELIOT. Cloth. Illustrated. Pp. 210. Price $0.50.

First Year in Number. By FRANKLIN S. HOYT and HARRIET E. PEET. Cloth. Illustrated. Pp. 129.

MACMILLAN CO.

Auvergne and Its People. By FRANCES M. GOSTLING. Cloth. Illustrated. Pp. 291.

Experimental Psychology and Pedagogy. By R. SCHULZE. Translated by RUDOLF PINTNER. Cloth. Pp. 364.

STURGIS & WALTON CO.

Genetic Philosophy of Education. By G. E. PARTRIDGE. Cloth. Pp. 401. Price $1.50.

Story-Telling in School and Home. By EMELYN NEWCOMB PARTRIDGE and GEORGE EVERETT PARTRIDGE. Cloth. Pp. 323. Price $1.25.

THE PEOPLE'S UNIVERSITY

Vocation and Learning. By HUGO MÜNSTERBERG. Cloth. Pp. 289.

J. P. BELL CO.

A Study of Mental Fatigue. By W. H. HECK. Cloth. Pp. 28.

GOVERNMENT PRINTING OFFICE

Annual Report of the Board of Regents of the Smithsonian Institution, for the Year Ending June 30, 1911. Cloth. Pp. 688.

CURRENT EDUCATIONAL LITERATURE IN THE PERIODICALS[1]

IRENE WARREN[2]
Librarian, School of Education, the University of Chicago

Abercrombie, D. W. Honesty in school work. Educa. 33:289–99. (Ja. '13.)
Shows the causes of dishonesty on the part of students, and the suggested remedies.

Anderson, Roxanna E. A preliminary study of the reading tastes of high school pupils. Pedagog. Sem. 19:438–60. (D. '12.)
A study by means of questionnaire blanks filled out by the pupils.

Ash, Isaac Emery. The correlates and condition of mental inertia. Pedagog. Sem. 19:425–37. (D. '12.)
Reports a method of testing the originality and mental alertness of pupils by offering pairs of alternative problems or tasks. The results are correlated with general school standing and efficiency.

Ashley, M. L. Education as growth. Educa. Bi-mo. 7:149–52. (D. '12.)

Barnes, Earl. The education of a partially paralyzed muscle. Pedagog. Sem. 19:518–21. (D. '12.)
A brief description of the form of treatment and exercise by which a case of infantile paralysis was greatly ameliorated.

Brown, J. C. An investigation on the value of drill work in the fundamental operations of arithmetic. II. J. of Educa. Psychol. 3:561–70. (D.'12.)
Conclusion of the study showing the advantage of drill over non-drill methods.

Bruner, Frank G. What shall we teach the subnormal child? Educa. Bi-mo. 7:112–23. (D. '12.)
An argument for training of the subnormal child which shall center in specific and concentrated drill in an industrial process.

Buckham, John W. Study of religion in the university. Educa. R. 45:44–57. (Ja. '13.)

[1] *Abbreviations.*—Cent., Century; Educa., Education; Educa. Bi-mo., Educational Bi-monthly; Educa. R., Educational Review; El. School T., Elementary School Teacher; Harp. W., Harper's Weekly; J. of Educa. Psychol., Journal of Educational Psychology; Lit. D., Literary Digest; Man. Train. M., Manual Training Magazine; Outl., Outlook; Pedagog. Sem., Pedagogical Seminary; Pop. Sci. Mo., Popular Science Monthly; Psychol. Clinic, Psychological Clinic; School R., School Review; School W., School World; Sci. Am. Sup., Scientific American Supplement.

[2] Annotations by Dr. F. W. Bobbitt and Dr. F. N. Freeman.

Burnham, William H., and Fitzsimmons, M. Evelyn. The educational museum at Clark University. Pedagog. Sem. 19:526–52. (D. '12.)

A catalogue of the articles in the new educational museum which illustrates the development of school hygiene.

Chapman, Maxwell. The honor system at Princeton. Educa. 33:312–14. (Ja. '13.)

A brief statement of methods employed in effectively operating the honor system at Princeton.

Chauncey, Alexander Wallace. The honor system of Sheffield Scientific School. Educa. 33:315–17. (Ja. '13.)

Figures to show class sentiment, and the actual pledges signed.

"Cramming" for civil service examinations. School W. 15:7. (Ja. '13.)

Cutting, Starr Willard. The teaching of foreign modern literatures in our schools. Educa. Bi-mo. 7:97–103. (D. '12.)

The kind of literature and mode of treatment suitable in teaching modern foreign languages in the secondary schools.

Dolbear, Katherine E. Precocious children. Pedagog. Sem. 19:461–91. (D. '12.)

A critical study of the recently exploited cases of precocious children to determine how far their unusual development is due to special training. With a large bibliography.

FitzGerald, Ellen. Writers to read—Montaigne. Educa. Bi-mo. 7:104–7. (D. '12.)

The value of a study of Montaigne's writings to the teachers of composition.

Flower, E. Little village actors. Child (London) 3:328–33. (Ja. '13.)

An account of a play given by children from eight to twelve years of age.

Forbes, Charles H., and Fowler, Henry Thatcher. The degree for college plus school work. Educa. 33:263–75. (Ja. '13.)

Defense of college autocracy and of the classical program. Emphasizes the idea of continuity of secondary and collegiate work, and of the need of integration of courses.

Frazer, Norman L. English texts for schools. School W. 15:1–3. (Ja. '13.)

Grady, William E. Age and progress in a New York City school. Psychol. Clinic 6:209–21. (Ja. '13.)

Hadley, Arthur T. Methods of ascertaining and apportioning cost of instruction in universities. Educa. R. 45:58–69. (Ja. '13.)

Heald, Lucy. George Meredith's interest in education. School R. 21:112–33. (Fe. '13.)

By means of citations and quotations, shows Mr. Meredith's thorough appreciation of educational purposes and needs.

Henderson, Wilson H. What the manufacturer should expect of the manual training school graduate. Man. Train. M. 14:245–47. (Fe. '13.)

Hillix, Foster F. Record and cost keeping in school shops. Man. Train. M. 14:223–28. (Fe. '13.)

Hutchinson, Jean. Textile industries and their practical application to education. Educa. Bi-mo. 7:173–78. (D. '12.)

Some practical suggestions.

Kendall, Calvin N. The training of high-school teachers. School R. 21:92–102. (Fe. '13.)

Discusses in connection with the training of secondary teachers: academic training, professional study of education, observation of teaching, and practice teaching.

Kirkland, Chancellor J. H. The Association of Colleges and Secondary Schools of the South. School R. 21:103–11. (Fe. '13.)

Considers purposes of the association, college-entrance requirements, examinations, standards, and recent advances.

Lewis, E. E. The present status of vocational subjects in the high schools of California. Man. Train. M. 14:229–34. (Fe. '13.)

(The) "Literary Digest" as a textbook. Lit. D. 46:81. (11 Ja. '13.)

Lyons, Marian C. An argument for business English. Educa. Bi-mo. 7:108–11. (D. '12.)

Macdonald, Arthur. Diffusion of education and knowledge. Sci. Am. Sup. 75:27. (11 Ja. '13.)

MacDougall, Robert. The child's speech. III. Speech without words. J. of Educa. Psychol. 3:571–76. (D. '12.)

The use of inarticulate sounds as means of expression of emotions and meanings.

———. The child's speech. IV. Word and meaning. J. of Educa. Psychol. 4:29–38. (Ja. '13.)

A continuation of the previous study.

MacGillivray, D. The state leaving certificate of Scottish schools, with special reference to the qualifying examination of the primary stage. School W. 15:5–7. (Ja. '13.)

McManis, John T. The study of children in the normal school. Educa. Bi-mo. 7:124–31. (D. '12.)

Metzler, William H. Problems in the experimental pedagogy of geometry. J. of Educa. Psychol. 3:545–60. (D. '12.)

An elaborate set of proposed tests of the efficiency of geometry teaching.

Milne, William P. The teaching of scholarship mathematics in secondary schools. School W. 15:8–11. (Ja. '13.)

Mitchill, Theodore C. Loss of efficiency in the recitation. Educa. R. 45:8–28. (Ja. '13.)

Morton, William Henry Stephenson. Retardation in Nebraska. Psychol. Clinic 6:222–28. (Ja. '13.)

A general discussion with bibliography.

(The) most notable school books of 1912. School W. 15:15–17. (Ja. '13.)

New England Association of Colleges and Preparatory Schools. Educa. 33:257–62. (Ja. '13.)

Program; records of the business meeting; entrance requirements and the college degree.

Parmenter, Charles W., and Sanford, Edmund C. The degree for college work only. Educa. 33:276–88. (Ja. '13.)

Presents the reasons for recognizing modern courses as equal to the older ones for college preparation. Emphasizes the need of variety and continuity in studies, and of scientific study of the problems as a basis of judgment.

Paton, Stewart. College or university. Pop. Sci. Mo. 82:192–201. (Fe. '13.)

Phelps, William Lyon. Student honesty in college. Educa. 33:300–302. (Ja. '13.)

Plans for a greater University of Montana. Science 37:170–71. (31 Ja. '13.)

Pott, William S. A. The honor system of the University of Virginia. Educa. 33:303–11. (Ja. '13.)

Shows how the honor system has worked in a university that has longest employed it.

(The) Presidents and deans of various colleges for women. Fraternities in women's colleges. Cent. 85:526–32. (Fe. '13.)

Prosser, C. A. Practical arts and vocational guidance. Man. Train. M. 14:209–22. (Fe. '13.)

(The) public school up to date. Dial 54:81–83. (1 Fe. '13.)

Ryan, Johanna V. Library conditions in American cities. Educa. Bi-mo. 7:157–72. (D. '12.)

Statistics of high-school libraries based on a questionnaire.

(The) Roosevelt professor and the Harvard exchange professor at the University of Berlin. Educa. R. 45:70–86. (Ja. '13.)

Shallies, Guy-Wheeler. The distribution of high-school graduates after leaving school. School R. 21:81–91. (Fe. '13.)

Considers the relative ability of the groups of high-school graduates that enter college, normal schools, teaching without further training, business, industry, and housework, as shown by relative standing in class.

Shepherd, John Wilkes. Some suggestions for the teaching of nature study. II. Educa. Bi-mo. 7:132–48. (D. '12.)

Topics and methods suitable for the various grades.

Smith, David Eugene. The international commission on the teaching of mathematics. Educa. R. 45:1–7. (Ja. '13.)

(The) Society of College Teachers of Education. School R. 21:124–33. (Fe. '13.)

Staples, Clarence Leonard. A critique of high school Latin. Pedagog. Sem. 19:492–509. (D. '12.)

The author maintains that Latin in the high school should aim not at culture nor discipline but at an understanding of the derivation and grammatical structure of English.

Stone, C. W. Problems in the scientific study of the teaching of arithmetic. J. of Educa. Psychol. 4:1–16. (Ja. '13.)

A detailed outline of problems relating both to the value of arithmetic and to the methods of teaching it.

Storey, Thomas A. A follow-up system in medical inspection. Pedagog. Sem. 19:522–25. (D. '12.)

Describes the system used in the College of the City of New York of enforcing individual advice given concerning medical and hygienic treatment.

Teachers' certificates of proficiency. School W. 15:3–5. (Ja. '13.)

(A) theatre all for children. Lit. D. 46:74–75. (11 Ja. '13.)

Town, Clara Harrison. Language development in 285 idiots and imbeciles. Psychol. Clinic 6:229–35. (Ja. '13.)

The author finds a close relation between degree of mental defect and deficiency in language.

(The) universities. Harp. W. 57:34. (11 Ja. '13.)

Webster, Edward Harlan. Verse making in our schools. Pedagog. Sem. 19:510–17. (D. '12.)

It is argued that children can versify and that the practice would be valuable in a number of ways. Methods of teaching are suggested.

Weintrob, Joseph, and Weintrob, Raleigh. The influence of environment on mental ability as shown by Binet-Simon tests. J. of Educa. Psychol. 3:577–83. (D. '12.)

A comparison of the intelligence of children in the Horace Mann School, the Speyer School, and an orphan asylum, as measured by the Binet scale.

Who broke the window? Outl. 103:75–78. (11 Ja. '13.)

Wilkinson, M. O. B. The executive values in education. Educa. R. 45: 29–43. (Ja. '13.)

Winch, W. H. Mental adaptation during the school day as measured by arithmetical reasoning. Pt. 1. J. of Educa. Psychol. 4:17–28. (Ja. '13.)

The report of an experiment to compare the adaptability to mathematical problems of pupils who work in the early and in the latter part of the forenoon.

VOLUME XIII NUMBER 8

THE ELEMENTARY SCHOOL TEACHER

APRIL 1913

EDUCATIONAL NEWS AND EDITORIAL COMMENT

The Department of Superintendence

The most important educational gathering of the year is the winter meeting of the Department of Superintendence and its affiliated organizations which assembled in Philadelphia during the last week of February. Among the affiliated organizations were the National Council, the Society of College Teachers of Education, the National Society for the Study of Education, the International Kindergarten Association, and a half-dozen other national societies and general committees. The discussions of these various bodies cannot be reported here. Two general comments on the significance of this meeting apply to all of the organizations.

First, this winter meeting has clearly outstripped all other meetings in importance. The summer meeting of the association does not bring together as representative or influential a group of educators as does this meeting. The committees which report at this meeting are also of greater significance and influence in the aggregate than are the committees which report at the summer meeting. The total registration at Philadelphia was over 2,500 and there were a great many in attendance who were not formal members of the association.

Second, the very striking emphasis in all of the meetings on discussions of a scientific type marks a great advance upon the informal, inspirational programs of a few years ago. Here and there a voice was raised in protest against the effort to measure educational products, but in the main there was the most cordial sympathy with scientific studies of every type. Even the protests were encouraging, both because they warn the scientific worker of the necessity of caution against overhasty generalization and also because they show that even the reluctant are beginning to realize that the era of exact evaluations in education has arrived.

Summer Meeting of the N. E. A.

Official announcement was made at the Philadelphia meeting that the National Education Association will be held in Salt Lake City from July 7 to July 11. The general plan which is in view for the association is an eastern meeting in 1914 and a meeting in California in connection with the Panama Exposition in 1915.

A Co-operative School Survey

The Upper Peninsular Educational Association of Michigan established at its last meeting in October a bureau of research. The purpose of this bureau is to make an educational survey of the district covered by the association. The bureau has issued two elaborate blanks on which it seeks to secure information, first, from the superintendent or county commissioner, and second, from the individual teacher.

The blank addressed to superintendents and commissioners makes inquiry with regard to the buildings and their janitorial care; with regard to the course of study, emphasizing especially the newer subjects, as manual training, trade training, science, agriculture, etc. Third, questions are raised with regard to consolidation of schools, medical and physical inspection, and scientific tests undertaken to determine the success of instruction. Finally, a financial statement is requested.

The blank addressed to the teacher seeks to get together, first, information with regard to the teacher's own training and experience; second, with regard to the number and characteristics of students; third, with regard to all of the subjects of instruction in the school and the methods and equipment for the presenting of these subjects. The blanks are very suggestive and will be of assistance to anyone who is attempting a similar co-operative survey of a large district.

The example of this association in attempting through a co-operative committee to give the association a perfectly definite problem and at the same time to secure results that will be of large general interest cannot be too highly commended. The trouble with most educational associations is that they have no definite end in view and consequently waste the time and energy of those in attendance. The local school situation is undoubtedly the most important subject for consideration of any association, and the stimulus and training which will come to all members of the association from an investigation of such topics as those mentioned will be one very important outcome of the work of the committee.

The Wisconsin Rural School Survey

A good example of the difficulties that arise from the type of school inquiries which are now possible is to be found in the recent action of the County Superintendents Association held in Madison, Wis. It will be remembered that a report on the conditions of Wisconsin rural schools was made by the State Board of Public Affairs. The county superintendents at their meeting expressed the view that the investigation was made by men who were novices in the work of education. These men, it is asserted, know nothing of country schools and country-school conditions. They worked in less than one-half the counties in the state and in many of these counties their visits were extremely brief.

It is not the purpose of the present editorial to attempt to decide whether the criticisms of the inquiry are valid or not. The point which is to be emphasized is that school inquiries if they are to be of the highest advantage must be carried on systematically and must be broad and complete enough to command the respect of the community. The report which was issued on Wisconsin rural schools has not, as a matter of fact, led to desirable legislation during the present session of the Wisconsin legislature. It has aroused much antagonism; and as indicated by the references made above to the association of county superintendents, it has failed to serve as a constructive basis for the improvement of Wisconsin education.

The Ohio School Survey

An interesting situation and one that is very significant for school people has arisen in the state of Ohio. The governor and the legislature are fully convinced that the public schools of that state, especially the rural schools, are inefficient. They are therefore organizing a careful inquiry to ascertain just how inefficient their schools are.

The following extract from the *Columbus Journal* of March 1 sets forth clearly the attitude of that journal toward the proposed school survey:

> The act of the legislature providing for a school survey may be regarded as radical legislation. And such it is, if it is carried out in the spirit that the situation demands. The school system of this state does not enjoy the full confidence of the people. It is manned and womaned by talent sufficient to make it a success; but there is something the matter with the system, with the way things are done, and with the theories that underlie that system.
>
> To secure the modifications needed, and to put the schools upon a plane of greater efficiency, is the purpose of this act. To secure this, the personnel of that committee should be the first and most important thing to consider. What is wanted is a new departure, an essential change in the doctrine governing common-school education. We are not going to secure this by the sway of reactionary ideas, or under the advice of men who are satisfied with the *status quo*. There should be no inbreeding in the formulation of the new plans. We have had enough of the promulgation of the old theories of public instruction and now we need some men who are prepared with new and advanced ideas.
>
> This whole project is a part of the progressive tendency of the age, at the bottom of which is the exaltation of humanity instead of the promotion of professionalism and the old régime.

About a year ago attention was called in this journal to the fact that the immediate predecessors of the present Ohio legislature had so reduced the available public funds of the state that the schools of Ohio were in serious danger of suffering beyond the point of public endurance. When this fact is recalled in connection with the present provision for an inquiry, one wonders whether the legislature will succeed in getting at the real causes of deficiency in the Ohio schools through the agencies which will be employed for the conduct of this inquiry. There can be no question whatever that Ohio rural schools, like all other schools, are defective. There can be no question at all that any investigation committee will discover some of these defects. Are the educational people going to be satisfied to allow legislators thus to criticize the work of the schools without in turn drawing attention pointedly to the external influences which are continually operating to handicap the teacher and the school supervisor? There ought to be somewhere in the educational world an agency which would anticipate any governor and legislature by pointing out both the defects and the virtues of schools and the extent to which former legislation in the given state has interfered with the operations of the schools. Perhaps the inquiry which is to be made will bring out these facts, but there is great danger, as indicated by some of the inquiries which have already been made, that the real causes of the difficulty will not come to the surface.

A National Council Committee on Standards

The committee of the National Council on Standards and Tests of Efficiency of Schools and Systems of Schools rendered a report through its chairman, Professor Strayer, summarizing the work which has been done up to this time in the different parts of the country in standardizing various subjects and types of organization.

In connection with this report there was a vigorous discussion of the desirability of attempting to standardize the work of schools. There can be no doubt that many members of the council are skeptical as to the possibilities of measuring some of the most important products of school work. On the other hand, those who were in attendance were evidently keenly aware of the fact that school surveys and inquiries are rapidly increasing in number and influence. They were also aware that there must be some constituted educational commission which can undertake in an authoritative way to offer advice to those who are launching upon such inquiries. The committee recommended that its membership be enlarged in such a way that it should represent the most significant scholarship and best administrative practice known to the profession. The functions of this committee were then defined in the report which follows:

1. To encourage those who are engaged in the derivation of scales or units of measurement or in the application of such units to schools or systems

of schools for the sake of establishing standards which may be commonly accepted.

2. That this committee should be made known to the profession as a body ready to give advice or counsel with respect to the nature and scope of school surveys, investigations, or inquiries.

3. That on occasion this committee might be expected to respond to the request of those engaged in the administration of public education for significant help in the organization of a scientific and professional evaluation of the accomplishment of any school or system of schools. This third function can be exercised only when the work of this committee has been sufficiently well established to create the belief in the public mind that our profession is, through its accredited representatives, willing and able to pass in judgment upon the accomplishment of any one of its members. Any such action as is contemplated in this suggestion will, of course, require considerable financial support as well as professional zeal.

In keeping with the general skepticism about measurements, there was some opposition to this committee. Furthermore, there was some opposition on the ground that it would be assumed in some quarters that this committee had arbitrary and wholly artificial powers. It was feared that so small a collection of educators could hardly represent the general profession. The answer to these objections which was offered and accepted by the council was that the committee was not intended to be a court of final resort, but rather an organizing commission which should bring together information and agencies which can be of use in educational inquiries in any part of the country. It is not intended that this committee shall perform through its present membership all of the work which the council has in view. It is intended rather that this committee shall be a center around which activities of this type shall be focused.

The enlarged committee consists of the following persons: Dr. George D. Strayer, chairman, Superintendent William H. Maxwell, Superintendent James H. Van Sickle, Dr. Edward L. Thorndike, Professor E. P. Cubberley, Professor Edward C. Elliott, Professor Paul Hanus, Professor Charles H. Judd, Hon. Calvin N. Kendall, Miss Adelaide Steele Baylor, Hon. Ben Blewett, Mrs. Ella Flagg Young, Hon. John H. Phillips, Miss Katherine D. Blake, Superintendent Frank Spalding.

New York's Reception of the Hanus Report

Two important items of educational news come from New York City. First, the reports of Professor Hanus' committee are appearing in rapid succession. A short section of Professor Hanus' personal report appears with each report by an expert. These documents contain much material that is of universal interest, as well as the description and discussions of New York conditions. In due time each report will be reviewed. In the meantime it is to be noted that New York teachers are making a careful study of the reports and all the other interested parties are being heard at great length on each report. The following article from the *New York Globe* indicates in some detail what is going on:

Through representatives of their various associations, united in a central council, principals and teachers in the local schools have begun a thorough, exhaustive, and impartial study of the reports so far announced by the Committee on School Inquiry of the Board of Estimate. At the meeting of the council yesterday some twenty of the associations were represented, and good progress was made in outlining plans for the study contemplated. It was the prevailing opinion that steps should be taken to increase the representation of teachers, and the Executive Committee was authorized to present a plan to the next meeting.

Upon the recommendation of the central committee it was agreed that all of the reports, including those on the business side, should be studied, and that the report of the Committee on Studies of the Board of Education ought to be included. The scope of the reports was considered, and it was decided that they should not be exhaustive treatises, but clear, concise statements as to the recommendations approved or disapproved, and the reasons therefor. Latitude was given to the committees to report plans where plans suggested by the experts in their reports are not agreed to as outlined.

New York City School Legislation

Our second item of important educational news from New York City refers to certain bills which are before the legislature in Albany to transfer to the Board of Education powers which now belong to the superintendent. The whole matter is so clearly and justly presented in an editorial in the *Evening Post* of February 27 that the statement of the situation may be repeated in the terms of that editorial:

CHAOS IN THE SCHOOLS

It cannot too soon or too sharply be said that the bills pending at Albany to amend the city charter in matters vitally affecting the public schools are thoroughly mischievous. The fact that the Board of Education yesterday gave its approval to these measures does not disprove this. It rather confirms it. For the plain truth is that an attempt is being made to do indirectly and piecemeal what last year it was sought to do directly and wholesale. The Gaynor charter of 1912, with its rash tearing-up of the whole school system, met such strong opposition on the part of skilled educators and intelligent friends of the schools that it had to be dropped. But now some of the same things are to be compassed by means of a series of pop-gun bills. In favor of them, as Dr. Abraham Flexner asserts in a letter to the *Times*, "no single educator of standing can be quoted." They fly in the face of experience and of the best knowledge we have. With the reports on our school methods just obtained from experts by the city, they are in flat contradiction.

Let us take, for example, Assembly bill No. 1212. It would give to the Board of Education the power to "change the grades of all schools," and to "adopt and modify courses of study for all schools." The board can do that now, it is said. Yes, but only "upon the written recommendation of the Board of Superintendents." Those words are in the present law. They are stricken out by the bill. What would be the result? Why, that special knowledge and practical knowledge would be thrown out of the window, and that any member of the Board of Education who had energy enough and log-rolling cleverness enough could cause sweeping changes to be made in the grades and the courses of study, over the protests of the superintendents, and though the alterations might be born of ignorance or prejudice. Now, this is to stand the whole school system on its head. It would employ experts, but hamstring them. As Dr. Flexner states the case with authority: "The unbroken experience of every American city conclusively demonstrates that nothing but disaster results when duties belonging to trained educational experts are transferred to or usurped by a Board of Education, or any of its officers."

Two other bills are almost equally objectionable. One of them calls for the appointment of three additional district superintendents. Whether they are needed or not, we cannot say. But it is ominous that they are to be appointed, not, as now, "upon the nomination of the Board of Superintendents," but direct by the Board of Education. And there is in the same bill a provision that directors of special branches shall be taken from the supervision of the city superintendent and be under no authority but that of the Board of Education. This is a fine touch of chaos. Another one is to be found in Assembly bill No. 1214, which provides that "the president of the board shall have power to designate any member of the supervising or teaching staff to inspect and report upon any subject of which the board has cognizance or over which it has legal control." This may sound very innocent, but what does it imply? Why, that subordinates are to sit in judgment on their superiors. A district superintendent might undertake to pass upon the work of the city superintendent. A teacher would "inspect and report upon" her principal. Was there ever such a topsy-turvy scheme?

If it is a question of investigating the schools, what more do the board and the legislature want than the exhaustive inquiry carried on for two years by Professor Hanus and his corps of able assistants? The results of their patient labors have been coming from the press. But they might as well never have been printed if the haphazard and upheaving policy now indorsed by the Board of Education is to be put into force. Why invite the judgment of experts if it is at once to be flouted? Why go to great expense to get competent investigators if their conclusions are to be contemptuously ignored? On the whole matter of the functions of superintendents, the board has before it a particularly vigorous and suggestive report by Professor Edward C. Elliott, of Wisconsin University. One of his strongest pleas is that the superintendents should be set free from clerical labor so that they may do with full energy the vital work of overseeing instruction, fixing grades, changing courses of study. But these last duties are the very ones which the Board of Education would take away from them, while not lifting a finger to relieve them from the deadening routine of vast masses of correspondence and detailed reports. The force of ignorant audacity could scarcely go farther.

It is a time for protest and a time for action. The legislature and the governor should be given to understand that sappers and miners cannot be allowed to work in the dark beneath our educational structure. If reforms and reconstructions are necessary, they must be undertaken in the light of day and by hands fitted for the work. Certainly, the happy-go-lucky and subversive methods light-heartedly indorsed by the Board of Education deserve the severest condemnation.

School Nurses

The employment of school nurses is becoming a regular part of school organization. It is so common that it hardly constitutes a new item to call attention to the employment of a school nurse in any given community. In order that a record may be made of the steady growth of this movement, however, it is well to note from time to time such items as the following from the *Journal* of Marquette, Michigan:

Recognizing its responsibility in planning for a healthier Menominee, the board of education of that city has decided to appropriate funds for the employment of a visiting school nurse to be a member of the city's corps of instructors. The acquisition of a health pedagogue has long been considered by the board and its action now is considered an important step in the direction of civic advancement. While not altogether an innovation, the cities of Menominee's population supplied with visiting nurses are not many. Cities fortified with visiting nurses have found their services invaluable and many cases are cited where outbreaks of contagious diseases have been frustrated. The duties as outlined for the nurse will be instruction of the children in health matters generally, the care of pupils in ill health, and instruction in hygiene. The selection of a person to occupy the new position has been delegated to Superintendent of Schools Davis.

This item could undoubtedly be duplicated from week to week from various parts of the country. It is a clear indication of the gradual and widespread development of a better medical inspection and management of public schools.

Teachers' Courses in St. Louis

The City Teachers' College of St. Louis is performing a large service for the schools of that city. In the first place, it trains the teachers who are to go into the elementary schools from year to year. In the second place, it conducts under the name Extension Work a number of classes for teachers in active service. In the third place, it provides in a Saturday morning class conducted by Dr. Withers, head of the Teachers' College, an agency for scientific study of the St. Louis system. This Saturday morning class is attended regularly by a body of principals and supervisors and is pursuing a series of important studies. For example, studies are being made by reference to the individual records of children in the schools of the exact number of days which a child spends in each grade. This study is of great significance, first, because it recognizes the only legitimate basis for studies of retardation in actual attendance, and second, because the St. Louis school system has a method of securing acceleration in a relatively large number of cases. The work of the schools is organized in short quarters. Certain of these quarters are devoted in larger measure to reviews. Bright children and children who are well advanced in the work are allowed to omit the review quarters. This method of securing acceleration would invalidate all conclusions drawn from general statistics. Hence the special importance of the type of study which is being made.

This one example serves to show what a group of students of education can undertake when properly organized and encouraged. The example of the St. Louis Board of Education in organizing courses for teachers in service and thus keeping alive interests that will reflect themselves in the schools is worthy of wide recognition and imitation.

THE BLACKBOARD CALENDAR

ROBERT M. BROWN
State Normal School, Worcester, Mass.

The blackboard calendar is an extensively used device for teaching the rudimentary lessons in the science of the weather. It is known in many instances that the benefit derived from the calendar has fallen far short of any clearly defined result, and furthermore it is presumed that in the larger percentage of cases the use is limited to the fleeting period of time when the record for the day is entered in the proper square. Most of the reasons given for the daily task of noting the weather conditions may be summed up in trite phrases concerning the powers of observation or in platitudes about the appreciation of Nature's marvelous ways. It is doubtful whether much of the calendar work is more than a perfunctory performance—one of the chores in the day's work. The instances are numerous where the minds of the pupils are callous to this observance. The blackboard calendar as a device is excellent. The fault lies generally in a lack of appreciation on the part of the teacher of any application of the data recorded and especially of the power which lies in anticipating the conditions of any day or month. The main error is found in the pernicious habit of destroying the calendars, erasing them from the blackboard at the end of the months, to make room for the followimg month's calendar. The calendar represents a collection of facts and one is no more justified in throwing away the items which have been so carefully gathered than he is in leaving an inductive lesson with the "preparation," omitting entirely the more important steps which bring the lesson to a fruitful conclusion. The first lesson to be learned in the matter of the calendars is the value of them; the second is how to use the calendars so that the greatest amount of good can be gleaned from them. It is advised as a first step to preserve the calendars of every month. These may be copied from the blackboard upon large sheets of brown paper, or, better still, the original copy may be made on paper large enough so that the conventional signs may be seen from any part of the room. The legend to be used on the calendar becomes now an object of greater attention. There is no universally accepted set of signs which may be used and a large variety are now in use in the schools. There is no objection to using any code which a teacher prefers, but it will be necessary for the teachers in any single district where the pupils are to be promoted from one room to another to use the same set of symbols in order to increase the facility in the use of the calendars by the pupils as they go from room to room. There are two sets of symbols which may be used with authority:

1. The circle colored as follows: clear days in red; cloudy days in blue; partly cloudy days, upper half of circle in white, lower half in blue; rainy days in yellow; snowy days, a letter *S* as is shown on the October, 1911, calendar for Saturday, the seventh, colored yellow. These are the symbols which are used by the Weather Bureau on the large synoptic weather charts of the United States displayed in certain public places. In the calendars illustrating this article, for convenience in the reproduction, the reader will note that the circles which are cross-lined represent precipitation, the horizontally lined circles stand for cloudy days, and the sunny days are not lined. If these were in colors as indicated above, they would be much more effective. When the day has been mostly clear but some rain or snow has fallen during the night or early morning, an *R* for rain and an *S* for snow have been inserted in the circle, as may be noted for October 6, 1911. The arrows show the direction of the wind and in every instance fly with the wind. Frost is indicated by short vertical lines at the base of the squares (see October 25, 1911). On the October, 1911, calendar, the halo around the moon is indicated on the third in the upper right-hand corner. The crescent moon is indicated on the September, 1911, calendar on the twenty-sixth. It is possible as time goes on to add many more signs to the calendars, but for the purpose of this article only a few were reproduced.

2. In some localities where the weather flags are displayed and a knowledge of the various flags and combinations of flags is considered important, it is possible to use, instead of the circles, facsimiles of the flags. These flags are:

(1) A square white flag, alone, indicates fair weather, stationary temperature.
(2) A square blue flag, alone, indicates rain or snow, stationary temperature.
(3) A square white-and-blue flag (parallel bars of white and blue, the white above the blue), alone, indicates local rain or snow, stationary temperature.
(4) A black triangular flag is a temperature pennant. If above No. 1, it indicates fair weather and warmer; if below, fair weather and colder. If No. 4 is displayed above No. 2, it indicates rain or snow and warmer; if below, rain or snow and colder. If No. 4 is displayed above No. 3, it indicates local rain or snow and warmer; if below, local rain or snow and colder.
(5) A white flag with a black square in the center indicates a cold wave.
(6) A red flag with a black center indicates a storm of marked violence.
(7) A white triangular flag indicates westerly winds.
(8) A red triangular flag indicates easterly winds.

Nos. 7 and 8 are displayed with most of the above flags. No. 7 above a flag indicates a northwest wind; below, a southwest wind. No. 8 above a flag indicates a northeast wind; below, a southeast wind.

It is probable that the first calendar, because of the immaturity of the pupils, cannot be used to any large extent beyond the simple lessons which the different events suggest. In a year or two, the stage of the pupils permits more intricate processes and the accumulation of the facts over the previous years opens devious lines which may be pursued with profit. The work may begin with such a calendar as the September, 1911, which shows state of sky and precipitation only. A first investigation might be to determine the number of clear days in the month; of rainy days; of cloudy days. With the addition of another month's calendar, a comparison is offered. When the September, 1912, calendar has been completed, a monthly average for September is begun. A simple exercise which would bring into play a number of factors would be to determine the average number of rainy days per month, and the average number of clear days for each month. It may be worth while to know how many September months it takes to approximate an average which is fairly constant. Besides furnishing a very definite conception of one or two of the elements of our weather, the process has the advantage of concentrating and stimulating the interest in future calendars. On the October, 1911, calendar, the wind direction has been added and the avenues of procedure become at once multiplied. Is there any relation between state of sky and wind direction? Do east winds always bring rain? How many days in the month was the wind from a westerly direction? What percentage of winds were westerly? How does this percentage compare with the following October's record? Can we find an average percentage of days per month when the winds are westerly? If now in time the temperature be added to the records, then wind velocity, amount of precipitation, and cloud forms, the number of problems becomes at once too large to undertake, so that the teacher must select those which are directly related to issues which must be understood before the climates of the world can be approached with any degree of success.

Again, the use of the weather sayings which are prevalent in any locality makes an excellent subject for investigation and allows the pupils a basis for discrimination between the true and the false doctrines of the science. Thus for the September month the following sayings are current:

1. As September, so the coming May.
2. Heavy September rains bring drought.
3. September 15 is said to be fine six years out of seven.

The first invites a comparison between the calendars of the two months. It will be found to be somewhat unsatisfactory, however, because of its indefiniteness, and the pupils will soon be willing to drop it from the list of reputable sayings. The second is also indefinite, and as soon as any attempt is made to define it by means of the calendars, it also will be dropped. The third will be disproved by a number of September calendars. In addition to the current sayings for the months, many questions will arise from sayings which have their origin in some feature which happens to arise because of special conditions; thus from the September, 1911, calendar a number of additional queries arise:

1. The time of first killing frost. When it occurred on September 14, 1911, it was generally remarked that the first frost was early. Was it? If we had the 1910 calendar, the first frost would be found to have occurred on October 12 of that year. The 1912 calendar shows first frost on October 16. An attempt might be made to find the average time of first frost. The average time of first killing frost in Worcester is about September 23.

SEPTEMBER				1911		
SUN	MON	TUE	WED	THU	FRI	SAT
					1	2
3	4	5	6	7	8	9
10	11	12	13	14	15	16
R 17	18	19	20	21	22	23
24	R 25	26	27	28	29	30

OCTOBER				1911		
SUN	MON	TUE	WED	THU	FRI	SAT
1	2	3	4	5	R 6	7
8	9	10	11	12	13	14
15	16	17	18	19	20	21
22	23	24	25	26	R 27	28
29	30	31				

2. The question of the equinoctial storm. The autumnal equinox during 1911 was on September 23. Apart from a brief shower during the night of the 25th, the nearest rain occurred on the 27th. During 1912 the autumnal equinox occurred also on the 23d, and the nearest rain was on the 20th. Rain occurred at other times during the month. By means of a study of the intervals between rainy days and the number of rainy days on a series of September calendars, a proper appreciation of the value of this belief can be reached.

3. The wet and dry moon. On September 26, 1911, the crescent moon is added in position.

If the new moon appear with the points of the crescent turned up, the month will be dry. If the points are turned down, it will be wet.

This also can be settled without much trouble. All these form part of the common conversation on weather topics among a large class of people and it will not take a very long while nor very careful investigation to place the pupil alive to the power within his reach by which he may understand a few of the simple meteorological principles which are at the basis of a true and appreciative knowledge of atmospheric phenomena. In the October list are found sayings which futilely attempt to forecast the weather for the months to come. In many instances this desire to foretell weather features crops out and frequently the line between the good and the bad may be shown by the simple test of whether the immediate future or the more distant future is the object. In all of the following the distant future weather is predicted:

1. Much rain in October, much wind in December.
2. Warm October, cold February.
3. If October brings heavy frosts and winds, then will January and February be mild.
4. As the weather in October, so will it be in the next March.
5. There is often about October 18 a fine spell of fine dry weather and this has received the name of St. Luke's little summer.

The October, 1911, calendar suggests more fruitful lines of investigation than these.

1. It was rainy on the first Sunday of the month. The saying is common:

> If it rains on the first Sunday of the month, it will rain every Sunday of the month.

This, it is noted, is not true for the October of 1911. With a series of calendars the evidence would soon be conclusive.

2. The lunar halo is entered on the third, the fifth, and again on the thirtieth.

> A ring around the moon brings rain.

It rained on the fourth, the sixth and seventh, and again on the thirty-first. A good beginning of evidence in favor of this saying is at hand but more should be collected.

3. Snow fell for the first time during the fall on October 7. Is this early or late? What is the average time for the first snow? About this time the town character who also poses as the local "weather sharp" predicts the number of snow storms which the winter will yield. Both in the public print and through the medium of the itinerant forecaster many statements concerning the weather are expressed which the pupils ought to have some way to understand aright, and there is no way unless the events are recorded and preserved and used as data in teaching. The reason why so many unscientific remarks about the weather persist is that people do not take the trouble to follow them up. If the teacher attempts to teach weather science, she must begin with the current notions about the weather, and unless she wishes to have the wise-sounding but utterly foolish doggerel of some weather wiseacre to have more influence than her teaching, she must prepare her pupils against the fallacies of the science.

It is a common tendency to compare one season with another, and it is noticeable that the memory of people concerning weather events is fickle. This is not strange. It is the expectable thing, as events make their impressions of varying degrees according to circumstances. Consequently the comparison of one month with the corresponding one of another year and, better still, the corresponding ones for a series of years, will do much to overcome the tendency of misrepresenting, to oneself at least, the conditions of the seasons, and at the same time an estimate may be gained of the limits of variations of the seasons. Many lessons about the weather are poorly taught because the teacher has no evidence on hand, no data for the problem, or no facts to lead toward a generalization, and so the memory is invoked and comparisons are made until it were better if the subject had not been begun. And thus it is commonly the case that when November comes, every year there is a feeling that the days are unusual for the time of year. Our literature enforces the belief for we have read in the schools,

> November's sky is chill and drear
> November's leaf is red and sear.

or

> When chill November's surly blast
> Made fields and forests bare.

The November conditions in the land of Scott and Burns are not necessarily the features of our November weather. The November calendars for 1911 and 1912 show a preponderance of sunny days, nineteen each. During 1911 there were seven rainy days and during 1912 there were six. Traces of snow are shown on the 1911 calendar, while on the 1912 calendar, two snowy days, the 25th and the 28th, are recorded. If the temperature had been reproduced, a slight difference would be apparent and this is indicated somewhat by the wind direction. During November, 1911, there were three days with a southwest wind which gives us the genial weather of the Indian Summer type; during November, 1912, there were ten. If the three fall months are considered, there will be found to have been more days with a southwest wind during 1912 than during 1911. One more lesson can be taken from these two calendars. On Thursday, November 28, 1912, Thanksgiving Day, it snowed. About this time, the oldest inhabitant is telling about Thanksgiving Days when he was a boy, and the believer in the "old-fashioned winter" has much to say about the snow and ice which used to exist on Thanksgiving Day. In this direction also our calendars if they are saved can be of service.

This article is printed in the hope that the material may be suggestive; that some teachers who are struggling vainly toward some method of gaining interest in the weather may be moved to fresher trials, and that the teachers who have in a desultory way, month after month, gone through the form of making the calendar may find inspiration in their labor and in the facts which have been so slowly gathered.

A STRONG MOTIVATION FOR ARITHMETIC WORK

CASSIE L. PAINE
Boston, Massachusetts

In a certain school, a class of twelve sixth-grade children were allowed to work in a group by themselves. These children were not defective mentally, but were somewhat slow and indolent, and had little in their home life to stimulate vigorous intellectual activity. They had lagged more or less through the grades, all having failed of their last promotion, and several having failed at other times. They were generally deficient in all school subjects and particularly deficient in arithmetic and language.

In attacking the problem of having the children make up their deficiencies, there seemed to be two courses that might be pursued. One was to compel each child by coercion to complete a minimum amount of the required work, and another way was to arrange situations so that the children would see the need of obtaining knowledge, and therefore have a desire to do so.

The arithmetic work was at the stage where the four fundamental operations in common fractions, decimal fractions (U.S. money), and denominate numbers should be fixed. Problems of two or three steps involving these operations should be interpreted and performed, and the subject of percentage begun. The children disliked the ordinary drills in reading and writing decimals, in computing fractions, etc., and frankly said so. When given a problem involving reasoning, they began to work on it with no intelligent interpretation of its purpose, and half-heartedly tried one operation after another until in some way or other the correct answer was obtained.

The idea was conceived that if those children could realize the value in their own daily lives of accurate and intelligent computation, it would give them an incentive to acquire the necessary information. It was therefore decided to let them practice running a grocery store, and get the motive for their work in arithmetic that way. The plan was laid before the children and they entered into it with great enthusiasm.

The place selected for the store was a set of shelves upon which the schoolroom supplies were kept. It involved considerable work to move these supplies to other places, to clean the shelves, to find and hang curtains to cover the unused part, etc. But the children were willing to take any amount of time out of school hours and to go to any trouble for this purpose. Several firms, such as the National Biscuit Co., The Sunshine Biscuit Co., Heinz Pickle Co., were reported to be very willing to furnish samples of goods, empty cartons, etc., to schools to be used in this way. Consequently, the children were allowed to write to the several firms in regard to the matter. This was excellent practice in writing business letters.

As there was considerable delay in getting the goods, the children suggested that they bring things from their own homes to use while waiting for the others. This was allowed, and the accompanying photograph shows the result. Without direction from the teacher in charge, the children brought empty bottles, boxes, cans, etc., from their homes, mended the mutilated places, filled the transparent receptacles with materials that were similar in appearance to the original contents, wrote the prices in inconspicuous places, and arranged the goods on the shelves as in the picture. A money drawer was made, and measures and baskets of various kinds were procured.

The children decided upon the name of their store and made the sign. In order to do this, accurate measurements had to be taken and followed; rather careful arithmetical computations were also necessary in order to divide the space correctly. In the manual-training room, the boys made blocks of wood to represent cakes of soap to fit various soap wrappers that were brought. Wooden yeast cakes were also manufactured in the same way. A file was made for the sale slips and a hook upon which to hang the paper bags. The head of a butter firkin was covered with yellow paper, to represent butter and a block of wood covered with the same material represented the piece to be sold. For the sale slips a long strip of paper that came from a roll of ribbon was folded

SOUTH SALEM
GROCERY STORE
SALE
Salt
Butter
Eggs
Coffee

into uniform-sized pieces, and put into a box, through the cover of which one end protruded.

In order to keep up with the market prices, the children were obliged frequently to interview the various near-by grocers for the latest prices of the goods they carried. A slate was brought from one of the playrooms at home, upon which some child arranged and printed daily a price list that was hung in sight for the convenience of the customers. The children took turns in being storekeeper, bookkeeper, and store boy, and could actually "deliver the goods" in return for (toy) money. The other children, and frequently the teachers, were customers, and often a rather knotty problem in fractions would occur as a result of the transactions.

The storekeepers usually gave a discount for cash payments, and occasionally there would be discounts on all the sales during a limited period of time. Special sales for certain days were arranged and announced, as the accompanying photograph shows. Here the practical work in accurate computations in decimal fractions, in profit and loss, and in percentage took on a real meaning, and it was very interesting to see how seriously the children discussed the pros and cons of selling the different articles at a reduction.

The wholesale side of storekeeping was also attacked, and this involved work with larger numbers. The children took an inventory of goods on hand, and made an invoice of goods (that might have been) received from other firms. They planned a "supply" garden and made an estimate of the new stock for the store that might reasonably be expected from the garden. They kept weekly accounts of the running of the store, and reckoned up their "financial standing" every Friday.

All this represented the interesting "play" side of the work, but the educational problems did not stop there. After actually going through the bargaining at the store, each child wrote out his individual transaction in the form of a problem. This problem at a later date was given the other members of the class to do. This gave the children an intelligent appreciation of the purpose of a problem, and it formed an apperceptive basis for the interpretation of other arithmetical problems. It also gave the children needed practice in stating clearly the main facts of the trans-

South Salem
Grocery
Special
Sale

Jar of Jelly	25¢
Strickly Fresh Eggs	27¢
Evaporated Apples	13¢
Pickles	22¢
Sugar 2 LBS	12¢
Tea a LB	43¢
Codfish 3 Boxes	25¢

With Every
Purchase
Of Jelly
a
Box of Soap

South Salem Grocery
Marblehead Road
SPECIAL SALE !!!!

Jelly Per Jar 1 bar of soap with each purchase	25¢
Strictly fresh eggs	27¢
Regular price 30¢	30¢
Star Brand Evaporated apple Regular price 15¢	13¢
Granulated sugar 2 lbs for Regular price 13¢	12¢
Codfish 3 boxes for Regular price 09¢ a box	25¢
All 35¢ coffee cut down to	32¢
Best quality of tea Regular price 45¢	43¢

action. Below are some of the problems made out by the children in this way.

I went to the store and bought 1½ lbs Confectioner's sugar @ 8 ¢ lb. 1½ lbs Brown sugar @ 7 ¢ lb. 5 lbs granulated sugar @ 6½ ¢ lb. Find total cost. How much change will I receive from $2?

On a Bargain Day I bought 3 lbs butter at 34½ ¢ 4 boxes of Butter thin @ 9½¢. They allowed 10% on cash.

A woman bought 1 can cocoa @ 22 ¢ and 2 qts. milk @ 8 ¢ qt. She gave the clerk $1 and received $.72 in change. How much extra change did she receive?

If 2 boxes of butter thins cost 10 ¢ per box and ½ lb of butter at $.35 per lb. Cost?

If I pay the bill at once he will give me a discount of 7 per cent and I give him a ten dollar bill what was the change I got back?

If I go to the store with a dollar bill and buy 1 can of Tea @ 45 ¢, and 1 can of Backing Powder @ 25 ¢, 2 pounds of Sugar @ 13 ¢, 1 doz. Eggs 33 ¢, and 1 pkg Quaker Puffed Rice 10 c. How much more did I owe him.

Find the cost:

1 bag salt @ .10
1 box candy @ .35
1 box Uneeda @ .05
1 box White House coffee @ .25 can
Change from 1.00

I went to the store and bought 1 bottle Ammonia @ 10 ¢ bottle, 1 can Baker's Cocoa @ $.22 can, 1 pkg. Quaker Oats @ $.10 pkg., 1 bottle Malted Milk @ $ 25 ¢ bottle, 1 pkg. Not-A-Seed raisins @ $.10 ¢ pkg. and 1 doz. eggs @ $.33 doz. How much will I pay after 10 per cent has been taken off?

If I buy 1 box of chocolates at 1.00, and a Jar of Jam at .25, an a can of sugar of Milk at $.33,. How much will I pay if I get 3 per cent off from all the goods that I have bought.

The running of the store gave material for some of the written work in English. The children usually disliked writing compositions, but these copies of their first drafts will show how spontaneously they could write when the subject was something in which they were really interested.

Our Grocery Store

Everett

April 11, 1912.

We started a store in our room. All of us children brought boxes from home, and stuck them together with mending tissue and after we had a great many boxes. One day Aruthur and I came in early and put the store in condition. Miss P. came in and she thought it just grand. She asked us if we evered decorated a window in a store. We opened our store Tuesday morning at nine o'clock. I was the keeper the first day. We had a price list on our goods. The children were the customers. The gave me the money and I gave them the change. We made problems from what we bought.

Our Grocery Store

Edith

April 17, 1912.

The first thing we did was to send letters to the large biscuit companies. We have not received any thing yet. The store is in the front of the room. Mr. W. took some pictures of it. We have paper money. The store is open at nine o'clock. There are chocalates, cocoa, Quaker oats, malted milk and a grate many more things that I can not name. Everrett was the first store-keeper. Miss P. has been in and bought things. Our store is called the "South Salem Grocery Store." Each one of us made one or to letters. It was open April 1, 1912.

Our Grocery Store

Arthur

April 16 1912

We sent to three different places for sanple boxes and not receiving any, we brought boxes from home. We cleared off the shelves and Everett and I placed the boxes on the shelves. We opened the store the second day of April. Everett was the store keeper. We each bought something, and then Miss P. came in and bought something. We made up examples on the good we bought. We are making a sign. The name of the store is the South Salem Grocery Store.

Our Grocery Store

Auguste

april 12 1912

We wrote to the National Biscuit Co to have some sample boxes of biscuit be did not have any answer so we bought things from home, empty boxes of Uneeda biscuit, Baker's cocoa, Baking powder and other things. Everett and Arthur fixed the things on the shelvs and now we buy things.

I was store keeper the first day. I knew how to run a store because i had one last summer. When they bought for a big sum I allowed discount, and then we made problem. We use paper money. I enjoyed very much my first day in the store. The name of our store is South Salem Grocery Store. We made our own letters and we pasted them on the paper. We had the picture taken and it came out good.

(These problems and compositions are exact copies of the children's uncorrected first drafts. They are given, not to show accuracy of form, but evidence of thought on the part of the writers.)

It would be almost impossible to tell of the different ways in which the children showed the benefit of this kind of *live* arithmetic work. In the first place, they had a genuine desire to attend school and to work after they got there. They could exercise their creative ability in providing make-believe goods. They had practice in transacting business courteously. They gained much in speed and accuracy of computation without pencil and paper. They acquired confidence and intelligence in stating their wants and in judging the value of what they received. They had a feeling of responsibility in the care of the store, and saw the value of neatness, order, attractive arrangement of goods, etc. They realized the necessity of knowing how to write business letters, make out bills, receipts, and various other common business forms. They saw the importance of clear, legible writing and printing. They had the satisfaction of being able to state and perform problems, the conditions and results of which were concrete and actual. In their written English periods they had something to write about and a desire to make what they wrote interesting. But, perhaps, best of all, was the joy they experienced in originating ways of supplying actual needs. These children had never before had the feeling that their contributions to a class were of much use. Now they saw the actual value of what they could give, and this knowledge gave them a hitherto unknown feeling of encouragement and confidence in themselves.

THE STATUS OF SCIENCE TEACHING IN THE ELEMENTARY SCHOOLS OF THE UNITED STATES

PERCY E. ROWELL
Berkeley, California

One of the unsettled questions of the day concerns itself with the importance of science teaching in the grammar grades. There are many reasons why science should be taught in the grades, and there are but two reasons given why it cannot be taught. The latter are the crowded curriculum and the unpreparedness of the teachers, both of which may be remedied and gradually abolished.

The reasons for science in the grades fall under two heads: the personal and the economic. There is more to learn now than formerly, and the need for scientific education is becoming more pressing. Seventy-eight per cent of those who enter the grades do not go to high school, and if there is no scientific study given during these years the 78 per cent will never receive any real instruction in science. Again, science is so stimulating that its general introduction into the grades could do more toward retaining in the schools some of the 78 per cent than can any other study, and, in addition, it might arouse the ambition of some to take up a more advanced study of science.

The child cannot be aware of his need for science. The need becomes more apparent as scientific knowledge increases. It is society, however, which benefits most by the child's knowledge of science. The nature of scientific training is such that the child acquires habits of orderly and creative thinking; of reasoning from cause to effect. These habits will outlive the scientific facts which have led to their formation. Dewey has said: "We need to develop a certain active interest in truth and its allies, a certain disposition of inquiry, together with a command of the tools which make it effective, and to organize certain modes of activity in observation, construction, expression, and reflection." Science teaching may be made the study pre-eminently fitted for producing these results.

That community in which a large proportion of its citizens has had some scientific training will be well advanced economically.

In an attempt to ascertain the status of science teaching in the grades throughout the United States, a questionnaire was prepared and sent to all of the states, according to their population. Approximately one questionnaire was sent for each one hundred thousand inhabitants, or 872 in all. Of these, there were received 282 replies, making 32 per cent of returns. The list of questions follows:

1. Do you believe in science teaching in the elementary grades?
2. Should science be taught as a separate subject?
3. In what grade do you think science teaching should begin?
4. What object should be sought in the teaching of science in the grades?
5. How may this object be attained?
6. What should the science material consist of?
7. Do you think that science in the grades should lead toward the industries or toward general information and development?
8. How early should the pupils be required to make formal experiments?
9. How early should the pupils keep a formal record of their work?
10. What science or sciences does your school give in the grades?
11. What are the grades in which science is taught and what science is taught in each grade?
12. What is the method of presentation of the science in your school?
13. Do pupils tend to reason from one fact to another or is their knowledge more like a series of facts which are unrelated?
14. What interest do the boys show in the science work?
15. What interest do the girls show in the science work?
16. Does science aid in the other studies, either in time or understanding?
17. Does science work tend to keep the pupils in school longer?
18. Does science work tend to increase the number of pupils who go to high school?

Early in the work it was found necessary to reduce the number of kinds of answers, in order to draw any conclusions from the replies. Although there were but eighteen questions, soon the number of varieties of answers reached 287. By careful adjustments this number was reduced to 147, the later replies being filed under the headings which corresponded the closest with them. The information, which was received from the whole United States, is given in the form of summary tables. There is added a list showing the sources of the information.

KEY 1

Do you believe in science teaching in the grades?

Answers:

	Base 282 Number	Percentage
A. Yes	234	83
B. Yes—as nature-study	22	8
C. Not as a definite subject—as correlation	12	5
D. No	14	5
	282	Base

KEY 2

Should science be taught as a separate subject?

Answers:

	Base 277 Number	Percentage
A. Yes	110	40
B. Yes—as geography	8	3
C. Yes—as nature-study	19	7
D. Yes—as physiology and hygiene	8	3
E. Yes—in sixth, seventh, and eighth grades	31	11
F. Both separate and as correlation	18	6
G. No—as correlation	82	30
H. Not with a text	1	..
	277	Base

KEY 3

In what grade should science teaching begin?

Answers:

	Base 264 Number	Percentage
A. Kindergarten—as nature-study	18	7
B. First grade	117	44
C. First grade—as nature-study	20	8
D. Third or fourth grade	40	15
E. Fifth grade	23	9
F. Sixth grade	17	6
G. Seventh grade	22	9
H. High school	7	3
	264	Base

KEY 4

What object should be sought in this science teaching?

Answers:

		Base 406	
		Number	Percentage
A.	Information concerning common things and phenomena. Laws	107	26
B.	Observation and explanation of phenomena, training in observation	99	24
C.	Broadening of interests	52	13
D.	Habits of thought, reasoning power, scientific spirit, exactness	57	14
E.	Appreciation and love of nature	38	9
F.	The place of self in the environment	17	4
G.	Practical knowledge	19	5
H.	Preparation for high school or for future work	9	2
I.	Culture	8	2
		406	Base

KEY 5

How may this object be attained?

Answers:

		Base 262	
		Number	Percentage
A.	Good teaching—teach the child *as* a child—good syllabus	91	35
B.	By experiments by the pupils—real objects.	60	23
C.	Observation *and* application—assembling facts, explanations; clear and accurate statements	47	18
D.	Observing *living* animals and plants with *guidance*	28	11
E.	By selecting general informational subjects	12	5
F.	By excursions, visits to manufacturing plants, etc.	13	5
G.	By readings and lantern lessons	6	2
H.	Textbook in the hands of pupils	5	2
		262	Base

KEY 6

What should the science material consist of?

Answers:

		Base 247 Number	Percentage
A.	Phenomena of the environment	124	50
B.	Objects, specimens, especially alive, pictures, simple apparatus	30	12
C.	Nature-study—elementary science in the seventh and eighth grades	40	16
D.	*All* sciences	19	8
E.	Products of man's work—industries	9	4
F.	The relations of self to the rest of the world	7	3
G.	The use of textbooks	5	2
H.	Good teaching and much laboratory work	10	4
I.	Agriculture, physiology, biology, gardens	3	1
		247	Base

KEY 7

Should science lead toward industries or general information and development?

Answers:

		Base 260 Number	Percentage
A.	General information and development	147	57
B.	Industries	12	5
C.	Industries in upper grades	11	4
D.	Both	70	27
E.	Both—emphasis on industries	10	4
F.	Both—emphasis on general information	10	4
		260	Base

KEY 8

How early should pupils make formal experiments?

Answers:

		Base 240 Number	Percentage
A.	At the beginning of science work	29	12
B.	No time can be set	16	7
C.	First grade	20	8
D.	Third grade	13	5
E.	Fourth grade	14	6
F.	Fifth grade	18	8
G.	Sixth grade	26	11
H.	Seventh grade	57	23
I.	Eighth grade	19	8
J.	High school	28	12
		240	Base

KEY 9

How early should pupils keep a formal record of experiments?

Answers:

		Base 236 Number	Percentage
A.	From the beginning of science work........	42	18
B.	No time can be set......................	12	5
C.	First grade..........................	4	2
D.	Third grade..........................	17	7
E.	Fourth grade..........................	14	6
F.	Fifth grade..........................	18	8
G.	Sixth grade..........................	23	10
H.	Seventh grade..........................	53	22
I.	Eighth grade..........................	21	9
J.	High school..........................	32	14
		236	Base

KEY 10

What sciences does your school teach?

Answers:

		Base 401 Number	Percentage
A.	Agriculture..........................	30	7
B.	Biology..............................	11	3
C.	Botany..............................	18	4
D.	Elementary science (physics and chemistry)	38	9
E.	General science........................	61	15
F.	Geography...........................	40	10
G.	Hygiene (sanitation)...................	21	5
H.	Incidental...........................	7	2
I.	Meteorology..........................	5	1
J.	Nature-study.........................	79	20
K.	None, or very little....................	25	6
L.	Physiology...........................	66	16
		401	Base

KEY 11

In what grades are the different sciences taught, or is the work general?

Answers:

		Base 270	
		Number	Percentage
A.	Nature-study in all grades	47	17
B.	Nature-study in lower grades	21	8
C.	General science in all grades	61	23
D.	General science in lower grades	10	4
E.	General science in eighth grade	7	3
F.	Physics in upper grades	25	9
G.	Physiology in all grades (hygiene and sanitation)	25	9
H.	Physiology in fourth to eighth grades	25	9
I.	Geography in all grades	9	3
J.	Geography in fourth to eighth grades	9	3
K.	Incidental	7	3
L.	Agriculture in fourth to eighth grades	24	9
		270	Base

KEY 12

What is the method of presentation of science in your school?

Answers:

		Base 214	
		Number	Percentage
A.	Experiments by teacher *and* pupils	62	28
B.	Experiments by teacher, observation and record by pupils	17	8
C.	Object method	37	17
D.	Observation and deduction	14	6
E.	Oral—inductive	31	14
F.	By book and experiment	27	12
G.	Talks, grades 1–3; text, grades 4–8	6	3
H.	Various methods; depends upon the teacher	20	9
		214	Base

KEY 13

Do pupils reason or is their learning a series of facts?

Answers:

		Base 191	
		Number	Percentage
A.	Series of facts	71	37
B.	Progressive reasoning	43	22
C.	Both	10	5
D.	They learn to relate slowly	31	16
E.	Try to teach reasoning	16	8
F.	It depends upon the teaching	14	7
G.	Not prepared to answer	6	3
		191	Base

KEY 14

What interest do boys show in the science work?

Answers:

		Base 179 Number	Percentag
A.	Excellent	41	23
B.	Good	60	33
C.	Experimental work liked best—the doing	26	15
D.	More than in any other subject	6	3
E.	Same as in any other study	21	12
F.	More than the girls	13	8
G.	Everything depends upon the teacher	12	7
		179	Base

KEY 15

What interest do girls show in the science work?

Answers:

		Base 177 Number	Percentage
A.	Excellent	20	11
B.	Good	18	10
C.	Good in adapted work	21	12
D.	More than the boys	3	2
E.	As much as the boys	68	39
F.	Hardly less than the boys	9	5
G.	Less than the boys	29	16
H.	More *lively*—less real interest than the boys	4	2
I.	Same as in any other subject	5	3
		177	Base

KEY 16

Does science aid the other studies in time or in understanding?

Answers:

		Base 198 Number	Percentage
A.	Yes, in one or the other	102	52
B.	Both	31	16
C.	Understanding	15	8
D.	Yes, in geography	7	4
E.	Yes, especially for oral and written expression	6	3
F.	Somewhat, in one or the other	7	4
G.	Like other studies if well taught	9	5
H.	No	6	3
I.	Hard to tell	15	8
		198	Base

KEY 17

Does science tend to keep pupils in school longer?

Answers:

		Base 195	
		Number	Percentage
A.	Yes	73	37
B.	Probably—I think so—I believe so	26	13
C.	Think not	12	6
D.	Not to a marked degree (like other subjects)	18	9
E.	No	15	8
F.	Don't know—can't tell—hard to tell	51	26
		195	Base

KEY 18

Does science work increase number of pupils going to high school?

Answers:

		Base 194	
		Number	Percentage
A.	Yes	76	39
B.	Probably—I think so—I believe so	29	15
C.	True of any subject well taught	7	4
D.	No	23	12
E.	Don't know—no evidence—hard to tell	59	30
		194	Base

There can be no doubt that educators believe that science should have a place in the curriculum of the grades. While 83 per cent of the replies are unqualifiedly in favor of science teaching, 8 per cent limit science teaching to nature-study and 4 per cent believe that it should be given as correlation. A small minority, 5 per cent, are decidedly opposed to science teaching in the grades, and their opposition is based upon the fact that the curriculum is already too crowded and that teachers are not prepared to take up science teaching.

That science should be taught as a separate subject is believed by 40 per cent; that it should be geography by 3 per cent, nature-study by 7 per cent, physiology and hygiene by 3 per cent, and that it should be taught only in the upper grades by 11 per cent. This makes a total of 64 per cent who are in favor of science as a separate subject. It will be noticed that 30 per cent are in favor of science

DISTRIBUTION OF QUESTIONNAIRES AND REPLIES

Number	State	Number Sent	Number Received	Percentage Received	Number Normals	Percentage Normals
1	Alabama	24	7	28	0	0
2	Arizona	6	1	17	1	100
3	Arkansas	14	3	21	0	0
4	California	59	26	44	4	15
5	Colorado	9	2	22	1	50
6	Connecticut	10	5	50	2	40
7	Delaware	3	0	0	0	0
8	Dist. of Columbia	10	4	40	1	25
9	Florida	5	1	20	0	0
10	Georgia	13	3	23	0	0
11	Idaho	4	1	25	1	100
12	Illinois	62	23	37	5	21
13	Indiana	33	12	36	0	0
14	Iowa	19	7	39	1	14
15	Kansas	13	5	38	2	40
16	Kentucky	18	6	33	2	23
17	Louisiana	9	5	55	2	40
18	Maine	9	3	33	2	66
19	Maryland	5	0	0	0	0
20	Massachusetts	35	10	29	2	20
21	Michigan	29	10	34	0	0
22	Minnesota	24	5	21	2	40
23	Mississippi	14	1	7	0	0
24	Missouri	22	7	32	0	0
25	Montana	6	1	17	0	0
26	Nebraska	16	6	37	2	33
27	Nevada	3	2	67	2	100
28	New Hampshire	4	4	100	1	25
29	New Jersey	27	11	41	2	18
30	New Mexico	6	2	33	1	50
31	New York	64	18	28	2	11
32	North Carolina	7	1	14	0	0
33	North Dakota	9	1	11	1	100
34	Ohio	62	21	34	2	10
35	Oklahoma	8	2	25	1	50
36	Oregon	7	1	14	0	0
37	Pennsylvania	50	18	36	3	17
38	Rhode Island	5	2	40	0	0
39	South Carolina	7	2	29	1	50
40	South Dakota	9	5	55	2	40
41	Tennessee	14	3	21	0	0
42	Texas	29	4	14	2	50
43	Utah	5	3	60	0	0
44	Vermont	4	2	50	1	50
45	Virginia	14	1	7	0	0
46	Washington	16	7	44	1	14
47	West Virginia	11	4	36	2	50
48	Wisconsin	35	12	34	4	33
49	Wyoming	5	1	20	0	0
	Totals for United States	872	282	32	58	21

teaching as correlation, although in Question 1 only 4 per cent so indicated their belief. This is probably due to the division of their replies and 30 per cent may be taken as the correct percentage of teachers who believe in correlation of science work. Be this as it may, a large majority of teachers are in favor of science as a separate subject in the grades. The crowded condition of the curriculum does not seem to prevent the introduction of science as a new subject.

The grade in which science teaching should begin is undoubtedly the first, 52 per cent so believing. Of these 8 per cent would limit the science to nature-study. A second maximum is reached in the third or fourth grade with 15 per cent. It is quite apparent that the majority of teachers believe that there should be instruction in science throughout the entire grammar-school course. A small percentage believe that it should begin, as nature-study, even in the kindergarten.

The object of science teaching in the grades would seem to be information concerning common things, a proper observation of them, and a reasonable explanation for their occurrence. Those in favor of information concerning everyday phenomena number 26 per cent, while 24 per cent believe that training in observation and the explanation of phenomena are the desired objects. Broadening of interests, as an object to be sought in science teaching, is indicated by 13 per cent, and reasoning power, as a goal, is stated by 14 per cent of the replies. Practical knowledge, as a desired aim of science teaching, wins the support of but 5 per cent. This seems odd in this age of utilitarianism, and will be taken up again in Question 7.

Though rather decided that science should be taught so as to give information and to develop powers of observation, there is not much information given in regard to methods of obtaining this result. Good teaching as a method is given by 35 per cent, but all educators are in favor of good teaching. The question is, What is good teaching in science? It must be different from the usual methods of teaching in the other subjects of the grades. The answer that the object of science teaching may be attained by observation *and* application, by assembling facts, and giving explanations in clear and accurate statements, while receiving but 18 per cent of the replies in its favor, is probably the truest solution. Experiments by the pupils, excursions, and readings, in fact all of the devices of teachers of science, are of little value without the use of this method. Mere observation is useless unless it can be fixed by the concrete example, by many concrete examples. The acquisition of facts is incomplete unless they can be grouped according to the child's idea, to be sure, around some central fact, while clear and accurate statements of fact are the only evidences of real knowledge. Unless a child can explain phenomena, he does not know their reason for existing. There is too much learning of word formulas and too little learning of ideas. Good teaching *is* necessary, but good teaching can be given only by good teachers.

As science material, the phenomena of the environment leads with an even 50 per cent. This is as it should be. Our knowledge, especially when we are young, should be concerned with a good understanding of our immediate surroundings. Later the sphere of knowledge may be enlarged, and that sphere is the most stable which has the solidest core. Closely connected with the environment, objects and specimens as science material meet the favor of 12 per cent. Nature-study and elementary science meet the approval of 16 per cent, while 8 per cent believe that all of the sciences should contribute material for a science course in the grades. As a source of material, 4 per cent mention the industries. The fact that only 1 per cent believe in agriculture and garden work is the most surprising answer of all.

There seems to be much indefiniteness in regard to the content of nature-study. Naturally a complete study of nature must embrace nearly all scientific knowledge. The definition that nature-study is limited to plants and animals seems best. If that is accepted there need be no doubt as to the material which is to be studied. To study the phenomena of the environment in a satisfactory manner necessitates the introduction of material from all of the sciences. Note that this is not the same as saying that it is necessary to teach all of the sciences in the grades. The different sciences are but artificial, man-made divisions of phenomena, and in the grades—if not also in the high school—the phenomena should be studied irrespective of the sciences of which the scientist deems that they are a part. Such a collection of everyday, useful phenomena may well be given the name of general science.

The question whether science teaching in the grades should lead toward general information and development or toward the industries is answered in favor of the former by 57 per cent, while but 5 per cent lean toward the industries. That both should be the goal of science teaching is believed by 27 per cent. These replies must cause some surprise in this so-called commercial age. It was noted in Question 4 that practical knowledge as an object of science teaching is favored by but 5 per cent. It is interesting to see that 5 per cent also believe in the industries. It is still more interesting to discover, by reference to the original replies, that only one individual who believes in practical knowledge is found among those who believe in the industries. We must conclude that by practical knowledge is meant, not money-making ability, but real mental development which shall be lasting and beneficial to its possessor and also to the community. There is no reason why general information and development may not produce the most practical education possible. The poorest preparation for a given occupation is the one which ignores the interrelations of all lines of work, and concerns itself with but the one. Just as the rays of light diverge from their source, so must the lines of thought spread out and envelop all things, until the lens of specialization brings to a focus those lines of thought which are strongest and clearest. Woe be to him who holds his lens too close to the source.

The place where formal experiments should be performed seems to be in the seventh grade, 23 per cent so indicating their belief. This percentage is small, due to the fact that each grade has its advocates. That formal experiments belong in the high school is indicated by 12 per cent. In both Questions 8 and 9 there seems to be considerable misunderstanding in regard to the word "formal." "Formal experiments" and "formal records" were intended to mean experiments and records having definite or regular form, but both being adjusted to the capacity of the child and therefore natural. It is possible that it was this misinterpretation of the question which led to such diverse answers.

The seventh grade also leads with 22 per cent as the place where formal records of experiments should be kept. While in Question 8, 12 per cent believe that formal experiments should be made at the beginning of science work, in Question 9, 18 per cent believe that formal records should be kept from the beginning. This is explained when it is noticed in Question 12 that many experiments are performed by the teacher while the pupils make the record. Thus the records by the pupils may easily precede the performance of experiments by them.

The answers to Questions 8 and 9 strongly indicate that there is a decided break in the grades between the sixth and seventh years. Some of the other answers also point this same way, and there can be no doubt that the introductory high school, or, as it is also called, the intermediate high school, is based upon correct principles. If science is taught in no other grades, it surely should be part of the curriculum of the seventh and eighth grades, and its nature should be broad and general.

The answers to Question 10 are greater in number than the number of questionnaires which were returned because many of the replies gave two or more different sciences. A comparison of the popularity of the various sciences is nevertheless possible. Nature-study still leads, receiving 20 per cent, but it is on the decrease, due to a growing dissatisfaction because it does not seem to meet the requirements of the child. There are so many other things which he wishes to know in science that information concerning plants and animals, although desirable, is not sufficient. Physiology comes next to nature-study with 16 per cent, while general science is a close third with 15 per cent. If, however, elementary science is taken to be the same as general science, then the latter leads all, having 24 per cent. When we remember that, in the replies to Question 6, 50 per cent are in favor of phenomena of the environment as a source of science material, and when we consider that these phenomena must of necessity be the manifestations of all of the sciences, it seems quite evident that general science is the coming study for the grades.

Referring again to the answers of Question 6, it is seen that only 1 per cent believe that the science material should be drawn from agriculture, physiology, biology, and garden work, while in the replies to Question 10, 7 per cent state that they are teaching agriculture, 3 per cent biology, 4 per cent botany, and 16 per cent physiology, making a total of 30 per cent. The natural conclusion is that 29 per cent are teaching these studies, although they do not believe that they are the best sources of science material. This conclusion is a little offset by the fact that a larger percentage of city schools than country schools replied. This doubtless explains why only 7 per cent of the schools from which replies were received are teaching agriculture. Even if this is the reason, it seems strange that such an important subject is not gaining ground faster in the elementary schools, since it is winning such a strong hold upon the high schools of this country. It may be that it is a study which is too highly specialized for the grades.

Although required and taught in most schools, geography receives in its favor but 10 per cent of the answers. Probably most teachers do not consider geography as a science. The smallness of the number of schools in which no science is taught, namely 6 per cent, is a good sign and strengthens the replies to Question 1.

The answers to Question 11 show that elementary science and general science were considered as being the same. Grouping answer A with answer B, and combining answers C, D, and E, general science has 30 per cent in its favor and nature-study has 25 per cent. Comparing answer A with answer C, it is seen that general science leads nature-study *in all the grades* in the ratio of 23 to 17. The variations in the percentages of the replies to Questions 10 and 11 are due to the different number of answers. While 401 replies were given for Question 10, only 270 replies were received for Question 11. It might not be out of place to suggest that in the comparison of the answers to different questions the number replying should be noted as well as the percentage.

As a method of presentation of science in the grades, experiments by teacher *and* pupils leads with 28 per cent, while the object method, which is doubtless the same as the experimental method, comes next with 17 per cent. It is quite evident that science, even in the grades, has outgrown the memoriter method. However, as many of the replies suggested, the experiments to be performed by the pupils should be simple, and those which do not require exact measurements or much detail work. The experiments should direct the child's *activity* and not tend to cramp him in his quest for scientific knowledge. Better a few self-discovered facts that live and have a meaning than many teacher-imposed "facts" which are but word formulas, and affect the child but little.

That the knowledge which the pupils of the grades acquire is a series of more or less unrelated facts is indicated by 37 per cent of those who replied. Besides these, 16 per cent believe that children only slowly learn to relate a new fact with facts previously known. On the other hand, 22 per cent think that such pupils possess progressive reasoning power. The 7 per cent who believe that the results depend upon the teacher, and the 8 per cent who state that reasoning power should be taught as far as possible, while not directly answering the question, do point the way to better things. Reasoning power can be developed in no way better than by means of science work, or through the application of scientific methods to the other work of the grades. Since science teaching has not been given in the grades long enough for the other subjects to be affected by its methods, it should be given a more important place in the curriculum, not alone for its own sake but in order that it may exert an energizing influence upon the whole course of study. All lines of study should encourage the child's What? How? and Why? to the fullest extent—and then satisfy him with ideas, not give him words as empty as sounding brass.

The answers to Questions 14 and 15 show that the interest in science work in the grades is very good. Only 12 per cent believe that science work attracts no more interest than the other studies. The evidence that boys show more interest in science than is shown by girls is not very strong, although 16 per cent so state, since 39 per cent believe that girls show as much interest as the boys. It is doubtful if there is much differentiation in educational interest before the high-school age.

The evidence that science aids the other studies both in time and in understanding is decidedly conclusive. Combining the first six replies, it is seen that 87 per cent consider that its effect upon the other studies is very beneficial. In comparison with this, the 3 per cent who think that science does not aid the other studies seem to be in the hopeless minority. In justice to them, as well as to the 8 per cent who found it a hard question to answer, it must be said that several stated that if the science teaching in their schools could be improved it would aid the other studies. This again brings up the matter of better prepared teachers who can teach science.

The answers to Questions 17 and 18 must prove of great interest to all educators. If 50 per cent believe that science work in the grades tends to keep the pupils from leaving school, and if 54 per cent believe that it tends to increase the number of pupils who go to high school, then surely every grammar school should give a course in science. Pupils leave school more because they cannot see the good of the education which they are receiving than for any other reason. Science seems to show them that there is some advantage in attending school. Then again there is so much repetition of the work in the grades, so much of the overworked "spiral" method (with the distance between the convolutions almost microscopic), that active children rebel and break away. It may truthfully be said that much repetition is necessary in order that the facts may be fixed in the minds of the pupils, but that is because there is very little interest in the work and their minds are not in a condition to assimilate new thoughts. Give them work in science, and, if the replies to Questions 16, 17, and 18 are true, there will be the greatest of interest, the other studies will be learned in far less time, and a larger and growing percentage of pupils will graduate from the grades and go to high school.

The crowded condition of the curriculum of the grades has been mentioned many times in the replies to this questionnaire. It is usually offered as a reason why new subjects should not be added. The crowded condition of the curriculum is due more to repetition and to the method of teaching which exalts the *tools* of education to the dignity of *subjects*, than to the number of subjects which are being taught. The introduction of general science can furnish the basis for the employment of all of the tools of education. English composition, writing, spelling, oral expression, arithmetic, all would have in the minds of the pupils an excuse for existing. These studies would develop and have a truer significance, through their active use, than would otherwise be possible. Education is drudgery only to one who does not understand whither it is leading.

To teach such a science course would not be difficult to the teacher who has received instruction in general science, as defined elsewhere in this article. When the immense value of science in the grades is considered, the desirability and even the necessity for giving teachers such training is very apparent. The average teacher in the grades is not prepared to teach such a course in science. This is natural and not to the discredit of the teacher. There has been no special demand for science teaching in the grades, and the teacher who has prepared herself to teach science is teaching in the high school. The teaching of a general science course in the grades requires a different training than is necessary for the teacher of some specialized science course in the high school. Without a doubt the latter would fail completely as a teacher of science in the grades. As far as is known there is practically no instruction being given in the normal schools of the country whereby teachers may be prepared for science work in the grades, with the exception of nature-study and agriculture.

While nature-study has its place, and instruction in agriculture is certainly most desirable in the grades, these studies are naturally self-limited and do not supply the needs of the child in this pre-eminently scientific age. General science, which embraces both nature-study and agriculture, as well as including material from all of the sciences, not only supplies the needs of the child but, by showing him undreamed-of possibilities, stimulates him to higher and better things. Instruction in general science, and in the methods of teaching general science in the grades, should be given in every normal school of the United States.

BOOK REVIEWS

Correlated Courses in Woodwork and Mechanical Drawing. By IRA S. GRIFFITH, A.B. The Manual Arts Press. Pp. 238.

Essentials of Woodworking. By IRA S. GRIFFITH, A.B. The Manual Arts Press. Pp. 190.

Projects for Beginning Woodwork and Mechanical Drawing. By IRA S. GRIFFITH, A.B. The Manual Arts Press. 51 plates.

Advanced Projects in Woodwork. By IRA S. GRIFFITH, A.B. The Manual Arts Press. 51 plates.

The books on woodworking which are listed above represent a very comprehensive attempt to make the shopwork in the last two years of the elementary school systematic and progressive. One of the great virtues of the foreign systems of manual training, namely the Russian system and the Lloyd system, was that these systems were worked out completely, so that the teacher of limited training knew how to proceed step by step through a series of class exercises. With a reorganization of manual training and the injection of many demands for an industrial type of training, the regular progression of this work has lost somewhat. Even teachers who have seen the importance of introducing manual training into the school work have been unable to organize their good intentions and the enthusiasm of the students into anything which would constitute a regular progressive scheme.

In the first book, *Correlated Courses in Woodwork and Mechanical Drawing*, Mr. Griffith has given, in detail, lessons for each of the different grades. He has also given some discussions of the methods of grading the work and of the different materials necessary for the successive grades. The normal-school student and the teacher will find in these discussions the best possible stimulus to a careful and systematic consideration of the lines of work which children can profitably take up.

The second volume, *Essentials of Woodworking*, contains very good descriptions of the tools which are needed for a manual-training course and also a discussion of how each tool is to be used. The book also contains an account of the principles of simple joinery and cabinet-work and an account of the different kinds of wood that can be employed for ordinary shopwork.

The two volumes entitled *Projects for Beginning* and *Advanced Projects* give drawings which can be used for classroom work. These drawings repeat the sketches that are presented in the first volume and are convenient in this form for the use of students in classes.

This series of books is certainly a very genuine contribution to the work of manual training. One of the gravest difficulties with the technical subjects in the school course is that they lack that kind of progression which is characteristic of academic courses. Because of this lack of systematic organization there is also in many cases a lack of genuine educational utility in the courses. Mr. Griffith is a teacher of experience. He has also been in contact with the normal classes at Bradley Polytechnic Institute and has trained them in the presentation of materials. The book shows a broad view of the subject-matter of manual training adequate for advanced students as well as for immature children who begin the shopwork in the grades. The work is progressive but not formal. The student is given the idea of a real project, but is at the same time guided in his work so that he will get the fundamental processes necessary to a general training in the use of tools.

C. H. J.

The Children's Reading. By FRANCES JENKINS OLCOTT. Boston: Houghton Mifflin Co., 1912. Pp. 344. $1.25 net.

Miss Olcott has so well stated the aim and scope of her book in the prefatory note to readers that I can do no better than quote it here.

"The aim of this book is to meet in a simple and practical way the following questions often asked by parents:

"Of what value are books in the education of my children?

"What is the effect of bad reading?

"How may I interest my children in home-reading?

"What kind of books do children like?

"What books shall I give my growing boy and girl?

"Where and how may I procure books?

"These questions are answered in fourteen chapters, each followed by a descriptive list of books helpful to parents and to child-study clubs, or suitable for the children's own reading. All juvenile books recommended are selected by standards based on Christian ethics, practical psychology, and the literary values of generally accepted good books. Instructions are given for procuring books by purchase or from public libraries. Special suggestions are made for parents living in the country.

"To make the information in the book of practical use, suggestions are given as to ways and means of interesting children in home-reading, and developing their literary tastes gradually and pleasantly—for, as the greatest of our English poets says: 'No profit grows where is no pleasure taken.'"

Miss Olcott, for many years the Director of the Children's Department of the Carnegie Library in Pittsburgh, has had exceptional opportunities for developing the use of good books among children. Her wide experience has most admirably suited her to the task she has undertaken. The teacher and librarian, as well as the parent, will find it very convenient to have so much information of a practical nature in a single volume. It is a mine of information published in attractive form.

IRENE WARREN

BOOKS RECEIVED

AMERICAN BOOK CO., CHICAGO

Founders of Our Country. By FANNY E. COE. Cloth. Illustrated. Pp. 320. Price, $0.50.

Latin Subordinate Clause Syntax. By M. A. LEIPER. Flexible cloth. Pp. 55. Price, $0.30.

Outline for Review in Civics. By ARTHUR MAYER WOLFSON. Cloth. Pp. 80. Price, $0.25.

Representative Essays in Modern Thought—A Basis for Composition. Edited by HARRISON ROSS STEEVES and FRANK HUMPHREY RISTINE. Half-leather. Pp. 547. Price $1.50.

Aus vergangener Zeit. Edited by ARNOLD WERNER-SPANHOOFD. Cloth. Pp. 278. Illustrated, with notes, conversational questions, and vocabulary. Price $0.50.

Deutsche Heimat. Edited by JOSEFA SCHRAKAMP. Cloth. Pp. 404. Illustrated, with notes, conversational questions, and vocabulary. Price $0.80.

Hannah of Kentucky. By JAMES OTIS. Cloth. Pp. 149. Illustrated. Price $0.35.

RAND McNALLY & CO., CHICAGO

The Autobiography of Benjamin Franklin. Edited by GEORGE B. AITON. Cloth. Illustrated. Pp. 314. Price $0.45.

Abraham Lincoln, the Man of the People ("Little Lives of Great Men Series"). By WILLIAM H. MACE. Cloth. Illustrated. Pp. 191. Price $0.35.

TEACHERS COLLEGE, COLUMBIA UNIVERSITY, NEW YORK

Industrial Education. By JAMES E. RUSSELL and FREDERICK G. BONSER. Pp. 50. Cloth $0.65; paper $0.30.

A Syllabus of a Course on Elementary Woodworking. By WILLIAM NOYES. Paper. Pp. 47. Price $0.30.

C. K. & H. B. TAYLOR, PHILADELPHIA

The Moral Education of School Children. By CHARLES KEEN TAYLOR. Cloth. Pp. 77. Price $0.75.

GINN & CO., CHICAGO

Cyr's New Primer. By ELLEN M. CYR. Cloth. Illustrated. Pp. 121. Price $0.30.

The Beacon Primer. By JAMES H. FASSETT. Cloth. Illustrated. Pp. 120. Price $0.35.

GINN & CO., BOSTON

Busy Builders' Book. By BERTHA B. and ERNEST COBB. Cloth. Illustrated. Pp. 68. Price $0.30.

HENRY HOLT & CO., NEW YORK

Sprach- und Lesebuch. By W. H. GOHDES and H. A. BUSCHEK. Cloth. Pp. 370. Price $1.15.

L. A. RANKIN & CO., BOSTON

Walks and Talks. By WILLIAM HAWLEY SMITH. Paper. Pp. 224.

SUPERINTENDENT GOVERNMENT PRINTING, CALCUTTA, INDIA

Report of the Conference on the Education of the Domiciled Community in India, Simla, July, 1912. Cardboard. Pp. 202. Price Re. 1, or 1s. 6d.

CAMBRIDGE UNIVERSITY PRESS, ENGLAND

Macbeth ("The Granta Shakespeare"). Edited by J. H. LOBBAN. Cloth. Illustrated. Pp. 148.

L. K. CAMERON, TORONTO

The Montessori Method. An Exposition and Criticism. By S. A. MORGAN. Bulletin No. 1, Ontario Department of Education. Paper. Pp. 72.

Industrial, Technical, and Art Education. Bulletin No. 2, Ontario Department of Education. Paper. Pp. 181.

THE MANUAL ARTS PRESS, PEORIA

Manual Training Toys for the Boy's Workshop. By HARRIS W. MOORE. Cloth. Pp. 111. Price $1.00.

D. C. HEATH & CO., BOSTON

Plant and Animal Children and How They Grow. By ELLEN TORELLE. Cloth. Illustrated. Pp. 230. Price $0.50.

WARWICK & YORK, BALTIMORE

Experimental Studies of Mental Defectives. By J. E. WALLACE WALLIN. Cloth. Pp. 155. Price $1.25.

LONGMANS, GREEN & CO., NEW YORK

The English Teacher's Manual. By L. A. PITTENGER. Paper. Pp. 116. Price $0.25.

J. BIELEFELDS VERLAG, FREIBURG

The Little Yankee. By ALFRED D. SCHOCH and R. KRON. Cloth. Pp. 192. Price 3 M.

OXFORD UNIVERSITY PRESS, AMERICAN BRANCH, NEW YORK

Gobseck et Jesus Christ en Flandre. By HONORÉ DE BALZAC. Edited with Introduction, Notes, and Index by DR. R. T. HOLBROOK. Cloth. Pp. 197. Price $0.60.

UNIVERSITY OF CHICAGO PRESS, CHICAGO

The Twelfth Yearbook of the National Society for the Study of Education. Paper. 2 volumes. Pp. 119; 114.

CURRENT EDUCATIONAL LITERATURE IN THE PERIODICALS[1]

IRENE WARREN[2]
Librarian, School of Education, University of Chicago

America lagging behind in aero-schools. Lit. D. 46:225. (1 Fe. '13.)

Bachrach, William. The two-year stenographic course at the Parker High School. Educa. Bi-mo. 7:229–35. (Fe. '13.)

Boyd, William R. How the Iowa state colleges are getting together. R. of Rs. 47:209–11. (Fe. '13.)

Bracq, Jean Charlemagne. French in the college course. Educa. R. 45:122–139. (Fe. '13.)

The author presents his opinions as to the many values of teaching French in colleges and the best methods to employ.

Buck, Gertrude. Some preliminary considerations in planning the revision of grammatical terminology, English J. 2:11–17. (Ja. '13.)

Caldwell, Otis W. The laboratory method and high-school efficiency. Pop. Sci. Mo. 82:243–51. (Mr. '13.)

Discusses the advantages of directed supervised study over the usual home study.

Canby, Henry Seidel. The undergraduate. Harper 126:592–98. (Mr. '13.)

Chapman, John Jay. Charles Eliot Norton. Harp. W. 57:6. (1 Fe. '13.)

Chubb, Percival. Education for play. Relig. Educa. 7:699–704. (Fe. '13.)

Clapp, John M. Oral English in the college course. English J. 2:18–33. (Fe. '13.)

Clark, Herbert F. Constructive morals and school life. Psychol. Clinic 6:252–55. (Fe. '13.)

Davis, Jesse B. Vocational and moral guidance in the high school. Relig. Educa. 7:645–53. (Fe. '13.)

Farley, George L. Causes of non-promotion. Psychol. Clinic 6:256–59. (Fe. '13.)

A brief statistical study.

[1] Abbreviations.—Educa. Bi-mo., Educational Bi-monthly; Educa. R., Educational Review; El. School T., Elementary School Teacher; English J., English Journal; Harp. W., Harper's Weekly; J. of Educa. Psychol., Journal of Educational Psychology; Lit. D., Literary Digest; Pop. Sci. Mo., Popular Science Monthly; Psychol. Clinic, Psychological Clinic; Relig. Educa., Religious Education; R. of Rs., Review of Reviews; School Sci. and Math., School Science and Mathematics; Sci. Am. Sup., Scientific American Supplement; Teach. Coll. Rec., Teachers College Record.

[2] Annotations by Dr. J. F. Bobbitt and Dr. F. N. Freeman.

Harris, James H. An inquiry into the compositional interests of pupils in the seventh and eighth grades. English J. 2:34–43. (Ja. '13.)

A study of the kinds of composition and of subjects for composition preferred by seventh- and eighth-grade pupils.

Hatch, Henry D. Some observations on Scottish public educational provisions for promoting the life careers of pupils leaving school. Educa. Bi-mo. 7:203–21. (Fe. '13.)

Hedges, William. A year of prevocational work. Educa. Bi-mo. 7:191–202. (Fe. '13.)

Johnson, Franklin W. Preliminary study in moral education. Relig. Educa. 7:621–25. (Fe. '13.)

An inquiry into certain aspects of the practice of high-school students in certain types of moral conduct.

Jones, Elmer E. Individual differences in school children. Psychol. Clinic 6:241–51. (Fe. '13.)

The variation among a small group of children as determined by tests of association, reaction, observation, memory, perception of form, mathematics, and reading.

King, Irving. The opportunity afforded by the social life of the school. Relig. Educa. 7:604–11. (Fe. '13.)

An account of the resources at hand and of the requirements in utilizing them.

Kingsley, Sherman C. The newest interest in the mother and child. Child (Chicago) 1:13–16. (Fe. '13.)

Koeppel, George. Observations concerning the organization of schools and certain phases of educational work in Germany. III. El. School T. 13:287–93. (Fe. '13.)

The reform of school systems.

Leathes, Stanley. Modern languages in education. Educa. R. 45:155–66. (Fe. '13.)

Looking regretfully back at the good old days when Latin and Greek held beneficent sway, he considers the possibilities of using modern languages to equally good purpose.

Looking school facts in the face. Lit. D. 46:278–79. (8 Fe. '13.)

McAndrew, William. Social education in high schools. Relig. Educa. 7:597–603. (Fe. '13.)

A general statement of the worthlessness of the high school, as at present constituted, for social education.

MacDougall, Robert. The child's speech. V. The mastery of the tongue. J. of Educa. Psychol. 4:85–96. (Fe. '13.)

The development of control over the articulatory processes.

MacLear, Martha. The latest thing in education. Educa. R. 45:140–45. (Fe. '13.)

Presents two or three illustrations to show that the much-lauded schools of the past were probably not so efficient as sometimes painted.

McManis, John T. The study of children in the normal school. Educa. Bi-mo. 7:236–43. (Fe. '13.)

Maxwell, William H. The attitude of the American parent toward education. Educa. R. 45:167–83. (Fe. '13.)

Deals with the various types of parents in their attitudes toward the work of the schools.

Miles, H. E. Work and citizenship. Survey 29:682–85. (15 Fe. '13.)

Presents on the basis of Wisconsin experience a vigorous plea for industrial education separate and apart from public-school systems.

Monroe, Walter S. Analysis of Colburn's arithmetics. V. El. School. T. 13:294–302. (Fe. '13.)

Motoring books to the people. Lit. D. 46:230. (1 Fe. '13.)

National Education Association Committee course for moral instruction in high schools. Relig. Educa. 7:681–91. (Fe. '13.)

O'Shea, M. V. Recent contributions to the literature of education. Dial 54:142–44. (16 Fe. '13.)

Pyle, William H. Mental and physical examination of school children in rural districts. Psychol. Clinic 6:260–62. (Fe. '13.)

Pyle, W. H. Standards of mental efficiency. J. of Educa. Psychol. 4:61–70. (Fe. '13.)

Some miscellaneous results from tests given to children of various ages.

Roman, F. W. Control of industrial schools of Germany. El. School T. 13:269–73. (Fe. '13.)

Gives the historical reason for the separate control of industrial schools.

School-books that ruin eyesight. Lit. D. 46:394. (22 Fe. '13.)

School of Education. A seven-year elementary school. El. School T. 13:274–86. (Fe. '13.)

Describes by a detailed analysis of the subjects of instruction how one year between the University Elementary and High Schools has been saved.

Scott, Colin A. Personality and purpose of high school students. Relig. Educa. 7:626–30. (Fe. '13.)

Proposes making the work of the high school the expression of purposes cherished by the pupils.

Scott, Fred Newton. Our problems. English J. 2:1–10 (Ja. '13.)

Sharp, Frank Chapman, and Neumann, Henry. A course in moral education for the high school. Relig. Educa. 7:653–80. (Fe. '13.)

Shepherd, John Wilkes. Some suggestions for the teaching of nature study. III. Educa. Bi-mo. 7:247–63. (Fe. '13.)

Showerman, Grant. Life and letters. Educa. R. 45:109–121. (Fe. '13.)

A mediation on the relations and interactions of literature and active human experience.

Smith, David Eugene. Number games and number rhymes. Teach. Coll. Rec. 13:1–110. (N. '12.)

The description of a number of different sorts of number recreations with some discussion of their application to the teaching of number.

Smith, Harlan J. The educational work of a great museum. Sci. Am. Sup. 75:86–87. (8 Fe. '13.)

Swift, Edgar James. School organization and social growth. Relig. Educa. 7:612–16. (Fe. '13.)

The use of the gang spirit in promoting wholesome social organization.

Tufts, James H. The study of public morality in high schools. Relig. Educa. 7:631–36. (Fe. '13.)

Shows that at least in the field of public morality there is much that can and should be taught in the school.

Wells, Dora. Beginnings in the Lucy L. Flower Technical High School. Educa. Bi-mo. 7:222–28. (Fe. '13.)

Whitney, Worrallo. Science in the high schools, an investigation. School Sci. and Math. 13:183–196. (Mr. '13.)

A study by the questionnaire method which indicates that high schools in the Middle West are modifying their science teaching so as to connect it with everyday experience.

Wilson, H. B. Vocational self-discovery. Relig. Educa. 7:691–98. (Fe. '13.)

Winch, W. H. Mental adaptation during the school day as measured by arithmetical reasoning. Pt. 2. J. of Educa. Psychol. 4:71–84. (Fe. '13.)

Wolfe, L. E. The many-book versus the few-book course of study. Educa. R. 45:146–54. (Fe. '13.)

An excellent article that should be widely read, showing that, for the sake of concreteness, vividness, interest, and effectiveness, there should be a large amount of reading in connection with each subject instead of the usual condensed textbook plan.

Wyche, Richard T. The story tellers' league. World's Work 25:588–90. (Mr. '13.)

VOLUME XIII NUMBER 9

THE ELEMENTARY SCHOOL TEACHER

MAY 1913

EDUCATIONAL NEWS AND EDITORIAL COMMENT

Radical modifications in the organization of the elementary school are sure to appear within the next few years. The following general announcement from Superintendent Chadsey of Detroit is interesting as indicating one line of cleavage which is likely to be followed in many school systems. He is reported to have said: "Our plans call for a series of schools located in all sections of the city at which special attention shall be given to industrial and economic subjects, especially after the sixth grade. We hope that the plans of the school board may be realized during the next three years." The course up to the end of the sixth grade will deal with the fundamental subjects of instruction. Beyond this point there will be specialization. In one of these special courses emphasis will be laid upon commercial subjects, in another upon industrial forms of training, and the third special course will be designated an academic course. This is the one which will naturally be taken by the students who are going forward to higher schools. Girls have not been overlooked in the plans made by the board; the industrial and economic school centers will give special courses for the girl who is preparing to go into business and earn her living or for the girl who is preparing to take charge of a home. Domestic science will therefore be a part of these elementary courses and certain industrial lines of training will also be given.

Detroit Plans a Six-Year Elementary Course

Differentiation of the elementary schools beyond the sixth grade will mean the earlier beginning of the type of work which heretofore has been common in the high school. There is in this plan of reorganization a clear recognition of the fact that the last two years of the elementary school as now conducted are in need of thoroughgoing revision if the time of the pupils is to be economically and advantageously employed.

Kansas Decision on Textbooks

The state of Kansas has for some time been listening to discussions for and against the practice of certain school boards which have neglected to obey the textbook law in that state. The law is very rigid in its prescription of books. These books must be definitely adopted by the board and must be of a certain stipulated price. The practice of certain boards of education has been to introduce supplementary books in different subjects and under this guise to displace some of the cheaper and, on the whole, less satisfactory books which are required under the state adoption. The case has been carried from court to court until finally the Supreme Court was reached. This court holds that it is illegal to use supplementary readers. The state, according to the decision, must name all the books to be used in the schools of the state and fixes the prices at which they shall be sold. The law must be interpreted to mean that no other books shall be used in the schools. It is alleged by the plaintiff and admitted by the board in the test case that supplementary books have been used in certain of the lower grades. The board urged that the children had completed the books prescribed by the state first and that the other books were found necessary in order that the work might continue. The court, however, finds that the practice of introducing these supplementary books is contrary to the letter and spirit of the law, and consequently holds that an injunction shall be issued against the use of such supplementary books. The rest of the country will look for the consequences of this ruling with great interest. If the law is of such character that it is impossible under it to introduce supplementary reading-material in the grades, it is probably better that the meaning of that law should be clearly brought out in order that the law itself may be modified. In the meantime the teachers of Kansas will have the hearty sympathy of educational people everywhere. To work in schools without suitable textbook helps is like trying to conduct a modern business establishment without telephones or elevators. It can be done, but not with advantage to the business.

Cost of Textbooks in Michigan Cities

The *Journal* of Lansing, Mich., has been carrying on a campaign of education of the people of that city in favor of free textbooks. The following table, which is quoted from the issue of March 15, may be of interest to those who are gathering information regarding the actual cost of textbooks.

The state *Journal* has gone into the question of the average cost per year for each child in cities using free textbooks. It has received communications direct from members of the school boards in these cities and these show that the average cost in free textbooks cities is 55 cents.

A table follows which sets forth the average cost a year for each child:

Battle Creek, all grades	$0.66
Negaunee, all grades	.48
Flint, all grades	.75
Holland, eight grades	.50
Owosso, eight grades	.43
Muskegon, eight grades	.40
Saginaw, all grades	.53
Sault Ste. Marie, all grades	.90
Grand Haven, eight grades	.33
Cheboygan, eight grades	.43
Alma, all grades	.69
Menominee, eight grades	.56
Detroit, eight grades	.40
Average cost	$0.55

The general problem of textbooks is under vigorous discussion in all parts of the country. It is said that the book companies are beginning to feel the effects of state legislation which provides for the local printing of schoolbooks. The labor unions have taken a great deal of interest in the general problem of the making of schoolbooks and many citizens have written pro and con with regard to the desirability of furnishing textbooks at public expense. There seems to be no doubt in the minds of most of the editorial writers that the cost of textbooks is a subject of large importance in public-school economy.

Minneapolis Inquiry into School Elimination

A committee of citizens of the city of Minneapolis have made a study of the reasons for withdrawals from the public schools of that city. A number of matters of general importance are brought out in the tables given in the report, but the present reference to this report must be limited to a single table.

TABLE NUMBER 7

REASONS FOR LEAVING SCHOOL

Aggregate Family Income	Ill-Health	Had to Go to Work	Child's Desire to Earn Money	Kept Vacation Work	Disliked or Not Interested in School	Trouble with Teacher	Failure to Pass	Further Public School Not Worth	Total
No one earning	....	9 4 3 * 1 0	1 *	....	....	....	....	....	 17
$18–24	....	7 1 * 1	....	....	1 *	....	....	....	 9
$25–29	....	6 1 1 * 1 0	1 0	1 0	1 0	....	....	....	 10
$30–39	....	6 1 * 1	....	....	....	....	....	....	 8
$40–49	1 1 1 0	11 1 * 0	....	....	2 2 * 0	1 0	....	2 0	 21
Independent small income	1 3 1 0	2 4 2 * 1 0	1 1 1 * 1 0	....	1 2 1 * 1 0	2 1	....	3 2 * 0	 26
$50–74	2 3 * 0	19 2 3 * 1 0	3 2 5 * 1 0	2 1 * 1 0	8 2 8 * 1 0	....	1 0	2 2 * 1	 65
$75–99	1 *	6 6 3 * 1 0	1 2 * 0	1 1 1 0	3 3 7 * 1 0	1 1 1 * 1 0	....	1 6 1 * 1 0	 45
$100–149	1 1 1 * 1 0	4 6 8 * 1 0	2 2 3 * 1 0	1 1 1 0	5 12 23 * 1 0	2 0	2 1	9 3 7 * 1 0	 92
$150	1 2 1 0	4 2 3 * 1 0	1 0	....	2 2 2 * 1 0	1 0	1 0	4 1 2 * 1 0	 33
Independent large income	2 0	....	2 1 * 1	1 1	6 3 4 * 1 0	1 1 * 0	....	1 4 1 0	 26
Total	20	125	29	9	104	11	4	50	352
Percent of 352	5.7	35.5	8.2	2.6	29.6	3.1	1.1	14.2	....

NOTE.—*–14 years. 1–15 years. 0–16 years.

Comment is not necessary. The vivid presentation of the educational problem which this table makes justifies the energy spent in the investigation. It is understood that the Board of Education intends to follow up the matter with an inquiry of its own.

The Progress of Compulsory Education

The state of North Carolina has adopted a compulsory education act and has lengthened the minimum school term to six months. This leaves only five states in the Union without compulsory education.

Supervision by Grades Rather than by Schools

The city of East St. Louis has been trying for a little over a year an experiment in school administration. Instead of leaving the supervision of schools to principals in the various buildings, supervisors were appointed to organize the work of certain grades throughout the whole city. One of these supervisors was given charge of the seventh and eighth grades, another of the sixth and fifth, another of the fourth and third, and still another of the first two grades. The principals of the buildings are put in charge of only the strictly local necessities, such as discipline, and matters relating to building supplies. They have no supervision over the course of study or of the work of the teachers in the lower grades. They are given instructorial charge of the highest grade, and devote their whole time to teaching. The plan was adopted in order to render more uniform the work of the different schools throughout the city. Prior to the adoption of the plan some schools had been notably more efficient than others. It was thought that the work could be brought to a high level in all of the schools by cultivating a more immediate interrelation between like grades. Furthermore, the plan seemed to be financially much more economical, because a single supervisor could do the work of several principals.

The plan has been in operation for a year and two months. The discussion of this plan has been so vigorous and the objections to it so strong that it has become an issue in the present election of the school board. The objections which are raised to the plan call attention to the fact that the amount of supervision which is given to the different supervisors is very unequal. The primary supervisor has charge of nearly three times as many teachers as the supervisor of the upper grades. Furthermore, it is pointed out that the pupil's transition from grade to grade is rendered difficult by the lack of common aims and modes of organization in the different parts of a single school. The supervisors meet once a week for general conferences, but each one has his own views with regard to the organization of his part of the school. Further than this, it is pointed out that the supervisors have no such opportunity to become acquainted with individual children as would the principal of the building. The child's progress through the school is therefore dependent on the judgment of a number of different teachers and supervisors who come in contact with him for only a short period at a time.

The matter is likely to be settled before this announcement appears in the *Elementary School Teacher*. The record of the experiment is, however, of interest whatever the final outcome in East St. Louis. Similar modes of organization have undoubtedly been tried in other quarters. It would be of interest to learn whether the supervisory plan has succeeded and been retained in any school system.

Educating the People in Domestic Matters

During the month of February last the department of home economics of the University of Texas held an open school of home economics for the women of that state. Lectures, demonstrations, and exhibits constituted the program of this week's session of the special school. The work was open without entrance requirements, age limits, or examinations, and emphasized the economic, hygienic, and aesthetic aspects of food, shelter, and clothing in their connection with the home and institutions directly related to the home.

A number of lecturers of national importance contributed to the program, and the regular members of the department of domestic economy of the university gave courses and demonstrations. Besides the lectures there was an exhibit in the rooms of the Domestic Science Building and in a tent erected for this purpose. The exhibit was arranged and classified under three divisions: food, clothing, and shelter.

In the food exhibit the subject was treated from the point of view of the municipality as well as of the individual. With a quart of milk as a text the process of procuring this important product was traced back to its source, showing side by side sanitary and unsanitary methods of handling. In this same exhibit also were shown sample nursing bottles, those of a type easy to clean and others dangerous because of the difficulty of keeping them fit for use. Dietary charts showing typical meals for children and adults of various ages and under varying conditions of labor were on exhibition. Charts showing good and bad buying of materials were among the most important of the exhibits.

In the textile exhibit appeared material from other institutions which had loaned charts and other materials for this purpose. Under the head of shelter were given models showing how the problems of sanitation, comfort, and convenience have been solved in the building of houses and in the carrying-out of municipal improvements and improvements in rural districts.

The attendance on this week of home economics was from all parts of the state. Women's clubs sent their delegates, schools sent their home economics teachers, and many housewives throughout the state sought this opportunity of becoming acquainted with improved methods of domestic economy.

Foreign Languages in Elementary Schools

From San Francisco, Cal., comes an account of the activities of the Cosmopolitan Educational Association. This association met on March 6 to discuss the teaching of foreign languages in elementary schools. The report made by the officers of the association showed that over 16,000 citizens had signified their readiness, in answer to written requests, to send their children to schools where they can be trained in either elementary French, German, Italian, or Spanish.

There are two general reasons why the introduction of foreign languages into the elementary schools is likely to become a topic of increasing importance. First, practical conditions of commercial life are driving all those who are interested in foreign trade to see the importance of at least a reading-knowledge of some foreign language. In the second place, it is becoming increasingly obvious that the early years of childhood are the best years for a cultivation of a knowledge of a foreign language. Children take up the pronunciation and the grammatical forms in the early years much more readily than they will in later years when their habits of English expression are much more fixed.

The activities of the Cosmopolitan Education Association show that the issue can be made a practical issue and that the purposes of this society can find a large support if properly presented.

Indiana Legislation on Industrial Education and Truancy

The legislature of Indiana recently passed a very comprehensive law on industrial education. This law provides that a deputy state superintendent of public instruction is to be appointed by the state superintendent with the approval of the State Board of Education. The duty of this deputy shall be to take charge of vocational work in the state. Under the law he may organize elementary agriculture in the grades in all towns and township schools. He may organize elementary industrial work in the grades of all city and town schools and elementary domestic science shall be taught in the grades of all the schools. The State Board of Education is to prepare a course of study for such work. After September 1, 1915, all teachers required to teach in the above-named subjects shall have passed an examination and secured a license in such subjects.

Further steps in a similar direction were taken in the section which provides that when a county makes an annual appropriation of $1,500 and when twenty or more residents of a county who are actively interested in agriculture shall file a petition with the County Board of Education for a county agent together with a deposit of $500, the County Board of Education shall apply to Purdue University for the appointment of a county agent, whose appointment is made subject to the approval of the County Board of Education and the State Board of Education. The state is authorized to pay one-half of the salary of this county agent.

These enactments help to furnish the machinery for a thorough organization of industrial education in the state of Indiana in immediate relation to the work of the public school. The influence of these various special officers will undoubtedly be felt in remodeling the course of study in the subjects which are usually taken up in the grades as well as in the special industrial lines.

The Indiana legislature also adopted a truancy law which provides that children between the ages of fourteen and sixteen must attend school if they have not completed the fifth-grade work. Such a law as this recognizes the fact that the usual method of defining the age limit of elementary-school work is not altogether satisfactory. It is probably the beginning of a clearer recognition in all of the states that legislation shall be drafted in such a way as to secure a certain number of grades of training for each pupil. If the common form of compulsory legislation is intended to carry the pupil through the eight grades of the elementary school, it is, of course, a decided failure. The Indiana law is very low in its prescription of the fifth grade as the minimum that will be accepted for a pupil. Later legislation will undoubtedly bring this to the sixth or even to later years of the elementary school.

Normal Course in the Montessori Method

Information begins to come back from Rome with regard to the success of the courses organized by Dr. Montessori and the probabilities of an invasion of this country by a number of persons fully trained to introduce this work into the United States. We are now told that seventy teachers from all parts of the world have enrolled in these courses, having been permitted to do so by Dr. Montessori. Over fifty of these are Americans. Two American teachers have gone so far as to organize at Rome a separate school for English-speaking children, which they will conduct under the personal supervision of Dr. Montessori.

The normal course will cover a period of four months. In these courses the students will have the opportunity of hearing several lectures a week by Dr. Montessori, and there will be daily practical training and observation in a school which she is maintaining especially for the purpose of training these students. We are told that some American teachers have been in Italy for a year studying Italian in order that they may "personally understand" the lectures and explanations. Presumably the other teachers will get some indirect understanding of what is done, and it is to be hoped that a normal course of four months will give them a thorough grasp upon the methods of this new treatment of young children. The time has passed in the United States when any great system of education would venture to launch itself through a four months' course of normal training, but doubtless this new method can be sufficiently understood in that period—at least to permit the fifty American teachers to start institutions in the United States on their return.

Already there are indications that subsidies will be available for these teachers when they come back, and we shall undoubtedly be instructed through articles and discussions, once more reviving the interest which has during the last few months been somewhat less keen than it was a year ago.

Congress on School Hygiene

Attention has once before been called to the meeting of the International Congress on School Hygiene to be held in Buffalo during the last week of August of this year. The prospects of a large and important meeting at that time grow with the development of the program and the registration of those who are to be in attendance. The Bureau of Education at Washington is taking an active part in the distribution of information regarding this meeting. All teachers and supervisors interested in this phase of school work should secure this information by addressing the bureau.

The Ohio School Inquiry

The following editorial clipped from the *Journal* of Hamilton, Ohio, is very typical of the discussions which usually attach to a school inquiry.

THE INVESTIGATION OF THE PUBLIC-SCHOOL SYSTEM BY DISINTERESTED EXPERTS

In steering clear of the maelstrom of public-school politics and factions and selecting persons not actively engaged in the state educational system for the public-school survey commission, Governor Cox is sure to obtain a disinterested report of conditions in this most important subject. A disinterested report is always preferable to one that is drawn up by one who has investigated his own work.

The high ideals of the state executive in this matter were further reflected in the caliber of the appointees. Representative Oliver J. Z. Thatcher, of

Wilmington, is a man of scholarly attainments augmented by years of practical experience as a successful educator in one of the country's greatest universities —that at Chicago. He is now living in retirement on a farm in Clinton County. Miss Edith Campbell, an instructor of economics in the University of Cincinnati, is a thorough student of all things that pertain to education, and she is said to be one of the best-equipped women in the country. The administrative details of the commission will be looked after by William L. Allendorf, a banker and successful business man of Sandusky. He always has been interested in civic, social, and educational problems and he has kept pace with advanced thought.

The commission will have the services of a corps of experts, experienced in such surveys, which will be provided by the Municipal Research Bureau of New York City.

A review of what has been done in this connection discloses that the governor has acquitted himself with distinction. It is one of the most important undertakings ever launched by an Ohio executive.

This clipping shows several interesting aspects of the Ohio situation. First, note the personal qualifications of the judges. Second, note that the New York Bureau, well known in connection with the New York Inquiry, is here to do the real work. Finally, note the only matter on which extended comment is here offered. This article shows that there is a very clear assumption on the part of the ordinary editorial writer that there is something wrong with the schools which cannot properly be judged except by a wholly impartial jury. There seems to be an assumption that the expert educator would gloss over a situation that is corrupt or even criminal. This attitude on the part of the public is undoubtedly due to the fact that educators have not up to this time succeeded in explaining clearly what they are undertaking to the citizens who support the schools. It is time that some energy of school officers be devoted to the task of giving publicity to the achievements of the school and to its purposes. School people also should be entirely willing to face mistakes and failures. There can be no doubt at all that there are elements in our school situation which can be improved and corrected. Very frequently the public ought to share with the school officer the blame where blame is to be attached to any school mistakes. At all events, this general attitude that the school is on the defensive and that somebody must judge of its doings who will be candid and frank rather than those who are intimately interested, reveals a situation which should be cured by more intimate contact between the educational expert and the people interested in the development of the school.

The Reorganized State Association in Illinois

The Illinois Teachers' Association has been organized by the federation of all the sectional associations. For some years the sectional associations have been, in point of enrolment and in program, of greater importance than the central annual meeting of the state association. At the last meeting of each of these sectional associations votes were passed in favor of federation, also providing by the adoption of higher membership fees for the support of the central association, so that it is now possible to employ a permanent secretary and issue a monthly bulletin dealing with matters of general interest to all of the teachers in the state. The first bulletin, entitled *The Illinois Teacher*, appeared on April 1. It contained some discussion of the organization which is to publish it, some discussion of the vocational bills which are being taken up in the state, and also other matters of legislation, especially the two-mill tax. There is also a brief statement regarding the normal schools of the state. The news items are rather meager in this first issue of *The Illinois Teacher*, but evidently a medium has been established whereby the members of the various associations throughout the state are to receive ultimately information with regard to legislation and other current educational matters of general importance. It is to be hoped that this new organization will see the possibility of preparing a list of all the teachers in the state and carrying on other activities which will demonstrate the feasibility of a central organization which shall represent much more adequately than most teachers' organizations do the interests of all of the teachers throughout the state.

DRAMATIZATION IN HISTORY TEACHING

HORACE G. BROWN
Normal School, Worcester, Mass.

We hope for a steady and healthy increase in dramatization in and out of school. We ask its promoters to prepare themselves in order to see and secure real values. This can be done by thoughtful analysis of results of certain things. For instance, much loose talk about dramatization does not put it in a school. Much play, with marching, singing, posing, may never total dramatization. There are dramatic elements which, when properly combined, form the true dramatization. Some of these every teacher knows. What the teacher lacks may be his judgment of these combined elements. These elements may be color, form, action, sound, light, suggestion, thought, contrast, conflict, and so on to the end of a long list. The problem is how to get an effective combination. I would suggest the following essentials.

1. *Motif and effect.*—Every story and picture has one effect upon us stronger than all others. Before we can dramatize it, we should decide what this leading effect is to be and plan to secure it.

2. *Unity.*—If the effect is worth giving, it is worth giving in its full power. Hence, we should study to remove everything, no matter how good in itself, that lessens the one effect we seek.

3. *Harmony.*—We may have unity in one aspect and lack of harmony in others. For instance, we may have the three fates grouped showing unity of idea, but so dressed as to promote strife among the colors.

4. *Spirit.*—"The letter killeth, the spirit giveth life." Dramatization is to touch life with life so that it goes forth more lively than before, and so less conquerable by forces of evil effect. To select the one spirit in a story, episode, or noble personality, the one which has the life-giving touch, is to be dramatically skilled and endowed. Yet this skill and endowment can be had by intelligent searching, reflection, decision; searching especially in the

world's storehouse of dramatic experience, the works of undisputed genius, and the world of human activity around us.

With these essentials in mind for future study and application, let us pass to consider forms of dramatization in teaching. I think we can easily divide them into formal and informal groups.

The formal group will contain plays (professional and amateur), dialogues, pantomimes, tableaux, pageants, folk dances (and other group dancing), marching, singing, especially antiphonal in rendering. Let us consider each briefly from the school standpoint.

THE FORMAL GROUP

Plays.—Plays are, for the most part, found in the secondary school, though playlets, simple and good, are occasionally produced by grammar-school pupils at fairs, sales, and celebrations.

Dialogues.—This is one of the oldest essentials of the drama but dialogue is something more than exchange of talk. Dialogue has all four essentials; unity, harmony, spirit, effect, and must keep them all appealing to the listener. In the following dialogue, often used in grade one, one can almost feel the values approach zero they become so infinitesimally small.

The Little Red Hen: "Who will eat my bread?"
The Duck: "I will."
The Goose: "I will."
The Turkey: "I will."
The Little Red Hen: "I will not give you any. I will eat it myself."

It would seem desirable to select a tale of more substance to display the riches of dramatization and to "stir the souls of pupils to appreciation." That the child would prefer to call himself a duck or a goose to say those words over and over in the reading-class, is probably true, but that is small praise.

Pantomimes.—The pantomime is not used nearly enough. It calls for action, expression of thought and feeling, without words. Thus it calls for keenest attention, analysis, and conveyance of thought. It *must* bring out the points or the exercise fails. If we take the dramatic tale of the little red hen and throw away the words and have it silently acted with facial and other expressions both actor and observer *must* see the situation, the appeal, and the droll, although selfish, climax.

The pantomime reveals clearly the good dramatic values of a tale, and often gets rid of a load of silly words. Words should be of dramatic value, but very often they are not, and only hide other values that do exist.

Tableaux.—The tableau is one of the most formal and difficult kinds of dramatization. It demands all four essential qualities: unity, harmony, spirit, effect, and in addition much of proportion, grace, color, and suggestive symbol. The fact that it is still-life makes it very difficult to render and not so satisfactory to children, who like activity; and the fact it is so rich in possible color, form, symbol-effect, makes it almost impossible in the short time allowed for preparation. It is not to be wondered at that it is not a regular part of our school activity. When used, it is very costly in time, nervous energy, artistic taste, imagination, and often clearly shows its points of failure. When well done, it is beautiful, instructive, satisfying.

It seems a wiser procedure to use a more informal kind of tableau such as children may devise, and, while getting the full effect of their analysis and impression, allow the fun of the thing to atone for the many accompanying faults and incongruities. *In fact, here lies the benefit of the whole matter of dramatization; namely, in letting the children work out their own dramatic sensations and impressions with childish freedom.* The teacher introduces her higher aims and principles in a pleasant offer of suggestive experiment.

Large, overloaded, inharmonious scenes may dazzle for the instant but they have very little real value in the development of those who look on, or of those who take part. The simpler, the more natural, the more self-expressed the tableau is, the better it is for the development of perception and the refining of taste.

Pageants.—I like to use this word to describe a scene which has movement, more or less vocal expression, and several parts joined to make a whole. Others use the word to mean a spectacle. As I have used it, it becomes the great *composite* of the types of dramatization already described. As a composite, little or much of any type may be used. Hence it can be made to fit any dramatic situation. I urge its use by teachers and others. Having motion, it is freer in its execution, therefore easier for the participants and more enjoyable. It can be used without platforms, curtains, or scenery (although these add to the effectiveness); hence it is perfectly adapted to any school. In the larger schoolhouse, the dressing-room with the corridor gives ample room for its display. In the country one-room schoolhouse, out-of-doors affords the most desirable of all effects. One can wait for favorable weather without disturbance of any other school appointments.

In history or literature, although the course of study is crowded and teachers are busy, each month may bring out a topic for a pageant. Let the children select what they prefer and decide how they can show it. When these suggestions of theirs are assorted and arranged, it will be found they can be used grouped in a procession. The teacher and pupils can plan together and carry out the pageant in details—as to music, marching, placards, symbols, costumes, etc. Let the teacher keep the expectant attitude, and she will get some surprises, some of them surprisingly good. Prescribed dramatics will often fail, while those spontaneously and naturally produced will grow in quality and popularity. After some experience, children can be trusted to select the essential picture-stories from their history and literature, and for these they may devise pageants as fast as they occur. Materials can mostly be brought from homes, sometimes made, seldom bought. All three of these ways are excellent in their effects. This monthly exhibit may be added to from time to time until, at the close of the year, the pupils will have seen pass before them the year's story, not once, but several times; some parts always new; all parts increasingly effective.

Here is a way *to review and drill on essentials in a thorough, clear, delightful way.* It is understandable. It has become a part of the child's possession, for he has created it; he has seen it. It is a moving-picture and a living-picture show in which every pupil joins his own life in explaining and picturing the life of the past out of which our present life comes. This is as near the ideal education as we can come. How unlike the literal words the pupil might have remembered instead!

To illustrate the above, I here outline a year's pageant for the seventh grade, which we call "The Meaning of America." The parade formed in a lower corridor, marched up and into the room to lively music. The divisions came in the following order.

I. The First Inhabitants:

An Indian group in costume with appropriate symbols of Indian life, as hunter, warrior, fisher, child-life, etc.

II. The Coming of the Spaniard (in these subdivisions):

Military explorers, and enslaved Indians, in symbolic costume, and bearing gold and silver ore; palm leaves, the banana, the cocoanut are to symbolize the nature of the region occupied.

An outline map, showing a colored area which the Spanish occupied, may also be carried.

Also placards reading, "No Industry"; "No Schools"; "No Town-meeting"; "Monarchy"; "Religious Intolerance," should appear.

III. The Coming of the French (in these subdivisions):

The French and Indian trappers, with pack, traps, furs, canoes, and other symbols.

The missionary, in religious garb.

The soldiers, with the despotic governor, in military garb.

Branches of birch, maple, pine, fir, with snow to suggest the climate of the region occupied.

An outline map, showing in color the area France occupied, may be carried.

Placards reading, "No Public School"; "No Self-Government"; "Religious Zeal"; "Benevolent Despotism," are shown.

IV. The Coming of the English (in these subdivisions):

A. *Virginia:*

Gentlemen, and convicts, with John Smith as leader.

The later Cavaliers, and Puritans in Virginia, in contrasted costume.

Pocahontas, and other Indians, and John Rolfe.

Specimens of tobacco and corn are carried, symbolizing the important products.

Slaves (men, women, and children), with hoe, or basket, or other symbol.

Placards reading, "The First Colony"; "The First Legislature in America"; "The First Negro Slaves in America," are carried.

B. *Massachusetts:*

The Puritans and Pilgrims (men, women, and children) in suggestive garb, carrying the Bible, and the spelling-book, as symbols.

Indians with their corn, beans, furs, fish, as symbols of their industries.

Small dishes of sand, pebbles, and living twigs of native trees, specimens of native flowers are carried to suggest the nature of the region occupied.

Small bits of wood, miniature ships, water-wheels, fish-lines are to suggest products and industries.

Placards reading, "Self-Government"; "Religious Freedom"; "Religious Tolerance"; "The Public School," are carried.

C. *The Quakers* (in symbolic attire):

Pictures of Quakers may be carried; also a map showing the location of Pennsylvania.

Group of Quakers and Indians, mingling in a friendly way.

William Penn, impersonated by some pupil.

Placards reading, "Pennsylvania or Penn's Woods"; "Philadelphia, Place of Brotherly Love," and others, appear.

V. THE COMING OF THE DUTCH:

A group of Dutch men, women, and children in Dutch attire, Dutch fur merchants, and Indians with furs. Peter Stuyvesant is impersonated.

VI. COLONIAL LIFE, WITH SUGGESTIVE SYMBOLS:

The Colonial minister, doctor, lawyer, school teacher.

The Colonial knitter, cobbler, blacksmith, boat-builder.

Pictures of the Colonial houses, ships, wagons, etc., can be carried.

The slave-driver, the slave, the Virginia gentleman and lady.

VII. REVOLUTIONARY HEROES; IMPERSONATED BY PUPILS:

Washington, Lafayette, Samuel Adams, Franklin, Jefferson, Patrick Henry, and others.

(Pupils to select their own hero and the symbols which will make them known.) Each may carry a card with some famous saying by the man they represent; or carry a portrait of the hero.

Also appear placards, reading, "E Pluribus Unum"; "We must hang together or be hanged separately"; "Taxation without representation is tyranny," and other quotations pupils may select.

A group of Minute-men, in symbolic attire, complete the division.

VIII. THE CONSTITUTION:

A group suggesting the President, Congress, and the Supreme Court, to be impersonated. Another group bears placards, reading, "To form a more perfect union, establish justice, insure domestic tranquillity, provide for the common defense, promote the general welfare, and secure the blessings of liberty to ourselves and our posterity," and other quotations, giving tribute to the Constitution, to be selected by the pupils themselves.

IX. INVENTIONS:

Miniatures, *constructed by the pupils*, to be borne in the processions; steamboat, canal-boat, locomotive, telegraph, telephone, electric light, etc.

X. PRODUCTS THAT HAVE MADE US GREAT:

Pupils to devise simple exhibits and carry them in the procession. Specimens of coal, iron, petroleum, gold, silver, copper, etc. Specimens of apples, peaches, oranges, grapes, etc. Specimens of beef, butter, wool, leather, etc.

Placards giving statistics, or historic facts, about the products may be carried.

XI. The Pioneers:

The trapper and hunter, the settler and farmer, the herdsman, the miner, mountain guide, Indian guide, the preacher and teacher, to be impersonated with suggestive symbols.

XII. American Ideals (in symbolic costume):

Liberty, Justice, Law, Religion.

Here are twelve numbers and we have covered suggestively only about half of our American history, touching only the essentials. The eighth grade can work out the rest.

Of course the above is simply suggestive to the pupil. Any teacher may choose her own topics and symbolize them in her own way.

The one important thing is that *each pupil think out what each group and symbol means—what the whole together means.*

It is to be noted that very little *complete* costuming is called for. Much use is made of the *suggestive*, the *symbol*, the *idea*, rather than the complete picture.

Songs, marches, and dances.—The three remaining topics of dramatic value need but little comment. All three in themselves are dramatic in spirit and expression, and are the oldest accompaniments of other dramatic expressions which we have. As accompaniments their use has been somewhat limited. When one recalls the large part the Greek chorus had in the Greek play, we get a glimpse of what we can do with singing, marching, dancing in our dramatizing in the schools. In expressing the religious, warlike, or simply festive life of a people, we cannot afford to neglect them.

Take the Indian. Note how the song and dance enters into his war and worship festivals. The military spirit has in all times been expressed more or less in the measured tread and regular movements of the body, especially when in company with others. Hence, the *clan spirit* as well as the *national spirit* is especially well expressed by marches. Much varied effect can be obtained by group-marching in all sorts of combinations. Dancing, folk-dancing particularly, is having a revival. It is well if we see in it expression of an earlier *folk-feeling*, not a show by some of our twentieth-century children.

The use of the dance, the march, the song, not *as dances, songs, and marches*, but *as expressions of social pictures* and *social spirits of a people or a period*, will prove very profitable to a thoughtful teacher in the development of dramatization.

THE INFORMAL GROUP

We now take up the less formal ways of dramatizing. Under this head I mention, first, simple informal dramatization, as in reading in the lower grades. There is little or no preparation. "I am he." "I am it." Dramatization has begun. This is spontaneously expressed in words from the lesson and in such facial expression, gesture, and posture as the child is moved to use. This is simple and excellent. The first value to secure in it is the *sure and real identification*, in the child's mind, *of the character and himself*. Of course full expression of what the child has seen, felt, thought about the part is much to be desired.

I would call attention, in the second place, to the value in the *dramatic sentence*. We are all aware of the fun in a single word, as in punning. Similarly, we often find the whole situation pictured for us in a single sentence. This, for example, is found in the really good short yarn or anecdote. It is also occasionally found in the sayings of small children in the home, and the answers of pupils in schools. One can collect many in the school year. They are so small we usually let them come either unnoticed or unvalued. Yet they are, perhaps, the diamonds among dramatic values. It is these we should prize *as beginnings* and which we should develop into a considerable dramatic expression. The teacher can do much to encourage this by showing dramatic situations by her own use of language. In her own matter-of-fact questions, she can, if she wishes, stimulate dramatic seeing and feeling. Let me illustrate.

The lesson is on the discovery of America.

Question: "What Asiatic products are mentioned in connection with trade routes?"

Here the dramatic value is zero. Let us revise it.

"If you were an Arab, what animal would you use on the desert? What articles would you load on his back? Where would you go to get these articles? How would you dress in that climate? What would you take with you to trade for these new products? Why would you want to trade anyway?"

Notice, by impersonation, and vivid mental picturing, and actual *imaginative thinking*, we have got at the heart of the whole matter, and what is more, it will not be forgotten. Thousands of similar situations are found throughout the history.

The Constitution is considered by most to be the driest, hardest topic to be found in history for upper grades. Yet it has been proved that by impersonation of the men in the Constitutional Convention, and by *imaginative* travel to the very halls in Philadelphia, and by working out these ideas in actual discussion in a mimic convention, a dry topic becomes a most interesting, helpful, and lasting one.

The last informal item I would suggest is the sentence-picture of natural scenery that surrounds the incident or the fact. Let me illustrate this. Take a lesson on the French in America.

Question: "Who founded Quebec, and when?"

Answer: "Quebec was founded in 1608 by Champlain."

Here the dramatic value is zero; the history value, ditto. Let me revise it.

"Here is a picture of a kind of ship they used about 1600. Here is another picture of a man named Samuel Champlain. Will you be Champlain? Now, if you sailed up this river, how many miles would you go? [Measure by scale of miles on the map.] How long do you *think* it would take you on a modern steamer? If it were the winter time, how would the country look? Were there forests, or prairies, along the banks? What kind of trees would you see? When you planned to build Quebec, did you build it on sandy shore? or prairie? or on a cliff? How does Quebec look today? Look at these pictures of Quebec. When did you found Quebec? Why?"

These are suggestions merely to invite teachers to enter a large field and, for the most part, unexplored. The pleasure of original pioneering, sometimes called initiative, is one essential to vigorous teaching. It adds the touch of eager leadership, to displace much driving of the herd, rendered so prevalent today by the machinery of supervision and instruction.

PRACTICE TEACHING IN MODEL SCHOOLS

E. E. LEWIS
State Normal School, Charleston, Illinois

In 1909 the accrediting committee of the California State Board of Education sent a questionnaire to every state normal school in the United States. Among the questions asked were a number concerning the practice teaching and observation work required of students before graduation. The data obtained from these replies came into the hands of the writer through the courtesy of Dr. M. E. Dailey, president of the State Normal School, San Jose, Cal., who was a member of that committee. The facts pertaining to practice teaching and observation work are here compiled and briefly interpreted with the hope that they may stimulate further inquiry concerning current methods in normal schools.

RELATION OF PRACTICE TEACHING TO COURSES IN METHODS

From the replies to the first question, "How much time intervenes between the study of methods and the practice teaching?" we find the following facts: (1) Practice teaching follows the courses in methods immediately in 47 of the 115 state normal schools replying, or in 40 per cent of them. This group includes all schools in which the student-teacher begins his practice teaching immediately upon the completion of the work in methods. In many normal schools the courses in methods are completed in the Junior year and practice teaching comes in the Senior year. Other schools have the courses in methods in both the Junior and the Senior years, with practice teaching in the Senior year only. Courses in general methods as well as in special methods precede the practice teaching in all schools of this group. (2) Practice teaching is taken simultaneously with methods in 28 of the 115 schools, or in 24 per cent of those replying. (3) Less than one term of twelve weeks intervenes between the study of methods and practice teaching in 12 normal schools, or in 10 per cent of the group studied.

(4) The study of methods precedes practice teaching by more than one term of twelve weeks, and less than three such terms, in 14 schools, or 11 per cent. (5) More than one year intervenes between the courses in methods and the practice teaching in but one institution. Fourteen per cent of the schools wrote the vague answer, "varies," and are, therefore, not considered in the above figures.

The two prevailing tendencies are, first, to have practice teaching taken simultaneously with methods, and second, to have practice teaching follow immediately the courses in methods. The second plan is the more common.

AMOUNT OF PRACTICE TEACHING REQUIRED

The next question asked is: "How much practice teaching is required of each student before graduation?" The replies reveal a wider range of variation than would seem possible in institutions all maintained for the one purpose of training teachers for the elementary schools. Pupil-teachers are required to teach anywhere from two weeks to two years, the length of time varying with the size of the training school, the number of student-teachers, and the pedagogical view of the administrative officers in charge.

The replies to this question were given by different schools in varying units, such as weeks, months, hours, and terms, making the computation of averages difficult. This may be illustrated by quoting at random the following answers: "one hundred and twenty hours"; "five months"; "one period a day for twenty weeks"; "two terms of room teaching"; "one-fifth of the course." I have managed to use most of these answers by reducing the time given in each case to school terms of twelve weeks with one period of forty to forty-five minutes of teaching each day.

The following replies are from schools requiring less than one term of teaching: "four periods per week every two weeks for one year"; "twenty full days"; "one-fifth of the course"; "six weeks"; "part of the time for six weeks." The remaining schools are divisible into three groups with respect to the length of time required for practice teaching: (1) those schools requiring less than two terms of twelve weeks each, one period daily, but more than one such term; there are 10 institutions in this group; (2)

those schools requiring at least two terms or twenty-four weeks, one period daily; there are 42 institutions in this group; (3) those schools requiring the equivalent of one year, that is, three terms, one period daily; there are 66 institutions in this group.

To summarize: 53 per cent of the state normal schools replying require the equivalent of three terms or one full year of practice teaching; 34 per cent, the equivalent of two terms; 8 per cent, the equivalent of one term, and 5 per cent less than one term. There are possibly two institutions that require more than one year of practice teaching. The median institution requires three terms or one year.

SCHOOLS IN WHICH PRACTICE TEACHING IS REQUIRED

The third question is: "Is any or all of the practice teaching done in schools other than practice schools under your supervision?" In 95 of the 117 replying all the practice teaching is done in a practice school connected with the normal school. Twenty-two institutions use local town and city schools. When outside schools are used, the practice teaching is almost without exception supervised by the faculty of the normal school. There is only one normal school in the list in which student-teachers are allowed to teach in outside schools under outside supervision alone. In 10 of the schools studied, practice teaching is required in city and town schools as well as in the training school more immediately under the control and supervision of the normal school. Usually practice teaching in outside schools is merely a temporary makeshift necessary until a training school can be established.

GRADES IN WHICH PRACTICE TEACHING IS REQUIRED

The fourth question asked is: "In how many grades does each student-teacher do practice teaching?" A number of general answers were received, for example: "several"; "no specific number"; "varies"; "three to eight"; "all possible"; "usually in one department." However, most of the answers were more specific. I have recorded them in the following table. This table shows the number of grades in which students are required to teach.

Number of Grades	1	2	3	4	5	6	7	8	9*
Number of schools	3	10	24	20	3	7	2	15	3
Percentage of total schools replying	2	9	23	19	2	6	2	14	2

* These numbers do not refer to the grade, as the ninth grade, but to the number of different grades in which each student is required to teach during his practice experience. Thus, 3 schools require teaching in only one grade; 10 in two grades; 24 in three grades, etc.

The range is from one to nine grades. Which means that in some normal schools, pupil-teachers are required to teach in only one grade, while in other schools they are required to teach in all nine grades. Eight schools require teaching in the primary, intermediate, and grammar departments. A number of indefinite answers were received which are here eliminated. Evidently the most common practice is to require teaching in three or four different grades.

SUBJECTS IN WHICH PRACTICE TEACHING IS REQUIRED

Question five, "In what subjects does each student do practice teaching?" is closely related to the preceding one. The following answers are quoted as exceptional: "varies, but must have one of music, nature-study, drawing, or manual training"; "four to six branches"; "nearly all"; "no regulation"; "any two, in all but special"; "several"; "all possible"; "determined by the supervisor of practice"; "six selected." The remaining replies I have listed under four groups:

1. Those requiring all subjects: 58 institutions;
2. Those requiring any three, preferably one in each of the three departments: 9 institutions;
3. Those leaving it to the option of the student and supervisor: 9 institutions;
4. Those specifically indicating the subjects: 12 schools.

Eleven of the 12 schools that specifically answer this question require arithmetic; 10 require reading; 6 history; 6 music; 5 language; 5 geography; 4 writing; 4 grammar; 3 nature-study; 2 drawing; 2 manual training; one domestic science, and one agriculture.

Again, 2 of the 12 schools in question require practice teaching in seven different subjects; 4 require practice teaching in six subjects, 2 in five; one in four; 2 in three, and one in two.

These institutions require students to teach an average of five different subjects during their course. And the six subjects taught in their order of preference are: arithmetic, reading, language, history, music, and geography. These figures must not be taken too seriously, however. The reader must remember that we are arguing upon the basis of what prevails in only 12 institutions. But I find upon checking back that these 12 schools are among the very best in the list when all points are considered. They represent the very best practice that appears in the whole group of normal schools.

THE AMOUNT AND KIND OF OBSERVATION WORK REQUIRED

The sixth question concerns the observation work required of practice teachers: "Do students observe the teaching of other persons? If so, what persons?" To the first part of the question 115 schools replied "yes," and only one replied "no." To the second part 78 replied "critic teachers," and the rest named one or more of the following: room teacher, experienced teacher, method teacher, supervisor, principal, departmental teacher, student teacher, student assistant, expert students, regular professors, city, town, and village teachers, normal-school teachers, and heads of departments. The most common practice seems to be for the students to observe the critic teachers.

Question seven is: "If so, do they observe before, during, or after their practice teaching?" In 18 state normal schools, or in 15 per cent of the group studied, students observe before their work in teaching begins, and continue observing during their term of teaching and also after their teaching is done. Eight schools, or 7 per cent, require observations during the time of teaching only. Eight schools, or 7 per cent, require observations both during and after the teaching period. Twenty-five schools, or 22 per cent, require observations before the time of teaching only. Fifty-five schools, or 49 per cent, require observations both before and during teaching. A few of the answers cannot be placed in any of these groups. Examples are: "take little stock in observation work"; "observe only when need arises"; "each student has observation period assigned on program." The most common practice is to observe both before and during the teaching period. Over 70 per cent of these schools follow this plan.

In reply to question eight, "How much observation work is required?" we have various and puzzling answers such as: "one week out of six"; "no rule"; "twenty hours"; "one hour per week"; "much"; "little"; "one hour a day for a term"; "no minimum and no maximum"; "about three times as much as teaching"; "perhaps three weeks in two years"; "two hundred to two hundred and fifty hours"; "one week in five in the Junior year"; "one year of teaching, about half of which is observation"; "one hour per week for one-half year"; "possibly one-tenth of the time devoted to teaching"; "twenty weeks in special subjects." The only conclusions to be drawn from such replies are that local circumstances govern the amount of time given to observation work, and that, in general, observation work is considered less valuable than practice teaching.

In almost every institution in question some observation work is required. In the few schools in which no practice teaching is required the amount of observation work is naturally much greater than in those requiring practice teaching. In schools that require one year of practice teaching it is common to have from 20–30 observations along with the teaching. The student observes the recitations of a critic teacher until he feels competent to take charge of the class himself. The observation of 6 or 8 lessons at the beginning of each term of teaching is usually all that is necessary. In a few schools one period a week throughout the year is set aside for observation work. The entire group of practice teachers meet with the supervisor or with one of the method teachers and observe the recitation of a critic teacher. In this way 30–40 group observations are made during the year covering all the subjects in all the grades. Each of these model lessons is discussed by the class and usually each student criticizes the lesson in a written report.

TEACHING IN THE KINDERGARTEN

To determine the amount of practice work normal schools give teachers in the kindergarten, question nine was formulated: "Are students given any practice teaching in the kindergarten?" Most of the answers to this question fall into one of the following groups: (1) 38 schools, or 33 per cent of the 113 schools replying, answer this question in the affirmative but do not specify just what students are required or permitted to teach in the kindergarten; (2) 25 schools, or 22 per cent, reply, "to specialists only"; (3) 50 schools, or 45 per cent, do not offer any practice teaching in the kindergarten. Evidently state normal schools have been slow to accept the responsibility for the training of kindergarten teachers.

DOES THE TRAINING SCHOOL REPRESENT ACTUAL WORKING CONDITIONS?

To determine whether or not the training schools in connection with our normal schools represent actual working conditions question ten was asked: "What attempt, if any, is made to have the training school represent actual working conditions outside?" The answers fall into two groups:

1. Twenty-eight frankly state that they make no attempt to duplicate the working conditions of the outside common schools.

2. Sixty schools claim that they make all possible attempts to do so. A few of the replies indicating the feeling there is on this question follow: "some, but conditions make much impossible"; "we conform to the state course of study"; "none, except in the seventh, eighth, and ninth grades"; "all possible except size of classes"; "all possible, making plans, disciplining children, and test reports to supervisors are required on outside work"; "by having the same subjects taught in the same way"; "we set standards that are better"; "we make no attempt, we aim at perfect conditions"; "just such as you will find plus high ideals"; "always attempting with little success"; "impossible, do the best we can"; "we try to set standards"; "try to make our school best type"; "our object is to meet and better conditions."

There are 17 institutions that use city and town schools for observation and practice teaching, thus meeting actual conditions. If we add these 17 to the 60 in the second group, we gain a fair appreciation of the extent of the attempt to make the model schools represent actual conditions. Such an attempt has been made in at least 73 per cent of our state normal schools.

TRAINING FOR SPECIAL TEACHERS AND SUPERVISORY OFFICERS

The eleventh question is: "What facilities, if any, are offered for departmental or special teachers to secure training?"

1. Twelve schools, or 10 per cent, reply, "little."
2. Forty-two schools, or 39 per cent, reply, "none."
3. Forty-seven schools, or 43 per cent, reply, "for special teachers."
4. Six schools, or about 5 per cent, reply, "for departmental teachers."

The following exceptional replies should also be noted; "none, but a little graduate work is offered"; "we are establishing a department for that purpose"; "there is no demand for it." A number of normal schools are training teachers in the special subjects of music, drawing and art, manual training, and domestic science, and a very few are attempting to train departmental teachers. The training provided for teachers of the special subjects greatly exceeds the training provided for departmental teachers.

Question twelve is: "Is there any training for supervisory officers or principals?" Eighty-seven schools, or 18 per cent, replied, "no," and 20 schools, or 19 per cent, replied, "yes." The extent of such attempts may be seen by a glance at the following answers: "yes, a training class is conducted for principals by the superintendent of the local schools"; "yes, for principals of rural schools"; "yes, for those taking the B.A. degree"; "yes, especially with men"; "yes, summer school offers a course"; "yes, a course in superintendency"; "no, not yet, but will"; "no, but encouraged"; "no, only incidentally"; "no, will offer a course next year"; "nothing special, but individually some." State normal schools make practically no attempt to train supervisory officers.

SUPERVISORS OF PRACTICE TEACHING

The last question which we will consider is: "Who supervises the practice teaching?" There are 129 replies to this question. From a study of these answers we should be able to determine the prevailing methods of supervising practice teaching. First of all we find a wide range of official supervisors ranking from the president of the normal school to student-assistants. They may be classified in groups according to their respective powers and functions.

1. Principal, president, or superintendent of the normal school.
2. Principal, director, supervisor, or superintendent of the model, observation, practice, or training school.
3. General supervisor, director of training, or superintendent of practice teaching, other than principal of training school.
4. Grade teacher, sometimes called room teacher, department teacher, grade supervisor, or critic teacher.
5. Heads of departments in normal schools.
6. Professors of psychology, pedagogy, or education in such schools.
7. Teachers of general methods.
8. Teachers of special methods and special subjects.

We will consider these in the order listed above. In every state normal school it is one of the implied duties of the president or principal to supervise the practice teaching of students. However, there are only 9 institutions in the United States in which the president of the normal school directly exercises the function of supervisor. In the rest of the schools the duty of supervising practice work is delegated by the president to a subordinate. As normal schools have grown in size the administrative force has gradually been separated from the teaching force.

In about 20 schools the principal of the training department is the chief supervisor of practice teaching. But the principal neither of the normal school nor of the training school is the type supervisor of practice work today. Several other ways of handling this work are in vogue, as a further examination of the data shows.

Among these is the appointment of a general overseer of practice teaching subordinate only to the two principals. This person is variously called general supervisor, director or directress of training, and superintendent of practice teaching. There are 27 normal schools in the list studied that have an overseer of practice work in addition to the two principals above mentioned. The position of overseer of practice work has been created because of the inability of the principals on account of increased administrative duties adequately to supervise such work. Improvements in methods of teaching have also demanded an especially trained person for such work. The establishment of such a position is in keeping with the departure from general to special courses in methods, the growing tendency toward a departmental as opposed to a grade or room plan of organization and instruction, and also with the increased size of normal and training schools.

This plan is not, however, the most common method of supervising practice and observation work. The supervision of practice teaching is done by the grade teachers to a much greater extent than by all other groups combined. It is not possible to give figures in percentage setting forth this fact, as in scarcely a single place is one group doing supervisory work to the exclusion of all other groups. The most common ways may be briefly described as follows: (1) to have one grade in a room under a regularly employed room, grade, or critic teacher; (2) to have two grades in a room under one or two such teachers; (3) to have three departments, primary, intermediate, and grammar, with one or more departmental teachers in each. Practice teachers in schools having the first or second plan take charge of the room, or of one portion of the children in that room, for from one period a day to full time. Under the department system the practice teacher usually takes a single class one hour a day during the period of teaching. In every instance without exception the critic teacher supervises the work of the student, though in possibly thirty schools the critic teacher is helped by other supervisors as well.

In a few normal schools those who are at the head of departments in the normal school supervise the teaching of their subjects in the training school. This is especially true of the newer and more recently introduced subjects, such as drawing, music, domestic science, sewing, and manual training. In fact, practice teaching in the special subjects is almost entirely supervised by the teachers of those subjects.

In 7 schools in the list the professor of education, pedagogy, or psychology also has supervision over practice teaching. Quite frequently this person is the overseer of practice work. There are three institutions in which he is declared to be the sole supervisor. The teacher of general methods appears as a supervisor in but two institutions in the list.

The tendency is to have competent critic teachers who take charge of the students teaching in their grades; and a general overseer of practice teaching who supervises the work of the critic teachers, and also teaches general methods and the fundamental professional courses in education.

THE DECLINE OF THE ENGLISH APPRENTICESHIP SYSTEM

JONATHAN FRENCH SCOTT
Madison, Wisconsin

As was shown in a former article, the English apprenticeship system under the control of the gilds was something of a success, this success being largely due to the personal relationship existing between master and apprentice, and to the effective supervision of their relationship by the craft gild. Eminently suited as the institution was to the conditions of the Middle Ages, however, it was not equally well suited to all times and all conditions. In the present article, an attempt will be made to show: first, that the custom of apprenticeship was continued by the English government after the decline of the gild system; secondly, that the institution lost its strength as a result of the changed social and economic conditions of the seventeenth and eighteenth centuries; and thirdly, that a revival of the apprenticeship system would prove inadequate as a solution of the present problem of industrial education.

Neither bombastic by-laws nor prosecution for offenses against them could save the gilds from decline. In some of the old corporate towns they may have retained even in the eighteenth century a considerable hold upon the local market,[1] but they had little or no control in the newer industrial centers of England, such as Manchester and Birmingham, where manufactures developed rapidly upon a capitalistic basis. In a word, the gilds, retaining the form and spirit of the Middle Ages, could not adjust themselves to the conditions of the modern era.

Though the gilds declined, apprenticeship persisted, achieving a new importance in Elizabeth's reign (1558–1603) as a part of

[1] Adam Smith, *Wealth of Nations* (Cannan, ed.), I, 131: "If you would have your work tolerably executed, it must be done in the suburbs, where the workmen having no exclusive privilege, have nothing but their characters to depend upon, and you must then smuggle it into the town as well as you can."

British economic policy. Two laws were passed which greatly affected the history of the institution. The first of these, the Statute of Artificers or Apprentices,[1] forbade any one henceforth to exercise any craft then existing in England, unless he had previously served at least seven years thereto as an apprentice. This law made more general the seven-years' requirement, previously dependent chiefly on local custom and gild regulation.[2]

The second law, an act of 1601,[3] attempted to deal with the curse of pauperism. Towns and villages had fallen into decay, agriculture was giving way to sheep-farming, and the land was full of "rogues, vagabonds, and sturdy beggars." To prevent the rising generation from growing up in idleness the law of 1601 provided that the parish authorities might bind out beggar children as apprentices "where they shall see convenient."[4] By means of laws such as these two, Parliament hoped to bring about greater stability in industrial life and thus to increase the strength and prosperity of the realm of England.

Thus the institution of apprenticeship was vitally affected by the two acts of the fifth and forty-third years of Queen Elizabeth. In the first place, the number of apprentices must have been very greatly increased. In the second place, these apprentices were drawn very largely from a lower stratum of society than formerly. And finally, as has been already indicated, the institution of apprenticeship was continued under new auspices at a time when the gilds were dying out.

To the parish apprenticeship system the attempt was made to extend the idea of the personal relationship between master and apprentice. The master was still expected to perform the duties of a parent toward the indentured child, and sometimes to provide him with the elements of education. Many of the American colonies passed laws insisting upon the instruction, especially the religious instruction, of apprentices. Thus the Connecticut Code of 1650 made it incumbent upon masters to catechize their children

[1] 5 Eliz. c. 4.

[2] The law was by no means a dead letter, though enforced irregularly. From a study of local records and law reports I find this to be so.

[3] 43 Eliz. c. 2.

[4] Sec. 5.

and servants once a week at least, "in the grounds and principles of religion," and to teach "by themselves or others their children and apprentices so much learning as may enable them perfectly to read the English tongue and knowledge of the capital laws."[1] In England no general law to compel masters to provide apprentices with this sort of instruction is to be found before the Act of 1802, of which mention will be made later; but individual masters sometimes agreed to see to the schooling of children bound out to them.[2]

The personal relationship, however, was being gradually undermined. The very nature of the parish apprenticeship system was such as to create a gulf between the master and his fledgling workmen. The children were from the lowest grade of society, were apt to be idle and immoral, and therefore likely to receive little consideration from their masters. A law of the latter seventeenth century widened the gulf by compelling persons, willing or unwilling, to receive parish children as apprentices at the pleasure of the authorities.[3] Not rarely the apprentice thus forced upon a parish resident must have become an object of distaste to him.

The growth of capitalism also weakened the personal relationship between master and apprentice.

The typical craftsman of the Middle Ages was a man of small means, keeping but one or two apprentices; besides, the number was limited by gild ordinance. But from the fifteenth century on, there was an increasing tendency on the part of masters possessed of capital to disregard these rules. The laws of the Framework Knitters' Company, for example, forbade more than three apprentices to be taken to one journeyman; in Queen Anne's reign (1701 to 1714) some masters took ten or more to one journeyman,[4] while later in the century a certain master "always had a staff of twenty-

[1] Clews, *Colonial Educational Legislation*, p. 59; see also Hening, *The Statutes at Large* (Virginia), 4 Anne c. 33; *Records of the Massachusetts Colony*, II, 6; Clews, *op. cit.*, *passim.*

[2] Bateson, *Leicester Records*, III, 197; Markham and Cox, *Records of Northampton*, II, 323.

[3] 8 and 9 Will. III, c. 30. In one instance a girl was bound out to a clergyman, who was compelled "to teach her the art and mystery of husbandry" (Cox, *Derbyshire* I, 243).

[4] W. Felkin, *History of the Machine Wrought Hosiery and Lace Manufactures*, p. 23.

five apprentices, more or less, and never employed a journeyman for more than thirty years."[1]

The impossibility of keeping up the old family relationship under these conditions, the impossibility of giving apprentices adequate trade instruction, is obvious. The capitalist manufacturer would not stand *in loco parentis* to twenty or thirty ragged children nor would he take pains to teach them their trade properly. Even had he had the time and inclination to instruct them, it was becoming less and less to his economic interest to do so. For as the number of apprentices and other operatives increased, the tendency was to confine workmen to one or two processes of manufacture, in which they might become especially skilled.[2] Such a practice was, of course, subversive of any adequate industrial education.

In general, then, the manufacturer failed to care properly for the social and economic interests of his apprentice; his predecessor, the mediaeval gild master, under the supervision of the craft gild, had equipped the youth for life in a far better way.

These conditions, affecting so seriously the lives of apprentices, were aggravated by the growth of cut-throat competition and the increased use of labor-saving machinery. For their own advantage, capitalists "used all their power to oppress the laborers, and drove down wages to starvation point,"[3] and after Adam Smith's *Wealth of Nations* appeared (1776) manufacturers used his *laissez-faire* theory to justify intellectually and morally their policy of unrestricted competition and control of industry.[4] Thus capital and competition brought antagonism between employer and employee, between master and apprentice.

The epoch of invention, beginning about the middle of the eighteenth century, while it marks an enormous advance in economic progress, marks also the last stage in the history of the old apprenticeship system. The invention of labor-saving machinery increased the tendency to the division of labor,[5] and thus hindered

[1] W. Felkin, *op. cit.*, p. 75.

[2] Cunningham, *Growth of English Industry and Commerce*, "Modern Times," Part II, p, 615.

[3] Toynbee, *Industrial Revolution*, p. 66.

[4] Webb, *History of Trade Unionism*, p. 49.

[5] Cunningham, *op. cit.*, "Modern Times," Part II, p. 615; Baines, *History of Cotton Manufacture*, p. 184.

workers from attaining a thorough knowledge of their trades. Sometimes it rendered possible the substitution of unskilled labor, thus making a long apprenticeship unnecessary from the economic viewpoint of the master. In many instances children were now able to attend machines and carry on work which had formerly required the attention of adults.[1] Thus was the institution of apprenticeship metamorphosed into the practice of child labor; the children might retain the name of apprentices, but they were practically wretched, unintelligent little factory hands.

The decay of the apprenticeship system is also due, in part, to the lack of an adequate supervision, to take the place of that once supplied by the gilds. There was no gild court to see that the master treated his apprentice properly, no adequate system of examinations to test the results of the apprentice's work and the master's teaching. In a word, there was no institution vitally interested, as the gild had been, in the welfare of the apprentice and in his relation to his master.

Legislation did, indeed, attempt to set up a system of supervision for parish apprentices. The parish authorities were supposed to see that master and apprentice did their duty to each other;[2] but their oversight was inefficient.[3] A writer of 1732 says: "Parish officers . . . . to save expense, are apt to ruin children by putting them out as early as they can, to any sorry masters that will take them, without any concern for their education or welfare."[4] Apprentices might be neglected, ill-treated or starved by their masters; they might lead lives of idleness or wickedness, with little or no interference from the authorities.[5]

To the neglect of the parish officers, then, and to their failure to exercise a proper supervision over the relationship of master and

[1] Baines, *History of Cotton Manufacture*, p. 239.

[2] 43 Eliz. c. 2; 8 and 9 Will. III, c. 30; 17 Geo. II, c. 3; etc.

[3] Cunningham, *op. cit.*, "Modern Times," Part II, p. 629; Acts of Parliament, 7, Geo. III, c. 39, and 33 Geo. III, c. 55.

[4] Hutchins and Harrison, *History of Factory Legislation*, p. 6.

[5] *Ibid.*, pp. 6, 14; Felkin, *op. cit.*, p. 79. "Sir Samuel Romilly says in his *Diary* (II, 374) that he has known cases where the 'apprentices were murdered by their masters in order to get fresh premiums with new apprentices'" (Hutchins and Harrison, p. 14).

apprentice, may be in part attributed the wretched and uninstructed condition of the children in the factories.

In 1802 the government roused itself to a more vigorous effort to remedy the evils clustering around the apprenticeship system. An act was passed for the "Preservation of the Health and Morals of Apprentices and others, employed in Cotton and other Mills, and Cotton and other factories."[1] This law ordered every master or mistress of a mill to supply every apprentice "with suitable linen, stockings, hats, and shoes," one complete new suit to be delivered once a year. No apprentice was to be compelled to work more than twelve hours in any one day, nor to work between nine at night and six in the morning. It was also enacted that every apprentice should be instructed during a part of every working-day in reading, writing, and arithmetic by some person provided and paid by the master and mistress. Furthermore, religious instruction was to be given and masters were to see to it that their apprentices attended divine service regularly. It is clear that this act is an attempt to make the master responsible, as of yore, for the moral and physical welfare of his young charges. But manufacturers could not be made to accept this responsibility; this and later "factory acts" failed in their purpose.[2] Shortly afterward the apprenticeship clauses of the Act of Fifth Elizabeth were abolished, first for those engaged in the woolen manufactures,[3] and in 1814 for all trades.[4] The day of apprenticeship as a system was past. Social progress had failed to keep pace with economic advance and the twentieth century is therefore attempting to solve problems created by the seventeenth and eighteenth.

It is evident from all this that during the seventeenth and eighteenth centuries the English apprenticeship system was by no means a success. Neither the social nor the economic interests of the apprentice were cared for properly. In mediaeval times the master had received the boy into the family life, looked after his moral and religious, as well as his physical, welfare, and in teaching him his craft, had given him the advantage of individual instruction. If the master were negligent in his teaching, if he failed in his social

[1] 42 Geo. III, c. 73.

[2] Hutchins and Harrison, p. 17.

[3] 49 Geo. III, c. 109.

[4] 54 Geo. III, c. 96.

duty toward the lad, he was called to account by the authority of the gild. In general the mediaeval apprentice was not ill-prepared to take his place in society. In the seventeenth and eighteenth centuries manufacturers were outgrowing the gild system and paid less and less attention to restrictions made upon the number of apprentices by either the gild or the government. With a large number of apprentices the manufacturer could not sustain the same personal relations as with one or two. Craft instruction and moral training suffered accordingly. Furthermore, with the employment of large numbers of apprentices came the temptation to the master to perfect each apprentice in one or two processes instead of teaching him the whole trade. Finally, as the use of machinery increased, the need for skilled labor decreased and not infrequently the apprentice became merely the unskilled operative of a machine. On the other hand, the manufacturer needed not only a wide knowledge of his craft, but a considerable amount of capital as well to succeed in his business. Thus it came about that the apprentice in many branches of manufacture could not look forward to becoming a master as a matter of course, but was forced to remain a factory operative all his life.

The social gulf between the master and his apprentices, which was in many cases created by the rise of capital, was further increased by the parish apprenticeship system. Apprentices drawn from the lowest portion of society could not expect always to be received on terms of equality into their masters' houses, especially where the masters were forced by the authorities to receive these apprentices. There was indeed an attempt to preserve the old personal relation between master and apprentice, but there was no institution like the gild to see that the right relation was preserved. In general the attempt was not a success and the condition of the parish apprentices was frequently wretched indeed. This is true not merely of the factories, but of the handicrafts as well. In its latter days, then, the apprenticeship system was a failure.

Would it be a success if it were generally revived at the present time? There can be no doubt that many of the factors instrumental in breaking down the old apprenticeship system are dominant in industrial life today. Capital is a prime moving force, the factory system is firmly fixed, the captain of industry deals with large numbers of operatives, not with a few journeymen and apprentices. The social gulf between employer and employee is as great as ever, the economic difficulties preventing the operative from rising into the manufacturing class are greater than ever. More than this, there is a distinct antagonism between the employing and the employed classes. These conditions would make it impossible to bring back the old personal relationship and identity of economic interest between master and apprentice, which formed so important an element of the success of the old system.[1] If the apprenticeship system is to be revived, then, it must be revived in some form totally different from that of the Middle Ages.

It must be remembered that the problem of industrial education is both economic and social in character. It means not merely that the youth should be trained to become an efficient workman with a skilled knowledge of all branches of his trade, but it means also that there should be implanted in him high ideals in regard to his work, that his growing moral nature should be developed at a period in his life when temptation is most likely to assail him; in a word, that he should be made an efficient and high-minded member of society.

If the problem were merely the economic one of supplying manufacturers with skilled labor, it might possibly be left to the employing class for solution. Just now there is a growing demand among employers for skilled labor; consequently enterprising manufacturing concerns are paying more attention to the apprenticeship system, and are establishing apprentice schools which have met with some success.[2] There can be no doubt, too, that certain specialized branches of manufacture can never be well taught save in the concerns carrying on these industries.[3] On the other hand, the demand of employers for skilled labor affects but a small proportion of the industrial classes, for employers need thoroughly trained mechanics for only a comparatively small number of posi-

[1] This would not apply to those trades which still remain largely on a handicraft basis, such as those of barber and custom tailor.

[2] Carroll D. Wright, *The Apprenticeship System in Its Relation to Industrial Education.*

[3] *Ibid.*, pp. 33, 35, 41.

tions, while the question of industrial education concerns some 90 per cent of the population. Already the advisability of giving apprentices a thorough knowledge of the principles underlying its manufacture is being questioned by at least one concern which has established a school for apprentices. Principal J. D. Burks, of the Teachers Training School, Albany, N.Y., writes:

> A few weeks ago I was inspecting one of the largest manufacturing establishments in New York state, which had recently organized a school for apprentices, provided it with a thoroughly modern equipment, and placed in charge a well-educated man of high ideals and practical ability. Here, I thought, I had found an enterprise that might have something to teach the schools concerning their effort to meet concrete social needs. The master-mechanic, to whose initiative this school was due, told me, however, that he had serious doubt as to the practical value of his apprentice school. He thought he would direct the teacher to use the machines for demonstration purposes only, as the boys spent too much time "figuring out how to get a piece of work set up, and how to get the thing done." "These boys," he said, "will work all their lives for our company, and we want them to do things our way. We don't want the boys to draw; we want them to read drawings. We don't want them to figure; we want them to read figures. We don't want them to boss. We want them to be bossed." And he might have added, "We don't want them to think, but to become automatic machines."[1]

It is evident, then, that manufacturing establishments do not always feel it to their economic advantage to give apprentices a broad knowledge of the various processes of their branches of manufacture.[2]

It is hardly probable that the manufacturer will fully perceive the social significance of the movement for industrial education and

[1] Proceedings of the National Education Association, 1909, p. 293.

[2] "President Charles S. Howe, of the Case School of Applied Science, Cleveland, Ohio, in 1907, sent a letter to 400 manufacturers in the state of Ohio, making certain inquiries relative to the apprenticeship system, and received replies from 124, including nearly all the large concerns among the 400 addressed. Of the 124 who answered, 44 had no apprenticeship system, and were not especially interested in it; 24 had no system, but were interested. The superintendents of these 24 stated that they had no apprenticeship system because they had very few men employed, but they hoped as soon as their facilities increased, and their work expanded, to establish such a system at least to a limited extent. Fifty-six companies answered that they had apprenticeship systems more or less complete, but most of them gave the apprentices nothing more than was absolutely necessary to enable them to do their work in the particular trades engaged in with fair success."—Wright, *The Apprenticeship System.* etc., pp. 18,19.

co-operate with it. He has not done a great deal thus far to remove the deadening influences of factory labor, save where reforms have been forced on him from without. He views his employees from the economic rather than from the social point of view, and would be likely to consider the moral, aesthetic, and social training of the apprentices as more or less of a waste of time. Individual manufacturers of a philanthropic nature may do something to give their youngest workmen the right sort of industrial instruction from the social as well as the economic point of view, but not manufacturers as a class.

It is chiefly to the public school that we must look for a solution of the problem of industrial education. The public school can furnish, in greater degree than any other agency, those elements upon which the success of the mediaeval institution of apprenticeship so largely depended—an adequate system of supervision and the right personal relationship between teacher and taught. The public school has already developed a well-organized system of administration and supervision which it can easily extend to include industrial education. The thought of economic gain will not blind the eyes of the teacher to the social needs of his pupils, as it blinded the eyes of the master to the needs of the apprentice, and as it sometimes blinds the eyes of the manufacturer to the needs of the employee. More and more the public school is insisting that there be the right personal relationship between teacher and taught, for the ultimate aim of education must always be the welfare of the pupil. I doubt if there is any higher service that a teacher can perform for society than that of guiding boys in their formative years to high ideals of industrial work and of life.

BOOK REVIEWS

Theory and Practice of Teaching Art. By ARTHUR WESLEY DOW, Professor of Fine Arts in Teachers College, Columbia University. 2d ed., with additional text and illustrations. New York: Teachers College, Columbia University, 1912.

In his book, *Theory and Practice of Teaching Art,* the second edition of which appears this year, Professor Dow presents in attractive and helpful form a plan for developing aesthetic appreciation and expression.

He designates this plan as a "synthetic method"; a method of building up given material such as lines, shapes, tones, and colors into forms of aesthetic expression. This method is contrasted with what is termed the analytic or academic method, which consists in drawing from nature to acquire a knowledge of facts of appearance, and skill in representing these facts. Following the analytic method the student would begin by observing and recording facts of appearance, to be used later as a medium of expression. By the synthetic method the student begins by arranging lines, shapes, and tones so as to build up harmonious combinations. He accompanies this practice with drawing from nature in order to obtain data to render these lines and shapes significant in expression as well as beautiful in arrangement.

Professor Dow has rendered an important service to art education in thus sharply contrasting the interest in recording objective facts as they appear to the eye, with the interest in harmonious arrangement of forms so that they produce aesthetic satisfaction. He rightly insists that the principles of arrangement of lines, spaces, and tones have a logic of their own, which produces aesthetic pleasure, and which is in large degree distinct from any consideration of the subject-matter which those lines represent. He emphasizes the truth that no amount of industry or skill along the line of literal representation can by itself produce the full range of artistic expression.

The principles expressed in the book are concretely set forth in a series of exercises suitable for different grades and adapted to give acquaintance with, and ability to use, the elements of artistic expression.

While accepting Professor Dow's distinction between the interest in representing appearances and the interest in harmonious arrangement of form, one questions whether a certain loss to art would not result from limiting the value of literal drawing from objects merely to that of securing data to give significance to compositions which would otherwise be abstract, and whether practice in conscientious analysis of actual appearances has not made a contribution to art which the approach by principles of design does not include. The history of art seems to indicate that the close study of a bit of reality in order to lay hold upon its meaning and transcribe its characteristics without regard to artistic composition, often leads one beyond the scientific interest in securing information, and into an interest in the individual significance of that object, into a sympathetic attitude toward that particular portion of reality, and thus into a genuine aesthetic experience of a sort which initiates the style of expression and does not merely furnish data to make significant the otherwise abstract elements of a decorative convention.

Throughout the book the word art appears to be used in the sense of abstract design. In public education at the present time it is used, whether justifiably or not, in a more inclusive sense. The so-called teacher of art finds himself called upon to make his subject minister to other than the formally aesthetic ends which Professor Dow emphasizes and yet to ends with as important an educational significance. Whether one accepts the strict definition of art in education, or insists upon the wider significance, he will find the book a discriminating treatment of what all must consider to be one of the major aspects of the subject.

WALTER SARGENT

Experimental Psychology and Pedagogy. By R. SCHULZE. Translated by RUDOLF PINTNER. New York: Macmillan, 1912. Pp. 364.

This book differs somewhat from the other German treatises which deal with the subject in that it gives in detail the apparatus necessary for a number of experiments. The subdivisions of the subject are, however, chiefly psychological, so that the book does not differ from a manual of experimental psychology as much as some of the books on experimental education which have appeared in English.

The first chapter deals with the mathematical methods of computing experimental and statistical results. Then follow chapters on Sensations, Perceptions and Ideas, Feelings, and the Will. Then follow five chapters on more complex processes of Attention, Association, Memory, Apperception, and Speech. Following this are two chapters on Mental and Physical Work and Fatigue. Finally there is a chapter on Psychical Correlations.

To the teacher of educational psychology who wishes to introduce some experimental work into the class exercises the descriptive accounts of experiments will be very useful.

C. H. J.

CURRENT EDUCATIONAL LITERATURE IN THE PERIODICALS[1]

IRENE WARREN[2]
Librarian, School of Education, University of Chicago

Anthony, Willis B. Teaching real life in school. World's Work 25:695–98. (Ap. '13.)

Armstrong, A. C. German culture and the universities. Educa. R. 45:325–38. (Ap. '13.)

Babcock, Kendric C. Bibliographical instruction in college. Lib. J. 38:133–36. (Mr. '13.)

Baldwin, Bird T. Educational psychology at the Cleveland meeting of the American Psychological Association. J. of Educa. Psychol. 4:164–70. (Mr. '13.)

Barnes, Earl. Comparison of Froebelian and Montessori methods and principles. Kind. R. 23:487–90. (Ap. '13.)

Bawden, William T. Recent progress in the movement for vocational education. Voca. Educa. 2:318–33. (Mr. '13.)

Boggs, Anita U. M. Cultural schools or continuation schools. Pedagog. Sem. 20:71–77. (Mr. '13).

Protest against narrow vocational training.

Boutroux, Emile. The thought of America and of France. Educa. R. 45:269–88. (Mr. '13.)

Boyer, Jacques. A new method of educating deaf mutes. Sci. Am. 108:221. (8 Mr. '13.)

Butler, Nicholas Murray. Vocational preparation as a social problem. Educa. R. 45:289–97. (Mr. '13.)

Canby, Henry Seidel. The professor. Harper 126:782–87. (Ap. '13.)

Coleman, Norman F. The Bible as literature in the high school. School R. 21:246–49. (Ap. '13.)

Collateral work in connection with the study of American literature. Educa. 33:448–50. (Mr. '13.)

[1] *Abbreviations.*—Educa., Education; Educa. R., Educational Review; El. School T., Elementary School Teacher; J. of Educa. Psychol., Journal of Educational Psychology; Kind. R., Kindergarten Review; Lib. J., Library Journal; Liv. Age., Living Age; Outl., Outlook; Pedagog. Sem., Pedagogical Seminary; Pop. Sci. Mo., Popular Science Monthly; Psychol. Clinic, Psychological Clinic; R. of Rs., Review of Reviews; School R., School Review; Sci. Am., Scientific American; Teach. Coll. Rec., Teachers' College Record; Tech. World M., Technical World Magazine; Voca. Educa., Vocational Education.

[2] Annotations by Dr. F. N. Freeman.

Cook, W. A. Vocational training for the Indians. Voca. Educa. 2:289–98. (Mr. '13.)

Corbin, Alice M. How to equip a playroom—the Pittsburgh plan. Playground 7:8–15. (Ap. '13.)

Courtis, S. A. The reliability of single measurements with standard tests. El. School T. 13:326–45. (Mr. '13.)

Curtis, Henry S. The boy scouts the salvation of the village boy. Pedagog. Sem. 20:78–85. (Mr. '13.)

Dana, John Cotton. The supreme importance of reading. Pegagog. Sem. 20:17–22. (Mr. '13.)

Thinks we do not know how to read properly.

DeBusk, B. W. Height, weight, capacity, and retardation. Pedagog. Sem. 20:89–92. (Mr. '13.)

Finds a positive relation between height, weight, vital capacity, and advancement in school.

Education: a keynote of the Panama Pacific Exposition. R. of Rs. 47:309.

Educational rank of the states. Lit. D. 46:772. (5 Ap. '13.)

Elliott, Edward C. The report of the New York school inquiry. El. School T. 13:320–25. (Mr. '13.)

Forbes, George M. Organization and administration of industrial schools. Voca. Educa. 2:278–88. (Mr. '13.)

Franklin, Robert. Schoolhouses as employment agencies. Tech. World M. 19:268–70. (Ap. '13.)

Furney, Oakley. Education with an aim to service. Voca. Educa. 2:299–317. (Mr. '13.)

Gayler, G. W. Elimination from a different angle. Psychol. Clinic 7:11–16. (Mr. '13.)

Methods by which elimination was reduced in one town.

Gerrans, H. T. Oxford University finance. Educa. R. 45:376–87. (Ap. '13.)

Gilbertson, Albert N. A Swedish study in children's ideals. Pedagog. Sem. 20:100–106. (Mr. '13.)

Gillette, John M. Sociology as a high school subject. Educa. R. 45:256–62. (Mr. '13.)

Harley, Harrison L. The physical status of the special class for bright children at the University of Pennsylvania, summer session of 1912. Psychol. Clinic 7:20–23. (Mr. '13.)

Heilig, Matthias R. A child's vocabulary. Pedagog. Sem. 20:1–16. (Mr. '13.)

A catalogue of words used by a girl of three years.

Hodge, Clifton F. Preparation of teachers for nature study and civic biology. Pedagog. Sem. 20:58–70. (Mr. '13.)

Jamgotchian, Mesrob K. Sparrow language the secret language among the Armenian children. Pedagog. Sem. 20:98–99. (Mr. '13.)

Jones, W. Franklin. The vitality of teaching. Psychol. Clinic 7:1–10. (Mr. '13.)

Motivation as the central problem in teaching.

Kaempffert, Waldemar. The industrial need of technically trained men. Sci. Am. 108:252–54. (15 Mr. '13.)

Kimball, Dorthy E. Convent schools in America. Educa. R. 45:263–68. (Mr. '13.)

Koeppel, George. Observations concerning the organization of schools and certain phases of educational work in Germany. IV. El. School T. 13:346–52. (Mr. '13.)

Krause, Carl A. Modern language instruction in the United States. Educa. R. 45:237–48. (Mr. '13.)

Levin, Samuel M. Improvement of elementary evening schools. Educa. 33:399–409. (Mr. '13.)

Lippert, Emanuel. Child study in Bohemia and Moravia. Pedagog. Sem. 20:107–8. (Mr. '13.)

———. Report of the Bohemian National Committee for Protection of Children. Pedagog. Sem. 20:109–11. (Mr. '13.)

Lurton, Freeman E. Reducing retardation. Pedagog. Sem. 20:86–88. (Mr. '13.)

The reduction of the amount of retardation accomplished largely by the reduction of time lost from school.

MacDougall, Robert. The child's speech. IV. Word and speech. J. of Educa. Psychol. 4:29–38. (Ja. '13.)

MacLear, Martha. The fact of personality in the development of an atypical child. Pedagog. Sem. 20:93–97. (Mr. '13.)

Methods of treatment in an individual case.

McKee, Ralph H. Ancient vs. modern languages as a preparation for English. Pedagog. Sem. 20:45–47. (Mr. '13.)

Comparison of grades in college of those having different amount of ancient and modern foreign language in their preparatory work.

McLane, C. L. The junior college;, or upward extension of the high school. School R. 21:161–70. (Mr. '13.)

Mackie, Ransom A. Progressive high school reorganization. Educa. 33:420–27. (Mr. '13.)

Magni, John A. The decline of the classics and their place in future curricula. Pedagog. Sem. 20:23–44. (Mr. '13.)

Argues that the classics have suffered on account of a false and temporary utilitarian aim in education.

Miller, George J. A high-school course in field geography. School R. 21:171–79. (Mr. '13.)

New York public school controversy. Outl. 103:575–76. (15 Mr. '13.)

Parkinson, William D. Equal pay or equal service. Educa. R. 45:249–55. (Mr. '13.)

Pyle, W. H. Economical learning. J. of Educa. Psychol. 4:148–58. (Mr. '13.)

Rapeer, Louis W. The problem of formal grammar in elementary education. J. of Educa. Psychol. 4:125–37. (Mr. '13.)

Rendall, E. D. John Smith at Harrow. Liv. Age 58:602–12. (8 Mr. '13.)

Richter, Leonard. Educational surveys and vocational guidance. Teach. Coll. Rec. 14:3–43. (Ja. '13.)

Robertson, C. R. The training of secondary-school teachers. School R. 21:225–34. (Ap. '13.)

Rowell, Percy E. The status of science teaching in the elementary schools of the United States. El. School T. 13:387–404. (Ap. '13.)

Russell, James E. Professional factors in the training of the high school teacher. Educa. R. 45:217–36. (Mr. '13.)

Sanders, W. H. A study of professional work as presented in the state normal schools of the United States. Pedagog. Sem. 20:48–57. (Mr. '13.)

A study of the lack of uniformity in the work of the state normal schools.

Smith, Preserved. The unity of knowledge and the curriculum. Educa. R. 45:339–44. (Ap. '13.)

Snow, William B. Modern language in American public schools. Educa. R. 45:362–75. (Ap. '13.)

Starch, Daniel, and Elliott, Edward C. Reliability of grading work in mathematics. School R. 21:254–59. (Ap. '13.)

Starkey, Alice G. A plea for more moral training in the colleges. Educa. 33:437–39. (Mr. '13.)

Stevenson, John J. Some random thoughts concerning college conditions. Pop. Sci. Mo. 83:397–411. (Ap. '13.)

Stockbridge, Frank Parker. A university that runs a state. World's Work 25:699–708. (Ap. '13.)

Stone, C. W. Problems in the scientific study of the teaching of arithmetic. J. of Educa. Psychol. 4:1–16. (Ja. '13.)

Terman, Louis M., and Hocking, Adeline. The sleep of school children: its distribution according to age, and its relation to physical and mental efficiency. J. of Educa. Psychol. 4:138–47. (Mr. '13.)

Tesson, Louis J. Oral instruction in modern languages. Educa. 33:428–36. (Mr. '13.)

Thompson, Grace. High-school reading: the Newark plan. School R. 21:187–90. (Mr. '13.)

Washington, Booker T. New type of rural school. Survey 29:837–38. (15 Mr. '13.)

Wheeler, George. The six-year high school. School R. 21:239–45. (Ap. '13.)

White, Frank R. Industrial education in the Philippine Islands. Voca. Educa. 2:265–77. (Mr. '13.)

Wild, Laura H. Training for social efficiency. Educa. 33:440–47. (Mr. '13.)

VOLUME XIII NUMBER 10

THE ELEMENTARY SCHOOL TEACHER

JUNE 1913

CONTROL OF GERMAN INDUSTRIAL SCHOOLS

EDWIN G. COOLEY
Educational Adviser of the Commercial Club of Chicago

Dr. Roman's article in the February number of the *Elementary School Teacher* is at hand. Dr. Roman's book *Die deutschen gewerblichen und kaufmännischen Fortbildungs- und Fachschulen* contains nothing that is not in accordance with the general positions taken in the reports and recommendations of the present writer.[1] The publication of this article changes the situation, and I should like to make a few comments on its statements.

The table on p. 270 of Dr. Roman's article is a translation of one found on p. 23 in Lexis' *Das technische Unterrichtswesen*. This book was printed in 1904, and is not up to date in its description of the industrial school systems of Germany. In fact, this table contains one or more small inaccuracies in its description of the situation at the time the book was written. Further confusion has been introduced by the fact that, while Dr. Roman seemed to be quoting the table literally, he has omitted one or two facts found in it, and seems to be unaware of a number of changes that have taken place since the book was written.

It ought to be remembered that the discussion of the facts found in this table does not touch the real question at issue in Illinois. The table deals with the higher supervision of the technical schools of Germany; the supervision that all parties in Illinois

[1] See especially *Vocational Education in Europe*, report to the Commercial Club of Chicago, Chicago, 1912.

agree to refer to an industrial commission or state board. Further, there has been no radical difference of opinion here as to the composition and authority of this state board or commission. The discussion of the question of higher supervision in Germany, therefore, casts no light on the controversy in Illinois. It is interesting, however, as a statement of fact and as expressing a frame of mind.

In Professor Lexis' table the schools of Baden are stated to be under the control of the Ministry of Education, although at the time the book was written they were under the Ministries of Justice and of Education, and were directly managed by a national industrial commission whose president was a representative of the Ministry of the Interior. In this commission were always to be found representatives of the industries. Since this book was written, these schools have been taken entirely away from the Ministry of Education and placed under the Ministry of the Interior. This change took place on April 28, 1905.

In Professor Lexis' table, p. 23, the statement is made that part of the schools—industrial continuation schools, building-trade schools, art-trade schools, and higher commercial schools—are under the Ministry of Education. The next item states that the technical schools for the textile industries and fine mechanics are under the Ministry of the Interior. Dr. Roman omits this latter statement from his table on p. 270. The actual higher supervision is exercised by an industrial upper school council whose presiding officer and actual head is the president of the Central Department of Commerce and Industry. This gentleman, Herr Mosthaf, is the man to whom you go if you wish information about the industrial schools of Württemberg. He is not a schoolmaster, but a trained man of business. Other representatives of the Department of Commerce and Industry, school men, and men of affairs in this school council are under him. Dr. Roman contents himself with the statement that these schools are under the Ministry of Education, and that the director of the schools is always a member of the council. That means, he says, that he practically controls these schools. As the director of these schools is almost invariably a member of these boards in all Germany, it would appear from Dr. Roman's reasoning that they controlled all such schools in

Germany. The facts are that great care is taken to prevent the undue influence of the school man by the organization of the boards or commissions having the schools in charge.

Dr. Roman's statements with reference to Bavaria are also likely to confuse the reader. He states, p. 270: "In Bavaria the director of the high school and the district school directors have direct charge of the industrial schools. This accounts for the fact that Dr. Kerschensteiner has been able to bring Munich to the front in the trade-school development." The facts are that in Bavaria, including Munich, the high schools (secondary schools) are not under the management of Dr. Kerschensteiner or Dr. Kerschensteiner's board. The building-trade school and art-trade school in that city are under still another board. Leaving out the schools of college grade in Munich, there are three distinct bodies of school officials exercising control over different systems of schools, Dr. Kerschensteiner having the elementary and continuation schools under his charge.

I frankly admit the excellence of Dr. Kerschensteiner's work in Munich and consider him a wonderful man. I believe, however, that he has succeeded in his work with the continuation schools, not on account of his connection with the general schools, but in spite of it.

It should be noted in the first place that he is separated from the control of the secondary schools. It should also be remembered that Dr. Kerschensteiner has been in a constant struggle with the school authorities of Munich for many years over these schools, and that he has succeeded largely on account of his co-operation with local trade and business organizations. Dr. Kerschensteiner was under investigation in 1910, and the question was openly discussed in the leading papers of Munich as to whether he would be forced into retirement on account of the opposition of the authorities. Munich is not a case proving the advantages of having the same authorities control the cultural and vocational schools; it is the exception which brings out the advantage of the other plan. A further reason for making this statement lies in the fact that Munich is the one place in Bavaria that has exceptional vocational continuation schools, Bavaria, as a whole being behind the other countries of Germany. Dr. Roman himself, p. 62, calls attention to the fact that "Bavaria is still far back in the supplying of industrial schools for girls."

The question of higher supervision is not the one agitating the people of Illinois. We are divided on the question of local boards of control. In Germany the only place where these schools are under the ordinary local board of control is Bavaria, and there the secondary schools—academic and technical—are under separate boards. The local bodies controlling these schools in Prussia, Saxony, Württemberg, Bavaria, and Hesse are always different bodies from the ones controlling the cultural school of the community. A typical local board is the one in Karlsruhe, Baden, which is made up as follows: (1) the burgomeister, or mayor, as president; (2) another representative of the state council; (3) the director of the industrial schools; (4 and 5) two representatives of employers; (6 and 7) two representatives of employees. This typical school celebrated its seventy-fifth anniversary in 1909.

Dr. Roman states that the administration of the schools of Prussia was taken out of the hands of the Ministry of Education and placed in the hands of the Ministry of Commerce and Industry in 1885. He intimates, if he does not state, that Bismarck did this on account of difficulties over religious matters. The official statement, however, was that it was done owing to the complaints of some of the practical men of Prussia, representatives of the gilds, etc. The schoolmasters of Prussia have continued to believe ever since that they could run these schools better than they are now being run. No one else seems to think so, however. The upper house of the Prussian parliament recently voted unanimously against putting them into the hands of the Ministry of Education. At a recent conference of teachers of industrial schools where Director Haese (quoted with approval by Dr. Roman) was present, and I think the presiding officer, it was voted by an overwhelming majority to retain the present organization. One prominent speaker spoke with great emphasis of their obligation to Prince Bismarck for taking these schools out of the hands of the Ministry of Education in 1885. I found no one connected with the management of practical affairs who thought the present dual arrangement should be changed.

The man of affairs everywhere believes that separation from the general type of school is necessary to success.

It is misleading to try to make it appear, as in Dr. Roman's article, that the question at issue in Germany is a religious one. We know that the Prussian continuation school does not teach religion and that the Munich and other South Germany schools do. At the present time the schools of Munich and other places of South Germany where they do teach religion appear to be superior to many of those in Prussia. My observations lead me to believe that the teaching of religion has little to do with the matter. Some of the best continuation schools I saw were in Prussia, and some of the poorest schools I saw were in South Germany, and yet as a whole I am inclined to think that the continuation schools of Baden are superior to those of any other country of Germany.

A further reason for my belief that the religious question does not "cut any figure" in this matter is the fact that in Switzerland, where there is complete separation of Church and State, the authorities appear to be equally insistent upon a separate board of control for each of the various types of schools. You will find different bodies controlling the industrial school, the commercial school, and the academic school. In Dr. Biefer's *Methodik*, a recent authority on vocational schools, the statement is made that this question of separation is absolutely fundamental. He urges that the boards be made up of practical men—employers and employees—and educators, with the practical men in control. In Austria, where all the schools teach religion, the industrial schools have been placed under the control of the Ministry of Public Works. Here again some of the schools are of a very superior order and some of them distinctly inferior to those of Prussia. I think it is misleading for Dr. Roman to inject the question of religious instruction into the question of success or lack of success of the various systems of management.

In the beginnings of the movement for vocational schools every community has to some extent made use of the general school buildings and equipment and the ordinary school faculty, but everywhere experience has shown the necessity of getting away from the general buildings and faculties and control. In Munich the continuation schools have their own buildings and equipment, and they are making every effort to hasten the day when the full-time teachers will devote their entire energies to the vocational school, and when the day-school teachers will be retired from service in them. It is significant that in Munich, where the one board is said to control, the movement for separate buildings and separate faculties is as pronounced as it is in Württemburg and Baden where they have separate boards of control. Anyone who will deliberately put forward as a reason for leaving these schools in the hands of the ordinary board that they wish to avoid having separate buildings, equipment, and special practically trained teachers betrays a lack of knowledge of the movement and a very imperfect conception of the problem of providing vocational education for our boys and girls. No one who understands the question will try to use the fag-ends of our present school system, in buildings, equipment, or faculty, for the assistance of the fourteen- to eighteen-year old boys and girls who are in search of practical education. No one who knows boys and girls of fourteen will believe they ought to be compelled to rely upon the fag-end of their energies after doing a day's work in the shop, in their efforts to secure a practical education.

In Dr. Roman's article and others there is talk about "class division in society," and about the "undermining of democracy." Suppose we analyze this proposition a little. Under either form of administration the boys and girls are cared for in schools supported by public taxation, administered by school authorities selected in the same way. Under either system you will find them placed in separate rooms, in many cases in separate buildings, and, where efficient, under especially trained teachers. No one seriously proposes to put all of the boys between fourteen and eighteen together in one building; no one seriously supposes that democracy would require us to have the carpenter apprentice taught by the same teacher who prepares another boy for the University of Chicago. He ought to be taught, of course, by just as good a teacher. The difference seems to lie in the fact that the local board to whom the teachers and principal of the schools are responsible would be a separate one, made up of practical men or women, with the superintendent of schools. It is hard to say how this organization could endanger democracy or bring about a "class division in society."

The real question before us is this: Under our present school organization, perhaps through no fault of the schools, there are, in a community like Chicago, in the neighborhood of 40,000 young people between fourteen and eighteen who are not in school. Of this number about one-half are employed in remunerative occupation. Society and the school have faced this situation in the past with considerable complacency, now and then offering these boys and girls a chance to get some vocational training in any evening school. The proposition is now made to care for all of these young people, employing the same general public agencies, and we are torn to pieces over "the attempt to overturn the American public-school system." I hardly think it worth while to discuss the criticism further.

The real reason for division of opinion is that many people believe these boys and girls would be made more efficient by placing them in schools directly responsible to a body of practical men and women, men and women with whom and for whom the boys or girls will work in their future life. We are simply anxious to secure individual efficiency, and through this, social efficiency and good citizenship; and we believe the proposed organization will be best adapted to secure this end. The attempt to inject the question of "class division" is far-fetched.

Referring again to German experience, I will say that I have visited about two hundred schools in Germany, Austria, and Switzerland, and have never found any division of interest among the people on account of the separate system of management. I did not find any lack of co-operation in the common use of school property; in fact, I found this common use more general in Prussia where they have separate boards than I did in Munich where they have one. I found, too, that the continuation schools of Munich cost more than they do in any other place in Germany.

My investigation in Germany with my experience in America convinces me, as I have said, that "these schools should be separate, independent, compulsory day schools, supported by special taxes, carried on usually in special buildings, administered by special boards of practical men and women, taught by specially trained practical men from the vocations, and securing the closest possible co-operation between the school and the factory, the school and the farm, the school and the counting-room, or the school and the home. Adaptation and co-operation are the watch-words for the new type of schools."

[This number of the *Elementary School Teacher* is devoted entirely to two topics: first, the general topic of industrial education; second, Mr. Courtis' tests. Both matters are so urgent that the editorial department is being omitted in order to bring out these papers before the summer months. The *Elementary School Teacher* does not in general enter into controversial matters and it has no judgment to offer with regard to the merits of the case under discussion by Mr. Cooley and Mr. Roman. The main point which impresses the editorial reader is the difficulty of disentangling the German situtation from itself, to say nothing of applying it to the American schools. In earlier numbers of this Journal the present writer has expressed very definite opinions with regard to the desirability of separating American schools. The present discussion certainly does not modify in any wise the belief which he has reached on the basis of such evidence as has been submitted up to this time.—C. H. J.]

CONTROL OF THE INDUSTRIAL SCHOOLS OF GERMANY ONCE MORE

FREDERICK W. ROMAN
University of South Dakota

The article by Dr. Cooley on "Control of German Industrial Schools" is before me. I, too, should like to make a few comments on its statements.

In my previous article I referred the reader to Lexis, *Das technische Unterrichtswesen*, pp. 17–25. The table in my article is patterned after Professor Lexis' table, p. 23. It was not planned to be a translation, hence I omitted the items which Dr. Cooley mentions. My reason for doing so was the fact that the schools which are under the Ministry of the Interior include one single institution for *Feinmechanik*, which is purely a state school. Such a school would not throw much light on our problem. The other schools included the *Fachschulen für Textilindustrie*. These schools have absolutely nothing to do with our question. To bring them into this discussion only obscures. It should be remembered that pupils on leaving the German public schools are in no wise prepared to enter a *Fachschule*. Dr. Cooley states that the Lexis' table contained one or more inaccuracies at the time the book was written, and that a number of changes have been made since 1904. Such statements are likely to be quite misleading. German schools have made great advancement since 1904, but no significant or marked changes have been made in the control since that date.

Further, Dr. Cooley states that the table deals only with the higher supervision of the technical schools of Germany. In this he is mistaken.

The criticism with reference to the schools of Baden is partly correct. There should have been added to my table the industrial continuation schools, which were put under the Minister of the Interior in 1905. The criticism implies that all the industrial schools were put under the Department of the Interior. Only the one type of schools was affected by the change. The control of the commercial continuation schools, the continuation schools for agriculture, and schools for domestic science was not changed.

We must add that the industrial continuation schools of Baden are governed in the main by a board called the *Landesgewerbeamt*. This is not a local board. This board is composed of certain state officials and members appointed by the Ministry of the Interior. Direktor Sierck, editor of the school journal (*Zeitschrift für das gesamte Fortbildungsschulwesen in Preussen*), says that the local board is quite limited in its power. Speaking of the local board he says: "Seine Befügnisse sind durch die bestehenden detaillierten Vorschriften und durch das weitgehende Aufsichtsrecht der vorgeordneten Behörden ziemlich beschränkt."[1] Hence we see that local control by a separate board gets meager encouragement, even from this one type.

The change was made to establish a closer connection between these schools and the *Gewerbe und Fachschulen*. The latter are recruited to a limited extent by the former. The former aims to teach the mass of workers, the latter prepares foremen, superintendents, and captains of industry. Now if in this country we could put our industrial schools under the same control that such schools have in Baden, there would be some good sense in separating them from public-school management, because in that case one could be sure of intelligent supervision. It is not possible to establish such a connection with our privately endowed technical schools. The machinery of our state-supported higher technical school is not yet prepared to undertake the task either.

The organization in Baden can do this. There are quite a number of higher industrial schools supported by the state. The boards controlling them are specialists, and not politicians. There is nothing in the Baden law to justify a two-school board system here. One ignorant school board in an American city is quite sufficient. Two would be superfluous.

Whereas no great change has been made in control of the industrial schools in the last decade, it will be interesting to note a tendency to do away with the dual system in Saxony. The journal

[1] Sierck, *Das deutsche Fortbildungsschulwesen*, p. 68 (published 1908).

Die Fortbildungsschule (Leipzig), April, 1911, contains an article on "Der Dualismus im gewerblichen Unterrichtswesen." There the *Sächische Fortbildungsschulverein* and the *Sächische Leherverein* have both come out for a union of the two types of control. After giving the usual arguments for union, the paragraph closes by stating, "Ein Verschmelzung beider Schularten kann allen Beteiligten nur zum Segen gereichen." Then the article continues to give examples where the union has recently been carried through in such cities as Chemnitz, Plauen, Annaberg, and Zittau. The article closes by stating "Also der Weg zur Beseitigung des Dualismus ist gezeigt und beschritten."

What I said about the control of the schools of Württemberg was correct. But let us go more into detail this time. The highest authority is the Ministry of Schools and Churches. The next in rank is a board called the *Gewerbeoberschulrat.* This is composed of a member of the Department of Commerce and Industry and other members appointed by the King. The law requires this board to look after the higher supervision, as may be directed by the Ministry of Schools and Churches. The next in authority is the *Beirat,* which is composed of eighteen members appointed by the Ministry of Schools and Churches. This board is composed of certain officials of the district, directors and officers of higher trade schools, higher commercial schools, public schools, art schools, and representatives of various trades. Below this, each school has an advisory board.

In discussing the control of the industrial continuation schools, Sierck says (p. 68) in the book already mentioned above, "Wie aus dem vorstehenden ersichtlich, ist hier nicht das Ministerium für Handel und Gewerbe, sondern das für Kirchen- und Schulwesen die höchste entscheidende Instanz." He adds, "In Baden ist die Verwaltung des Fortbildungsschulwesens in ähnlicher Weise organisiert."

As stated in my previous article, the director of the public schools, being on both boards, wields an enormous influence. He has a life position, and politics do not influence his actions. He is always a well-trained scholar, and is usually the most influential man in the community. When disputes arise in everyday life, the quarreling parties not infrequently decide to bring their witnesses and evidence to the schoolmaster instead of the court. Both sides argue their points of view. The schoolmaster renders a decision. That usually ends it. Thus without any legal authority whatever, he exercises an immense control over the grown-up folk. Why not? They were once his pupils and learned to respect his judgment, and to believe that his word was law.

My statements with reference to Bavaria have also been challenged. Let me quote again from Sierck (p. 70): "Die Sonn- und Feiertagsschule partizipiert an der Verwaltung der Volksschule, die gewerbliche und kaufmännische Fortbildungsschule steht als Nebenanstalt unter dem Rektorat der Realschule und die selbständigen Anstalten dieser Art stehen unter einem Lokalschulvorstand, beide unter der mit weitgehenden Befugnissen Ausgestatteten Kammer des Innern der Kreisregierung und in letzter Instanz unter dem Staatsministerium des Innern für Kirchen und Schulangelegenheiten." This proves that not all the schools are organized in connection with the elementary schools. Some are put under the rector of a *Realschule* ("secondary school"), others are organized independently under a separate board. All types are found in Munich. When I was in Munich I secured an official permit from Dr. Kerschensteiner to visit continuation schools, high schools, commercial schools, an art school, and a teacher's seminar. In all cases the boards including the rectors of the secondary schools were under Dr. Kerschensteiner. That date was 1910.

The functions of all these local boards are largely advisory. They have no such powers as are exercised by local school boards in this country. They can neither appoint nor dismiss teachers. They cannot plan the curriculum. Their chief duties consist in making arrangements with the constituents whom they represent to levy taxes, furnish buildings, heat, and light. The reader must understand that the Germans have little local authority in anything. They are accustomed to a paternal government. They are ruled by a highly centralized régime. Even the schools of all classes have the military air. Dr. Cooley says it is misleading for me to try to make it appear that the question at issue is a religious one. Let me refer the American reader to an authority that is easily accessible. Read *Beginnings in Industrial Education* (Houghton Mifflin Co.), by Professor Hanus of Harvard University. On p. 150, he quotes a state school inspector who said, "The domination of the church is our greatest obstacle in the path of educational progress." Other similar quotations follow. Then again on p. 185 Professor Hanus says, "One of the most serious questions, which Bavaria and indeed all Germany has to deal with, is the one of freeing the public rural school from the incubus of ecclesiastical control." It is just this condition which led to the statement in my own book (p. 62) which Dr. Cooley cites. Dr. Cooley says that he thinks the continuation schools of Baden are superior to those of any other state in Germany. Many Germans have told me the same thing. When I would ask them how they explained it, the answer was invariably, "Baden is the most free from church control."

Dr. Cooley calls attention to the Prussian Conference of Teachers of Schools, that voted to retain the present dual organization. I have already stated that I talked with prominent industrial-school directors, who told me that the reason why they favored the dual organization was because that seemed the only way to keep the church from getting increased control. When I was in Germany, Massachusetts had the industrial commission to manage the schools. That led me to investigate the question of dual organization. I went to these same men who favored dual organization in Prussia to ask what they thought about the dual plan. They thought that a country not divided on the religious question would undoubtedly do better to have only one board. Further reasons have already been noted in the previous article.

Dr. Cooley mentions the official statement, which was given as the reason for separating the schools in 1885. The official statement was that the work of the industrial schools had a closer connection with the Ministry of Trade and Commerce than with the Ministry of Education (see *Zeitschrift für das gesamte Fortbildungsschulwesen*, May, 1911, p. 356). I was once confused over that official statement too, but these same directors assured me that the real reason was the existence of a constant fight between Bismarck and the clergy. Bismarck himself was at that time Minister of

Trade and Commerce of Prussia. The argument in his official statement helped him get the schools away from the clergy. The journal which I have just cited (pp. 356–75) gives a long list of extracts from speeches made in the lower house of the Prussian Parliament in 1911. These speeches prove beyond all doubt that the religious question is the main one at issue. Let me quote a characteristic extract from a member of Parliament: "Wir fürchten eben wenn Sie einmal den kleinen Finger in dem obligatorischen Religionsunterricht haben, dass Sie dann auch die Leitung der ganzen Fortbildungsschule in die Hand bekommen wollen." Toward the close of the article we read, "Vor allem wird der Religionsunterricht der Punkt sein, über den man schwerlich zu einer Einigung kommen wird."

In Bavaria it was the clerical party that forced the investigation of Dr. Kerschensteiner's work in 1910.

To argue for a two-board system in this country because of Germany's example, without giving the full causes for the separation, seems to me to be unfair to the American public.

May I add that Dr. Kerschensteiner mentions in his reports frequently that in the different stages of developing the industrial schools, it was found necessary to improve the elementary schools. Is it not clear that he would have been greatly handicapped if he had not had the elementary schools under his charge? Prussian reports state frequently that the industrial schools have improved only as the efficiency of the elementary schools has been raised.

If we had two boards in this country, there would at once be a dispute as to the cause of the inefficiency of the industrial schools. Each board would place the blame on the other. The people would join the contest. Instead of a united community fighting ignorance, we should have the scene of well-meaning people fighting each other.

There is no reason to believe that a second school board would know more about industrial schools than the ones we now have. In the last analysis the same power that elects the first board will have to elect the second. This whole movement of dual organization looks to me like a political scheme to increase the number of officers at the expense of efficiency and economy.

GERMAN SCHOOLS

A REJOINDER

EDWIN G. COOLEY

In Dr. Roman's reply he relies, as in his former article, on the published opinions of certain schoolmasters in Germany. It is unnecessary for him to heap up proof that many German schoolmasters are perfectly confident of their ability to handle vocational education and general education both. We are familiar in Illinois with the same point of view. But vocational education is at least as much a problem of commerce and the industries as of general education, and the men and women, employers and employees, who are actually at work in the various trades and other employments must also be consulted as to the kind of training that is best for the new applicants for places in the particular occupation chosen.

In the "relatively small space" to which the editor's communication of May 5 not unreasonably restricts my reply, I cannot take each statement of Dr. Roman's and answer it in detail. I shall therefore refer only to two or three points. My difficulty in answering within a small space may be illustrated from the second and fourth paragraphs of Dr. Roman's reply. In the second paragraph he excuses the omission of certain types of vocational schools from his former table by saying that his concern is not with them, but with industrial continuation schools; while in his fourth paragraph he belittles an error of his in the same table by saying that this second omission did not concern all vocational schools, but involved industrial continuation schools only. He devotes much space in his reply to arguments which have to do solely with the division of authority between state and local boards (both vocational), which is not an issue at all in our present discussion; what we are talking about here is the division of authority between two local school boards, one general and one vocational. In his account of the administration of the industrial schools of Württemberg he neglects to state that the Gewerbe Oberschulrat, which, as he says, is "composed of a member of the Department of Commerce and Industry and other members appointed by the king," is the real governing body, although responsible to the Ministry of Schools and Churches; and that this member of the Department of Commerce and Industry is the chairman, and the actual head of the whole organization.

Not to follow Dr. Roman up point by point, I may content myself with directing attention to the fact that, while details differ everywhere, there is throughout Germany a universal recognition of the necessity for some sort of separate organization for the vocational schools; and everywhere, but in Bavaria, as I showed above, these schools are directed by a board or committee on which the commercial or industrial interest is given the controlling power. Wherever the American visitor goes—to Baden, Württemberg, Hesse, Saxony, Prussia, Austria—he naturally applies to the Department of Education for his permit to visit schools, and everywhere but in Bavaria he finds that he has gone to the wrong department—that the work of industrial education is carried on under the Department of Commerce and Industry or of the Interior, or by a special commission, and that it is there he must go for information about these schools. My own personal experiences to this effect are confirmed by the results of the study of vocational education in Germany by the two most important commissions that have undertaken this work—the Wisconsin commission of 1908–11 and the Swedish commission of 1907–12. Both carried away the same impression that I received —namely, that vocational schools cannot succeed unless practical men of affairs—employers and working-men—are given a decisive part in their management. Charles C. McCarthy, who drafted the report of the Wisconsin commission, summarized its observations by saying that "the Germans have established, almost universally, local committees of business men, manufacturers, and workmen, who control these schools wherever they are." This is also the net result of the facts reported by Dr. Roman himself.

Dr. Roman goes even farther than most school men. He

evidently distrusts any management of any schools, whether general or vocational, by persons who are not school men. The seventh paragraph of his reply, as printed above, indicates the two steps in his program. First, we must drop the idea of a separate and specially qualified management for the new vocational schools. Next, we must drop the general board of education. This will leave us Dr. Roman's ideal—a system of schools with no interference from citizens. "One ignorant school board in an American city," he says in the paragraph just referred to, "is quite sufficient. Two would be superfluous." Here is the bureaucracy that so many secretly believe in. The only trouble with this doctrine is that it is grossly undemocratic and absolutely unacceptable to any American (or German) community.

I shall not analyze further the reply of Dr. Roman. Let me, however, speak of one of his comments on the situation in Germany. "The director of the public schools," he says, "being on both boards, wields an enormous influence." The proposed vocational school law in Illinois, which Dr. Roman criticizes, provides that every board of control for these schools, state or local, shall always have as one of its members *ex officio* the chief school officer, the superintendent of schools. Why does Dr. Roman not trust these superintendents to exercise the "enormous influence" on both general and vocational boards that he saw them exercise in Germany? Besides distrusting the management of public schools, by the business men, the workman, and the citizen in general, does he also distrust the American school-man? And, if so, on whom is he relying? The college professor?

INDUSTRIAL EDUCATION IN THE EARLY NINETEENTH CENTURY

F. R. ALDRICH
Russell, Kansas

One of the most important topics before the people today in the educational field is the subject of industrial training. We are often given to the idea that attention to industrial arts in the common or public schools is a late development. There is often more or less of a hesitancy upon our part to introduce work of the kind into the curriculum, fearing that it is too much of an innovation, too radical a departure from the established traditions. Men of deep thought and long experience are generally conservative. Particularly is this true of the school man. But that conservatism is often based upon ignorance is easily shown when the causes of the opposition to this element upon the part of school men is carefully investigated. Training along lines other than the old established classics is by no means new in the history of the public schools of America. It has come down in one form or another almost since the establishment of the very first schools, and while perhaps it has never accomplished all the good which its authors have hoped for it, still it has certainly done enough to justify a further consideration, and its retention in our school system. It has never been, generally, in any period of our school history, a failure.

It is not the purpose of this article to go into a detailed history of industrial training even in the United States, but merely to note some of its phases during the early part of the nineteenth century. And there can probably be no better place to begin that investigation than in Boston, since it is here in the New England states that we find a very early and a comparatively original development of the school system. Here as elsewhere in this country, even down into the nineteenth century, schools were not as a whole free, and consequently not for the whole public. One peculiar feature was that there was no provision in the public- or free-school system for the education of the child before entering the grammar schools. It was the custom to send the child to private schools at varying rates of tuition from the age of four to seven, when, having acquired a knowledge of reading sufficient to permit the reading of a testament, he might enter a public grammar school where tuition was free. These private schools naturally varied widely in their efficiency, in their manner of teaching, and in just what they taught besides reading. Some undoubtedly introduced more or less of the industrial element. But as a class it is evident that there was no great regularity, and as a whole, along industrial lines, if not in the regular work, probably not very much was accomplished. Every child of the better class received some instruction of this sort at home. Indeed, it was a long-established custom for the girls of the houeshold to be taught and to become expert in such arts as sewing and knitting, since a knowledge of both of these arts was of vastly greater importance to the home-builder in those days than now in an age of factories and machine production.

Some time within the first two decades of the century there began to grow up in Boston a feeling that primary schools also should be free and a part of the general public-school system. Many believed that the illiteracy of the city was due to the indifference of the poorer classes toward education, which was an ornament of the rich, or at least of the well to do, in their estimation, and a luxury, not a necessity, for the poor man. But gradually the belief in the utility of an education for every individual grew until, in 1818, primary schools were for the first time established by the city of Boston. At first the schools were in session the year around, but girls were allowed to attend only in the summer, when most of the boys did not attend. To the girls alone during this summer term industrial arts were taught, principally sewing and knitting. But then, as now, there were misgivings, as the half-apologetic, half-defensive report of a visitor shows: "I believe that a little manual exercise will induce the children to learn more and better and faster, and will give a spirit and an animation to whatever they perform." Not a word about the benefit of what is actually learned, but attention was centered wholly upon the general disciplinary training.

But, nevertheless, industrial training in Boston increased rapidly. It is true that the work was by no means considered upon a level with the other school work, but merely supplementary. A report of some of the work done mentions the following articles: 30 shirts; 12 pairs of sheets; 6 pairs of pillow cases; 26 pocket handkerchiefs; 8 cravats; 10 infant socks; 3 pairs of mittens. Many other small articles were noted, all of a very practical and useful nature. One cannot but speculate upon the comparative utility of the knowledge thus gained and the benefit which accrued to society at large.

In 1824 it was noted that the poor of the city were very deficient in a knowledge of sewing and knitting. One cause seems to have been that it was customary for the pupil to furnish all material. Many parents were too poor to furnish the requisite amount and quality, and many who were not too poor still were careless and indifferent about giving any aid that required any exertion or expenditure. The city, therefore, determined to furnish the material free, where it was found necessary. What a change of front in six years, when a committee had reported adversely to a proposition to make the primary schools free! It was in this period also that girls were allowed to attend school in the winter, and there thus came about a further extension of the industrial work. But this was undoubtedly the high tide of manual work in the Boston schools of this general period, for we find that four years later, while needlework is still strictly maintained in some schools, in general there has been a decline in this branch of education. From time to time there was agitation in regard to it. In 1839 the Grammar School Committee desired to have the work of knitting and sewing extended farther in that department, but the authorities were conservative, saying that as these arts were already taught in the primary grades, they saw no need of farther extension. In 1847 a resolution was passed for a more general introduction of sewing and knitting into the primary grades, but we are led to infer that this was more of an attempt to regain ground lost than to establish anything radically new. It is probable that the age of factories and machine work was already making its influence felt in Boston, and special industrial skill was beginning to replace general industrial skill, especially in the making of garments and such articles as have been noted above.

Such, then, were the conditions in New England.

The school history of New York is unlike that of Boston. Schools and education in general were more backward. The history of education in New York in the early part of the nineteenth century is principally the history of the Public School Society. We may note, however, that as early as 1820 samples of sewing by the girls of the public schools were exhibited. In general this policy of industrial training to girls was defended upon the ground that none of the professions were then open to women. On the other hand, all the professions were open to the boys, and indeed a choice of some profession was deemed essential to worldly success. Therefore there seemed less need for manual training for any but the girls. And such reports as we have of the work actually done along industrial lines show that it was the work of the girls, and very similar to the work done in Boston, as an enumeration of the following articles will show. There were to be found shirts, shifts, sheets, samplers, cravats, night caps, thread cases, stockings, diaper towels, handkerchiefs, pillow cases, table cloths, towels, aprons, infants' shirts, neck gussets, wristbands, curtains, and ruffles. But here again we note that there is a feeling that the industrial element has for its purpose not alone the tangible product of industry, but to a great degree its disciplinary effect upon the mind of the student, as note the report of a committee in 1820: "The practical instruction in the industrial arts to which females must mainly look for subsistence at the present time . . . . has doubtless exerted a quiet but refining influence over many minds and hearts."

In Pennsylvania we find similar conditions. In some places we see a spirit manifested in advance of either of the two localities already discussed, as may be evidenced by some of the industrial work done in Lancaster. One school in particular advertised the following branches of work: needlework, tambour work in shading in gold and silver, filigree work, openwork, plain sewing, and sample work with painting and drawing. Here more than in the two centers considered above this industrial work was valued as having for its purpose the fitting of the individual for his life-work, whatever it might be, whether of the professions or of a more lowly calling. Here also there was less distinction made between the boys and girls. In fact in the rules for the Boys' High School may be found these significant words: "The studies for pupils designated for college shall be directed accordingly; and in all cases, so far as consistent with the rules of the school, the study of each pupil shall be shaped to suit the occupation or profession for which he is designed." Who would suppose that this was a dictum laid down nearly three-quarters of a century ago, in 1849, and not the utterance of a modern champion of industrial training?

As we go westward, it would seem the ideas of industrial training become more liberal in form. In Boston it is in the primary schools and for girls alone; in New York still for girls, but for those of a more mature age; in Pennsylvania for both sexes, fitting for some definite life-calling. And as we go on westward, we shall find that ideas of industrial education in states, for example like Indiana, were broader still and extended strongly toward agricultural training and instruction. In the West and South we get a very practical application of the idea that industrial training should be such that a student might at the same time gain the mental benefits, the preparation for future life-work, and finally gain entire or partial support while at school from his labors. Boone says that "the idea of the Hofwyl institution in Switzerland had but recently been imported into this country and already the Fellenberg schools had been planted in a number of states, notably one each in Connecticut and in South Carolina, that were the precursors if not the progenitors of our later agricultural colleges." Several schools had been founded in New York before 1835 which tried to combine manual labor with the cultivation of the mind. In Ohio Oberlin Collegiate Institute, which afterward became Oberlin College, there was a plan by which both boys and girls could partly support themselves by daily manual labor, either within the buildings or in the fields.

The movement spread rapidly when it reached Indiana. One of the principal causes was doubtless the fact that this was purely an agricultural state and the idea that special agricultural training should come with training in other subjects made a stronger appeal than in older regions of the East. Probably the frontiersman felt little need of a purely literary training, but like all other individuals, hailed with delight an indication that at last his special occupation was being recognized as all-important and worthy of having definite instruction given in it. Many schools sprang up which took the significant name of "farmers' academies." These schools seem to have been like other classical schools, with greater emphasis upon the industrial, particularly the agricultural. Soon the idea ran to an extreme, however, and numbers of schools got no farther than incorporation, while others sprang up with a mushroom growth, only to suspend operation within a few months. In general all these schools were but unsuccessful attempts to meet a little understood, but nevertheless recognized, need. The only institutions which seemed to meet success at all along these lines were the schools established for the benefit of the colored people, and in them, then as today, the industrial element was the great need and the essential life-spark that kept them alive.

So much, then, for the general conditions in representative states which stand for school progress throughout the North. As a whole we cannot but note some peculiar things in connection with this industrial training wherever it is found. As deep as the feeling for it seems to be where the work is found, still the sentiment for it does not seem to be altogether sincere. There is hardly a state where the work has not been undertaken to a limited extent, but its history seems to stop with those beginnings. No community or state during the whole first half of the nineteenth century actually took up the work as if it were considered the end of important instruction, but generally merely a side-line. The movers of the work are nearly always open to a suspicion of a lack of genuine and complete sincerity, because while professing to place this work in the forefront of importance they still cling to the idea of the superiority of the classical schools. This feeling may for a time be hidden, but sooner or later it appears when it comes to a question of educating their own children. Only for the Negro is it a panacea for all ills. Is it not possible that the deeply imbedded prejudice against this form of education has risen, for the most part unconsciously, but nevertheless truly, from an attempt to reconcile their minds to equal race rights if not to race equality? One thing strengthens this feeling. In the investigation of the history of education throughout the southern states for this general period there is little or no mention of any industrial element in public education, except, perhaps, here and there the briefest reference to a public charge, an apprentice, or an orphan. But considering the social conditions during the whole of this period in the South, and the existence of the institution of slavery, it is not at all strange that the idea of industrial education was unpopular, since it was, in theory at least, putting the white child upon the level with the Negro, which was an unthinkable action.

The whole movement during this period was, however, founded upon the same basis that is generally believed today to be the only one which can promise success. That is, every such movement must be built upon community need. The phases of the problem have been and will continue to be the recognition of this need and the wise and proper satisfaction of it. The need has been there through all our national life. It was there during the special period with which this article has dealt. It is there today. Events today seem to point to a much more definite grappling with the problem in the near future than has ever been undertaken before. And in the attempted solution there can be little doubt but that the experiences of those who have tried and failed, perhaps, along these lines, will stand out like beacon lights, pointing out not alone the dangers, but as well the routes of safety.

BIBLIOGRAPHY

The Academician, Vol. I.
Pole and Lancaster. *Education.*
American Journal of Education, Vols. I and IV.
Annals of Education, Vols. II, III, IV.
Griscomb. *Monitorial Instruction.*
Reports of the Regents of the State of New York, 1835.
Report of the Superintendent of Common Schools, New York, 1834.
Report of the Visitors of the Common Schools, New York, 1834.
American Institute of Instruction, Boston, 1830.
Bourne. *History of the Public School Society of New York.*

Wickersham. *School History of Lancaster, Pa.*
New Jersey School Report, 1847.
Connecticut Common School Journal, 1839.
American Educational Society, *Annual Reports*, Nos. 18 and 19.
American Educational Society, *Quarterly Register*, 1829, 1833.
Boone. *A History of Education in Indiana.*
Educational Reports, Massachusetts, I and II.
Annual Reports of the Comptroller of Public Schools, Philadelphia, 1835–42.
Martin. *Evolution of the Massachusetts Public School System.*
Higginson. *History of the Public School System of Rhode Island.*
State School Report of Rhode Island, 1875.
Brayley. *Schools and School Boys of Old Boston.*
Wightman. *Annals of the Boston Primary School Committee.*
Dabney. *Education in the South.*
Lewis. *History of Higher Education in Kentucky.*
Merriam. *Higher Education in Tennessee.*
Bernard's Journal of Education, Vol. XXVII.
Graves. *Great Educators*, Pestalozzi, Fellenberg, Lancaster, Bell.
Lancaster. *The Lancastrian System of Education.*
Steiner. *History of Education in Connecticut.*
Pierson. *History of Education in Delaware.*
Ward. *History of Education in Connecticut.*
Bush. *History of Education in Florida.*
Parker. *History of Education in Iowa.*
Reed. *History of Education in Kentucky.*
Fay. *History of Education in Louisiana.*
Steiner. *History of Education in Maryland.*
Murray. *History of Education in New Jersey.*
Coon. *History of Education in North Carolina.*
Smith. *History of Education in North Carolina.*
Yetter. *History of Higher Education in Pennsylvania.*

THE RELIABILITY OF SINGLE MEASUREMENTS WITH STANDARD TESTS[1]

S. A. COURTIS
Liggett School, Detroit, Mich.

The question of the reliability of a single measure of a child's ability to write the answers to the addition combinations seems to the writer better shown by repeated measurements at intervals over a long period of time than by the creation of an artificial practice series. Accordingly he presents in Fig. 8 the scores of certain members of an eighth-grade class under his control. The period of time represented is three school years. The test the first year differed from that shown in Fig. 1 above in that it contained no zero combinations; that is, the test was slightly more difficult. For the other two years one or another of the three editions of Test 1 were used. Variations in external conditions were reduced to a minimum through mechanical timing and uniform procedure.

It will be noted that the curve based upon the class averages show marked fluctuations. Through October, November, and December, 1909, the curve is level. During this period the class was drilling on the combinations in the other operations, and the work did not influence the scores in addition; did not "transfer" in other words. Accordingly this is a good period to study the fluctuations in the scores of individuals. During the remainder of this school year there was direct practice on the addition combinations and the scores show corresponding increases. The first week in October, 1910, the addition test was given each day of the week, and during the following eight weeks, once each week, thus forming a direct practice series. As a whole the 1910–11 curve of progress after the first rise is fairly level during this period, with gain as before during the two remaining thirds of the year. The last year the tests were given but three times, little attention was

[1] Continued from Vol. XIII, No. 7, March, 1913.

paid to direct work on the tables, and most of the gain was made the first third.

Tabulation of the November to December differences (19 cases) gave an average variation of 6 points and a maximum of 13; of the December to January differences (Christmas vacation) an

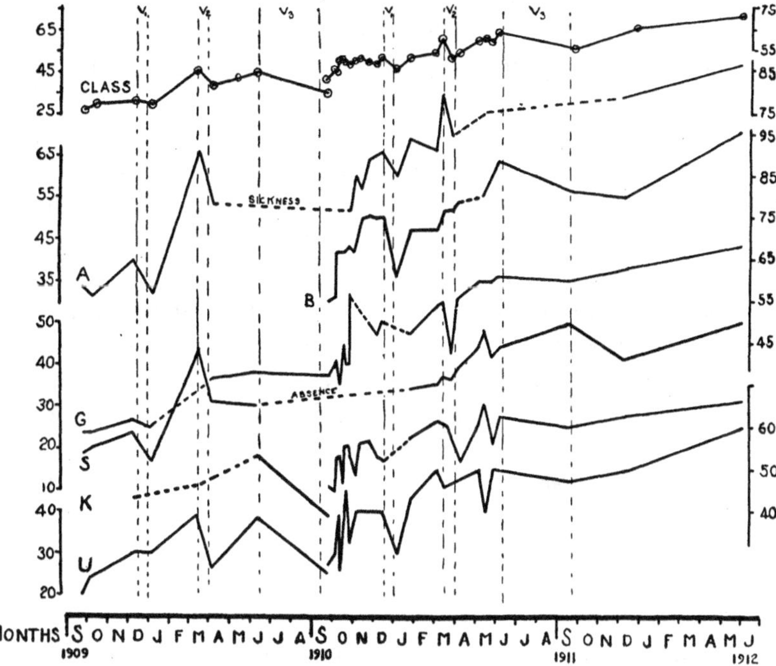

FIG. 8.—Curves based upon the average scores in Test 1, addition combinations, made by a class, and upon the individual scores of certain members in the class. Time scale, months from September, 1909, to June, 1912. Small circles upon class curve indicate the dates at which tests were given. V_1, V_2, V_3 represent the Christmas, spring, and summer vacations respectively. Scales at the right and left give number of answers written per minute. Note that a unit space in the class scale has twice the value of the unit in the other scales. For explanation of the curves see text.

average variation of 5 points. The average difference from one score to the next was for the practice week (97 cases), 4.7 points; 63 per cent of the differences were 5 or under; 25 per cent from 6 to 10 points, and 11 per cent from 10 to 17 points. For the eight-week period (124 cases) the average variation was 3.9 points;

74 per cent of these differences were less than 5 points; 23 per cent from 6 to 10 points, and 5 per cent from 10 to 17 points.

These figures agree very well with the results of the article under discussion and show that in general a single measurement of an individual will yield a value that will not differ more than 5 points from his true ability at the time. For two-thirds of the children the differences will be 5 or less. About one child in ten will have a markedly unreliable score, the amount of the deviation ranging from 10 to 30 points.

So far, the results fully confirm the data from the other study and with such general statements the writer has no quarrel. His contention, however, is that the fact of the great range in the nature and amount of individual variation makes such statements of little value unless rightly interpreted. The child is a plastic, developing organism. Its performance in any test is determined by a large number of factors. The nature of some of these factors, and the degree of the effects of all are entirely unknown. If the child's mind is in stable equilibrium, a single measurement (barring external accidents) will yield a reliable result, and a series of measurements will show but small chance variations from the score of the first test. If, however, the child's mind is in unstable equilibrium so that it is easily modified by experience, any one score may differ markedly from any number of previous or later measurements that may be made, and a practice series may yield results that it will be as foolish to combine into a single measure of ability as it is to express the sum of three apples and two potatoes by a single figure with the name of either. In one sense each and every measurement is absolutely unreliable in that it is impossible to predict, on the basis of any number of past measurements, what score an individual will make in the next test, owing to possible changes made in the mind of the individual by that past work. In another sense each independent measurement is also absolutely reliable; for it records the actual achievement of the individual at the time and under the conditions of the test. In other words, the writer believes each mental measurement should be treated only as symptom of internal conditions. An unusual score is a sign that a cause or causes are at work which must be evaluated before the score can be rightly interpreted, but the score itself is a true measure of conditions at that instant, and, if the conditions continue, the score of a second test will agree with the first within two or three points. But no general rule can be made that will cover all the facts of individual variation, and the interpretation of one or more measurements of an individual must remain a matter of individual judgment.

A consideration of the individual curves given in Fig. 8 will make these points clear. Individual A the first week of school made a score of 33 and two weeks later of 31. In December before the Christmas vacation her score was 40, after vacation 32. The class average during the same period shows little variation. One may interpret these differences in these scores as chance variation, or one may see from the rest of the curve that this individual is easily affected by her experiences. When the class is gaining, she gains a great deal; during vacation she loses consistently. It is probable, therefore, that the change from 31 to 40 in December represents a real internal change, a "transfer" from the regular work in arithmetic. Her actual score at the end of any practice series will be unreliable by 10 or more points, since, during any period of disuse, her ability to add decreases by that amount. On the other hand, it is interesting to note that a large part of the gain made during the midyear term, 1909–10, was permanent, as her scores after vacation and after a long and serious illness agree. This individual makes a fine showing under drill, but the gain is largely specific and misleading.

Individual B, on the other hand, is of quite a different type and her curve is given as representing that of a girl of unusual ability. The opening week of school her score was 55, the Monday of the following week it was 56. On Tuesday it jumped without warning to 67, and on the remaining days of the week her scores were 67, 67, 67. The following Monday it was still 67, and in the three tests during the following month her scores were 67, 68, 67, a series of seven scores practically without variation. The second week in November her score again increased suddenly, this time to 75, and from this time on to April her scores were 75, 76, 75, 75, 61, 72, 72, 77, 77, 79. The low score, 61, marks the effect of the

Christmas vacation, but the loss was quickly made up. The remaining scores for May and June were 81, 86, 89, and for the next year 82, 80, 96. Such constancy and such sudden gains are by no means unusual. The writer can show many cases where the same score has been repeated week after week for five or six weeks at a time. It would seem, too, that in many children there are "psychological moments" when a little practice will produce marked gains which are held forever after, while even a large amount of practice at other times produces little or no apparent effect. Whether this is merely the much-discussed "plateau effect," or whether it reflects certain inner physiological changes, the writer does not know.

The other curves were chosen to illustrate various types of children. G is that of a stable individual of average ability; S shows the effect of absence and travel (a little tutoring was done on the trip but no school was attended during this period); K, a variable individual of more than average ability; U, of the member of the class weakest in addition. U gained steadily during the first two-thirds of the year. The March (1910) vacation and the summer vacation following both show large losses. The practice series, 1910, was marked by violent fluctuations in score, while for the succeeding five weeks a perfectly constant score of 40 was made each week. It should be noted that 40 is the level nearly reached at the two previous high points of the curve.

One cannot follow the score of many individuals in successive tests of addition, subtraction, multiplication, and division through several years without realizing that the number of factors determining any one score is very large, and that the question of reliability is not as simple a question as it might seem. It is certain that the possible unreliability of any single measurement must always be kept in mind; it is equally certain, also, that nine times out of ten a single test reflects the true conditions accurately. It is granted that a series of twenty-five tests will reveal additional facts in regard to an individual, but it is also to be remarked that it may take many other related tests and much experimentation to make the meaning of the additional facts clear. As a practical expedient, twenty-five tests of each individual in the hundreds of abilities that must eventually be measured if there is to be efficient classroom teaching is out of the question. The writer is sorry the conclusions of the authors should have taken this form, and hopes that no teacher or superintendent just awakening to the value and possibilities of measurement and standardization will be discouraged by the statement. For the purpose of the study was based upon a misconception of the purpose of the tests, and the methods used are applicable only to more stable mental conditions than are found in the minds of growing children.

In this connection it is necessary to remind the reader that Test 1 is but one of a series of eight related tests and that, as used by the writer, the scores in all these tests are interpreted together. To quote from the folder of instructions describing the use of the comparative graph sheet, "The general plan is, therefore, to interpret any curve in the light of all the knowledge of the individual that can be obtained, and to check conclusions reached by further tests at the first opportunity."

Thus in Fig. 9 are given the curves of two seventh-grade individuals of extreme types. In the interpretations of such curves the scores made in Tests 7 and 8 should be considered first. For Test 7 the standard scores for the seventh grade are 13 examples attempted and 8 right. Individual A's score is unsatisfactory, as she has attempted 14 examples and has but 4 of the 14 right. Individual B's score, on the other hand, represents exceptional ability, for although she attempted but 11 examples, 10 of these were right, indicating unusual accuracy. Now it should be evident at once that since B actually has the ability to add, subtract, multiply, and divide in Test 7, it is of little consequence whether he knows his tables or not. The fact that in the addition combinations his score is that of a fourth-grade child has no significance whatever. He can actually add in long-column addition at a higher rate of speed than he can write the answers to the single combinations, and on the basis of much experience in this type of work, the writer is able to state that any attempt to increase his score in Tests 1 to 4 by practice is likely to act adversely upon Test 7. Yet it is certain that the low score of 35 in addition is not an "unreliable" score; for it is confirmed by the scores in the other speed tests. Even the higher score in division is probably not due to chance variation, but to the greater ability of the individual in this process.

The unsatisfactory scores of individual A in Test 7, however, are not due to "tables" either; for her scores are two grades above standard in all except division, and are double those of individual B. Again these scores are reliable, for the four scores agree closely.

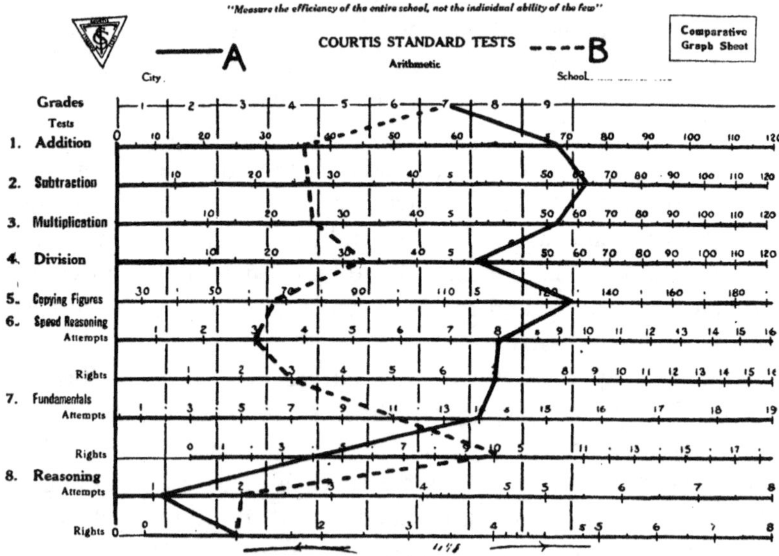

FIG. 9.—Curves of two individuals of extreme types. A (solid line) knows her tables very well, but works inaccurately in Test 7 (abstract examples in the four operations), getting but four examples right out of the 14 attempted. B (broken line) has only 4th-grade scores in the tables, but is able to work ten examples out of eleven correctly. Neither A nor B would profit by drill on the tables.

The apparent drop in division is due to the character of the scale at this point where the maximum of the development curve occurs, and the real difference is so small that it falls within the range of chance errors (5). A has been overdrilled on the tables. It should be evident that no amount of further drill on the tables could benefit A in the slightest, *unless* her past drill has been wholly written, so that the score is an indication of the specific ability to write the answers and not of ability to make ready response.

An oral test could be used to answer this question. It is probable, however, that A's defect is to be found in some of the other abilities involved in the longer computations, such as ability to "borrow and carry," to copy figures accurately, etc. Whatever the cause, it must be remedied by special work at the weak point, and no other remedial work will be efficient. The actual cause could easily be determined from an analysis of the mistakes made.

It should be noticed that in the interpretation of such departures from standard, balance of scores is more important than absolute size of score, and that so small a difference as ten points is without great significance. The average yearly progress is about seven points. Accepting the author's own figures, the scores of eight children out of nine will fall within ten points or within a grade and a half. More than two-thirds of a class will differ less than a grade. How accurately a single measurement thus places an individual on the scale of status and how great the need for measurement in teaching is shown by the statistics for the range of individual variation within the grades under present inefficient conditions.

In Fig. 10 is given the distribution of 7,625 eighth-grade scores in Test 1, also for comparison, the distributions of a number of groups of children in single classes from various cities, and of 118 eighth-grade class averages. It will be seen that the range is very great and fairly constant from city to city. The eighth-grade average score in addition is about the same everywhere.[1] As long as the differences between individuals in the same class amounts to as much as the entire average progress during the whole school life, a test that will enable a teacher to place a child on the scale of status as accurately as within ten points and on the basis of a single measurement, must be of very great value to the intelligent teacher. As long as present conditions continue, the need for the refinements of measures derived from practice series of twenty-five or more measurements of each individual is not apparent.

Such curves as those of B above raise a very important question, "What is the ideal form of the individual development curve?"

[1] The larger cities tend to emphasize the abstract at the expense of the reasoning work, and the average scores in Test 1 are from ten to fifteen points higher, with a corresponding range of individual variation.

In Fig. 11 is given the actual development curve for knowledge of the fundamental combinations in addition based upon the standard scores derived from the measure of many thousands of children (light solid line). A form in accordance with the suggestion made

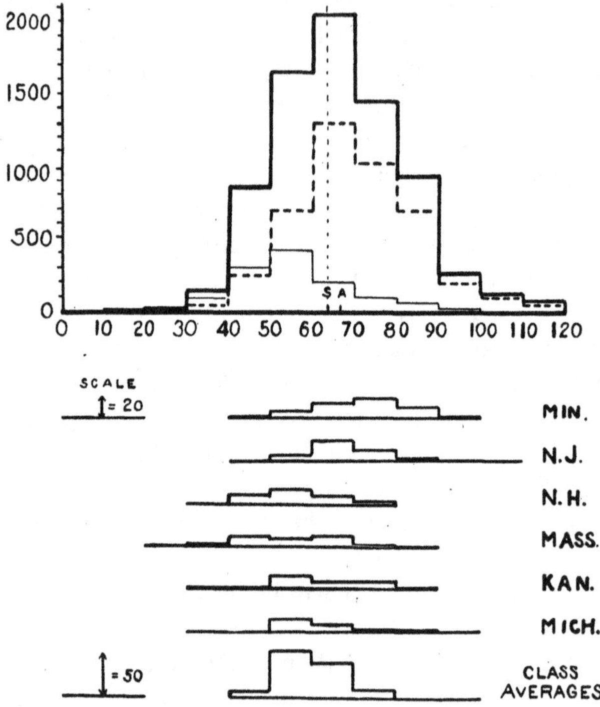

Fig. 10.—Upper part of figure, distribution of scores of 7,625 eighth-grade children in Test 1. Collected from schools in many states. Vertical scale = number of children making each score. Horizontal scale = number of answers written per minute. The range of the scores is from 15 answers per minute to 115 per minute. A = average score of the entire group; S = standard eighth-grade score.

Middle figures = distributions of individual scores in typical classes from various states.

Lower figure = distribution of 118 eighth-grade class averages; 80 per cent fall within a range of 20 points.

by the writer above—that the growth occurs suddenly and at certain periods only—is indicated by the broken line. The dotted line is a variation of this same idea; i.e., that the child should learn his table early and all at once. Slowly gathering evidence has led the writer to suspect, however, that the ideal form for efficient teaching is that represented by the heavy line; that is, that under ideal conditions a child would acquire through concrete experience and oral drill a working knowledge of the simpler combinations. He would put this knowledge to immediate use in working abstract examples and perfect his knowledge by repeated use. But as there would be no drill on the separate combinations, before long higher habits of grouping, of unconscious short cuts, etc., would begin to form and ability to recall the separate combinations would

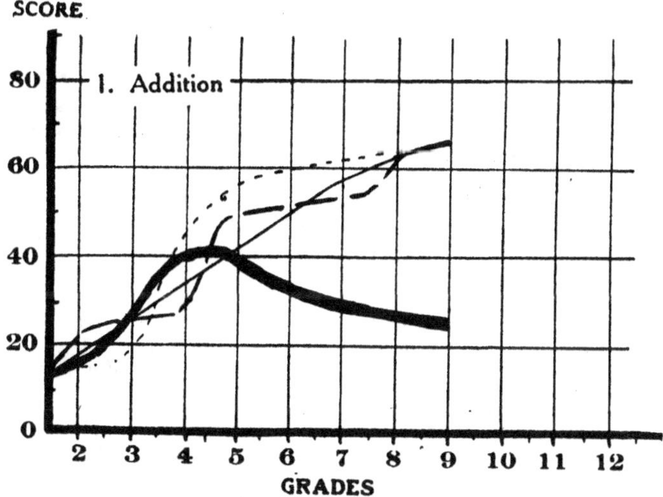

FIG. 11.—Various types of development curves for the ability measured by Test 1. Light, solid line=actual curve derived from measurement of many children. Heavy line=possible ideal form. For meaning of other lines see text.

decline. Whether this is the true explanation or not, it affords a working basis for valuable experimental work. At least two things are certain: (1) many children able to do eighth-grade work in Test 7 with fourth-grade knowledge of the tables are found, particularly among those who are exceptionally accurate: (2) a very great deal of useless, ineffective drill work on the tables is done in our schools. In Fig. 10, 762 or 10 per cent of the whole group have scores higher than the standard by 20 or more points, although very few of these really use the tables at anything like the standard rate.

One last point remains to be discussed; the question as to the correlation that exists between ability in Test 1 and ability in column addition. Fortunately in his attempt to derive units of measurement, the writer has had occasion to give a series of tests designed to measure the relative difficulty of various addition examples and that data is presented herewith.

In Table V is given a sample example from each of the series of tests. Tests A and H were the speed test shown in Fig. 1. Test B was composed of single combinations—practically the test shown in Fig. 1 with different spacing and the zero and 1 combinations omitted. Test C consisted of examples containing four figures, thus requiring three additions except as a person was able to "see" the sum of the four at once. Each of the other tests contained one type of examples, the examples increasing in length up to columns of 13 figures (12 additions). The examples in Tests I, J, K, L are all composed of columns of 8 additions each but increase from single columns up to examples of four columns. Such a series unquestionably measures the "ability to add."

TABLE V

SAMPLE EXAMPLES FROM A SERIES OF TESTS IN COLUMN ADDITION. EACH TEST WAS COMPOSED WHOLLY OF EXAMPLES OF ONE TYPE, AND WAS OF SUCH LENGTH THAT NO ONE FINISHED IN THE TIME ALLOWED

A	C	E	F	G	I	J	K	L
8	5			7				
3	6			5				
	2			8				
	7			9				
(B)			4	4	8	3	4	8
			7	3	3	49	557	9,659
7	(D)	9	2	9	4	66	892	3,778
4		3	2	7	4	75	347	9,484
	7	6	4	9	7	32	562	5,247
(H)	6	4	9	7	8	96	738	8,470
	2	8	2	8	7	85	658	7,966
9	7	2	5	5	6	64	273	6,323
2	4	3	2	2	2	59	797	3,277

The tests (except the speed tests) were mimeographed and given in regular class time by the class teacher. The time allowances varied from one minute for the simpler tests to three minutes for the more difficult. Mechanical timing was used. Tests A to H were given on one day in rapid succession, from one to two minutes' rest being allowed between each trial. The remaining tests were given some weeks later. The scores were expressed as number of additions made per minute. The mistakes were scored as number of "columns wrong." The individual results are given in Table VI, also the averages for the class. Individuals A to U are eighth-grade girls and the letters represent the same individuals as in Fig. 8. Individuals X, Y, Z are teachers tested at the time the class was tested and also a year later for the purposes of this article. Y is the writer himself. Z is his assistant in charge of his statistical work, a bookkeeper with a business-college training and a year and a half of practical experience, an exceedingly rapid and efficient worker.

Even a casual inspection of the table will show that the correlation between ability in Test 1 and ability "to add" is no simple thing and like most other such relations between mental tests is wholly an individual matter. The results cannot properly be expressed in a single coefficient. For instance, individual A who stands highest in the speed Tests A, B, and H—the single combinations—falls to a rank of fifteenth when there are even three additions in a column and varies from eleventh to nineteenth in succeeding tests. B, on the other hand, is second in the speed tests and first in all other tests. At the other extreme, individual Q was seventeenth in the speed tests but is second highest in the four most difficult tests, and individual T was twentieth in the speed tests and was fifth in the last test. Between these extremes every degree of correlation is found. The correlation coefficient based upon the relative ranks of the 21 individuals in the first and last tests is $r = +0.43$.

The essential facts of the table and additional data derived from the same tests in other grades are presented graphically in Fig. 12. Test H is placed next to Test A in order that comparison may be easily made. A and H, it should be remembered, are two trials with the test shown in Fig. 1, one trial before and one after the first five tests in adding columns; that is, before and after eleven minutes' actual work in column addition. Every grade but the sixth grade shows an increase in score and in the eighth grade the practice effect is comparable to previous results, 75 per

TABLE VI

COLUMN ADDITION

Scores in Number of Additions per Minute of 21 Eighth-Grade Girls

Test No.	A	B	C	D	E	F	G	H	I	J	K	L
A.......	85	60	33	26	23	24	22	86	36	30	25	25
B.......	77	54	50	52	54	50	42	82	70	60	58	56
C.......	77	50	30	36	33	24	24	75	36	28	32	29
D.......	73	53	48	47	40	48	39	80	46	44	39	40
E.......	72	41	37	41	45	44	42	88	44	36	38	28
F.......	71	37	33	40	30	34	28	72	36	17	30	29
G.......	69	43	36	37	31	31	28	72	36	38	29	24
H.......	69	42	37	30	29	22	22	67	40	28	26	26
I........	65	41	36	50	24	24	24	67	28	28	26	24
J........	65	42	33	37	31	20	20	68	28	28	33	21
K.......	65	39	32	31	24	34	30	62	40	40	38	32
L.......	64	43	39	38	38	32	34	67	40	36	39	40
M......	62	40	42	34	34	34	32	60	44	36	33	29
N.......	62	47	40	47	43	34	37	64	36	26	34	27
O.......	62	40	36	35	37	30	26	64	44	33	29	26
P.......	55	39	29	19	17	18	14	62	36	20	22	18
Q.......	55	40	42	46	42	46	36	56	49	49	45	43
R.......	52	41	30	30	23	24	28	58	32	26	23	21
S........	52	24	27	22	21	28	27	47	24	20	30	24
T.......	48	31	38	37	37	42	42	52	44	36	29	32
U.......	39	30	32	29	23	20	26	49	36	22	26	26
Average .	63	41	36	35	31	33	29	66	39	32	33	30
W^1......	84	63	62	76	60	58	50	93	..	..	..	..
W^2......	87	67	66	78	71	64	58	86	62	52	59	..
X^1......	..	65	69	64	70	66	58	..	..	..	..	..
X^2......	70	65	63	68	66	58	53	85	64	52	55	..
Y^1......	..	70	72	67	72	69	69	..	..	..	..	..
Y^2......	87	71	77	71	76	79	76	93	67	50	47	62
Y^3......	85	67	78	70	68	65	60	90	70	51	55	58
Z^1.......	105	87	114	120	113	112	108	110	116	89	101	111
Z^2.......	112	90	120	116	108	120	111	113	128	96	99	115
Average for W, X, Y.......	83	69	70	71	69	66	61	89	66	51	54	..

NOTE.—W, X, and Y are teachers, Z a bookkeeper.

cent of the children varying five or less points, 19 per cent between 6 and 10, 5 per cent between 11 and 16. A feature of the results is that 26 per cent of the fifth-grade differences, 57 per cent of the sixth-grade, 18 per cent of the seventh-grade, and 19 per cent of the eighth-grade differences were negative. This, together with the decline in the curves, would seem to indicate the effect of a fatigue factor. In this connection the recovery on Test I should be noted. Test I was of course the same as Test F, but in the case of the children was given first of the Tests I, J, K, and L a few weeks

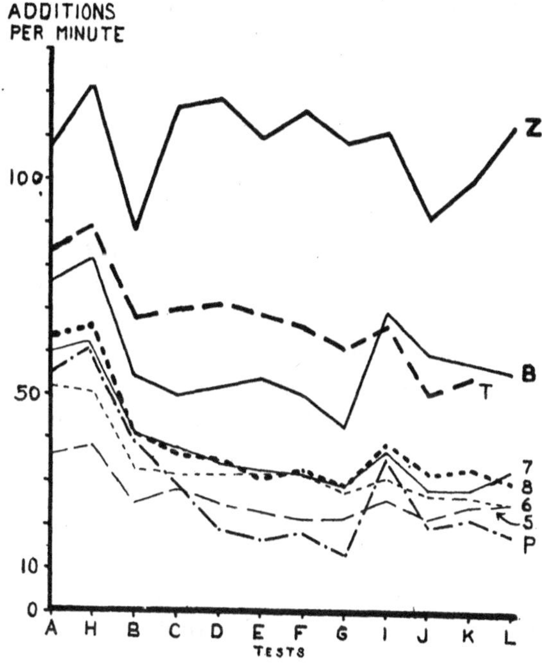

FIG. 12.—Graph of relative scores in tests of column addition. Vertical scale = number of additions per minute. Horizontal scale = tests corresponding to examples shown in Table V. Z = curve of bookkeeper; T = average scores of three mathematics teachers; B = best individual in the class; P = poorest individual. 7, 8, 6, 5 = curves of corresponding grade averages.

after the previous series. For individual Z and for the teachers (T), however, the two series were given one after the other on the same day.

In considering the results, the difference between Tests A, H, and B should be noted first. B is slightly harder than A and H because the zero and one combinations were omitted, but the real cause of the difference in score is the greater distance the hand must travel in writing the answers. B was constructed to conform to the spacing in the succeeding tests. In Tests A and H the combinations were printed twenty on a line while in B there are but ten on a line. Even Z who is able to think the answers at a very high rate of speed cannot overcome the physical handicap of greater number of figures to be written and the greater space to be covered. The differences between the scores for A and B and between B and the other tests are quite constant. Therefore in general the individual who has a high score in the speed tests will show a corresponding score in "adding."

The general statement of the correlation between the two abilities will not be true of individuals as was shown above. In the figure, B is the curve of the best individual in the class and P of the poorest, and these two differ more in Tests E and F than they do in Tests A and H, that is, the difference between their ability in column addition is greater than the difference shown by their scores in the combinations. This does not mean, however, that the tests of the combinations do not measure abilities used in column addition; for even on the basis of the analysis of the abilities involved in column addition given by the authors, readiness of association is but one of several factors and the lack of correlation may be due to a defect in one of the other factors. The writer would add two factors to those given by the authors of the study being discussed, (1) attention span, (2) fatigue, and in this case the extreme drop of the curve of P is probably due to the effects of fatigue.

The relative level of the curves of the different grades is very significant. The seventh grade has overtaken the eighth and the sixth the seventh. The writer of course believes this due to changes in methods that have been made based upon the results of the testing work and expects to produce very much greater changes through knowledge and control of the various factors involved. It is impossible to teach efficiently a child to "add" when neither the teacher nor the children have more than such a vague general aim before them. At the same time the separation between the eighth-grade average and the curve of the teacher's score and between the teacher's and professional ability in addition show that conditions are far from satisfactory. It is a relatively simple matter to develop "readiness of response," but to teach column addition is quite a different matter.

Some of the individual results from such tests, however, throw light upon the factors determining a score. In Fig. 13 are given a

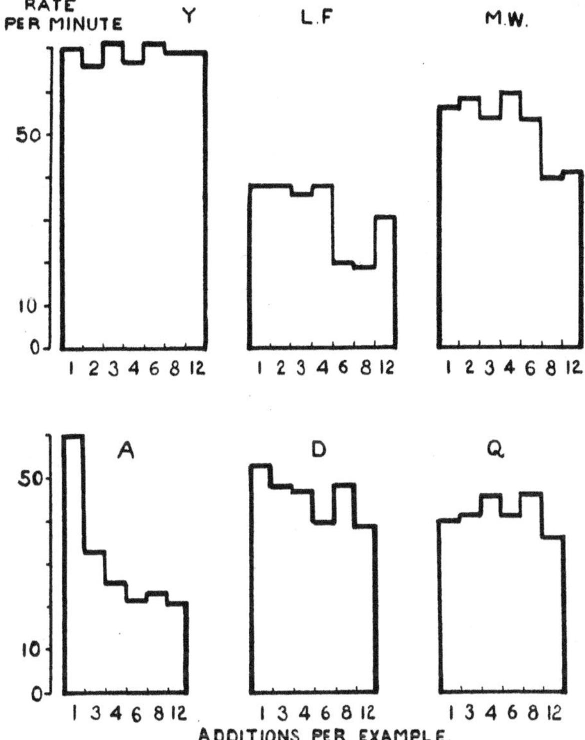

FIG. 13.—Change of rates with columns of varying length. Vertical scale = number of additions per minute; horizontal scale = number of additions in each example of the test. Test 1 corresponds to B in Table V, Test 2 to C, etc. Y, A, D, and Q represent the same individuals as in previous tables.

number of individual curves, so drawn as to make clear the changes in rates through the series. For curves Y, L, F, M, W the tests used were the same as those described above but the time allowance was just a minute for each test, and a longer rest was allowed between the tests. For during the second and third minutes of continuous work the scores even of adults begin to fall off rapidly. Curves A, D, and Q are from the results given in the table. LF was seventh grade, and MW fifth grade. Individual Y (the writer) worked at a uniform rate, whatever the length of a column; the variations are of the order of chance variations. LF also worked a uniform rate for columns involving 1, 2, 3, and 4 additions, but an increase in the length of the column to 6 additions decreased the rate nearly one-half. In this case the cause is known; for the writer, watching, saw the girl when nearing the top of a column, hesitate, lose her place, and begin again. The limit of her attention span had been reached and it required an unusual effort, an extra grip on her attention, to reach the top of the column. Nearly every column was added twice with the consequent decrease in her rate. For MW much the same thing was true, but the drop came at 8 figures instead of 6 and the effect was not so marked.

In many cases causes were not as evident as in these two and all sorts of individual variations were found. A's curve has already been described. For minds of this type, the scores in the speed test give a totally false idea of the real ability in column addition. D represents a common type. Q illustrates the type that "warms up" to its work, but in all sooner or later a point is reached to go beyond which calls for greater effort, more inaccurate work, and rapid fatigue.

Out of 21 members of the eighth-grade class, the mistakes made were as follows:

Number of Test	Number of Individuals Making Errors	Number of Columns Added Incorrectly	Number of Test	Number of Individuals Making Errors	Number of Columns Added Incorrectly
Test A.....	2	2	Test E....	12	38
Test B.....	8	23	Test F.....	17	31
Test C.....	16	31	Test G....	21	61
Test D.....	17	44			

That is, here, as before, to make errors consumes time and the rate changes to correspond.

In bringing this discussion to a close, the writer feels that the evidence shows plainly that so far as chance variations are concerned, the result from a single measurement will ordinarily not vary more than 5 points from the true score. That, on the other hand, the possibility of external accidents (breaking of pencil points, etc.) and of peculiar physical and mental condition radically modifying the achievement must *always* be kept in mind. That no attention should be paid to small variations from the standard, and that all large differences should be checked both by repeating the test and by comparison with similar scores in other tests; that the need for repeating measurements will occur at the most in about one case in ten. That if properly used, Test 1 measures one of the factors directly concerned in column addition and that the results rightly interpreted have a diagnostic value.

Finally, that the supreme thing in education is the fact of the very great variation in the abilities and needs of individuals. It is true that the writer urges the necessity for the measurement of the efficiency of the entire school, but it is also true that in no other way will the facts of the individual variation and of present gross inefficiency be revealed. The poorest school and the weakest teacher will, if they but keep at work enough years, turn out some naturally gifted individual to whose achievement they can forever afterward proudly point as a sample of their products. But at the present time no school has yet been found in which if the entire school be measured with standard tests under uniform conditions, the product of teaching is not shown to be so widely variable that so far as the particular ability is concerned, the school must be regarded as having failed utterly in accomplishing its purpose. At the present time the school is able to teach only those fitted by nature to respond readily to its teaching but if it were organized to detect and minister to the special need of the individual, vastly more could be accomplished. Definite aims, i.e., to render every child in the eighth grade able by June to add in four minutes 35 examples each a single column of 9 figures—and diagnostic tests—i.e., tests that will enable a teacher to determine exactly why a child can work but 23 such examples in the time allowed—and the experimental determination of efficient methods, are the lines along which progress will be made. The basic factor in education is thus the fact of individual differences in natural ability, and the supreme problem of future is the working out of administrative methods of dealing with large masses of children, yet at the same time giving to each child the special attention and the special courses it needs, without sacrificing the benefits of class work and group instruction. Only as the Courtis Tests aid in this "discovery of the individual" and the laws of his development will they have accomplished their purpose.

BOOK REVIEWS

Manual of Moral and Humane Education. By FLORA HELM KRAUSE, Chicago: R. R. Donnelley & Sons. 8vo, pp. 271.

Educators are coming more and more to recognize the importance of moral education. Humane education is an important part of moral education and may very properly be made the starting-point for the same.

Mrs. Krause had in mind in writing this book the desire to demonstrate that the subject of moral and humane education can and should be taught not in a sentimental but in a truly educational way, that is, by correlating it with other subjects of the curriculum and working out for it a clear program, bringing together a body of literature to make it a real discipline.

For the teacher the most valuable part of the book is the carefully constructed outlines for teaching this subject in the grades. Not only is there a wealth of literature both prose and poetry, but the rich bibliographies, the great number of suggested themes make the book extremely handy for the teacher.

The course is made out for each month of the school year. There is work planned out for each grade in connection with four subjects of the curriculum: nature-study, art, literature, and civics.

This material the teacher may use to enrich his teaching of the subjects, thus not only doing his set work better, but incidentally inculcating valuable lessons in morals. And it seems to us that as a rule the most effective teaching of morals is that which is done incidentally in connection with the study of varied phases of life.

The book has already been put on the library and supplementary lists of the Chicago schools and is largely used in the schools of Illinois where humane education has been made part of the curriculum.

Every teacher in the grades should know this book.

C. H. HANDSCHIN

BOOKS RECEIVED

AMERICAN BOOK CO., NEW YORK

Household Science and Arts. By JOSEPHINE MORRIS. Cloth. 12mo. Pp. 256, With illustrations. Price $0.60.

Martha of California. By JAMES OTIS. Cloth. 12mo. Pp. 142. With illustrations. Price $0.35.

Mighty Animals. By JENNIE IRENE MIX. With an introduction by Dr. FREDERICK A. LUCAS. Cloth. 12mo. Pp. 144. With illustrations. Price $0.40.

High School Agriculture. By D. D. MAYNE and K. L. HATCH. Cloth. Pp. 432. Illustrated.

Schatzkästlein. By J. P. HEBEL. Edited with Notes and Vocabulary by MENCO STERN. Cloth. Pp. 179.

MACMILLAN, NEW YORK

Human Behavior; A First Book in Psychology for Teachers. By STEPHEN S. COLVIN and WILLIAM C. BAGLEY. Cloth. Pp. 336. With illustrations. Price $1.00 net.

The Posture of School Children. By JESSIE H. BANCROFT. Cloth. Pp. 327. With illustrations. Price $1.50 net.

School Hygiene. By FLETCHER B. DRESSLAR, Ph.D. Cloth. Pp. 369. Price $1.25 net.

HENRY HOLT & CO., NEW YORK

Modern Geography for High Schools. By ROLLIN C. SALISBURY, HARLAN H. BARROWS, and WALTER S. TOWER. Cloth. 12mo. Pp. 418. With illustrations and maps.

GINN & CO., CHICAGO

School and Home Gardens. By W. H. D. MEIER, A.M. Cloth. 12mo. Pp. 318. With illustrations. Price $0.80.

The Peirce Spellers. Book One and Book Two. By WALTER MERTON PEIRCE. Cloth. Pp. 131.

Minimum Essentials: Sheets of Graded Questions in Arithmetic and Language. By THOMAS E. THOMPSON. Paper. Pp. 44.

UNIVERSITY PRESS, CAMBRIDGE

A Source Book of English History. Volume I, 597–1603 A.D. Edited by ARTHUR D. INNES, M.A. Cloth, large crown 8vo. Pp. viii+384. With 31 illustrations. Price 4*s*. 6*d*.

Burke's Reflections on the French Revolution. Edited by W. ALISON PHILLIPS, M.A., and CATHERINE BEATRICE PHILLIPS. Cloth. Pp. 311. Price $1.25 net.

FREDERICK A. STOKES CO., NEW YORK

A Guide to the Montessori Method. By ELLEN YALE STEVENS. Cloth. Pp. 240. With illustrations. Price $1.00 net.

CHRISTOPHER SOWER CO., PHILADELPHIA

Culture, Discipline and Democracy. By A. DUNCAN YOCUM, PH.D. Cloth. Pp. 320. Price $1.25.

J. B. LIPPINCOTT CO., PHILADELPHIA

Noted Pennsylvanians. By WALTER LEFFERTS. Cardboard. Pp. 252. With illustrations.

The Princess and the Goblin. Simplified by ELIZABETH LEWIS. Cloth. Pp. 124. With illustrations in color. Price $0.50 net.

HOUGHTON MIFFLIN CO., BOSTON

Language Teaching in the Grades. By ALICE WOODWORTH COOLEY. ("Riverside Educational Monographs.") Cloth. Pp. 88. Price $0.35.

New Ideals in Rural Schools. By GEORGE HERBERT BETTS, PH.D. ("Riverside Educational Monographs.") Cloth. Pp. 128. Price $0.60.

Preparing for Citizenship. By WILLIAM BACKUS GUITTEAU, PH.D. Cloth. Pp. 238. With illustrations.

Seventh Reader. By JAMES H. VAN SICKLE and WILHELMINA SEEGMILLER assisted by FRANCES JENKINS. ("The Riverside Readers.") Cloth. Pp. 276. With illustrations. Price $0.55.

The Japanese Twins. By LUCY FITCH PERKINS. Cloth. Pp. 178. With illustrations. Price $0.50.

The Second Book of Stories for the Story-Teller. By FANNY E. COE. Cloth. Pp. 209. Price $0.80.

THE CENTURY CO., NEW YORK

Jataka Tales. Re-told by ELLEN C. BABBITT. Cloth. Pp. 92. With illustrations. Price $0.40 net.

Panama, Past and Present. By FARNHAM BISHOP. Cloth. Pp. 271. With illustrations. Price $0.75 net.

RAND MCNALLY & CO., NEW YORK

Cromwell, England's Uncrowned King. By Esse V. Hathaway. ("Little Lives of Great Men Series.") Cloth. Pp. 177. With illustrations.

MANUAL ARTS PRESS, PEORIA

Inexpensive Basketry. By William S. Marten. Paper. Pp. 45. With illustrations. Price $0.25.

Leather Work. By Adelaide Mickel. Paper. Pp. 53. With illustrations. Price $0.75.

SOCIAL CENTER PUBLISHING CO., DETROIT

Bedrock: Education and Employment, the Foundation of the Republic. By Annie L. Diggs. Cloth. Pp. 70. Price $0.25.

SURVEY ASSOCIATES, INC., NEW YORK (RUSSELL SAGE FOUNDATION)

Medical Inspection of Schools. By Luther H. Gulick, M.D., and Leonard P. Ayres, Ph.D. Cloth. Pp. 224. With illustrations.

CARNEGIE FOUNDATION FOR THE ADVANCEMENT OF TEACHING

Seventh Annual Report of the President and of the Treasurer. Paper. Pp. 194.

UNIVERSITY OF MISSOURI, COLUMBIA, MO.

Geography of Missouri ("Education Series," Vol. I, No. 4). By Frederick V. Emerson. Paper. Pp. 74.

PUBLIC EDUCATION ASSOCIATION, PHILADELPHIA

The German System of Industrial Schooling. By Ralph C. Busser, LL.D., American Consul, Erfurt, Germany. Paper. Pp. 63.

RUSSELL SAGE FOUNDATION, NEW YORK

Psychological Tests in Vocational Guidance. By Leonard P. Ayres, Ph.D. Paper. Pp. 5. Price $0.05.

The Effect of Promotion Rates on School Efficiency. By Leonard P. Ayres, Ph.D. Paper. Pp. 13. Price $0.05.

STURGIS & WALTON CO., NEW YORK

The Education of To-Morrow. By ARLAND D. WEEKS. With an Introduction by M. V. O'SHEA. Cloth. Pp. 232. Price $1.25 net.

WARWICK & YORK INC., BALTIMORE

Variations in the Grades of High School Pupils. By CLARENCE TRUMAN GRAY, A.M. ("Educational Psychology Monographs.") Cloth. Pp. 120. Price $1.25.

CURRENT EDUCATIONAL LITERATURE IN THE PERIODICALS[1]

IRENE WARREN[2]
Librarian, School of Education, University of Chicago

Arnold, Felix. Politics, efficiency, and retardation. Psychol. Clinic 7:35–38. (Ap. '13.)

Art schools for girls. Lit. D. 46:1010–11. (3 My. '13.)

Atkinson, Eleanor. Lincoln's alma mater. Harper 126:942–47. (My. '13.)

Ayres, Leonard P. Psychological tests in vocational guidance. J. of Educa. Psychol. 4:232–37. (Ap. '13.)

A brief summary of what has been done and of the prospects of future work.

Baldwin, Bird T. The boy of high school age. Relig. Educa. 8:23–32. (Ap. '13).

The type of religious and moral training suited to the adolescent boy.

Blankenburg, Rudolph. The municipal need of technically trained men. II. Sci. Am. 108:342–43. (12 Ap. '13.)

Blount, Alma. Normal school training for the teaching of English in elementary schools. English J. 2:215–20. (Ap. '13.)

Bredvold, Louis L. Suggestions for reconstruction in high school English. Educa. 33:492–98. (Ap. '13.)

Brown, F. C. Scholarship and the state. Pop. Sci. Mo. 82:510–15. (My. '13.)

Brown, Horace G. Dramatization in history teaching. El. School T. 13:425–33. (My. '13.)

A classification of different sorts of dramatization with their uses, and an outline for dramatic illustration of early American history.

Calfee, Marguerite. College freshman and four general intelligence tests. J. of Educa. Psychol. 4:223–31. (Ap. '13.)

Low correlations were found between college grades and card-sorting, card-dealing, alphabet-sorting, and the minor test.

[1] *Abbreviations.*—Educa., Education; El. School T., Elementary School Teacher; English J., English Journal; J. of Educa. (Bost.), Journal of Education (Boston); J. of Educa. Psychol., Journal of Educational Psychology; Lit. D., Literary Digest; Pop. Sci. Mo., Popular Science Monthly; Psychol. Clinic, Psychological Clinic; Relig. Educa., Religious Education; School R., School Review; Sci. Am., Scientific American.

[2] Annotations by Dr. Frank N. Freeman.

Clancy, George C. The weak student in freshman English composition. English J. 2:235–40. (Ap. '13.)

Colvin, Stephen S. The practical results of recent studies in educational psychology. School R. 21:307–22. (My. '13.)

Cox, John Harrington. Preparation for teaching college English. English J. 2:207–14. (Ap. '13.)

Dearborn, Walter F. The practical results of recent studies in educational statistics. School R. 21:297–306. (My. '13.)

(The) decline of book-reading. Lit. D. 46:829–30. (12 Ap. '13.)

Fargo, Lucile F. The place of the library in high school education. Educa. 33:473–77. (Ap. '13.)

Foster, William T. The college president. Science 37:653–58. (2 My. '13.)

Gayler, G. W. Vocational training as a preventive of crime. Psychol. Clinic 7:39–46. (Ap. '13.)

A general plea for vocational training.

Heck, W. H. A second study of mental fatigue in relation to the daily school program. Psychol. Clinic 7:29–34. (Ap. '13.)

Finds slight amount of decrease in efficiency in afternoon as measured by arithmetic tests.

Hendrick, Burton J. Six thousand girls at school. McClure 41:46–57. (My. '13.)

Hilton, Henry H. Cost of textbooks per pupil. J. of Educa. (Bost.) 77:369. (3 Ap. '13.)

Immodest college advertising. Lit. D. 46:950. (26 Ap. '13.)

Jones, H. Bedford. The personal influence of the teacher. Educa. 33:499–502. (Ap. '13.)

Lakenan, Mary E. The whole and part methods of memorizing poetry and prose. J. of Educa. Psychol. 4:189–98. (Ap. '13.)

A retrial of the two methods of memorizing resulting to the advantage of the whole method.

Lewis, E. E. Practice teaching in model schools. El. School T. 13:434–44 (My. '13.)

A statistical study of the organization of practice teaching.

Maurer, Elizabeth King. The school and the advertiser. Craftsman 24:84–85. (Ap. '13.)

Moore, Ernest C. Improvement in educational practice. School R. 21:323–33. (My. '13.)

Neglected educational material. Lit. D. 46:1004. (3 My. '13.)

Pedersen, Victor Cox. Sex hygiene in the public schools. Good Housekeeping 56:532–34. (Ap. '13.)

Rapeer, Louis W. The secondary school teachers of Prussia. Educa. 33:478–87. (Ap. '13.)

Richardson, Charles F. The problem of waste in the college lecture. School R. 21:334–43. (My. '13.)

Riordon, Raymond. A new idea in state schools that will build up character and body as well as brain: a suggestion for California. Craftsman 24:52–60. (Ap. '13.)

Scott, Jonathan French. The decline of the English apprenticeship system. El. School T. 13:445–54. (My. '13.)

The continuation of the discussion in a previous article.

Shaer, I. Special classes for bright children in an English elementary school. J. of Educa. Psychol. 4:209–22. (Ap. '13.)

A system of flexible promotion.

Shull, Charles A. Recent legislation affecting educational institutions in Kansas. Science 37:622–24. (25 Ap. '13.)

Discusses the law consolidating the educational administration of the state.

Stevens, Ellen Yale. The Montessori movement. McClure 41:182–86. (My. '13.)

Terman, Lewis M., and Hocking, Adeline. The sleep of school children, its distribution according to age, and its relation to physical and mental efficiency. J. of Educa. Psychol. 4:199–208. (Ap. '13.)

Discusses low correlations which were found between amount of sleep and intelligence, school success and nervous traits.

Thomas, C. E. English for industrial pupils. English J. 2:241–46. (Ap. '13.)

Todd, Helen M. Why children work. McClure 40:68–79. (Ap. '13.)

Children's confessions to a factory inspector.

Wetzel, William A. The old and new systems of education, a contrast. Educa. 33:503–12. (Ap. '13.)

Wilson, Jessie Woodrow. What girls can do for girls. Good Housekeeping 56:437–45. (Ap. '13.)

The Summer Quarter

of

The University of Chicago

1913

PRELIMINARY LIST OF COURSES

A Circular giving complete information will be issued about March 1 and will be sent on request

GENERAL INFORMATION

The Organization of the University includes: the Graduate School of Arts and Literature; the Ogden (Graduate) School of Science; the Colleges (Senior and Junior) of Arts, Literature, and Science; the Divinity School, the Law School, Courses in Medicine, the College of Education, the College of Commerce and Administration.

Faculty, Endowment, and Equipment.—The faculty numbers three hundred and thirty-seven; the libraries contain 381,351 books and 195,000 pamphlets (estimated). The University owns 90 acres of land in Chicago and has 35 buildings.

Location of the University.—The University grounds lie on both sides of the Midway Plaisance between Washington and Jackson parks, six miles south of the center of Chicago. Electric cars, elevated trains, and the Illinois Central suburban service reach all railway stations.

The University Year is divided into quarters: the Autumn (October to December); the Winter (January to March); the Spring (April to the middle of June); the Summer (middle of June to August). Students are admitted at the opening of each quarter; graduation exercises are held at the close of each quarter.

Admission to Colleges and Schools.—Students must present satisfactory evidence of the completion of a four years' course in an acceptable high school or academy in order to be admitted to candidacy for the Bachelor's degrees. Graduate students must possess Bachelor's degrees from accredited colleges. Qualified students over twenty-one may be admitted as unclassified students.

The Unit of Work and of Credit is a major, i.e., a course of instruction involving four or five recitations or lecture hours per week for a full quarter, or double that number of hours for a term of six weeks. A minor is one-half a major. Normal work is three majors per quarter, or nine per year of three quarters.

Degrees.—In the Graduate Schools are conferred the degrees of Doctor of Philosophy and Master of Arts, of Science, and of Philosophy; in the Colleges, the degrees of Bachelor of Arts, of Science, of Philosophy; in the Divinity School, the degrees of Bachelor of Divinity, Master of Arts, and Doctor of Philosophy; in the Law School, the degrees of Doctor of Laws and Bachelor of Laws; in the College of Education, the degrees of Bachelor of Arts, Philosophy, or Science, in Education.

Tuition, Fees, etc.—The regular fee for three major courses in Arts, Literature, and Science, and in the College of Education is $40 per quarter. All students pay once a matriculation fee of $5. In Law and Medicine, the fees are $50 and $60.

Cost of Living.—In University dormitories rooms rent from $25 to $75 per quarter. The charge for table-board in the women's halls is $4.50 per week. At Hutchinson Hall (à la carte service) board costs from $3.50 per week upward. Board and lodging may be had at the same or even lower rates outside the University.

Fellowships, Scholarships, Student Service, etc.—By virtue of endowments and special appropriations, fellowships and honor scholarships and service afford stipends or free tuition to a number of able and deserving students. Further information is contained in a circular entitled *Assistance to Students*, which will be sent upon request.

THE SUMMER QUARTER

These Announcements are provisional and incomplete. A detailed circular will be issued about March 1.

The Calendar for 1913.—The First Term begins Monday, June 16, and closes Wednesday, July 23; the Second Term begins Thursday, July 24, and ends Friday, August 29, the Autumn Convocation being held on the afternoon of that day.

A Quarter of Regular Work for Credit.—In the personnel of the teaching staff, in scope and methods of instruction, and in credit-value the work of the Summer Quarter ranks with that of the other quarters of the academic year.

Precaution about Gaining Admission.—Undergraduate students should make sure that they are eligible for admission before they leave home for Chicago. Persons thus failing to make arrangements in advance may be rejected or directed to the University High School. Graduate students should inquire in advance as to their eligibility for registration in the Graduate Schools. Application in writing should be made to the University Examiners.

Limitation of Work, etc.—The student is limited to three minor courses for each term, or to three major courses for both terms. In special cases permission may be obtained from the deans to pursue an additional course, for which in the case of undergraduate students, a supplementary fee must be paid. Graduate and Law students are given larger privileges, and students in the College of Education may add one of the arts without additional fee.

Graduate Study.—College professors and school teachers, clergymen, and members of other professions, holding Bachelor's degrees from accepted colleges, may avail themselves of the facilities of the University to pursue advanced studies under the guidance of research professors in all the chief departments of investigation.

Biblical and Theological Study.—The Divinity School offers to professors of theology, to theological students, to ministers, to religious workers, and to others interested in biblical and theological study, introductory and advanced courses in all its departments. See p. 11.

Professional Courses in Law.—Students beginning the study of law, those in the midst of their professional studies at Chicago or elsewhere, and practicing lawyers are offered work of a thorough and systematic character. See p. 14.

Courses in Medicine.—College seniors planning to study medicine, students in medical schools, and practitioners will find the summer course in medicine admirably adapted to their needs. The Summer Quarter is of especial value to students who need to review and to make up work. See p. 16.

Educational Principles and Methods.—The courses of all departments have a bearing upon the work of teaching, but the courses of the College of Education are peculiarly adapted to the professional needs of teachers, both in primary and secondary schools. The work in the various shops affords unusually complete instruction in the industrial arts and crafts. See. p. 11.

Public Lectures.—A series of public lectures, concerts, and other forms of entertainment is scheduled throughout the Summer Quarter, and affords opportunity to students to hear speakers of eminence and artists of distinction.

Chicago in Summer.—An agreeable summer temperature, spacious parks, notable libraries and museums, great industrial plants, typical foreign colonies, a number of Settlements, and other significant social institutions make Chicago a peculiarly appropriate center for study and investigation.

Cobb Hall and Men's Dormitories

Women's Halls

HUTCHINSON COMMONS, MITCHELL TOWER, AND THE REYNOLDS CLUB

BARTLETT GYMNASIUM

Excursion Parties.—It has been customary, especially in the South, to organize special excursion parties for the journey to Chicago. The University will be glad to put inquirers into communication with the organizers of such parties.

ARTS, LITERATURE, AND SCIENCE

NOTE.—The following condensed paragraphs contain hardly more than titles of courses. No systematic attempt is made to indicate (*a*) the character of the courses; (*b*) to what types of students they are open; (*c*) what prerequisites are demanded; or (*d*) at what hours the classes meet. All details are given in the complete announcements, which will be mailed promptly to all who apply to the UNIVERSITY OF CHICAGO, CHICAGO, ILLINOIS.

Philosophy, Psychology, and Education.—Courses will be offered in Metaphysics, in Ethics, and in the History of Philosophy; in Elementary and Advanced Psychology, in Genetic and Experimental Psychology, in Educational Psychology, in the History of Education, in School Organization and Administration, in the Formation of the Curriculum, in the Relation of the Arts to the Course of Study, in Industrial Education, in Child-Study, and in the Pedagogy of the various subjects of the school course.

Political Economy, Political Science, History, Sociology and Anthropology, and Household Administration.—Courses will be offered in the Principles of Political Economy, in Transportation, in Taxation, in Public Finance, in Statistics, in Values, in Distribution of Wealth, and in Money; in Constitutional Law; in Ancient History, in Mediaeval and Modern History [Church and State], in English History, Political and Industrial, in American Constitutional History, and in various periods of Political and Industrial History, also Teacher's Course in American History; in Archaeology and Anthropology, in the Fundamental Ideas of Sociology, in the Growth of Sociological Method, in Rural Sociology, in Social Technology; in the Chemistry of Food Preparations, in Home Economics, in House Sanitation, and in the Legal and Economic Aspects of Household Administration.

Semitics and Biblical Greek.—Courses will be offered in the Interpretation of the Old Testament, in Elementary and Advanced Hebrew, in Assyrian and Egyptian Languages, and in History; and in New Testament History.

Comparative Religion.—Courses will be offered in the Outline History of Religion and in the Philosophy of Religion.

History of Art, Sanskrit, Greek, and Latin.—Courses will be offered in Prehistoric Art in Greece, in Greek Architecture, in Roman Sculpture, in Roman Coins, in an Introduction to the Study of Art, and in Flemish and Dutch Painting; in Elementary Sanskrit, in the Study of the Veda, in Hindu Religion, in Indo-European Comparative Philology, in an Introduction to the Study of Language, and in Outlines of Latin Historical Grammar; in Beginning Greek, in Anabasis, in Homer, Iliad and Odyssey, in Plato's Apology, in an Introduction to Greek Tragedy, in Aristotle's Poetics, in Lyric Poetry, in Isocrates, and in the Public Orations of Demosthenes; in Cicero, De Senectute, De finibus, Academica, and De Natura deorum, in Terence, the Phormio, in Livy, in Horace, Odes and Epodes, in Catullus, in Juvenal, in Virgil's Aeneid, with especial reference to the technique, in Ovid, Metamorphoses, in Horace, Satires, in Roman Private Life, in Colloquial Latin, and in the Training of Teachers, first-year work in the Training of Teachers, course in Caesar, and in the Comparative Syntax of the Greek and Latin Verb.

Modern Languages.—Courses will be offered in Old English, in Middle English, in various periods of English Literature, and in English Composition; in Elementary and Intermediate French, in Old French Literature, in various periods of later French Literature, in Phonetics, in French Grammar, in Spanish, and in Italian; in Elementary and Intermediate German, in the History of German Literature, in Recent German Literature and Drama, in Gothic, and in Middle High German; in Dante in English, and in the Short Story in various literatures.

Mathematics, Astronomy, Physics, and Chemistry.—Courses will be offered in Trigonometry, College Algebra, Plane Analytic Geometry, Graphic Analysis, Differential and Integral Calculus, in Advanced Calculus, in Theory of Functions, also Synoptic Course in Higher Mathematics; Definite Integrals, Differential

AUDITORIUM OF LEON MANDEL ASSEMBLY HALL

Geometry, Theory of Physical Units, Theory of Numbers, Vector Analysis, General Analysis, and Reading and Research in Pure and Applied Mathematics; Descriptive Astronomy, Introduction to Celestial Mechanics, Analytic Mechanics, Research work at the Yerkes Observatory; Theoretical Optics, Light Waves and Their Uses, Advanced Spectroscopy, Relativity, Electron Theory, Research, work, Graduate laboratory work, Electric Waves, Mechanics, Molecular Physics and Heat, Electricity, Sound, and Light, and Physical Manipulation, two Courses for Teachers; Elementary General Chemistry; General Inorganic Chemistry, Elementary and Advanced Qualitative and Quantitative Analysis, Special Methods of Analysis, Elementary Organic Chemistry, Advanced Organic Preparations, Advanced Inorganic Preparations, Elementary and Advanced Physical Chemistry, Advanced Physico-chemical Measurements, Research in Organic, Inorganic, and Physical Chemistry.

WILLIAM RAINEY

MEMORIAL LIBRARY

Geology and Geography.—Courses will be offered in Physiography, in General Geology, in Economic Geology, in Elementary Mineralogy and Petrology, and several Field Courses for students of different stages of advancement; in the Conservation of Natural Resources, in the Geography of Europe, in Geographic Influences on American History, in Advanced and Elementary Commercial Geography, and perhaps in Anthropogeography.

The Biological Departments.—At the Marine Biological Laboratory, Woods Hole, Mass., courses in Zoölogy, Embryology, Botany, Physiological Chemistry, General and Comparative Physiology, and Biological Research, will be offered, for which credit is allowed in the University.

At the University of Chicago courses will be offered in Elementary Zoölogy, in Elementary Economic Field Zoölogy, in Experimental Behavior and Ecology,

HULL BIOLOGICAL LABORATORY AND MITCHELL TOWER

in Animal Geography, in Vertebrate and Invertebrate Zoölogy, in Genetics and Experimental Evolution, in Microscopical Technique, and advanced work in Zoölogy, including research, and in Embryology; in Introductory Anatomy; in Topographical Anatomy, Histology, in Anatomy of the Ear, Nose, and Throat, and in advanced research work; in Introductory Physiology, in Physiology of Digestion, Metabolism, Absorption, etc., in Physiology of Mammals, in Physiology of the Organs of Internal Secretion, in Research, and review courses in Physiology; in Teaching Botany in the High School, in Research in Morphology, in Special Morphology of Gymnosperms, in Research in Ecology, in Elementary Ecology, in Research in Taxonomy, in Classification of Vascular Plants, in General Morphology of Thallophytes, in Methods in Plant Histology, in Growth and Movement, in Research in Plant Physiology, in Elementary Plant Pathology, in Elementary Botany, and in Ecological Anatomy; in General Pathology and

Pathological Histology, in the Pathogenic Bacteria, in Sanitary Water Analysis, and in Research in Pathology and in Bacteriology.

Public Speaking.—Courses will be offered in Elementary and Advanced work in Public Speaking, with particular stress on the Vocal Interpretation of Literature, Oral Composition, and the pedagogy of both subjects as applied to High-School and College curricula.

THE SCHOOL OF EDUCATION

The School of Education of the University of Chicago consists of four divisions: (1) The Graduate Department of Education; (2) The College of Education; (3) The University High School; (4) The University Elementary School.

The Graduate Department of Education gives advanced courses in principles and theory of education, educational psychology, history of education, and social and administrative aspects of education. The Master's degree and the degree of Doctor of Philosophy are conferred.

The College of Education is a College of the University, with all the University privileges, and in addition provides the professional training of elementary and secondary school teachers and supervisors. It offers undergraduate courses in professional subjects and in the methods of arranging and presenting the various subject-matters which are taken up in the elementary and secondary schools. Certain of these courses can be completed in two years and lead to certificates; other courses cover a period of four years and lead to a Bachelor's degree.

The University High School with the fully equipped shops of the Manual Training School is in session during the Summer Quarter. Opportunity is offered to take beginning courses in Latin and German and to review courses in Mathematics, English, and History. The regular shopwork supplemented by discussions of methods is open to teachers pursuing these courses.

The University Elementary School.—Only the kindergarten department of the Elementary School is in session during the first term of the Summer Quarter. This offers an opportunity for observation.

COURSE OF INSTRUCTION IN THE GRADUATE DEPARTMENT AND IN THE COLLEGE

Courses in the Pedagogy of History and Literature in the Grades, in Home Economics, in English, in Mathematics, Physics, Geography, the Biological Sciences, School Library Economics; also in Oral Reading and in Hygiene and Physical Education, in Kindergarten Theory and Practice, in Children's Reading, in Aesthetic and Industrial Arts, in Household Art, and Review Courses in various subjects in the High School, will be offered, in addition to those named on p. 3.

THE DIVINITY SCHOOL

Admission.—The Divinity School is open to students of all denominations. The instruction is intended for ministers, missionaries, theological students, Christian teachers, and others intending to take up some form of religious work.

The English Theological Seminary is intended for those without college degrees. It is in session only during the Summer Quarter.

The Graduate Divinity School is designed primarily for college graduates. Pastors, theological teachers, students in other seminaries, and candidates for the ministry with requisite training are admitted in the Summer Quarter.

Ryerson Physical Laboratory

Hull Botanical Laboratory

YERKES OBSERVATORY

THE UNIVERSITY PRESS

Expenses.—No tuition fee is charged in the Summer Quarter. Incidental and library fees to the amount of $5 are charged, and matriculants pay the usual $5 fee. Dormitory rooms cost $8.75 to $12.75 per quarter; table-board about $3 per week in clubs or families.

In addition to the courses referred to on p. 3 there will be offered courses in Old and New Testament, in Biblical Theology, in Systematic Theology, in Church History, in Homiletics, in Religious Education, in Ecclesiastical Sociology, in Music, and in Public Speaking. Courses will be offered also in the Disciples' Divinity House.

THE LAW SCHOOL

Scope of Work.—The work of the Law School is intended for students whose education and maturity have fitted them to pursue serious professional study. The method of instruction employed—the study and discussion of cases—is designed to give an effective knowledge of legal principles, and to develop the power of independent legal reasoning. The three-year course of study offered constitutes a thorough preparation for the practice of law in any English-speaking jurisdiction. By means of the quarter system students may be graduated in two and one-fourth calendar years.

The Summer Quarter.—Regular courses of instruction counting toward a degree are continued through the Summer Quarter. Either advanced or beginning students may enter the school in the summer, and continue in the Autumn or in the next Summer Quarter. The courses are so arranged that students may take one, two, or three quarters in succession in the summer only, before continuing in a following Autumn Quarter. The summer work offers particular advantages to teachers, to students who wish to do extra work, and to practitioners who desire to study special subjects.

Building and Library.—The Law School occupies a building erected especially for it within the University quadrangles, and is equipped with a law library containing about 38,000 volumes.

Admission Requirements and Degrees.—Only college graduates or students who have had college work equivalent to three years in the University of Chicago are admitted as regular students, candidates for the degree of Doctor of Law (J.D.). The University permits one year of law to be counted as the fourth year of college work, making it possible to obtain both degrees in six years.

Students over twenty-one years old who have completed at least a four-year high-school course may be admitted as candidates for the degree of Bachelor of Laws (LL.B.), but must maintain a standing 10 per cent above the passing mark. In rare instances students over twenty-one who cannot meet these requirements will be admitted as unclassified, not candidates for a degree.

Fees.—A matriculation fee of $5 is required of every student entering for the first time. The tuition fee is $50 a quarter ($25 a term).

All correspondence concerning the Law School should be addressed to James P. Hall, Dean of the University of Chicago Law School, Chicago, Ill.

Courses Offered.—During the Summer, 1913, the Law School will offer courses in: Contracts, Criminal Law, Title to Real Estate, Damages, Constitutional Law, Mortgages, Wills, Sales, and Trusts.

THE SCHOOL OF EDUCATION

COURSES IN MEDICINE

First Two Years of the Medical Course.—Courses in Medicine constituting the first two years of the four-year course in medicine of Rush Medical College are given at the University of Chicago. For the majority of students taking up medical work for the first time, it is of decided advantage to enter with the Summer or the Autumn Quarter. For the student who is lacking in any of the admission courses, or who seeks advanced standing, it is of especial advantage to enter for the Summer Quarter.

Requirements for Admission.—The requirements for admission comprise (*a*) fifteen units of high-school work, demanded for admission to the Junior Colleges of the University, and (*b*) two years of college work, which must have included at least four majors of college chemistry, including both inorganic and organic, and qualitative analysis (in addition to the year of high-school chemistry), one major of college biology with laboratory work, two majors of college physics, and a reading knowledge of German or French. Admission to advanced standing is granted students from other recognized institutions under suitable restrictions. *The inclusive fee in the Medical Courses is $60 per quarter.*

Courses for Practitioners.—All the courses offered are open to practitioners of medicine, who may matriculate as unclassified or as graduate students. No student may register for a particular course unless he has had the prerequisite work. Attention is called to the fact that certain courses of special value to practitioners are given in the summer. Practitioners taking this work are free to attend the clinics at Rush Medical College without charge.

Courses in Medicine will be found listed on p. 10.

VARIOUS UNIVERSITY ACTIVITIES

UNIVERSITY PUBLIC LECTURES

By means of public lectures and entertainments of an educational character the University presents many opportunities for culture and instruction apart from the work of the laboratory and the classroom. The lectures are delivered by eminent scholars. Concerts or recitals will be given Tuesday evenings and popular lectures Friday evenings throughout the Summer Quarter.

CORRESPONDENCE-STUDY DEPARTMENT

The teachers and students who for any reason cannot come into residence during the summer or other quarters may study under the direct personal guidance of University instructors who conduct by correspondence more than three hundred and twenty-five of the classroom courses. The tuition fee is $16 for one major, $30 for two, and $40 for three. Work may begin at any time.

Bulletin of Recent Publications of *The University of Chicago Press*

1913

AGENTS

The Baker & Taylor Company, New York

The Cambridge University Press, London and Edinburgh

Th. Stauffer, Leipzig

The Maruzen-Kabushiki-Kaisha, Tokyo, Osaka, and Kyoto

Bulletin of Recent Publications of *The University of Chicago Press*

The Courts, the Constitution, and Parties. Studies in Constitutional History and Politics. By Andrew C. McLaughlin, Professor of History in the University of Chicago.

308 pages, 12mo, cloth; $1.50, postpaid $1.63

A volume of peculiar interest at this time, when the courts and political parties are subject to general criticism. The discussion is especially significant as coming from a lifelong student of constitutional questions, whose work at the University of Michigan, the Carnegie Institution of Washington, and as head of the Department of History in the University of Chicago, is so widely known. The point of view is historical. Though the articles are scientific they are directed to the reader who is interested in public affairs rather than to the professional student. The work consists of five papers, the first of which discusses the power of a court to declare a law unconstitutional. Two of the papers deal with the growth and essential character of political parties, and are followed by one on the history of differing theories of the federal Union. The work concludes with a discussion of the written constitution in some of its historical aspects, taking up the origin of these documents and the problems of their maintenance and interpretation in the development of the modern popular state.

The Mechanistic Conception of Life. Biological Essays by Jacques Loeb, Head of the Department of Experimental Biology, Rockefeller Institute for Medical Research.

238 pages, 12mo, cloth; $1.50, postpaid $1.65

The achievements of Professor Jacques Loeb in the field of experimental biology have made him so widely known as to insure any book of his a large circle of readers. His experimental work at the universities of Chicago and California, as well as in his present position, gives this volume an especial significance.

In his latest work, *The Mechanistic Conception of Life*, Professor Loeb presents many of the current problems in biology, and discusses the question whether the phenomena of life can be explained by physical and chemical laws. He finds it possible to control by physical or chemical means not merely the processes of reproduction, but also the conduct of animals with reference to environment.

The New York Medical Journal. The profession, as well as everyone interested in biology, will thank the author and the publishers for collecting these essays and placing them before the reading public.

The Chicago Tribune. It is refreshing to contemplate the wonderful exactitude, clearness, honesty, and unanswerable logic of Dr. Loeb.

Heredity and Eugenics. By John M. Coulter, William E. Castle, Edward M. East, William L. Tower, and Charles B. Davenport.

312 pages, 8vo, cloth; $2.50, postpaid $2.70

Leading investigators, representing the University of Chicago, Harvard University, and the Carnegie Institution of Washington, have contributed to this work, in which great care has been taken by each contributor to make clear to the general reader the present position of evolution, experimental results in heredity in connection with both plants and animals, the enormous value of the practical application of these laws in breeding, and human eugenics. The volume is profusely illustrated.

The Nation, New York. "Heredity and Eugenics" may be heartily recommended to readers seeking, as beginners, to get in touch with the discussion of these subjects. . . . . In most of the lectures there is an admirable reserve, not to say skepticism, in the treatment of large questions which the public is often misled to regard as already and finally settled.

Railway Economics. A Collective Catalogue of Books in Fourteen American Libraries. Prepared by the Bureau of Railway Economics, Washington, D.C.

450 pages, 8vo, cloth; $3.00, postpaid $3.28

Much of the literature relating to railways is widely scattered. The student of railway transportation finds it impossible to secure access to any all-embracing sources of information in any one of even the largest general libraries.

In the present work the Bureau of Railway Economics has undertaken to list the works relating to the economics of railway transportation that are catalogued in thirteen of the principal libraries of this country, together with those in its own collection.

The volume can fairly lay claim to being a representative bibliography in the field of railway economics.

It is confidently believed that the work will prove valuable to all interested in the literature of railway transportation, and particularly to the economist and practical railroad man.

The Evening Post, New York. Of all these invaluable aids to the student which the librarians of the country are producing, this is the most exhaustive and workmanlike of any that has been issued in the economic field.

American Permian Vertebrates. By Samuel Wendell Williston, Professor of Paleontology in the University of Chicago.

152 pages, 39 plates, 8vo, cloth; $2.50, postpaid $2.68

This work comprises a series of monographic studies with briefer notes and descriptions of new or little-known amphibians and reptiles from the Permian deposits of Texas and New Mexico. The material upon which these studies are based was for the most part collected during recent years by field parties from the University of Chicago. The book is offered as a contribution to knowledge on the subject of ancient reptiles and amphibians, with such summaries and definitions—based chiefly on American forms—as our present knowledge permits. The work is illustrated by the author.

Athenaeum. The paleontologist will welcome the work as a solid contribution to our knowledge of a fauna which is of exceptional interest to the student of evolution, inasmuch as it includes forms that help to bridge over some of the differences between reptiles and amphibians.

Morphology of Gymnosperms. By John M. Coulter, Professor of Botany, and Charles J. Chamberlain, Associate Professor of Botany, in the University of Chicago.

470 pages, 462 illustrations, 8vo, cloth; $4.00, postpaid $4.22

This work is a revised and enlarged edition of the book brought out by Professors Coulter and Chamberlain in 1901. Each of the seven great groups is here presented in detail, and a final chapter discusses the problem of phylogeny and points out the evolutionary tendencies. The extinct groups, notably the primitive "seed-ferns," are now included for the first time; and vascular anatomy is fully recognized as a morphological subject of first importance. The entire presentation is thoroughly and systematically organized and arranged with a view to the greatest possible clearness. The illustrations are numerous and in large part original.

Nature. The book is an invaluable record, admirably illustrated, of our present knowledge of the older type of seed-plants.

The Historicity of Jesus. A criticism of the contention that Jesus never lived, a statement of the evidence for his existence, an estimate of his relation to Christianity. By Shirley Jackson Case, Assistant Professor of New Testament Interpretation in the University of Chicago.

360 pages, 12mo, cloth; \$1.50, postpaid \$1.62

Did Jesus ever live, or is he a mythical personage like the deities of Greece and Rome? is to many people a somewhat startling question. But in recent years his actual existence has been vigorously questioned, and the subject is being given wide notice and discussion. The negative opinion has found supporters in America, England, Holland, France, and Germany. To present a complete and unprejudiced statement of the evidence for Jesus' actual existence is the aim of the author of *The Historicity of Jesus.*

The Nation, New York. It is creditable to American scholarship that the first survey of the entire debate should have been made by a representative of an American divinity school, and that the treatment of the question is adequate and fair in the presentation of the arguments on both sides, and marked by discernment both of the underlying principles and the consequences involved for the religious life.

Sociological Study of the Bible, Showing the Development of the Idea of God in Relation to History. By Louis Wallis, formerly Instructor in Sociology in the Ohio State University.

One volume, bound in cloth; \$1.50, postpaid \$1.68

This book is written on the basis of the modern scientific interpretation of the Bible; but it approaches Bible-study from a new point of view, using the sociological method of research. The ancient Hebrew nation is treated as a social group originating at the point of contact between Amorite city-states and Israelite clans from the Arabian desert. The great struggle within the nation was primarily between the legal usages of the constituent races. This conflict found expression very slowly in terms of antagonism between the gods of the Israelites and the Amorites. Mr. Wallis' papers on the subject have been appearing for some years in the *American Journal of Sociology;* but they are entirely recast and revised for book publication.

The Dial. A significant and closely reasoned work.

The Scotsman. Whether or not one agrees with Mr. Wallis, the originality and freshness of his views and the marked ability with which they are propounded cannot be denied.

The Minister and the Boy. By Allan Hoben, Associate Professor of Homiletics in the Divinity School of the University of Chicago.

Illustrated, 180 pages, 12mo, cloth; $1.00, postpaid $1.10

From the first chapter on "The Call of Boyhood," through one on "The Approach to Boyhood," the author leads us by suggestion and informing principle to realize the remarkable opportunity afforded by the raw material "boy," on which the minister may work. Later chapters on play and vocational choice show how to train the boy for citizenship, how responsive he is to the right sort of impetus, and how his religious life may indirectly, and even unconsciously, be stimulated by the proper appeal to his manly instincts, while furnishing him with a normal outlet for his natural enthusiasm. The book is practical throughout, and each chapter is filled with concrete suggestions which are vitalized by the author's actual experience as a basis.

Mr. Hoben's book is not only enlightening and entertaining, but is wonderfully practical. It should be in the hands of every probation officer, pastor, teacher, and parent.—JUDGE BEN B. LINDSEY.

Scientific Management in the Churches. By Shailer Mathews, Dean of the Divinity School in the University of Chicago.

66 pages, 12mo, cloth; 50 cents, postpaid 55 cents

Why not apply "scientific management" to the varied activities of the church? is the question asked by Dr. Shailer Mathews in his book. The crying need for it is almost startlingly portrayed, and the broad lines of the plan—the adaptation of "scientific management" to an institution such as the church—are inspiring in their suggestiveness.

The book is of the utmost value to all who belong to the active organization in their church—or who are, in the language of the author, "spiritual workmen."

The Independent. A small volume containing matter of large practical value.

The Continent. Dean Mathews' treatment of the subject is practical, and his suggestions are exceedingly useful.

The Ethics of the Old Testament. By Hinckley G. Mitchell, Professor of Hebrew and Old Testament Exegesis in Tufts College.

420 pages, 12mo, cloth; $2.00, postpaid $2.15

The aim of the author is to present a faithful and, as nearly as possible within the limits of a manual, a comprehensive view of the development of ethical ideas among the Hebrew nation. To this end he takes the books, or parts of books, of the Old Testament in the order of their origin, and discusses their teaching, whether direct or indirect, on the duties that men owe to themselves, their families, and the larger world of which they are a part. This is the first volume to be issued in the series of "Handbooks of Ethics and Religion" edited by Shailer Mathews.

Congregationalist and Christian World. It goes far to popularize the results of modern Biblical scholarship, and in general is within the comprehension of ordinary Bible students.

Old Testament Story. Teacher's Manual and Pupil's Notebook. By Charles H. Corbett.

Manual, $1.00, postpaid $1.09; Notebook, 50 cents, postpaid 59 cents

This latest addition to the Constructive Bible Studies, covering the period from Moses to Solomon, is designed for teachers of pupils from ten to twelve years of age corresponding to grades five and six of the public school. The pupil's equipment consists of a loose-leaf notebook containing a page for each lesson. It includes pictures, maps, outlines, paper models, and an occasional written lesson, thereby providing considerable opportunity for handwork.

The Churchman, New York. Teachers will find much that is helpful in Mr. Corbett's manual.

Unity, Chicago. The unique and really valuable part of the Corbett work is his Pupil's Notebook that accompanies it.

American Poems. Selected and Edited with Illustrative and Explanatory Notes and a Bibliography. By Walter C. Bronson, Litt.D., Professor of English Literature in Brown University.

680 pages, 12mo, cloth; $1.50, postpaid $1.68

The book offers a most carefully chosen and well-balanced presentation of the poetic works of Americans, covering the entire period of our history. For the teacher as well as the student the value of the work is greatly enhanced by the comprehensive Notes, Bibliography, and Indices. It is believed that the book will have the wide popularity of Professor Bronson's earlier collection, *English Poems,* which has been adopted by all leading American colleges.

The Dial. The resources of the special collections of Brown University have supplied the editor with the best authorities for accurate texts, and have made possible the widest range of selections.

San Francisco Call. A notably successful attempt to produce a useful book, against which the charge of injudicious inclusions and exclusions commonly urged against similar works cannot be made.

English Poems. Selected and Edited with Illustrative and Explanatory Notes and Bibliographies. By Walter C. Bronson, Litt. D., Professor of English Literature in Brown University.

I. Old English and Middle English Periods
436 pages, 12mo, cloth; School edition, $1.00, postpaid $1.15
Library edition, $1.50, postpaid $1.65

II. The Elizabethan Age and the Puritan Period
550 pages, 12mo, cloth; School edition, $1.00, postpaid $1.15
Library edition, $1.50, postpaid $1.66

III. The Restoration and the Eighteenth Century
541 pages, 12mo, cloth; School edition, $1.00, postpaid $1.15
Library edition, $1.50, postpaid $1.66

IV. The Nineteenth Century
635 pages, 12mo, cloth; School edition, $1.00, postpaid $1.15
Library edition, $1.50, postpaid $1.68

This series of four volumes is intended primarily to afford college classes and general readers a convenient, inexpensive, and scholarly collection of the most important English poetry.

The selections, so far as possible, are complete poems. The notes, though concisely expressed, occupy nearly a hundred pages in each volume. They contain explanations of words and allusions which the average college student might find obscure; statements by the poet or his friends that throw light on the poem; the poet's theory of poetry when this can be given in his own words; quotations which reveal his literary relationships or his methods of work; and extracts from contemporary criticism to show how the poet was received by his own generation. The last-mentioned feature has contributed much to the remarkable success of the series, which is the best general collection of English poetry that has yet been offered at a reasonable price.

The Journal of Education. These volumes are of supreme importance because of their completeness as to material and the scholarly way in which the poems have been annotated.

Questions on Shakespeare. By Albert H. Tolman, Associate Professor of English Literature in the University of Chicago.

The exercises on each play follow a logical order, embracing general questions, questions on individual acts and scenes, character-study, the relation of the play to its sources, and questions concerning the text or meaning.

The questions upon the following comedies are being issued in pamphlet form: A Midsummer-Night's Dream, Much Ado about Nothing, I Henry IV, II Henry IV, The Merchant of Venice, As You Like It, Twelfth Night, The Tempest.

Price 15 cents each, postpaid 17 cents each

Two bound volumes have appeared in this series as follows:

Questions on Shakespeare Part I, Introduction; 75 cents, postpaid 81 cents.

Questions on Shakespeare Part II, contains exercises on the three parts of Henry VI, Richard III, Love's Labour 's Lost, The Comedy of Errors, The Two Gentlemen of Verona, A Midsummer-Night's Dream, and all the Poems with the exception of the Sonnets. $1.00, postpaid $1.09.

Dr. Horace Howard Furness, Editor of the New Variorum Shakespeare. It is fairly astonishing what a deal of information in all departments of Shakespearian study you have compiled, and set forth alluringly—no small consideration where young people are concerned—within so small a space.

The Elementary Course in English. By James Fleming Hosic, Ph.M., Head of the Department of English in the Chicago Teachers College.

152 pages, 16mo, cloth; 75 cents, postpaid 82 cents

The constantly growing use of this book offers convincing testimony to its value as a practical guide for teachers, supervisors, and parents. It presents in outline a working theory of elementary English, with selected references to the recent literature of the subject. In this way the book is especially adapted to individual study and to group discussions in normal schools, teachers' reading circles, teachers' institutes, and parents' associations. The book contains also a suggestive course of study in composition, grammar, word-study, reading, and literature. Definite standards of attainment in these subjects are indicated for each year. Graded lists of material include stories for reading and for telling, poems for study and memorizing, supplementary reading-books classified by subjects, and selected literary studies for higher grades. The Appendix contains a list of books to be read to the children, a list of verse collections, and a list of prose collections. The author's long connection with the Department of English in the Chicago Teachers College qualifies him to speak with authority on the subject. The book has been endorsed by the *Course of Study*, the official publication of the Chicago public schools.

Educational Review. A good book. . . . . The thoughtful and studious teacher of elementary English will find it full of helpful suggestions and advice.

Agricultural Education in the Public Schools. By Benjamin M. Davis, Professor of Agricultural Education in Miami University.

170 pages, 8vo, cloth; $1.00, postpaid $1.12

In this book Professor Benjamin M. Davis has attacked the problem of the co-ordination of all the agencies now at work on the problem of agricultural education. He has performed a service which will be appreciated by all who have any large knowledge of the problem and of the difficulties which the movement encounters. He has made an effort to canvass the whole field and to give a detailed exposition of the forces employed in building up a rational course of agricultural education. He has presented more fully than anyone else the materials which define the problem and which make it possible for the teacher to meet it intelligently. The annotated bibliography at the end of the book will do much to make the best material available for anyone desiring to get hold of this material through independent study. The book serves, therefore, as a general introduction to the study of agricultural education.

Nature. Professor Davis may be congratulated on a most valuable and thoughtful expert contribution to the literature of his subject.

A Descriptive Catalogue of Manuscripts in the Libraries of the University of Chicago. Prepared by Edgar Johnson Goodspeed, Associate Professor of Biblical and Patristic Greek and Assistant Director of Haskell Oriental Museum.

140 pages, 8vo, cloth; $1.00, postpaid $1.11

This catalogue containing the description of ninety-nine manuscripts in the possession of the University of Chicago was published in connection with the dedication of the Harper

Memorial Library, June 11, 1912. At that time the manuscripts were transferred to permanent quarters in the Manuscript Room of the new Library. Not all the manuscripts of the University are here included, the Greek papyri in Haskell Oriental Museum and the East Indian and other oriental manuscripts being reserved for separate treatment. Most of the manuscripts described in the catalogue came to the University with the Berlin Collection in 1891. The languages of the manuscripts include Latin, Greek, Italian, Spanish, French, German, English, Dutch, Icelandic, Hebrew, and Arabic.

Outlines of Economics, Developed in a Series of Problems. By Members of the Department of Political Economy of the University of Chicago.

160 pages, interleaved, 12mo, cloth; $1.00, postpaid $1.13

This book is an attempt on the part of its authors to make some advances in the direction of improving the current methods of teaching the elementary course in economics. The ideals which have shaped the character of the book are: (1) A belief that the elementary course in economics offers exceptional opportunities for training in thinking and reasoning—a sort of training the importance of which can hardly be exaggerated. The inductive-problem method here used is believed to be the one best adapted to accomplish this end. (2) A desire to connect the theoretical principles of economics with the actual facts and with problems of the business world, and to induce the student to apply his knowledge of that world to the subject of study.

The result is a careful, analytical syllabus of the subjects usually covered in the introductory course, accompanied by some 1,200 questions and problems, designed: (*a*) to afford set problems for written work; (*b*) to guide the student in his reading, while fostering independent thinking; (*c*) to give direction to classroom discussion. It is expected that the *Outlines* will be used in connection with some textbook.

Nation. In their *Outlines of Economics, Developed in a Series of Problems*, three members of the Department of Political Economy in the University of Chicago have performed with remarkable thoroughness and grasp a task of great difficulty. The book consists in the main of sets of searching questions, dealing successively with every phase of the great subject, the order being determined by the attempt of the authors "not only to link economic theory with descriptive material, but in a measure to build the theory up out of the familiar events of economic life"; an attempt in which, we believe, they have succeeded as completely as the case admits.

Pragmatism and Its Critics. By Addison Webster Moore, Professor of Philosophy in the University of Chicago.

296 pages, 12mo, cloth; $1.25, postpaid $1.36

The general discussion of the philosophical movement known as "pragmatism" has awakened so spirited a controversy that the present volume is especially timely and significant. Professor Moore lays stress on three phases of the question: (1) the historical background of the movement; (2) its relation to the conception of evolution; (3) the social character of pragmatic doctrines. *Pragmatism and Its Critics* is a good example of the modern type of philosophical exposition. It is in a free, conversational style, is profound without being difficult, and simple without sacrificing accuracy.

Philosophical Review. No student is likely to read these chapters without receiving valuable help. The last chapter of this group, "How Ideas Work," is especially noteworthy as containing one of the most attractive and forcible presentations of the pragmatist theory of truth and error.

The Theology of Schleiermacher. By George Cross, Professor of Christian Theology in the Newton Theological Institution.

356 pages, 12mo, cloth; $1.50, postpaid $1.65

Professor Cross's book attempts to introduce the English-speaking student to Schleiermacher himself. It consists principally of a condensed "thought-translation" of his greatest work, *The Christian Faith.* The exposition is introduced by the interesting story of Schleiermacher's life, with emphasis on his religious experience. This is accompanied by a luminous account of the changes in Protestantism that necessitated a reconstruction of its doctrines. The work closes with a critical estimate of Schleiermacher's contribution to the solution of present religious problems, which in the judgment of scholars will stand as an extremely valuable portion of the book. Taken together, the translation, the analysis, and the critical estimate reveal Schleiermacher as a pioneer in modern religious thought.

The Christian World, London. This work is as timely as it is able. It is remarkable that, considering the enormous influence of Schleiermacher on modern theology, the English-speaking world has hitherto had such meager opportunity of studying the man and his teaching.

PUBLICATIONS IN SERIES

Publications of the National Society for the Study of Education (Formerly the National Herbart Society).

The annual reports (each issued in two parts) contain important papers and discussions on pedagogical subjects, concerning which detailed information will be furnished on request. The Yearbooks for 1895–99, for 1902–6, and for 1907–11 have been bound together, the price of each volume being $5.00, postpaid $5.30.

Publications of the American Sociological Society.

Six volumes of Papers and Proceedings have been issued. Price per volume, $1.50, postage extra.

The School Review Monographs.

This is a series of educational papers recently begun under the supervision of the editors of the *School Review.* The first number, *Research within the Field of Education, Its Organization and Encouragement,* will be sent postpaid for 53 cents; the second number, embracing articles on various educational subjects, for 56 cents. Both have been prepared by the Society of College Teachers of Education.

Yearbooks of the Superintendents' and Principals' Association of Northern Illinois.

Seven Yearbooks have been issued. Price 50 cents each, postage extra.

Publications of the Western Economic Society.

Vol. I, Part I, of the Proceedings, *Reciprocity with Canada,* has been issued. Price 75 cents, postpaid 83 cents.

Philosophic Studies (Edited by James Hayden Tufts).

Three numbers have been issued. Price 50 cents each, postpaid 54 cents.

Papers of the Bibliographical Society of America.

Six volumes have been published. Detailed list on request.

The Bulletin of the Bibliographical Society of America.

Published at intervals by the Society. $1.00 per volume, postage extra.

Historical and Linguistic Studies in Literature Related to the New Testament.

FIRST SERIES: TEXTS (4 numbers published).
SECOND SERIES: STUDIES (9 numbers published).

Proceedings of the Baptist Congress.

The Proceedings of the last meeting will be sent postpaid for 58 cents. Many of the back numbers can also be supplied.

Annual Tables of Constants and Numerical Data, Chemical, Physical, and Technological. Issued by an International Commission Appointed by the Seventh International Congress of Applied Chemistry.

We are distributing agents for this publication in the United States. Full information on request.

PERIODICALS

The Biblical World. SHAILER MATHEWS, Editor in Chief. Published monthly, with illustrations. Subscription price, $2.00 a year; single copies, 25 cents; foreign postage, 68 cents.

The School Review. Edited by the Department of Education in the University of Chicago. Published monthly, except in July and August. Subscription price, $1.50 a year; single copies, 20 cents; foreign postage, 52 cents.

The Elementary School Teacher. Edited by the Faculty of the Elementary School of the University of Chicago. Published monthly, except in July and August, with illustrations. Subscription price, $1.50 a year; single copies, 20 cents; foreign postage 46 cents.

The Botanical Gazette. Edited by JOHN M. COULTER. Published monthly, with illustrations. Subscription price, $7.00 a year; single copies, 75 cents; foreign postage, 84 cents.

The Journal of Geology. Edited by THOMAS C. CHAMBERLIN. Published semi-quarterly, with illustrations. Subscription price, $4.00 a year; single copies, 65 cents; foreign postage, 53 cents.

The Astrophysical Journal. Edited by GEORGE E. HALE, HENRY G. GALE, and EDWIN B. FROST. Published monthly, except in February and August, with illustrations. Subscription price, $5.00 a year; single copies, 65 cents; foreign postage, 62 cents.

The American Journal of Sociology. Edited by ALBION W. SMALL. Published bimonthly. Subscription price, $2.00 a year; single copies, 50 cents; foreign postage, 43 cents.

The Journal of Political Economy. Edited by the Faculty of Political Economy of the University of Chicago. Published monthly, except in August and September. Subscription price, $3.00 a year; single copies, 35 cents; foreign postage, 42 cents.

The American Journal of Theology. Edited by the Divinity Faculty of the University of Chicago. Published quarterly. Subscription price, $3.00 a year; single copies, $1.00; foreign postage, 41 cents.

The American Journal of Semitic Languages and Literatures. Edited by ROBERT FRANCIS HARPER. Published quarterly. Subscription price, $4.00 a year; single copies, $1.25; foreign postage, 26 cents.

Modern Philology. JOHN M. MANLY, Managing Editor. Published quarterly. Subscription price, $3.00 a year; single copies, $1.00; foreign postage, 41 cents.

The Classical Journal. FRANK J. MILLER, ARTHUR T. WALKER, and CHARLES D. ADAMS, Managing Editors. Published monthly, except in July, August, and September. Subscription price, $1.50 a year; single copies, 25 cents; foreign postage, 24 cents.

Classical Philology. PAUL SHOREY, Managing Editor. Published quarterly. Subscription price, $3.00 a year; single copies, $1.00; foreign postage, 23 cents.

The University of Chicago Magazine. Edited by a Board of Alumni. Published nine times a year. Subscription price, $1.50 a year; single copies, 20 cents; foreign postage, 27 cents.

Journal of the Association of Collegiate Alumnae. Published by the Association at the University of Chicago Press. Issued in January, March, April, and May of each year. Subscription price, $1.00 a year; single copies, 25 cents; foreign postage, 16 cents.

The English Journal. JAMES FLEMING HOSIC, Managing Editor. Published monthly, except in July and August, by the National Council of Teachers of English, at the University of Chicago Press. Subscription price, $2.50 a year; single copies, 30 cents; foreign postage, 45 cents.

Bibliography of Social Science. Edited by Dr. Hermann Beck, Berlin, and Dr. Charles Kinzbrunner, London, in co-operation with the Department of Political Economy in the University of Chicago. Published monthly. Annual subscription, $6.00. We are exclusive agents for the United States and Canada. Full information on combination rates with other journals on request. Complete sets of back numbers can be furnished at special rates.

Arrangements have been completed by which the American agency for the following journals of the Cambridge University Press will be in the hands of the University of Chicago Press, beginning January 1, 1913:

Biometrika

Parasitology

Journal of Genetics

The Journal of Hygiene

The Modern Language Review

The British Journal of Psychology

The Journal of Agricultural Science

Correspondence regarding details of service on these journals is invited.

The University of Chicago Press
Chicago, Illinois

PUBLICATIONS OF THE CAMBRIDGE UNIVERSITY PRESS

THE **University of Chicago Press** has become the American agent for the scientific journals and the following books issued by the Cambridge University Press of England:

BOOKS

The Genus Iris. By William Rickatson Dykes. With Forty-eight Colored Plates and Thirty Line Drawings in the Text.

254 pages, demi folio, half morocco; $37.50, postpaid $38.36

This elaborate and artistic volume brings together the available information on all the known species of Iris. The account of each includes references to it in botanical literature and a full description of the plant, together with observations on its peculiarities, its position in the genus, its value as a garden plant, and its cultivation. As far as possible the account of the distribution of each species is based on the results of research in the herbaria of Kew, the British Museum, the Botanic Gardens of Oxford, Cambridge, Berlin, Paris, Vienna, and St. Petersburg, and the United States National Museum at Washington.

The most striking feature of the book is the forty-eight life-size colored plates, reproduced from originals drawn from living plants—making it a volume of great beauty as well as of scientific importance.

Byzantine and Romanesque Architecture. By Thomas Graham Jackson, R.A. Two Volumes, with 165 Plates and 148 Illustrations.

Vols. I and II, each 294 pages, crown quarto, half vellum; two vols. $12.50, postpaid $13.25

This work contains an account of the development in Eastern and Western Europe of Post-Roman architecture from the fourth to the twelfth century. It attempts not merely to describe the architecture, but to explain it by the social and political history of the time. The description of the churches of Constantinople and Salonica, which have a special interest at this time, is followed by an account of Italo-Byzantine work at Ravenna and in the Exarchate, and of the Romanesque styles of Germany, France, and England. Most of the illustrations are from drawings by either the author or his son, and add great artistic value to the volumes.

The Duab of Turkestan. A Physiographic Sketch and Account of Some Travels. By W. Rickmer Rickmers. With 207 Maps, Diagrams, and Other Illustrations.

580 pages, royal 8vo, cloth; $9.00, postpaid $9.44

A record of exploration of a little-known region, combined with some elementary physiography. The book discusses the various geographical elements in the natural organic system of the Duab of Turkestan (or Land between the two Rivers) between the Oxus and the Jaxartes, the information being strung on the thread of an interesting story of travel and mountain exploration. The author was at great pains to obtain typical views of physical features such as mountains, valleys, and glaciers, and also of vegetation, village life, and architecture; and there are many diagrams for a clearer understanding of the text.

The book is especially suitable for colleges, libraries, and schools, and for all students or teachers of physical geography and natural science.

JOURNALS

Biometrika. A journal for the statistical study of biological problems. Edited by Karl Pearson. Subscription price, $7.50 a volume; single copies, $2.50.

Parasitology. Edited by G. H. F. Nuttall and A. E. Shipley. Subscription price, $7.50 a volume; single copies, $2.50.

Journal of Genetics. Edited by W. Bateson and R. C. Punnett. Subscription price, $7.50 a volume; single copies, $2.50.

The Journal of Hygiene. Edited by G. H. F. Nuttall. Subscription price, $5.25 a volume; single copies, $1.75.

The Modern Language Review. Edited by J. G. Robertson, G. C. Macaulay, and H. Oelsner. Subscription price, $3.00 a volume; single copies, $1.00.

The British Journal of Psychology. Edited by W. H. R. Rivers and C. S. Myers. Subscription price, $3.75 a volume.

The Journal of Agricultural Science. Edited by Professor R. H. Biffen, A. D. Hall, and Professor T. B. Wood. Subscription price, $3.75 a volume; single copies, $1.25.

The Biochemical Journal. Edited by W. M. Bayliss and Arthur Harden. Subscription price, $5.25 a volume.

The Journal of Physiology. Edited by J. N. Langley. Subscription price, $5.25 a volume.

Note.—Prices on back volumes vary, and postage from London is charged on back volumes and single copies.

PERIODICALS PUBLISHED BY THE UNIVERSITY OF CHICAGO PRESS

The Biblical World. SHAILER MATHEWS, Editor in Chief. Published monthly, with illustrations. Subscription price, $2.00 a year; single copies, 25 cents; foreign postage, 68 cents.

The School Review. Edited by the Department of Education in the University of Chicago. Published monthly, except in July and August. Subscription price, $1.50 a year; single copies, 20 cents; foreign postage, 52 cents.

The Elementary School Teacher. Edited by the Faculty of the Elementary School of the University of Chicago. Published monthly, except in July and August, with illustrations. Subscription price, $1.50 a year; single copies, 20 cents; foreign postage 46 cents.

The Botanical Gazette. Edited by JOHN M. COULTER. Published monthly, with illustrations. Subscription price, $7.00 a year; single copies, 75 cents; foreign postage, 84 cents.

The Journal of Geology. Edited by THOMAS C. CHAMBERLIN. Published semi-quarterly, with illustrations. Subscription price, $4.00 a year; single copies, 65 cents; foreign postage, 53 cents.

The Astrophysical Journal. Edited by GEORGE E. HALE, HENRY G. GALE, and EDWIN B. FROST. Published monthly, except in February and August, with illustrations. Subscription price, $5.00 a year; single copies, 65 cents; foreign postage, 62 cents.

The American Journal of Sociology. Edited by ALBION W. SMALL. Published bimonthly. Subscription price, $2.00 a year; single copies, 50 cents; foreign postage, 43 cents.

The Journal of Political Economy. Edited by the Faculty of Political Economy of the University of Chicago. Published monthly, except in August and September. Subscription price, $3.00 a year; single copies, 35 cents; foreign postage, 42 cents.

The American Journal of Theology. Edited by the Divinity Faculty of the University of Chicago. Published quarterly. Subscription price, $3.00 a year; single copies, $1.00; foreign postage, 41 cents.

The American Journal of Semitic Languages and Literatures. Edited by ROBERT FRANCIS HARPER. Published quarterly. Subscription price, $4.00 a year; single copies, $1.25; foreign postage, 26 cents.

Modern Philology. JOHN M. MANLY, Managing Editor. Published quarterly. Subscription price, $3.00 a year; single copies, $1.00; foreign postage, 41 cents.

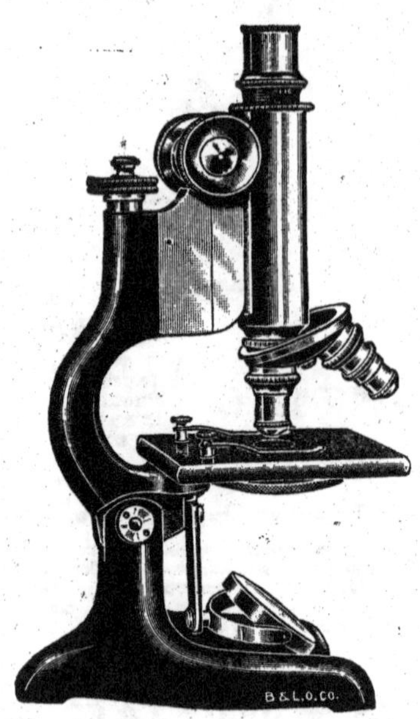

F2—$31.50
Special Price to Schools

There is the very best reason for inviting your confidence in the

Bausch and Lomb Microscopes

In optical equipment and construction they represent the extensive experience and close touch with laboratory workers enjoyed by makers, who through consistent effort, year after year, have made possible a reliable microscope at a reasonable price.

Write today for new Supplement to Microscope Catalog.

Bausch & Lomb Optical Co.
421 ST. PAUL STREET ROCHESTER, N.Y.

6

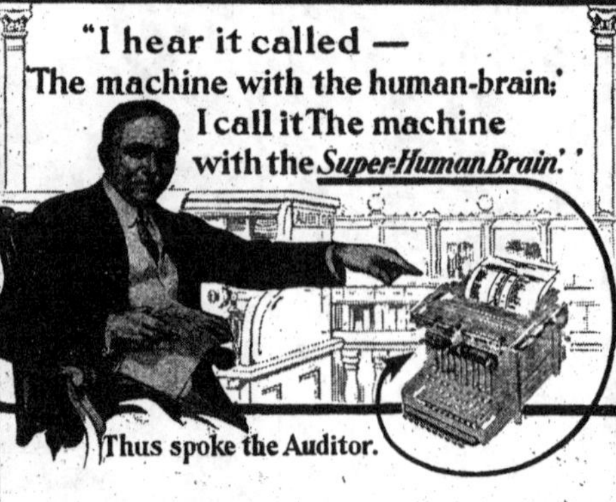

He was speaking of the

Remington
Adding and Subtracting
Typewriter
(Wahl Adding Mechanism)

This machine does something that only the brain, directing the hand, has hitherto been able to do—that is, *write and add (or subtract) on the same page.*

But this is not all. It does such work *more easily, more rapidly, and more accurately* than the human brain has ever performed similar labor.

Thus the machine is *human* in what it does and *super-human* in the way it does it.

Illustrated booklet sent on request

Remington Typewriter Company
(Incorporated)
325-331 Broadway, New York
Branches Everywhere

Typewriter Agents Wanted
SAMPLES AT WHOLESALE

Get in Business for Yourself

Big commissions—monthly payments—trial shipments—new stock—visible models

Typewriters from $28.50 up that formerly sold for $100

Write today for Agency offer. Mention UNIVERSITY OF CHICAGO JOURNALS

Michigan Typewriter Exchange
GRAND RAPIDS, MICH.

Use the Coupon

FROM U. OF C. JOURNALS

Name ______________________

Address ______________________

4

The Elementary School Teacher

EDITED BY

THE FACULTY OF THE SCHOOL OF EDUCATION

WITH THE CO-OPERATION OF

THE FACULTY OF THE FRANCIS W. PARKER SCHOOL

Vol. XIII CONTENTS FOR JUNE 1913 No. 10

The Elementary School Teacher is published monthly from September to June. ¶The subscription price is $1.50 per year; the price of single copies is 20 cents. Orders for service of less than a half-year will be charged at the single-copy rate. ¶Postage is prepaid by the publishers on all orders from the United States, Mexico, Cuba, Porto Rico, Panama Canal Zone, Republic of Panama, Hawaiian Islands, Philippine Islands, Guam, Tutuila (Samoa), Shanghai. ¶Postage is charged extra as follows: For Canada, 30 cents on annual subscriptions (total $1.80); on single copies, 3 cents (total 23 cents). For all other countries in the Postal Union, 46 cents on annual subscriptions (total $1.96); on single copies, 6 cents (total 26 cents). ¶Remittances should be made payable to The University of Chicago Press, and should be in Chicago or New York exchange, postal or express money order. If local check is used, 10 cents must be added for collection.

The following agents have been appointed and are authorized to quote the prices indicated:

For the British Empire: The Cambridge University Press, Fetter Lane, London, E.C., England. Yearly subscriptions, including postage, 8*s.* each; single copies, including postage, 1*s.* each.

For the Continent of Europe: Th. Stauffer, Universitätsstrasse 26, Leipzig, Germany. Yearly subscriptions, including postage, M. 8.25 each; single copies, including postage, M. 1.10 each.

For Japan and Korea: The Maruzen-Kabushiki-Kaisha, 11 to 16 Nihonbashi Tori Sanchome, Tokyo, Japan. Yearly subscriptions, including postage, Yen 4.00 each; single copies, including postage, Yen 0.50 each.

Claims for missing numbers should be made within the month following the regular month of publication. The publishers expect to supply missing numbers free only when they have been lost in transit.

Business correspondence should be addressed to The University of Chicago Press, Chicago, Ill.

Communications for the editors and manuscripts should be addressed to the Editors of THE ELEMENTARY SCHOOL TEACHER, The University of Chicago, Chicago, Ill.

Entered October 12, 1903, at the Post-office at Chicago, Ill., as second-class matter, under Act of Congress, March 3, 1879

Volume XIII JUNE 1913 Number 10

The Elementary School Teacher

THE UNIVERSITY OF CHICAGO PRESS
CHICAGO, ILLINOIS, U.S.A.

AGENTS
THE CAMBRIDGE UNIVERSITY PRESS, LONDON AND EDINBURGH
TH. STAUFFER, LEIPZIG
THE MARUZEN-KABUSHIKI-KAISHA, TOKYO, OSAKA, KYOTO

www.ingramcontent.com/pod-product-compliance
Lightning Source LLC
LaVergne TN
LVHW010521100826
845148LV00001B/63

* 9 7 8 1 4 2 5 5 7 3 8 0 5 *